OXFORD EARLY MUSIC SERIES

THE LUTE IN BRITAIN

THE LUTE IN BRITAIN

A HISTORY OF THE INSTRUMENT AND ITS MUSIC

BY

MATTHEW SPRING

OXFORD

UNIVERSITY PRESS

OXFORD
UNIVERSITY PRESS

Great Clarendon Street, Oxford OX2 6DP

Oxford University Press is a department of the University of Oxford.
It furthers the University's objective of excellence in research, scholarship,
and education by publishing worldwide in

Oxford New York

Athens Auckland Bangkok Bogotá Buenos Aires Cape Town
Chennai Dar es Salaam Delhi Florence Hong Kong Istanbul Karachi
Kolkata Kuala Lumpur Madrid Melbourne Mexico City Mumbai Nairobi
Paris São Paulo Shanghai Singapore Taipei Tokyo Toronto Warsaw
and associated companies in Berlin Ibadan

Oxford is a registered trade mark of Oxford University Press
in the UK and in certain other countries

Published in the United States
by Oxford University Press Inc., New York

© Matthew Spring 2001

The moral rights of the author have been asserted

Database right Oxford University Press (maker)

First published 2001

British Library Cataloguing in Publication Data

Data available

Library of Congress Cataloging in Publication Data
Spring, Matthew.
The lute in Britain: a history of the instrument and its music / by Matthew Spring.
p. cm.—(Oxford early music series)
Includes bibliographical references and index.
1. Lute—Great Britain—History. 2. Lute music—History and criticism.
3. Music—Great Britain—History and criticism.
I. Title. II. Oxford early music series (Unnumbered)
ML1010.S77 2000 787.8'3'0941—dc21 00-032699

ISBN 0-19-518838-1

1 3 5 7 9 10 8 6 4 2

Typeset by Hope Services (Abingdon) Ltd.
Printed in Great Britain
on acid-free paper by
Bookcraft Ltd
Midsomer Norton, Somerset

Dedicated to the memory of my father,
George Henry Thomas Spring (1929–96),
who bought me my first lute and the
complete works for solo lute of John Dowland

PREFACE

The lute was one of the most important instruments in use in Europe from late medieval times up to the eighteenth century, as a solo instrument, in combination with other instruments, or with the voice. Despite its acknowledged importance there is, as yet, no comprehensive book on either the instrument or its music, apart from performance studies or bibliographical and reference publications. Books on the guitar are plentiful. There are a number on the viol. Even relatively obscure instruments like the early mandolin can boast a dedicated book. Yet the lute languishes in seeming neglect, probably because of the vastness of its literature and repertory. For this reason any book is bound to attract criticism for lack of scholarship or balance. My hope is that any deficiencies in this book will be made up by its strengths. There will certainly be books to follow this, in particular Douglas Alton Smith's history of the lute from antiquity to the renaissance, and Ian Harwood's forthcoming book on the mixed consort.

I have chosen to focus on the lute in Britain, the area with which I am most familiar. Yet there are disadvantages to treating lute developments in Britain in isolation. With this in mind I have included two chapters on Continental changes in the instrument and its technique, as well as passing references to developments outside Britain throughout the book. Through the work of Diana Poulton, John Ward, and others, the music of John Dowland is well represented in publication and widely appreciated. To a lesser extent this can be said of the English lutenist-composers of Dowland's generation. The lute was played in Britain for well over four hundred years before its revival this century, and very little has been written about the lute in medieval or eighteenth-century Britain. Few would question that the achievements of Dowland and his contemporaries eclipsed those that preceded or followed. Yet my concern has been to cover all periods and to emphasize the continuity of traditions over time, even when source information is not plentiful. I realize that, for some readers, I may have gone too far in redressing the balance away from the late Elizabethan/early Jacobean times, from which music sources are most abundant.

This book is aimed at a readership that spans the player, maker, and lute enthusiast on the one hand, and the general music student and serious listener on the other. It is intended to fill a gap that I believe exists between what is known and available in specialist journals and theses, and what is for sale in music shops. Through the activities of the Lute Society and its counterparts in other countries, articles on lutes and sources of lute music in Britain are now numerous. Much of the English lute music of the period 1580–1660 is available in facsimile or modern editions. In the last twenty years lute music has become an established feature in the programming of many of the country's foremost music venues, and the lute in various contexts is regularly heard on the radio. Yet the instrument still suffers from being regarded by many as 'specialist', liked and understood by a small number of enthusiasts. It is my hope that this book will go some way towards integrating the lute and its music into the mainstream of our musical culture.

To a large degree a history of the lute in Britain is a history of surviving musical sources. It is here that we find the most easily accessible and abundant information on what music lutenists were playing and on what types of instruments. The lute player of today, more than perhaps any other type of instrumentalist, is aware of the range of individual primary musical sources and their different characters. This has much to do with the nature of tablature. Once mastered it is easy to read, and has changed little since the sixteenth century. Most modern players are happy to perform from published facsimiles of original sources. This book attempts to inform the reader about the lute sources from each period, and to build up a picture of the totality of source survival from each period. But a word of caution here: it may be a mistake simply to equate plentiful source survival from a particular period with the popularity of lute playing within that period. Manuscripts and old books survive as a matter of chance and fashion. Much lute playing may have been done without music, or from music on separate unbound pieces of paper that were soon after destroyed or used again for some other purpose.

Together with the musical and non-musical information gleaned from lute sources, most of the chapters include some discussion of the social background to lute playing, the changes to the instrument itself, and the development of playing technique. Some biographical information on the main players, composers, or commentators of each period has been included—but deliberately kept short. In periods from which musical source information is scarce, individual sources may have inevitably received more attention than they would otherwise merit. For such periods I have had to rely more on literary and iconographical information to build up a picture of lute development.

Each of the chapters dealing directly with the lute in Britain, except the last, summarizes the position of lutenists at the English court. The court was the greatest employer of musicians until the eighteenth century, and most lutenists aspired to a royal post. Dowland's failure to secure one until late in life made him an embittered man. Changes of fashion at court normally set the course that the rest of the country then tried to follow. For work on my own thesis I trawled through court records at the Public Record Office. Now the task has been made much simpler and more agreeable through the publication of Andrew Ashbee's *Records of English Court Music* (*RECM*).

The chapter divisions of the historical narrative all presented themselves quite logically with the exception of the separation of the period 1580–1625 into late

Elizabethan and Jacobean. To split up the sources from this period is arbitrary, since they logically form one entity, as covered in the theses of David Lumsden and Julia Craig-McFeely. Not to have divided the period would have produced an unacceptably large chapter. As originally conceived the book covered only solo lute music. I then decided that two bridging chapters were needed to explain the changes to the instrument and its playing technique that happened around 1480–1530 and 1600–50; these developments occurred first on the Continent and were then introduced to England. Lastly I included three chapters on the lute in consort, lute song, and the theorbo. For the book to be inclusive and balanced these areas seemed vital, especially as they are closely linked with the development of the solo lute. However, the subjects covered in these three chapters are underrepresented, especially so in the case of lute songs, which have never been entirely forgotten, and for which the surrounding literature is enormous. My approach here has been to ignore the literary dimension of the songs entirely, and discuss the songs from the point of view of the lute and its development.

The last chapter is devoted to the lute in Scotland. Scotland had her own court until 1603. Source material from Scotland in the period 1630–1710 is arguably as plentiful and important as that from England in the same period. Several of the Scottish sources contain a high proportion of Scots melodies that set them apart from anything produced in England. For this reason I have dealt with Scotland separately, though some sources, in particular those from the Panmure collection that contain a repertoire that is French in origin, have also been touched on elsewhere in the book.

M.S.

Oxford
January 2000

ACKNOWLEDGEMENTS

The primary research on which much of the material in the book is based was undertaken by others. In particular important source-related work has been done by Christopher Page, John Ward, Diana Poulton, Ian Harwood, David Lumsden, Julia Craig-McFeely, Warwick Edwards, Lyle Nordstom, Tim Crawford, Robert Spencer, David Greer, and Ian Spink. To these and many others I am grateful. I have tried in the text and footnotes to mention those who have significantly contributed to the primary research in the field. Inevitably some will remain inadequately acknowledged. To them I apologize.

My interest in the lute was kindled some twenty years ago by the late Diana Poulton, with whom I learnt the instrument while at Keele University. Work on this book originated with my Oxford University thesis, during the research for which I received help from John Caldwell, Tim Crawford, John Harper, and Ian Spink. Special thanks are due to the Leverhulme Trust for funding a three-year fellowship based at the London Guildhall University which enabled me to expand my knowledge of the sources of British lute music, to visit and inspect at first hand all the important manuscripts, and to write this book. A debt is owed to Lewis Jones for help at this stage. More recently I am particularly grateful to the late and much lamented Robert Spencer for encouragement, access to his unparalleled music collection, and for help in collecting the plates and illustrations in this book—many of which are from his own collection. I also thank Jill Spencer for continuing support after Robert's death. During the final preparation of this book Robert Spencer's collection was removed from Woodford Green to its new home at the Royal Academy of Music, though at present the material remains uncatalogued and not generally available for study.

Special mention must be made of the invaluable and painstaking service paid by Stewart McCoy, who over the years has spent an enormous amount of time reading, correcting, and commenting on my work in its various drafts. His contribution, often delivered with considerable wit, has greatly improved the accuracy and enriched the content of this book at every stage. His task has been Herculean, and to him I am very grateful. Thanks are due to Peter Forrester for bringing to my attention a good number of pictures with lutes which I did not otherwise know, and to Jon Banks, who helped with the production of the book. I am grateful for financial help from the Department of Music at Bath Spa University College towards the completion of the final stages of this book. Other people to whom I owe special thanks for reading my various drafts, and offering comments, help, and support are: Peter Holman, Andrew Ashbee, and Ian Harwood; to Bonnie Blackburn for her excellent copy-editing; and to Bruce Phillips, Helen Peres da Costa, Dorothy McLean, and all at Oxford University Press for their care in publishing the work.

I am grateful to the following institutions and individuals for permission to reproduce the illustrations: Biblioteca del Monasterio de El Escorial, Madrid (Pl. 1.1); Wartburg-Stiftung, Eisenach (Pls. 1.2–3); The Public Record Office (Pls. 2.1, 5.2(*a*) and (*c*)); Board of Trustees of the Victoria and Albert Museum (Pls. 2.2, 3.2(*b*)); Vicar and Churchwardens of Steeple Aston, Oxfordshire (Pl. 2.2); Vicar and Churchwardens of St Agnes, Cawston and of St Martin's Church, Hindringham, Norfolk (Pls. 2.3–4); Bibliothèque Nationale de France (Pl. 3.2(*a*)); Trustees of The National Gallery, London (Pls. 4.1 and 10.2); Staatliche Museen Preußischer Kulturbesitz, Gemäldegalerie, Berlin (Pl. 4.2); National Portrait Gallery (Pls. 4.3 and 6.2); Lord Berkeley (Pl. 4.5); the British Library (Pls. 4.6, 7.6, 8.1, 10.9); Statens Museum for Kunst, Copenhagen (Pl. 5.1); Lord Hotham and the Librarian of the Brynmor Jones Library, University of Hull (Pl. 5.2(*b*)); the Syndics of Cambridge University Library (Pl. 5.3); Shakespeare's Birthplace Trust (Pl. 6.1); the Marquis of Bath (Pl. 10.5); Manchester City Art Gallery (Pl. 10.6); Bodleian Library, University of Oxford (Pl. 10.10); Viscount De L'Isle (Pl. 11.1); English Heritage, Eastern Region (Pl. 11.2); The Columbus Museum of Art, Columbus, Ohio (Pl. 11.3); Mr and Mrs Lloyd-Baker (Pl. 12.2); the Duke of Roxburghe (Pl. 13.2); Lady Georgina Coleridge (Pl. 13.3); Historic Scotland (Pl. 13.4); Lord Crawford (Pl. 13.5).

The following plates are from the collection of the late Robert Spencer: 5.4, 6.3, 7.1, 7.2, 7.3, 7.4, 7.5, 8.2, 10.1, 10.3, 10.4, 11.4, 11.5, 13.1. They are reproduced with the kind permission of Jill Spencer and The Royal Academy of Music. Plates 4.4, 10.7, 10.8, and 12.5 are reproduced with kind permission of their private owners.

Lastly my heartfelt thanks to my family, particularly my brother Peter for financial help in times past, and my wife Sara and son Lewis for putting up with me in recent years while I have been involved with this project.

CONTENTS

LIST OF ILLUSTRATIONS

LIST OF TABLES

LIST OF MUSICAL EXAMPLES

NOTE TO THE READER

Quotations from books, manuscripts, and other documents have been reproduced as they appear in the original but with some modernizations of spellings. Thus þ has been changed to *th*, *i* to *j*, and *u* to *v* (occasionally the reverse in the case of *u* and *v*). The long *s* appears as a standard *s*. Contractions have been expanded within square brackets. I have not attempted to reproduce all italic type when it appears in original source documents, though I have reproduced it in some cases, as with excerpts from Mace, where they are so much part of the style. Quotations in other languages have been translated within parentheses. In general proper names follow forms adopted in *New Grove* with some exceptions; for instance I have preferred 'Jacques Gaultier' to 'Jacques Gautier' as the former is the spelling most used by the man himself.

In 1582 the Gregorian calendar was adopted by much of Continental Europe. Britain continued with the old style Julian calendar until 1752. By this date there was a separation of eleven days between the calendar systems. The English civil year under the Julian calendar began on 25 March. Thus any particular year ran from 25 March of one year to 24 March of the next. Where a documentary date falls between 1 January and 24 March it is rendered with the given year date, followed by a slash and the year date as it would be under the present calender system, e.g. 1625/6.

Pitch is indicated by the letter system in which middle C is *c′*, C above is *c″*, C below is *c*, and C two octaves below middle C is *C*. The term 'course' with reference to a lute or other similar plucked instrument denotes either a single string or double strings (even treble strings in the case of some citterns) that are placed so close to each other that they are normally plucked and sounded as one. Pitches for different tunings are given from the first course downwards. This is better for comparative purposes as all lutes have a top course but not all lutes have more than six courses. Almost all the examples involve tablature together with a simultaneous piano score transcription. The tablature has been copied in the form that it appears in the source. I have aimed at a minimum of editorial interference; thus rhythm signs appear in a variety of types, most of which are particular to the period from which they come.

One major problem that I have never fully resolved concerns the many ornamentation signs that occur in tablature sources from *c.*1575 onwards. I have faithfully reproduced these in my tablature (though occasionally approximating their position) but, with one important exception, omitted them from the piano score transcription. I have tried a variety of approaches in early drafts of this book, ranging from exactly reproducing the ornament signs in both tablature and transcription, to attempting to realize the ornament signs as they might actually be played. Any realization of the signs is highly problematic as few sources give directions, and the same tablature signs clearly meant different things in different sources and across different periods. For this reason I have chosen simply to reproduce them in the tablature only, with the important exception of pieces by Thomas Mace. Mace is exceptional in that he provides an exact description of every sign he uses. In his pieces a realization of the signs seemed both justified and meaningful. For the other examples I would refer the reader to Martin Shepherd's article, 'The Interpretation of Signs for Graces in English Lute Music', *LSJ* 36 (1996), 37–84. This article will alert the reader to the main problems and provide some pointers for their resolution.

The spellings 'coranto' and 'almain' have been adopted to designate English dance-types in British sources (which are often similar to their Italian counterparts) and thereby to distinguish them from the French 'courante' or 'allemande' which appear in British sources after 1620 and in some cases earlier.

Table of Tunings

The following table indicates relative pitches only and takes the fourth course as being a constant *f*. Only the top six strings are shown, although lower strings and diapasons may also vary.

A. Renaissance or 'vieil ton' tunings

1. g', d', a, f, c, G

B. *Cordes avalées*

This term, which simply means 'lowered strings', was used in Morlaye's guitar books of 1552 and 1553, but came to be associated with retunings of the middle and lower courses of the lute *c*.1600–10. For example, the tuning g', d', $b\flat$, f, $B\flat$, F, $[E\flat]$ used by Besard in *Thesaurus harmonicus* (1603).

C. Transitional tunings or 'nouveau ton'

6. f', c', a, f, c, G = 'Harp Way' tuning

7. f', c', $a\flat$, f, c, G = 'Harp Way Flat' or 'Lawrence' tuning

8. e', c', a, f, c, G = 'English Gaultier's', 'Sharp', or 'Mersenne's extraordinary' tuning

9. $e\flat'$, c', a, f, c, G = 'Flat with the third sharp'

10. $e\flat'$, c', $a\flat$, f, c, G = 'French Flat' or 'Flat' tuning

D. D Major/D minor tuning

Standard D minor tuning = f', d', a, f, d, A, G, F, E, D

D major tuning = $f\sharp'$, d', a, $f\sharp$, d, A, G, $F\sharp$, E, D

This table is taken from the first part of the table in Wallace B. Rave, 'Some Manuscripts of French Lute Music 1630–1700: An Introductory Study' (Ph.D. thesis, University of Illinois at Urbana-Champaign, 1972), pp. xi–xii, which itself is based on the list in Hans Radke's 'Beiträge zur Erforschung der Lautentablaturen des 16.–18. Jahrhunderts', *Die Musikforschung*, 16 (1963), 41–2.

ABBREVIATIONS

Manuscripts

Add. 4900	*GB-Lbl* Add. MS 4900
Add. 15117	*GB-Lbl* Add. MS 15117
Add. 29246	*GB-Lbl* Add. MS 29246 (Paston MS)
Add. 31392	*GB-Lbl* Add. MS 31392
Add. 31698	*GB-Lbl* Add. MS 31698 (Straube MS)
Add. 31992	*GB-Lbl* Add. MS 31992 (Paston MS)
Add. 31698	*GB-Lbl* Add. MS 31698
Add. 38539	*GB-Lbl* Add. MS Add. 38539
Basle 53	*CH-Bmi* F.IX 53
Balcarres	*GB-En* MS Acc. 9769 84/1/6 on loan (Balcarres lute book)
Ballet	*EIRE-Dtc* MS MS 408/1 and MS 408/2 (Ballet and Ballet companion lute book)
Berlin 40165	*D-Bsb* Mus. MS 40165
Berlin 40264	*D-Bsb* Mus. MS 40264
Berlin 40641	*PL-Kj* Berlin Mus. MS 40641
Blaikie	Dundee, Central Library, Wighton Collection
Bodley 410–414	*GB-Ob* MS Mus. Sch. c. 410–414
Board	*GB-Lam*, The Robert Spencer Collection (Margaret Board lute book)
Bowie	*GB-En* MS Acc. 5412 (on deposit)
Brogyntyn	*GB-AB* MS 27 in the Brogyntyn Collection, National Library of Wales
Browne	GB-*Lam*, The Robert Spencer Collection (Browne bandora and lyra viol MS)
Burwell Tutor	Ingham, Norwich, Captain Anthony Howard's private collection (Burwell lute tutor)
Chicago	*US-Cn* Case MS 7 Q.5
Cosens	*GB-Cu* MS 3056
Creyghton	*GB-Lbl* Add. MS 37074
Dallis	*EIRE-Dtc* MS 410/1
Danby	*US-R* MS Vault M2.1.D172
Dd.2.11	*GB-Cu* MS Dd.2.11
Dd.3.18	*GB-Cu* MS Dd.3.18

Dd.4.22	*GB-Cu* MS Dd.4.22
Dd.5.78.3	*GB-Cu* MS Dd.5.78.3
Dd.9.33	*GB-Cu* MS Dd.9.33
Euing	*GB-Ge* MS R.d.43
Folger	*US-Ws* MS V.b.280 (*olim* MS 1610.1)
FVB	*GB-Cfm* Mu. MS 168 (Fitzwilliam Virginal Book)
Giles Lodge	*US-Ws* MS V.a.159 (*olim* MS 448.16) (Giles Lodge's lute book)
Guthrie	*GB-Eu* MS Laing III.3
Hainhofer	*D-W* MSS Guelf.18.7 and 18.8.Aug. (Philipp Hainhofer's lute books, volumes III and IV)
Haslemere	*GB-HAd* MS II.B.1
Herbert	*GB-Cfm* Mu. MS 689 (Lord Herbert of Cherbury's lute book)
Hirsch	*GB-Lbl* MS Hirsch M.1353
Houghton 174	*US-CA* Houghton Library, MS 174
Königsberg	*LT-Va* M. 285-MF-LXXIX
Krems L 81	Kremsmünster, Benedictine Abbey Library, MS L 81
Lawes Duets	*GB-Ob* MS Mus. Sch. b. 2 (William Lawes autograph score)
Leyden	*GB-En* Adv. MS 5.2.19
Longleat	Warminster, Longleat House, Old Library, Recess VI, Mus. MS 7
Lowther	*GB-Cfm* Mu. MS 688
Marsh	*EIRE-Dm* MS Z3.2.13
Montbuysson	*D-Kl* MS.4to Mus.108(1)
Mynshall	*GB-Lam* The Robert Spencer Collection (Mynshall lute book)
Nanki	*J-Tn* MS N-4/42
Nn.6.36	*GB-Cu* MS Nn.6.36
O.16.2	*GB-Ctc* MS O.16.2
Osborne	*US-Wc* MS M2.1.T2 18B Case
Osborn Commonplace Book	*US-NH* Osborn Collection Music MS 13
Ox 576	*GB-Ob* MS Mus. Sch. f. 576
Pan 4	*GB-En* MS 9451
Pan 5	*GB-En* MS 9452
Pan 7	*GB-En* MS 9494
Pan 8	*GB-En* MS 9449 (Lady Campbell's music book)
Pickeringe	*GB-Lbl* Egerton MS 2046 (Jane Pickeringe's lute book)

Poznań	*PL-Pu* MS. Rkp. 7033
Prague IV.G.18	Prague, Národní Muzeum, Hudebni Oddělení, MS IV.G.18
RA 58	*GB-Lbl* MS Royal Appendix 58
Reymes	*F-Pcrs* Lute MS without shelf number
Robarts	Llanhydrock House, Cornwall, owned by the National Trust
Ros 54	*D-ROu* Mus. saec. XVII-54
Rowallan	*GB-Eu* MS Laing III. 487 (Sir William Mure of Rowallan's lute book)
Ruthwen	*F-Pn* Fonds du Conservatoire National, MS Rés. 1110
Sampson	*GB-Lam*, The Robert Spencer Collection (Sampson lute book)
Schele	*D-Hs* MS M.B/2768 (Ernst Schele's lute book)
Sibley Vault	*US-R* M 140.V.186/S
Sinkler	*GB-En* MS 3296 (Margaret Sinkler's MS for violin and keyboard)
Skene	*GB-En* Adv. MS 5-2-15
Stobaeus	*GB-Lbl* MS Sloane 1021
Stowe 389	*GB-Lbl* MS Stowe 389
Straloch	Robert Gordon of Straloch's lute book (lost)
Straloch/Graham copy	*GB-En* MS Adv. 5.2.18
Swan	St Petersburg, Biblioteka Akademii Nauk, MS O No. 124
Tabley	Tabley House, Knutsford, Cheshire (Tabley Lute MS)
Thistlethwaite	*GB-Eu* MS Dc.5.125
Thysius	*NL-Lt* in Bibliotheek der Rijksuniversiteit, MS 1666
Trumbull	*GB-Cu* Add. 8844 (*olim* Reading, Berkshire Record Office, Trumbull Add. MS 6)
Ulm 132	*D-Us* Schermar Collection, MS 132
Vm⁷ 6211	*F-Pn* MS Vm⁷ 6211
Welde	Willey Park, Shropshire, Lord Forester's private collection
Werl	*GB-Lam* The Robert Spencer Collection (Albrecht Werl's lute book)
Wemyss	*GB-En* Sutherland papers, Dep. 314 no. 23 (Lady Margaret Wemyss lute book)
Wickhambrook	*US-NH* Special Collections MS Ma.21.W.623
Willoughby	*GB-NO* MS Mi LM 16
Wilson	*GB-Ob* MS Mus. Sch. b. 1 (John Wilson autograph songbook)

Libraries

France

F-Pcrs	Paris, Bibliothèque du Centre National de la Recherche Scientifique
F-Pn	Paris, Bibliothèque Nationale de France

Germany

D-Bsb	Berlin, Staatsbibliothek zu Berlin—Preußischer Kulturbesitz
D-Hs	Hamburg, Staats- und Universitätsbibliothek
D-Kl	Kassel, Landesbibliothek
D-Mbs	Munich, Bayerische Staatsbibliothek
D-ROu	Rostock, Universitätsbibliothek
D-Sl	Stuttgart, Württembergische Landesbibliothek
D-Us	Ulm, Stadtbibliothek
D-W	Wolfenbuttel, Herzog August Bibliothek

Great Britain

GB-AB	Aberystwyth, National Library of Wales
GB-Cfm	Cambridge, Fitzwilliam Museum
GB-Ckc	Cambridge, Rowe Music Library, King's College
GB-Cmc	Cambridge, Magdalene College
GB-Cu	Cambridge, University Library
GB-Ctc	Cambridge, Trinity College
GB-En	Edinburgh, National Library of Scotland
GB-Eu	Edinburgh, University Library
GB-Ge	Glasgow, Euing Music Library
GB-HAdolmetsch	Haslemere, Dolmetsch private collection
GB-Lam	London, Royal Academy of Music
GB-Lbl	London, British Library, Reference Division
GB-Lcm	London, Royal College of Music
GB-Lgc	London, Gresham College (Guildhall Library)
GB-Lwa	London, Library of the Dean and Chapter of Westminster Abbey
GB-Mr	Manchester, John Rylands Library
GB-NO	Nottingham, University Library
GB-Ob	Oxford, Bodleian Library
GB-Och	Oxford, Christ Church Library

Ireland

EIRE-Dm	Dublin, Marsh's Library
EIRE-Dtc	Dublin, Trinity College

Italy

I-Bu	Bologna, Biblioteca Universitaria
I-PESo	Pesaro, Biblioteca Oliveriana

Japan

J-Tn	Tokyo, Music Library, Ohki private collection

Lithuania

LT-Va	Vilnius, Central Library of the Lithuanian Academy of Science

The Netherlands

NL-Lt	Leiden, Bibliotheca Thysiana
NL-Uu	Utrecht, Bibliotheek der Rijksuniversiteit

Poland

PL-Kj	Kraków, Biblioteka Jagiellońska
PL-Pu	Poznań, Biblioteka Uniwersytecka

Spain

E-E	El Escorial, Real Monasterio de S. Lorenzo

Switzerland

CH-Bmi	Basle, Musikwissenschaftliches Institut der Universität

United States of America

US-CA	Cambridge, Harvard University Music Libraries
US-Cn	Chicago, Newberry Library
US-NH	Yale University, School of Music Library
US-NYp	New York, Public Library at Lincoln Center, Library and Museum of the Performing Arts
US-R	Rochester, Eastman School of Music, Sibley Library
US-Wc	Washington, DC, Library of Congress Music Division
US-Ws	Washington, DC, Folger Shakespeare Library

Bibliographical

Biographical Dictionary	Andrew Ashbee and David Lasocki, assisted by Peter Holman and Fiona Kisby, *A Biographical Dictionary of English Court Musicians 1485–1714*, 2 vols. (Aldershot, 1998)
CMM	Corpus mensurabilis musicae
DNB	*Dictionary of National Biography*
EETS	Early English Text Society
EETS/ES	Early English Text Society/Extra Series
EETS/OS	Early English Text Society/Original Series
EM	*Early Music*
FoMRHI	*Fellowship of Makers and Researchers of Historical Instruments*
Grove Instruments	*The New Grove Dictionary of Musical Instruments*, ed. Stanley Sadie, 3 vols. (London, 1984)
GSJ	*Galpin Society Journal*
JAMS	*Journal of the American Musicological Society*
JLSA	*Journal of the Lute Society of America*
LS	Lute Society
LSJ	*Lute Society Journal*, also *The Lute*
MB	Musica Britannica
M&L	*Music and Letters*
MED	*Middle English Dictionary*, ed. Hans Kurath, 10 vols. (Ann Arbor, 1954–)
New Grove	*The New Grove Dictionary of Music and Musicians*, ed. Stanley Sadie, 20 vols. (London, 1980)
PMA	*Proceedings of the Musical Association*
PRMA	*Proceedings of the Royal Musical Association*
PRO	Public Record Office
RECM	Andrew Ashbee, *Records of English Court Music*, 9 vols. (Snodland, 1986–)
RISM	Répertoire International des Sources Musicales
RMARC	*The Royal Musical Association Research Chronicle*

Chapter One

Introduction

Contrary to popular belief, the lute was never the natural instrument of the troubadour or trouvère. It does not feature in French or English iconography or literature before the thirteenth century. This introduction traces the appearance of the lute before its arrival in northern Europe. It serves to differentiate, at an early stage, the lute from other popular plucked instruments like the gittern and citole. It is intended to do no more than lay down some general markers on the early history of the lute, a huge subject quite outside the scope of this book.

Plucked string instruments with long thin necks and relatively small bodies are thought to be of considerably greater antiquity than those with short necks.[1] Long-necked lutes are found depicted on Mesopotamian seals dating as far back as the period 2340–2198 BC, and appear in ancient Egyptian iconography.[2] Such ancient long-necked lutes have modern-day descendants in the Turkish saz, the Indian tambura, the Pakistani tanbur, and in many Islamic, African, and Central Asian folk instruments.[3] Short-necked lutes were known in Egyptian times and in classical antiquity. One of the most successful and long-lasting short-necked lutes is the Arabic ʿūd. The exact origins of the ʿūd are remote and undocumented, but it has been suggested that it was developed by the Arabs from the Persian barbat during the seventh to ninth centuries, into a form still recognizable as the ʿūd today.[4] The pre-Islamic Arab lute had a tapering neck and a small body covered in skin.[5] Laurence Picken has suggested that this instrument, in turn, had its origins in the short-necked lute known to the Central Asian Turco-Mongols of the first-century kingdom of Kusanas.[6]

The medieval European lute is closely related to the Arabic ʿūd, indeed the name 'lute' is said to have been derived from the Arabic 'al ʿūd'. The word ʿūd simply means 'wood', the material from which the instrument is made. Many instruments were made of wood. The name ʿūd may have come about through a need to highlight the instrument's wooden soundboard, so as to distingush it from instruments

---

[1] Diana Poulton, 'The Early History of the Lute', *JLSA* 20–1 (1987–8), 1–21 at 1.

[2] Harvey Turnbull, 'The Origin of the Long-Necked Lute', *GSJ* 25 (1972), 58–66 at 59–60.

[3] Jean L. Jenkins, *Musical Instruments* (Horniman Museum and Library Publication; London, 1970), 73–4.

[4] Henry G. Farmer, 'The Origin of the Arabian Lute and Rebec', *Studies in Oriental Musical Instruments* (London, 1931), 95–6.

[5] Jenkins, *Musical Instruments*, 74.

[6] Laurence Picken, 'The Origin of the Short Lute', *GSJ* 8 (1955), 32–42 at 40.

with fronts made of skin, parchment, or any other material. The centuries after the rise of Islam (c.670) saw a cultivation of the ʿūd by the Arabs, such that by the tenth century it had inspired long treatises covering tunings, technique, and musical theory.[7] Much work was done by Henry Farmer in the inter-war years on the early Arabic ʿūd, its origins, and introduction into Europe.[8] Though the subject remains little understood, there has been a recent revival of interest in the area.[9]

A variety of plucked-instrument types which have features in common with the lute can be found in medieval European iconographical sources from the ninth to the twelfth century. Examples are in the Utrecht Psalter, Stuttgart Psalter, and Beatus Apocalypse MSS.[10] However, as Emanuel Winternitz suggested, their ancestry may be connected to the classical kithara, and their descendants are more likely to have been the medieval citole and later the Renaissance cittern than any type of lute.[11] These instruments usually have slender bodies which taper to a bulbous pegbox. The ʿūd, by contrast, appears in medieval iconography of the thirteenth century as a distinctly larger instrument, with a plump round body, and a bent-back pegbox.[12]

The earliest known ʿūd player in Europe was Ziryāb, a virtuoso player from Baghdad, whose real name was Abu ʾl-Hasan ʿAlī ibn Nāfiʿ. He crossed into Al-Andaluz in 821, and entered the service of ʿAbd al-Raḥmān II (822–52), the Caliph of Córdoba. Ziryāb's fame preceded him, and the Caliph is said to have ridden out of Córdoba to welcome the musician personally, and paid him 40,000 pieces of gold annually.[13] Moorish power in the Iberian Peninsula gradually declined from its zenith in the tenth century to the final expulsion in 1492 of the Moors from Granada, their last remaining stronghold. During this time Christian courts grew in power and absorbed Moorish lands. Much Arabic influence remained, not least in the music and instruments at the expanding Christian courts.[14]

The famous miniatures in the *Cantigas de Santa Maria* (c.1260) of Alfonso el Sabio, King of Castile and Leon (1221–84), depict a great variety of instruments

[7] Farmer, 'The Origin of the Arabian Lute and Rebec', 88. See also id., 'The Influence of Music: From Arabic Sources', *PMA* 52 (1925–6), 89–124.

[8] Curtis Bouterse, 'Reconstructing the Medieval Arabic Lute: A Reconsideration of Farmer's "Structure of the Arabic and Persian Lute"', *GSJ* 32 (1979), 2–9.

[9] For recent writings on the subject see Monika Burzik, *Quellenstudien zu europäischen Zupfinstrumentenformen* (Kassel, 1995), and Eckhard Neubauer, 'Der Bau der Laute und ihre Besaitung nach arabischen, persischen und türkischen Quellen des 9. bis 15. Jahrhunderts', *Zeitschrift für Geschichte der arabisch-islamischen Wissenschaften*, 8 (1993), 259–378.

[10] *NL-Uu* 32, Pss. 43, 71, 92, 150; *D-Sl*, Bibl. fol. 23, fo. 125ʳ; *GB-Mr* Lat. 8, fo. 89ʳ.

[11] Emanuel Winternitz, *Musical Instruments and their Symbolism in Western Art* (London, 1967), 57–65.

[12] For three drawings taken from 12th- and 13th-c. iconography, see Bouterse, 'Reconstructing the Medieval Arabic Lute', 3.

[13] Henry G. Farmer, *A History of Arabian Music to the XIIIth Century* (London, 1929), 128–30.

[14] Higinio Anglés, *Historia de la música medieval en Navarra* (Pamplona, 1970), 341–54.

played by both Moorish and Christian musicians.[15] Two of the pictures show large-bodied instruments with large bridges and several sound holes. These instruments are recognizable as the ʿūd in a form not far removed from that seen today in Arab countries (see Pl. 1.1). In one of these miniatures the ʿūd is played together with a rebab, which also is seen in a form little altered from that still found today in parts of the Arab world.[16] In the other miniature, two ʿūds are seen together; one is played, and the other held while its owner listens.[17]

The Arabic origin of both the ʿūd and rebab may account for their joint depiction, and these two instruments may have formed a common ensemble. The ʿūd in this miniature is so large that its near-circular front almost completely obscures the player's chest, and the neck extends outside the frame of the picture (Pl. 1.1(*a*)). Nine pegs are depicted, suggesting a five-course instrument with a single top or bottom string, and with the remaining strings grouped in octave or unison pairs. It is plucked by a plectrum held in the right hand. The player's right arm cradles the instrument from below, and thus supports it.

In the second miniature one ʿūd has eight pegs, and the other twelve (Pl. 1.1(*b*)). There is probably some confusion in these depictions. On both instruments the pegs are not equally distributed on either side of the pegboxes, nor do their numbers tally with the number of strings. On one of the instruments the nine strings that appear are clearly grouped into four pairs with a single string on the bass. According to the ninth-century theorists, the ʿūd had four strings corresponding to the four humours of the body. From top to bottom the strings were coloured: yellow for bile; red for blood; white for phlegm; black for melancholy. Ziryāb's contribution was to add a fifth string, also red, symbolizing the soul, which he introduced between the second and third.[18] It would appear from the Cantigas miniatures that both four- and five-course ʿūds were known in thirteenth-century Spain, and that courses were normally paired rather than single. Unfortunately, the miniatures tell us nothing about the backs of the ʿūds. All surviving old lutes and ʿūds have backs constructed by gluing separate ribs together to form a curved shell. Arab manuscripts from as early as the tenth century show that a ribbed construction was the norm.[19] We must suppose that the early European ʿūds, as depicted in the Cantigas miniatures, also had a ribbed back, but we cannot be sure.

---

[15] For a facsimile of the original, *E-E* b.I.2, with a critical edition of music and text see Higinio Anglés, *La música de las Cantigas de Santa María del Rey Alfonso el Sabio*, 3 vols. (Barcelona, 1943–59). For a study of *E-E* t.I.1 with reproductions of the miniatures see José Guerrero Lovillo, *Las Cántigas: estudio arqueológico de sus miniaturas* (Madrid, 1949).

[16] *E-E* b.I.2., fo. 162ʳ.

[17] Ibid., fo. 54ʳ.

[18] Julián Ribera y Tarragó, *La música de las Cantigas, estudio sobre su origen y naturaleza* (Madrid, 1922); trans. Eleanor Hague and Marion Leffingwell in *Music in Ancient Arabia and Spain* (Stanford, 1929; repr. New York, 1970), 103.

[19] Bouterse, 'Reconstructing the Medieval Arabic Lute', 3.

PL. 1.1. Miniatures from the
Cantigas de Santa Maria (*c.*1260): (a)
rebab and ʿūd; (b) two ʿūds; (c) two
gitterns; (d) fiddle and citole; (e) citole
and oval-bodied lute. El Escorial, Real
Monasterio de S. Lorenzo, MS b.1.2.
Copyright Patrimonio Nacional

Two other important plucked instruments that appear in the Cantigas miniatures are the gittern and citole. Laurence Wright has conclusively shown that the term 'gittern' should be applied to the small plucked instrument with a rounded back and sickle-shaped pegbox.[20] The gittern is shown in the Cantigas miniatures with a body which merges into the neck (suggesting a single-piece carved construction), leading to a sickle-shaped pegbox terminating in a bulbous crest or carved head (Pl. 1.1(c)).[21] Like the ʿūd, the gittern is of Arabic origin.[22] It is fortunate that a mid-fifteenth-century gittern by Hans Ott has survived.[23] Ott was active in Nuremberg from 1434 to 1463, during which time the instrument was probably produced (Pls. 1.2, 1.3). It seems that by the mid-fourteenth century the lute and gittern were an extablished ensemble in Italy.[24]

According to Wright the term 'citole' should be applied to the instrument that Winternitz has identified as having its origin in the classical lyre or kithara, and its descendant in the Renaissance cittern.[25] This instrument would appear to have been carved from a solid piece of wood, and is depicted in medieval iconography in several shapes. One such shape has been likened to a holly-leaf. Winternitz has suggested that the 'wings' of the holly-leaf shape developed from the kithara's yoke, and that they persist in a vestigial form on the cittern. The citole is depicted in three Cantigas illustrations. In the picture of King Alfonso with his court, two citole players appear on one side opposite two fiddle players on the other.[26] In a later miniature the combination of fiddle and citole reappears (Pl. 1.1(d)), and in a further depiction the citole is played alongside an instrument with an oval belly, a sickle-shaped pegbox, and a neck that is thin and quite long relative to the body length (Pl. 1.1(e)).[27]

The citole's period of most common use in Europe was from 1200 to 1350.[28] Unlike the lute and gittern, it is not thought to be of Arabic origin, although it was popular in fourteenth-century Spain. We are fortunate that a magnificently carved English citole survives. According to Mary Remnant it should be dated c.1300–40.[29] This instrument was altered to carry a violin neck and strings at a later stage, but its original body form is intact. Both the surviving gittern and citole have carved

[20] Laurence Wright, 'The Medieval Gittern and Citole: A Case of Mistaken Identity', *GSJ* 30 (1977), 8–42.

[21] *E-E* b.I.2, fo. 104ʳ.　　　　　　　　　　[22] Wright, 'The Medieval Gittern and Citole', 11.

[23] For a description and photograph see Friedemann Hellwig, 'Lute-Making in the Late 15th and the 16th Century', *LSJ* 16 (1974), 24–38. The instrument today forms part of the Wartburg Stiftung, Eisenach (Cat. no. KH 50).

[24] Howard Mayer Brown, 'St Augustine, Lady Music, and the Gittern in Fourteenth-Century Italy', *Musica disciplina*, 38 (1984), 25–65 at 43.

[25] Wright, 'The Medieval Gittern and Citole', 23; Winternitz, *Musical Instruments*, 57–65.

[26] *E-E* b.I.2, fo. 29ʳ.　　　　　　　　　　[27] Ibid., fos. 39ʳ, 147ʳ.

[28] Wright, 'The Medieval Gittern and Citole', 24.

[29] Remnant calls this citole 'the Warwick gittern'. Mary Remnant, 'The Gittern in English Medieval Art', *GSJ* 18 (1965), 104–9; Mary Remnant and Richard Marks, 'A Medieval Gittern', in *Music and Civilization: The British Museum Yearbook*, 4 (1980), 83–134 at 101.

PL. 1.3. Detail of the rose of the Hans Ott gittern

PL. 1.2. The Hans Ott gittern. Wartburg Stiftung, Eisenach (Cat. no. KH 50)

backs. This feature, which we must assume to be the norm for gitterns, citoles, and many other medieval stringed instruments, sets them apart from the ʿūd and lute of ribbed construction. That no medieval lute survives may be due to the fragility of ribbed construction, and the instability of glue in the often cold and wet conditions of Europe.

The oval-bellied, long-necked lutes appear elsewhere in the Cantigas miniatures[30] and in other iconography of the period. They may have a variety of belly shapes and pegbox constructions, but all have long necks. Such instruments no doubt developed from the ancient Mesopotamian instruments mentioned at the outset, which have plentiful modern descendants in Arabic and Asian countries. It is also possible that such long-necked lutes were known in fourteenth-century

---

[30] *E-E* b.1.2, fos. 125ʳ, 140ᵛ, 147ʳ.

France as the 'guiterne moresche'.[31] Long-necked instruments, while maintaining a presence in southern Europe, seem never to have been popular in the north.

Other instruments besides the ʿūd and gittern were also successfully introduced to Europe via the Arab world from the twelfth to the fourteenth century. The shawm, another import from north Africa, had, by the beginning of the fifteenth century, become the basis for the dance-band ensemble of loud or 'haut' instruments found throughout Europe. The nakers were similarly successful as percussion instruments. These instruments of Arabic origin immensely enriched the stock of instrumental colours and techniques open to medieval musicians. Once introduced they were adapted in response to the rise of polyphonic music in the later Middle Ages. By the fourteenth century lutes in central and northern Europe were clearly different from the ʿūds seen in thirteenth-century Spanish iconography.

[31] Wright, 'The Medieval Gittern and Citole', 10–11. The Spanish term occurs in a poem of *c*.1330 by Juan Ruiz, where the Moorish gittern is differentiated from the Latin gittern. Guillaume de Machaut's two poems 'La Prise d'Alexandrie' and 'Remède de Fortune' mention the 'morache', probably the long-necked lute by another name.

Chapter Two

The Lute in England before 1500

Quod Resoun: 'In age of .xx. yeer
Goo to oxenford, or lerne lawe.'
Quod Lust: 'harpe and giterne there may y leere,
And pickid staffe therewith to plawe,
At tauerne to make wommen myrie cheere,
And wilde felawis to-gidere drawe.'

From *The Mirror of the Periods of Man's Life*
(*c*.1450)[1]

No actual lute music from Britain survives before the earliest sixteenth-century tablatures. We must rely on literary and iconographical evidence to build a picture of lute practice in the medieval period. This chapter surveys what material there is. Conclusions are few and questions are many.

There is no trace of the lute or gittern in Britain before 1285. Certainly these instruments were largely unknown, or at best insignificant, before the fourteenth century. They may have been introduced directly from Spain: the medieval English court had good contacts with those of Spain, and Plantagenet kings often intermarried with the northern Spanish to bolster themselves against the French. Richard I, the son of Henry II and Eleanor of Aquitaine, married Berengaria, daughter of Sancho VI of Navarre, in 1191. Another of Henry II's offspring, his daughter Eleanor, married Alfonso VIII of Castile in 1169. Perhaps more important was the unusually happy marriage of Edward I to Eleanor, sister of Alfonso X of Castile in 1254. This Alfonso was the king for whom the Cantigas manuscripts were compiled. Indeed it may be more than coincidence that it was during Edward's reign that the lute is first mentioned in England. Alternatively, the instrument may have been introduced via France. The terms 'leüt' or 'leüz' appear in the French language around 1270.[2] Many of the English aristocracy had extensive lands and connections in France, and many did not begin to speak English as their first language or think of themselves as primarily English until the thirteenth century. French was the language at court until the late fourteenth century. Once established in France,

---

[1] Lust: worldly pleasure; leere: learn; pickid: pointed; plawe: play. From *Hymns to the Virgin and Christ*, ed. Frederick J. Furnival (EETS/OS, 24; London, 1867), 61, ll. 89–94. See Christopher Page, 'String-Instrument Making in Medieval England and Some Oxford Harpmakers 1380–1466', *GSJ* 31 (1978), 44–67 at 51.

[2] Wright, 'The Medieval Gittern and Citole', 10.

new fashions, like the cultivation of novel instruments, would have quickly become known in England.

Apart from a mutilated twelfth-century church sculpture from the monastery of Cluny which may include a lute, the oldest iconographical evidence for the lute in France dates from the thirteenth century.[3] A six-string lute appears in a manuscript of the *Roman de Troie* by Benoist de Sainte-More. Here the lute is being played with the fingers.[4] Another thirteenth-century lute appears in the stained-glass windows of the monastery church at Bon-Port in Normandy.[5]

The best-known early literary reference to the lute in French occurs in the continuation by Guillaume de Lorris of the *Roman de la Rose* written by Jehan de Meung. The original has been dated *c.*1240, but the continuation is some years later. Guillaume de Lorris mentions:

> Et fet ses estrumanz soner
> qu'en ni oïst pas Dieu toner
> qu'il an a de trop de manieres;
> e plus an a les mains manieres
> c'onques n'ot Amphion de Thebes:
> harpes a, gigues e rubebes,
> si ra quitarres e leüz
> por soi deporter elleüz;[6]

In the somewhat later romance *Cleomadès* of *c.*1285, the trouvère poet Adenet le Roy includes the lines: 'Harpes et gigues et canons, Leüs rubebes et kitaires.'[7]

In French inventories, royal accounts, poems, pictures, and carvings, lutes appear with increasing frequency, indicating that during the fourteenth century they became accepted instruments for royal minstrels, amateurs, and lower-status itinerant musicians.[8] Clearly the lute did become reasonably well known in France in the last decades of the thirteenth century. There is good information, outlined below, to show that it had been successfully introduced into England by the first decades of the fourteenth century.

In 1306 one 'Janin Le Lutour', was among the 180 minstrels who attended a great feast at Westminster Hall (see Pl. 2.1).[9] The feast took place on Sunday 22 May,

[3] Michel Brenet (Marie Bobillier), 'Notes sur l'histoire du luth en France', *Rivista musicale italiana*, 5 (1898), 6 (1899); repr. (Geneva, 1973), 3.

[4] An engraving appears in Eugène-Emmanuel Viollet-le-Duc, *Dictionnaire raisonné du mobilier français*, 6 vols. (Paris, 1858–75), ii. 277.

[5] Henri-Marie F. Lavoix, *Histoire de l'instrumentation depuis le seizième siècle jusqu'à nos jours* (Paris, 1878), 61.

[6] Félix Lecoy (ed.), *Le Roman de la Rose*, 3 vols (Paris, 1965–70), iii, 131, ll. 20995–1002.

[7] Adenet le Roy, *Cleomadès*, ed. A. Van Hasselt (Brussels, 1865–6), ll. 17274–5. See Wright, 'The Medieval Gittern and Citole', 38, for a more substantial quotation.

[8] For references to lutes and lutenists in 14th-c. France see Lionel de La Laurencie, *Les Luthistes* (Paris, 1928), 9.

[9] Constance Bullock-Davies, *Menestrellorum multitudo: Minstrels at a Royal Feast* (Cardiff, 1978).

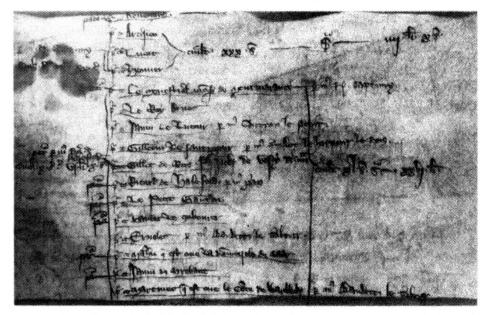

PL. 2.1. Westminster Festival Roll (PRO E101/369/6), showing payment to 'Janin le Lutour'

after a ceremony in which Prince Edward (later Edward II), who had been knighted
himself earlier that day by the king and granted the Duchy of Aquitaine, went on
to dub some 300 aspirant knights. These men had been lured to London by a royal
proclamation that all who wished to receive knighthood 'should come to London
this side of Whitsunday next to receive the necessary equipment from the King's
Wardrobe and at his gift, so that they might receive knighthood from him on the
same day'.[10] Edward I had an ulterior motive in this seemingly magnanimous ges-
ture. John Comyn, one of Edward's 'counsellers' of Scotland, had recently been
murdered. Edward wished to raise and equip a large force of knights, whose ranks
had been seriously depleted in previous campaigns. With this force he hoped to
avenge the murder of Comyn and suppress the rebellion of Robert Bruce, the man
responsible. According to accounts of the period, the minstrels entered the great
feast carrying a pair of swans draped in green silk, in front of which the knights were
encouraged to take vows, swearing to perform deeds of honour in the forthcoming
Scots campaign.[11] Most numerous among the musicians present were twenty-six
harpers, followed in numerical strength by nineteen trumpeters, thirteen vielle
players, and nine crowders.[12] The presence of both a single lutenist and a single git-

---

[10] Constance Bullock-Davies, *Menestrellorum multitudo: Minstrels at a Royal Feast* (Cardiff, 1978), p. xv.

[11] Ibid., p. xxxiii.   [12] Ibid. 10.

ternist must indicate their relative novelty at this time. All the minstrels were attached to various aristocratic households.

The lute player, 'Janin Le Lutour', was among the king's minstrels, and is the earliest lute player in England whose career can be traced. He first appears in royal accounts in 1285 as 'Johann Le Leutour'. He is listed among the Prince of Wales's minstrels for the years 1295–1303, and thereafter remained in royal service until Edward I's death in 1307. Janin was a most favoured minstrel. He was exempt from all taxes and burdens, and received the wages of a squire within the royal household (that is 7*d.* a day, instead of 4½*d.* like most other minstrels). He also received considerable sums in the form of 'largesse' on important festivals. At the great feast in 1306 he received 40*s.*[13] He travelled widely in the service of the king, and had a close association with the earls of Lancaster and Lincoln. In 1300 and 1305, for instance, he journeyed to France in the company of the earl of Lincoln. By 1307, when he disappears from Wardrobe accounts, no doubt to retire from service on the death of his royal patron, he was a man of considerable standing and substance.[14] His conspicuous success may have done much to establish the acceptability of the lute among the minstrelsy of England.

With the exception of the reigns of Richard II, Henry VI, Edward IV, and Richard III, there was, among the royal minstrels, at least one member specified as a lute player at some point in every reign during the period 1295–1509.[15] Many minstrels had no specific instrumental appellation, but certainly played one and possibly several instruments. It may be that the lute featured among the instruments played by royal minstrels without specific designation. Lute-playing minstrels normally appear among the king's household in this period. This contrasts with psaltery players, who seem to have been considered more suitable for a queen's entertainment. A psaltery player appears regularly in the lists of minstrels of the queen's household in this period.[16]

The year 1306 is also the earliest date for the appearance in royal household accounts of a minstrel designated 'Le Gitarer'. Certainly the lute and gittern entered the list of instruments used by royal minstrels at around the same time.[17] Gittern players among royal minstrels are last heard of in the period 1413–22 during the reign of Henry V, when one, 'Hans', was employed in that capacity.[18] (See Table 2.1.) The citole, by comparison, is first heard of as early as 1269, but is last

[13] The payroll in which this is noted is PRO E101/369/6.

[14] Bullock-Davies, *Menestrellorum multitudo*, 113–15.

[15] Richard Rastall, 'The Minstrels of the English Royal Households, 25 Edward I–1 Henry VIII: An Inventory', *RMARC* 4 (1964), 1–41.

[16] Richard Rastall, 'Some English Consort-Groupings of the Late Middle Ages', *M&L* 55 (1974), 179–202 at 184.

[17] Bullock-Davies, *Menestrellorum multitudo*, 94. The gitternist named was 'Peter', who was one of the Prince of Wales's household in 1306.

[18] Rastall, 'The Minstrels of the English Royal Households', 28.

Table 2.1. *English royal minstrels designated as lute or gittern players*

Monarch	Player	Date
Edward I	Janin (lute)[a]	1303–7
	Peter (gittern player to Prince of Wales)	1306
Edward II	Peter (lute)	1311
	Berdric (lute)	1311
	Dominic (gittern player to the queen)	1316
Edward III	John (lute)	1329–30
	Richard Bottore (gittern)	1331–41
Henry IV	William (lute)	1406–7
Henry V	William (lute)[b]	1414
	Hans (gittern)	1414
Henry VII	Guilliam (lute)[c]	1499
	Giles	1502–9
	Kennar (lute)[d]	1503
	Watt	1504

Note: There is no mention of lute or gittern players for the reigns of Richard II, Henry VI, Edward IV, or Richard III.

SOURCE: Rastall, 'The Minstrels of the English Royal Households'.

[a] Also luter to Edward, Prince of Wales, 1295–1303.

[b] Probably the same William who served Henry IV.

[c] Also in the household of Prince Arthur.

[d] Also in the household of Princess Margaret.

mentioned in 1361/2.[19] A certain 'Janyn Le Citoler' performed at Edward I's great feast, receiving one mark. Two citole players, Thomas Dynys and Ivo Vala (also referred to as Jiron or Yorri), were long-serving minstrels to both Edward II and Edward III. There are many English carvings and manuscript depictions of the citole from the period 1260–1360, but they are markedly less frequent after this period.[20] During the early fourteenth century the well-established citole was eclipsed in popularity by the newly introduced lute and gittern.

[19] Wright, 'The Medieval Gittern and Citole', 24. The 1269 reference is in *MED*; the 1361/2 one in Rastall, 'The Minstrels of the English Royal Household', 17.

[20] The many citoles in the Walter de Milmete MSS of 1326/7 are indicative of its popularity. For example, *GB-Lbl* Add. MS 47680 contains two pictures of citoles (fos. 9ᵛ and 16ᵛ). For citole iconography, see Remnant and Marks, 'A Medieval Gittern', pls. 54, 56–60, 63, 68–9, and 71.

The players of the lute, gittern, and citole appear in Royal Wardrobe accounts in a non-specific section of instrumental minstrels in the company of bagpipers, organists, and players of the flute, hornpipe, psaltery, fiddle, and cornemuse. Other more numerous and better established classes of minstrels were grouped by instrument. Such were the trumpeters, nakerers, taborers, harpers, violists, and gigatores (players of bowed string instruments), together with the non-instrumental 'kings of minstrels', vigilatores (night-watchmen, some of whom may also have played instruments), waferers (those who baked special wafers which were served after a meal with a sweet wine called hippocras), and falconers.[21] The king's trumpeters were of special symbolic importance, as they were held to reflect his majesty. They announced the king's presence, specific times of day, and his whereabouts when on the move.

England had long been famed for her harpers. They were appreciated at the Spanish courts, where a number of their names are mentioned in court accounts.[22] Until the late fifteenth century the harp was the most favoured courtly instrument, after which time the lute took its position of pre-eminence.[23] Harpers had a special role as guardians of oral history. Many were blind. They maintained a centuries-old tradition of singing and playing 'gestes', both traditional and in honour of their patrons and their forebears.[24] Edward I and Edward II employed many harpers: up to three at any one time. Edward II styled two of his harpers 'Master', and another became a minstrel-king as *Roy de North*.[25] The custom of maintaining royal harpers continued up to the death, in 1565, of blind William More, harper to Henry VIII.[26] In theory this tradition continued, though with some gaps, until the nineteenth century. As late as the reign of George IV the Crown employed a harpist. The last holder of the title, Edward Jones, was something of an antiquarian, and at one time owned the Herbert lute MS.[27]

Fourteenth-century references to lutes and lute players in documents that do not relate to the royal court are relatively rare, but they do occur. Christopher Page has drawn attention to the mention of one John 'le luter' in a subsidy roll of 1319.[28] He was probably a merchant, and in a document of 1344/5 is styled as 'de Aconia'. Page suggests that this reference to Acre, the crusading port in the Holy Land, may link him to the making or importing of lutes, which at this time were still similar in

[21] Rastall, 'The Minstrels of the English Royal Households', 1–4.

[22] Anglés, *Historia de la música medieval en Navarra*, 379–82.

[23] Rastall, 'Some English Consort-Groupings', 183.

[24] John Southworth, *The English Medieval Minstrel* (Woodbridge, 1989), 87–101.

[25] Rastall, 'Some English Consort-Groupings', 183.

[26] Peter Holman, 'The Harp in Stuart England: New Light on William Lawes's Harp Consorts', *EM* 15 (1987), 188–203 at 188.

[27] Thurston Dart, 'Lord Herbert of Cherbury's Lute Book', *M&L* 38 (1957), 136–54 at 136.

[28] Page, 'String-Instrument Making', 48, from B. O. E. Ekwall, *Two Early London Subsidy Rolls* (Lund, 1951), 301.

many respects to the Arabic ʿūd from which they had developed. The hosteller's accounts for Durham Priory 1361–2 refer to a payment to a lutenist and his wife: 'In uno viro ludenti in uno loyt et uxori ejus cantanti apud Bewrpayr, 2s' ('To a man playing the lute and his wife singing at Bewrpayr [probably Bear Park in Durham, known as Beaurepayre in 1267]).[29] Galpin suggests that this lutenist could be 'John Mumford', royal minstrel to Richard II.[30]

Evidence of more widespread ownership of lutes and gitterns in England is apparent around 1400. In 1381 three men, John Swetenham, William Garlthorp, and John Pycard, were committed to prison for making a disturbance with 'giternes'.[31] The association of gitterns with taverns and unruly behaviour was well established, not only in England, but also in France, where legal prosecutions resulted with some frequency.[32] The will dated 1404/5 of John Bount, a Somerset landowner with property in Bristol, lists a 'great harp' and a gittern with a woman's face ('quinternam . . . cum facie damisell'), which was presumably carved at the end of the pegbox.[33] The will of Robert Wolvedon, treasurer of the Church of York, proved in 1432, lists 'iiij li., unum claivicimbalum et j lute' ('a claivicembalum and a lute together valued at £4').[34] It is likely that the infrequent mention of instruments such as the lute and gittern in wills of the period is because they were not of sufficient value to be listed, unless they were of unusually high quality or specially featured like the gittern with a carved head mentioned above. A somewhat later example of a lute's value is provided by an inventory of the possessions of William Braggs, an Oxford Master of Arts. In 1468 Braggs owned a lute priced at 10*d*. This was a small sum even then.[35]

It is in the late fourteenth century that the lute and gittern first appear in Middle English literature. In William Langland's 'The Vision of Piers Plowman' (*c*.1362–99), 'Love' sings to the lute in the lines:

> Truthe trumpede tho and song *Te Deum laudamus*;
> And thanne lutede Love in a loud note,
> '*Ecce quam bonum et quam iocundum &c*'.[36]

---

[29] *Account Rolls of Durham Priory*, ed. J. T. Fowler (Surtees Society, 99; 1898), 127. My thanks to Bonnie Blackburn for the translation and suggested identification of the place.

[30] Francis W. Galpin, *Old English Instruments of Music* (London, 1910) 42; Jeffrey Pulver, *A Dictionary of Old English Music and Musical Instruments* (London, 1923), 132.

[31] *MED* iv. 137.

[32] Wright, 'The Medieval Gittern and Citole', 14–15.

[33] Christopher Page, 'The 15th-Century Lute: New and Neglected Sources', *EM* 9 (1981), 11–21 at 19; from *Somerset Medieval Wills 1383–1500*, ed. F. W. Weaver (Somerset Record Society, 16; 1901), 11–14.

[34] Page, 'The 15th-Century Lute', 20; from *Testamenta Eboracensia*, ed. J. Raine (Surtees Society, 45; 1936), 91–2.

[35] Page, 'String-Instrument Making', 52; from *Registrum Cancellarii Oxoniensis, 1434–1469*, ed. H. E. Salter, 2 vols. (Oxford Historical Society, 93–4; 1932), ii. 326; also in A. B. Emden, *A Biographical Register of the University of Oxford to A.D. 1500* (Oxford, 1957), i. 247.

[36] William Langland, *The Vision of Piers Plowman: A Critical Edition of the B-Text*, ed. A. V. C. Schmidt (London, 1978), 234, Passus xviii, ll. 424–6.

Earlier in the same work Langland has 'Haukyn the Actif Man' remark that he, Haukyn, is a minstrel, although he:

> kan neither taboure ne trompe ne telle no gestes,
> Farten ne fithelen at festes, ne harpen,
> Jape ne jogele ne gentilliche pipe,
> Ne neither saille ne sautrie ne synge with the gyterne.[37]

This list of accomplishments that might be expected from a minstrel of the time confirms that singing to the gittern was common practice. The licentious associations of the gittern are evident in a Lollard tract of *c*.1393. It originated from the followers of Wyclif, and was aimed at the custom of friars playing instruments on holy days: '[they indulge in] veyn songis and knackynge and harpynge, gyternynge & daunsynge, & othere veyn triflis to geten the stynkyng loue of damyselis'.[38]

The theme of riotous behaviour and carousing with instruments present in the Lollard tract and the above-mentioned court case is echoed by Chaucer in *The Canterbury Tales*. The 'Pardoner's Tale' (*c*.1390) opens with a description of an idle and dissipated company of Flemish young folk who occupy their time in vice and ribaldry, riot and gambling, in stews and public-houses:

> Where as with harpes lutes and gyternes
> They daunce and pleyen at dees bothe day and nyght[39]

In 'The Miller's Tale', Nicholas, the fashionable and gallant Oxford student, keeps 'a gay sautrye' [psaltery] above his bed with which he sings and plays 'Angelus ad virginem'.[40] The parish clerk, Absolon, who is also young and foppish, but of a lower social status (he works a trade as a barber and clerk), plays the gittern and rebec/rebab. He could:

> And pleyen songes on a smal rubible
> Therto he song somtyme a loud quynyble
> And as wel koude he pleye on a gyterne
> In al the toun nas brewhous ne tauerne
> That he ne visited with his solas.[41]

Nicholas and Absolon are rivals for the love of the Miller's comely young wife. They epitomize the age-old 'town versus gown' conflict. Their contrasting characters are mirrored by their chosen instruments: the courtly psaltery sung privately at night, against the more raffish gittern so suitable for taverns and stews. The

[37] Ibid. 154, Passus xiii, ll. 230–3.

[38] 'Of the Leaven of Pharisees' (*c*.1383), in John Wyclif, *The English Works of Wyclif Hitherto Unprinted*, ed. F. D. Matthew (EETS/OS, 74; London, 1880), 9, quoted in Page, 'String-Instrument Making', 52.

[39] VI (C) 466–7. I have used *The Text of The Canterbury Tales, by Geoffrey Chaucer*, ed. John M. Manly and Edith Rickert, 8 vols. (Chicago, 1940).

[40] I (A) 3213 16.   [41] I (A) 3331 5.

character of Absolon is comparable to that of Perkyn Revelour, the apprentice in 'The Cook's Tale', who loved dancing, dice, music, and wenches. He similarly could 'pleye on gyterne or ribible'.[42]

In the 'Manciple's Tale' the lute and gittern are listed among Phebus' instruments of minstrelsy. On being tricked by the crow into slaying his wife he destroys his instruments in his grief:

> For sorwe of which he brak his mynstralcye
> Bothe harpe and lute gyterne and sawtrye[43]

This suggests some versatility with string instruments. Royal minstrelsy is evoked in the 'Tale of Sir Topas' in the lines:

> Heere is the queen of fayerie
> With harp and lute and symphonye
> Dwelying in this place.[44]

The playing of instruments by Chaucer's Nicholas the scholar and Absolon the parish clerk would suggest that in later medieval Oxford instrumental skills were quite widespread among the students and younger members of the town society. There is some additional evidence of this. In 1438 Brasenose Hall owned an old harp and a broken lute.[45] A Sir W. Lydbery appears in a register kept by the Chancellory of the University. The inventory of his property lists 'a lewt price vi d'.[46] In the anonymous text *The Mirror or the Periods of Man's Life* (*c*.1450), quoted at the head of this chapter, the author reflects on the dissipated student life at Oxford and the Inns of Court.[47] We know the names of at least six Oxford harp makers during the period 1380–1466, indicating both a high level of musical activity and the popularity of the harp at this time.[48]

A more dignified picture of the use of the lute and gittern is painted in the works of John Lydgate. In *Reson and Sensuallyte* (*c*.1408) he describes a pleasure garden in which the gods honour Cupid with the sound of 'mynstalcye':

> And Instrumentys that dyde excelle,
> Many moo than I kan telle:
> Harpys, fythels, and eke rotys,
> Wel accordyng with her notys,

---

[42] I (A) 4396.   [43] IX (H) 267–8.

[44] VII *2004–6; 814–16. Some MS versions have pipe in place of lute.

[45] Page, 'String-Instrument Making', 52.   [46] Ibid.

[47] Is it possible that the 'pickid staffe' referred to in this text is a 'pricked stave', i.e. notated music? If so, this would be early evidence of some form of notation being used to learn music on the harp and gittern.

[48] Ibid. 46–8.

> Lutys, Rubibis, and geterns,
> More for estatys than taverns,
> Orgnys, cytolys, monacordys.[49]

Unusually, Lydgate employs the much exploited gittern/tavern rhyme to disassociate the two. He suggests instead that lutes, rebecs/rebabs, and gitterns are more suitable for noblemen's houses ('estatys') than taverns.

In *The Pilgrimage of the Life of Man* (*c*.1430), a translation of a poem by Guillaume de Deguileville, Lydgate reverts to tradition when presenting Miss Idleness, daughter of Dame Idleness. Miss Idleness teaches lovers to dance, play games such as chess and backgammon, and:

> To pleye on sondry Instrumentys,
> On harpe, lut, & on gyterne,
> And to revelle at taverne,[50]

The gittern is mentioned again in the same work in a description of music inspired by Pride:

> Ther ys harpë nor gyterne,
> Symphonyë, nouther crowde,
> Whan ye lyst to syngë lowde.[51]

A further moralizing text of the mid-fifteenth century, *Jacob's Well* (*c*.1450), speaks of the lute as an instrument of idleness. All manner of sports, dancing, going to wakes, and wrestling matches all result in idleness, as do playing the harp and lute.[52] In a final Lydgate reference the lute is mentioned in *A Kalendare*:

> For this holy daunce mynstralcy ys goode,
> Now, *Seynt Bruce*, helpe with thy sounded lute[53]

Lydgate's evocation of music, Cupid, and courtly love is pre-dated by a similar scene in John Gower's *Confessio Amantis* (*c*.1393), where, in a vision, a company of lovers appears with Cupid. They dance softly to low music, smiling, not laughing:

> With Harpe and Lute and with Citole.
> The hovedance and the Carole,
> In such a wise as love hath bede,
> A softe pas thei dance and trede;[54]

[49] John Lydgate, *Lydgate's Reson and Sensuallyte*, ed. Ernest Sieper (EETS/ES, 84; London, 1901), i. 146, ll. 5577–83.

[50] *The Pilgrimage of the Life of Man*, ed. Frederick J. Furnivall (EETS/ES, 83; London, 1901), part II, 316, ll. 11616–17.

[51] Ibid. 386, ll. 14264–7.

[52] *Jacob's Well*, ed. Arthur Brandeis (EETS/OS, 115; London, 1900), part I, 105, ll. 23–35.

[53] Lydgate, *The Minor Poems*, ed. Henry Noble MacCracken (EETS/ES, 107; London, 1911), part I, 374, ll. 316–17.

[54] John Gower, *The English Works*, ed. G. C. Macauley (EETS/ES, 82; London, 1900), 459, ll. 2679–82.

References to lutes as instruments of minstrelsy occur with increasing frequency in fifteenth-century romances.[55] In *Sir Cleges*, a Middle English metrical romance from *c*.1400, the knight hears a sound 'Of dyvers mynstrelsé; Of trompus, pypus, and claraneris, of harpis, luttis, and getarnys, A sitole and sawtré'.[56] In 'Octavian Imperator', which originated at the same time, the lute is included in a list of minstrel instruments.[57] In the *Laud Troy Book* (*c*.1400), a paraphrase of the Trojan War, the Greeks sing, dance, and hold a banquet after a temporary truce with the Trojans. Here again the lute is mentioned alongside other instruments.[58] A knight, Sir Degrevant, the subject of a mid-fifteenth-century romance, plays a number of instruments, including the harp, gittern, rote, and citole.[59]

The rising popularity of the lute as a favoured minstrel instrument, as suggested by mid- and later fifteenth-century literature, can be corroborated. A Patent Roll of 1451 records a pardon granted to William Luter of Selby, whose profession was 'luter' and 'mynstrell'.[60] On 14 July 1483 a local minstrel was paid 2*s.* 4*d.* for mending a lute belonging to the household of John Howard, Duke of Norfolk.[61] *The Coventry Leat Book* (*c*.1499) describes a town pageant staged in 1474 involving town waits and actors to welcome Prince Edward (aged 3) to Coventry. The prince and his entourage stopped at various places in the town to hear music and speeches by actors representing saints and past kings. A short 'pagiont' was staged at the Broadgate, 'and seint Edward beyng therin with x a-states with hym, with mynstralcy of harpe and lute'.[62]

Lexicons and dictionaries of the fifteenth century regularly include the lute, showing the word was firmly established in the language by then.[63] Page has found possible references in Poll Tax returns and other documents to two London lute

[55] *Three Middle English Sermons from the Worcester Chapter MS F.10*, ed. D. M. Grisdale (Leeds University School of English Language Text & Monographs, 5; Kendal, 1939), 1–21: '[th]er schuld melodie of no minstracie, no nou[th]er harpe, nor luet . . . glade . . . [th]in herte as schulde [th]is harpe of Goddis . . . mercy'.

[56] *Middle English Metrical Romances*, ed. Walter Hoyt French and Charles Brockway Hale, 2 vols. (New York, 1964), ii. 877–95, ll. 100–2.

[57] G. Sarrazin (ed.), 'Octavian Imperator', *Altenglische Bibliothek*, 3 (Heilbron, 1885), 4, ll. 67–70. 'Ther myzt men here menstralcye, Trompys, tabours, and cornettys crye, Roowte, gyterne, lute and sawtrye, Fydelys and othyr mo; . . .'

[58] *The Laud Troy Book*, ed. J. Ernst Wülfing (EETS/OS, 121; London, 1902), 242, l. 8216. Other contemporary references to banqueting minstrels occur in *The Early English Versions of the Gesta Romanorum*, ed. Sidney J. H. Herrtage (EETS/ES, 33; London, 1879), 247, and *Lyrics in Anglia* (*c*.1500), ed. Frederick Morgan Padelford (Anglia, 31; 1908).

[59] *The Romance of Sir Degrevant*, ed. L. F. Casson (EETS/OS, 221; London, 1949), 4, ll. 36–9: 'And gytternyng full gaye; Wele to playe on a rotte, To syng many newe note, And of harpyng, wele I wote.'

[60] W. H. Grattan Flood, 'Entries Relating to Music in the English Patent Rolls of the Fifteenth Century', *Musical Antiquary*, 4 (1912–13), 225–37 at 230; from Cal. Pat. Rolls, 1446–52 Henry VI, vol. v.

[61] *Household Books of John, Duke of Norfolk and Thomas, Earl of Surrey (1481–1490)*, ed. J. P. Collier (London, 1844), xxiii, 218: 'Item, to the menstrellis for the mendynge of a lewte, ij.s iij.d.'

[62] *Two Coventry Corpus Christi Plays*, ed. Hardin Craig (EETS/ES, 87; London, 1902), 115, ll. 25–7.

[63] e.g. *Promptorium parvulorum*, ed. Albert Way (Camden Society, 25, 54, 89; 1843–65) from *GB-Lbl* Harley MS 221. 'Lute, instrument of musyke: Viella, samba, lambutum.'

makers. In one of 1433/4, a certain John Thomas is clearly identified as 'Lut maker', and another, 'Lodowycus', may by inference also have been a lute maker.[64] This reference to lute-making in England is particularly important, given the very few references to English manufacture of lutes in the sixteenth and seventeenth centuries.

The earliest iconographical evidence of the lute in England, like the literary and documentary evidence, dates from the beginning of the fourteenth century. Possibly the earliest representation of a lute in Britain is to be found on a cope from Steeple Aston, where a lute is played by an angel on horseback (see Pl. 2.2). The cope, a magnificently embroidered clerical outer garment, is dated 1310–40 by the Victoria and Albert Museum, to which it is on loan.[65] The lute has four pegs on one side only of the pegbox, which is bent back at 90 degrees. The belly is oval-shaped with sides that taper in towards the neck intersection, and has a large central rose. Only three strings are visible. The threads that portray the strings have deteriorated around the bridge, but originally they ran over the bridge to the base of the belly. The lute is played with a long thin plectrum about the length of the player's middle finger. The horse observes the performance with a bemused expression. The plectrum is clearly attached to the player by a string, presumably an essential precaution against loss during equestrian performance.

To judge from carvings of instruments in churches and from manuscript illuminations, the gittern was more popular than the lute in fourteenth-century England. Depictions of lutes at this time are relatively rare. An illuminated manuscript made by Walter de Milemete includes a gittern played by a half-man, half-beast grotesque, and an instrument with some lute characteristics played by a similar creature.[66] This instrument has a long oval shape, a single rose, four to five strings, and is played without a plectrum. Its trefoil pegbox suggests it may be a plucked fiddle, although this feature is shared by the gittern on the previous folio. A miniature, in a copy of the *Romance of Alexander* produced in England *c*.1380, shows three, or possibly four, lutes among a variety of instruments being played by minstrels who form part of a nobleman's procession.[67] By contrast, the citole appears in fourteenth-century musical iconography with some frequency. For example, the de Milemete manuscript mentioned above, a treatise on kingship made for, and presented to, Edward III, includes a great many instruments in its border decorations and pictures. Among them are four citoles.[68]

[64] Page, 'String-Instrument Making', 45 and 47; from *GB-Lgc* 9171/3, fos. 374ᵛ and 390ᵛ.

[65] *The Medieval Treasury: The Art of the Middle Ages in the Victoria and Albert Museum*, ed. Paul Williamson (London, 1986), 198–9, pl. 19; see also Mary Remnant, 'Notes and Queries: "Opus Anglicanum" ', *GSJ* 17 (1964), 111–13, and pl. 12.

[66] *GB-Och* 92. The gittern is found on fo. 50ʳ and the lute or plucked fiddle on fo. 51ʳ.

[67] *F-Pn* fr. 22547, fo. 245ᵛ. A facsimile is printed in *New Grove*, xii. 349.

[68] *GB-Och* 92, fos. 14ᵛ, 18ᵛ, 31ᵛ, and 43ᵛ. For further examples of citoles in English iconography see Remnant, 'The Gittern in English Medieval Art' (she calls citoles 'gitterns'), and Wright, 'The Medieval Gittern and Citole', 36 n. 68.

PL. 2.2. Detail from the Steeple Aston Cope. London, Victoria and Albert Museum, on loan

An important carved representation of a gittern survives in the Exeter Cathedral minstrels' gallery from *c.*1325–50.[69] Here a relatively large gittern is played by one of the twelve musicians represented. A citolist is also among the minstrels. The gittern has a sickle-shaped pegbox with a solid head at its extremity and a body which slopes into the neck. The strings run over the bridge and are attached to the base of the instrument. In all the fourteenth-century representations of gitterns that are listed in Table 2.2 the players are all angels, except at Exeter Cathedral and St Mary's, King's Lynn, where the players are mortal minstrels, and at Hereford, where the musician is a goat.[70] In each case the instruments are identified as gitterns

Table 2.2. *English medieval lute and gittern iconography*

Date	Place	Description
1310–40	Steeple Aston Cope (V&A)	Silk embroidered cope. Angel musician on horseback
*c.*1325–50	Exeter Cathedral, minstrel's gallery	Gittern played by one of 12 stone-carved minstrels
1326	GB-Och 92, fo. 51ʳ	Illuminated MS; beast playing an instrument with some lute-like features
*c.*1337–50	Gloucester Cathedral, choir vault	Carved gittern
*c.*14th c. (early)	Hereford Cathedral, misericord	Carved gittern
1344	GB-Ob 264, fo. 21ˇ	Gittern in miniature by Jehans de Grise illustrating *Romans d'Alexandre*
1364	Church of St Margaret, King's Lynn	Gittern and other instruments played by minstrel
*c.*1370–80	Bohun Psalter, GB-Lbl Egerton 3277, fo. 160ʳ	Gittern played by angel
*c.*1380	F-Pn fr. 22547, fo. 245ˇ	Miniature with lutes played in procession
*c.*14th c.	GB-Lbl Add. 47680, fo. 9ˇ	Illuminated MS; gittern
*c.*14th c.	Beverley Minster, Yorks.	Stone-carved gittern, north nave aisle arcade
*c.*14th c.	Church of St Botolph, Boston, Lincs.	Two gitternists on misericords
*c.*14th c.	Church of St Mary, Happisburgh, Norfolk	Gitternists carved on font
*c.*14th c.	Church of Burgh St Peter, Norfolk	Gitternists carved on font
1384	The Litlyngton Missal, GB-Lwa 37	Illuminated MS; angel with gittern

[69] Charles John P. Cave, *Medieval Carvings in Exeter Cathedral* (London, 1953).

[70] Gloucester Cathedral carving (*c.*1337–50), choir vault; King's Lynn brass (1364), Mary Remnant *English Bowed Instruments from Anglo-Saxon to Tudor Times* (Oxford, 1986), pl. 101; de Milemete MS (1326–7); GB-Lbl Add. 47680, fo. 9ˇ; Bohun Psalter (*c.*1370–80), GB-Lbl Egerton 3277, fo. 160ʳ (Remnant, ibid., pl. 103); Litlynton missal (*c.*1383–4), GB-Lwa 37; Hereford Cathedral misericord (early 14th c.), Remnant, ibid., pl. 63; Beverley Minster carving (14th c.), north nave aisle arcade —see Joscelyn Godwin, '"Main divers acors": Some Instrument Collections of the Ars Nova Period', *EM* 5 (1977), 148–59 at 148.

Table 2.2. *cont.*

Date	Place	Description
c.1400	Chapter House, Westminster Abbey	Wall painting of the Elders of the Apocalypse. Three of the 12 square panels show respectively a lute, a gittern, a lute and gittern
c.1400	Church of the Holy Sepulchre, Cambridge	Wood-carved angel lutenist in the roof
c.1400–6	Sherborne Missal, Alnwick Castle (*GB-Lbl* Add. MS 74236)	Lute and gittern among balcony of angels playing instruments
c.1400–40	Rattlesdon Church, Suffolk	Stained glass window in tower with an angel lutenist
c.15th c.	*GB-Ob* Illum MS e Museo, fo. 83ᵛ	Drawing of a lutenist
c.15th c.	*GB-Ob* Bodley 770, fo. 25ᵛ	Drawing of three angel musicians, one with a lute
c.15th c.	Church of All Saints, Besthorpe, Norfolk	Stained-glass window with minstrels playing a lute and rebec
c.15th c.	*GB-Lbl* Harley 2838, fo. 44ᵛ	MS illumination of an angel playing a lute with four courses; another angel plays a fiddle. The lute is played with a plectrum
c.15th c.	*GB-Ob* Lat. Liturg. g. 5, p. 217	Lute played by female angel
c.15th c.	Church of St Agnes, Cawston, Norfolk	Stained glass (not *in situ*) contains three lutes and one gittern
c.15th c.	Church of St Mary Magdalen, Warham, Norfolk	Stained glass with two lutenists
c.15th c.	Church of St Mary the Virgin, N. Elmham, Norfolk	Stained glass lute or gittern
c.15th c.	Church of St Mary the Virgin, Linton, Cambs.	Stained glass west window with an angel lutenist
c.1405	Winchester Cathedral, south aisle of nave	Roof boss with angel lutenist
c.1450	Church of St Mary, Braughing, Herts.	Stone-carved angel lutenist holding a four-course lute
c.1460	Church of St Mary, Diss, Norfolk	Stone-carved lute with gittern in porch played by angels
c.1460–4	Church of St Mary, Shrewsbury	Roof boss with angel lutenist
c.1493	Church of All Saints, Hillesdon, Bucks.	Plaster frieze of musicians includes two lutes
later 15th c.	Church of St Martin, Hindringham, Norfolk	Lute played by angel in stained-glass window
later 15th c.	Beauchamp Chapel, Church of St Mary, Warwick	Stained glass includes two lutes played with two gitterns
later 15th c.	Little Hadham Church, Herts.	Carved lute and gittern in porch

Note: This table includes only a sample of medieval lute and gittern iconography. There is no exhaustive study on this subject. For a longer list of English carved lute/gittern iconography, see Jeremy and Gwen Montagu, *Minstrels and Angels* (Berkeley, 1998), 96–120.

by their sickle-shaped pegbox and by their slim 'tear-drop'-shaped bodies, suggestive of a single-piece carved body construction. Some are small in relation to their players, but several are not significantly smaller than one would expect for a lute, as in the case of the Exeter Cathedral and Bohun psalter gitterns.

In the fifteenth century depictions of lutes in English churches and cathedrals outnumber those of gitterns. In particular, carvings of angel lutenists are common. Holy Sepulchre Church, Cambridge, contains a wood-carved angel lutenist in the roof. A stone-carved angel in St Mary's, Braughing, holds a lute with four courses, and plays with a plectrum. The porch stone carvings at Pelham St Mary, Diss, include a 4-course lute and gittern played together by angels.[71] A Winchester Cathedral nave roof boss features an angel lutenist, as does a roof boss in St Mary's, Shrewsbury.[72] The remarkable frieze of angel musicians at All Saints, Hillesdon, includes two lutenists. In one corner the lute is grouped with a rebec, harp, and portative organ; in the other with fiddle, harp, and portative organ. Both lutes are large with rounded bellies. The right-hand position of both players, with their arms extending up from below the instruments and their hands in a clenched postion, suggest a plectrum technique.[73]

Lutes are increasingly common in surviving fifteenth-century stained-glass windows that depict minstrels and angel musicians. The famous windows of the Beauchamp Chapel of St Mary's, Warwick, include two lutes and two gitterns.[74] The stained-glass window at Rattlesdon church includes an angel playing a lute with a complicated central multi-rose, and at least two subsidiary roses, three courses, and a body that tapers into the neck like a gittern.[75] All Saints, Besthorpe, has a window containing minstrels playing a rebec together with a lute which has six strings and three pegs on the top side of the pegbox. The well-dressed minstrel plays with a long plectrum.[76] Plates 2.3 and 2.4 show stained glass from the Norfolk churches of St Agnes, Cawston and St Martin, Hindringham, which feature winged lute-playing angels. Norfolk churchs are particularly rich in fifteenth-century lute iconography.

Among fifteenth-century manuscript lute depictions is a 'doodle' at the back of a book of commentaries on St Augustine's rules.[77] The instrument is clearly

---

[71] Holy Sepulchre Church, Cambridge (c.1400); St Mary's, Braughing, Herts (c.1450); St Mary's Church, Diss, Norfolk (c.1460).

[72] Winchester Cathedral boss, south aisle of nave (c.1405), Charles John P. Cave, *Roof Bosses in Medieval Churches* (Cambridge, 1948), 8; St Mary's Church, Shrewsbury (c.1460–4)—see Lawrence Wright, 'Medieval Carvings of Musical Instruments in St. Mary's Church, Shrewsbury', *FoMRHI* 12 (1977), Comm. 74.

[73] Remnant, *English Bowed Instruments*, pls. 137, 138 (c.1493).

[74] Jeremy Montagu, *The World of Medieval and Renaissance Musical Instruments* (Newton Abbot, 1976), pl. 55, 70–1.

[75] Rattlesdon Church window in church tower (c.1400–40).

[76] All Saints Church, Besthorpe; Remnant, *English Bowed Instruments*, pl. 126.

[77] GB-Ob Illum MS e Museo I 39, fo. 83'. The MS contains excerpts from commentaries on the 'Regula beati Augustini doctoris' by Hugh of St Victor and Nicholas Tryvet. While the drawing cannot be dated precisely, the costume, instrument, and hand suggest the 15th c.

PL. 2.3. Lute-playing angels in a stained glass window from the Church of St. Agnes, Cawston, Norfolk

PL. 2.4. Lute-playing angels in a stained glass window from the Church of St. Martin, Hindringham, Norfolk

drawn, complete with the full figure of a male musician. It has three strings and is near-circular in shape. Perhaps a medieval reader, bored by the impenetrable text, allowed his mind to wander to thoughts of music, and then expressed his idea in the drawing. Another drawing in a manuscript of religious prose, the *Pilgrimage of the Soul*, serves to illustrate the text.[78] Above the picture of five angels bringing the departed soul to the gates of heaven are the lines: 'melody of angels'; and below the picture the further lines: 'angels which having in hands som lusty instruments as harp, organs and sawtry [psaltery]'. Of the five angels three play instruments: a harp, lute, and trumpet. The lute has a single rose and a sharply angled pegbox. Among other manuscript depictions of lutes listed in Table 2.1,[79] the Sherborne Missal shows a balcony of angels all playing different instruments. Among them are a gittern player and a lute player standing next to each other.[80]

In summary it would appear from the fourteenth- and fifteenth-century English iconographic evidence that after its arrival the lute developed from an almond-shaped form with belly sides sloping into the neck and often multiple soundholes, to a more rounded or oval body shape with a distinct neck and normally a single, central rose.[81] Some of the fifteenth-century lute depictions listed above preserve characteristics of the medieval Arab 'ūd, particularly multiple roses and a neck which slopes to some degree into the neck. No extant English depiction conclusively proves that the back was built up from several ribs, or carved from a block of wood like a gittern. The only extant working drawing of a lute, produced around 1450 by Henri Arnault of Zwolle, physician and scholar at the Court of Philip the Good, Duke of Burgundy, specifies nine ribs of identical size.[82] From this it is possible to speculate that the medieval lute was normally of ribbed rather than carved construction, although there may have been exceptions. From the earliest writings by Arab theorists it seems that 'ūd and lute construction conformed to strict arithmetical and geometrical principles. Numerical perfections are the basis for Arnault's description, in which no measurements are given, but the whole is worked out according to proportions.[83] There is every reason to believe that this approach was widespread throughout medieval Europe.[84]

No English medieval lute is clearly depicted with frets on the neck. This may be due to lack of detail in the pictures and carvings, but we cannot discount the possibility that some medieval lutes were unfretted. We know that the Arabs had frets on their lutes in the medieval period, and frets are visible in a variety of Continental

[78] *GB-Ob* Bodl. 770, fo. 25ᵛ (early 15th c.).
[79] *GB-Lbl* Harley 2838, fo. 44ᵛ. Here the lute is played with a fiddle; it has four courses and is played with a plectrum; *GB-Ob* Illum MS Lat. liturg. g. 5, p. 217, where the angel is female.
[80] Sherbourne Missal (*c*.1400–6), *GB-Lbl* Add MS 74236, p. 276; Remnant *English Bowed Instruments*, pl. 114.
[81] Bouterse, 'Reconstructing the Medieval Arabic Lute', 3.
[82] *F-Pn* Lat. 7295, p. 132.
[83] Ian Harwood, 'A Fifteenth-Century Lute Design', *LSJ* 2 (1960), 3–8.
[84] Gerhard Christian Söhne, 'On the Geometry of the Lute', *JLSA* 13 (1980), 35–54 at 35.

lute depictions.[85] The number of frets varies from as few as four to as many as eight; and the long neck of the Arnault design would allow twelve.[86] Although there are a number of lutes in English medieval iconography which suggest only three courses, we may assume that four or five courses were the norm. These courses could be either double or single. If double they could be tuned either to the unison or octave. In the early 1480s Tinctoris mentions tuning strings at the octave except for the top string. This is technically improbable for the second and third courses unless the lute were large. However, it seems likely that the practice of octave stringing for some courses was widespread for much of this period.[87]

No specific directions on how to tune the lute survive from England before the late fifteenth century. There are a number of Continental sources on the subject which may cast some light on English practice. When considering any aspect of lute tuning it should be stressed that the actual pitch of the top string of the lute is normally determined by the string length and string material (usually gut), and that lute tuning is better thought of in terms of interval patterns rather than pitches, even though sources may state actual pitches. As a starting point Farmer suggests that the original Arab tuning of the ʿūd was *a, g, d, c* (from top to bottom) for a four-course instrument.[88] As always, these pitches should be taken as relative, not actual. Under Persian influence this tuning was altered to one of consecutive fourths, first at the bottom and later at the top, to give a resulting *c′, g, d, A*. Christopher Page has drawn attention to the similarity of this development to that of the gittern described in a late fourteenth-century music treatise, which he suggests is by the French priest and music teacher Jean Vaillant.[89] The treatise gives a tuning, ascribed to one 'Thebus the Arab', of *c′, g, d, A*. To arrive at this, in the words of the treatise, the 'Arab loosened the lower string adjusting a fourth between it and its neighbour'. It may be that in the fourteenth century the lute, like the gittern, was tuned in rising fourths, which indeed is the normal tuning of the Arabic ʿūd both today and in medieval times.

We know that by the end of the fifteenth century the tuning by fourths had given way to a tuning of fourths around a major third. An English tuning instruction for the lute survives in a document which contains formulae on various learned subjects, including how to set out warrants, letters of attorney, and obligations, as well

---

[85] Henry G. Farmer, 'Was the Arabian and Persian Lute Fretted?', *Journal of the Royal Asiatic Society*, 103 (1937), 453–60.

[86] Peter Danner, 'Before Petrucci: The Lute in the Fifteenth Century', *JLSA*, 5 (1972), 4–17 at 12.

[87] Anthony Baines, 'Fifteenth-Century Instruments in Tinctoris's *De Inventione et usu musicae*', *GSJ*, 3 (1950), 19–26 at 21.

[88] Henry G. Farmer, *An Old Moorish Lute Tutor* (Glasgow, 1933), 26; also 'The Origin of the Arabian Lute and Rebec', 97.

[89] Christopher Page, 'Fourteenth-Century Instruments and Tunings: A Treatise by Jean Vaillant? (Berkeley, MS 744)', *GSJ* 33 (1980), 17–35.

as listing psalm tones and solmization syllables.[90] The document probably originally belonged to a university man. Among the formulae is one headed 'To sette a lute'. Christopher Page suggests this section of the manuscript dates from the last decades of the fifteenth century.[91] The tuning is for a 5-course lute, and the individual strings are named 'Trebill', 'Seconde trebill', 'Meene', 'Tenor', and 'basse'. The resulting tuning gives the relative pitches g', d', a, f, c (assuming a first course at g' pitch). This is the tuning specified by Tinctoris in his famous *De inventione et usu musicae*.[92] Tinctoris also allows for a sixth string, which he states was adopted first by the Germans. That other lute tunings were known in the fifteenth century is attested to by two other contemporary tuning instructions, one published in Bologna in 1482, the other in Salamanca *c.*1495, both by Spaniards.[93] The first suggests a tuning d', a, f, c, G (with the interval of a third between the second and third courses) but allows for further variant tunings of which only the three lowest string pitches are stated (a, d, A). The second, according to Page, gives the tuning a', d', a, f, c.[94]

From the meagre evidence we have we may surmise that during the fourteenth and fifteenth centuries the interval of the third was introduced into the series of fourths. As the lute with five courses became the norm, the third settled into its position between the third and fourth courses, yet throughout the fifteenth century variants were known.

The single most helpful source of information on lute playing in fifteenth-century Britain occurs in a booklet of expenditure accounts written by George Cely. Cely was an educated young middle-class wool merchant and a member of the Staple Company at Calais, a town then in British hands. The booklet includes accounts for a course of lessons with a professional musician, Thomas Rede, in the years 1474–5. Rede taught Cely not only the lute, but dancing and the harp. On 14 November 1474 Cely paid Rede 3*s.* 6*d.* for 'a byll ffor to lerne to tevne the levte'.[95] This seems a huge sum if we reflect that Sir Lydbery's lute was valued at 6*d.* in 1462/3, and in 1468 William Braggs's lute was worth 10*d.* One could have had a week's board and lodging in Calais for 3*s.* 4*d.* at that time, and for 2*d.* one could have purchased a servant's dinner in London.[96] This 'byll', in all probability, constituted more of a handwritten tutor than a set of tuning instructions like those in the

[90] *GB-Ctc* O.2.13, fo. 97⁻. See Page, 'The 15th-Century Lute', 13–14.

[91] Ibid. 13.

[92] Baines, 'Fifteenth-Century Instruments', 22: 'the two middle strings are tuned to a major third, and the rest in fourths'.

[93] Page, 'The 15th-Century Lute', 14–16. The two sources are Elio Antonio de Nebrija, *Vocabulario Español-Latino* (Salamanca, *c.*1495), and Bartolomé Ramos de Pareja, *Musica practica* (Bologna, 1482).

[94] Page, 'The 15th-Century Lute', 16.

[95] PRO C.47/37/11, fos. 1–5. See Alison Hanham, 'The Musical Studies of a Fifteenth-Century Wool Merchant', *Review of English Studies*, 8 (1957), 270–4 at 270, and Page, 'The 15th-Century Lute', 17–19.

[96] Hanham, 'The Musical Studies', 273.

Trinity College manuscript mentioned above. The purchase, as part of a series of closely supervised lessons, of a loose-leaf tutor and music copied out by the teacher from his exemplars and stock of pieces, may have been the normal method for teaching literate amateurs. If so, then it conforms closely with what we know of lute teaching in the sixteenth and seventeenth centuries.[97]

Cely mentions learning to play forty dances in the course of his studies. Of these, twenty-six are specified as on the harp, and fourteen on the lute.[98] For these fourteen dances, plus 'a horne pype' also on the lute, Cely paid 4s. 10d. Another item lists payment of 16d. for 'an lytyll ffyngyr hyng [o]n the lewte' [a little fingering on the lute].[99] Does this suggest tablature? Tablature was not well established at this time, and we can only speculate as to what form of fingering instruction this bill refers.

Quite apart from these large payments Rede received a flat-rate retainer of one 'plack' a week. A plack was a small Brabant coin worth either 2¼d. or 8d., depending on whether this was an old or new plack.[100] Of special interest are the names of seven pieces that Cely was taught to play: 'O Freshest Flower', 'O Rosa Bella', 'Mine Heart's Lust', 'Of Such Complain', 'Go Heart Hurt with Adversity', 'My Daily (or Doly) Woe', and 'Toujours'. It is very significant that of the titles which refer to known pieces, all are polyphonic songs, rather than pieces from a purely instrumental tradition. All are in English, apart from the popular 'O Rosa Bella', and one in French, a language which Cely was also learning.[101] Whether Cely sang these songs to the harp or lute, or played them instrumentally, is not known. He was certainly concentrating on the lute in December 1474, when three of them are mentioned, as the account follows the two November bills for lute dances and fingering. The song titles are particularly important as they are the only firm indication that we have of the sort of repertory that a British lute player might have performed prior to 1500.

It is evident from this survey of iconographical and literary evidence that the lute and gittern were quickly accepted by professional English minstrels after the introduction of these instruments to England around 1300. One possible explanation for this easy acceptance was that both instruments required a basic playing technique that was easily transferred from the citole, which was well established in the late thirteenth century. This transference of interest may have contributed to the citole's decline by the mid-fourteenth century. The lute and gittern, by the late fourteenth century, were played not only by professional minstrels, but by students, men in trade, and others from the emerging middle class, and possibly even by the

---

[97] Page, 'The 15th-Century Lute', 18.

[98] Hanham, 'The Musical Studies', 271: 'Item the ffurst day of Novembyr I payd vn to the sayd Thomas ffor to lerne xiiij davnsys and an horne pype on the levt . . . iiijs xd.'

[99] Ibid. 271, 272.   [100] Ibid. 273.   [101] Ibid. 272–3.

knightly class too. Gitterns, in particular, are listed among the property and accoutrements of raffish young men who used them for carousing after dark, a facet of their use highlighted in literature of the Chaucerian period. References to the gittern subside after 1450. In place of the gittern the lute is more often associated with the harp, whose dominant position among courtly instruments the lute assumes by the end of the century.

In formulating ideas on how the lute was played in late medieval/early Renaissance Britain a certain amount can be gleaned from iconography. Most English lute iconography shows the instrument played standing and held almost at right angle to the body, with the right arm cradling the instrument from below. In the great majority of cases the right hand holds a quill or plectrum which is often as long as the player's middle finger or longer. The quill or plectrum is seen to be held in a variety of ways. Often it is between the thumb and index finger, like a modern guitar plectrum, or between the index and middle finger, or even the middle and ring finger. Yet there are exceptions at all stages which show the instrument plucked directly with the fingers.[102]

In the absence of any lute music from the medieval period in England, this review of literature and iconography has severe limitations, and prevents us from piecing together a more detailed picture of how the lute was played, its repertory, and in what ensembles it featured.[103] Nor is it possible to discern any English traits, either in the playing or making of lutes, in which English practices can be differentiated from those on the Continent. Account-books and financial transactions of the period include the lute among the 'still' instruments.[104] The English words 'loud' and 'still' correspond to the Continental 'haut' and 'bas'.[105] These terms grouped together on the one hand noisy instruments (trumpets, horns, shawms, percussion), and on the other hand quiet instruments (portative organ, flutes, string instruments). Different circumstances required different minstrel music, and the two groups were normally kept separate.

Rastall describes the lute as a solo instrument from among the 'still' instruments. It is used to accompany the voice, and is commonly referred to in consort with other quiet instruments.[106] Most iconography from the period shows the lute with other instruments. 'Still' instruments were symbolic of divine order, of heaven and paradise, and are normally depicted played by a host of angels, each of which holds a representative instrument type.[107] This is typically seen in English church carvings.

---

[102] e.g. see *GB-Och* 92, fo. 51ʳ.

[103] See Alexander Blachly's review in *Musical Quarterly*, 57 (1971), 330–41 for problems in interpreting iconography and literary references.

[104] Rastall, 'Some English Consort-Groupings', 183.

[105] Edmund A. Bowles, 'Haut and Bas: The Grouping of Musical Instruments in the Middle Ages', *Musica disciplina*, 8 (1954), 115–40.

[106] Rastall, 'Some English Consort-Groupings', 183–6.   [107] Ibid. 197.

In medieval drama 'still' instruments, including the lute, were used to create a setting of inner heaven.[108] This symbolism is fully apparent in medieval English literary references. A Continental poem by Eustace Deschamps refers to the lute as having a 'very soft delicate tone quality', which conforms with the instrument's heavenly symbolism.[109] It also suggests that the lute would not be heard in a large group of instruments, and that such mass 'still' consorts as appear in literature and iconograpy are unlikely to have occurred in practice. More likely the lute was used in the medieval period as a solo instrument, to accompany the voice in combination with one other plucked instrument, typically a gittern, harp, or another lute, or in some other small ensemble of 'still' instruments. The titles of the Cely pieces indicate that by 1500 lutes in England did participate in the performance of a polyphonic repertory of music.

[108] Edmund A. Bowles, 'The Role of Musical Instruments in Medieval Sacred Drama', *Musical Quarterly*, 45 (1959), 67–84 at 74.

[109] Bowles, 'Haut and Bas', 127: 'Leuths . . . trestous instrumens coy.'

Chapter Three

From Medieval to Renaissance: A Continental Excursus, 1480–1530

besides all Bolonia Lutes are in the shape of apare and those are the best Lutes
but there goodnes is not attributed to there figure but to there antiquity to the
skill of those Lutemakers to the quality of the wood and seasoning of it and to
the varnishing of it . . . which is darkish red[1]

Towards the end of the fifteenth-century lute technique underwent a fundamental
change from one suited to playing a single line to one which allowed a solo player
to play two or more parts at once. The new technique may have originated first
among lutenists at the Burgundian court in the 1460s and 1470s, but was then
developed in Italy in the closing decades of the fifteenth century and early years of
the sixteenth. During the first half of the sixteenth century the technique was
adopted throughout western Europe, and the old monophonic style, normally associated with the use of a plectrum, was gradually discontinued. This development is
part of the general move from monophony to polyphony that characterizes the transition from the Middle Ages to the Renaissance, a transition that saw the emergence
of new families of string and wind instruments that were specifically designed to
play polyphonic music.

Memorizing a single melodic line should present few problems to a lutenist, and
performing from memory may have advantages if he wants to improvise freely.
However, memorizing two or more contrapuntal parts is a far more difficult
prospect, and it is easier to perform such music reading from some form of tablature. It is quite understandable that the earliest surviving lute tablatures date from
this period of technical transition. As regards England there is little real information on how the lute was played before the mid-sixteenth century, the approximate
date of the oldest surviving English lute sources. Instead we must turn to
Continental commentators and sources of lute music to give us some idea of how
lute technique was developing, and assume that in England a similar development
took place some time afterwards.

---

[1] *The Burwell Lute Tutor*, facs. with an introduction by Robert Spencer (Reproductions of Early Music, 1;
Leeds, 1974), ch. 2, fo. 3r. For a version in modern English see Thurston Dart, 'Miss Mary Burwell's Instruction
Book for the Lute', *GSJ* 11 (1958), 3–62.

Much of what is known about fifteenth-century lute technique comes from Johannes Tinctoris's *De inventione et usu musicae*. This work was produced in the Aragonese Kingdom of Naples in the years 1481–3 by a Walloon with a wide knowledge of European musical developments. He refers to the lute as the 'lyra', and sees its ancestry in the Apollonian lyre, an association strong in the Renaissance and Baroque periods. Tinctoris speaks of the lute as a 5-course instrument, but also knows of 6-course instruments, a development he attributes to the Germans. Germans are also credited with using brass for the lowest strings, and with developing the ability to play two-, three-, or four-part compositions on a single lute. In this capacity he names two players in particular, one 'Orbus, the German'; the other, 'Henri', lutenist to Charles, the last Duke of Burgundy (d. 1477).[2] Henri may be Henri Büchlin, a lute player in the duke's service in 1469.[3] 'Orbus' simply meant blind, and the most notable blind German musician of the age was Conrad Paumann of Nuremberg (*c*.1410–73).[4] Paumann, though famous as an organist, was also a lutenist. Tinctoris discusses another method of playing in which a pair of musicians play together, one taking the tenor line (he mentions the bowed viola in this respect), and the other taking the treble part on the lute and improvising 'marvellously upon it with such taste that the performance cannot be rivalled'.[5] For improvisation in this manner he names Pietro Bono as pre-eminent. Pietro Bono de Burzellis was the most famous lutenist of his age, a German by birth who became lutenist to Ercole, Duke of Ferrara. A long poem by Lippo Brandolini describes Pietrobono's technique in some detail. Using a plectrum of ivory Pietrobono would decorate a tenor line using metric development, ascending and descending scale passages on all parts of the fingerboard, sequences and rhythmic variation.[6]

The differentiation of the two styles of playing in the later fifteenth century—on the one hand the older monophonic improvisatory style using a plectrum and suitable for both gittern and lute, with an accompanying *tenorista* playing a lower part; on the other, a newer Germanic solo polyphonic style suggestive of finger-plucking technique—is corroborated by other writings of the period.[7] We know of several *tenorista*/lutenist pairs working in Italy before 1500, particularly in Mantua, Ferrara, Verona, and Milan.[8] Many of these musicians were intimately connected with the development of the frottola at these courts. It is probable that many of the

---

[2] Baines, 'Fifteenth-Century Instruments', 24.

[3] Danner, 'Before Petrucci', 14.

[4] I am grateful to Peter Holman for this suggestion.

[5] Baines, 'Fifteenth-Century Instruments', 24.

[6] Alberto Gallo, *Music in the Castle* (Chicago, 1995), 114–35.

[7] Peter Danner, 'Before Petrucci', 15. In particular Paolo Cortesi's *De cardinalatu libri tres* (1510) mentions Pietro Bono as an improviser and the Germans Balthasar and Joannes Maria as polyphonists. See also Lewis Lockwood, 'Pietrobono and the Instrumental Tradition at Ferrara in the Fifteenth Century', *Rivista italiana di musicologia*, 10 (1975), 115–33 at 121.

[8] The most famous are Pietro Bono/Francesco de la Gatta and Marchetto Cara/Roberto d'Avanzini. See William F. Prizer, 'Lutenists at the Court of Mantua in the Late Fifteenth and Early Sixteenth Centuries', *JLSA* 13 (1980), 5–34 at 15.

generation of lutenists in Italy working around 1490–1500 could play with both techniques, but gradually the polyphonic finger-plucking technique supplanted that of the plectrum. Many of the most illustrious lutenists of the later fifteenth century in Italy also sang to the lute. Pietro Bono, Marchetto Cara, Giovanni Angelo Testagrossa, and Giacomo de San Secondo are all mentioned as singers, as well as lute virtuosi.[9]

The earliest surviving sources of lute music reflect these developments. The first printed books of lute music, published by Petrucci, were of music composed or arranged by Francesco Spinacino (two books of 1507), Joan Ambrosio Dalza (1508), and Franciscus Bossinensis (1509 and 1511). There was also another book, probably by Giovan Maria (1508), which has not survived. Bossinensis's books are concerned with frottole, but also contain short ricercars marked as suitable for preceding certain songs. Spinacino's books contain a high proportion of ricercars, many of which are long and based on polyphonic vocal compositions. They also contain a few duets with an embellished monophonic upper part over a slower *tenorista* lower part. Dalza's book is more concerned with solo dance music, but includes some intabulations of vocal pieces, all of which require finger plucking. There are also two duets with a monophonic upper part suitable for plectrum technique, played over a simple tenor part for a second lute. In the first of these duets the *tenorista* simply plays a drone. In the second, a 'Calata', the *tenorista* repeats a simple tenor (see Ex. 3.1). While the first piece is entirely playable with plectra, there are a few instances in both parts of the second piece where players are required to strike non-adjacent strings simultaneously.[10] These printed pieces are among the few good examples of a mainly improvisatory genre that was clearly very popular in the fifteenth century.

It seems that some lutenists were also playing single-line music directly from mensural notation in this period. There is a significant amount of complex music from the decades around 1500 which requires such a large range that performance by voices or wind instruments would seem unlikely if not impossible. Such pieces are often related to vocal compositions that may have been their starting point, and may contain a few words of text, but remain otherwise textless. A source which contains such music is the famous Segovia Codex.[11] Here there are sections which contain elaborate textless two- and three-part compositions by Agricola, Tinctoris, Obrecht, Roelkin, Adam, and others, some of which would appear to have been

[9] Prizer, 'Lutenists at the Court of Mantua'. See also Nino Pirrotta, 'Music and Cultural Tendencies in 15th-Century Italy', *JAMS* 19 (1966), 127–61 for a discussion of Paolo Cortesi's *De cardinalatu libri tres*, and Antonio Cornazano's *Sforziade*, which also deals with Pietro Bono as a player and singer.

[10] Joan Ambrosio Dalza, *Intabulatura de lauto libro quarto* (Venice, 1508; repr. Geneva, 1980), fos. 39ʳ–42ᵛ, *Piva* and *Calata*.

[11] Jon Banks, 'A Piece of Fifteenth-Century Lute Music in the Segovia Codex', *LSJ* 34 (1994), 3–10.

EX. 3.1. *'Calata', bars 1–13, lutenist/tenorista duet from Joan Ambrosio Dalza,* Intabulatura de lauto libro quarto *(Venice, 1508), fos. 41ʳ–42ᵛ*

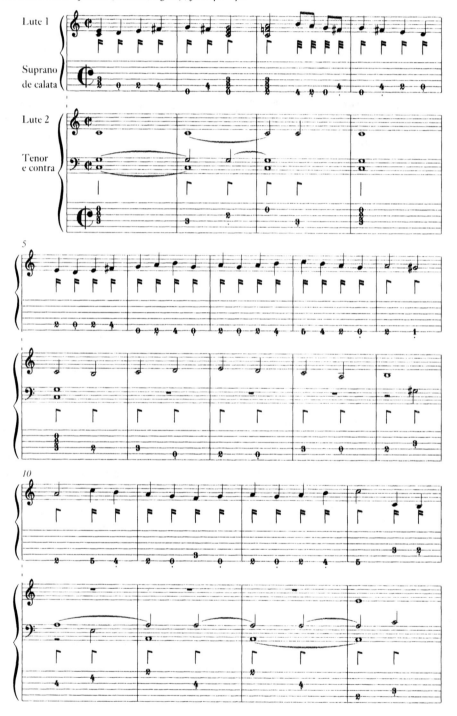

intended for lutes or gitterns of differing sizes. The likelihood that lutes and associated instruments played complicated notated music in this period has only recently been seriously considered.[12] However, it is clear that these pieces in the Segovia Codex work best on lutes and associated plucked instruments, and connect with the early tablature duet repertoire exemplified by Ex. 3.1. The Segovia Codex pieces are all in mensural notation and this opens up the exciting prospect for lutenists today that the very considerable corpus of elaborate two, three and four part music of the late fifteen and early sixteenth centuries may have been intended for lute esembles.

There are several early manuscript sources of lute tablature that pre-date the first printed lute books. The earliest surviving tablature occurs in a manuscript of German poetry from *c*.1470–3. It includes four simple melodies written in German tablature symbols placed after the poems for which they are intended.[13] The melodies have no rhythm signs. This early date is entirely plausible in the light of the remarks of Sebastian Virdung, who published the earliest example of printed German tablature in 1511 (see Pl. 3.1). Virdung's example is unlike most German tablature in that the four parts are kept distinct, as in the mensural and organ notation it follows, though it could be played by four lutes, each playing a single line.[14] However, to combine the lines into a single tablature is a simple procedure. Virdung states that Paumann invented German lute tablature.[15] It is not so surprising that the German tablature system was devised by a blind musician, since it is ideal for dictation: two pieces of information (course and fret position) are communicated quickly and unambiguously in one symbol.

The connection between organ and lute music seems to have been strong in Germany at this time, and there are similarities between early organ tablature systems and German lute tablature. As originally conceived, German lute tablature uses the numbers one to five for the open courses, and then the letters of the alphabet for each fret position on each of the five courses. Organ tablature has the upper part (right-hand) in mensural notation, and the lower parts in alphabetic form. For the lower part or parts in alphabetic notation, the white notes of the keyboard are simply written as alphabetical letters. Thus the note *a* is written as the letter 'a'.

---

[12] Jon Banks, 'Performing the Instrumental Music in the Segovia Codex', *EM* 27 (1999), 295–309.

[13] David Fallows, '15th-Century Tablatures for Plucked Instruments: A Summary, a Revision and a Suggestion', *LSJ* 19 (1977), 7–33 at 8–9. The Königstein songbook is published as *Das Königsteiner Liederbuch*, ed. Paul Sappler (Münchener Texte und Untersuchungen zur deutschen Literatur des Mittelalters, 29; Munich, 1970). Page has suggested a possible 14th-c. source of French tablature, although this has been discounted. See Christopher Page, 'French Lute Tablature in the 14th Century?', *EM* 8 (1980), 488–92, and Jonathan Bates and Stewart McCoy, 'Mercury's Tetrachord', *EM* 10 (1982), 213–15.

[14] Uta Henning, 'The Lute Made Easy: A Chapter from Virdung's *Musica Getutscht* (1511)', *LSJ* 15 (1973), 20–36. A example of printed German lute tablature playable on one lute appeared in Arnolt Schlick's *Tablaturen etlicher lobgesang und lidlein uff die orgeln und lauten* (Mainz, 1512).

[15] Sebastian Virdung, *Musica getutscht* (Basle, 1511), sig. K3ʳ. Virdung is an important source of information on the lute at the time. The story is reiterated by Martin Agricola in *Musica instrumentalis deudsch* (Wittenberg, 1529), fo. 29ʳ.

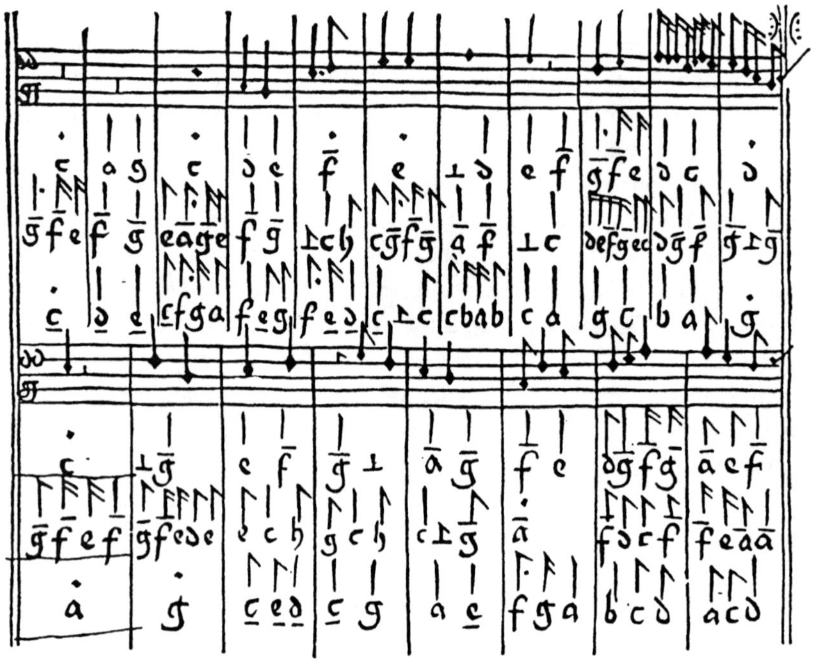

PL. 3.1. 'O haylige onbeflecte', from Sebastian Virdung, *Musica getutscht* (Basle, 1511): (a) German organ tablature (sig. I^v); (b) lute tablature (sig. M2^v)

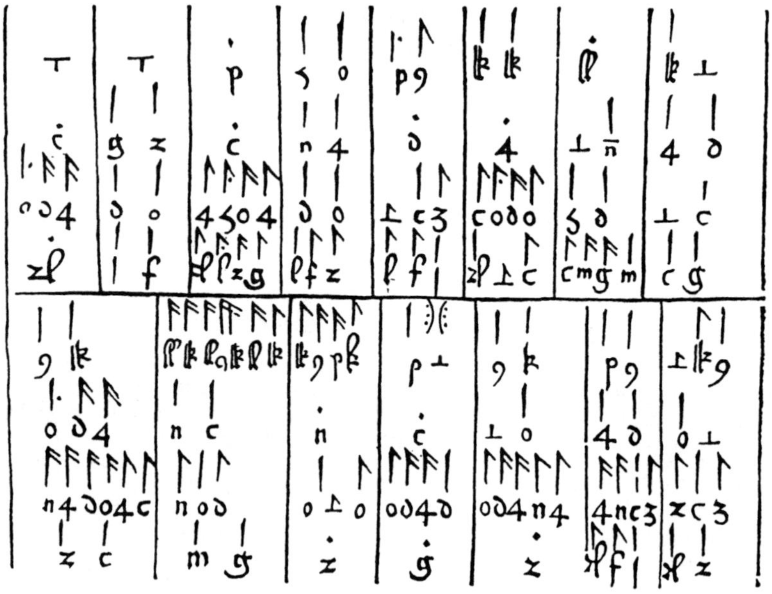

Extra symbols are then incorporated for accidentals and for upper or lower octaves. The lower part or parts in alphabetic form also have 'flags' above each letter to denote rhythm. They are in fact no more than the mensural notation stems without note heads. They may have one or more short lines drawn at an angle to the top of the stem to indicate doubled speed like a quaver or semi-quaver (⁀ ⁀ ⁀), or they may be 'beamed' together into a grid (⊓). Dots are also used to extend the length of the note by half its original value in the normal way. This method of denoting rhythm is exactly that used in German lute tablature. Paumann, famous for his keyboard music in the Buxheimer Orgelbuch (*c.*1460) and the *Fundamentum organisandi*, may have invented German lute tablature as an extension of his involvement in organ tablature. It may be that, just as Cabezón and Henestrosa in the next century expected harpists and vihuelists to read keyboard tablature, so late fifteenth-century German lutenists may have read organ tablature. German keyboard music of the late fifteenth century is easily transcribed for the lute. It has been suggested that at least one of the pieces in the Buxheimer Orgelbuch may be for lutes.[16] The books of Virdung (1511) and Schlick (1512), which contain the earliest German printed lute tablatures, also include related German organ tablatures.[17] The invention of tablature no doubt facilitated the development of playing polyphony on a single lute, and the finger-plucking techniques that then became unavoidable. Plectrum strokes can only play single or adjacent strings at any point in time. With independent strokes using the fingers and thumb, the simultaneous plucking of any combination of strings becomes possible.

German tablature was used in German-speaking countries for much of the sixteenth century, and even into the seventeenth. By 1600 it had lost popularity and was giving way to the so-called French system, which was used from the first in France and England, but may have originated in Italy. In the French system of tablature only alphabetic symbols are used. Parallel lines are drawn across the page (a tablature stave), one for each course, and the alphabetic symbols are placed on, or above, the lines. Tablature letters for the notes plucked on the first course occupy the top tablature stave line, the second course the second line down, and so on. Open courses are denoted by the letter *a*, the first fret uses *b*, the second *c*, and so on. During most of the sixteenth century the method of notating rhythm was fundamentally the same as for German tablature. In the seventeenth century lute tablature did not normally use the grid system, although there is plenty of overlap of methods. Instead a stem with the appropriate note-head appeared above the stave only when there was a change of rhythm.

The earliest surviving lute tablature in French tablature is found in the famous heart-shaped Pesaro manuscript. The first pieces in the manuscript consist of song

---

[16] Fallows, '15th-Century Tablatures', 29–33.   [17] Danner, 'Before Petrucci', 13.

arrangements, ricercars, and basse dances.[18] The source contains twenty-four lute solos in the sections of the manuscript which probably date from shortly before 1500. Most revealing are some of the unusual symbols found in the manuscript, and in particular the so-called 'T-sign'. Vladimir Ivanoff has suggested that this may be an abbreviation for the term *Tactus*, which is used in at least some German organ manuscripts of the fifteenth century to denote a stereotypical melodic formula of four semibreves. Understanding of the implications of this symbol help to make sense of the rhythm of the music (rhythm signs are largely absent), and of the processes the fifteenth-century player used to construct his music.[19] It is note-worthy that a piece for a 7-course instrument appears among the twenty-four solos, and a later section of the manuscript includes another piece, a version of Hayne's 'De tous biens plaine', suggestive of plectrum technique.[20] This piece contains polyphony but can be played with a plectrum, as only adjacent strings are ever sounded together. This is proof of an intermediate stage when polyphony was attempted, but the plectrum retained (see Ex. 3.2.)

The earliest lute music in the so-called Italian tablature occurs in the Bologna and Thibault manuscripts.[21] These sources are roughly contemporary with the Pesaro manuscript, and suggest that the 'Italian' and 'French' systems both evolved inde-pendently in Italy at much the same time. The Italian system is fundamentally the same as the French, but with two differences: numbers are used in place of letters (i.e. *0* for the open string, *1* for the first fret, *2* for the second, and so on); the tab-lature-stave line is read from the bottom up, so the top-course numbers are placed on the bottom tablature-stave line, the second-course numbers on the second from bottom, and so on up. This reflects the position in which the lute is held, with the lowest string at the top. Compare the two tablature systems in Exs. 3.1 and 3.2.

The Bologna manuscript is a three-folio fragment which shows considerable Spanish influence, and may have originated from the Spanish court in Naples in the last years of the fifteenth century.[22] One page is entitled 'La mano a la viola', sug-gesting the viola da mano, the Italian equivalent of the Spanish vihuela. The viola da mano was accepted in Italy wherever Spanish cultural influence was strong.[23] The Bologna manuscript is in 'Neapolitan' tablature. This system is the same way up as French tablature but uses '1' for the open string, and then each fret up the fingerboard is consecutively numbered from 2 upwards. The manuscript contains a version of a rondeau by Vincenet (Vincent du Bruecquet, organist and singer at the

[18] I-PESo 1144, fos. 1ʳ–32ᵛ and fos. 78ᵛ–81ʳ. Danner, 'Before Petrucci', 12.
[19] See Vladimir Ivanoff, 'An Invitation to the Fifteenth-Century Lute: The Pesaro Manuscript', in Victor Anand Coelho (ed.), *Performance of Lute, Guitar and Vihuela: Historical Practice and Modern Interpretation* (Cambridge, 1996), 1–15.
[20] Danner, 'Before Petrucci', 12–15. See also Walter H. Rubsamen, 'The Earliest French Lute Tablature', *JAMS* 21 (1968), 286–99.
[21] I-Bu 596 HH 24 and F-Pn Rés. Vmd. 275.   [22] Fallows, '15th-Century Tablatures', 26.
[23] Ian Woodfield, *The Early History of the Viol* (Cambridge, 1984). See ch. 5, 80–99.

Ex. 3.2. *'De tus biense', bars 1–15, from Pesaro MS, no. 13, fo. 21ʳ; plectrum polyphony*

Savoy chapel, 1450–64),[24] 'Fortune par ta cruaulté', with the two lower voices
intabulated and an upper voice in mensural notation without words. Performance
was probably by a combination of a *tenorista* playing the lower two entabulated parts
on a viola da mano or lute, with the upper part in mensural notation being used by
a soloist on lute, viola da mano, or gittern, as the basis for fast 'plectrum-style'
embellishment.[25]

[24] See David Fallows, *A Catalogue of Polyphonic Songs, 1415–1480* (Oxford, 1999), 724.
[25] Fallows, '15th-Century Tablatures', 27.

The earliest source of Italian lute tablature proper, the Thibault manuscript, probably belonged to a lutenist-singer with a Venetian background, and was compiled in the years after 1500.[26] It contains as wide a variety of repertory as the Petrucci books of 1507–11. Intabulations of both fifteenth-century French chansons and the newer Italian frottola co-exist with some dance music. In spite of the unusual chord alignment problems encountered in the tablature, the book was compiled for a player using finger-plucking techniques rather than a plectrum.[27]

Seventeenth- and eighteenth-century written authorities on the lute had, in general, only a vague awareness of lute music and lute practice in the earlier part of the sixteenth century, yet were agreed on one thing: that, as the Burwell Tutor quotation at the head of this chapter shows, lute makers from this early period, and especially those from Bologna, produced lutes that were never surpassed.[28] The author of the Burwell Tutor names the German makers Laux Maler and Hans Frei as 'the two chiefest Lutemakers that have lived at Bologna'.[29] The instruments made by these makers were of a classic body form that was admired and copied by later generations of lute makers.[30] Instruments that survived into the seventeenth and eighteenth centuries became enormously valuable, and, like Stradivari violins in the nineteenth and twentieth centuries, were repeatedly renecked and restrung, so that they could play music of a later age. The two Maler instruments in the Prague Národní Muzeum are a case in point. Both were converted into 13-course lutes by Thomas Edlinger in the 1720s, although earlier seventeenth-century neck alterations were probably undertaken prior to Edlinger's work.[31] The perfection of lute design in Italy in the first decades of the sixteenth century, together with the new polyphonic right-hand finger techniques, helped to establish the lute as perhaps the leading 'art music' instrument of the sixteenth century throughout Europe.

It is remarkable that from the evidence we have today, with a few exceptions, early sixteenth-century lutes of quality were made exclusively by Germans.[32] The

---

[26] The MS is available in facsimile edition as *Tablature de luth italienne . . . Fac-similé du ms. de la Bibliothèque nationale, Paris, Rés. Vmd. ms. 27* (Geneva, 1981). For a discussion of the MS see Lewis Jones, 'The Thibault Lute Manuscript: An Introduction', Part I, *LSJ* 22 (1982), 69–87 and Part II, *LSJ* 23 (1983), 21–6.

[27] Ibid., Part I, 72–4.

[28] Such later authorities include Jacques Gaultier, Thomas Mace, John Evelyn, Ernst Gottlieb Baron, and Alessandro Piccinini.

[29] *Burwell Lute Tutor*, fo. 3ʳ.

[30] In particular, the 18th-c. school of Martin and Johann Christoph Hoffman, who modelled their design on that of Maler and Frei.

[31] The 13-course conversions were no doubt for Prince Philip Lobkovitz, as the instruments were found in 1872 in the old chapel of Schloss Eisenberg, which had belonged to the Lobkovitz family.

[32] Hellwig, 'Lute-Making in the Late 15th and 16th Century', 24–38. The only exceptions to the monopoly of German makers are Italians in Italy before the arrival of the German makers, and possibly also Spanish instrument makers who may on occasion have made lutes. See Prizer, 'Lutenists at the Court of Mantua', 18–19, for references to Lorenzo da Pavia *c.*1500, instrument maker to Isabella d'Este, who made lutes and surely was Italian. In 16th-c. Spain the making of a lute was a requirement in the examination of viol makers. See Diana Poulton, 'The Lute in Christian Spain', *LSJ* 19 (1977), 34–49 at 39–40.

craft was especially well established in southern Germany in the fifteenth century
in the regions of Innsbruck, Augsburg, and Füssen. Füssen in Bavaria is of great
significance to the history of lute-making, as it was close to the forests containing
the rare yew wood that was deemed the best material for lute ribs, as well as spruce
for the soundboards, and because several of the most illustrious lute-making families originally came from the town. In the second half of the fifteenth century some
German lute makers migrated to north Italian cities, where they set up workshops.[33] Such makers kept their links with southern Germany, whence wood, and
possibly also lute parts that were semi-finished, were obtained for use in the construction of lutes in Italian workshops prior to distribution throughout Europe.

Laux Maler is the best-known maker of the early sixteenth century. His career
development may have been paralleled by other less well known German lute makers. The son of a lute maker, of 'Alemania alta', Maler had set up a workshop in
Bologna by 1518. His will of 1552 shows him to have been a man of some wealth,
owning four houses, three shops, and employing at least four men (all German).
Sigismund Maler, a famous mid-century lute maker working in Venice, may have
been a son or relation of Laux. The most surprising entries in Maler's will of 1552
relate to 998 finished lutes of every description contained in his workshop, plus 127
others in various stages of completion.[34] This huge number of lutes gives us an idea
of the scale of his operation, and Maler was not alone. As already mentioned, Hans
Frei had a workshop in Bologna at much the same time as Maler, as did another
German, Nikolaus Schonfeld.[35]

During the sixteenth century other German lute makers set up workshops in
Italian cities other than Bologna: in Venice, Marx Unverdorben, possibly a student
of Laux Maler; in Venice and Padua, the famous Tieffenbrucker/Venere family,
who came originally from the village of Tieffenbruck near Füssen, and Michielle
and Andreas Harton; in Rome, Mattaeus Bueckenberg.[36] Inventories and tax assessments of the Tieffenbrucker workshop in Venice show that their production of lutes
was on a scale similar to that of the Maler workshop in Bologna, and that hundreds
if not thousands of lutes or lute parts in various stages of assemblage were found in
the workshops at the time of stock-taking. These lutes were sold both retail and
wholesale. The income produced was sufficient for the family to be 'far more com-
fortable financially than most other Venetian craftsmen'.[37] Surviving evidence suggests that these makers, together with those that remained in Germany, successfully

---

[33] German lute makers had been resident in Siena for some time before 1465: see Frank A. D'Accone, *The Civic Muse: Music and Musicians in Siena during the Middle Ages and the Renaissance* (Chicago, 1997), 655–7.

[34] Michael J. Prynne, 'The Old Bologna Lute-Makers', *LSJ* 5 (1963), 18–31.   [35] Ibid. 29.

[36] For information on Venetian makers see Stefano Toffolo, *Antichi strumenti veneziani: 1500–1800* (Venice, 1987); for the latest information on the Tieffenbrucher family see Giulio M. Ongaro, 'The Tieffenbruckers and the Business of Lute-Making in Sixteenth-Century Venice', *GSJ* 44 (1991), 46–54.

[37] Ibid. 48–51.

monopolized the manufacture of lutes for much of the sixteenth century. The superiority of their instruments, the scale of their operations, and their control of the
market was such that it seems that little professional specialist lute-making took
place elsewhere in Europe until well into the century.

While no doubt the older, medieval type of lute, perhaps more suitable for
single-line plectrum playing, continued to be made in more isolated areas, it seems
that only Germans could produce lutes in the new Renaissance design. Countries
like England and France, where Renaissance lutes suitable for polyphony became
popular during the century, were thus, at first, largely reliant on imported lutes.

Very few lutes by early sixteenth-century makers survive. The oldest is probably
that by Matheus Pocht of 'Artzell pey Innsbrugg', dated 1519.[38] Some four by
Maler and five by Hans Frei exist, together with three by Unverdorben.[39] None
survive by Sigismund Maler or Nicholas Schonfeld. This low incidence of survival,
despite the large numbers that were produced, is probably due to their continuous
use by later generations.[40] However, from the few that do survive, together with
accurate contemporary drawings, paintings and *intarsie*, we have a good idea of the
general shape of these instruments. Lutes of the fifteenth century, as typified by the
Arnault design (see Pl. 3.2), tend to have a 'plump' round body shape. According
to Arnault this shape was produced by drawing a half-circle for the lower part of
the body, and then opening the compass up to the diameter of the circle to draw
two arcs which curve in on either side of the neck for the upper part of the body.[41]

As lute technique developed from the monophonic plectrum style to the polyphonic finger-plucking style, so lute design altered to meet the new requirements
of players. The pear-shaped body developed by Maler, Frei, and others is much
longer, with the circular lower body shape flattened out at the base of the instrument. This shape was achieved using three radii (see Fig. 3.1). First the compass
was opened out to the length of the body and a small arc inscribed for the bass of
the lute. Then the line was continued round to the widest point of the outline
using a short radius. Finally the compass was opened out to a length up to twice
the previous diameter, and then used to continue the line by arcing up to the neck
end.[42]

[38] This instrument was formerly owned by the British Lute Society, but is now owned by the lutenist Anthony
Bailes.

[39] Prynne, 'The Old Bologna Lute-Makers'. Prynne lists five by Maler, but the Vienna instrument can be discounted as it is almost certainly a fake. See also id., 'A Note on Marx Unverdorben', *LSJ* 1 (1959), 58.

[40] Alessandro Piccinini, in his *Intavolatura di liuto et di chitarrone* (Bologna, 1623), p. 5, cap. xxvii, 'Dell'origine
del chitarrone', relates that the French came especially to Bologna to take lutes back to France, paying anything
that was asked for them, so that very few were left.

[41] Harwood, 'A Fifteenth-Century Lute Design', 3.

[42] For a full description of this process together with a concise overview of historical lute construction, see
Robert Lundberg, 'Historical Lute Construction: The Erlangen Lectures, Day One', *American Lutherie*, 12
(Winter, 1987), 37–47.

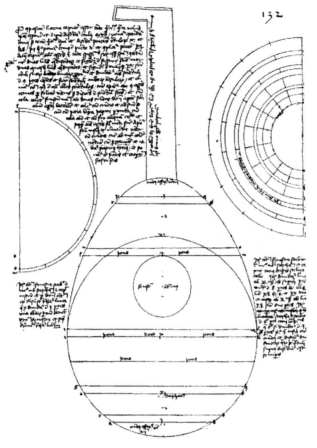

132

PL. 3.2. (a) Henri
Arnault de Zwolle's
diagram of a lute, mid-
fifteenth century, from
Paris, Bibliothèque
Nationale de France, lat.
7295, p. 132; (b) the back
of two Renaissance pear-
shaped lutes, *left* by
Laux Maler of Bologna,
early sixteenth century;
right by Marx
Unverdorben of Venice,
mid-sixteenth century;
Victoria and Albert
Museum

(*a*)

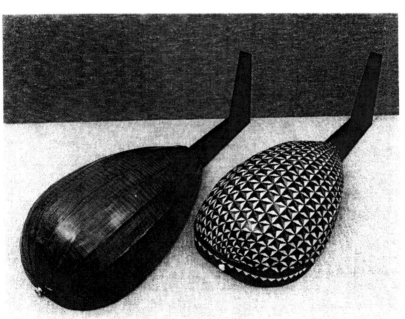

(*b*)

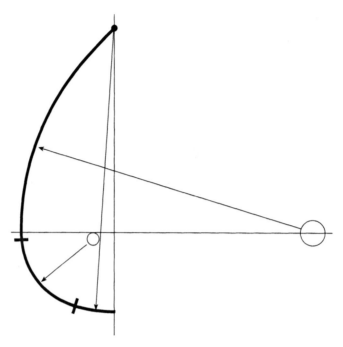

FIG. 3.1. *Diagram of the three arcs used to produce the pearl-shaped mould used by Italian makers of the early sixteenth century*

Lutes of the early sixteenth century normally had nine or eleven ribs and eight frets. Typically these instruments had six courses, the top being a single string, the lower courses double, with unisons on the second and third courses, and octaves for the lowest three courses. Seven-course lutes were not unknown, as one of the earliest surviving sources shows, and contemporary authorities confirm.[43] Like most other favoured instruments of the Renaissance era, the lute was being built in a variety of sizes by the mid and later sixteenth century, from a great bass to a small octave. Approximate top-string pitches for the Renaissance lute family are: small octave *g″*; descant *d″*, alto *a′*; tenor *g′*; bass *d′* or *c′*; great bass *a*.[44] The solo member of the lute family was often the tenor or 'mean' lute tuned *g′*, *d′*, *a*, *f*, *c*, *G*, a tuning that became known in the next century as the *vieil ton* or 'old tuning'. This 'classic' lute remained the norm until late into the sixteenth century, when, in the final decades, lute design again began a period of rapid change.

---

[43] The Pesaro MS of *c.*1500 contains music for a 7-course instrument. Virdung in his *Musica getutscht*, sig. I3ʳ, mentions lutes with seven courses.

[44] Lundberg, 'Historical Lute Construction', 34–5.

In summary, it is clear from German and Italian sources that lute playing on the Continent from the mid-fifteenth century onwards was undergoing a fundamental transition. The improvisatory monophonic plectrum style, performed with a second instrument to provide a tenor line or chordal accompaniment, was giving way to a harmonically self-sufficient polyphonic style, using the fingers of the right hand to pluck the strings directly. There is every indication that the two techniques overlapped well into the sixteenth century, when plectrum playing became less common. Inextricably linked to the development of polyphonic intabulations of vocal music is the first appearance of lute tablature. No English tablature survives from before the mid-sixteenth century so it is impossible to say with certainty when these developments reached England. The lute was increasing in popularity around the close of the fifteenth century, while interest in the harp was decreasing. One reason for this may have been that the diatonic limitations of the early harp meant it could not keep pace with musical developments.

John Stevens points to the absence in the Cely papers of any indication that Cely could read music, and suggests that Rede had to 'lerne' him to play by ear.[45] I have argued that learning and memorizing this way is easy and logical if playing only a single line. To learn a two- or three-part texture by rote, without the benefit of tablature, is a very much more difficult exercise. A ballad like 'Myn hertis lust sterre of my comfort', which we know Cely learnt, and which survives in the Mellon Chansonnier, perhaps works best with a lute intabulating the two lower parts, and a voice on the top line.[46] This would allow for the 'ficta' chromaticism that the piece requires, which on the diatonic harp would be difficult, and would enable Cely to perform all three parts unaided. Such a solo arrangement would be much facilitated with some form of tablature, though there is no actual evidence for this. Other evidence that lute music was being written down in England in the fifteenth century appears in a list of music possessed by an unknown musician, scribbled down on the back of an ecclesiastical document.[47] Among them is the item 'all songys for the leute'. This could mean songs or dance music, but does suggest polyphony and finger plucking for the music to have required writing down in some form.

The English royal household at the turn of the century still employed only one or two specialist lutenists, just as it had in the late medieval period. Henry VII did, however, take care to have all his children taught the lute, and there are odd references to lutes and lute playing in royal circles in the 1490s, such as the payment in 1492 of 6s. 8d. to 'one that pleyed on the lute', and twice in 1496 of 13s. 4d. to 'Hugh Denes for a lute'.[48] A quickening of interest in the lute at the English court is much

[45] John Stevens, *Music and Poetry in the Early Tudor Court* (Cambridge, 1961; rev. edn., 1979), 284.

[46] New Haven, Yale University, Beinecke Rare Book and Manuscript Library, MS 91. For an edition see *The Mellon Chansonnier*, ed. Leeman L. Perkins and Howard Garey, 2 vols. (New Haven, 1979).

[47] *GB-Lbl* Add. 38163. [48] *RECM* vii. 151, 155.

more apparent in the early years of the sixteenth century, no doubt due to the introduction of the new polyphonic lute technique. There is no musical evidence that the new style of lute playing using the fingers had reached England before the sixteenth century, but there are strong indications that some people in cosmopolitan circles were playing polyphonic intabulated music on the lute in late fifteenth-century England.

Chapter Four

The Early and Mid-Renaissance Periods 1500–1580

Bewaile with me all ye that have profest
Of musicke tharte by touche of coarde or winde:
Laye downe your lutes and let your gitterns rest,
Phillips is dead whose like you can not find
Of musicke much exceadying all the rest,
Muses therfore of force now must you wrest.
Your pleasant notes into another sound,
The stringe is broke, the lute is dispossest,
The hand is cold, the bodye in the ground.
The lowring lute lamenteth now therfore,
Phillips her frende that can her touche no more.

'On the death of Philips', lamenting the death
of Philip van Wilder[1]

The first eighty years of the sixteenth century would appear to lack coherence as a chapter unit of English lute history. The period is not circumscribed by any change of monarch, specific historic event, or easily defined stylistic change. Yet we have seen that, as regards the lute, fundamental change was occurring on the Continent, particularly in Italy, with the introduction of new making and playing techniques in the years up to and around 1500. It is after this point that these changes took hold in England, as they did throughout much of western Europe. The years 1578–9 saw the appointment of Mathias (or Mathathias) Mason and John Johnson as royal lutenists and, in the following years, the appointment of several more lutenists of note, and the instigation of a specific consort of lutes among the Queen's Musick. Johnson is the first native English lutenist composer of real merit, and his appointment marks a turning point.

The earliest surviving sources of English lute music date from around the mid-sixteenth century. They are mostly commonplace books compiled by amateurs who had only modest musical and technical skills. Sources from the 1570s are both more numerous and of more consistent quality, indicating that lute playing was more popular, and that lute skills were becoming more widespread. Clearly the court took

[1] From *Songs and Sonnettes* (1557). The poem is quoted in full in Jane A. Bernstein, 'Philip van Wilder and the Netherlandish Chanson in England', *Musica disciplina*, 33 (1979), 55–75. *Songes and Sonnettes* (1557) is published in *Tottel's Miscellany 1557–1587*, ed. Hyder E. Rollins (rev. edn., Cambridge, Mass., 1965).

the lead. The ability to play intabulated polyphonic music, which entailed plucking
the strings directly with the fingers, was almost certainly introduced by foreign-
born musicians. Henry VII's court was visited by many Continental musicians, and
Henry VIII actively recruited foreigners, particularly from Italy, in his bid to
develop London as a European centre of the arts. Instruments like the viol and violin were introduced this way. The lute had been present in England for two centuries before 1500, but the 6-course lute in the form developed by makers working
in the northern Italian cities probably first appeared in England at court around
1500. This type of lute remained the norm throughout the eighty years that followed. During this time Continental playing and compositional techniques were
absorbed and developed, such that by 1580 a truly English style of lute playing was
ready to flower.

It has been noted that in fifteenth-century England the term gittern referred to
an instrument like the medieval lute in many respects, though normally smaller in
size and carved from a solid piece of wood. John Ward believes that by 1550 the
term 'gittern' referred to a rather different instrument, namely a small 4-course
cittern with the tuning 4th–3th–4th, though there is scant evidence for such an
instrument before the seventeenth century. This instrument may be seen as a continuation of the old medieval English gittern, but was strung in metal and was
played with a quill like the cittern.[2] Confusion surrounds the use of the term 'gittern' in England at this time due to the presence of the gut-strung 4-course guitar,
which was particularly popular in France around the mid-century. This gut-strung
guitar also had the tuning 4th–3th–4th and was termed the 'guiterne' by Le Roy in
his lost instruction book published in Paris in 1551. An English translation of this
book, of which a fragment survives, appeared in England as *An instruction to the
Gitterne* (1569), published by James Rowbotham.[3] This confusion over names
means that the references to the gittern in the sixteenth century (or its many variant spellings, i.e getarn, getron, getterne, gytern, gytryn, etc.) must always be
treated with caution. The mention of 'gitterns' in the quotation above from the
lament on the death of Philip van Wilder is a case in point.

Sometime shortly before 1550 Thomas Whythorne 'learned to play on the
Gyttern, and Sittern. which ij instruments wer then strange in England, and ther-
for the mor dezyred and esteemed'.[4] We may assume Whythorne means the cittern
and the 4-course guitar, not the old English gittern, but we cannot be sure. What
do we make of the item listed in the royal inventory of musical instruments of
1542/3 that mentions 'four Gitterns with 4 Cases to them', or in the same inven-

---

[2] John Ward, 'Sprightly and Cheerful Musick: Notes on the Cittern, Gittern and Guitar in Sixteenth- and
Seventeenth-Century England', *LSJ* 21–2 (1979–81), 6; *Music for Elizabethan Lutes*, 2 vols. (Oxford, 1992), 28.
[3] Ward, 'Sprightly and Cheerful Musick', 16.
[4] Thomas Whythorne, *The Autobiography of Thomas Whythorne*, ed. James M. Osborn (Oxford, 1961), 19.

tory 'oone Gittern and oone Lute beinge in a case Chest'.[5] A further confusion arises in the case of the 'Four Gitterons with 4 cases to them: they are caulled Spanishe Vialles' in a royal inventory of 1547, which, it has been suggested, refers to bridgeless drone viols of the type developed in Spain in the fifteenth century as a bowed version of the *vihuela de mano*.[6] In truth we cannot be sure if the old gut-strung medieval gittern, the gut-strung 4-course guitar, Ward's metal-strung cittern, or some other type of instrument altogether, is being referred to in any one of these references. By 1580 interest in the gut-strung guitar had decreased, and there are far fewer references to gitterns to trouble us. By contrast, the lute was gaining in popularity around 1580, playing skills were improving and the wealth of the repertoire circulating in manuscripts ever increasing.

Iconographical evidence of the new Renaissance pearl-shaped lute in England made by the Bologna makers survives from around 1530. There are a number of pictures by Hans Holbein the Younger that include a lute of the new Italian type. Most famous perhaps is that of the French ambassadors, Jean de Dinteville and Georges de Selve, painted in 1533, now in the National Gallery. Here the lute is included, with a book of music and some wind instruments, to illustrate the musical pursuits of these worldy men. The lute has eleven T-shaped pegs, typical of Italian lutes in iconography of the late fifteenth and early sixteenth centuries (see Pl. 4.1). As with several lutes in Italian *intarsie*, a string is broken. In this case it is the thin octave string of the fourth course. The broken string reflects not only the reality of gut stringing, but, together with other artefacts in the picture, such as the crucifix and the distorted skull, is symbolic of death and disharmony. It has been suggested that the picture is a meditation on the embassy of the two ambassadors, that the pillar dial gives the date as Good Friday, 11 April 1533, the deadline set by Henry VIII for Pope Clement VII to agree to his divorce, and that the ominous symbols are portents of the forthcoming fragmentation of Christendom.[7]

Another Holbein portrait now in Berlin prominently features a lute (see Pl. 4.2).[8] The subject is a bearded man who holds a lute in his left hand and a letter in the other. This 6-course lute may be of slightly later manufacture than *The Ambassadors*'s lute, as the pegs are now heart-shaped. The progression from T-shaped to heart-shaped pegs can be seen in Italian iconography *c*.1500–20. John Ward has suggested that the subject of the portrait may be Philip van Wilder.[9] Philip van Wilder was a Fleming who rose to an exalted position in Henry's household as lutenist, composer, and Gentleman of the Privy Chamber to both Henry and his son Edward VI. Holbein died in 1543, so if it is Philip's portrait, and there are

[5] *RECM* vii. 387.   [6] Ibid. 393; Woodfield, *The Early History of the Viol*, 206–7.

[7] Richard Foster and Pamela Tudor-Craig, *The Secret Life of Paintings* (Woodbridge, 1986), 75–95.

[8] Berlin, Staatliche Museen Preußischer Kulturbesitz, Gemäldegalerie.

[9] Ward, *Music for Elizabethan Lutes*, i. 2.

PL. 4.1. Detail from
Hans Holbein the
Younger, *The
Ambassadors*, 1533.
London, National
Gallery

PL. 4.2. Hans
Holbein the Younger,
Man with a Lute.
Berlin, Staatliche
Museen Preußischer
Kulturbesitz,
Gemäldegalerie

arguments aginst this,[10] the picture must have been painted before this date. Two other pictures by Holbein include lutes. One, a drawing of Apollo and the Muses, was designed for the coronation of Anne Boleyn in 1533, and includes a lute together with a number of other instruments surrounding Apollo playing his harp.[11] The other, the 'More Family' portrait, the original of which no longer exists, includes a lute together with a viol. A copy of the original was made by Rowland Lockey in the 1590s, and is now in Nostrell Priory, Wakefield.[12] A further copy is owned by the National Portrait Gallery (see Pl. 4.3). Again the lute depicted has nine ribs but only six frets.

Some English iconography from the first quarter of the sixteenth century shows lutes of the medieval type. The stone carving of a lute-playing angel in King's College Chapel (c.1508–16) and the minstrel lutenist among the five minstrels on the 'Minstrel's Pillar' at St Mary's Church, Beverley (1520–4), a church associated with the guild of minstrels, both show lutes of the medieval 'rounded' type. They are played standing up, with a right-hand position suggestive of plectrum technique.[13] A woodcarving dated c.1540 in the collection of Guy Oldham shows a very different left-hand position with the fingers directly plucking the strings,[14] as do a bench end at Sloley church, Norfolk, and a corbel of a lutenist also at St Mary's Church, Beverley, both of which also date from the early sixteenth century. There is a woodcut of a medieval-type lute in an Oxford manuscript illustrating the 'Beautie of Women', which is dated c.1525.[15] *GB-Och* illuminated MS 101, commissioned by Cardinal Wolsey and executed in the Netherlands, also contains two interesting lute portrayals, though since the manuscript was put together abroad it may have little relevance to England. Folio 27ᵛ shows a lute and recorder played together by angels. The lute is played with the fingers but is round in shape and has five or six strings. On fo. 35ᵛ another angel lutenist appears playing a similar lute together with a harpist. Here five gold strings are visible. The most interesting features of both these illustrations are the bridge-like bars on the belly near the body/neck intersection. These features usually appear on fiddles and citoles of the fourteenth and fifteenth centuries. The function of such bars has never been explained, but their inclusion together with the instrument's shape is clearly archaic.

Sixteenth-century English lute iconography is rare in comparison with Continental, especially Italian, iconography. However, there are sufficient

---

[10] I am grateful to David van Edwards for pointing out to me that the lutenist wears a boatswain's whistle around his neck. This was the insignia of the Lord High Admiral, an office held by John Dudley, Viscount Lisle from 1543, and the future Duke of Northumberland.

[11] Remnant, *English Bowed Instruments*, pl. 149.

[12] Ibid., pl. 174. Another copy exists in the Victoria and Albert Museum.

[13] Ibid., pls. 142, 145.   [14] Lute Society Picture Collection.

[15] 'Beautie of Women' (c.1525), *GB-Ob* Rawl D. 1220, fo. 31ᵛ.

representations from the first three decades to show the continuation of the medieval-type lute, alongside that of the newly imported Renaissance lute known in court circles, and depicted by Holbein in works from the 1530s. A little-known wall-painting survives at Brammell Hall which shows a typical minstrel with a medieval-type lute. Lute iconography in the first two decades of Elizabeth I's reign is no more plentiful. Undoubtedly the most important representation is that on the Hardwick Hall 'Eglantine' table (*c.*1568), in which a lute, cittern, and 4-course guitar are portrayed in different shades of wood, along with other instruments and music books, one of which contains tablature.[16] Here the lute is the classic 6-course Renaissance lute that we would expect for the period of the table's construction. Of particular interest is the portrait of a young girl by Hans Eworth (fl. *c.*1540–73) tentatively dated *c.*1565 (see Pl. 4.4). The splendidly dressed girl has a small quarto tablature book open on her lap. Her instrument is a 6-course lute (single first course) with heart-shaped pegs. The fretboard of her lute appears to extend onto the belly, and covers the area over the block. This unusual feature is seen in some early and mid-sixteenth century Italian pictures of lutes.

References to the lute at the court of Henry VIII confirm that the instrument had replaced the harp as the courtly instrument par excellence, and a fit and proper instrument for princes and princesses to play; this despite the impression given by the famous manuscript illumination of Henry playing the harp to his fool.[17] Henry VII had seen to it that all his children were given lutes: Prince Henry at the age of 7 in 1498; and the princesses Margaret and Mary at 7 (1501), and 12 (1505) respectively.[18] Each lute was bought for the same amount, 13*s.* 4*d.* This may have been a standard sum for minor court expenses, as Giles Duwes was given the same amount in 1507 'for strynges for my Lady Mares lute'.[19] Although there is no reference to Arthur receiving a lute, 'Guyllam', one of the king's musicians, is described in January 1498/9 as 'my Lorde Prince luter', and may have instructed him on the instrument.[20] Glowing reports of the lute playing of Princess Mary and Prince Henry are recorded.[21] The Venetian ambassador, Magnifico Piero Pasqualigo, wrote in 1515 of Henry, who at the age of 23 had been king since 1509: 'He speaks French, English and Latin, and a little Italian, plays well on the lute and

---

[16] David Collins, 'A 16th-Century Manuscript in Wood: The Eglantine Table at Hardwick Hall', *EM* 4 (1976), 275–9.

[17] *GB-Lbl* Royal 2.A.xvi, fo. 63ᵛ. A photograph appears in Southworth, *The English Medieval Minstrel*, 152.

[18] *RECM* vii. 163, viii. 171, 177. Also see Sydney Anglo, 'The Court Festivals of Henry VII: A Study Based upon the Account Books of John Heron, Treasurer of the Chamber', *Bulletin of the John Rylands Library*, 43 (1960–1), 12–45 at 33, 36, 40. For a summary of the lute-playing activities of the Tudor royal family see John Ward, 'A Dowland Miscellany', *JLSA* 10 (1977), 5–151 at 112–14.

[19] *RECM* vii. 185.   [20] Ibid. 165.

[21] For an account of Mary's playing at the reception of Philip, King of Castile, at Windsor Castle in 1506, see *Historia regis Henrici septimi*, ed. James Gairdner (London, 1858), 288–9; also see Sebastian Giustinian, *Four Years at the Court of Henry VIII*, trans. Rawdon Brown, 2 vols. (London, 1854), i. 86.

PL. 4.3. Rowland Lockey
(partly after Holbein
153–?), *Sir Thomas More
and his Descendants*, 1593.
London, National Portrait
Gallery, no.2765

PL. 4.4. Portrait of a girl
with a lute by Hans
Eworth, *c*.1565. Private
collection

harpsichord, sings from books at sight, draws the bow with greater strength than any man in England, and jousts marvellously.'[22]

Like his father, Henry VIII also had all his children taught the lute, including his bastard son Henry Fitzroy, Duke of Richmond, his son by Elizabeth Blount.[23] The Princess and future Queen Mary may have received instruction from Giles Duwes, one of the king's luters who attended on the Princess in 1525–6, and she certainly did receive lute tuition from Philip van Wilder.[24] Princess Mary was encouraged to practise the lute and virginals by her mother Katherine of Aragon.[25] Katherine herself was no musician, but was well educated, and was an important patron of humanistic scholarship.[26] When Mary became Queen she continued to practise, as Giovanni Michiel noted in his letter to the Venetian Senate on 13 May 1557: 'She also practises music, playing especially on the claricorde (*manicordo*) and on the lute so excellently that, when intent on it (though now she plays rarely), she surprised the best performers, both by the rapidity of her hand and by her style of playing.'[27]

The teaching of the lute by Philip van Wilder to Prince Edward, the future Edward VI, was also successful, so much so that Edward was able to entertain the Mareshal St Andre with his lute in July 1551.[28] In 1553, Christopher Tye, in the dedication of his *Actes of the Apostles* to Edward, suggested that instead of love songs, the king should perform Tye's pieces on the lute:

> That such good thinges your grace might move,
> Your lute when ye assaye:
> In stade of songes of wanton love
> These stories then to playe.[29]

Tye's title-page also states they are 'supplied with notes to eche chapter, to synge and also to play upon the lute'. The implication here is that Edward should either sing one of the parts of Tye's four-part settings of the verses from the first fourteen chapters of the *Actes* to his own lute accompaniment, a known mode of private performance of psalms at this time, or perform them as lute solos. Against this it must be said that the *Actes* would be difficult, if not impossible to play, if literally intabulated, and would need simplification to be made playable in any form.

---

[22] Giustinian, *Four Years*, i. 86

[23] In May 1531 Henry paid 20s. to 'Arthur [Duwes] the lewter for a lewte for the duke of Richemond'; see *RECM* vii. 367.

[24] PRO E. 101/420/11, fo. 1; see *The Privy Purse Expenses of the Princess Mary*, ed. F. Madden (London, 1831).

[25] *Letters and Papers, Foreign and Domestic, of the Reign of Henry VIII*, ed. John S. Brewer, vi (London, 1882), 472.

[26] Maria Dowling, *Humanism in the Age of Henry VIII* (London, 1986).

[27] *Calendar of State Papers and Manuscripts, Relating to English Affairs Existing in the Archives and Collections of Venice, and in other Libraries of Northern Italy*, ed. Rawdon Brown, vi, part 2: 1556–57 (London, 1881), no. 884, p. 1055.

[28] Noted by the king in his journal. See J. G. Nichol, *Literary Remains of King Edward the Sixth* (London, 1857), ii. 332–3, or *The Chronicle and Political Papers of King Edward VI*, ed. W. K. Jordan (London, 1966).

[29] M. C. Boyd, *Elizabethan Music and Musical Criticism* (Philadelphia, 1940), 69.

PL. 4.5. Nicholas Hilliard,
miniature of Queen Elizabeth
playing the lute *c.*1580.
Berkeley Castle

We know that Princess Elizabeth was playing the lute during her residence at Hatfield from 1551 to 1552, as there is a payment to 'John Baptist [Bassano?], for lute stringes for her grace'.[30] There is a needlework picture of the young princess surrounded by artefacts symbolic of the arts and crafts she learnt.[31] Among them is a lute-like instrument held by a lady-in-waiting. The famous miniature of Elizabeth holding a lute by Nicholas Hilliard now at Berkeley Castle probably dates from around 1580, but may be earlier (see Pl. 4.5).[32] In the summer of 1559 Baron Breuner, emissary of the Archduke Charles, heard Elizabeth play while travelling in a boat on the river Thames. 'She spoke a long while with me, and invited me to leave my boat and take a seat in that of the Treasurer's. She then had her boat laid alongside and played upon the lute.'[33] Charles of Styria (1540–90) was the younger brother of the emperor Maximilian II. Through emissaries he was effectively courting Elizabeth by proxy. The possibility of this marriage was a political expedient for

---

[30] *RECM* vii. 382.

[31] Private collection of Irwin Untermeyer. See David Scott, 'Elizabeth I as Lutenist', *LSJ* 18 (1976), 45.

[32] Reproduced in Christopher Hogwood, *Music at Court* (London, 1977), 35.

[33] Victor von Klarwill, *Queen Elizabeth and Some Foreigners*, trans. T. H. Nash (London, 1928), 96.

the Queen at this time, as a means of deflecting native suitors. Her lute playing was intended to show off her accomplishments as a future wife.

There is a report that in 1565 Henry Lord Berkeley bought a lute of mother-of-pearl for his wife, for which Queen Elizabeth had offered 100 marks.[34] In the summer of that year another emissary of the Archduke Charles, Adam von Zwetkovich, Baron von Mitterburg heard the Queen play '. . . very beautifully upon the clavichord and the lute'.[35] Camden in his *Annales* says that Elizabeth could sing and play on the lute 'prettily and sweetly'.[36] John Playford tells it differently, and stated, in an edition of *An Introduction to the Skill of Musick* (1687), that she '. . . did often recreate herself upon an excellent Instrument called the Polyphant, not much unlike a Lute, but strung with wire'.[37] Donald Gill has suggested that the instrument referred to in this Playford quotation was the orpharion rather than the polyphant, an instrument not invented in Elizabeth's lifetime.[38] It is clear that such lute playing as the Queen did was confined to her youth and early maturity, and that with the onset of middle age in the 1570s and 1580s such activities were curtailed.

As well as Henry VIII's children, at least two of his wives played the lute, and their relationships with professional musicians played a part in the downfall of both queens. Anne Boleyn could play the lute and accompany herself on the instrument. Her close association with the virginalist Mark Smeaton, a musician of the Privy Chamber, led to accusations of adultery to which Smeaton confessed under torture.[39] Catherine Howard's early study of the lute at 14 in 1534 may have indirectly played a part in her disgrace. At her trial it was claimed that she had had lovers while living at Horsham in the house of her step-grandmother, the Dowager Duchess of Norfolk, among them her lute teacher Henry Mannox.[40]

The sixteenth century saw the final stages in the transformation of the medieval English minstrel into the Renaissance musician. As a nominal retainer and all-round entertainer a minstrel might probably have been proficient on a number of instruments, worn the livery of his patron, and spent much of his time travelling around to regional fairs and visiting other great houses.[41] With the importation of a number of prominent families of foreign musicians, mainly Italian, by Henry VIII, the function of minstrels changed into that of household music teachers, performers, and composers, with a much improved status and access to family members. This process was slow, and, outside the royal household and that of a few select mag-

---

[34] T. D. Forsbroke, *Berkeley Manuscripts* (London, 1821), 102.   [35] Klarwill, *Queen Elizabeth*, 228.

[36] William Camden, *The historie of . . . princesse Elizabeth, late queene of England*, trans. R. Norton (London, 1635), 7.

[37] John Playford, *An Introduction to the Skill of Musick* (14th edn., London, 1687).

[38] Donald Gill, 'The Orpharion and Bandora', *GSJ* 13 (1960), 14–25 at 22.

[39] David Starkey (ed.), *Henry VIII: A European Court in England* (London, 1991), 105.

[40] This allegation was passed to Cranmer by John Lassels on information from Mary Lassels, chambere to the Duchess. See Neville Williams, *Henry VIII and his Court* (London, 1971), 208. PRO *SP* 167, fos. 135–6.

[41] Southworth, *The English Medieval Minstrel*, 142–55.

nates, did not take place until Elizabeth's reign, but the change was set in motion by Henry himself. Probably the first important group to arrive were the three members of the Flemish van Wilder family, Matthew, Philip, and Peter, some of whom were present at court as early as 1515.[42] The van Wilders were primarily lutenists who also played viols, and may have been the first to introduce the viol to England. Matthew might have played the viol in England as early as 1506, when he visited this country unexpectedly as a result of being shipwrecked while part of the entourage of Philip of Castile. Several of the King of Castile's minstrels played for the English King and were paid for their service on 20 February 1505/6.[43]

The next group of foreign musicians to be taken into royal service were two Germans, Hans Highorne and Hans Hassenet, specialist viol players who arrived in the 1520s.[44] Peter Holman has shown that in 1540, as part of the preparations for the Cleves wedding, a new consort of violins was instituted, drawn from four inter-related families of Sephardic Jews recruited in Italy.[45] Although described in accounts as players of 'Vialles', Holman has shown that, for the most part, they played violins, instruments then thought especially appropriate for dance music. This consort was an addition to the existing consorts for flutes and sackbuts. Thus during Henry's reign a new, larger 'King's Musick' took shape in which specialist pre-formed consorts of like instruments performed for specific functions. The increased revenues available to the Crown as a result of monastic seizures helped to make this possible. Musicians from abroad were more privileged than the old royal minstrels, and normally commanded greater respect and salaries. Their instruments and music were, in the main, drawn from northern Italian cities, where, as with the lute, new Renaissance musical ideas, instrumental techniques, and designs had first become popular.

In the 1490s Henry VII had established the Privy Chamber along French lines as part of his financial and political overhaul of government.[46] Up to this time all royal musicians were members of the Presence Chamber. With the establishment of the Privy Chamber, as laid down in statute in the Elthan Ordinances of 1526, some musicians, particularly those of the 'bas' or 'still' type (which included lute players), now gained access to the new Chamber while those of the 'haut' or 'loud' type remained outside.[47] (For a list of the professional lutenists in the royal household 1500–78 see Table 4.1.)

---

[42] Remnant, *English Bowed Instruments*, 73, 94. Quoted from Revel Accounts for 7 and 6 Jan. 1515 for the court at Greenwich.

[43] Peter Holman, *Four and Twenty Fiddlers: The Violin at the English Court 1540–1690* (Oxford, 1993), 73. Also Remnant, *English Bowed Instruments*, 73.

[44] Holman, *Four and Twenty Fiddlers*, 75.

[45] Peter Holman, 'The English Royal Violin Consort in the Sixteenth Century', *PRMA* 109 (1983), 39–59, and *Four and Twenty Fiddlers*, 78–100.

[46] David Starkey, *The English Court, from the Wars of the Roses to the Civil War* (London, 1987).

[47] Starkey, *Henry VIII: A European Court in England*, 105–6.

Table 4.1. *Professional lutenists in the royal household, 1500–1578*

Lutenist	Dates	Instruments and position	Salary
Giles Duwes	–1501–35	Lewter and Mynstrel of the chamber	£13. 6s. 8d. p.a. 1506–9, then 40s. per month
Arthur Duwes	1510–40	Lute	10s. 4d. p.m. (= 4d. a day)
Peter de Brescia	1512–c.1536	Lute	£40 p.a.
Matthew van Wilder	1516–17	Lute and viol	20 marks p.a. (= 22s. 2½d. p.m. or £17. 15s. 6d. p.a.)
Peter van Wilder	1519–62	Lute and viol; Groom of the Privy Chamber from 1553	£10 p.a. in 1519 increased to 31s. p.m. by 1525. Annuity paid from 1558 to 1562
Philip van Wilder	–1525–53	Lute, musician of the Privy Chamber in 1529, and Gentleman of the Privy Chamber from 1539	£40 p.a. annuity of £80 p.a. in 1551/2
Henry van Wilder	1553–7	Musician of the Privy Chamber[a]?	
Anthony Conti	1550/1–75[b]	Luter	£30. 8s. 4d. p.a. (= 20d. per day)
Thomas Lichfield	–1547–82 or later	Groom of the Privy Chamber	£2.6 13s. 4d. plus £40. 0s. 6d. livery
Alfonso Ferrabosco I	1562–78	Gentleman of the Privy Chamber[a]	£100 p.a.

[a] Possibly not a lutenist.

[b] With a possible period of absence 1557–64.

Until 1500 English kings had normally employed one, or possibly two minstrels designated 'luters'. Henry VII gave employment to 'Giles Duwes', a lutenist among the still minstrels (1501–35), who is often referred to in accounts as 'Giles' or 'Master Giles'. Other possible lutenists are: 'Watt' (also a fool), who we know was employed in 1504; 'Guillim', mentioned above in possible connection with Prince Arthur, who appears in accounts from 1492 to 1513; and 'Kenner', minstrel to Princess Margaret, the Queen of Scots, in 1503.[48] Henry VIII gave long-standing employment to Giles Duwes, who had continued in royal service from the previous reign, and to his son Arthur Duwes (1510–40). It was Arthur who was the probable lute tutor to the Duke of Richmond.[49] Giles was the recipient of many royal

[48] *RECM* vii. 176; 151, *passim*.

[49] See Andrew Ashbee, 'Groomed for Service: Musicians in the Privy Chamber at the English Court, c.1495–1558', *EM* 25 (1997), 185–97 at 189; Rastall, 'The Minstrels of the English Royal Households'; also *RECM* vii. 16, *passim*; 194, *passim*.

favours, including several lucrative licences to import tons of Toulouse woad and Gascon wine, 'custom from the port of Bristowe', and the posts of 'keeper of the place called "le Prince Warderobe"' in the city of London, and 'keeper of the King's library at his manor of Richemounte [Richmond]'.[50] Giles had first entered royal service as French tutor to the children of Henry VII, and may have been of French origin or extraction. His important post as librarian indicates that he was a man of considerable learning, quite apart from his musical accomplishments.[51]

Several important Italian lutenists were present at the Tudor court in the early years of Henry's reign. The most important was John Peter de Brescia who is mentioned first in 1512 as receiving an annuity of £40 p.a., and was still serving the Princess Mary in 1533.[52] This man appears with some frequency in accounts between 1514 and 1518 as John Peter de Brescia, John Piero, Zuan Piero, and Giovanni Pietro de Bustis (as he once signed himself). He was a particular favourite of the king at this time and is referred to in one letter as the King's 'confidential attendant'.[53] According to an account by the Venetian ambassador's secretary, Nicolo Sagudino, which is addressed to Alvise Foscari the Signory of Venice, Henry gave a dinner for foreign ambassadors at Greenwich on May Day 1515, after which music was performed. Sagudino relates that: 'Among the listeners was a Brescian, to whom the King gives 300 ducats a year for playing the lute, and who took up his instruments and played a few things with him [Sagudino].'[54] Sagudino goes on to describe his own organ playing at the same event as superior to that of any in the king's service. He notes that the king himself practised the organ day and night. Finally he asks to have sent from Italy compositions by 'Zuane Maria'. This request shows Sagudino to have been aware of recent developments in Venetian lute music, as Gian Maria was one of the foremost lutenists in Italy at this time. Another letter by Sagudino dated 19 May 1517 discusses events at Richmond, and shows that John Peter was upset by a rival lutenist: 'the King made them listen to a lad who played upon the lute, better than ever was heard, to the amazement of his Majesty, who never wearies of him, and since the coming of this lad, Zuan Piero is not in such favour as before, and complains, and is quite determined on returning to Italy . . .'.[55] Holman connects this lad with Peter van Wilder who, as mentioned above, may have been at court from 1512.[56]

John Peter did return to Italy, as he was sent by Henry as an official messenger to Mantua and Ferrara in 1517, and returned to Henry with a lute and a letter of 13 October 1517 from Duke Alfonso d'Este of Ferrara.[57] This letter accompanied a gift

---

[50] *RECM* vii. 47, 62, 66, 30, 31, 64.   [51] I am grateful to Andrew Ashbee for this information.

[52] *RECM* vii. 39, 70.   [53] Ashbee, 'Groomed for Service', 189.

[54] Giustinian, *Four Years*, i. 78–81; also in *RECM* vii. 46.

[55] Giustinian, *Four Years*, i. 75; extracts also in *RECM* vii. 50.

[56] Holman, *Four and Twenty Fiddlers*, 72.

[57] Ivy L. Mumford, 'The Identity of "Zuan Piero"', *Renaissance News*, 11 (1958), 179–82.

of a 'cithern, called in Italy a lute' from Duke Alfonso to Henry, and was borne by
'John Peter, the duke's physician'. John Peter de Brescia is clearly identified with
Zuan Piero in this letter, which praised John Peter's 'skill in the art of music', no
doubt to draw attention to his perceived neglect by the king:[58]

when amongst other things I pointed out to the aforesaid John Peter a lyre of that type which
in Italy we call a lute, he immediately said that he thought this would please your Majesty.
I replied that I would believe it had come from heaven if it would please your Majesty and
handed it over to the same John Peter to be taken to your Majesty.[59]

Evidently John Peter knew the king's likes and dislikes well enough to suggest the
lute as a gift from Alfonso to Henry. The suggestion that John Peter was also a
physician is not corroborated in English accounts. While he continued to serve until
at least 1536, references to his activities diminish by the 1520s. John Peter did, however, also serve the Princess Mary, and his wife was among her ladies and gentle-
women.[60]

The great Albert da Ripa, one of the foremost lute virtuosi of the age, visited
England in 1529 in the train of Cardinal Campeggio. The following entry is in court
accounts: 'Item, the xijth day of February, to Alb[t] de Ripa, luter mynstrell, and servant to the Cardinall of Mantua, in rewarde xxxiij[li] vj[s] viij[d] [£33. 6s. 8d.].'[61] Da Ripa
did not stay in England, but by the summer of 1529 was employed by Henry's rival,
Francis I of France, and was richly rewarded with money and lands, occupying a
position of prominence at court similar to that of Philip van Wilder in England.[62]
According to one account, Henry had tried to entice the Neapolitan Luigi Dentice
into his service with an offer of a yearly salary of 1,000 crowns (£240). He may have
made a similar unsuccessful offer to da Ripa.[63]

Philip van Wilder (c.1500–53) rose to a position of unusual distinction, becoming the highest ranking musician of his time. He provides the best example of the
heightened status of musicians in the more secular society of Reformation England.
Philip is first listed as a royal musician in 1525, but had probably been in the King's
Musick for some time.[64] In January 1516/17 Matthew van Wilder was paid 20
marks for a year's salary as 'oon of our mynstrelles and player upon lewte and
veoldes'.[65] He was paid for a year from December 1516, but thereafter payments
cease, and he is not mentioned again in accounts. Holman connects him with

[58] *RECM* vii. 50.
[59] *GB-Lbl* Cotton Vitell. B. III, fo. 148[r], original in Latin, translated in Mumford, 'The identity of "Zuan Piero"', 181. Other references to John Peter are in *Letters and Papers*, ed. Brewer, ii, pt. 1: *1515–16*, no. 1761, 12 Apr. 1516: 'Peter de Bustis'; and ii, pt. 2: *1517*, no. 3751, 17 Oct. 1517, 'John Peter de Bustis'.
[60] Ashbee, 'Groomed for Service', 188–9.
[61] J. Payne Collier (ed.), *Trevelyan Papers Prior to AD 1558* (Camden Society, 68; London, 1867), 147.
[62] Lyle Nordstrom, 'Albert de Rippe, Joueur de luth du Roy', *EM* 7 (1979), 378–85.
[63] Ward, 'A Dowland Miscellany', 17, 96.
[64] *GB-Lbl* Egerton 2604, fo. 5[r]; *RECM* vii. 254; Holman, *Four and Twenty Fiddlers*, 72.
[65] *RECM* vii. 410.

'Matthys de Widre', a musette player at the Burgundian court in 1501, and suggests that Peter and Philip were Matthew's sons.[66] In 1544 Peter claimed to have been in royal service for twenty-nine years (i.e. from 1515), and to have been born in 'Millom in the dominion of the Emperor'.[67] His salary was established at £10 per annum from February 1518/19. He remained in service as a viol player throughout Mary's reign, and was granted an annuity by Elizabeth until 1562.[68] Peter probably played the lute early in his career. He is always listed as a lute player in the Treasurer of the Chamber Accounts, but transferred his attention to the viol at some point.

It is significant that there are a number of instrumental pieces in the famous Henry VIII manuscript, including some attributed to Cornish, Isaac, and Agricola, and that they can be played on lutes. Could these pieces have formed part of the repertory the Van Wilder trio were playing on lutes around 1515, and might some of the pieces have been brought by them from the Continent to England? Given that we now believe there was a tradition of playing complex contrapuntal music on lutes and gitterns on the Continent in this transitional period, with each instrument taking a single line and playing from mensural notation, it is likely that foreign musicians introduced it to England.

Of the three van Wilders, special favour was shown to Philip. In the course of his career he received several licences to import 'wyne and woad'.[69] An entry for 14 December 1529 in a book of privy purse expenses mentions Philip as 'phillip wylde of the pryvay Chambre'.[70] In 1539 he was granted denization by the king, which allowed him to own land, and be styled Gentleman of the Privy Chamber.[71] His first of several grants of land also occured in 1539. In it he received lands formerly belonging to the dissolved monastery of Christchurch, near the Tower of London. He exchanged these lands in the same year for a large holding of land and buildings that had belonged to Cerne Abbey, Dorset, for an annual rent of £12. 3s. 0d.[72]

These extraordinary favours made Philip a rich and influential man. He was put in charge of the nine 'Synginge Men & Children' of the Privy Chamber, which was no doubt specially formed to perform the French chansons that Philip himself composed.[73] Philip had been authorized to impress children throughout the country for service among his singers. He bought instruments for the Crown, and it is clear

[66] Holman, *Four and Twenty Fiddlers*, 71, 73.

[67] *Letters of Denization and Acts of Naturalisation for Aliens in England (1509–1603)*, ed. William Page (Publications of the Huguenot Society of London, 7; Lymington, 1893), vol. 1/viii; Ward, *Music for Elizabethan Lutes*, i. 2. Ward suggests that 'Millom' is the present day village of 'Millam' in French-speaking Belgium, which in 1500 was still part of the Empire.

[68] *RECM* vii. 241. Established by warrant of 21 Apr. 1519. For his annuity see *RECM* vi. 84.

[69] PRO C 66/649, m. 21; *RECM* vi. 84, vii. 69.   [70] *RECM* vii. 362.

[71] PRO C 82/751; *RECM* vii. 77, 82.

[72] PRO C 66/689 m. 35; copy at Winchester College, MW WCM 142/7a-c; *RECM* vii. 78, 88.

[73] See Bernstein, 'Philip van Wilder'; David Humphreys, 'Philip van Wilder: A Study of his Work and its Sources', *Soundings*, 9 (1979–80), 13–36.

from Great Wardrobe inventories of 1542/3 and 1547 that he had care of the royal instrument collection.[74] The second of these inventories is entitled 'Instruments at Westminster in the charge of Philipp Van Wilder', and was compiled after Henry's death in 1547.[75] One item in the inventory is for twenty-three lutes with the same number of cases. Another is for a 'Gitteron and a Lute beinge in a Case Cheste fashion of Timbre couered with leather'. A third mentions 'a litle Venice' lute, and a fourth 'at Newhall' . . . 'One olde Lute'.

Some lute pieces, none of which occurs in sources that date from his lifetime, can be ascribed positively or tentatively to Philip.[76] In his own time he was evidently a composer of some importance, and from what does survive we can be sure he was fully able to compose music for the lute in the Italian polyphonic style. Philip maintained his pre-eminent position during the reign of Edward VI (1547–53), dying a few months before the king. A poem bewailing his death appeared in Tottel's *Songes and Sonnettes* (1557) (reproduced at the head of this chapter). A Henry van Wilde, probably Philip's son, became a musician to Queen Mary and a member of the Privy Chamber, but does not appear to have served Elizabeth.[77]

After the arrival of the van Wilders and the permanent employment of Philip, the numbers of royal musicians designated as 'luters' increased to four (or five if we include Peter de Brescia) in the years 1528–33.[78] With the death of the second Duwes in 1540 the numbers drop to two, Peter and Philip van Wilder. Philip died in 1553, but Peter continued in service until 1562. The only lutenist regularly identified as such in the first two decades of Elizabeth's reign was Anthony Conti, first mentioned in accounts in 1550/1.[79] In 1578 the number of lutenists began to rise again with the recruitment of Mathias Mason, followed by John Johnson in 1579, and stabilized at between four and six in the 1580s. From this number a specific consort of lutes developed, the lute thus taking its place alongside the other consorts of 'like' instruments.[80] Normal court attendance for royal lutenists might have required them to provide vocal accompaniments, play in mixed instrumental consorts, and possibly play solo music.

---

[74] PRO E315/160; *GB-Lbl* Harley 1419.

[75] *GB-Lbl* Harley 1419, fo. 200ʳ; printed in Raymond Russell, *The Harpsichord and Clavichord* (London, 1959), 155–60; Galpin, *Old English Instruments of Music*, 215–22; and *RECM* vii. 383–98.

[76] See Ward, *Music for Elizabethan Lutes*, 5–6. Arrangements of van Wilder's chansons for solo lute occur in: Osborn commonplace book, fos. 17ᵛ–18ʳ: Brogyntyn MS, p. 14 ('Je file quand Dieu'); Dd.2.11, fo. 17ʳ; Dallis MS, no. 47; Wickhambrook MS, fo. 12ᵛ ('Ma poure bourse'); Willoughby MS, fos. 9ʳ–10ᵛ ('Por vous aimer'); Wickhambrook MS, fo. 13ʳ; Dd.2.11, fos. 24ᵛ–25ʳ; Trumbull MS, fos. 21ᵛ–23ʳ ('Si vous voules'). Possible solo lute pieces are: Osborn Commonplace Book, 'Philips song'; Willoughby MS, fos. 11ᵛ–12ʳ, 'Pauyon philips'; Dd.5.78.3, fos. 26ᵛ–27ʳ, Fantasia, 'Mr Phs'; Marsh MS, pp. 426–8, 'Dump philli'.

[77] *RECM* vii. 132, 147.

[78] e.g. in Oct. 1529 Brian Tuke, the king's Treasurer of the Chamber, listed payments to four 'lewters' for their monthly wages: 'Maister Giles' 40s.; 'Arthur Dewes' 10s. 3d.; 'Phillip Welder' 66s. 7d.; 'Peter Welder' 31s. See Collier, *Trevelyan Papers*, 138. Other miscellaneous payments to these lutenists are recorded in the accounts from Oct. 1529 to May 1531. See also *RECM* vii. 254–67.

[79] *RECM* vii. 313.   [80] John Ward, 'A Dowland Miscellany', 107–12.

Anthony Conti (de Conti or de County), who is sometimes listed among the virginalists but probably was not one, joined the King's Musick in 1550/1, and went on to serve Mary and then Elizabeth as lutenist up to 1579, although there is period (1557–64) when he disappears from view.[81] Once the van Wilders had died he is the only identifiable royal lutenist until 1579. According to David Lasocki he may have been a Spanish musician of Jewish descent, as he was listed as a Spanish subject among the returns of 'strangers' in London.[82] It is more likely that he was Italian, as he had an Italian wife, Lucretia, and he lodged with another Italian, Francis Jetto, a perfumer of gloves, in the parish of St Dionis, Backchurch, between 1565 and 1571. He and his wife received denization in 1571, and Anthony received various grants and gifts from Elizabeth.[83] No music survives by Conti that can be firmly ascribed.[84] During Mary's reign two minstrels were given places which were later occupied by lutenists. There is no information to confirm that Richard Pike (a member of the King's Musick 1553–68) played the lute, other than that his place was revived for John Dowland in 1612. Probably he was an old-style minstrel, who may have included the lute among the instruments he played. Robert Woodward (King's Musick 1557–98) was probably not a lutenist, according to John Ward.[85]

An important but little-known court musician was Thomas Lichfield, a Groom of the Privy Chamber from at least 1558, and possibly earlier, to *c*.1582. It is likely that he was the groom with responsibility for the overall supervision of court music, a duty that had initially belonged to Philip van Wilder until his death, and which had probably passed to Peter van Wilder in the years 1553–8. Lichfield began his long court career as one of the singing men and boys directed by Philip van Wilder, but was probably more a lutenist than a singer during Elizabeth's reign. For New Year's Day 1578/9 he presented the Queen with 'a very fayre lute, the backeside and necke of mother-of-perle, the case of crymson vellat, enbrawedered with flowers, and the inside of grene vellate'.[86] The responsibilities and favours that he accumulated at court show that he was a successful and influential musician.[87] The fine galliard ascribed to 'Lychfy' in the Marsh manuscript must surely be by this man.[88]

Of all the Italian musicians who found favour at the English court none was more highly esteemed than Alfonso Ferrabosco the Elder. He served Elizabeth I as musician and spy during the years 1562–78, acting on her behalf on several trips

---

[81] Ibid. 109; *GB-Lbl* Royal 18.C.xxxiv, fo. 133ᵛ.

[82] David Lasocki, 'Professional Recorder Players in England' (Ph.D diss., University of Iowa, 1983), ii. 545–55, 584–91.

[83] *Biographical Dictionary*, i. 286.

[84] Spencer, in the inventory to the Boethius Press facsimile of the Willoughby MS, suggests that the 'Anthony Pauyn', fos. 14ᵛ–15ʳ, might refer to Conti.

[85] Ward, 'A Dowland Miscellany', 109.

[86] *Biographical Dictionary*, ii. 723.

[87] Ibid. 722–4.

[88] Marsh MS, no. 28; Thistlethwaite, fos. 35ᵛ–36ʳ.

abroad.[89] He became a Gentleman of the Privy Chamber to Elizabeth, and was well rewarded with an annuity of £100 p.a. and a number of gifts.[90] Seventeen pieces for solo lute, along with one duet, and five pieces for bandora survive in post-1580 sources. It seems that some if not all his pieces were not originally conceived for the lute, and it has been suggested that Ferrabosco was not a lutenist.[91] This point may never be proved conclusively either way. He certainly performed on something, as he was rewarded, along with other Italian musicians, for 'Playing before her highness' in February 1575/6.[92] He had an excellent reputation as a contrapuntist and particularly as a composer of madrigals and sacred vocal music. His contrapuntal skills made a deep impression on contemporaries like Byrd and Morley, and his compositions probably influenced contemporary lutenists, who intabulated and played transcriptions of his music.[93] Lute versions of his pieces remained in circulation in the period 1580–1610.

As Renaissance humanistic ideals in education permeated English society from the court outwards, so musical competence, as exemplified by Henry VIII, became desirable for the accomplished courtier. The medieval minstrel retainer was likely to have been musically illiterate. Now household musicians were required who could instruct their patrons in music. Sir Thomas Hoby's *The Booke of the Courtyer*, a translation of Baldassare Castiglione's manual on the behaviour appropriate to a Renaissance courtier, was published in 1561. Castiglione had visited England himself in 1506 to receive the garter on behalf of Duke Guidobaldo della Rovere of Urbino, the patron who inspired his original book, and was an early facilitator of Anglo-Italian cultural exchange.[94] In Hoby's translation singing to the lute is praised over the ability to sing part-songs.[95] Sir Thomas Elyot's *The boke named the governour* (1531), a treatise on how to educate a prince and dedicated to Henry, is less enthusiastic about music. He allows it to be a harmless recreation, but not to be taken seriously by persons of rank.[96]

Explicit exhortations to learn to play instruments as a desirable accomplishment for persons of quality first appear in Elizabethan sources on education. Humphrey Gilbert drew up a plan for the 'Erection of an Academy in London for education of

[89] Alfonso Ferrabosco the Elder, *Opera omnia*, ed. Richard Charteris (CMM 96; Neuhausen-Stuttgart, 1988), introduction to vol. i. See also Richard Charteris, 'New Information about the Life of Alfonso Ferrabosco the Elder (1543–1588)', *RMARC* 17 (1981), 97–114, and id., *Alfonso Ferrabosco the Elder (1543–1588): A Thematic Catalogue of his Music with a Biographical Calendar* (New York, 1984).

[90] *RECM* viii. 34; vi. 19.

[91] Alfonso Ferrabosco, *Collected Works for Lute and Bandora*, ed. Nigel North (Music for the Lute, Book 8, part 1; Oxford, 1974), p. viii.

[92] *RECM* vi. 115.

[93] Thomas Morley attests to his 'deep skill' in *A Plain and Easy Introduction to Practical Music*, ed. R. Alec Harman (London, 1952), 294.

[94] Starkey (ed.), *Henry VIII: A European Court in England*, 11.

[95] Thomas Hoby, *The Book of the Courtier* (London, 1561; mod. edn. London, 1928).

[96] Sir Thomas Elyot, *The boke named the governour* (London, 1531), i. 42. See Stevens, *Music and Poetry*, 272–5.

her Maiestes Wardes, and others of the youth of nobility and gentlemen' (1564) with provision for 'one Teacher of Musick, and to play one the Lute, the Bandora and Cytherne'.[97] Roger Asham, tutor to Edward VI, and fellow of St John's College, Cambridge, includes among the 'passtimes that be fitte for Courtlie Gentlemen' in his book *The Scholemaster* (1570), 'To daunce cumlie: to sing, and playe of instrumentes cunnyngly'.[98]

Musical literacy among nobles and other educated people rose dramatically during the sixteenth century. Some families followed the royal example as early as the 1530s and 1540s, obtaining lutes, viols, and teachers to instruct the family. During the mid- and later sixteenth century the old aristocracy underwent a crisis, many dying out or remaining on the wrong side of the religious divide. New upstart gentry families, enriched by the dissolution of the monasteries, took their places at court. However, Elizabeth raised few new families to the peerage and let many titles lapse, and this period saw many rich families falling into debt, while others became yet richer.[99] Increasingly, noble and even gentry families came to own or rent a permanent London home, enabling the diffusion of court fashions to became quicker and more direct.[100] By the 1570s and 1580s musical literacy and instrumental and vocal proficiency were certainly increasing. However, Morley may have been exaggerating the situation in Elizabethan England when, in his *A Plaine and Easie Introduction to Practicall Musicke* (1597), he relates that a guest who declined to sing at sight after supper had his upbringing and education questioned.[101]

Expense accounts for wealthy households exist which prove the increased ownership of lutes, and are an indication of the quickening pace of domestic music-making activity. In the early years of the century great households, like those of the Dukes of Northumberland and the Earls of Rutland, employed several minstrels, at least one of whom probably played the lute.[102] There is increased evidence for the ownership and study of the lute by nobles and gentry after 1530. In 1525 John, Lord Marney, left his daughter Kateryn his 'grete lute'.[103] Richard Cromwell's son Gregory was taught the lute in 1530.[104] According to Erasmus, Sir Thomas More's first wife learnt 'every kind of music', and his second, in middle age, was persuaded 'to learn to play upon the gittern, the lute, the clavichord and the recorders', and to

---

[97] *Queene Elizabethes Achademy, a Booke of Precedence*, ed. Frederick J. Furnivall (EETS/ES, 8; London, 1869), 7.

[98] Roger Ascham, *The Scholemaster* (London, 1570), facs. repr., selected and ed. R. C. Alston (Menston, 1967), fo. 19ᵛ.

[99] Lawrence Stone, *The Crisis of the Aristocracy (1558–1641)* (Oxford, 1967). The Elizabethan age saw a rising mobility of land and economic change among the aristocracy that peaked in the Jacobean period. See pp. 22–3, 93–5.

[100] Ibid. 183–91. [101] Ed. Harman, 9.

[102] H. W. King, 'Ancient Wills', *Transactions of the Essex Archaeological Society*, 3 (1863–5), 160.

[103] Ibid. [104] David C. Price, *Patrons and Musicians of the English Renaissance* (Cambridge, 1981), 13.

practise daily.[105] Such domestic music-making might account for the inclusion of instruments in the More family portrait (see above, Pl. 4.3). Evidence shows that lutes and viols were acquired and played in the 1530s by the families of the Earls of Rutland, the Marquis of Exeter, and the Earls of Hertford (Seymour).[106] In 1538 a Venetian lute was bought from Philip van Wilder for 45s. by the Seymour family. The family bought more lutes and strings the following year, and it seems from an inventory of 1539 that they were used by Edward Seymour and his wife Anne Stanhope. Edward Seymour was created Earl of Hertford in 1537 and later, in Edward VI's reign, Duke of Somerset and Lord Protector. He held these titles until his downfall and execution in 1552.[107]

The tradition of young men learning the lute at university or the Inns of Court continued on from the medieval era into the Renaissance. Sir William Petre sent his ward John Talbot to Oxford in February 1559 with a 'Colen lute' [i.e. a Cologne lute].[108] In the 1560s Henry Howard, 8th Earl of Northampton, was taught the lute while at King's College, and some colleges even bought their own instruments for in-house entertainments.[109] A full set of accounts exists for the maintaining and buying of lutes for John Petre, son of Sir William Petre of Ingatestone Hall, Essex, while a student at the Middle Temple (1567–77).[110] The accounts mention a 'Mr Petro' who was the main provider of lutes and strings, and was rewarded with 20s. for 'a booke for the lute and prycking song within'. The cost of lute strings was high relative to the cost of the instrument. For four 'knots of lute strings' Petre paid 12d. A lute could cost as little as 6s. 8d., or as much as 50s.[111] Sir William Petre had paid 13s. for a 'Cullen' lute in 1561, which may have been an average price for a lute imported from Germany at this time.[112]

By 1570 many leading families were equipped with instruments for solo and consort use, and with household musicians to play and teach them. Robert Dudley, Earl of Leicester, Elizabeth's early suitor, had his own lute in 1558, and later had three lutes among his instruments at Kenilworth House.[113] Other great families who showed particular interest in domestic music-making were the Kytsons of Hengrave Hall, the Berties of Eresby, and the family of Sir Henry Sidney, Vice-Treasurer of Ireland, which produced the poet and hero Sir Philip Sidney.[114]

[105] Stevens, *Music and Poetry*, 276.

[106] Price, *Patrons and Musicians*, 13 n. 1; Stevens, *Music and Poetry*, 276–7; Price, *Patrons and Musicians*, 122.

[107] Price, *Patrons and Musicians*, 122–3. The lutes are described as 'a lute of my lorde' and 'a little lute for the lady Anne'.

[108] Ibid. 26.   [109] Ibid. 22.

[110] F. G. Emmison, 'John Petre's Account-Books, 1567–77', *GSJ* 14 (1961), 73–5.

[111] Ward, 'A Dowland Miscellany', 116–17. Petre also paid Mr Petro or Pietro 13s. 4d. 'for the exchange of a lute'. This musical factotum may be the same 'Mr Petre' credited with a galliard in the Willoughby MS, fo. 30'.

[112] F. G. Emmison, *The Tudor Secretary: Sir William Petre at Court and Home* (Cambridge, Mass., 1961), 212.

[113] Price, *Patrons and Musicians*, 167, 169.

[114] Ibid.: Kytson, 71–83; Bertie 140–2; Sidney, 171. For the Petre family see 28, 83–91.

Two important families left lute books which cast some light on how the lute was used in wealthy households. The lute books of the Catholic Edward Paston are the more remarkable and may date in part from the 1590s. The surviving lute book of Sir Francis Willoughby (*c*.1547–96) was begun possibly as early as about 1560 when he was 13 and completed no later than *c*.1585.[115] Sir Francis, the man responsible for the building of Wollaton Hall near Nottingham, is representative of the aristocracy that developed after the political and religious upheavals of the mid-century. Coming from a junior branch of the Willoughby d'Eresby family, Francis had become rich through mining interests, and was anxious to impress the Queen with his courtly endeavours. Both the building of the extravagant Wollaton Hall (1580–8) and his musical studies should be seen in the light of this drive for higher social acceptability.[116]

Willoughby accounts show that by 1560 Sir Francis had taken singing and virginal lessons. In the 1570s and 1580s, he employed a resident 'musisson', John Edlin (1573–4), who was paid £5 p.a. Another family servant who played the lute, Richard Grene, was asked to find Francis 'any treble lutes fit for his purpose' while in London. A Wollaton inventory of 1609 included a 'whyt lute of bone'.[117] Another inventory of 1601 included instruments for the East Tower Chamber: '2 lutes, 3 instruments with wyer strings, 1 base vyall', strongly suggesting there had been mixed consort music at the house. The many visitations of the Nottingham Waits, and the musicians of Peregrine Bertie, Lord Willoughby (Francis's cousin), and those of Lord Arundel his brother-in-law, together with the household's own musicians and family members, meant there would have been a steady stream of people available to play in such a consort.[118]

We may assume that the Willoughby lute book was produced for Sir Francis's own use, as it has his initials embossed on the front and back cover, and he himself played the lute. The book has a few pieces in the hand of Sir Francis himself, and, it has been suggested, in the hands of his wife and one or more of his daughters. Two pieces were 'sett owt' by one of the family musicians, Richard Grene. Visiting professional musicians or amateur lutenist friends may also have contributed. The book includes eight pieces for cittern and one for keyboard, a setting of Philip van Wilder's 'Je file quand Dieu', along with thirty-eight pieces for lute. It is a testament to the close interaction between household musicians and professionals with amateur family members in many leading families at this time.

---

[115] *The Willoughby Lute Book*, facs. with an introduction by Jeffrey Alexander and Robert Spencer (Musical Sources, 13; Kilkenny, 1978).

[116] John Buxton, *Elizabethan Taste* (London, 1963), 51 3.

[117] *The Willoughby Lute Book*; see Alexander and Spencer's introductory study. Grene copied two pieces into the lute book, and he is mentioned on fos. 11ᵛ and 33ᵛ.

[118] Ibid.; Price, *Patrons and Musicians*, 149–51.

Thomas Whythorne's autobiography gives us some insight into the life and career of a household musician during the turmoil of the mid-century years and the early years of Elizabeth's reign.[119] Whythorne was sent to Magdalen College School, Oxford, in 1538 at the age of 10, passing on to the College itself in 1544. On the death of his uncle and patron in the following year, he undertook an apprenticeship with the court poet and musician John Heywood. While living with Heywood, Whythorne 'learned to play on the virginals, the lute, and to make English verses'. He also copied out many verses by Surrey and Wyatt with the intention of imitating their poetic style. In 1548, his apprenticeship over, he established himself in London as a music tutor to the gentry, adding the gittern and cittern to the list of instruments he could teach. After Continental travels during the upheaval of Mary's reign, Whythorne returned to England in 1555, becoming music tutor to Ambrose Dudley, Earl of Warwick and brother to the Earl of Leicester, and several court ladies, whose advances (he says) he skilfully deflected. In the 1560s he worked both in a musical and business capacity for the rich merchant William Bromfield. His publication of *Songes for Three, Fower and Five Voyces* (London, 1571) led to his appointment as Master of Music in the chapel of Archbishop Parker. Whythorne's autobiography, written *c*.1576, is the earliest extant full-length autobiography in English. It provides a unique insight into the circumstances of a domestic musician at this time, and is also notable as it is written in phonetic script (similar to Hart's 'New Orthography'), and contains much poetry intended to be sung with instrumental accompaniment.

The relative value of lutes in England during the Elizabethan period can be established from entries in the London Port Book for the years 1567/8. In ten months between 1567 and 1568, eighty-six lutes were legally imported—six small, twenty-four 'coarse', six in cases, twelve from Antwerp, fourteen from Cologne, twenty-four from Venice—together with 13,848 lute strings, fourteen gitterns, and eighteen citterns.[120] Venetian lutes were much the most expensive, being valued at £1 each, with Cologne ('Cullen') lutes valued at a mere 5*s*. Strings were expensive: 'Minikins', for instance, cost 10*s*. for 144.[121] The mention of Antwerp lutes suggests that by the later half of the sixteenth century Germans had ceased to monopolize lute manufacture. Antwerp lutes made by members of the Hofmans family have survived from the early years of the seventeenth century.[122] Alternatively, they

[119] *Autobiography*, ed. Osborn.

[120] *The Port and Trade of Early Elizabethan London: Documents*, ed. B. Dietz (London, 1972), viii. 1972, quoted in Ward, 'A Dowland Miscellany', 116.

[121] *A Tudor Book of Rates*, ed. Thomas Stuart Willan (Manchester, 1962), quoted in Ward, 'A Dowland Miscellany', 116.

[122] A fine but now badly damaged lute by 'Jacques Hoffman der Jonghen' is owned by the Bavarian National Museum (Mu 16) and a small lute labelled 'mateu hofmans le plues anne en anvers 1605' is owned by the Brussels Conservatoire. I am grateful to M. Awouters for information on the Hofmans family. See M. Awouters, 'Snaarinstruementenbouw te Antwerpen: de family Hofmans in de 17de eeuw', in L. Janssens and M. Kin (eds.),

might simply have been lutes whose provenance could not be established and were labelled Antwerp lutes as the ships came from that city.

There is some evidence that lutes were being made in England after the mid-century. In 1556 Queen Mary was given a 'faire lute, edged with passamayne of gold and silke' by the instrument maker Browne as a New Year's gift.[123] John Ward has unearthed several references to lute makers active in England in the period 1560–90. Of the four names some, if not all, were foreigners: Melchior de Fombroker; the 'lute maker Mr Augustine in Crouched friers'; 'Mr Jerome', who is cited for repairing a lute in a will of 1588 (Ward suggests that both these last may have been members of the Bassano family); and John White, who is referred to as 'almaine [= German?] and lutemaker'.[124] Members of the Bassano family made viols and lutes. In 1571 they offered the Bavarian court six large 'viole da gamba' and a chest of three lutes ('nemblich ein Bass, ein Tenor und ein Discant') in ebony and ivory.[125]

The earliest English source of lute music to survive comes from the decades around the mid-century. Several of these sources include items of tablature for the 4-course guitar, the cittern, or metal-strung gittern. These tablatures appear in commonplace books along with recipes, poems, odd pieces of music for keyboard instruments, accounts, and all manner of other miscellaneous material. They show that the general amateur's repertory was heavily reliant on popular songs and ground basses, of poor quality and relatively easy to play. The sources of the 1570s reveal a marked improvement in handling tablature and the pieces show much greater artistry. A greater variety of forms is present, with pavans and galliards, chanson intabulations, and fantasias appearing, although popular song settings and pieces based on grounds still predominate.

RA 58 is probably the earliest British lute source that survives (see Table 4.2). It may originally have been a commonplace book belonging to a professional musician connected to Henry VIII's court. It contains much vocal music, and may have been one of a set of part-books. Included in its contents are eight pieces for lute and a number for keyboard. The keyboard pieces were probably composed and intended for performance at Henry's court.[126] The lute pieces have been variously dated as from the last years of Henry's reign, or the reigns of Edward VI (1547–53) and Mary

Handelingen van het eerste Congres van de Federatie van Nederlandstalige Verenigingen voor Oudheidkunde en Geschiedenis van België te Hasselt, 19 22 Augustus 1982 (1990), 319–30.

[123] Gerald Hayes, *King's Music* (London, 1937), 53.   [124] Ward, *Music for Elizabethan Lutes*, 25.

[125] Holman, *Four and Twenty Fiddlers*, 121; David Lasocki, 'The Anglo-Venetian Bassano Family as Instrument Makers and Repairers', *GSJ* 38 (1985), 112–32 at 120–1.

[126] Arthur W. Byler, 'Italian Currents in the Popular Music of England in the Sixteenth Century' (Ph.D. diss., University of Chicago, 1952), 43 51. The keyboard pieces include 'Hugh Aston's Hornepipe', the anonymous 'My lady Carey's dompe', and 'The short measure off my lady wynfylds rounde'. See John Caldwell, *English Keyboard Music before the Nineteenth Century* (Oxford, 1973), 46–7. The vocal music is a selection of single voice parts in Latin, French, and Italian, both secular and sacred.

Table 4.2. *English sources of solo lute music before 1580*

PRINCIPAL MS SOURCES	
RA 58	*c.*1540–55
Stowe 389	1558
The Osborn commonplace book	*c.*1560
The Giles Lodge commonplace book	*c.*1560–75
The Thistlethwaite lute book	*c.*1565–75
The Willoughby lute book	*c.*1575
FRAGMENTARY SOURCES	
GB-Lbl Royal App. 76	*c.*1550–60
GB-Lbl Sloane 2329	*c.*1550–60
GB-Lbl 1242.g.1	*c.*1560
GB-Lbl Add. 60577	*c.*1540
USA, New Jersey, private library of Michael d'Andrea	*c.*1570
PRINTED SOURCES	
Le Roy, *A Briefe and easye instrution* (1568)	
Le Roy, *A brief and plaine Instruction to set all Musicke* (1574)	
Le Roy, *A brief instruction how to play on the Lute by Tablatorie* (1574)	
Le Roy, *The thirde booke for the Lute* (1574)	

(1553–8), or even the first years of Elizabeth's.[127] The controversy centres on the title of one of the pieces, 'The Duke of Somersettes Dompe'. 'Dumps' were often musical lamentations in honour of some deceased person.[128] Edward Seymour was made Duke of Somerset in February 1547 and executed in January 1551/2, and this has led to the dating of this part of the manuscript as from the 1550s. Julia Craig-McFeely has pointed out that there was an earlier Duke of Somerset, Henry Fitzroy, who died in 1536, and that the lute music connects with music that was around much earlier than the 1550s. She dates the lute part of the manuscript *c.*1530.[129] I would suggest the 1540s as a more reasonable compromise date, given that there are lute versions of poems by Henry Howard that were popular well into the 1540s and 1550s, and that a date in the 1540s could refer to either of the Dukes.

Stowe 389 began as a manuscript copy of certain legal statutes dating from the fifteenth century, to which a certain Ralphe Bowle somewhat incongruously added eleven lute pieces, and one for 4-course guitar. Bowle's pieces can be precisely dated, as he wrote above the first piece 'The xiij Daie of maye the same written by me Ralphe bowle to Learne to play on his Lutte in anno 1558.'

[127] Ward, *Music for Elizabethan Lutes*, 13–15; Byler, 'Italian Currents', 46; Stevens, *Music and Poetry*, 279.

[128] John Ward, 'The "Doleful Dumps" ', *JAMS* 4 (1951), 111–21 at 120–1.

[129] Julia Craig-McFeely, 'English Lute Manuscripts and Scribes 1530–1630', 3 vols. (D.Phil. thesis, University of Oxford, 1994), ii. 562.

The Osborn and Giles Lodge commonplace books contain lute music that was probably added sometime after that in RA 58 and Stowe 389. The Osborn commonplace book contains lute, gittern, and 4-course guitar music. No names or clues as to its original ownership are present in the manuscript. The Giles Lodge manuscript contains several names, including one on the reverse side of the first folio at the head of a list of 'money owinge to Giles Lodge, 1591'. Three hands added lute music to this manuscript, the third of which noted the debt to Lodge, who otherwise may have had no connection with the rest of the manuscript's contents. Both books contain a mixture of music and miscellaneous writings, including remedies and recipes. This mixture was typical of commonplace books of the time, like the famous Mulliner book, which contains keyboard music as well as gittern and cittern music.[130]

The Osborn commonplace book contains a selection of poetry. Some of it is drawn from broadside ballads, which in some cases may have been sung to the tune settings found among the instrumental pieces. That the singing of broadside ballads to popular tunes was a normal practice is indicated in the publication of *A Handefull of pleasant delites* (1584), the next poetical anthology to survive after *Songes and Sonnettes* (1557), where specific tunes are named for most of the ballads.[131] Three hands also added to the Osborn commonplace book, but only one hand, the first to own the book, added the thirty-one lute, fifteen gittern, and six 4-course guitar pieces in the manuscript, most probably during the 1560s.

Two important sources survive whose contents probably date, in the main, from the 1570s, the Willoughby and Thistlethwaite manuscripts. The Willoughby manuscript is representative of the lute books compiled by courtiers and gentry of the generation of Sir Francis Willoughby (*c*.1547-96), and contains pieces that were widely circulated, plus a few that may have been produced locally. The Thistlethwaite manuscript, named after the 'Thisstllethwaite' who added his name to the last piece in the book,[132] contains an altogether more professional repertoire. Ward has conjectured that this manuscript dates from the late 1560s and early 1570s, and that its main contributor composed much of the music he wrote into the manuscript.[133] The initials on the front and back cover, 'I. B.', have prompted the suggestion that it might have initially belonged to a member of the Bassano family,[134] possibly Jaspar Bassano, or Baptista Bassano, who must be the John Baptist who gave Elizabeth as princess lute strings in 1552, and as queen a 'vennise Lute'

---

[130] Thomas Mulliner Book, *GB-Lbl* Add. 30513, published as *The Mulliner Book*, ed. and transcr. Denis Stevens (Musica Britannica, 1; London, 1951). See Byler, 'Italian Currents', 68–75.

[131] John Ward, 'Music for *A Handfull of pleasant delites*', *JAMS* 10 (1957), 151–80. The single surviving copy in the BL, 'by Clement Robinson and divers others' (1584), was printed by Richard Jones and contains thirty-two ballads, for which twenty-seven have specific tunes.

[132] *GB-Eu* Dc.5.125, fo. 95ᵛ.   [133] Ward, *Music for Elizabethan Lutes*, i. 51.

[134] Ibid. 59.

in 1564/5.[135] Both these men played in the recorder consort from around 1540 to their deaths in 1577 and 1576 respectively. The book contains a very cosmopolitan repertoire, much of it technically advanced. This is the sort of music we might expect a professional musician moving in court circles to have played.

The Thistlethwaite manuscript is the most substantial source so far encountered, containing fifty-eight items spread over 190 pages, all but sixteen pages of which have lute tablature. Unlike other contemporary sources, it contains only lute music. As many as eleven scribes added to the manuscript at some stage, and it is clear that within these scribes lie a variety of musical personalities. The largest contribution is made by the scribe who Ward has suggested may have been an Italian professional lutenist. The intabulations are from standard mid-century published sources of works by Josquin, Arcadelt, Verdelot, Lasso, Rore, and Berchem. The style is austere, with little attempt at idiomatic figuration to enliven the transfer from a vocal medium to that of a solo lute. The manuscript is important as an indication of the professional's repertoire, and contrasts with the amateur sources so far encountered. It stands as a reminder of the presence of Italian lute music in England at this time.

The considerable increase in technical demands and musical literacy in the Willoughby and Thistlethwaite manuscripts over earlier sources is such that there is seldom any confusion of intention, despite errors, when compared to the many inconsistencies and omissions in the earlier sources. This increase in musical competence may be due, in part, to the influence of Le Roy's tutors for the lute and associated instruments, such as the 4-course guitar and cittern, published in England in the 1560s and 1570s. One piece in the Willoughby manuscript, and a large part of the Thistlethwaite manuscript, dispense with the 'grid' system of notating rhythm signs, using instead the single 'flag' rhythm sign only where there is a change of rhythm.[136] On the strength of these two sources it appears that the 1570s saw an advance in musical standards and in particular in the handling of tablature.

The Willoughby manuscript contains much music in the style of the 1570s and early 1580s, typified by the pavans and galliards of John Johnson It also has music that is much older. It includes the same two Francesco da Milano fantasias as the Osborn commonplace book, the same van Wilder chanson 'Je file quand Dieu' (here in a version for virginals), and also variations on the harmonic ground 'Conde Claros'.[137] The pieces are, however, often concordant with the sources of the 1580s and 1590s, particularly the Marsh and Ballet manuscripts. Of the thirty-nine lute pieces, sixteen are also present in the Marsh manuscript in some form.

---

[135] *RECM* vii. 382; vi. 14.

[136] Willoughby MS, fo. 31ʳ ˅, *Jonsons Gallyard*; Thistlethwaite MS, hands A, C, D, E, G, H.

[137] 'Conde Claros' was a harmonic ground on the progression I–IV–V–I that Spanish composers used as a basis for the composition of continuous *diferencias* (elaborative divisions).

The titles and attributions to some of the pieces in the Willoughby manuscript are lacking. Perhaps much lute music circulated anonymously among players. A few titles do appear and are exceptional in that they identify other sources. Thus, for example, no.7 is entitled 'a pauyn Bruzter owt of grennes Booke pag 7', indicating that Richard Grene, an old and trusted servant of Willoughby, owned a lute book himself, from which Sir Francis gained his version. Number 26 is entitled 'Hawles Galiard sett owt p[er, i.e. by] Ry[chard] Grene', proving that Green himself wrote in nos. 9, 25, and 26. Apart from the pieces by Narváez, Francesco da Milano, van Wilder, and John Johnson, the titles suggest attributions to several little-known composers; no. 23, 'A galiard of Mr petro', may refer to the 'Mr Pietro' who helped John Petre with his lute studies while a student at the Middle Temple, and was probably a musical servant in the same capacity as Richard Grene to Sir Francis. Other composers named are 'Brewster', 'T.A.', 'Hawles', and 'Anthony'.[138]

Other than the six important manuscript sources discussed above, there are a number of fragmentary English lute sources that survive from the period up to 1580. *GB-Lbl* RA 76, fo. 37ᵛ contains part of a lute piece in Italian tablature; a copy of 'The Maister of the Game' in *GB-Lbl* Sloane 2329 has no actual music, but the flyleaf lists twenty pieces, many of which are known from existing sources; *GB-Lbl* 1242.g.1, a book printed by Wyllyam Myddylton, contains a handwritten version of the 'Holloyne p dye' (no. 6 of the Osborn commonplace book); *GB-Lbl* Add. 60577, a fifteenth- and sixteenth-century literary anthology associated with William Way and a circle of Catholic sympathizers and clerics at Winchester, includes two pieces in lute tablature without rhythm signs, one entitled 'La galantyne', the other indecipherable.[139] *GB-Lbl* Add. 4900 is of considerable importance as a source of early song accompaniments, but contains no solo music.

The earliest surviving[140] printed work for the lute in England is Adrian Le Roy's tutor, *A Briefe and easye instru[c]tion to learne the tablature to conducte and dispose thy hande unto the Lute* (1568).[141] The book was 'englished by J. Alford Londenor' and 'Imprinted by Ihon kyngston for Iames Rowbotham . . . to be solde at hys shop in paternoster rowe'. The book makes it clear that Alford was responsible for the translation only. Le Roy is never mentioned as the author. This tutor was reprinted with some alterations as Book II of a composite of three books also published by

---

[138] It may be that 'T.A.' refers to Thomas Aytkinson, another Willoughby servant. See Ward, *Music for Elizabethan Lutes*, i. 46.

[139] Fo. 190ʳ⁻ᵛ; *The Winchester Anthology*, a facsimile reprint of *GB-Lbl* Add. 60577 with an introduction and list of contents by Edward Wilson, and an account of the music by Iain Fenlon (London, 1981), 43–4.

[140] Thurston Dart, 'A Hand-List of English Instrumental Music Printed before 1681', *GSJ* 8 (1955), 13–26. Dart lists the 'Science of Lutyng' (1565) and Ballard's 'Exortation . . . how to play the lute'(1567), which do not survive, or were never printed.

[141] Single surviving copy in *GB-Lbl*. Facs. edn. entitled *Fantaisies et danses*, ed. and trans. by Pierre Jansen, with a study of concordances by Daniel Heartz (Paris, 1962; 2nd rev. edn., 1975).

Rowbotham, and printed by Kingston in 1574.[142] Book I of this set was an instruction manual for the intabulation of vocal music entitled *A briefe and plaine Instruction to set all Musicke of eight divers tunes in Tablature for the Lute*. Book II of the set was the 1568 work now called *A briefe Instruction how to play on the Lute by Tablature, to conduct and dispose thy hand unto the Lute, with certain easie lessons for that purpose*. With these two books came Book III, *The thirde booke for the Lute, conteinyng diverse Psalmes and many fine excellente Tunes, sette forthe by A.R. the aucthour thereof*. This work acknowledges it was 'ALL FIRST WRITTEN IN FRENCH BY ADRIAN LE ROY, AND NOW TRANSLATED INTO ENGLISH by F. ke. GENTELMAN' and was dedicated to Lord Edward Seymour, Viscount Beauchamp and Earl of Hertford, and heir to the beheaded Lord Protector.[143] The Lord Protector had been a notable patron of music, and a likely lute player himself. His son, after two decades of political and financial difficulty following his father's execution in 1552, also became a great music patron and a noted judge of music.[144]

Le Roy's lute tutor had probably appeared first in 1567, as the lost *Breve et facile instruction pour apprendre la tablature, à bien accorder, conduire et disposer la main sur le Luth* published in Paris. The intabulation manual had probably first appeared in 1570 as *Instruction de partir toute Musique des huit divers tons en tablature de Luth*.[145] This book, which is also lost, contained twelve examples of intabulated vocal pieces from another Le Roy publication entitled *Mellange d'Orlande de Lassus* of 1570. These intabulation examples appear in the English 1574 translation. Book III of the 1574 London edition contains twenty French chansons, eight metrical psalms, and one English tune. The chansons were drawn from yet another book by Le Roy, his *Livre d'airs de cour* of 1571 for voice and lute.[146] Le Roy's activities as a producer of instrumental tutors did not stop at the lute. He also produced similar tutors for the cittern and the 4-course guitar, this last being published in an English translation of 1569 as *A Briefe and plaine instruction for to learne the Tablature, to Conduct and dispose the hand unto the Gitterne*, of which only four pages survive.[147] Clearly Le Roy was moved to produce these tutors to provide a means of self-instruction for the reader, and thereby facilitate an outlet for the humanistic desire for self-improvement, evidently as deeply felt in England as in France in the 1560s and 1570s.

[142] There are three surviving copies of the 1574 edition: *GB-Lbl* (imperfect); *GB-Ob*; *F-Pn*.

[143] For a modern edition see Adrian Le Roy, *Œuvres d'Adrian Le Roy: Les Instructions pour le Luth (1574)*, ed. J. Jacquot, P. Y. Sordes, and J. M. Vaccaro, 2 vols. (Paris, 1977). See p. 1 for a plate of the title-page.

[144] Price, *Patrons and Musicians*, 121–9.

[145] Ian Harwood, 'On the Publication of Adrian Le Roy's Lute Instructions', *LSJ* 18 (1976), 30–7. The details of these titles and dates are conjectural, though very likely.

[146] *Œuvres d'Adrian Le Roy*, ed. Jacquot, Sordes, and Vaccaro, pp. ix–xiv.

[147] A unique copy of the Le Roy cittern book, entitled *Breve et facile instruction pour apprendre la tablature, a bien accorder, conduire, et disposer la main sur le cistre*, exists in the Trier Stadtbibliothek. The 1551 original of the gittern book is lost. The 4-page fragment of the English translation surfaced in the University of Pennsylvania library. See Ward, 'Sprightly and Cheerful Musick', 16.

Le Roy's tutor for the lute consists of twenty-five rules, divided into five sections dealing with the tablature, the left hand, the right hand, other non-tablature symbols, and tuning. This subdivision is exactly paralleled in his surviving cittern tutor, and was no doubt also followed in his lost 4-course guitar tutor.[148] The rules give a concise explanation of tablature and the technique developed to play polyphonic music. Central to this technique is rule 9, which explains that tablature letters without dots are musically articulated by striking 'dounewarde with thy thombe', but if there is a dot under the letter it should be 'striken upwardes with one of the fingers'.[149] This downward pluck with the thumb and upward pluck with the fingers for all scale passages developed directly out of the up-and-down motion of the plectrum.

Other significant points of interest for the left hand are the provision for stops up to the letter 'n', or twelfth fret, while frets were only present up to letter 'i', the eighth fret. These higher positions have to be stopped 'as cunnyngly as if thei had frettes'.[150] The requirement in the 20th and 21st rule for the first finger and occasionally the second finger of the left hand to stop two courses, while the other fingers hold down other strings, may be a surprise to modern players, as is the preference for the fourth finger over the third in close-position chords. All the rules for the right hand are admirably logical and consistent. Chords of four notes are struck with the three fingers and thumb, while the little finger 'serveth but to keepe the hand firm upon the beallie of the Lute'. Six-note chords are plucked with the thumb striking the sixth and fifth courses, the index finger the fourth and third, and the top two courses with the remaining second and third fingers. Five-note chords are plucked with the thumb striking the sixth and fifth (or fifth and fourth if they are consecutive), or the index finger striking the third and fourth if the fifth is not present in the chord.[151]

The relative infrequency of intabulations of vocal music in surviving sources by native English composers suggests that Book I of Le Roy's 1574 publication may have provoked little response. This book instructs the reader in how to intabulate music in the eight Gregorian modes, and how to transpose the vocal parts so that they lie comfortably within the compass of the lute. Le Roy admits that occasionally notes will descend below the compass and will have to be omitted, but points out that 'Lutes of the newe invention with thirteen strynges, bee not subjecte to this inconvenience'.[152] This provides evidence of the 7-course lute in France around 1570. We know such instruments were in existence in Italy and Germany much earlier. English manuscript sources, however, provide no evidence of their presence before *c.*1580.

[148] Daniel Heartz, 'An Elizabethan Tutor for the Guitar', *GSJ* 16 (1962), 3–21. Heartz attempts a reconstruction of Le Roy's tutor for guitar.

[149] 1574 edn., fo. 65; modern edn., 52.   [150] 1574 edn., fo. 64ʳ; modern edn., 51.

[151] 1574 edn., fo. 66ʳ; modern edn., 54.   [152] 1574 edn., fo. 33ʳ; modern edn., 31.

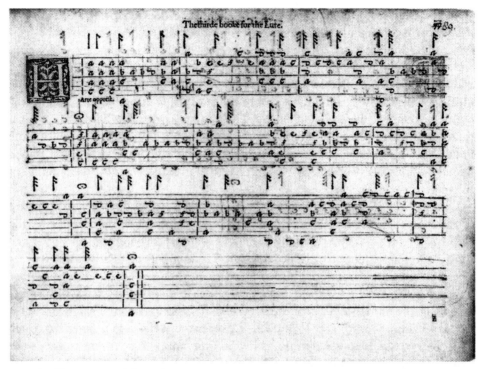

PL. 4.6. 'Harte opprest' from Adrian Le Roy, *A briefe and plaine Instruction . . . for the Lute*
(London, 1574), Book III, *The thirde booke for the Lute*, sig. ZI

The 'divers Psalmes and many fine excelent tunes' of Book III of Le Roy's 1574
publication include the earliest surviving published English lute music. The twenty
'airs de cour' intabulated for solo lute in Book III of the 1574 London publication
had originally been published in Paris by Le Roy as songs for voice and lute.
However, the eight psalms and the song, 'Hart opprest' (see Pl. 4.6) are not found
among any of the other works he produced. Could Rowbotham have assembled
these last intabulations? 'Harte oppressyd with desp'rat thought' is possibly a poem
by Sir Thomas Wyatt which was set as a four-part song during the Henrician
period.[153] The style of this intabulation and those of the psalms is indistinguishable
from the chansons. Their presence is a reminder of the primary use of the lute in
England in the performance of sung or recited poetry and other vocally inspired
music, secular and sacred, for much of the sixteenth century.

Among the pieces in Stowe 389 and RA 58 perhaps the most significant are the
arrangements of part-songs, popular ballad tunes, and tunes associated with recita-

---

[153] The poem appears in *Collected Poems of Sir Thomas Wyatt*, ed. Kenneth Muir and Patricia Thompson
(Liverpool, 1969). See John Ward, 'Barley's Songs without Words', *LSJ* 12 (1970), 5–22 at 15.

tion schemes for the performances of poetry. These vocal tune settings were probably the basis of the amateur's repertory in the early and mid-sixteenth century. We
can imagine that this was the sort of material that Thomas Whythorne would have
provided his gentry pupils with in the 1550s and 1560s for the singing or recitation
of the poetry of Surrey and Wyatt that was so popular at this time, or for the enjoyment of the tunes on their own without the words.[154] Many of the poems by Surrey
and Wyatt published in *Songes and Sonnettes* have associated tunes. Indeed a copy
of the book formerly in the library of Sir William Watkins Wynne, now lost, had
twelve tunes written into the margin next to the poems for which they acted as word
carriers.[155] The next step was to add a lute accompaniment to support the voice.
This accompaniment could also be played for its own sake. A good example of this
process is the setting in both RA 58 and Stowe 389 of Surrey's 'If care do cause men
cry, why do not I complaine?', no. 265 in *Songes and Sonnettes* (see Ex. 4.1). Both
settings are simple, consisting in the main of three-part chords with the top part
carrying the tune.

During Elizabeth's reign the process of intabulating tunes associated with popular poetry as accompaniments or solos for the lute was increasingly extended to
broadside ballad tunes. Broadside ballads were becoming popular at this time, and
were printed in large numbers in the Elizabethan era, making their associated tunes
hugely popular too.[156] The practice of harmonizing these tunes as lute solos, coupled with the English variation technique developed over the next half-
century, became England's most original contribution to the corpus of lute music.

The large proportion of pieces based on Italian grounds (the passamezzo antico
and moderno, and their stock variants; the romanesca, folia, and Ruggiero) is typical of the first generation of English lute composers, led by John Johnson, who
developed a style of composition largely based on these forms (see Ex. 4.2).[157]
These grounds themselves may have originally been used as word carriers for
recitation of poetry. An example of such a piece from Stowe 389 shows the simple
but rhythmic textures woven over such ground basses in these early manuscripts,
the ground in this case being the 'romanesca' (see Ex. 4.3). Here the
III–VII–i–V–III–VII–i/V–I ground is stated twice, first in common time and then
in triple time, with similar melodic material in both, thus forming a piva–saltarello
type pair. The fact that in both these early manuscripts only two tablature rhythmic signs are used in the main, and the scribes were apparently unable to handle

---

[154] *Autobiography*, ed. Osborn, 165. Whythorne taught a gentleman's daughter to play 'somewhat on the virginals and the lute, and also to sing pricksong . . . [and] . . . to teach her to sing to the lute also'.

[155] The tunes are found in a copy of George F. Nott's unpublished 'Songs and Sonnets' (1814?) in the library
at Arundel Castle.

[156] Claude M. Simpson, *The British Broadside Ballad and its Music* (New Brunswick, NJ, 1966), pp. ix–xxii.

[157] Byler, 'Italian Currents', 13–41.

Ex. 4.1. *Settings of 'If care do cause men cry': (a) Stowe 389, fo. 120ʳ; (b) RA 58, fo. 52ʳ, bars 1–6*

1. MS has ⌐ ⌐ ⌐ ⍑ for bar 3.
2. MS has ⌐ ⌐ for bar 2.
3. MS has ⌐ ⌐ ⌐ for bar 3.
4. MS has ⌐.
5. MS has ⌐ ⌐ ⌐⌐ for bar 5.

NB. All rhythm sign dots and most barlines are editorial.

Ex. 4.2. *Italian grounds and their variants*

1. Passamezzo antico

2. Passamezzo moderno

3. Romanesca

4. Folia

5. Rogero

6. Quadro Pavan

7. Bergamasca

dotted notes or triple-time rhythm, means that there are always a number of possible editorial solutions to these pieces.[158]

Despite the limited quality of the music in these earliest two sources, they contain, in microcosm, all the forms and characteristics of mature Elizabethan lute music, except the contrapuntal fantasia. The most interesting early piece is the 'The Duke of Somersettes Dompe' from RA 58. There are strong similarities between the piece and Vincenzo Capirola's 'Paduana Bellissima', suggesting that this Dump is based on an Italian model.[159] Both Capirola's piece and the Dump require the

[158] For a different solution see ibid. 132.
[159] See Capirola, *Compositione di messer Vincenzo Capirola*, ed. Otto Gombosi (Neuilly-sur-Seine, 1955).

Ex. 4.3. *Untitled piece based on the romanesca ground, Stowe 389, fo. 120ᵛ*

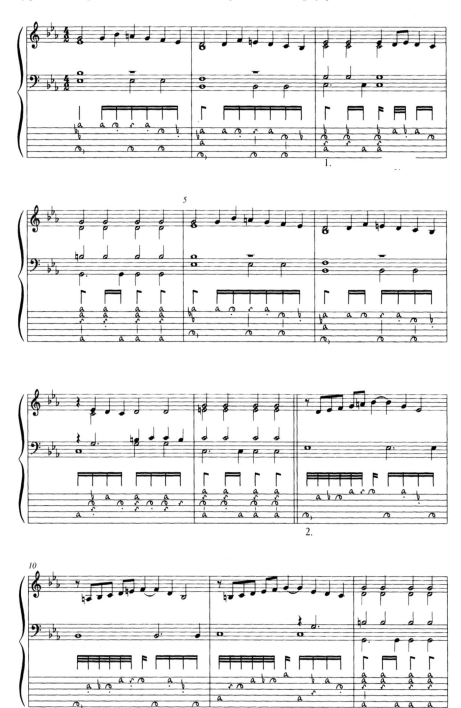

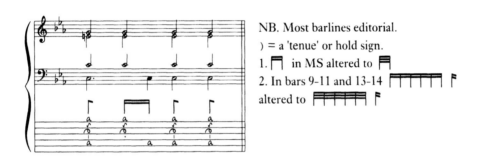

NB. Most barlines editorial.
) = a 'tenue' or hold sign.

retuning of the bottom course down a tone, resulting in an open fifth between the sixth and fifth courses, giving a strong tonic/dominant/tonic basis to both pieces. 'Somersettes Dompe' has six variations. The first three eight-bar sections are rigorously organized, each section consisting of two balanced four-bar phrases, the first with a I–I–IV/II–V harmonic base, the later I–I–V–I (Ex. 4.4). The next section introduces new melodic material and running divisions. This section is unbalanced, with a four-bar phrase answered by a six-bar one, though this may have resulted from corruption that has crept in through aural and manuscript circulation. The following section is characterized by parallel sixths and then running passages and repetition at the octave. Finally, the last eight-bar section reverts back to the original melody with increased harmonic movement. As the scribe uses only two rhythm signs in the main, and no dots, any editorial solution to this piece is problematic. This Dump contains many of the characteristics of mature English variation technique, being episodic in nature, and moving from the simple to the more complex, the later sections being characterized by different rhythmic figurations and running passages with a return to the opening idea at the close.

The music of the Osborn commonplace book is technically more advanced than that in RA 58 and Stowe, and the pieces are more extended. Most significant is the inclusion of several pieces from foreign sources. These include two fantasias by

Ex. 4.4. *'The Duke of Somersettes Dompe', RA 58, fos. 51ᵛ–52ʳ*

6th course tuned at F

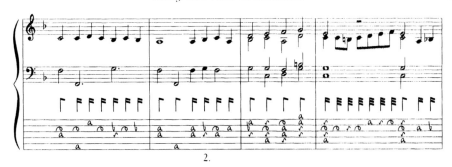

2.

1. Soprano and bass notes on separate beats in the MS, here combined onto second beat.

2. Bass part Gb altered to G♮.

NB. Original barring has the anacrusis on the first beat. The MS does not use tablature rhythm signs for quaver beats (𝄻). All quaver beats are editorial reconstructions.

Francesco da Milano and two divergent versions of pieces for vihuela by Luis de Narváez from his *Los seys libros del Delphin de musica de cifras para tañer Vihuela* (Valladolid, 1538). There are also two lute intabulations of French chansons, one by Claudin de Sermisy, 'C'est a grand tort', and one by the anglicized Philip van Wilder, 'Je file quand Dieu me donne'.[160] This last 'chanson rustique' (see Ex. 4.5) was van Wilder's most widely copied piece. It was most probably composed for performance by the singing men and boys of the Privy Chamber that first assembled sometime during the 1530s. It also survives in versions for keyboard and five-part viol ensemble, and was published by Le Roy and Ballard in *Mellange de chansons* (Paris, 1572), and reprinted in *Le rossignol musical* (Antwerp, 1598).[161] It was even turned into a 'bransle gay' by Claude Gervaise.[162] Three manuscript arrangements

[160] Ward, *Music for Elizabethan Lutes*, inventory of lute, gittern, and guitar pieces in the Osborn commonplace book, pp. 38–41.

[161] Humphreys, 'Philip van Wilder', 17; Bernstein, 'Philip van Wilder', 71.

[162] Claude Gervaise, *Sixième livre de danceries* (Paris, 1555), no. 48, 'Bransle Gay II'. I am grateful to Stewart McCoy for this information.

Ex. 4.5. '*Je file quand Dieu me donne de quoy*' *by Philip van Wilder from the Osborn common-place book, fo. 17ᵛ, bars 1–9, with the superius part from* Mellange de chansons *(Paris, 1572)*

NB. All barring is editorial

1. MS rhythm sign ⌐, altered to | 3. Tablature '∿' on the 4th course has been ignored

2. MS rhythm signs ⌐ ⌐, altered to ⌐⌐   4. MS rhythm sign ⌐, altered to ⌐

of the piece exist for performance of the lower parts on the lute, presumably with the top part sung. The Osborn commonplace book version and that of the near contemporary Add. 4900 share some of the same idiomatic figuration. The later Brogyntyn manuscript version is without figuration, but gives the piece in full, including the last eight bars absent in the earlier versions.[163] Both the Osborn and Add. 4900 versions were probably derived from the same original intabulation made by a professional musician, which became corrupted after some years of circulation in manuscript. The presence of these intabulations and foreign fantasias introduces a new strand into the repertoire of amateur lute music played in England. No doubt they were introduced by foreign professionals, and, at first, were available in limited number to amateurs with court connections.

By contrast, none of the pieces added by the earlier two hands found in the Giles Lodge is foreign. Like the compilers of RA 58 and Stowe 389 these scribes did not understand the use of the dot to extend duration, and the rhythmic groupings of notes are not regular. These pieces were probably added to the manuscript before 1570. Clearly the original owner of the Osborn commonplace book had access to more sophisticated cosmopolitan sources for the copying of music, and was better informed musically than the Giles Lodge manuscript scribes.

The foreign pieces apart, the Osborn commonplace book contains a similar repertoire to that of the other sources so far discussed, though in musically more sophisticated versions. Of the four song arrangements the two on the first folio are notable as they appear on the page with a vocal line in staff notation above the tablature.[164] The first, entitled simply 'A songe', may have been a utilitarian word carrier for any number of the poems in the manuscript. Among the other songs is another setting of the popular Surrey poem 'If care do cause men cry' (see above, Ex. 4.1). The manuscript also contains five pavans, four galliards (one of which, like the 'Somersettes Dompe', requires the sixth course to be lowered a whole tone), three versions of the passamezzo antico, a 'Passamezzo d'angleterre', one dump, two 'points'—i.e. short pieces of a contrapuntal nature—two fantasies other than those by Francesco da Milano, and one intabulation of a Sternhold and Hopkins setting of Ps. 4. The vocal settings, fantasias, and points aside, the most common element in the music contained in this book is the use of Italian grounds and English variation technique. Among the grounds, the passamezzo antico and passamezzo moderno, the romanesca, and the folia are present.

Of the sets of variations in the Osborn commonplace book perhaps the most notable is 'Artheres Dumpe' (see Ex. 4.6). Robert Spencer suggested this title might refer to Arthur Dewes, lutenist to Henry VIII.[165] The piece is built on a simple

---

[163] Osborn commonplace book, fos. 17ʳ–18ᵛ; *GB-Lbl* Add. 4900, fo. 62ʳ; Brogyntyn MS, p. 14.

[164] Osborn commonplace book, fo. 1ʳ, 'A songe'; *The tender love that dredethe losse.*

[165] *The Marsh Lute Book*, facs. with an introductory note by Robert Spencer (Musical Sources, 20; Kilkenny, 1981), p. xxii.

Ex. 4.6. *'Artheres dumpe', Osborn commonplace book, fos. 9ᵛ–10ʳ*

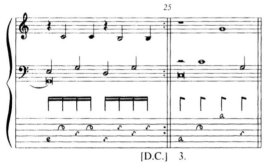

[D.C.]   3.

NB. All single barlines are editorial.
1. Tenor tablature sign ' ⱥ ' changed to ' ↄ '
2. Single barline altered to double.
3. There is a signum congruentiae above this tablature
letter indicating a return to the beginning at this point.

alternating tonic/dominant bass. The opening four-bar section, characterized by
the 'bell-like' overlapping of notes, contrasts with the arpeggiation of the succeeding four four-bar episodes, each of which is repeated and which exploit different
registers of the instrument. There is a suggestion that the opening passage should
then be repeated before the close. Two other versions of the piece survive in
the later Marsh manuscript (*c*.1595), the first of which is incomplete, though the

second, entitled 'Dump philli', lasts a full eighty-six bars.[166] This title prompts the conjecture that the piece was composed by, or for, Philip van Wilder. In its full form it is an astonishing tour de force, and certainly one of the most successful early English lute pieces. Like other mid-century sets of variations both for lute and keyboard, it builds with increasing rhythmic activity to return to the opening material at the close.[167]

The heavy reliance on ground-bass structure is also a feature of the Giles Lodge manuscript. Of the first twenty-seven pieces, four use the passamezzo antico, one the passamezzo moderno, one the bergamasca, and one the folia variant known as the 'Cara cosa'.[168] Among the ballad tunes are 'Will ye go walke the woods so wilde', 'Robin Hood', and 'Trenchmore'. Other pieces with vocal associations include a setting of Ovid's first epistle 'Hunc tua Penelope', 'Blame not my lute', and Surrey's 'In winters iuste return', found also in RA 58. In cases like 'Blame not my lute', where the title refers to a known poem (by Wyatt) and the piece is a simple ground (Cara cosa), the suggestion is that the performer(s) sang or recited to the lute ground.[169] Many of the pieces in this manuscript consist of no more than a single short statement of the tune or ground. Others, such as nos. 3, 9, 11, 14, 18, and 19, involve subsequent variations which show some tendency to elaboration as the piece progresses.

The last eleven pieces in the Giles Lodge manuscript date from the 1570s or the 1580s. They are notated with a full complement of rhythm signs so that it is possible to read the music at sight from the manuscript page with little difficulty. Several of the pieces are longer than anything in the earlier part, with varied repeat structures, left-hand fret stops up to the eighth fret, and *barre* chords up to the fifth fret.[170] In 'In Crete' the technical difficulty of the high frets is compounded by the tuning of the lowest course down a tone. While this music is still amateur, it is clearly not for a beginner. All but one of the eleven pieces concord with pieces in near contemporary English sources; five are structurally based on Italian grounds, two are French in origin, and four of the tunes were used as ballad tunes.[171] One of the ballad tunes, 'All of grene willowe' (no. 35), does not easily fit the words of Desdemona's song from Shakespeare's *Othello*, but was a well-known ballad with the same refrain.[172] The first piece of the eleven provides us with the best clue as to the dating of this section of the book. Entitled 'O heavenly god / my L. of Essex songs' and attributed to 'Wm hewese', it relates to Walter Devereux, first Earl of

[166] *The Marsh Lute Book*, 175-6; 426-8.
[167] Similar variation sets are the 'Sommersettes Dompe' and the 'Ashton hornepipe'.
[168] Passamezzo antico, nos. 7, 14, 17, 27; passamezzo moderno, no. 11; bergamasca, no. 9; Cara cosa, no. 4.
[169] *The Penguin Book of Early Music*, ed. Anthony Rooley (Harmondswoth, 1980), 135.
[170] Giles Lodge MS, no. 29, fos. 14ʳ-15ᵛ; no. 30, fos. 15ʳ-17ᵛ; no. 30, fos. 20ᵛ-21ʳ.
[171] Italian grounds, nos. 29, 31, 33, 35, 38; French pieces, nos. 30, 31; ballad tunes, nos. 31, 33, 34, 36.
[172] Frederick Sternfeld, *Music in Shakespearean Tragedy* (London, 1963), 36-7.

Essex, who died in September 1576. According to a contemporary account, on the night before the Earl died:

he willed William Hayes his musician to playe on the virgynalls, and to singe. 'Playe' said he, 'my songe, and I will singe yt my self.' And so he did most joyfullie; not as the howlinge Swan, still lookinge downe, wayleth her end, but as the swete lark, liftinge upp his hands, and castinge his eyes upp unto his God . . .[173]

The words of this song appeared as a poem ascribed to Francis Kinwellmarsh in *The Paradise of Dainty Devices* (1576), entitled 'The complaint of a Synner'.[174] It began with the words: 'O heavenlie God, O father deare, cast down thy tender eye.' Later editions have the words 'sung by the Earl of Essex upon his death-bed in Ireland'. This suggests that this piece could have been added to the manuscript no earlier than 1576. The song was popular around the 1580s as it appears in two versions in the Dallis manuscript with a voice part notated above the lute tablature.[175] Unlike the Dallis manuscript versions, the Giles Lodge tablature is complete in itself with the vocal line carried, for the most part, at the top of each chord, rather than the lute part being an intabulation of only the lower voices.

Of the forms in the Willoughby manuscript, the pavans and galliards are most numerous, and of these, several are based on grounds. Four such pieces are entitled 'quadro pavan', and one 'quadro gallyard'.[176] These titles refer to the passamezzo moderno ground in the major key using B *quadratum* (♮). Through common usage in the 1570s and 1580s this type of piece became almost a form in itself, often with a distinctive opening few bars of chordal reiteration; it could be played in any key, and was used as a framework for elaborate running divisions in repeated sections.

Typically the quadro pavan consists of a sixteen-bar chordal statement of the ground, followed by a varied repeat of the statement with running divisions. This is answered by an eight-bar section in the dominant key returning to the tonic, which is also repeated with its own variation. The inclusion of the final eight-bar section after the statement of the ground pattern became the factor that most differentiated the quadro pavan from the passamezzo moderno.[177] Most quadro pavans and galliards are anonymous, and their mechanical nature prompted Thomas Morley to remark in his *A Plaine and Easie Introduction to Practicall Musicke* (1597) that they were nicknamed 'Gregory Walker': 'That name in derision

[173] Byler, 'Italian Currents', 60. From an account by Edward Waterhouse, the Earl's friend and secretary, preserved in Richard Broughter's commonplace book. See Henry Elliot Malden (ed.), 'Devereux Papers with Richard Brouhton's Memoranda (1575–1601)', *Camden Miscellany*, 13 (1923), pub. in Camden 3rd ser., 34 (London, 1924), v, fos. 9–11.
[174] *The Paradise of Dainty Devices (1576–1606), by Richard Edwards and Others*, ed. Hyder E. Rollins (Cambridge, Mass., 1927), 87–8, 251–2.
[175] Dallis MS, nos. 180, 187, pp. 202–3, 212. [176] *The Willoughby Lute Book*, nos. 10, 18, 27, 28, 29.
[177] The Dallis MS e.g. always distinguishes 'passemesso', which is without the extra bars, from 'quadros', which have them.

Ex. 4.7. *'Quadro Pavan in C major', Willoughby MS, fos. 34ᵛ–35ʳ, bars 33–48*

they have given this quadrant pavane because, because it "walketh" amongst the barbers and fiddlers more common then any other.'[178] Example 4.7, the 'Quadro Pavan in C major' from the Willoughby manuscript, is typical of the genre. These pieces contain little that is melodically memorable, but have strong rhythmic drive. Like some jazz and blues their value lies more in their recognizable harmonic sequence and suitability as a framework for improvisation. The octave stringing that one would expect on lutes in this period has a considerable impact on a piece like the Willoughby manuscript quadro pavan. For instance, in bar 34 the tenor-line crotchets connect the melody line minim g's with the g' at the start of bar 35 by sounding at both octaves, and the parallel octaves between the bass and treble line in the second half of bar 39 are improved by the tenor line a also sounding an a', which is actually the heard melody-line note for the third minim of that bar.

Of all the pieces in the Willoughby manuscript the Pavan and Galliard to Delight by John Johnson are the most significant as they are probably the earliest versions of these excellent pieces. (See Exs. 4.8 and 4.9.) They constitute a milestone in the development of English lute music, as the first fully extended pieces by a known lutenist composer in a completely English idiom. Both dances have a tripartite form, with varied repeats of each section. Tripartite dance forms, and especially pavans and galliards, were to become the principle vehicles for the explosion of musical creativity in the 1590s. The phenomenon of paired dances, using the same musical material in the context of two contrasting rhythmic frameworks, is particularly a feature of instrumental music of the 1580s and 1590s, and is much less often encountered in music composed in the Jacobean period.

Unlike the impersonal, four-square nature of the quadro pavan above, the Pavan and Galliard to Delight show a new attention to detail. Melodic interest moves in places from the upper part to the middle or bass part, as for example in bars 5 to 6 of the Pavan. 7–6 suspensions are used to highlight points of special beauty, as in bar 5. Above all, the pieces show a new-found flexibility and variety in rhythm and

---

[178] Ed. Harman, 214.

Ex. 4.8. *'Pavan to Delight' by John Johnson, opening section with varied repeat, Willoughby MS, fos. 25ᵛ–26ʳ, bars 1–16*

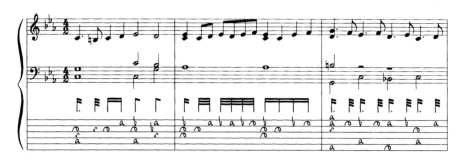

melodic figuration. The running quaver divisions in the Pavan do not always move predictably, and the piece freely intermixes four different tablature rhythms, together with dotted notes to add impetus. Johnson's Pavan and Galliard display a greater ability to maintain interest over a larger span of time than other pieces in earlier manuscripts.

English instrumental music was transformed in the forty years from 1540 to 1580. The importation and settlement in England of foreign musicians and their families in this period began a process that saw instrumental playing and composing skills, first developed on the Continent and in northern Italy especially, successfully transplanted to England. There are a number of pieces that survive from post-1570s lute sources that are attributed to Augustine, Lodwick, Ambrose, Anthony, and Petro that must relate to members of the Lupo, Bassano, and Galliardello family. Augustino Bassano, who entered royal service in 1550 as a wind player and remained in his post until his death in 1604, may have played the lute. Two of his seven instrumental pieces survive in lute sources and may tentatively be ascribed to him.[179] There is a lute piece attributed to Renaldo Paradiso, as well as fifteen pieces by Alfonso Ferrabosco I which exist in versions for solo lute. While it seems that none of these Italians was employed as a lutenist, their indirect influence

[179] Ward, 'A Dowland Miscellany', 110; id., *Music for Elizabethan Lutes*, 51.

Ex. 4.9. *'Galliard to Delight' by John Johnson, opening section with varied repeat, Willoughby MS, fo. 28ʳ, bars 1–16*

1. MS ⊕ altered to ⊕ to conform with bar 2.

may have been strong. The Thistlethwaite manuscript is very probably representative of their contribution. They were part of a generation of foreign musicians in England who produced and played a repertory of Elizabethan instrumental dance music that is largely lost. Lute versions of some of their consort pieces were made by these composers themselves, or others, and helped to establish the dance forms of pavans, galliards, etc. as the norm for solo lute music, rather than fantasias or pieces based on Italian grounds. The use of the lute for playing a tablature reduction of three-, four-, and five-part instrumental may have been important at this time in establishing the instrument's solo repertory. Composers may also have worked in the other direction, composing first on the lute and then developing the piece for ensemble.

By 1580 the expatriate musicians were giving way to a new generation of English composers, like Thomas Morley, Peter Philips, and Anthony Holborne, who absorbed and further developed the styles and forms the Italians had implanted. By the end of the 1580s, as England was entering a period of relative political isolation, it is clear that reliance on the technical and compositional skills of foreign lute players was no longer necessary. A new generation of English-born players had absorbed the skills and techniques of the foreigners and was ready to take over.

Chapter Five

The Golden Age, Part I: 1580–1603

for the play that is now, and the lessons (that are now a daies) are so curiouslie set, that we of the olde mine, are smoakt up like to sea-cole, and this age, hath the golden ore, and sparkling diamondes of divine Musitions, that for mine owne part, I am content, to give place both to youth, and the time, onelie content to be an auditore, and lover of the best.

Knight to Timotheus, in Thomas Robinson, *The Schoole of Musicke* (1603), sig. B

Ovid, in his first book of the *Metamorphoses*, describes the four ages of man, of which 'The Golden Age was first; which uncompelled, And without rule, in faith and truth exceelled'.[1] Under the reign of Saturn this age experienced no wars, no laws, no seasons, and there was no work to be done. Peace, justice, and equality were universal. Virgil in his fourth Eclogue spoke of the dawning of a new golden age for Rome under Augustus, when civilization and the arts would flourish. This poem was later reinterpreted by Constantine, with the virgin goddess Astraea, who ushers in the new golden age, identified as the Virgin Mary. John Foxe, in his *Book of Martyrs*, the most influential and popular book of Elizabethan times after the Bible, drew a parallel between Constantine's ending of religious persecutions, and the accession of Elizabeth after the repression and burnings of the Marian period.[2] The new Astraea was personified by Elizabeth I, whose favourite personal device was the phoenix. Like Augustus in the early days of Imperial Rome, she was seen to have re-established justice, and to have provided a rule under which peace and the arts could flourish. This point was made by Sir John Davies in his *Hymnes of Astraea* (1599), referring to Elizabeth as she who: 'Hath brought againe the golden dayes, And all the world amended.'[3]

This theme of the Golden Age restored permeates the poetry of the age. Edmund Spencer in *The Faerie Queen* and *The Shepheards Calendar*, and Sir Philip Sidney in *The Countess of Pembroke's Arcadia* and *Astrophel and Stella*, attempted to establish English as a language of epic poetry, and to produce works that could stand alongside those of Virgil and the classical writers. The Arcadian backdrop evoked for these works was an idealized portrayal of Elizabethan court life.

[1] Buxton, *Elizabethan Taste*, 8, quoted from the *Metamorphoses*, trans. George Sandys (1632).
[2] Ibid. 9. John Foxe, *Book of Martyrs* (Latin edn., Basle, 1559; English rev. edn., London, 1563).
[3] Davies, Sir John, *The Poems of Sir John Davies*, ed. Robert Krueger (Oxford, 1975), 71.

In spite of the efforts of Sidney and Spencer, the idea that English was a language of first-rate importance, capable of great poetry, would have been accepted by few people outside Britain before the eighteenth century. By contrast, England's contribution to the mainstream of European music is unlikely to have been so questioned. Tinctoris and Martin le Franc had special praise for English music during the age of Dunstable. Once again, in the last years of the sixteenth century and early seventeenth century, England became an exporter of music and musicians, and English styles and compositions were much admired abroad.

Some musicians, like Peter Philips and Richard Deering, left the country as Catholic recusants. Others were attached to English theatre companies which travelled abroad. Some companies left for good after the act of 1572, which had restricted their activities at home, unless they were licensed and could find a suitable patron.[4] Most expatriate musicians, however, like John Dowland, Thomas Robinson, William Brade, and Thomas Simpson, were primarily attracted by better career opportunities in the rich courts of northern Europe. As a result a considerable corpus of English string-consort music and lute music of the late Elizabethan and Jacobean periods was published and circulated in manuscript on the Continent, and, particularly in the case of English consort music, was widely imitated.[5]

That England was truly 'a nest of singing birds' during the late Elizabethan/Jacobean age was endorsed by Francis Meres in *Wits Treasury* (1598) when he compared a list of sixteen of the most famous English composers of the Tudor period with a list of seventeen from ancient Greece.[6] The high standing of English musicians at this time was underlined by Dr Case in his celebrated defence of music, and echoed in the quotation above from Thomas Robinson's *The Schoole of Musicke* (1603).[7] If the years 1580 to 1625 were a golden age for English lute music, the metaphor being uncomfortably transferred from the literary domain, they were also glorious in other areas of music.[8]

The two working generations from the appointment of John Johnson in 1579 to a place as a lutenist in the Queen's music to the death of his son Robert Johnson in 1633 encompass the maturity and decline of an identifiable native style, and its replacement by something quite different. These years coincided with the high point of the lute's popularity, not only in England but throughout Europe, and the

---

[4] Holman, *Four and Twenty Fiddlers*, 156.

[5] English music of Dowland and his generation was published in the Continental string-consort publications of the Englishmen William Brade (Hamburg, 1609 and 1617) and Thomas Simpson (Hamburg, 1621) and the Germans Samuel Scheidt (Hamburg, 1621) and Johann Hermann Schein (Leipzig, 1617). Ibid. 144–72.

[6] Francis Meres, *Palladis Tamia (Wits Treasury), Being the Second part of Wits Commonwealth* (London, 1598), fo. 288ᵛ.

[7] John Case, *Apologia musices* (Oxford, 1588).

[8] The first article to use the term Golden Age in connection with English lute music was Richard Newton's, 'English Lute Music of the Golden Age', *PRMA*, 45 (1938–9), 63–90.

period from which by far the most English source material survives. This age produced the complete output of English madrigals, of published English lute songs, of mixed-consort music, of the maturity of the virginal school, and a large proportion of English viol consort music.

The work of the madrigalists and virginalists, and to a lesser extent the lute-song repertoire, have been well known since the early decades of this century, yet it is only in the last forty years that a similar awareness of the achievements of English lute music of the late Elizabethan/Jacobean period has arisen. Source survival leads us to conclude that the zenith of the lute's so-called golden age in England was the 1590s. In part at least, this was because the lute was pivotal to the mixed consort which was flourishing at this time. In may also relate to the fact that the period of popularity for the viol among amateurs had yet to start. The creative energy in lute music of the late Elizabethan period outweighed that of the Jacobean, which produced less new music, and during which much of the old music remained popular.

Concrete evidence of a school of native English lute makers during this era has yet to be unearthed, although there were a number of foreign lute makers working in England whose names are known. The meagre lute iconography of this period, some of which is listed in Table 5.1, tells us a little about the circumstances in which the lute was played, and what instruments were played with it, but the depictions are so imprecise as to tell us little more. There are pictures of the lute being played along with the other instruments of a mixed consort group, one being the famous funeral portrait of Sir Henry Unton.[9] The painting of the *Courtiers of Queen Elizabeth* attributed to Marcus Gheeraerts the Elder (wrongly, according to Holman) showing a lute with a violin band providing music for outside dancing tells us more about the use of the lute at court than the lute itself.[10] As the dance band certainly played without written music, the addition of the lute is evidence of a use for the lute at court that is otherwise unrecorded. One feature that is noticeable is the 'plump' rounded outline of the soundboard when compared with the shape of the lute in the Hilliard miniature (see above, Pl. 4.5) or those of the Henrician period. This outline is also present in the miniature painting by Isaac Oliver that probably dates from the 1590s (see Pl. 5.1).

With such a dearth of information on the type of lute played in England at this time, we must turn to foreign sources and assume that in England lutenists either played imported instruments or lutes of English manufacture that followed Continental trends in design. Surviving lutes suggest that the traditional centres of lute-making, Germany and Italy (especially Venice), maintained their dominance in

[9] Unton funeral portrait (after 1596), National Portrait Gallery, London; other pictures include the great chamber frieze at Gilling Castle, Yorkshire, and a ceiling painted at Crathes Castle, nr. Aberdeen.
[10] Buxton, *Elizabethan Taste*, pl. 15; also Holman, *Four and Twenty Fiddlers*, 117 and pl. 3(b).

Table 5.1. *English lute iconography of the Golden Age period*

Representation	Date and place	Instrumentation
Miniature painting of Queen Elizabeth by Nicholas Hilliard	*c.*1580, Royal Collection	6-course lute being played by the Queen
Oil painting on panel, *Jepthah's Daughter*	1580–1610, Royal Collection	lute with triangle and pipe and tabor
Low relief carving Exeter Cathedral	1586, Tomb of Matthew Godwin	2 lutes with cornett, sackbut, and organ
Carved wood overmantel	late 16th c., Christchurch Mansions, Ipswich	a king (David?) with lute and 3 naked dancers
Carved wood fireplace surround	late 16th c., Guildhall, Barnstaple, Devon	male lute player
Oil painting, *Courtiers of Queen Elizabeth*	*c.*1600, present whereabouts unknown (reproduced in Holman, *Four and Twenty Fiddlers*, pl. 3*b*)	lute played with 3 violins for dancing
Miniature painting by Isaac Oliver	*c.*1610, Museum of Fine Arts, Copenhagen	lute played with a transverse flute, and possibly other instruments also
Mural	*c.*1615, Beaconsfield private house	standing male lute player
Ceiling plaster	completed 1620, Blicking Long Gallery Hall, Norfolk	male lute player accompanying a female singer
Carving on chimney piece	'Jacobean' room, Audley End, Essex	lute and violin

For representations of lutes as part of a mixed consort see Table 6.4. I have not included the many woodcut monumental title-pages of the period that include lutes as part of the devices and emblems employed, such as in Dowland's *First Booke of Songs* (1597), Morley's *Plaine and Easie Introduction* (1597), and Christopher Saxton's *Atlas of the Countries of England and Wales* (1579).

the field, although evidence of lute-making workshops in major European cities outside Germany and Italy is more plentiful than before the mid-century.[11]

The typical body outline of lutes by the most famous makers of this period, like the prolific Wendelio Venere (alias Wendelin Tieffenbrucker), Michael Harton (both of Padua), and Magno Dieffoprucher (or Magnus Tieffenbrucker) of Venice, was rounder and fuller, with the upper part of the belly wider than in earlier sixteenth-century lutes. The backs of these lutes were much rounder than earlier

---

[11] Gaspar Tieffenbrucker I was active in Lyon in 1533–64 and Gaspar Tieffenbrucker II established a workshop in Paris in 1582 (see Ian Harwood, 'Tieffenbrucker', *New Grove*). Also, the Hofmans family were making lutes in Antwerp *c.*1600.

PL. 5.1. Isaac Oliver, miniature *c.*1590–5, *Virtue Confronts Vice—An Allegory*. Statens
Museum for Kunst, Copenhagen, no. 6938

ones, a section cut through the belly at the deepest point approximating to a semi-
circle.[12] This near-circular bowl was achieved by increasing the number of ribs
from 9 or 11 to 21, 33, 35, or 37, with 33 and 35 being the most common numbers.
As before, yew was the favoured wood for the back, with many instruments appearing to have double the true number of ribs by using wood that was half 'heart' and
half 'sap' wood, and then cutting and planing them so that the junction between the
two ran along the centreline of each rib.[13]

Other modifications common to lutes at this time were the addition of a seventh
course and the use of unison double courses for some or all of the bass strings, particularly the fourth and fifth courses, in preference to octave stringing. Some early

[12] Lundberg, 'Historical Lute Construction', 38–41.

[13] Typical of such lutes are the bass and octave bass lutes in Nuremberg (Germanisches Museum); the Wendelio
Tieffenbrucker/Venere in Darmstadt (Hessiches Landesmuseum Kg. 67.106); and the Leipzig Magnus
Tieffenbrucker (Musikinstrumenten Museum, 492), which are all multi-ribbed with 'heart and sap' yew-wood
backs.

sixteenth-century pieces required the retuning of the sixth course down a whole tone (from *G* to *F*, assuming a lute tuned at nominal *g'* for the top course).[14] Clearly the advantages of having another course permanently pitched below the sixth led to its incorporation into the design of the instrument. Seven-course lutes were not altogether new. There are references to 7-course lutes on the Continent from as early as the Pesaro MS (*c.*1500). The length of the bridge, the width of the fingerboard, and the size of the pegbox were all increased to accommodate the extra string. Having made the addition, it could be used as an *F* or *D* bass, the latter gradually becoming the more common.

Once the 7-course lute was established, the advantage of an 8-course instrument (less retuning of the bass course) became likewise apparent. This process led to a gradual increase in the number of strings up to ten courses in the period before 1625, but with much overlap. Tablature which requires a 7-course lute first appeared in an English publication in Dowland's *First Booke of Songes* (1597), and also in a number of manuscripts that date from the 1590s.[15] However, most golden-age music was written for the 6-course lute. Only manscripts, or sections of manuscripts, that were primarily Jacobean suggest a lute of more than six courses as the norm. In this respect England lagged behind much of Europe.[16]

It seems that the practice of octave stringing was abandoned in the late Elizabethan period. In his *A new Booke of Tabliture* (1596), William Barley published a revised version of Alford's translation of Le Roy's 'Instructions to the Lute' (which had first appeared in England in 1568). Barley instructs the reader on how to tune a 6-course lute with octave stringing on the bottom three courses,[17] but he may have been out of step with current practice. Unison stringing is expected by Thomas Robinson in his *Schoole of Musicke* (1603), the next English printed lute book to appear, as is the use of double stringing for the first course, a characteristic of surviving instruments and of lutes in Continental paintings of this time.[18]

The effect of these changes in design was to increase the resonance of the bass response at the expense of the upper partials, and to lessen the explosive qualities of the upper courses, a 'stiffer' but more homogeneous sound emerging. There is little to suggest that the basic right-hand technique of thumb-and-index-finger

---

[14] e.g. the 'Somersettes dump' in RA 58, and 'Alleluya of M\(^r\) Taverner' in Add. 4900, require the bottom string to be tuned down a tone; Add. 4900 contains an instruction to do so: 'descendit Bassus'.

[15] William Barley published a selection of music that we know was primarily intended for lute, and which required seven courses, in his *A New Booke of Tabliture* (1596).

[16] Anthoine Francisque's *Le Tresor d'Orfée* of 1600 requires a lute with nine courses.

[17] Barley, *A new Booke of Tabliture*, 'The foure and twentieth Rule'; see Ward, 'A Dowland Miscellany', 125–6.

[18] Thomas Robinson, *The Schoole of Musicke* (1603) sig. B2, 'and upon the Lute everie string double, you shall understand, that two strings are in one tune, & also beare the name but of one string'. Surviving instruments with double top strings are 1592 Venere (Bologna); Hartung great bass (Nuremberg); Heber (Florence); M. Dieff (Florence).

alternation for running passages (save where chords occur), altered much before the close of the century. Barley reiterates Le Roy in this respect.

Those who played the lute at this time were from much the same social groups as earlier in Elizabeth's reign: wealthy amateurs (often women) with gentry or noble backgrounds; professional male musicians of a lower social status; and young men at court, the universities, and Inns of Court. What was new was the rise in technical standards of playing achieved by both professionals and amateurs, and the magnificent corpus of music produced. Eighteen major sources survive from the late Elizabethan period (though some may have been compiled over several years stretching into the Stuart period), far more than from any other time. (See below, Table 5.3.)

There is evidence of lutenists among men at the universities and Inns of Court in several of the sources. The Dallis manuscript is associated with Dr Dallis, a teacher at Cambridge University. The nine related volumes written out by Mathew Holmes, precentor of Christ Church Cathedral, Oxford, may reflect the musical activities of a circle of friends and pupils at Oxford in the 1590s. This was the decade when Lord Herbert of Cherbury attended Oxford University, and 'attained to sing his part at first sight in music and to play on the lute, with very little or almost no teaching', and when Dr Nicholas Bonde, President of Magdalen College, Oxford, owned two lutes, two bandoras, and two citterns at his death.[19] In 1601, while at Lincoln College, Oxford, John Pulteney paid 20s. to one 'that teacheth him on the lute for the whole quarter'.[20] Philip Gawdy maintained his lute playing while at Clifford's Inn in 1581, although he was anxious to play down his enthusiasm for it in his letters to his father.[21]

There are many more identifiable professional lutenists after 1580 than before. For the first twenty years of Elizabeth's reign the only designated royal lute player was Anthony Conti, though others, like Alfonso Ferrabosco I, Augustine Bassano, and Richard Pike, who are listed simply as musicians, may have included the lute among the instruments they played. The Court led the way in the years 1577–80, by augmenting the number of lutenists with the appointment of John Johnson to the place of Conti who died some time after 1579, and by the appointments of Mathias Mason and Thomas Cardell in 1578.[22] (See Table 5.2 for a list of royal lutenists, 1578–1625.) Mason and Johnson were both given two years' back pay in 1581, indicating they had been in royal service for at least two years.[23] Mason had the extra privilege of access to the Privy Chamber.[24] Although there is good evidence that Cardell was a lutenist, he is not normally mentioned in accounts with the other lutenists. This is because he had special duties as a dancing-master and had

[19] Ian Harwood, 'The Origins of the Cambridge Lute Manuscripts', *LSJ* 5 (1963), 32–48 at 45.
[20] Price, *Patrons and Musicians*, 26.   [21] Buxton, *Elizabethan Taste*, 189.
[22] *RECM* vi. 119 for Mason and Cardell.   [23] Ibid. 124.   [24] Ibid., p. viii.

Table 5.2. *Professional lutenists in the royal household 1578–1603*

Lutenist	Dates	Instruments and position	Salary
Mathias/Mathathias Mason	1578–1610	Lute; musician for the three lutes; musician of the Privy Chamber	£20 p.a. raised to £40 p.a. in 1589
John Johnson	1579–94	lute; musician for the three lutes	£20 p.a.
Francis Fiavet	1582?	lute	
Robert Hales	1582–1616	lute and voice; Groom of the Privy Chamber to Queen Anne of Denmark	£40 p.a.
Walter Pierce	1588–1604	lute; musician for the three lutes	£20 p.a.
Edward Collard	1598–9	lute	£20 p.a.
also:			
Thomas Cardell	1578–1621	dancing-master and lute; Groom of the Privy Chamber to Anne of Denmark	£20 p.a.; £40 p.a. from 1593; £100 p.a. from 1604; £140 p.a. from 1605
Francis Cardell	1604–5[a]		

[a] Was to succeed his father Thomas, but died so that Thomas then regained his place.

succeeded the Italian Jaspar Gaffoyne in that role.[25] Further appointments were made of the singer/lutenist Robert Hales in 1582, and Walter Pierce (or Piers) in 1588.[26]

It is not until 1590 that a group that is collectively designated 'lute' appears in Wardrobe accounts, and only in 1600 does such a group appear in Treasury of the Chamber accounts.[27] Before this time the known lute players are among a group listed simply as 'musicians'. During the 1580s accounts show that a specific consort of 'the three lutes' was in existence, and that Johnson, Mason, and Pierce were all members of it at various times.[28] We can also be clear from miscellaneous account entries that from the 1580s there was a group of musicians at court who were specifically designated lute players, and that this number varied from four to six players. The group consisted of John Johnson, Mason, Pierce, Hales, together with Alfonso Ferrabosco II, Cardell, and Francis Fiavet appearing on occasion.[29] John

[25] Gaffoyne was in royal service from 1542 to 1584 at £23. 6s. 8d. p.a., though this was probably a pension in the last years, which overlap with Thomas Cardell. See *Biographical Dictionary*, i. 452.

[26] Ward, 'A Dowland Miscellany', 108; Diana Poulton, *John Dowland* (London, 1972; rev. edn., 1982), 107–18.

[27] *RECM* vi, Wardrobe (1590), 54; Treasury of the Chamber (1600), 161.

[28] Ibid., p. viii; and for Johnson, 124; Mason, 126; Pierce, 145.

[29] *RECM* vi: Ferrabosco and Cardell, 59; Fiavet, 134.

Johnson died in 1594. His place was temporarily filled by Edward Collard in 1598–9.[30] He had apparently died by 1604.[31]

Among the great households there is evidence of music-making which included lutes at: Chatsworth, the home of the Cavendishes; Ingatestone, home of the Petres; and Belvoir, the estate of the Manvers family.[32] In each case, members of these families learnt the lute, and would have employed lutenists as teachers. Some lutenists received part-time employment, as in the case of Francis Pilkington from Ferdinando Stanley, Fifth Earl of Derby.[33] There was always the possibility of advancement from a leading household to a royal one, as with Robert Dowland and John Danyel, who first served in the Cavendish and Hertford families respectively prior to gaining their court positions.[34]

Musicians were ranked among the lowest of the officers that served above stairs. They were treated in the same manner as other resident servants, though they had a greater degree of intimacy with their patrons than fellow-ranking servants, and were marked out by their literacy.[35] There were also servants with musical skills who were principally employed in a non-musical capacity, chaplains for example. Such men usually go unrecorded, but their numbers may have been substantial.[36]

Professional lutenists would have been expected to wear their patron's livery when in attendance, to perform at specific times of the day and at special functions, to play within the various instrumental consorts, and to accompany voices. They might be called upon to compose music if known to be capable. They were normally provided with the tools of their trade, which for lutenists included instruments, strings, and books. At court, where the possibilities were greatest, they might be required to perform in the consort of three lutes, as soloist in the Privy Chamber, or with other instruments or voices. Royal lutenists earned between £20 p.a. as a musician 'for the three lutes', to as much as £40 p.a. as a 'chief luter', plus a standard allowance for livery.[37] Away from court professional lutenists might earn as little as £10 p.a. For royal lutenists there was always the possibility of incidental work for other patrons, as court appointments allowed the possibility of pluralism, a perk not enjoyed by musicians patronized by aristocratic households.[38]

---

[30] *RECM* vi. 159.

[31] *Biographical Dictionary*, i. 276. He was paid from Midsummer 1598 but appointed in June 1599.

[32] Price, *Patrons and Musicians*, 117, 89; 138–9 for Manvers.

[33] Lynn Hulse, 'Musical Patronage of the English Aristocracy c.1590–1640' (Ph.D. thesis, King's College, University of London, 1993), 47, 318. This service took place before 1594. Pilkington printed a piece for orpharion by the Earl in his *Second Set of Madrigals* (1624). See Francis Pilkington, *Complete Works for Solo Lute*, ed. Brian Jeffrey (Music for the Lute, 3; Oxford, 1969), p. vi.

[34] Hulse, 'Musical Patronage', 82.   [35] Ibid. 267.   [36] Ibid. 46.

[37] *RECM* vi. 147. Hales received the salary as a chief lutenist from his appointment. Mason had his raised from £20 p.a. to £40 in 1589.

[38] Hulse, 'Musical Patronage', 81–2. Ead., 'Hardwick MS 29: A New Source for Jacobean Lutenists', *LSJ* 26 (1986), 53–72 at 64.

Many of the growing number of professional lutenists in London lived in close proximity to one another. A large number of musicians, theatre people, printers, and booksellers lived between the river and Holborn, Temple Bar in the west, and the River Fleet in the east. This area centred on the parish of St Dunstans-in-the-West, and included Fleet Street, Fetter Lane, and Chancery Lane.[39] Dowland, Rosseter, and Campion lived in this area. This high concentration of talents would have helped a fast and fruitful exchange of ideas. Music by one composer would soon have been known by others. The establishment of the London season by the late sixteenth century meant that even provincial musicians were soon aware of musical activities in the capital, through their periodic presence or that of their patrons.

Most professional lutenists would have gained a musical education by serving an apprenticeship, the conditions of which were codified by the 1563 statue of artificiers.[40] As in the cases of Bacheler and Robert Johnson, whose indenture documents survive, the apprentice would have been indentured either to a professional musician, or to a man of means able to provide a teacher. Robert Johnson was bound to George Carey, second Baron Hunsdon, for the usual seven years by an indenture dated 2 March 1596.[41] In it Carey undertook 'to teach & enstruct or Cause to be taught and enstructed his said servaunt in the arte of Musicke . . .' as well as provide him with clothes and board, and to pay him a penny a year for seven years, and at the end to give him 'doble apparell both lynnen and wollen'.

In Daniel Bacheler's indenture document, dated 1586 (see Pl. 5.2(*a*)), his apprenticeship indentures were signed over from his uncle, the dancing-master and lutenist Thomas Cardell, to Sir Francis Walsingham. Walsingham promised to 'gyve, fynde and allowe to his said apprentize meate, drinke, apparell, lynnen, wollen hose, shoes, lodginge, wasshinge and all other things nedefull and necessarie for an apprentise of his degree to have duringe all the terme that the siad Danyell shall serve'. For his part Bacheler was 'not to playe at any unlawfull games, not to haunt taverns nor any lewde dyshonest companye nor contracte himselffe in matrymonye to any woman—but in all thinges as an honest, faythfull and diligente apprentyce shall gently, quietly and faythfully use, beare and behave him selfe towarde his said mayster and maysters'.[42] With this standard wording the 14-year-old Bacheler, who had already served seven of his original sixteen-year apprenticeship with his uncle, was bound for a further nine years to Walsingham.[43] (See Pl. 5.2(*a* and *c*).)

---

[39] John Jeffreys, *The Life and Works of Philip Rosseter* (Wendover, 1990), 69–85.

[40] Ward, 'A Dowland Miscellany', 7; Hulse, 'Musical Patronage', 296.

[41] Berkeley Castle, Select Charter 822. For a plate of this document see Ward, 'A Dowland Miscellany', 88–9.

[42] PRO, E 40/12979.   [43] Anne Batchelor, *A Batchelor's Delight* (Beverley, 1990), 39.

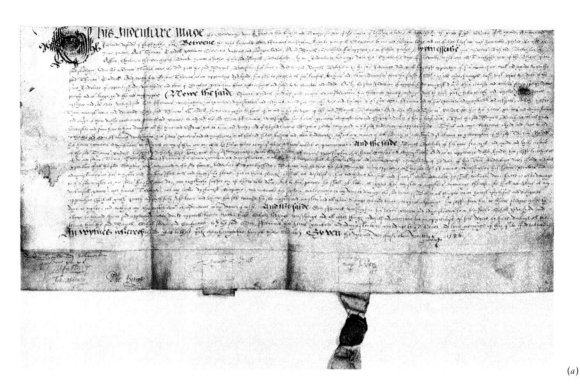

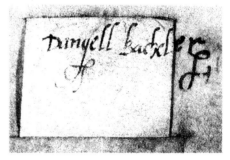

PL. 5.2. (a) Daniel Bacheler's 1586 indenture document, PRO E 40/12979; (b) the second page of the treble viol part of no. 3, 'Sir Francis Walsingham's Godmorrow', from the Walsingham Consort Books, the University of Hull, Brynmor Jones library (archives and special collections) DDHO/20/1 copied by Bacheler; (c) enlargement of signature from 1586 indenture document

(a)

(b)

(c)

All the leading lute composers were patronized by courtiers, and most became royal musicians. John Johnson is probably the earliest of the leading figures, though little is known of his life. He was very likely born around or before the mid-century, finished his apprenticeship(s) before 1570, and then worked for a patron who helped him gain his royal appointment in 1579. It has been suggested that Robert Dudley, the Earl of Leicester, may have assisted him in early life.[44] Tributes from fellow composers and contempories survive. In a 1586 book of emblems dedicated to Leicester, Geoffrey Whitney gave a Johnson special praise by favourably comparing his play to that of Apollo. As with all references that do not specify which Johnson, it is possible that this accolade may have been directed at Edward Johnson, though John is probably more likely, given his royal appointment. Also in 1588 John Johnson was listed by John Case in his *Apologia musices* as an honoured musician alongside Byrd, Bull, Morley, and Dowland.[45] The success of John's music, as measured by the large number of manuscripts in which it circulated and the several popular ballad tunes associated with him, is only matched by that of Dowland.

Francis Cutting was attached to the Howard family, the Earls of Arundel. He also had contact with the 1st Earl of Suffolk and received at least one gift from him.[46] He died in or before January 1595/6, was probably born around or soon after the mid-century, and may have had East Anglian connections. He is referred to as 'gentleman' in Arundel accounts, and left a small estate on his death to his wife, with whom he had produced at least ten children. Included among the offspring was the acclaimed lutenist Thomas Cutting, about whom more is known, though almost no music by him survives. Francis Cutting never gained a court appointment, though his music is extant in reasonable quantity, and is of a consistently high quality.

Anthony Holborne became a Gentleman Usher to Queen Elizabeth, and, although he did not have an appointment as a musician, we can assume that he was called upon to use his musical skills at court. He probably had this appointment by 1597 when *The Cittharn Schoole* was published, as in it he is styled 'Gentleman and servant to her most excellent Majestie'. In the last three years of his life, 1599–1602, he also worked for Robert Cecil, the 1st Earl of Salisbury, from whom Holborne's widow tried to get an appointment for one of her sons in 1606.[47] Holborne was a man of some substance, well able to versify, write in Latin, and most probably had an education at a university or Inn of Court, or both. He is significant as a composer of cittern and bandora music as well as lute music, and his published collection of

[44] Philip Brett was the first to make this suggestion in '*Musicae Modernae Laus*: Geoffrey Whitney's Tributes to the Lute and its Players', *LSJ* 7 (1965), 40–4. See also Ward, *Music for Elizabethan Lutes*, i. 66.

[45] Ward, *Music for Elizabethan Lutes*, i. 67.

[46] Lynn Hulse, 'Francis and Thomas Cutting: Father and Son?', *LSJ* 26 (1986), 73–4; Hulse, 'Musical Patronage', 322.

[47] Holborne, *The Complete Works of Anthony Holborne*, ed. Masakata Kanazawa, 2 vols. (Cambridge, Mass., 1967), i. 1–5; Hulse, 'Musical Patronage', 321.

Pavans, Galliards, Almains (London, 1597) is of immense importance, since it is the only collection of dance music published in Elizabethan England. This collection is dedicated to Sir Richard Champernowne of Modbury in Devon, a relative of Robert Cecil. Champernowne maintained a band of musicians at Modbury, and it seems that Holborne had written for, or at least arranged, some of the collection for this band.[48] There is a fascinating overlap between the published five-part consort dances and his surviving lute repertoire. In all, thirty-three of his lute solos appear in some form among the sixty-five consort dances. A further eight consort dances appear among his bandora or cittern pieces.

John Dowland's career was marked out by failure at home and time spent abroad. Dowland represents an extreme among English lutenists in his cosmopolitanism and the extent to which his life and music should be viewed in a European rather than English context. His early life and apprenticeship remain a mystery. In 1580, aged 17, Dowland took up service with Sir Henry Cobham, ambassador to France. He converted to Catholicism as a young man in France, and returned to England around 1583, when Cobham was relieved of his post. It may be that he entered the service of Henry Noel around this time. He was operating on the fringes of the court in the early 1590s, as he took part in two entertainments for the Queen in 1590 and 1592. His past religious sympathies may have created problems for him at court, and he was passed over a number of times when lutenist places became vacant. His failure to get John Johnson's place in 1594 prompted his return to the Continent, with travels in Germany and Italy. Dealings with English priests abroad aroused suspicion at home.[49] This produced a strong declaration of loyalty to the Protestant faith in a long letter to Sir Robert Cecil in 1595. In this letter Dowland relates that the Queen, on being spoken to of Dowland, had responded that 'I [Dowland] was a man to serve any prince in the world, but that I was an obstinate papist'.[50] Dowland hurried home after the letter only to be met with more failure, due in part to the death of his likely patron Sir Henry Noel in February 1596/7.[51]

Frustration prompted Dowland to accept a lucrative post as lutenist to Christian IV of Denmark in 1598. Here he remained until 1606, with extended periods of leave in England. By 1612 he was lutenist to Theophilus Howard, Lord Howard de Walden, and may also have served Lord Hunsdon during his career.[52] Only in 1612 did Dowland receive an English royal lutenist's post, in the long dormant place of Richard Pike. This place was revived specially for Dowland in recognition of his fame and the apparent injustice he had suffered.[53] The patronage of Lord Walden may have had a bearing on this appointment as Theophilus' father, Thomas

---

[48] Holman, *Four and Twenty Fiddlers*, 128.   [49] Poulton, *John Dowland*, 26–40.
[50] Ibid. 38.   [51] Ward, 'A Dowland Miscellany', 18–19.
[52] Poulton, *John Dowland*, 30–1, 52–63, 66.   [53] Ibid. 71.

Howard, Earl of Suffolk, was acting Lord Chamberlain in the years 1603–14, and was responsible for appointing royal musicians.[54] Dowland received at least one gift from the first Earl of Devonshire, into whose service his son Robert entered in 1612, and it may be that John also served the Earl.[55] Dowland maintained his teaching and performing activities well into the 1620s, but appears to have composed little after gaining his royal appointment in 1612.

Table 5.3. *English sources of solo lute music 1580–1625*

Source	Date	Courses	Comments
A. MAJOR MANUSCRIPT SOURCES			
Add. 2764(2)	c.1585–90	6	25 solo fragmentary items
Add. 31392	c.1600–5	6	31 solos. 1 t&g. Some pieces for bandora
Add. 38539	c.1615–20	10	83 solos. 4 t. Also variously known as the 'Sturt' or 'ML' lute book
Berlin 40641 (now in Kraków)	c.1615	10	27 solos. Also associated with John Sturt
Berlin 40143	c.1600	7	72 items, only a small number of which are solos by English composers. A Continental MS probably compiled by the Englishman D. Richard
Ballet (408/1)	c.1595	6	24 lute items (3 duets; 1 consort part; 17 solos; 3 fragments)
Ballet (408/2)	c.1600–03	6	64 lute items, all but 2 of which are solos
Board	c.1620–5	10	100 solos, 4 t&g, 1 consort treble
Brogyntyn	c.1595–1600	6	9 solos; 1 trio (incomplete); 24 consort song lute parts
Cosens	c.1606–10	7	70 lute solos
Dallis	c.1583–5	6	228 items. 198 solos; 19 songs with words; 8 bandora items; 1 cittern; 1 for 5 lutes
Dd.2.11	c.1590–95	6	264 solos; 54 bandora; 4 consort/duet items
Dd.4.22	c.1615	6–8	24 solos and 1 duet part
Dd.5.78.3	c.1595–1600	7[a]	159 solos
Dd.9.33	c.1600–5	7	156 solos; 6 bandora pieces
Euing	c.1605–10	6[b]	72 solos
Folger	c.1590–5	6/7	41 solos; 4 t&g; 2 consort parts

---

[54] Andrew Ashbee (ed.), *William Lawes (1602–1645): Essays on his Life, Times and Work* (Aldershot, 1998), 9 n. 11.

[55] Hulse, 'Hardwick MS 29', 64.

Table 5.3. *cont.*

Source	Date	Courses	Comments
Herbert	*c.*1625–40	9/10	242 solos
Hirsch	*c.*1595	6ᶜ	54 solos; 1 duet
Marsh	*c.*1595	6	159 solos; 9 bandora pieces
Mynshall	*c.*1597–9	6/7	36 solos; 4 duet (t&g); 1 consort
Nn.6.36	*c.*1605–15	8	78 solos; 3 bandora pieces
O.16.2	*c.*1620	10	29 solos in Renaissance tuning (14 in transitional tunings that are *c.*1630)
Pickeringe	*c.*1616	6	66 solos; 15 duets
Sampson	*c.*1609	7	17 solos; 9 duet parts; 1 consort
Trumbull	*c.*1600	6	26 solos; 10 duet parts; 2 consort
Welde	*c.*1600–5	6	36 solos; 3 duets (t&g)
Wickhambrook	*c.*1595–1600	6	20 solo; 2 duet parts; 15 lute duets

B. MINOR/FRAGMENTARY MS SOURCES

GB-Lb Add. 6402	*c.*1605	fragments containing 4 pieces
GB-Lb Add. 41498	*c.*1590	fragment of 1 piece (Watkin's Ale)
GB-Lb Add. 15117	*c.*1615	7 solo lute pieces in the 'Swarland' song book
GB-Occ 254	*c.*1600	fragment with 2 pieces
GB-Och Mus. 1280	*c.*1590	fragment with 2 pieces
GB-Omc 265	*c.*1605	fragments containing parts of 4 pieces
Westminster Abbey, Library	*c.*1615	recently discovered single leaf containing seven short pieces
US-LAuc M286 M4L 992	*c.*1600–10	version of 'Go from my window' bound in with Mansell lyra viol MS (*c.*1640)

C. MAJOR PUBLISHED SOURCES

William Barley, *A New Booke of Tabliture* (1597) 7 lute; 14 orpharion; 10 bandora (5 songs without words)

Thomas Robinson, *The Schoole of Musicke* (1603) 32 solos; 3 t&g; 3 equal duets

Robert Dowland, *Varietie of Lute Lessons* (1610) 49 solos

D. MINOR PUBLISHED SOURCES

John Danyel, *Songes for the Lute, viol and voice* (1606): 1 lute piece by Danyel

John Dowland, *First Booke of Songs or Airs* (1597, 1600, 1606, 1613): 1 piece by John Dowland. The 1600 edition only also contains a second piece for lute by John Dowland

John Dowland, *Second Book of Airs* (1600): duet for lute and bass viol by John Dowland

John Dowland, *A Pilgrim's Solace* (1612): contains 1 piece by John Dowland

Robert Dowland, *A Musicall Banquet* (1610): 1 piece by John Dowland

John Maynard, *The XII. Wonders of the World* (1611): 6 pieces by Maynard

Francis Pilkington, *First Book of Songs or Airs* (1605): 1 piece by Pilkington for lute and bass viol

Francis Pilkington, *Second Set of Madrigals*, Altus (1624): 1 orpharion piece by Pilkington

Note:

   1. Only sources originally from England, or which are clearly by Englishmen abroad are included.

   2. Music in later layers of the manuscripts have been excluded.

   3. Only music for plucked instruments is mentioned (lute, bandora, cittern).

   4. Lute music in transitional tunings is excluded.

   5. The number of courses relates to the majority of pieces. There are many exceptions to the generalized number given.

   6. t&g = treble and ground; t = treble

   a Up to 10 added.

   b 7 and 8 added.

   c 2 pieces for 7.

Table 5.3 of sources 1580–1625 shows that of the twenty-nine major sources, eighteen date more from the Elizabethan rather than Jacobean era. Although some were compiled over a period of years that traversed the two reigns, they are classed as Elizabethan due to content and starting date. Together the late Elizabethan sources contain over 1,500 solo lute items, about a third of which appear in more than one source, along with much music for two lutes, lute parts for mixed consort, plus pieces for bandora, orpharion, cittern, keyboard, viol, and voice.[56] Taking the golden age as a whole, there are over 2,100 solo pieces in Renaissance tuning by over a hundred known composers found in over 110 sources.[57]

The surviving solo lute sources of the late Elizabethan period are relatively numerous, and rich in content. Yet it must always be borne in mind that they may not be a representative sample of the lute manuscripts circulating at the time.[58] Certainly the music contained in the manuscripts cannot give us a balanced picture of the totality of lute music then played, much of which would have been memorized by the player/composer or improvised from set formulae such as grounds, and not committed to paper. Composers may have actively avoided transmission to prevent plagiarism and competition. Sources that do survive are strongly biased towards the amateur, and were often compiled as a result of a course of lessons or other pedagogical activity. Professional lutenists may have played without music in the normal course of their duties, and are likely to have been prompted to write down their pieces when teaching them to others, rather than for themselves.[59]

Differences in musical style between the music in one source and another, which is attributed to the same composer, are often much greater than between pieces by different composers within the same source. A version of a piece by Dowland in a

---

[56] These figures are based on my own listing of pieces in the MSS.

[57] David Lumsden, 'The Sources of English Lute Music (1540–1620)', 3 vols. (Ph.D. thesis, University of Cambridge, 1955). In the résumé of this thesis (i. 134), Lumsden lists 2,185 pieces in all the forty-five English lute MSS in Renaissance tuning known to him then. Craig-McFeely lists 2,100 solo pieces in 112 sources, of which sixty-eight are English, forty-four foreign in 'English Lute Manuscripts', i. 5, 10.

[58] Craig-McFeely challenges this view; see ibid. 71, 154.   [59] Ibid. 156.

rural amateur's book, such as Mynshall's, may bear little comparison with a version in the Cambridge manuscripts. It is clear also that pieces changed and evolved over time. A comparison of the Folger manuscript version of Dowland's galliard 'Can she excuse' (otherwise known as 'The Earl of Essex Galliard'), which must date before 1596 (it appeared in Barley's *New Booke of Tabliture* of that year) and which carries his signature, and the version in Robert Dowland's *Varietie of Lute Lessons* (1610), which John Dowland must have sanctioned, shows innumerable discrepancies throughout (see Ex. 5.1). They are particularly divergent in the varied repeats of each of the three sections.[60]

Some of the late Elizabethan sources listed above share characteristics with the early commonplace books (Osborn and Giles Lodge) in that they contain solo pieces, exercises, consort, and duet music, as well as other writings, inserted by music lovers who did not generally have great skill on the lute. The Mynshall, Brogyntyn, Trumbull, and Dallis manuscripts are in this mould. Others, like the Welde and Wickhambrook, may have been started as a selection of the most popular pieces with the greatest currency, prepared for sale by a professional scribe. A large number of manuscripts contain music inserted for teaching purposes. In some cases these teaching pieces were copied into the manuscript by the teacher himself, though normally they were entered by the pupil. Another category is manuscripts containing the personal collections of good players, either amateur or professional. One would assign to this group the manuscripts compiled by Mathew Holmes, the Hirsch, the Marsh, and Add. 38539 manuscripts. Most sources can only be imprecisely dated by means of musical content, the instrument required (the use of a seventh course suggesting a later date), and palaeography.

The normal method of instruction on the lute was for the teacher to visit the pupil at home, and leave a 'lesson' which the pupil would then copy into his/her book before the next visit, though sometimes the teacher would copy the piece in. The teacher might keep a set of unbound exemplars for this purpose, to which the individual 'lesson' would be returned after use.[61] In this way the student would build up a collection of pieces provided and sanctioned by the teacher. Craig-McFeely has suggested that the Trumbull manuscript was originally a teacher's exemplar that was later bound.[62] Lute books that were at least in part compiled by a student of the lute under the direction of a teacher or teachers account for a large number of all surviving lute books. The Dallis, Folger, Board, and Pickeringe manuscripts are cases in point.

Lute books from the period after 1585 are normally upright, rather than oblong like those before 1580, and consist of paper that was either ruled with a six-line rastrum or printed with a lute stave. Often the paper was bought unbound, and later

[60] *Varietie*, Galliard 3, sig. M2; Folger MS, fo. 16r.
[61] Craig-McFeely, 'English Lute Manuscripts', 80, 85.   [62] Ibid. 80.

Ex. 5.1. *Comparison of (*a*) John Dowland's 'Can she excuse' from the Folger MS, fo. 16ʳ with (*b*) his 'The Right Honorable Robert Earle of Essex, high Marshall of England, his Galliard',* Varietie, *sig. M2, bars 1–12*

1. Alto part *f*′ altered to *e♭*′

Ex. 5.1. *cont.*

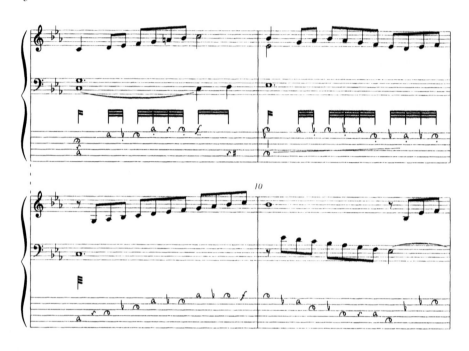

bound up as a book. The pupils were often young, between 15 and 20, and were typically young ladies from the leisured classes, who learnt as a pre-marriage accomplishment to advertise their gentility (Board, Pickeringe, Berlin 40641 manuscripts), or young men of a lower social standing who wished to improve their employment and social acceptability (Dallis and Mynshall).[63] The lute was one of the most popular instruments for the amateur in this period, and particularly so for women. Lute students often had clear and careful hands, when contrasted with the hands of known professionals, which are typically untidy. In general, manscripts associated with professionals have few titles, lack marginalia, and make use of printed paper.[64]

The nine related manuscripts housed in Cambridge University Library were described by Richard Newton in 1939 as 'the largest and most important body of Elizabethan instrumental music that has come down to us, not excepting even the famous Fitzwilliam Virginal Book',[65] and by Lyle Nordstrom in 1973 as 'the richest store of English lute music in the world'.[66] The identity of the fluent, untidy, but generally accurate scribe eluded researchers until Ian Harwood was able to show, through palaeographic analysis, that the books were the work of Mathew Holmes, precentor and singing man at Christ Church Cathedral, Oxford, from 1588 to 1597, and thereafter at Westminster Abbey until his death in 1621.[67] Holmes was in an unusual position in that he was a musical professional with a theoretical training, but one that did not play the lute for a living. As a precentor he had a church position that gave him a status above that of a normal musician, and greater social access and acceptability. It is to our good fortune that he had a practitioner's interest in the instrument and its music, and seems to have been able, through friends and connections, to compile a comprehensive collection of the best lute music current in England in his lifetime. Holmes's books have all the hallmarks of the professional, yet the collection exists as a result of amateur enthusiasm. A professional lutenist would not have bothered.

Of the nine volumes, four are mainly for solo lute: Dd.2.11, Dd.5.78.3, Dd.9.33, and Nn.6.36.[68] These manuscripts have been respectively dated *c.*1590–95, *c.*1595–1600, *c.*1600–5, *c.*1605–15, on the basis of their contents, the type of rhythm signs used, and the deterioration of Holmes's hand with age and illness.[69] Four of the remaining five books in the collection are part-books for lute, bass viol, recorder,

[63] Craig-McFeely, 'English Lute Manuscripts', 85–8. [64] Ibid. 125.

[65] Newton, 'English Lute Music', 72.

[66] Lyle Nordstrom, 'The Cambridge Consort Books', *JLSA* 5 (1972), 70–103 at 70.

[67] Harwood, 'The Origins'.

[68] Dd.2.11 contains 310 pieces for lute, plus 54 for bandora; Dd.5.78.3 has 156 for lute and one for lyra viol; Dd.9.33 has 150 for lute, one for bandora, one for lyra viol, and 5 lute duet or consort parts; Nn.6.36 has 90 pieces for lute, 3 for bandora, and 13 for lyra viol.

[69] Harwood, 'The Origins', *passim*, and Poulton, *John Dowland*, 98–100. I have slightly changed Harwood's dating of Dd.2.11 from *c.*1595 to *c.*1590–5.

and cittern, almost certainly from an original set of six for mixed consort, the violin and bandora books being missing.[70] The final book of the nine Holmes manuscripts is an important source for the solo cittern.[71]

The lute book from the mixed consort set (Dd.3.18) contains, along with pieces for consort, a sizeable collection of trebles to be played over some form of ground, including most of the Johnson duets that appear in the Marsh manuscript. It also contains five possible lute solos and music for an unusual consort of three orpharions (possibly together with three viols).[72] Twenty-four consort pieces plus four orpharion trios are attributed to Richard Reade, who joined the singing men at Christ Church in 1588, the same year as Holmes. Reade took his Oxford BA degree in 1592, and remained a singing man until his death in 1616/17.[73] One of Reade's pieces is titled 'Mr. Dr James, Deane of Christ Church, his Paven'.[74] In his will Reade left Dr William Goodwin (Dean of Christ Church 1611–20) a piece of gold to make him a ring. He also left a bass viol to Martha, the wife of William Gris, an Oxford Stationer who later became the College library keeper. This bass viol she already had in her keeping.[75]

From the information we have, it seems reasonable to suppose that Holmes compiled the mixed-consort books and the bulk of Dd.3.18 during the years 1588–97 while precentor at Christ Church, and that these books were used, at least in part, for the instrumental tuition of the choristers. At this time the solo cittern book and the first and largest lute book Dd.2.11 were compiled.[76] On moving to Westminster in 1597 Holmes continued collecting duets in Dd.3.18, and solo music in Dd.5.78.3 and Dd.9.33. This last mansucript also contains two prayers to be said by Holmes in his capacity as Abbey Precentor for sick and dying parishioners. One of the prayers is dated 28 February 1600.[77] The title of Francis Cutting's piece 'Sir Fooke [Fulke] Greville' (fo. 18r) could not have applied until after 25 July 1603 when Greville became a knight of the Bath, suggesting that Dd.9.33 was still being added to at this date.[78] The last book, Nn.6.36, contains music that is clearly later in style, and was worked on while Holmes was old and ailing.

Together Holmes's four solo lute books contain over 700 pieces, from which there are over 500 different compositions, since a sizeable number appear more than once. Versions of pieces in the Holmes manuscripts are often preferable to those in other sources for their accuracy and comprehensiveness. Technical difficulty was no

---

[70] Dd.3.18 (lute); Dd.5.20 (bass viol); Dd.5.21 (recorder); Dd.14.24 (cittern).

[71] Peter Danner, 'Dd.4.23 or English Cittern Music Revisited', *JLSA* 3 (1970), 1–12.

[72] Nordstrom, 'The Cambridge Consort Books', 74.   [73] Harwood, 'The Origins', 38.

[74] Dd.3.18, fo. 12r; Dd.5.20, fo. 7r; Dd.5.21, fo. 6v.   [75] Harwood, 'The Origins', 38.

[76] Poulton believes a substantial part was written before 1591. See *John Dowland*, 98.

[77] Dd.9.33, back flyleaf. The first concerns Davie Wier, who was buried at St Margaret's on 18 Mar. 1600/1. The second is for William Hooper, who was buried on 15 Apr. 1601 at Westminster. See Harwood, 'The Origins', 42–6.

[78] Poulton, *John Dowland*, 99.

deterrent to Holmes, whose versions of pieces that achieved large manuscript circulation are often the most demanding. He recopied pieces in a similar or identical version, sometimes within the same book.[79] This probably resulted from copying wholesale from other books that were lent to him, without worrying about any resulting duplication.

It might be that Holmes, who was an excellent scribe, compiled the lute books for some patron, or patrons. I believe that the collection contains so many personal touches—the prayers, legal documents, Dowland's signature, and the fact that it reflects his changing circumstances—that this cannot be the case. He was a careful and methodical man (as seen in the drafting of his will himself) whose professional responsibilities included participation in the musical development of boys. Thus his music manuscript collection was both personal and for teaching. It must be significant that the manuscripts have survived together, although there is no mention of them in his will.

Dd.2.11 is the single largest and most important of all English lute manuscripts. It is especially important for the number of pieces that are unique to it. The book is representative of the best lute music in circulation in the 1590s. It opens with a Latin epigram believed to be by John Case, the philosopher and fellow of St John's College, Oxford, who, very likely, was connected to Holmes's musical circle.[80] (See Pl. 53) Some of the pieces by Dowland that appear in Dd.2.11 ('Can she excuse' is an example), were later transformed into songs and published as such. This suggests that they had their origins as instrumental pieces and that Dowland composed the greater portion of his solo music by *c.*1595, although he may in some instances have continued to rework pieces to keep pace with changing fashions.[81] The manuscript suggests that many of Holborne's instrumental pieces published in *Pavans, Galliards, Almains* (1599) were known as lute solos years before publication, and may have been conceived as such on the basis of the melodic poverty of the inner parts of the consort versions. From Dd.2.11 we can also assume that Pilkington was a composer of lute music early in his career before his appointment as a lay clerk at Chester Cathedral in 1602, after which he probably composed little or nothing new for the instrument, as no works of his survive in Jacobean sources.[82]

The most popular forms in Dd.2.11 are tripartite galliards and pavans. This represents a significant departure from the sources of the 1580s (Dallis and Marsh particularly), where pieces based on variation technique over Italian grounds and their

[79] e.g. a John Johnson piece titled variously 'Johnsons Toy', 'Allmaine Jo Johnson', and 'Allins Jigg' appears twice in Dd.2.11 (fos. 20ᵛ, 56ʳ), and again in Dd.9.33 (fo. 28ᵛ) in versions which are similar. A John Dowland Almain appears in Dd.2.11 in identical versions on fos. 38ʳ and 47ʳ.

[80] Roger Harmon, 'Studies in the Cambridge Lute Manuscripts I: "Musica" ', *LSJ* 38 (1998), 29–42.

[81] Pieces by Dowland in Dd.2.11 that were later published as songs include 'The Frog Galliard' (fos. 40ᵛ and 93ʳ) and 'Can she excuse' (fos. 40ᵛ and 62ᵛ).

[82] Pilkington, *Complete Works*, ed. Jeffery, pp. iii–iv.

PL. 5.3. The opening page of Cambridge, University Library, Dd.2.11 copied by Mathew Holmes c.1590–5

derivatives, particularly the quadro pavan and galliard, were all-pervasive; and the tripartite structures with varied repeats, though popular, had yet to supplant other dance structures. Thus, of the pavans and galliards in Dd.2.11, only ten are clearly based on passamezzo antico and moderno basses, the great majority being tripartite in form.

The almain emerges in Dd.2.11 as another popular dance form, also with three sections, faster than the pavan, though Germanic and 'heavy', according to Morley.[83] Variation form is now confined to settings of popular ballad tunes of the day, with a small collection of tunes inspiring a large number of variation sets, in particular 'Walsingham', 'Robin is to the Greenwood gone', 'Go from my window', 'Lord Willoughby's Welcome Home', and 'Fortune my foe'. Dd.2.11 alone contains four sets of variations on Walsingham—by Collard, Cutting, Johnson, and anon.[84] The manuscript contains eighteen fantasias, including more than one by Ferrabosco, Holborne, Francesco da Milano, and some part-song arrangements, most of which were old established favourites like van Wilder's 'Ma poure bourse'. The number of foreign pieces, or arrangements of vocal pieces by Continental composers, is small.[85]

The music in Dd.2.11 is representative of the mature lute style of the Elizabethan era. It is at its most original, and least dependent on foreign models. A good example is Dowland's 'Lachrimae' Pavan.[86] The piece became internationally well known as a solo and song, and was the inspiration for his published consort collection (Ex. 5.2). 'Lachrimae' appears three times in Dd.2.11, twice for lute (versions in G minor and A minor with quite different varied repeats), and once for bandora. Poulton suggests that the Dd.2.11 version is the earliest 'good' version, and that the A minor version resulted from performance for viols and/or voices.[87] The G minor version was originally copied in Dd.2.11 as a piece for 6-course lute. At a later date Holmes, or someone else, added notes for a seventh course D in some places. The subtle melodic inflections and many changes of note value from the basic minim pulse (♩) up to semiquavers (♬) that are found in the varied repeats are features of the mature lute style, and were probably developed in the context of mixed consort music. Varied repeats in earlier English lute sources generally lack this degree of innovation, are more predictable, and do not normally enhance the first statement harmonically. The popularity of the mixed consort was at its height in the 1590s. The mixed-consort repertoire is overwhelmingly of tripartite pavans, galliards, and

---

[83] Morley, *A Plaine and Easie Introduction*, 181: 'The *Alman* is a more heavie daunce then this [the galliard] fitlie representing the nature of the people, whose name it carieth) . . .'

[84] Dd.2.11: Collard 96ᵛ–97ʳ; Cutting 96ʳ; Johnson 98ʳ; anon. 29ʳ.

[85] Folio 20ʳ, 'Avecques vous. Orlando'; fo. 20ᵛ, 'Ung Jour passe'; fo. 22ʳ, [no title, Emanuel Adriansen Fantasia]; fo. 24ʳ, 'Susanna. orlando'; fo. 24ᵛ–25ʳ, 'Si Vous Voulez'; fo. 25ʳ, [no title, Le Content est Riche]; fo. 27ʳ 'Jour desire'; 29ʳ, 'J'attend secours. Derick Gerard'; fo. 50ᵛ, 'Catins Orlando'; fo. 61ᵛ 'Au joly bois'; fo. 63ʳ 'Archdelt'.

[86] Dd.2.11, fo. 81ᵛ.   [87] Poulton, *John Dowland*, 127.

Ex. 5.2. *The first section of Dowland's 'Lachrimae Pavan' with its varied repeat from Dd.2.11,*
fo. 81ᵛ, bars 1–16

1. Holmes uses a hash (♯) here and elsewhere. This has been ignored as it is not an ornament but is used to show mistakes. Thanks to Rainer aus dem Spring for this discovery.

almains, in which the lute has the most interesting part, and plays divisions in the varied repeats. The shift in emphasis from the style of the 1580s as exemplified by the Marsh manuscript, to the 1590s as exemplified by Dd.2.11, must be due in some part to the influence of consort music.

Dd.5.78.3 and Dd.9.33 were probably largely compiled after Holmes had moved to Westminster in 1597, although they may have been started earlier. Dd.9.33 can be dated *c*.1600 by the two prayers found at the end. It is probably the later of the two, as Holmes, after the first twenty-two folios, largely abandons the 'grid' system of notating rhythm signs. Instead he uses the more economical and modern 'flag' signs, where only changes of rhythmic value are notated.[88] Dd.9.33 also includes more corantos, jigs, and volts, which were becoming fashionable throughout European lute music *c*.1600. The selection of pieces in these two manuscripts is of the highest quality, with many of the most weighty and technically difficult of the whole repertoire included. Bacheler's emergence and John Johnson's relative disappearance (with only three pieces) is the most obvious difference between the composers whose works are represented in these manuscripts and those in Dd.2.11. At Westminster Holmes would have been close to court circles, and able to collect a more recently composed and more cosmopolitan selection of pieces, in particular music by Bacheler and Robert Johnson (two of whose pieces are in Dd.9.33, one of which appears twice), Collard (1), and Allison (1).

Dd.5.78.3 contains a narrower selection of composers and forms than any of the other Holmes lute manuscripts. Two-thirds of the pieces are galliards (72) and pavans (34). There are only two identifiable fantasias (one by Dowland and one from Mertel's *Hortus musicalis novus*), eight almains, and five variations sets. Many of the finest pavans by Dowland and Cutting are here.[89] Only a few pieces by minor composers such as Kindersley can be identified. The tablature is particularly cramped and untidy, with most pages completely filled. Titles are mostly absent from the book, although it is noticeable that Dowland added his signature and the title 'Farewell' to a fantasy of his on fo. 44[r]. Presumably Holmes had direct access to the composer at some point, which might account for the large amount of Dowland's music in the source. Dd.9.33 contains a more even spread of forms. Together with 25 pavans and 36 galliards, there are 14 corantos, 8 jigs, and 3 volts, along with 14 almains and 6 variation sets, plus 9 fantasias, 3 of which are by Dowland, and a token quadro pavan. Most of the lighter forms are concentrated in the last five folios.

Dowland's two chromatic fantasias are each built on a six-note chromatic phrase, ascending in the case of 'Farewell' and descending in 'Forlorn Hope'.[90] (See Ex. 5.3.)

---

[88] Ibid. 98–9.   [89] e.g. Dowland's 'Mr John Langton's Pavan'.
[90] 'Farewell': Dd.5.78.3, fos. 43[v]–44[r], also in Euing MS, fos. 42[v]–42[r]; 'Forlorn Hope': Dd.9.33, fos. 16[v]–17[r], also in Elias Mertel's *Hortus Musicalis Novus* (Strasburg, 1615), no. 70, pp. 210–11.

Ex. 5.3. *Comparison of (a) the opening of John Dowland's 'Farewell Fancy' from Dd.5.79.3, fo. 43ᵛ with (b) his 'Forlorn Hope Fancy' from Dd.9.33, fo. 16ᵛ, bars 1–5*

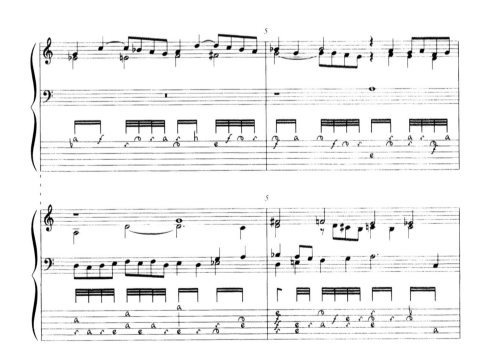

This phrase is introduced fourteen times in 'Farewell', and seventeen in 'Forlorn Hope', in ever-changing parts and positions to create a complex contrapuntal web. There are two other extended chromatic fantasias in the English repertoire (both on descending figures), one of which is ascribed to Rosseter in a foreign publication, and the other of which is anonymous.[91] These pieces are a great test of a performer's technique and have no equal in the English lute repertoire.

There are three important Elizabethan lute books found today in Dublin: the Dallis, Ballet, and Marsh manuscripts. The Dallis lute book was copied in the 1580s, though its repertoire is representative more of the 1570s.[92] It takes its name from an inscription on page 12: 'Incepi Nonis Augusti praeceptore M[agist]ro. Thoma Dallis. Cantabrigia Anno 1583', meaning 'I began on the Nones of August [5 August] with master Thomas Dallis as my teacher, Cambridge, 1583'.[93] Dallis was a musician and teacher at Trinity College in the 1580s and 1590s, becoming a doctor of music in 1594, and was mentioned by Whythorne in a scrap of paper found with his autobiography.[94] Instrumental activity at the college increased after the appointment of John Hilton as organist in 1594/5 and there are accounts for the purchase of lute strings by the college in 1596/7 and 1601/2.[95] Dallis was included by Francis Meres in his list of the most famous English musicians to be placed alongside those of ancient Greece.[96] A few items in the manuscript mention Dallis. One is the 'gailiard/all a greane willowe/Mr T. Dallis', an instrumental version of the song made famous by its appearance in Shakespeare's *Othello*.[97] From this we can infer that the hand and owner of the book was a pupil of Dallis, possibly a university student, and that Dallis supplied him with much of the music. The book starts with Latin instructions for tuning and holding the lute, and the first pieces are very simple. The influence of Dallis might explain the unusually eclectic repertoire of music it contains. Approximately a quarter of the pieces are based on ground basses and their derivative harmonic patterns: passamezzos antico and moderno, romanesca, Chi Passa, and quadro pavan.[98] In this respect it is akin to almost all the pre-1580 English lute manuscripts. Like them it also contains a number of tripartite pavans and galliards, and pieces related to ballad tunes.

[91] Pickeringe MS, fos. 23ᵛ–24ʳ, and J. D. Mylius, *Thesaurus gratiarum* (Frankfurt, 1622); Euing MS, fos. 42ᵛ–43ʳ. Printed in *The Collected Lute Music of John Dowland*, ed. Diana Poulton and Basil Lamb (London, 1974), nos. 71 and 72.

[92] Dublin, Trinity College Library, MS 410/1 (*olim* MS D.3.30/I). For a description and contents list see John Ward, 'The Lute Books of Trinity College Dublin: Preface', *LSJ* 9 (1967), 17–18.

[93] Dallis MS, p. 12.

[94] John Ward and Music 200, 'The Lute Books of Trinity College, Dublin: MS D.3.30/I, The So-called Dallis Lute Book', *LSJ* 9 (1967), 19–40 at 19.

[95] Ian Payne, *Provision and Practice of Sacred Music at Cambridge Colleges and Selected Cathedrals c.1547–c.1646* (New York and London, 1993), 138–9.

[96] Meres, *Palladis tamia*, fo. 288ᵛ.

[97] Sternfeld, *Music in Shakespearean Tragedy*, 37. This galliard is no. 21 in the Dallis MS. Other items which mention Dallis are nos. 22, 63, 95, 162, 192, and 193.

[98] Byler, 'Italian Currents', 92.

The Dallis manuscript is unusual among English lute sources in a number of ways: it is has a large number of pieces from Continental printed collections; it contains some thirty religious pieces, which may betray the influence of Dallis; and it has shorthand tablature rhythm signs for groupings of notes in place of the usual grid system. The printed collections in which the foreign Dallis manuscript pieces appear range in date from Spinacino's *Libro secondo* (1507), one of the four earliest printed books of lute tablature, through Giacomo de Gorzanis's *Il secondo libro* (1563) and *Il terzo libro* (1564), and Pierre Phalèse and Jean Bellère's *Theatrum musicum* of 1571 and 1574, to Emmanuel Adriaenssen's *Pratum musicum* (1584).[99] If the five pieces by Adriaenssen were taken from his book of 1584, as seems certain, it provides a 'terminus post quem' date for the manuscript.

The so-called Ballet lute book refers to two distinct manuscripts which were not bound together before the eighteenth century.[100] The first book (MS 408/1) contains a mainstream selection of popular lute pieces entered *c*.1590, together with sixty-four lyra viol pieces probably entered after 1610.[101] This book is titled 'William ballet his booke wittns william vines'. It has been assumed up to now that the main hand was that of William Ballet.[102] This hand was responsible for adding the sixteen solo lute pieces and two duets, plus part of a third duet. An unidentified adult hand added two short pieces, 'Pegaramsey' and 'Robin Reddock', on p. 26, and yet another hand a version of 'Bonny Sweet Robin' on p. 27. A child, or adult who could only write with difficulty, has tried to copy pieces and added flourishes at the bottom of several of the pages. Possibly the book was originally a selection of sixteen lute pieces plus some duets, written by a professional scribe to be sold. Later the book was passed to a child, William Ballet, whose teacher or guardian, William Vines, wrote the title of the book. Vines then added the extra pieces to the manuscript, which the child attempted to copy.

Of the solo pieces in the main scribe's hand, several were already current by 1580 and maintained their popularity well into the next century, for example the quadro pavan and galliard, and Johnson's flat pavan and galliard. The 'Passing measuers Pavin' uses the passamezzo antico, as does 'Queene Maries Dump'. This last had appeared in both RA 58 and the Dallis manuscript.[103] There are also pieces that date from the late 1580s and 1590s: Dowland's 'Fortune my foe to the consort', Bacheler's popular galliard related to the song 'To plead my faith', which was printed in *A Musicall Banquet* (1610); a piece attributed to Mathias Mason, but which is probably by Anthony Holborne ('Mr Southcote's galliard'); and an early version of Dowland's 'Sir John Smith his Almaine'.[104] There is also a number of

[99] Ward and Music 200, 'The Lute Books of Trinity College'; see the inventory, pp. 23–40.

[100] Trinity College, Dublin, MS 408/1 and 408/2 (*olim* MS D.1.21/I and MS D.1.21/II). See John Ward, 'The Lute Books of Trinity College Dublin, II: MS D.1.21 (the So-called Ballet Lute Book)', *LSJ* 10 (1968), 15–32.

[101] Ibid. 20.   [102] Ibid. 17.   [103] Ibid. 12–13, 5, 4–5.

[104] Trinity College, Dublin MS D.1.21, pp. 14, 17, 6.

easy tuneful pieces like the ballad tune setting 'Lost is my Liberty', and two sets of variations, one of which, 'The Horne Pipe', is based on the bergamasca; the other is a simple eight-bar ground with three following variations. The Ballet companion manuscript (*c.*1593–1603) is slightly later in date than the Ballet manuscript itself, and is remarkable for the approximately thirty simple ballad-tune arrangements it contains. It was used by researchers into ballad and folk tunes from William Chappell to Claude Simpson as a primary source for popular Elizabethan ballad tunes.[105] It is because these tunes are unelaborated that they have proved most valuable to researchers.

A fourth Elizabethan lute book is to be found in Dublin, this time in Archbishop Marsh's library, from which it takes its name.[106] It is a substantial source with 165 items spread over 429 pages. Unlike the great majority of pieces in contemporary manuscripts, many of those in the Marsh manuscript are long, some running to two or more pages. There are a few pieces from Pierre Phalèse's *Theatrum musicum* (Louvain, 1568) collection, including one set of variations that runs to six pages.[107] Spencer suggests that the book was bound up *c.*1595, and that some pages existed as loose sheets containing lute music well before that date.[108] Ward dates the work of the main hand in the book as *c.*1580. This hand contributed all 155 pieces for 6-course lute. A second hand, dated *c.*1600 by Ward[109] but quite possibly later, was responsible for the remaining ten pieces for 7-course lute. A high proportion of the pieces in the main earlier hand are unique, although fifteen pieces in the Willoughby manuscript and twenty pieces in the Thistlethwaite manuscript are to be found in the Marsh. Excepting the ten pieces for 7-course lute, the musical contents in this hand are suggestive of lute music current in England from 1560 to 1585, some of which was itself already decades old. Some of the pieces in earlier English lute books that appear in poor and erroneous versions reappear in the Marsh in longer and musically more developed forms.[110] Indeed, its contents could be said to summarize much of the best of English lute music up to the 1580s, before the arrival of Dowland and his generation. It also includes nine items for bandora, including a number of common grounds.

It seems that the main scribe of the Marsh manuscript was capable of composing his own music and intabulating the music of others, as many of the pieces show signs of the 'working out' of pieces. The presence of more than one version of the same piece gives this idea further credibility. Sometimes the scribe wrote the same

[105] William Chappell, *Popular Music of the Olden Time*, 2 vols. (London, 1859; repr. New York, 1965); Simpson, *The British Broadside Ballad*.
[106] *EIRE-Dm* Z3.2.13. Facs. pub. as *The Marsh Lute Book*.
[107] No. 132, also nos. 3, 84, and 133. Craig-McFeely, 'English Lute Music', ii. 508–16.
[108] *The Marsh Lute Book*, p. xi.
[109] John M. Ward, 'The Fourth Dublin Lute Book', *LSJ* 11 (1969), 28–46 at 29.
[110] e.g. 'Philips dump', no. 164.

piece out in different keys.[111] For instance there are the two earliest surviving lute arrangments of Robert Parsons's popular five-part 'In Nomine' for viols, one in G, the other A; the first is fully barred, the second almost entirely without barlines.[112] Sometimes the scribe abandons a piece, only to begin and complete it in a different part of the manuscript. While much of the contents are pedestrian, some pieces are elaborate and difficult to play. Almost half the pages in the book are empty, the others filled seemingly at random. This lack of organization may have resulted from the book being bound, in part, with sheets that were already filled with music. Most pieces are fully barred, but some have only the occasional barline, and a few none at all. The tablature is relatively free of errors, but where they do occur they are often uncorrected. Some of the sets of variations are so long that all semblance of form is lost.[113] Could it be that the scribe was the composer of some of the variations?

The most popular form in the book is the galliard (57), followed by sets of variations (45), some pieces being both. Variations on ostinato basses, particularly dumps, are a favourite, as are variations on a cantus firmus, passamezzo and related grounds (such as the quadro pavan), and ground-bass related tunes like Rogero, Chi Passa, and Sellingers Round. Other forms are pavans, fancies, In Nomines, almains, and intabulations of French chansons and other vocal music. The pieces that are sets of variations on pavans or galliards show considerable variety of organization. Some have one or two sections followed by any number of varied repeats, and one piece has a more complicated rondo form.

Most of the pieces in the Marsh manuscript are unattributed. By far the best-represented composer, where attribution by concordance is possible, is John Johnson. The ten popular pieces added by a later hand apart, most of the other English composers are relatively little known as producers of lute music: Newman, Weston, Lichfield, Fernyers, and Grene. This last may be the Richard Grene who also appears in the Willoughby manuscript. Cotton must be the Clement Cotton of the *FVB* who was Thomas Cardell's stepson. The names 'Mark Antoine' and 'Ambrose' may relate to Mark Anthony Galliardello and Ambrose Lupo, both long-standing royal musicians for the string consort brought to England by Henry VIII in the 1540s.[114] There is just one single piece by Anthony Holborne ('The New Year's Gift'). Holborne may have been born as early as 1547, and thus was of the same generation as John Johnson, though it seems his music did not become popular until the 1580s. Of pieces by foreign composers there are twenty by Francesco da Milano, including some not found in other English sources, six by Albert da

---

[111] Marsh, nos. 109 and 110, 51 and 131.
[112] Marsh, nos. 67 and 112. There are also intabulations of this piece in Dd.2.11 (fo. 73ᵛ) and the Pickeringe MS (p. 34).
[113] e.g. no. 114.
[114] Holman, *Four and Twenty Fiddlers*, 78–103; also id., 'The English Royal Violin Consort', 50–1, table II. Mark Anthony Galliardello was in royal service 1545–85, Ambrose Lupo 1540–91.

Ripa, and intabulations of chansons and madrigals by Claudin de Sermisy and Verdelot. The book contains nine pieces for 6-course bandora which are probably consort parts, and fourteen lute trebles.

The ten pieces for lute in the later hand are unexceptional versions of favourites by Dowland, Holborne, and a few other composers. Technically these pieces are modest in comparison with those in the earlier hand, many of which are peppered with fast turns and runs, particularly towards cadences and at the ends of phrases. 'Philips dump' is a case in point, with eighteen fast cadential turns in eighty-six bars. The predilection for such elaboration suggests a lutenist of considerable assurance, with a quick and easy hand.

There are some surviving sources, like the Wickhambrook and Welde manuscripts, that may have been prepared by professional copyists for direct sale to the public. The Wickhambrook manuscript gained its name from its purchase by Miss Dulcie Lawrence-Smith of Wickhambrook in Suffolk in the 1930s.[115] It survives in an incomplete form, having lost the first nine folios. Folios 10–17 contain twenty-five items: twenty-one for solo lute, two fragmentary or incomplete pieces, and two equal duets. It is beautifully written by two scribes whose hands share many characteristics, and who possibly worked together. The second hand adds pieces in spaces left by the first. The selection of pieces favours John Johnson (10) over Dowland (4). All the pieces have titles. The manuscript also contains three intabulations of chansons: two by van Wilder, and one by Lassus. Together with tripartite pavans (6) and galliards (5), the selection includes pieces based on ground-bass patterns: quadro pavans, a passymeasures pavan, and a Spanish pavan. The Spanish pavan uses a ground probably derived from the folia bass, and a tune above that became a popular ballad carrier. It inspired many sets of variations for solo lute.[116] The Wickhambrook version in C minor, entitled 'the oulde spannyshe paven', is a particularly fine set of eight variations which exploit very varied textures. The manuscript is entirely for 6-course lute and contains no ornament signs. The larger pieces are mostly of moderate difficulty and the page-fillers are very easy.

The Welde manuscript was discovered by Robert Spencer in 1960 at Willey Park, the home of Lord Forester.[117] It had belonged to an ancestor of Lord Forester, John Welde, whose name is stamped on the cover in gilt capitals. Welde was admitted to the Middle Temple on 2 August 1600, was Town Clerk of the City of London (1613–66), and bought Willey Park between 1612 and 1623.[118] The book also contains the signature of Dorothy Welde, who was probably John Welde's sister. Spencer posits that the book was produced by a professional scribe and bought by John Welde, most probably when he was a law student, and remained with the fam-

---

[115] Poulton, *John Dowland*, 102.   [116] Diana Poulton, 'Notes on the Spanish Pavan', *LSJ* 3 (1961), 5–16.
[117] Robert Spencer, 'The Weld Lute Manuscript', *LSJ* 1 (1959), 48–57. The Welde MS was not available to Lumsden when producing his thesis.   [118] Ibid. 54.

ily thereafter. In support of this, he points to the extremely neat, accurate, and upright tablature hand, and its dissimilarity to that of John Welde. Seven of the pieces require a lute with seven courses. This fact and the selection of pieces point to a date of *c*.1600–5. Of the thirty-nine pieces, two are John Johnson trebles for treble and ground and one has a bass part presumably for bass viol. Dowland (7) and Holborne (6) are the favoured composers, with contributions from Alfonso Ferrabosco I (2), Daniel Bacheler (2), John Johnson (3), Edward Collard (3), Mathias Mason (1), and arrangements of Byrd (2) and Phillips (1). One piece is titled 'Galliard sett forth by J.R' (possibly Philip Rosseter). No music by foreign composers is present, apart from the anglicized Ferrabosco. Like the Wickhambrook, the manuscript contains a selection of popular pieces and forms: ten pavans, eleven galliards, two almains, four sets of variations, and five ballad tunes. None of them is of more than moderate difficulty.

Holborne's fine almain entitled 'The Night Watch' (Ex. 5.4) appears in the Welde manuscript. Like many of Holborne's pieces it was published in his *Pavans, Galliards, Almains* in 1599 for a five-part consort. As with most of his pieces one can never be sure if it started off as a lute solo, or as an intabulation of an existing consort setting. As with other lute versions this solo has three moving parts with occasional four-part chords and some two-part texture. The five-part consort versions have an extra part, the Quintus, that is often superfluous and ungainly. The consort version is a fifth higher than the lute piece, a normal transposition to allow an expanded range to suit a full viol consort. While the treble and bass parts match reasonably well between the two versions, the inner parts show little connection. The lute solo setting of this piece fits so well on the instrument, one might be inclined to think it was written first for the lute.

Three manuscripts survive which were probably the product of amateur enthusiasm among the professional and gentry classes: the Brogyntyn, Mynshall, and Trumbull manuscripts. The Brogyntyn and Mynshall are provincial in character and origin, the first from Shropshire, near Oswestry, the other from Nantwich in Cheshire.[119] The Brogyntyn manuscript has lute music in a neat and upright hand and was probably produced *c*.1595. At some point in the 1620s the manuscript was used as a commonplace book by the lawyer-poet Thomas Thanet. The Mynshall manuscript is unusual in that it originated as a blank royal lute book, stamped with Elizabeth's arms on the covers, which somehow then became the property of the 15-year-old Richard Mynshall, and into which he copied forty-one items of music, the fourteenth of which is dated 1597. The presence in the book of a draft of a

---

[119] See the introduction to *The Brogyntyn Lute Book*, facs. with an introductory study by Robert Spencer and Jeffrey Alexander (Musical Sources, 12; Kilkenny, 1978). It is named after one of the homes of its present owner, Lord Harlech. The Mynshall Lute Book is in the private collection of Robert Spencer and is now in the Royal Academy of Music. For notes on provenance see the introductory study by Robert Spencer to *The Mynshall Lute Book* (Musical Sources, 6; Leeds, 1975).

Ex. 5.4. *Comparison of (a) Anthony Holborne's almain, 'The Night Watch', for solo lute in the Welde MS, fo. 6ᵛ, and (b) the five-part consort version published in* Pavans, Galliards, Almains *(1599), no. 55, bars 1–8*

1. Original barring of ³⁄₂ altered to ⁴⁄₂ throughout.

2. Rhythm signs ⌐ ⌐ altered to ⌐ ⌐ to fit other sources.

3. Dot added to fill bar.

famous letter dated 15 August 1598 from the Earl of Essex to Queen Elizabeth has never been fully explained.[120] The Trumbull lute book probably also resulted from a teenager's study of lute playing, in this case that undertaken by William Trumbull (*c*.1580–1635), secretary and envoy of James I at the Brussels court of the Archduke Albert of Austria in the years 1605–25.[121] Spencer suggests that Trumbull was himself the tablature scribe, and that he took the book with him while serving abroad.[122]

The Brogyntyn manuscript contains eight solo pieces, together with twenty-four consort-song intabulations, fourteen equal duet parts (all of which are incomplete in themselves as the second lute part is not present), and one part for a lute trio.[123] Among the solo pieces are three galliards, and pieces based on Italian grounds: Quadro pavans (3), a Passymeasures pavan, and Johnson's Medley (which may be a duet part). The solos and duets are entirely for 6-course lute, and are old-fashioned for *c*.1595, with Johnson the best represented.

The Trumbull and Mynshall manuscripts are similarly conservative in their selection of pieces, and were clearly pedagogical in purpose. The Trumbull contains twenty-six solos, ten duet parts, and two for consort, thirty-six of which are for 6-course lute, and two for 7-course. John Johnson is the best represented composer (8), followed by Holborne (5), Bassano (2), and Strogers (2). Composers with a single composition are Dowland, Morley, and van Wilder (chanson intabulation). Of the thirty-six solos, four duets (all treble and ground), and possibly one consort part in the Mynshall book, all save the last pieces are for 6-course lute. The pieces are strongly biased towards simple arrangements of popular tunes (12) without elaborate variations or divisions, and pieces based on grounds: Rogero, the Spanish pavan, Lavecchia, Quadro, and Passymeasures pavan. Tripartite galliards and pavans are comparatively few (5 and 2). Dowland's seven pieces appear in early simple forms lacking divisions and figuration. There are four pieces by John Johnson and one by Robert Johnson. The last piece in the Mynshall manuscript is in a different (later) hand for 7-course lute. Both the Mynshall and Trumbull are untidy and have many rhythmic errors, Richard Mynshall in particular displaying a lack of understanding of the notating of rhythm. Of all the sources these two books give the clearest picture of the pieces the young amateur might have been progressed through.

At the opposite end of the spectrum of difficulty are two fine manuscripts in the British Library which may have belonged to good amateurs or professionals: the Hirsch manuscript and Add. 31392. They can be classed as Elizabethan rather than Jacobean on the evidence of their contents and physical make-up. Both contain

[120] Robert Spencer, 'Three English Lute Manuscripts', *EM* 3 (1975), 119–24.
[121] *The Trumbull Lute Book*, facs. with an introductory note and guide to concordances by Robert Spencer (Musical Sources, 19; Clarabricken, 1980).
[122] Ibid., Introductory Note.
[123] Ian Davies, 'Replete for Three Lutes—The Missing Parts', *LSJ* 24 (1984), 38–43.

excellent music that is technically difficult, and, in the main, the work of practised hands. Add. 31392 has a more mainstream selection of pieces, akin to that of the Holmes manuscripts, with pieces by Dowland (7), Cutting (5), Pilkington (5), and Allison (4). Ferrabosco the Elder, Holborne, and Lodovicko [Bassano?] are also represented. Two copyists worked on this manuscript, one using the old 'grid' method for rhythm signs, the other the newer 'flag' type. Most of the pieces in this later hand require a seventh course, and most of those in the other do not. Pavans (17) are the most common forms in both sources. Add. 31392 has only token representation of galliards (4), vocal arrangements (2), fantasias (2), almains (2), variations (1), grounds (1). It also contains one treble and ground duet, five bandora pieces, and eighteen for keyboard.

Add. 31392 and Dd.2.11 together account for most of Pilkington's extant pieces. Pilkington is credited with his Mus.Bac. in the titles to each of the four pieces in the manuscript, which suggests a date after 1595. The dedication to 'Mrs Marie Oldfield' cannot have been made before 1600, when Mary Somerford married Phillipe Oldfield.[124] Pilkington's set of six variations on 'Go From My Window' is one of the most playable of all lute variations on this tune. It is built throughout on the idea of answering phrases inherent in the tune. The sixteen-bar tune can be divided into a pair of four-bar phrases (over chords of F major and then G minor), followed by an eight-bar phrase returning from G minor to F major. Variation I moves in conventional running divisions. In variations II and III the two-bar phrases are further subdivided into ever smaller phrases of contrasting tessituras, each echoing one another. (See Ex. 5.5.) As with so many English variation pieces, the penultimate variation features running passages, with a return to more sparse but harmonically richer texture in the last.

The Hirsch manuscript forms part of the Hirsch library acquired by the British Library in 1946. Five hands have contributed to the manuscript, but among the fifty-four solos and one duet for 6-course lute and two solos for 7-course lute, only three have attributions. Spencer suggests, on the basis of the contents, that it was started *c*.1595.[125] Among composers who have been identified, the most prominent are Dowland (7), Ferrabosco I (6), Cutting (5), Holborne (5), Allison (4). It is exceptional among English lute sources of this time in that it contains twenty-five fantasias, mostly to be found at the back of the book. Thirteen of the fantasias have yet to be identified. Of those that have been, four are by Ferrabosco I, two each by Francesco da Milano and Holborne, and one each by Paradiso, Adriaenssen, Byrd, and Marchant (duet part).

---

[124] Poulton, *John Dowland*, 105. Pilkington's galliard dedicated to Mrs Marie Oldfield is on fo. 22ᵛ of Add. 31392.

[125] *The Hirsch Lute Book*, facs. with an introductory study by Robert Spencer (Musical Sources, 21; Clarabricken, 1982), p. xiii.

Ex. 5.5. *Statement and three variations from Francis Pilkington's 'Go from my Window', Add. 31392, fos. 26ᵛ–27ʳ, bars 1–64*

1st. Variation

Ex. 5.5. *cont.*

2nd. Variation

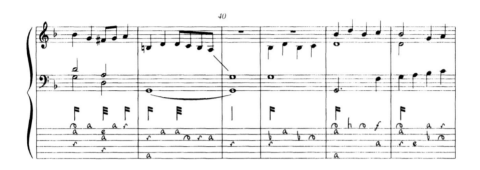

3rd. Variation

Ex. 5.5. *cont.*

The collection of music in the Hirsch manuscript is mainly serious and contrapuntal, and lacking in the lighter forms of toys, jigs, and ballad-tune settings, popular with the provincial amateurs like Mynshall. The general lack of ornamentation
and left- and right-hand fingering signs is an indication of the professionalism of the
Hirsch manuscript, a characteristic shared by the second Add. 31392 hand.
Ferrabosco's austere Fantasy on fo. 14ʳ is one of his easier pieces to play, and it is
far from easy. (See Ex. 5.6.) This fantasy appears unattributed in the Hirsch manuscript and in Besard's *Thesaurus harmonicus* (1603) fo. 32ᵛ, where it is attributed,
but in a different key. Like most of Ferrabosco's lute music it is probably an intabulation of a piece for three, four, or five-part consort, and does not fall very well
under the hand. The hand stretches in bars 9 and 10 are an example. Ferrabosco's
style and choice of forms is academic, and generally unlike that of contemporary
English lute music.

The lute manuscript in the Folger Library formerly known as the 'Dowland Lute
Book' is of exceptional interest. It was long thought to have originally belonged to
the Dowland family, and then to have remained with their descendants until the

Ex. 5.6. *Fantasia by Alfonso Ferrabosco I from the Hirsch MS, fo. 14ʳ, bars 1–10*

present century.[126] The Folger manuscript is now believed to have been the lute book of a student who took some instruction from Dowland, and during the nineteenth and early twentieth centuries was owned by a family with the name Dowland, who may or may not have been descendants of the composer.[127] The original student owner clearly took lessons with a number of teachers. Some twelve hands added to the Folger manuscript. John Ward has shown that the hands of John

[126] Poulton, *John Dowland*, 102–5.

[127] John Ward, 'The So-called "Dowland Lute Book" in the Folger Shakespeare Library', *JLSA* 9 (1976), 5–29.

Dowland and Robert Dowland, and the signature of John Johnson are present in the manuscript.[128] It is likely that the original owner took instruction from both the Dowlands, and also possibly from other professional lutenists.

The pieces in the Folger manuscript are suitable for beginners—short, simple, and attractive. There are forty-one solos, four duets (treble and ground), and two consort parts, plus fragments. Dowland is the best represented (10), with contributions from John Johnson (4), Robert Johnson (1), Allison (1), and Newman (1). Most numerous are the lighter forms: ballad-tune settings (4), almains (5), corantos (7), grounds (2), but there are also pavans (6) and galliards (8). Many of the pieces are unusually full of left- and right-hand fingering indications and ornaments. Quite possibly the book was used for several years, if the signature of John Johnson (d. 1594) and the hand of Robert Dowland (b. *c.*1591) are genuine. Lumsden suggested *c.*1610 as the most likely period for most of the manuscripts's compilation.[129] Ward's work would suggest that it was in use for a considerable period both before and after this date.

William Barley's *A new Booke of Tabliture* (1596) is the earliest printed collection of English lute music (see Pl. 5.4).[130] It consists of three separate books: one each for lute, orpharion, and bandora, containing seven, fourteen, and six solos, respectively. The bandora book also has four songs. It seems probable that *A new Booke* was published with a fourth book on music theory entitled *The pathway to musicke*,[131] as this is indicated on the title-page of the lute tutor and in the *The pathway* (1596).[132] Barley was an independent bookseller and publisher with a keen eye for the market. He had already ventured into the music-book trade with a tutor for the cittern in 1593, which was printed by John Danter.[133] Barley and Danter went on to produce a succession of books together on musical and non-musical subjects, and possibly collaborated on *A new Booke*. Barley may have been an interested amateur musician as, it seems, he himself prepared the brief instructions for the orpharion and bandora that preface those books. The instructions are admirably sensible,

---

[128] John Ward, 'The So-called "Dowland Lute Book" in the Folger Shakespeare Library', *JLSA* 9 (1976), 6, 16.

[129] Lumsden, 'The Sources of English Lute Music', 268.

[130] Modern edition: *Lute Music of Shakespeare's Time. William Barley: A New Booke of Tabliture, 1596*, ed. Wilburn W. Newcomb (University Park, Pa., 1966).

[131] Two copies of *The pathway* survive, one in the BL, the other at Helmington Hall bound up with the orpharion and bandora sections of *A new Booke*. It must be significant that this composite book has survived together with the Rose orpharion/small bandora, as part of the possessions of the Tollemache family. I am grateful to Ian Harwood for pointing this out to me.

[132] Ward, 'Barley's Songs without Words', 14 n. 2. The lute tutor describes *The pathway* as 'an introduction to Pricksesong, and certaine familliar rules of Descant, with other necessarie Tables plainely showing the true use of the Scale or Gamut, and also how to set any Lesson higher or lower at your pleasure'.

[133] No copy survives, but it was registered with the Stationer's Company on 19 Nov. 1593 and is listed in Andrew Maunsell's *Catalogue of English printed bookes* (London, 1595), part 2, p. 18. See Ward, 'Barley's Songs', 17 n. 3.

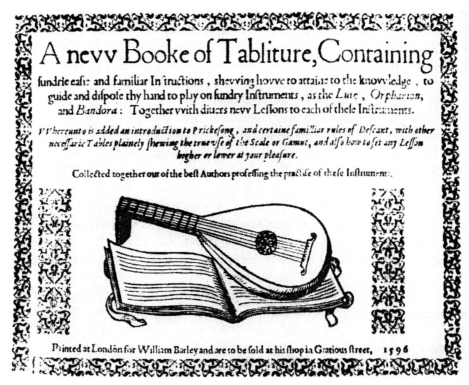

PL. 5.4. Frontispiece of William Barley's *A new Booke of Tabliture* (1596)

and emphasize the different approach that should be taken between the striking of the wire strings of the orpharion and bandora, and of the gut strings of the lute:

> the Orpharion is strong with wire strings, by reason of which manner of stringing, the Orpharion doth necessarily require a more gentle & drawing stroke than the Lute, I meane the fingers of the right hand must be easilie drawen over the stringes, and not suddenly griped, or sharpelie stroken as the Lute is: for if yee should doo so, then the wire stringes would clash or jarre together the one against the other, which would be a cause that the sounde would bee harsh and unpleasant.[134]

Barley's lute instructions present a new and more condensed version of the Le Roy rules that had first appeared in Alford's translation of 1568. These rules were most probably out of date by 1596. It is significant that the main criterion for deciding which pieces should be put into the lute tutor, and which into the orpharion tutor, is the number of courses required in the piece. All the lute pieces require only

[134] *A new Booke of Tabliture*, sig. A4ʳ (orpharion book).

six. Most of those for the orpharion require a seventh course tuned to *F*. Barley points out that pieces for lute and orpharion are interchangeable, but that the orpharion has 'more stringes than the Lute and also hath more frets or stops'.[135] There is, in fact, no other reason to believe that the orpharion pieces are any better suited to that instrument, and pieces like Dowland's 'Solus cum Sola' and 'Mistress Winter's Jump' appear in several lute sources.

Most probably Barley employed someone with a knowledge of the lute and bandora repertoire to choose and prepare the pieces. This editor's choice was excellent, and the organization within each section, from serious pavans to lighter forms, is thoroughly logical. Who this editor was is not known. Both Philip Rosseter and Francis Cutting have been suggested: Rosseter, because of the dedication of three of his pieces to the Countess of Sussex (who is also the dedicatee of the whole work), and Cutting, as he is by far the most favoured composer, with his name spelt out in full, while other composers are indicated by their initials only.[136] Cutting was dead by January 1595/6,[137] but the book could have been prepared a long time before going to press. My guess is that neither man was responsible. Barley's book has many mistakes. We know that the professional lutenist Edward Johnson was one of the proof-readers of John Dowland's *Second Book of Songs* and it is largely free of errors. Both Rosseter and Cutting were no less professional and I believe could not have done such a bad job.

All twenty-one pieces for lute and orpharion are by English composers. Cutting and Dowland apart, there are works by only two other composers: a single unique galliard by Edward Johnson, and the three Countess of Sussex galliards by Rosseter, two of which are unique.[138] Edward Johnson was a long serving-employee of the Kytsons of Hengrave Hall, and a composer of psalms, madrigals, and a variety of instrumental music.[139] This simple galliard is the only solo lute piece that can be ascribed to him. The three Rosseter galliards, like the Johnson piece, lack varied repeats. They are attractive and unusual, and though in unrelated keys, have a similarity of texture and rhythm such that they almost form a set. Circulation in surviving manuscripts shows that the seven pieces by Dowland in Barley's books were all very popular.[140] The versions here are generally simpler than those in Holmes's books, or later sources, but are of interest as they are dateable. Barley's version of Dowland's delightful 'Mistress Winter's Jump' is an excellent representative of jigs,

---

[135] *A new Booke of Tabliture*, sig. A4ʳ (orpharion book).

[136] Dart's review of Newcomb's edition in *JAMS* 20 (1967), 493–5, and Ward, 'A Dowland Miscellany', 124.

[137] Hulse, 'Francis and Thomas Cutting', 73.

[138] Rosseter's third galliard appears in Herbert fo. 21ᵛ entitled 'Gagliarda della Pavana' linking to the 'Pavana Ph: Johnson' on the previous page, with which it shares some harmonic material.

[139] See Price, *Patrons and Musicians*, 76–9, and Poulton, *John Dowland*, 51, 109, 247, 324, and 406.

[140] The pieces are 'Lachrimae Pavan', 'Piper's Pavan', 'Fortune', 'Can she excuse', 'Go from my Window', and 'Mrs Winter's Jump' in the lute book, and 'Solus cum Sola' in the orpharion book.

toys, volts, and other short light pieces that appear in solo lute manuscripts as page-fillers.

Cutting is the best represented composer in Barley's book, with ten pieces. His two pavans, an almain, and a galliard in the lute book all have varied repeats.[141] The almain repeats have running divisions like the identical Dd.2.11 version.[142] All other versions have slower-moving repeat sections instead of running divisions. Possibly the Barley/Dd.2.11 version was an earlier form of this piece.[143] Together with Cutting's justly popular variations on Walsingham and his version of Byrd's 'Pavana Bray', the orpharion book contains four lighter Cutting pieces which lack varied repeats and have few concordances. Could it have been that the editor knew and admired Cutting's music, and, in view of his recent death prior to 1596, paid him special homage by including so many of his pieces?

Cutting's version of Byrd's 'Pavana Bray' from the *FVB* is a particularly interesting piece as it constitutes a translation by a known master lutenist into lute music of a piece by an Elizabethan keyboard master. It is entitled 'Master Birds Pavan set by Francis Cutting' in Barley's book, where it appears without varied repeats. It also appears in Dd.9.33 without Barley's ornamentation, but with varied repeats and fewer errors. The three main statements of Cutting's pavan closely follow those of Byrd, but with some adjustment to, and loss of, inner-part texture. (See Ex. 5.7.) Cutting's varied repeats, however, are quite unlike those of Byrd's keyboard version, but are as intricate and interesting. As with other pieces by Cutting there are details in his music that seem to be suggestive of keyboard music. While Cutting may not have been a keyboard player he was clearly aware of contemporary keyboard technique.

Barley's books were heavily criticized by his contemporaries, including Thomas Morley, who condemned *The pathway* in his *Plaine and Easie Introduction to Practicall Musicke* (1597).[144] Clearly Barley appropriated music and published it without the consent of the composers. Both Holborne and Dowland complained of this.[145] Dowland in *The First Booke of Songes* (1597) spoke of 'divers Lute-lessons . . . lately printed without my knowledge, false and unperfect'.[146] In days before copyright such piracy was common, and Barley was no worse than many others in this respect.

[141] The varied repeats of the third and fourth sections of the galliard are especially welcome, as they are not present in the only other source (Euing MS, fo. 46ʳ).

[142] Dd.2.11, fo. 100ʳ.

[143] Early form Barley, sig. F1ᵛ–F2ᵛ; late forms: Add. 31392, fo. 26ʳ; Dd.5, fo. 31ʳ; Pickeringe, fos. 31ᵛ–32ʳ.

[144] Morley, *Plaine and Easie*, sig. *ʳ–*3ᵛ.

[145] Holborne in *The Cittharn Schoole* (1597), 'The Preface to the Reader', complained of a 'meere stranger . . . who . . . hath delivered in common to the worlds view certaine corrupt copies of my Idles . . .', most probably referring to Barley's 1593 cittern book.

[146] John Dowland, *The First Booke of Songes* (1597), sig. A1. Dowland promised also to 'set forth the choysest of all my lessons in Print', thus correcting Barley, something he never did.

Ex. 5.7. *Comparison of (a) Francis Cutting's arrangement for solo lute from William Barley's*
A new Booke of Tabliture *(1596), sig. D3ᵛ, bars 1–8 with (b) William Byrd's 'Pavana Bray'*
*(*FVB, *no. xci) for keyboard*

1. Barring of *Barley* (1596) has been altered to conform to that of FWVB. (ie from $\frac{2}{2}$ to $\frac{4}{2}$)

2. The second half of the lute part from bar 4 is missing in *Barley* (1596) and has been reconstructed from Dd.9.33,fo.12ᵛ

The charge made by several modern commentators that Barley's versions of pieces were inferior to, and more full of errors, than other publications of the period has been disputed by Ward.[147] Barley printed using woodblock, which was more difficult to correct than type, but may have been used to avoid the Byrd/Morley patent.[148] In fact most of the errors in the music are obvious and easily corrected. In the case of well-known pieces such as 'Lachrimae Pavan' and 'Piper's Pavan',

[147] Ward, 'A Dowland Miscellany', 123–33. Detractors were Lumsden and Poulton.
[148] I am grateful to Ian Harwood for this suggestion.

which are noticeably divergent from the majority of sources, Barley's versions have merit in themselves, and are of interest because they were published. Their presence underlines the fact that popular compositions altered over time, sometimes with the active participation of the composer. At a time when so little English lute music was published there was no such thing as a standard 'urtext' version, and deviation must be expected with a large circulation in manuscript copies.

Qualitative and stylistic assessments of the work of individual composers must always be tentatively made, given the vagaries of source survival. However, taking all the sources from the period 1580–1625, a general picture does emerge. The composers whose names we know may be divided into four groups: those for whom we have thirty or more attributed pieces; those with six or more; those with more than one; those with one. It is almost exclusively the first group that produced pieces with wide circulation. They comprise Dowland, with some seventy-five solo pieces (plus a further sixteen pieces of possible but uncertain ascription), followed by Daniel Bacheler (55), Anthony Holborne (52), Francis Cutting (43), and John Johnson (31).

In the second group are: Thomas Robinson (23), Robert Johnson (20), Alfonso Ferrabosco I (15), Francis Pilkington (15), Richard Allison (12), Edward Collard (9), Philip Rosseter (8), John Sturt (7), John Danyel (6), Thomas Dallis (6), and John Maynard (6). Of this group the pieces by Robinson, Dallis, and Maynard are almost exclusively found in single sources (*The Schoole of Musicke*, the Dallis manuscript, and *The XII. Wonders of the World* respectively).[149] There are also some fourteen arrangements for solo lute of pieces attributed to William Byrd (seven of which have doubtful connections with Byrd), and fifteen attributed to Peter Philips. These pieces were originally composed as keyboard or consort works, and were then adapted for the lute by an arranger.[150] In the third group of composers (for whom we have more than one attribution) are Augustine Bassano, Mathias Mason, Clement Cotton, Newman, Richard Green, R. Askue, Robert Kindersley, Nicholas Strogers, William Cavendish, Edward Pearce, John Marchant, and Thomas Smyth. None of those in the third and fourth groups has sufficient surviving works for any assessment to be made.[151]

The type of pieces into which the repertoire can be divided are remarkably few and uniform. These are fantasias, pavans, galliards, almains, the lighter forms of toys, jigs, and volts, sets of variations on popular tunes, and intabulations. In the Jacobean period increasing numbers of corantos, voltes, and masque dances were produced. Few intabulations of vocal pieces by English composers are present in

---

[149] Maynard's pieces are also published as duets for lute and bass viol, although the viol part is doubled in the bass by the lute, which is more or less complete in itself.

[150] Cutting was a known arranger of Byrd's music, and possibly Collard also. See *Music for the Lute 6, William Byrd*, ed. Nigel North (London, 1976), 54.

[151] For a list of these names see Lumsden, 'The Sources of English Lute Music', App. II, pp. 316–19.

the sources, as compared with Continental practice. Foreign composers like Francesco da Milano, da Ripa, Bakfark, and many others used intabulations of vocal music as vehicles for their own composition. It became an art form in its own right. England developed no comparable tradition. Intabulations were produced—the Paston manuscripts are a testament to this—but they were literal, and purely functional.

The lute fantasia would appear to have been more popular in England in the period before the 1590s than in the twenty years that followed. Dowland and Holborne apart, English composers in the period 1590–1610 produced few that survive, and those that circulated in manuscripts during this period are usually of foreign origin. Few native English composers produced more than two or three that survive, and many important lutenists, like Cutting, Pilkington, and Allison, have none at all. This contrasts with the early giants of Continental Renaissance lute music like Francesco, Bakfark, and de Ripa, who produced fantasias in great number. The later printed anthologies of the period 1584–1625 by Adriaenssen, Denss, Reymann, Rude, Van den Hove, Besard, Fuhrmann, Mertel, and Mylius give pride of place to the form (see above, Table 5.2). Mertel's great anthology of 1615 contains no fewer than 120 fantasias. It seems that the late Elizabethan dance forms were the overwhelming preoccupation of English lutenists in the 1590s, the decade in which by far the most English lute music was produced, and in which the mixed consort (for which the lute was central) was flourishing.

The presence of Alfonso Ferrabosco in England after 1562 may have done much to promote the fantasia form here at a time when the fantasias of Francesco da Milano were already being circulated. Ferrabosco produced at least five fantasias that survive as lute pieces, plus an 'ut, re, mi, fa, so, la' fantasia for three viols that is also known in a version for solo lute.[152] The Hirsh manuscript contains several fantasias which can be described as 'tablature short score' pieces, two of which have been published as three-part fantasias for viols.[153] Clearly the composition of fantasias and the intabulation of fantasias from other media did take place in England, but not to the extent that it did elsewhere in Europe.

Anthony Holborne wrote three surviving fantasias which show the influence of Francesco da Milano, particularly in their smooth polyphony, thin texture, and many points of imitation.[154] Among Golden Age English composers only Dowland significantly contributed to the form, writing at least seven but possibly more, as three further pieces titled 'fancy' or 'fantasia', which are of uncertain ascription,

[152] Ferrabosco, *Opera omnia*, ix: *Instrumental Music*, ed. Charteris, nos. 21a and 21b.

[153] *Anonymous Fantasias à3: VdGS anon. nos. 903, 904*, ed. Peter Trent (Sup. pub. 146; London, 1984). These pieces are nos. 36 and 37 in *The Hirsh Lute Book*, ed. Spencer.

[154] *The Complete Works*, ed. Kanazawa, nos. 1–3.

may be by him.[155] The great variety of texture and the multi-sectional nature of most of Dowland's fantasias place them favourably alongside the keyboard fantasias of Byrd. The fantasia that appears in Add. 31392 as 'A fantasie maister Dowland', was his most popular fantasia and probably a piece first composed in the 1590s, though one that he continually returned to.[156] In it the counterpoint of the memorable opening section gradually breaks down into short phrases that answer each other in different tessituras of the lute (Ex. 5.8). Eventually this section gives way to running passages and a time change into a fast bravura close.

The exuberance and virtuosic display Dowland infused into his multi-sectional fantasias set them apart from the rest of the lute fantasia tradition in England, which favoured a more unified, sober composition. His chromatic fantasias are more in keeping with this tradition, being generally monothematic and doleful in the extreme. Dowland's music has a cosmopolitan dimension lacking in most English lutenist-composers, and his interest in lute fantasias must surely connect with his Continental travels and work in Denmark.

Tripartite pavans, galliards, and almains are by far the most popular forms from the 1580s onwards. Pieces based on ground-bass patterns, in particular quadro pavans and galliards, remained in circulation throughout the period, but were less popular later, and can normally be dated back to the 1580s or before. Variations on popular tunes remain an important and peculiarly English part of the repertoire. Composers often reserved their most virtuosic and technically demanding music for such pieces. Bacheler's superb variations on 'Monsieur's Almain' are a case in point.

Of the composers in the second group listed above Ferrabosco stands out as being Continental in style and choice of forms (fantasias). Robert Johnson and John Sturt are clearly of a later generation and will be discussed in the next chapter. The compositions of Pilkington, Allison, and Rosseter are of consistently good quality, and stylistically similar. Those by Collard and Danyel are unusually inventive and individualistic. Collard's finely wrought pieces are very much part of the Elizabethan mainstream, Danyel's are more individualistic, and at times experimental. Only four pieces by Robinson are found in manuscript sources, the rest being unique to his published tutor. His lute pieces are attractive and tuneful, mostly of moderate difficulty, but not always suited to their didactic purpose.

It is only in the case of composers in the first group that there are sufficient surviving pieces for a real musical profile to emerge. John Johnson is the earliest lutenist-composer of importance, and some of his pieces maintained their

[155] Poulton, *John Dowland*, 113–18. For transcriptions see *The Collected Lute Music of John Dowland*, ed. Poulton and Lamb, nos. 72–4.

[156] The piece appears in six manuscript sources (Add. 31392, Euing, Pickeringe, Cosens, Add. 38539, and Per Brahe's lute book (Sweden, Skoklosters Castle Library, PB.fil.172)); and three printed books (*Varietie*, 1610; *Thesaurus harmonicus*, 1603; *Hortus musicalis novus*, 1615). The piece clearly developed over time. Compare *The Collected Lute Music*, nos. 1 and 1a.

Ex. 5.8. *Fantasia by John Dowland from Add. 31392, fo. 13ᵛ, bars 58–66*

1. Last tablature letter of bar 63 moved up from the third couse to the second to produce *d´* rather than *a*. This is to match the imitation and other sources.

popularity throughout the Jacobean period. Much of his music is thinner in texture, and his style closer to actual dance music than that of later composers. His pieces are stylistically diverse as they traverse the 1570s period, when ground-based lute music was popular, to the 1580s, when tripartite dance music became more the norm. A considerable amount of Johnson's surviving output exists as duets, some of which are also present in the sources as solos. It may be that some of his music originated as functional dance music to be performed by the royal consort of three lutes, for which no specific repertoire survives. If so, it transcended its original purpose, and maintained its popularity at a period when fashions had long since changed.

Francis Cutting's pieces best epitomize the English lute style of the late 1580s and early 1590s. From him we have no fantasias, no ground-based pieces, and only a few of the lighter forms. His close-textured pavans, galliards, and almains are contrapuntally precise and harmonically individual. They constitute many of the most perfectly balanced works of the repertoire. Best known among Holborne's pieces are the sparkling galliards and almains which have wonderful tunes, and subtle and intricate rhythmic patterns. Many of his pieces have evocative titles and are excellent at conveying a particular mood. He composed much solo music for the cittern and bandora, which like the consort music is often related to the solo lute music.

Bacheler's music is the least well known of the five composers, possibly because it is almost uniformly difficult to play, often needs nine or ten courses, and lacks a complete modern edition. While it is evident that he was already composing music in the 1580s when he was very young, many of his pieces were almost certainly not composed until well into the Jacobean period. This relatively long span of compositional activity has resulted in an output that is stylistically diverse. It includes the usual pavans, galliards, almains, and sets of variations, but also one fantasia, four courantes, and six preludes. These last items most clearly show the change in lute fashions in the Jacobean period. He seems to have had no interest in simple jigs and toys.

Only Dowland produced music in all the late Elizabethan forms in a sizeable number (excepting vocal intabulations, which were never much favoured by English lutenists). They range in mood from the frivolous to the most serious. His pieces are also very diverse in their technical requirements. A beginner can soon get some satisfaction from 'Mistress Winter's Jump'; only an exceptional player will master the chromatic fantasias. Dowland's solo lute music can be seen to have been the basic fulcrum for much of his vocal and instrumental music. It is perhaps no exaggeration to say that the revival of interest in English lute music is due in no small part to the exceptional range and accessibility of Dowland's music.

Chapter Six

The Lute in Consort

there was an excellent princely maske brought before hir [the Queen] after supper, by Mayster Goldingham, in the Privie Chamber; it was of gods and god-
desses, both strangely and richly apparelled . . . Then entred a consorte of
musicke; viz. sixe musitians, all in long vestures of white scarcenet gyrded
aboute them, and garlands on their heads, playing very cunningly.

Bernard Garter, *The Ioyful Receyving of the Queenes most excellent Maiestie
into hir Highnesse Citie of Norwich* (London, 1578)

The great majority of surviving lute pieces from England are for the solo lute, yet
this may not reflect the lute's common use, and its role as a consort and accompaniment instrument may be no less significant. During the Middle Ages it was
mainly used to play single lines, and combination with another instrument or
instruments, or a voice or voices, may have been the norm. Once technique had
changed to allow a single player to add a harmonic support to the melody line, the
lute became a leading solo instrument. Solo music apart, the instrument's new
capacity to play chords and polyphonic lines enhanced its suitability as an accompaniment instrument. Indeed the lute, in the form of the theorbo or archlute, was
still in use for this purpose until the eighteenth century, long after solo music had
ceased to be composed in Britain.

Within a consort of instruments the lute could either play a melodic line (with limited sustain) or provide chordal support—or a combination of both. The use of the lute
as a single-line melody instrument did not stop at the beginning of the sixteenth century, when, by discarding the plectrum and plucking directly with the fingers, harmonic and contrapuntal play became possible. A substantial and important repertoire
of duet and mixed-consort music survives from the 1570–1610 period, which makes a
feature of fast and agile single-line diminutions or divisions. Certain Stuart masques
required massed lutes, up to forty according to one account. Some masque musicians
designated 'treble lutes' may still have been using this type of play as late as the 1630s.

English sources of lute music of the period preserve a repertoire of over eighty
duets (see Table 6.1). There is an obvious division of the pieces into two categories:
the 'treble-and-ground duet' and the 'equal duet'.[1] In most treble-and-ground

---

[1] Lyle Nordstrom, 'The English Lute Duet and Consort Lesson', *LSJ* 18 (1976), 5–22. See also Richard
Newton, 'English Duets for Two Lutes', *LSJ* 1 (1959), 23–30.

duets one lute repeats a simple harmonic ground that may be anything from two to thirty-two bars in length. Grounds are normally a progression of homophonic chords with little melodic or rhythmic interest. Over this part the other lute plays a single-line melody, producing varied divisions for as many times as the ground is repeated. While there are a number of such duets in which both parts are relatively simple, the form normally involves the contrasting of a simple chordal ground with a more difficult single-line melody.

Table 6.1. *Principal English lute duets 1570–1625*

Note: Not included are the few Continental duets that appear in English sources, or grounds for which no matching trebles have been found. Titles have been standardized.

Title	Composer	Main sources (t = treble, g = ground)
TREBLE AND GROUND		
Chi Passa	John Johnson	Dd.3.18, fos. 7ᵛ–8ʳ (t); Marsh, pp. 151–3 (t)
Dump, no. 1	John Johnson	Dd.3.18, fo. 3ᵛ (t&g); Marsh, pp. 144–5 (t&g), Add. 31392, fo. 22ᵛ
Dump, no. 2 (Queen's Treble)	John Johnson	Dd.3.18, fos. 4ʳ–3ᵛ (t); Schele, pp. 138–9 (t); Pickeringe, fos. 8ᵛ–9ʳ (t&g); Folger, fos. 6ᵛ–7ʳ (t&g); Add. 38539, fos. 4ᵛ–5ʳ (t); Königsberg, fos. 61ᵛ–62ʳ (t&g), Brogyntyn, p. 7 (g)
Goodnight	John Johnson	Dd.3.18, fos. 15ᵛ–16ʳ (t); Marsh, pp. 26–7, 158–60 (t); Willoughby, fos. 3ᵛ–5ᵛ (t&g); Brogyntyn, p. 7 (g); Dallis, p. 16 (g)
The New Hunt is Up	John Johnson	Dd.3.18, fos. 13ᵛ–14ʳ (t); Trumbull, fos. 15ᵛ–16ʳ (t); Welde, fos. 13ʳ–14ʳ (t); Marsh, pp. 183–6 (t&g)
Rogero	John Johnson	Dd.3.18, fo. 1ʳ (t); Mynshall, fos. 3ᵛ (t); Trumbull, fo. 25ᵛ (t&g); Dallis, p. 92 (g)
The Short Almain, no. 1	John Johnson	Dd.3.18, fo. 10ᵛ (t); Pickeringe, fos. 13ᵛ–14ʳ (t&g)
The Short Almain, no. 2	John Johnson	Dd.3.18, fos. 9ᵛ–10ʳ (t); Pickeringe, fo. 14ʳ (g)
Trenchmore	John Johnson	Dd.3.18, fos. 12ᵛ–13ʳ (t); Welde, fos. 11ᵛ–12ʳ (t&g); Marsh, pp. 139–41 (t&g)
Wakefield on a Green	John Johnson	Dd.3.18, fos. 11ᵛ–12ʳ (t); Marsh, pp. 146–8 (t&g)
The Queenes good Night	Thomas Robinson	*Schoole of Musicke*, p. 13 (t&g)
Twenty waies upon the bels	Thomas Robinson	*Schoole of Musicke*, p. 14 (t&g)
Passemezzo Galliard	Thomas Robinson	*Schoole of Musicke*, p. 21 (t&g)

Title	Composer	Main sources (t = treble, g = ground)
The Sharp Pavan	Richard Allison	Pickeringe, fos. 11ᵛ–12ʳ (t&g); Folger, fos. 17ᵛ–18ʳ (t); Add. 38539, fos. 5ᵛ–6ʳ (t); Trumbull, fo. 17ʳ (g)
Spanish Measures	Richard Allison	Board, fos. 4ᵛ–5ʳ (t&g)
The Spanish Pavinge	Alfonso Ferrabosco	Dd.3.18, fos. 14ᵛ–15ʳ (t); Pickeringe, fos. 10ᵛ–11ʳ (t&g)
The Marygolde	Ellis Lawrey	Dd.3.18, fo. 23ʳ (t&g)
Passymeasures Galliard	John Danyel	Dd.3.18, fos. 62ʳ–63ʳ (t&g)
Short Almain	Francis Cutting	Dd.3.18, fo. 59ʳ (t)
Galliard	Robert Askue	Dd.9.33, fo. 88ᵛ (t)
Fortune my Foe	?John Dowland	Dd.9.33, fo. 89ʳ (t)
The Leaves be Green	Anon. (?J. Johnson)	Dd.3.18, fo. 17ᵛ (t); Dd.9.33, fos. 63ᵛ–64ʳ (t); Pickeringe, fos. 14ᵛ–15ʳ (t&g)
The Flatt Pavan	Anon. (?J. Johnson)	Dd.3.18, fo. 21ᵛ (t); Trumbull, fos. 17ʳ–19ʳ (t)
Galliard to the Flatt Pavan	Anon. (?J. Johnson)	Dd.3.18, fo. 22ʳ (t)
The Honsok/Hunts Up	Anon. (?J. Johnson)	Dd.3.18, fo. 4ᵛ (t); Board, fos. 2ᵛ–3ʳ (t&g); Folger, fos. 3ᵛ–4ʳ (t&g); Trumbull, fos. 1ᵛ–2ʳ (t&g)
Sellenger's Round	Anon. (?J. Johnson)	Dd.3.18, fo. 5ʳ (t), Marsh, p. 182 (t); Thysius, pp. 442–3 (t)
Greensleves	Anon. (?J. Johnson)	Dd.3.18, fos. 8ᵛ–9ʳ (t); Folger, fo. 5ʳ (g)
Cara Cosa	Anon. (?J. Johnson)	Marsh, pp. 162–3, 165 (t)
Passemeasures Galliard	Anon. (?J. Johnson)ᵃ	Marsh, pp. 154–6 (t&g)
Dump	Anon. (?J. Johnson)ᵃ	Marsh, pp. 150–1 (t&g)
Dump	Anon. (?J. Johnson)	Dd.3.18, fos. 71ᵛ–72ʳ (t); Thistlethwaite, fo. 2ʳ–3ʳ (t); Schele, p. 16 (t)
Passemeasures Pavan	Anon. (?J. Johnson)	Dd.3.18, fos. 1ᵛ–2ʳ (t&g); Marsh, pp. 142–4 (t); Mynshall, fos. 2ᵛ–3ʳ (t); Ballet, p. 85 (g)
Galliard to the Passemeasures	Anon. (?J. Johnson)	Dd.3.18, fo. 2ᵛ (t)
The French Galliard	Anon. (?J. Johnson)	Marsh, pp. 148–9 (t)
Go Merely wheele	Anon. (?J. Johnson)	Dd.3.18, fos. 40ᵛ–41ʳ (t)
Dump (Bergamasca)	Anon. (?J. Johnson)	Add. 38539, fo. 5ʳ (t); Board, fo. 1ʳ (t&g)
Green Garters	Anon. (?J. Johnson)	Dd.3.18, fos. 23ᵛ–24ʳ (t)
Callinoe	Anon.	Dd.3.18, fo. 3ʳ (t)
Quadro Pavan	Anon.	Dd.3.18, fos. 5ʳ–6ʳ (t); Pickeringe, fos. 9ᵛ–10ʳ (t&g); Trumbull, fos. 10ᵛ–11ʳ (t)
Quadro Galliard	Anon. (?J. Johnson)	Dd.3.18, fos. 6ᵛ–7ʳ (t); Pickeringe, fos. 8ʳ 12ᵛ–13ʳ (t&g); Trumbull, fos. 11ᵛ–12ʳ (t)
Dump	Anon.	Dd.3.18, fos. 6ʳ–7ʳ (t)
Robin is to the Greenwood	Anon.	Dd.3.18, fo. 11ʳ (t)
Passemezzo Galliard	Anon.	Dd.3.18, fos. 41ᵛ–42ʳ (t)

Table 6.1. *cont.*

Title	Composer	Main sources (t = treble, g = ground)
Passemazzo Pavan	Anon.	Dd.3.18, fos. 42ᵛ–43ᵛ (t)
The Galliard	Anon.	Dd.3.18, fos. 43ᵛ–44ʳ (t)
The Bodkin	Anon.	Dd.3.18, fo. 44ʳ⁻ᵛ (t)
Greensleeves	Anon.	Folger, fo. 5ʳ (t&g); Mynshall, fo. 3ʳ⁻ᵛ (t)
?Dump	Anon.	Add. 31392, fo. 22ʳ (t&g)
Rogero	Anon.	Marsh, p. 39 (t); Dallis, p. 92 (g)
A Treble	Anon.	Marsh, pp. 156–7 (t)
A Treble	Anon.	Ballet, pp. 85–6 (t)
Hart Opressed	Anon.	Mynshall, fo. 2ʳ (t)
John Come Kiss Me Now	Anon.	Welde, fos. 10ᵛ–11ʳ (t)
Malt's Come Down	Anon.	Dd.9.33, fo. 89ᵛ (t)
Mounsiers Alman	Anon.	Dd.9.33, fos. 53ᵛ–54ʳ (t)
A Treble	Anon.	Add. 38539, fo. 6ᵛ (t)

PIECES THAT CAN BE PLAYED AS DUETS ON LUTES A FOURTH APART
(s = superius, b = bassus)

Title	Composer	Main sources
Lady Rich's Galliard	John Dowland	Königsberg, fo. 21ʳ (s&b)
Philips Pavin	Peter Philips	Dallis, pp. 82–3 (s&b)
In Nomine Pavan	Nicholas Strogers^b	Dallis, p. 81 (b); Trumbull, fos. 16ᵛ–17ʳ (s); Hirsch, fo. 2ᵛ (s)
In Nomine Galliard	Nicholas Strogers	Dallis, pp. 93–4 (s&b); Trumbull, fo. 6ʳ (s); Hirsch, fo. 3ʳ (s), Dd.9.33, fo. 60ᵛ (s)
Chi Passa	Anon.	Willoughby, fos. 83ᵛ–85ʳ (s&b)

EQUAL DUETS

Title	Composer	Main sources
Flat Pavan	John Johnson	Pickeringe, fos. 4ᵛ–5ʳ (I&II); Trumbull, fo. 15ʳ (II)
Galliard to the Flat Pavan	John Johnson	Pickeringe, fos. 5ᵛ–6ʳ (I&II)
La Vecchia Pavan	John Johnson	Pickeringe, fo. 4ʳ (I); Ballet, p. 45 (I); Wickhambrook, fo. 14ʳ–15ᵛ (I&II); Brogyntyn, pp. 28–9 (II)
La Vecchia Galliard	John Johnson	Pickeringe, fo. 4ʳ˙ᵛ (I&II); Wickhambrook, fo. 16ʳ (I&II); Brogyntyn, p. 29 (II)
Galliard	John Johnson^c	Brogyntyn, p. 17 (II)
A Plaine song	Thomas Robinson	*Schoole of Musicke*, pp. 18–19 (I&II)
A Fantasie	Thomas Robinson	*Schoole of Musicke*, pp. 22–3 (I&II)
A Toy	Thomas Robinson	*Schoole of Musicke*, pp. 26–7 (I&II); Sampson, fo. 12ᵛ (II)
An allman/Eccho	John Marchant/ Francis Pilkington	Sampson, fo. 11ᵛ (II); Brogyntyn, p. 31 (I)
A Fancy	John Marchant	Hirsch, fo. 6ᵛ (I); Brogyntyn, p. 15 (II)
A Fancy	John Marchant	Thistlethwaite, fos. 77ᵛ–78ʳ (I)

Title	Composer	Main sources (t = treble, g = ground)
Lord Chamberlaine's Galliard	John Dowland[d]	*First Booke*, sig. L2ˇ (I&II); Dd.9.33, fo. 90ʳ (I&II)
Lord Willoughby's Welcome home	John Dowland	Sampson, fo. 11ˇ (II); Folger, fo. 9ˇ (I)
Now oh now/Frog Galliard	John Dowland[c]	Königsberg, fo. 21ʳ (II)
Pavan	Richard Reade[c]	Dd.3.18, fos. 54ˇ–55ʳ (I); Dd.3.18, fo. 54ʳ (II)
Pavan	Richard Reade[c]	Dd.3.18, fo. 55ʳ (I); Dd.3.18, fo. 54ˇ (II)
Pavan	Richard Reade[c]	Dd.3.18, fo. 55ʳ (I); Dd.3.18, fo. 54ˇ (II)
Pavan	Richard Reade[c]	Dd.3.18, fo. 56ʳ (I)
De la Tromba Pavan	Richard Allison	Pickeringe, fos. 6ˇ–8ʳ (I&II); Sampson fos. 10ˇ–11ʳ (II); Brogyntyn, pp. 26–7 (II)
Go From My Window	Richard Allison	Add. 2764(2), fo. 9ˇ (II)
A Fancy for 2 lutes	John Danyel[f]	Sampson, fo. 11ʳ (I)
Drewries accorde	Anon.	Pickeringe, fo. 6ˇ ʳ (I&II); Ballet, pp. 48–9 (I&II); Brogyntyn, p. 30 (II)
La Rosignall	Anon.	Pickeringe, fo. 8ʳ⁻ˇ (I&II); Board, fo. 6ʳ (I)
A Merry Mood	Anon.[f]	Sampson, fo. 12ʳ (I)
An Almayne	Anon.	Sampson, fo. 3ʳ; Folger, fo. 2ˇ (I&II)
Duncomb's Galliard	Anon.[f]	Sampson, fo. 12ˇ (I)
Galliard	Anon.[d]	Trumbull, fo. 32ˇ (I&II)
Galiard for 2 lutes/ Squires Galliard	Anon.[c]	Sampson, fos. 12ˇ–13ʳ (II)
Battel for 2 lutes	Anon.[g]	Pickeringe, fos. 52ˇ–54ʳ (I&II)
Alpha Pavan	Anon.[c]	Brogyntyn, p. 13 (II)
De la Trumba Galliard	Anon.[c]	Brogyntyn, pp. 27–8 (II)
Galliard after La Vecchia	Anon.	Ballet, pp. 46–7 (I&II)
Pavan to Delight	Anon.[h]	Folger, fos. 14ˇ–15ʳ (I); Brogyntyn, p. 13 (II)
Galliard	Anon.[f]	Trumbull, fo. 33ˇ (I)

[a] Ground on a lute tuned a fourth below.

[b] The Dallis bassus may be unrelated to the surviving superius.

[c] Lute II only.

[d] For two to play on one lute.

[e] For 2 orpharions tuned a fifth apart plus consort?

[f] Lute I only.

[g] Lutes a tone apart.

[h] Duet part that fits the solo version by John Johnson in Folger.

Trebles are ideally suited to the right-hand thumb-and-forefinger technique. This technique developed from plectrum playing, and such treble parts can be, and may have been, played using a plectrum.[2] This type of duet is older than the equal duet, which may have developed from it. The repertoire consists of many more duet trebles than equal duets (53 to 23).[3] Most treble-and-ground duets are sets of variations over a ground, but there are a number which are pavans, galliards, or some other popular dance form in which one lute 'descants' with fast divisions. Duet trebles were evidently very popular in the 1570s and 1580s, and connect with the large amount of solo lute music also based on grounds in sources like the Willoughby and Marsh manuscripts. It may be that some of this early solo music, such as the *Dump Philli* in the Marsh manuscript, developed in imitation of the effects and texture of a treble-and-ground duet.

The equal duet, by contrast, involves near equal technical difficulty for both players, and the sharing of musical responsibilities for melody and accompaniment. Some equal duets produce a treble-and-ground texture, in which the single-line melody is passed from player to player. While one player 'descants', the other accompanies with chords. Many of such 'alternating style' duets are based on tripartite dances (pavans, galliards, almains). A number of easier equal lute duets correspond to the lighter jigs and toys of the solo repertoire. These pieces, whether bipartite, tripartite or longer, consist of short answering phrases where the melodic material is passed from player to player, and is either reiterated exactly, or in a slightly altered form. This repetition of material can follow after a phrase is finished, or more quickly as an 'echo' effect, or as the type of canonic imitation known in the sixteenth century as 'reports'. These pieces connect with the considerable body of Renaissance duo material for two trebles. As with Morley's duets, such *bicinia* often had a pedagogical purpose.

Lute-duet trebles were produced in countries other than England in the sixteenth century. In Italy single-line trebles were composed and published throughout the century from Spinacino (1507) and Dalza (1508) to Galilei (1584) and Terzi (1593).[4] A variety of types of equal duets were published in Italy from Joannes Matelart's duet arrangements of fantasias by Francesco da Milano (1559) to the early seventeenth-century canzonas and toccatas by Melli (1614–20) and Piccinini (1623).[5] In general the emphasis in these equal duets is on the improvement in

---

[2] The use of a plectrum in connection with lute duets may have continued into the 17th c., as the engraving by Jacob Cats in *Sinne- en Minnebeelden* (1618) shows a plectrum on the smaller of the two lutes in the picture.

[3] The only study dedicated to the English lute duet is Jeffrey Alexander's 'The English Lute Duet, 1570–1610' (MA thesis, University of Nottingham, 1977).

[4] Francesco Spinacino, *Intabolatura de lauto* (Venice, 1507); Joan Ambrosio Dalza, *Intabulatura de lauto* (Venice, 1508); Vincenzo Galilei, *Fronimo: Dialogo* (Venice, 1584, rev. edn., 1584); Giovanni Antonio Terzi, *Intavolatura di liutto* (Venice, 1593).

[5] Joannes Matelart, *Intavolatura de leuto* (Rome, 1559); Pietro Paolo Melli, *Intabolatura di liuto* Libri I–V (Venice, 1614, 1616, 1616, 1616, 1620); Alessandro Piccinini, *Intavolatura di liuto et di chitarrone* (Bologna, 1623).

definition of musical ideas made possible with two lutes. Canonic imitation and echo effects are much clearer with two sound sources. Equal-duet music was published in quantity outside Italy in the sixteenth century, notably by the Antwerp publisher Phalèse, and in the late sixteenth and seventeenth century by the anthologists Adriaenssen, Van den Hove, and Besard. Later, in the Baroque period lute duets re-emerged with the French *contrepartie*—a piece composed for a second lute to combine with an existing lute solo in the manner of the Matelart/Milano pieces. There are some instances of this type of piece in the English repertoire—Dowland's 'Lord Wilobies Welcome home' is an example—but they are rare. Duets were still being produced in some quantity by the last generation of eighteenth-century German lutenist-composers.[6]

English sources suggest that the fashion for lute duets was strong in the years 1570–1610, but that duets were played well into the 1620s. The vogue was at its peak in the twenty years from 1570 to 1590, slightly before the most productive period for English solo lute music. The sixteenth-century combination of two lutes, one descanting and the other providing a simple accompaniment, must connect with the fifteenth-century combination of virtuoso lute or gittern performer with an

Table 6.2. *Principal sources of English lute duets*

Source	Number	Comments
Dd.3.18	43	35 trebles, only 3 of which have grounds attached. Of the 10 presumed equal duet parts, only two are complete and some may be consort parts
Marsh	15	All duet trebles, a few with grounds
Pickeringe	14	7 equal; 7 treble and ground
Brogyntyn	16	6 grounds; 10 equal duet parts
Trumbull	10	7 trebles, 5 with grounds; 2 lute-duet parts; 1 duet for two to play on one lute
Sampson	8	All equal duets, only one of which is complete
Folger	8	3 equal (only one of which is complete); 4 trebles (2 of which have grounds); one ground without treble
Ballet	7	4 equal duets (2 complete); 1 treble and ground; 2 grounds without trebles
Schoole of Musicke	6	3 trebles with grounds; 3 equal duets
Board	5	4 trebles (2 with grounds); 1 equal-duet part
Mynshall	5	4 trebles all without grounds; 1 equal-duet part

[6] Ernst Gottlieb Baron, 'Courante', *US-NYp* JOG 72–29, fasc. xiii; Leopold Sylvius Weiss, '4 Partien für zwei Lauten', *D-Dlb* MS Mus 2841/v/i; Joachim Bernhard Hagen, 'Konzert für zwei Lauten und Violine', *D-As* MS Tonkunst Schl. 290, fasc. ii, iii; Adam Falkenhagen, 'Duetto F-Dur für 2 Barocklauten', *D-As* MS Tonkunst Schl. 290, fasc. iii.

accompanimental 'tenorista'. This practice was well documented in Italy and may have been widespread in Europe. The combination must have been known in England well before the 1570s, from which point manuscript sources survive that contain duets.

The earliest English duet repertoire is quite sophisticated and reflects a developed genre. Possibly there was a written repertoire prior to 1570 that has not survived. More likely, the repertoire was the preserve of professionals able to improvise (or compose and memorize) descants over a simple accompaniment such as a well-known tenor or a stock chord progression. As the harmony was slow moving it gave time for the improviser to think. As professionals evolved from illiterate minstrels to trained musicians, so improvisation gave way to studied compositions committed to paper. The elaborate trebles of John Johnson in manuscripts of the 1570s and 1580s would be examples of this latter type. With the increasing number of good amateur players and the increased use of tablature and manuscript circulation of music, so the equal duet developed and technical demands became more moderate. Thomas Robinson may be referring to the descanting style of the 1570s and before when, in *The Schoole of Musicke* (1603), Timotheus the lute teacher berates the earlier generation of lute players, saying:

for in older times they strove (onelie) to have a quick hand upon the Lute, to runne hurrie hurrie, keeping a Catt in the gutter upon the ground, now true then false, now up now downe, with such painfull play, mocking, mowing, gripeing, grinning, sighing, supping, heaving, shouldring, labouring, and sweating, like cart Iades, without any skill in the world, or rule, or reason to play a lesson, or finger the Lute, or guide the bodie, or know any thing, that belongeth, either to skill or reason.

One basic difference between English duets of the 1570–1610 period and Continental duets is that English duets, with few exceptions, are for two identically pitched instruments.[7] A far greater proportion of Continental duets are for lutes of different pitches. Two of the Matelart/Francesco duets are for unison lutes; the rest, like many of the pieces published by Besard, Melli, and Piccinnini, are for instruments a tone apart. There are vihuela duets by Valderrábano that call for instruments a third, fourth, and fifth apart as well as at the unison.[8] Duets for lutes a fourth apart were particularly popular and would suit a treble and mean lute, or mean and bass. The large collection published by Heckel (1562) is for lutes a tone or a fourth apart, and Phalèse's 1552 set is for lutes at the unison, fourth, and fifth.

---

[7] The exceptions are found in the Marsh, Dallis and Pickeringe MSS. The Willoughby MS contains three solo settings of the 'Qui passa', two of which (nos. 7 and 36) can be played by two lutes a fourth apart, according to a footnote in the MS.

[8] Enriquez de Valderrábano, *Libro de música de vihuela, intitulado Silva de sirenas* (Valladolid, 1547), Libro IV.

The existence of lutes of different sizes in the sixteenth century is well documented. A good number of Renaissance bass lutes survive, many of them recycled as theorbos in the seventeenth century. Lutes of different sizes were played together as trios and quartets. Surviving plucked trio and quartet music in tablature spans the period from 1564, the date of Pacoloni's large collection for three lutes (to which Viaera added ad lib cittern parts, 1564),[9] to the anonymous suite published in 1645 entitled 'Conserto Vago' for lute, theorbo, and a small 4-course guitar.[10] The Thysius manuscript contains thirteen quartets for lutes in which pre-existing pieces are arranged for lutes of different sizes.[11] Music for two or more lutes, or for a number of lutes and voices, is an important ingredient of many of the Continental anthologies listed in Table 7.2. The opening two sections of Besard's *Novus partus* (1617) are devoted to music for three concerted lutes, the first of which also requires two or more other instruments or voices. The collections of Fuhrmann and Van den Hove also contain some lute duets.[12] Visual evidence is found in the anonymous French painting *Le bal des noces du duc de Joyeuse* (1581–2), in which a consort of four lutes provides court dance music.[13]

Adriaenssen's three books have sections devoted to concerted music for two to four lutes in various combinations.[14] In all lute-ensemble music, the upper lutes play divisions and are most active, while the lower parts are more functional and have a harmonic role. Adriaenssen's approach to arranging vocal music for a lute quartet at the nominal pitches a', g', e', and d' is quite straightforward. The soprano, alto, and tenor lutes play the soprano, alto, and tenor lines in their upper voices and all play the bass line in their lowest voice. The bass lute plays the bass part an octave lower and has the tenor in its upper part. Chords are filled out as required and melodic embellishments are normally given to the upper parts.

Concerted lutes were heard in England. Court accounts of the 1570s and 1580s occasionally mention lutenists as being of 'the three lutes'. John Johnson received his place 'in the room of Anthony de Counte, deceased, one of the musicians for the three lutes'.[15] This mention is a surprise, as until 1579 only one place (that of Anthony County) is specified as a lutenist. We could interpret the accounts as saying only that there were three lutenist places, and not that there was an ensemble

[9] Giovanni Pacoloni, *Longe elegantissima excellentissimi musici . . . tribus testudinibus ludenda Carmina* (Louvain, 1564); Frederic Viaera, *Nova et elegantissima in Cythara ludenda Carmina* (Louvain, 1564). Viaera provides a number of cittern pieces that can be played with Pacoloni's trios.

[10] Anthony Rooley and James Tyler, 'The Lute Consort', *LSJ* 14 (1972), 13–24.

[11] Todd Lane, 'The Lute Quartets in the Thysius Lute Book', *JLSA* 22 (1989), 28–59.

[12] Georg Leopold Fuhrmann, *Testudo gallo-germanica* (Nuremberg, 1615), 130–2; Joachim Van den Hove, *Florida* (Utrecht, 1601), fos. 72ʳ–76ʳ.

[13] Paris, Louvre, inv. 1817. There are several versions of this painting.

[14] In *Pratum musicum* (Antwerp, 1584) these sections are for: two lutes and three voices (fos. 40ᵛ–46ʳ, 57ʳ–58ʳ), three lutes (fos. 46ᵛ–49ᵛ), four lutes and four voices (fos. 49ʳ–51ʳ), two lutes and four voices (fos. 59ᵛ–60ʳ, 61ʳ).

[15] *RECM* vi. 124.

known as 'the three lutes'. Was there a court consort of lutes in existence by 1579? Accounts would confirm that there was, and the number of places was never fixed at three. Holman goes further and states that they were called 'of the three lutes', not because there were three players, but because the group used three different sizes of lute.[16] This is indicated in accounts which specify the size of lute used by particular players within the consort.[17] Mathias Mason, who was appointed at the same time as Johnson, was also mentioned as a 'musician for the 3 lutes'.[18] Walter Pierce's appointment in 1589 also specifies that he belonged to the group.[19] The warrant for Pierce's appointment contains the last mention of the group in royal accounts, and the appointment of Edward Collard to Johnson's place in 1599 makes no mention of the three lutes.

The consort of lutes did not die out at this stage but was expanded in the early seventeenth century. Robert Johnson and Philip Rosseter were both referred to in payments for strings for the bass lute, and in 1615 Johnson was 'one of the consorte of Lutes'.[20] In the 1630s the group was called 'his Ma[jes]tes fower Lutes'. The group may have got bigger again, as John Coggeshall was paid for supplying strings for 'the four lutes and theorba' in 1629 and 1630. In 1632 and 1633 he was responsible for 'provyding & maynteyning of his Ma[jes]tes Fower Lutes wth Stringes at all tymes of their meetings & practises'.[21] Outside court William Cavendish employed enough lutenists to make a lute consort a reality and purchased 'three bookes for three lutes'. On one occasion Cavendish paid Lord Dudley North's men who 'played on three lutes', suggesting another lute consort outside court.[22]

As for extant English lute music for concerted lutes we have only the title and one part of the piece 'Replete for three lutes' in the Brogyntyn manuscript.[23] The Dallis lute book contains a piece that can be played by four lutes, 'Era di maggio', and one for five lutes, 'Pavan si vous'.[24] The Dallis pieces are far from convincing. The parts of the eight-bar 'Pavan si vous' are written one below the other down the five tablature stave lines. The second, third, and fourth lines are marked 'Sup', 'Tenor', and 'Bassus' and the first line is almost identical to the second. The parts could be played by lutes at nominal pitch *g'*, *g'*, *d'*, *c'*, and '*a*'. Robinson promised, in his address to the reader in *The Schoole of Musicke* (1603), to follow it up with a book which included 'lessons for one, two and three Lutes', if the *The Schoole of Musicke* was well received. This he never did.

[16] Holman, *Four and Twenty Fiddlers*, 226–7.
[17] Robert Johnson and Philip Rosseter were at different times players of the bass lute; *RECM* iv. 87–8, 101.
[18] *RECM* vi. 126.   [19] Ibid. 145.   [20] Ibid., iv. 87–8, 98, 101, 109.
[21] Ibid., iii. 54, 57, 141, 146; Holman, *Four and Twenty Fiddlers*, 227.
[22] Hardwick MS 29, entry for Jan. 1616. See Hulse, 'Hardwick MS 29', 66.
[23] Brogyntyn MS, 18–19. For a reconstruction see Davies, 'Replete for Three Lutes'.
[24] Ward and Music 200, 'The Lute Books of Trinity College', 20.

The small amount of surviving English material for three or more lutes is all of inferior quality and in some cases may be reworkings of solo material in different keys, rather than music intended to be played together. The lack of source material may be because lute trios of this period performed duet material repertoire with a simple bass lute part added, rather than three independent parts. The trios in Hume's 1607 book can be played this way. It is certainly easy to concoct a bass lute part for most existing duets, and this transforms the sound into a richer and more balanced texture.

At court massed lutes were a feature of Stuart masques. Twelve lutes seems to have been a standard number for Jacobean masques, though *Love Freed from Ignorance and Folly* (1611) involved two groups of twelve lutenists, and twenty were organized by Robert Johnson for *Oberon* (1611). Their main role was to accompany vocal music but, as in *Hymenaei* (1606), the massed lutes did also accompany dancers.[25] A set of three pieces composed for the 1607 Lord Hayes Masque by Thomas Campion survive in arrangements for mixed consort in Rosseter's *Lessons for Consort* (1609). The pieces were published by Campion himself in *The Discription of a Maske* (1607) in versions for voice or voices, lute, and bass viol.[26] The first piece, 'Move Now', was originally performed as follows:

the foure *Silvans* played on their instruments [given on sig. B2 as 'two bearing meane Lutes, the third a base Lute, and the fourth a deepe Bandora'] the first straine of this song following: & at the repetition thereof the voices fell in with the instrumentes which were thus devided, a treble and a base were placed neare his Majestie, and an other treble and base neere the grove, that the words of the song might be heard of all.[27]

The resulting sound must have been familiar to the Stuart court and many others across Europe.

Table 6.1 shows that the English lute-duet repertoire is dominated by one man, John Johnson, and that while there are over twenty sources of English duets, only a handful of sources contain much of the music. Thomas Robinson's six finely crafted duets—three equal duets and three duet trebles—stand somewhat apart, as they were printed, and like Robinson's solo lute pieces, they do not appear to have circulated much in manuscript. The only other printed duet is Dowland's 'My Lord Chamberlaine his Galliard', 'an invention by the said Author for two to play upon one Lute'.[28] It is a good piece presented in a novel way, and allows the possibility of an intimate embrace between the two players. A similar two-on-one-lute duet is found in the Trumbull manuscript.[29] The idea was later copied by Hume in his 'Lesson for two to play upon one Viole'.[30]

[25] Peter Walls, *Music in the English Courtly Masque 1604–1640* (Oxford, 1996), 150–1.
[26] Thomas Campion, *The Discription of a Maske* (London, 1607), nos. II, III, V.
[27] Ibid., sig. C2.   [28] John Dowland, *The First Booke of Songs or Ayres* (London, 1597), sig. L2.
[29] Trumbull MS, fo. 32.   [30] Tobias Hume, *The First Part of Ayres* (London, 1605), no. 111.

The Lute in Consort

Of the lute-duet manuscript sources listed in Table 6.2 three are pre-eminent: Dd.3.18, Marsh, and Pickeringe. A further six manuscripts are important: Brogyntyn, Folger, Sampson, Trumbull, Board, and Ballet.[31] Dd.3.18 contains 109 compositions, including thirty-six duet trebles. Nordstrom suggests that Dd.3.18 was started earlier than the solo books in Holmes's hand as a collection of duet trebles, and that it was continually added to over a period of some twenty years.[32] Nordstrom divides the book into twelve sections, six of which contain trebles. The twelve sections are divided into those that contain mostly: consort lute parts; a mixture of duet trebles and consort parts; solos; equal duets; pieces for three orpharions. Most of the duet trebles in the opening section of the manuscript are either by John Johnson or are attributed to him by Nordstrom. Among the pieces in the second section is a unique treble by Ellis Lawrey entitled 'The Marygolde'.[33] Most of the trebles lack grounds, probably because they were so simple and well known. Lawrey's piece has its ground as it is more extended than most. The last sections with trebles include pieces by Cutting and Danyel. Many of the trebles in Dd.3.18 are unique. Of those for which concordances can be found, the Dd.3.18 versions are generally the most complete, and sometimes contain sections which are either absent or incorrect in other sources.

Like the earlier sections of Dd.3.18, the Marsh manuscript also dates from the 1580s, and contains many treble duets and no equal duets. Of the fifteen duet trebles, eight are by Johnson (including two versions of 'Goodnight'), and a further five are attributed to him by Nordstrom. All the eight Johnson pieces are found in some form in Dd.3.18, and some four of the possible Johnson pieces are unique to the Marsh manuscript. The Marsh manuscript contains a number of grounds for the bandora. Certainly the instrument was used as an alternative to a second lute to accompany lute trebles. Eleven of the trebles are placed together in one section of the manuscript.

The Pickeringe lute book probably dates from after 1600, and opens with a balanced group of seven equal duets and seven treble-and-ground duets. The selection of treble-and-ground duets contains popular favourites of an older generation. None is unique and none is excessive in length or technical demands. The book begins with the less antiquated equal duets, the first four of which are probably by Johnson, and all of which appear to have achieved some degree of popularity, to judge by manuscript concordances. In several cases the two parts cannot both be played together from the manuscript as they are written on different openings. Most probably this collection of fourteen pieces was copied as an entity from a friend's or a teacher's book. One senses that by the beginning of the seventeenth century the

[31] Lyle Nordstrom, 'The English Lute Duet', 5–6.
[32] Nordstrom, 'The Cambridge Consort Books', 73.   [33] Dd.3.18, fo. 23ʳ.

lute duet was no longer a form that interested lutenist-composers. Useful in teaching, it had become the preserve of the amateur.

Two Willoughby manuscript 'Qui passas' in different keys carry the note 'these tow qui passas agre one tow lutes the one set foure notes above the other'. The line alerts the player to the possibility of performing two solos based on the same ground as a duet on lutes a fourth apart.[34] The practice of creating duets, or possibly even trios, out of the simultaneous playing of different versions of standard grounds is lent support in the line in Holborne's *The Cittharn Schoole* (1597) where he states, 'I have conioyned the most usuall and familiar grounds of these our times, for consort or thine owne private selfe'.[35] Here the support of the bass viol is particularly needed as the cittern's tuning makes it impossible for it to play the bass line properly.

John Johnson's influence on the English lute duet cannot be overestimated. His duets were still being played and circulated decades after his death. Nordstrom, in his study of Johnson's duets, lists sixteen attributed pieces, and identifies a further sixteen that on stylistic grounds are likely to be by him.[36] Nordstrom's seven points of style characteristic of Johnson are: idiomatic use of all the resources of the lute; the exploration of the instrument's full range from the lowest notes on the sixth course to the highest note on the top string (g''); the preference for the high frets on the lowest three courses to contrast the octave stringing of these courses with the unison stringing of the upper courses; echo effects at the octave; cross-relations; triplets towards the close; extended sets of divisions. The trebles of 'Green Garters', the 'Short Almain 1', and 'The New Hunts Up' are long and virtuosic, and may reflect the material played by the royal lute consort. Example 6.1 exemplifies some of Johnson's points of style, particularly the exploitation of the full range of the lute (bar 49 descends to the lowest note on the lute, bar 62 ascends to the highest), echo effects (bars 49, 50, 63), and cross-relations (bars 55–6). It is interesting that the sources of this piece disagree on how to notate the two highest notes in bar 62. Dd.2.11 and the Marsh manuscript have them as 'm' and 'l'; the Welde manuscript as 'n' and 'l'; the Trumball manuscript as 'n' and 'm'. I believe they all imply the pitches g'' and f'' and that the confusion resulted from the fact that added frets on the belly of the lute to facilitate these notes had yet to be invented at the time of compostion.

No identifiable composer other than Johnson contributed significantly to the genre of the treble-and-ground duet. Stylistically Johnson's pieces are more diverse, varied, and less predictable than those of any other. Richard Allison's two

---

[34] Willoughby MS, nos. 36 and 37 for g' and d' lutes, fos. 83ᵛ–85ʳ.

[35] Anthony Holborne, *The Cittharn Schoole* (London, 1597), Preface to the Reader. I am grateful to Stewart McCoy for this suggestion.

[36] Lyle Nordstrom, 'The Lute Duets of John Johnson', *JLSA* 9 (1976), 30–42.

Ex. 6.1. '*The New Hunt is Up*' (*fourth variation of nine*), (a) *treble from Dd.3.18, fo. 13ᵛ;* (b) *ground from Marsh MS, p. 186, bars 48–63*

Ex. 6.1. *cont.*

1. Tablature letters altered to *n m n* as in the
Trumbull MS. fo.15ᵛ .

surviving duet trebles exist in versions for mixed consort. The 'Sharp Pavan' achieved some popularity, but it is conceivable that the Allison duets, like others in the repertoire, are anonymous arrangements of existing pieces for mixed consort or solo lute.[37] The Pickeringe version of Allison's 'Sharp Pavan' may suggest this in the manuscript note 'the treble to the pavinge of allasons'.[38] Robinson's modest trebles are pedagogical in purpose, and two are fully fingered for the left hand.[39] By 1603 when Robinson produced his book the genre may have seemed archaic, and suitable more for developing technical proficiency rather than musical expression.

The link with teaching is even stronger with equal duets. Many of the lighter duet pieces such as 'La rosignoll', 'An Allman/Eccho', and 'A merry moode' are simply exercises in 'reporting style'. In these pieces the alternation of roles between the two lutes of treble and accompaniment is rapid, and the musical material is swapped with little or no alteration. In 'An Allman/Eccho' the alternation of material is every two or four bars (see Ex. 6.2). Even the few fantasias for lute duet follow this pattern. Equal-duet pieces make excellent pedagogical exercises, as the pupil is able to copy the articulation and phrasing of the teacher.

The English duet repertoire is closely related to that of the mixed consort. Many pieces exist in versions for both combinations, and many of the sources that contain duets (Dd.3.18, Marsh, Folger, and Trumbull manuscripts in particular) also have lute-consort parts. Nordstrom put forward the plausible theory that the duet treble of the 1570s and 1580s gave rise to the consort lesson.[40] According to this theory the potential monotony of the ground was relieved by alternative instrumentation. The Marsh manuscript contains bandora grounds. Further instruments could join in—the bass viol on the bass line and the treble viol with a melody on top. With a larger ensemble, bipartite and tripartite dances were found to be more suitable, as the parts then had two or three sections of different material instead of one, and the lute could vary the sections by playing treble-line divisions on the repeats of each section.

Further expansion of the ensemble occurred with the addition of the cittern to supplement the harmonic framework supplied by the bandora, and the flute to play an inner part sounding an octave higher than written. The use of the flute in this way was known in France as early as the 1530s, and may well have been known in England. The lute then made the crucial move from doubling the soprano line in its upper part to playing a second inner line. In its mature form the music of the mixed consort can be divided into four parts. The soprano line is taken by the treble viol and the bass by the bass viol. Inner parts are taken by the flute and the lute

---

[37] *The Solo Lute Music of Richard Allison*, ed. John Robinson and Stewart McCoy, with a biographical sketch by Robert Spencer (Lute Society, Oldham, 1995), p. iii.

[38] Pickering MS, fo. 12[r].

[39] Robinson, *The Schoole of Musicke*: 'The Queenes good Night'; 'Twenty waies upon the bels'.

[40] Nordstrom, 'The English Lute Duet'.

Ex. 6.2. *'An Almain/ Eccho' for two lutes by Francis Pilkington/ Mr Marchant: (a) Lute 1, Brogyntyn, p. 31; (b) Lute 2, Sampson MS, fo. 11ᵛ, bars 15–20*

1. All the notes in this bar have been editorially altered to match the *Sampson* MS part.

(with its own supporting harmonies on the opening statements of the multi-partite dances, and divisions on the repeats). The cittern and bandora add rhythm and harmonic support, with the bandora doubling the bass with its bottom line.

Characteristic of the mature style of mixed consort pieces is the contrasting of different instrumental groupings. This is especially so in the last section of pavans and galliards where the lute and treble viol often answer each other in 'reporting style'. Nordstrom's contention is that this answering or echoing between pairs or groups of instruments is then mimicked in the equal duet. Thus the answering devices of so many equal duets developed out of the imitation found in mixed consort music. Possible examples of consort lessons being rearranged as equal-lute duets are 'Duncomb's Galliard', 'Squires Galliard', and the 'De La Tromba Pavan'. Where pieces exist in arrangements for several different genres the process of interactive development is difficult to disentangle and may only be guessed. Examples of this are Johnson's 'Flat Pavan' and Allison's 'De la Tromba Pavan', which exist in versions for solo lute, duet lutes, and for mixed consort.

John Johnson's 'Flat Pavan' is a fascinating example. Possibly the earliest form of this piece was the solo version in C minor as it exists in early sources (Giles Lodge and Dallis). It was from this that the treble-and-ground version in F minor probably developed, of which only the treble survives. These two forms were probably in circulation by the early 1580s.[41] The piece was expanded into a consort lesson in G minor by 1588 as the Walsingham consort books include the piece, and it was referred to in Anthony Munday's *A Banquet of Daintie Conceits* (1588), where one of his verses was to be 'sung after the note of the flat Pavin, which is playd in Consorte'. Probably the earliest consort version had the lute part following the tune, and such a lute part exists in the Folger manuscript.[42] At some point an alternative lute part developed within the consort arrangement, with the lute playing a line more independent of the tune.[43] Finally an equal-duet version developed in F minor that incorporated elements of the consort piece.[44] Suprisingly, an alternative treble-and-ground duet version appears in the Trumbull manuscript in G minor, which Nordstrom suggests could be played within the context of the consort.[45] (See Ex. 6.3.)

Nordstrom points to the 'De La Tromba Pavan' as a seminal piece. The piece takes its name from the trumpet-like answering phrases between viol and lute in the last section. A plausible line of development might have started with composition as a mixed-consort piece in the 1580s in the version found in the Cambridge and Walsingham part-books. An alternative to the treble viol part is provided in Dd.3.18, so that the answering is now between a pair of lutes within the consort.[46]

---

[41] Solo versions is Giles Lodge, Dallis, Dd.2.11, and Euing; treble in Dd.3.18.
[42] Folger MS, fo. 10ʳ.
[43] Trumbull MS, fo. 10ʳ.
[44] Trumbull MS, fo. 15ʳ, Pickeringe MS, fos. 4ᵛ–5ʳ.
[45] Nordstrom, 'The English Lute Duet', 15.
[46] Dd.3.18, fos. 45ᵛ–46ʳ.

This version is then the basis for a lute duet in which the trumpet calls are passed from one lute to another. The final version as published by Morley follows not the original consort version, but the lute-duet version, now with answering returned to lute and viol. Tromba effects are found in the final section of three of the Richard Reade pavans (nos. 2, 7, and 9), and it may be that Reade and his Oxford circle developed this technique with a didactic purpose in mind.

Ex. 6.3. *Comparison of versions of the 'Flat Pavan' by John Johnson, bars 1–4:* (a) *solo version from Dallis MS, p. 92;* (b) *duet version, Pickeringe MS, fos. 4ᵛ–5ʳ;* (c) *consort version from Walsingham consort books (bandora part from the Browne MS) with lute part from Folger MS, fo. 10ʳ, and an alternative lute part from Trumbull, fo. 10ʳ*

Ex. 6.3. *cont.*

There are four surviving sets of part-books for the English mixed consort which are purely instrumental: two in manuscript and two published. (See Table 6.3.) The fact that the two manuscript collections are earlier than the published ones may reflect the shift in the period 1580–1600 from the consort being associated with aristocratic private entertainments to association with waits and theatre musicians. Of the manuscript sources the Walsingham part-books are probably the earlier of the two, as two pieces are dated 1588.

Four books from the Walsingham set survive, and are marked 'for the treble viol', 'for the flute', 'for the cittern', and 'for the base viole'. The cittern book is in Mills

Ex. 6.3. *cont.*

Table 6.3. *The sources of English mixed-consort music*

A. PART-BOOK SETS

Walsingham Consort Books (1588)
    Treble viol: Brynmor Jones Library, Hull University, MS DDHO/20/1
    Flute: Brynmor Jones Library, Hull University, MS DDHO/20/2
    Bass Viol: Brynmor Jones Library, Hull University, MS DDHO/20/3
    Cittern: Mills College, Oakland, California

Cambridge Consort Books (*c*.1588–92)
    Bass viol: *GB-Cu* Dd.5.20
    Cittern: *GB-Cu* Dd.14.24
    Lute: *GB-Cu* Dd.3.18
    Recorder: *GB-Cu* Dd.5.21 (also contains some parts for flute and some for violin)

Thomas Morley, *The First Booke of Consort Lessons* (1599)
    Flute: *GB-Och* Mus 805 (olim K.4.19)
    Cittern: *GB-Ob* Douce MM.410
    Bandora: *GB-Och* Mus 806 (olim K.4.20)
    Bass viol: *GB-Lbl* K.1.i.21

Philip Rosseter, *Lessons for Consort* (1609)
    Cittern: *GB-Lcm* II.E.43 (lacking sig.C4)
    Lute: *GB-Ob* Mus 157 b.I (fragments only)
    Flute: *US-NYp* Drexel 5433.5

Thomas Morley, *The First Booke of Consort Lessons* (1611)
    Flute: *GB-Lbl* K.1.i.7
    Treble viol: *GB-Lcm* II.E.40 (copy also in *US-NYp*)
    Bandora: Henry E. Huntington Library, San Marino, California

B. LUTE AND BANDORA SOURCES CONTAINING CONSORT PARTS

Ballet: 1 lute consort part
Board: 1 lute consort part
Folger: 2 consort parts
Euing: 1 consort lute part
Schele: 2 consort lute parts
Königsberg: 2 bandora and 2 lute consort parts
Trumbull: 2 lute consort parts
Browne: 35 bandora consort parts
Dd.9.33: 1 lute consort part
Sampson: 1 lute consort part

College, Oakland, California, and was available to Beck and his predecessors in the field, but the find by Gwilym Beechey of the other three books in the 1960s greatly increased the surviving repertoire. The Walsingham books list thirty-four consort pieces copied out by what is now generally agreed to be the young Daniel Bacheler's elegant and remarkably error-free hand (see above, Pl. 5.2*b*). Bacheler was working as a page and apprenticed musician in the household of Sir Francis Walsingham in 1588. Two of the pieces mentioned in the contents list do not appear in any of the four books, and some pieces are present in only some of the books. Seven titles in the books refer to members of the Walsingham family—Sir Francis himself, Lady Walsingham his wife, and Lady Frances Sidney (the daughter who had been married to the poet and national hero, Sir Philip Sidney, from 1583 until his death at Zutphen in 1586).

The seven surviving consort pieces by Bacheler are found only in the Walsingham books.[47] As there is no lute book to the collection, and his pieces are all *unica*, we cannot be sure what Bacheler's lute writing for the mixed consort was like. In reconstructing the lost lute parts Warwick Edwards follows the style of Richard Allison, as he says Bacheler adopts 'many of the textures used by Allison'.[48] A further piece, 'The Lady Francis Sidney's Goodnight', is ascribed to Bacheler in the Walsingham books, but in the Morley consort collection and the Browne manuscript (formerly Braye Bandora and Lyra-Viol manuscript) it is ascribed to Richard Allison and called 'Response Pavan'. The confusion over this title and attribution, and the fact that the Walsingham collection contains thirteen out of the surviving total of eighteen consort pieces composed or set by Allison, has led to the suggestion that Allison and Bacheler worked together at this time, and that Allison may have also been attached to the Walsingham household.[49] Edwards goes so far as to suggest that Bacheler may have filled in the 'rhythm' parts to Allison's 'Response Pavan'.[50]

The other manuscript set, the Cambridge part-books copied by Mathew Holmes in Oxford in the years 1588–97, is discussed in Chapter 3 in relation to solo-lute music and duets. There is every indication that the consort books of the set were at least in part produced for the purpose of teaching the Christ Church choristers instrumental skills. Ian Payne's work on instrumental teaching provision at English cathedral churches makes it clear that the sixteenth-century letters patent of some cathedral organists included responsibility for the teaching of choristers, and perhaps other boys from the grammar schools, to play musical instruments. By the late sixteenth century this responsibility was often delegated to specially qualified lay clerks.[51] At Christ Church, Mathew Holmes, as precentor, had responsibility for all the singing; but another individual, the *informator*, was responsible for their general instruction, which included learning instruments. One of those who had this role

---

[47] Warwick A. Edwards, 'The Walsingham Consort Books', *M&L* 55 (1974), 209–14.
[48] *Music for Mixed Consort*, ed. Warwick A. Edwards (MB 40; London, 1977), p. xviii.
[49] Allison, *The Solo Lute Music*, p. viii.   [50] Edwards, 'The Walsingham Consort Books', 214.
[51] Payne, *Provision and Practice*, 134. There is some evidence that at Ely lutes and other plucked instruments were involved. The will of Edward Watson (1587), an Ely lay clerk, and possibly also the choristers' teacher of instruments, includes 'al my books for the Citteren, virginalls, bandora or lute'.

while Holmes was at Christ Church was the singing man John Mathew.[52] Mathew's 1602 probate inventory included eleven lutes valued together at £3 6s. 8d., and a chest of viols at £4.[53] These were cheap lutes even for the time and surely must have served for pedagogical purposes. I would suggest that Holmes was not just the scribe who prepared the books for the boys, but also selected the pieces, helped in their arrangement, and maintained the books. It may also be that he took the consort books with him to Westminster in 1597 with the intention of using them with the choirboys there.

The four surviving books are for cittern, bass viol, recorder, and lute; the bandora and violin books are missing. The cittern book is also important as a source of solo cittern music.[54] The recorder book has two pages of pieces labelled 'treble violan'. These pieces, accidentally copied into the wrong book, plus the several pictures of mixed consorts using violins, is the sum total of evidence for a violin being used instead of a treble viol, though Holman argues that the term 'viol' includes violin and viol.[55] The fact that this book is specified as 'the recorder parte' is the only instance among the sources for the replacement of the usual flute by the recorder. In some pieces a flute part is present as an alternative to the recorder. The Walsingham flute book calls for an instrument with a nominal range from *d* to *c'*. Most of the pieces could be played by a bass flute (lowest note *g*) at the written pitch, or by a tenor (lowest note *d'*) sounding an octave higher than written. Such a flute may be indicated by the moderately sized flutes in the pictures. A comparison of the flute part clefs used by Morley, Rosseter, and in the Walsingham books (alto and tenor), and that of the Cambridge recorder book (treble), plus the octave displacement that is discernable in concordant pieces, suggests that the Cambridge recorder book was for a tenor recorder. The octave displacements were to keep the recorder in its more unobtrusive lower range.[56]

Among the pieces in Holmes's four consort books there are quite a number for which parts are absent for one or more of the instruments, and in several pieces, for example 'Alysons Pauen', only the lute part survives. This may suggest that not all the pieces were for the full consort of six. The lute book (Dd.3.18) contains some sixty possible consort parts in addition to the duet trebles. As no lute book survives from the other sets, apart from the Bodleian Rosseter fragments, and consort lute parts from solo sources are few and often poor, this book is of vital importance to our knowledge of mixed-consort music. The book supplies lute parts to many of the pieces in the other collections, and the models for those that have to be reconstructed. Apart from the consort lute parts with no other surviving parts, there are

[52] My thanks to Ian Harwood for passing this information on to me.

[53] Michael Fleming, 'Some Points Arising from a Survey of Wills and Inventories', *GSJ* 53 (2000), 301–11 at 301.

[54] Ward, 'Sprightly and Cheerful Musick', 137–41. Nordstrom, 'The Cambridge Consort Books', 97–100.

[55] Holman, *Four and Twenty Fiddlers*, 136–7. [56] Nordstrom, 'The Cambridge Consort Books', 79.

pieces that may be duos or trios, and some lute parts that are simply repeated in the manuscript.

Of the four sets, the Holmes consort books contain the greatest diversity of piece types. The most frequently attributed composer is Richard Reade. Reade's attributions in Dd.3.18 includes twenty-four consort pieces, and four duets which, from comments in the book, appear to be intended for a trio of three wire-strung instruments (orpharions are mentioned), doubled by viols. Though no third tablature exists to expand these duets into trios, the third part may have been included in the lost bandora book.[57] Reade, a Christ Church singing man, received his B.Mus. degree on 7 July 1592. As he is never given this title by Holmes, it has been suggested that all the consort pieces attributed to him, and indeed most of Holmes's consort collection, were put together in the years 1588–92.[58] It seems that Holmes's meeting with Reade, together with the fact that Reade was evidently prepared to provide and arrange music for mixed consort, was the spur that got the Christ Church mixed consort project launched. Reade was evidently considered something of an expert on instruments as he was one of the appraisers of the will of Robert Mallet in 1612. Mallet combined being manciple of St Edmund Hall, Oxford, with being an instrument maker with a specialization in wire-strung instruments.[59]

Morley's *The First Booke of Consort Lessons* of 1599 is arguably the most influential source of the genre. It was reprinted in 1611, eight years after Morley's death, in a 'newly corrected and inlarged' edition published by John Brown, which argues strongly for its commercial success.[60] The title-page of the 1599 edition acknowledges the lessons were 'made by divers exquisite Authors', and that they were 'Newly set forth at the coast & charges of a Gentle-man, for his private pleasure, and for divers others his frendes which delight in Musicke'. None of the 'divers exquisite Authors' are named, but in his dedication to the Lord Mayor, Morley says the lessons are 'some few fruites of perfection of the most perfect men in their quality'. He says also that he has kept the composers' best interests at heart '. . . whose works that I might not abase in devoting them to a meane patron, nor abuse the workers in ioyning them discordes for their true descant'. Morley is at pains to say how carefully he has prepared the pieces, '. . . and not to disgrace my care and travaile, which at the instant request of my very good friend have beene very carefull, truly to set them out'.

It was suggested by Dart and Beck that the 'Gentleman' who paid the printing expenses was Richard Allison.[61] Robert Spencer rejects this idea for a number of

---

[57] Nordstrom, 'The Cambridge Consort Books', 95.   [58] Ibid. 77.

[59] Fleming, 'Some Points Arising', 302. Mallet's 'workhouse' held some furniture and '4 Orpharions, 5 Citternes whereof one in a case, 2 citternes unfinisht, a flatbackt lute & case, 2 chists, working tooles, with divers lumber', valued together at £5. 4s. 4d.

[60] Ward, 'Sprightly and Cheerful Musick', 30.

[61] *The First Book of Consort Lessons Collected by Thomas Morley 1599–1611*, ed. Sydney Beck (New York, 1959), 2; Thurston Dart, 'Morley's Consort Lessons of 1599', *PRMA* 74 (1947–8), 1–9.

reasons. Allison claimed the right to call himself a gentleman through inheritance, but was by his own admission 'a poore man'. He had been apprenticed to (or had served in the household of) Sir Ambrose Dudley, Earl of Warwick before 1589/90, and was not the dedicatee of Morley's *First Booke*.[62] Even if Allison was not Morley's sponsor, his musical contribution to the work outweighs that of any other. The first edition contained twenty-three pieces, five of which were by Allison, and the 1611 edition a further two new pieces, both by Allison. Five of these pieces, 'De La Tromba', 'Allisons Knell', 'Go from my window', 'The Batchelor's Delight', and 'Response Pavin', are among the most weighty and elaborate of the twenty-five, especially so in the case of the last two from the 1611 book. These pieces are different from the rest of the collection in that they were probably conceived first for mixed consort, rather than arranged from originals for other media.

The rest of the pieces in *The First Booke* appear to be either Morley's arrangements of existing works by known composers, Dowland (5), Byrd (2), Phillips (2), Nicolas Strogers (1); popular pieces (like 'Lavolto' and 'La Coranto'); popular songs arranged by Morley; or rearrangements of existing pieces by Morley. Among the songs is 'O Mistresse Mine', the melody of which is attributed to Morley, but which appears in a keyboard arrangement in *FVB* attributed to Byrd.[63] This melody is traditionally linked with verses from Shakespeare's *Twelfth Night*, though this has been challenged. The Shakespeare link with this setting started and maintained much of the interest in the mixed consort earlier in the last century, and attracted sponsorship for Beck's 1959 edition of *The First Booke*. 'Joyne hands' is a reworking of Morley's three-voice canzonet, 'See, mine own sweet jewel'. 'Sola Soletta' is an arrangement of a popular Italian madrigal by Girolamo Conversi 'Englished' to the words 'When al alone my bony love was playing'.[64]

In general Morley places the larger and more difficult pieces among the first twelve items in the *First Booke*, and then progresses to the simpler and more popular ones. The two Allison pieces added to the 1611 edition as numbers 24 and 25 are elaborate and far from simple. The cittern and bass viol books survive only from the 1599 edition. Apart from the lost lute book, copies of the other books (treble viol, bandora, and flute) survive from both editions. About a third of the pieces in *The First Booke* may be completed with lute parts from Holmes's manuscripts (mainly Dd.3.18), including five of Allison's seven.

Rosseter's *Lessons for Consort* (1609) has survived least well of all the sets.[65] Only the flute book has the complete twenty-five lessons. The cittern book has lost sig. C4 which contains nos. 22–5. Of the lute part, six fragments (from C2, D1, D2) have

[62] Allison, *The Solo Lute Music*, pp. ix, x.   [63] *FVB*, no. lxvi.
[64] *The First Book of Consort Lessons*, ed. Beck; see critical notes, 181–94.
[65] Ian Harwood, 'Rosseter's *Lessons for Consort* of 1609', *LSJ* 7 (1965), 15–23.

been recovered; C2 from a book binding in 1971. These turned out to contain parts of nos. 5–9. Referring to Morley's set, Rosseter says in his epistle to the reader that:

The good successes and francke entertainment which the late imprinted Set of Consort bookes generally received, hath given mee incouragement to second them with these my gatherings; most of the Songs being of their inventions whose memorie onely remaines, because I would be loth to rob any living men of the fruit of their owne labours, not knowing what private intent they may have to convert them to their more peculiar use. The Authours names I have severally prefixt, that every man might obtaine his right; And as for my industry in disposing them, I submit it to thy free censure.

In naming the authors Rosseter distances himself from Morley, who did not do so. Rosseter claims credit only for the arrangements of 'these flowers gathered out of diuers Gardens, and now by mee Consorted and divulged for the benefit of many'. Three of the pieces are by Rosseter himself. The other authors he names are: Allison (4), Anthony Holborne (4), Morley (3), John Baxter (2), Thomas Lupo (2), John Farmer (2), Dr Thomas Campion (1), Edmund Kete (1). Rosseter mentions in the epistle quoted above that most of the authors were dead by 1609. This is the clearest indication we have that Allison, who is last heard of in 1606, had died by 1609.[66]

Despite the loss of so much of the musical material from Rosseter's collection, both Harwood and Edwards working separately were able to reconstruct a majority of the lessons.[67] Like Morley's book, the pieces are a selection of dance-types, vocal music adaptations, and popular-tune arrangements. The book contains none of the newer dance forms (corantos or voltes), but does contain consort versions of two masque dances and a masque song. While it is difficult to make an assessment based on so little material, it seems that the collection contains fewer of the more elaborate pieces, such as those by Allison in the other sources, and includes more adaptations of popular tunes and songs. It also includes galliards that are musically related to 'Allisons Knell' and 'De la Tromba' pavans, at a time when matched pavans and galliards had ceased to be common.[68]

The existence of the English mixed consort in the period 1570–1610 is of great significance in the development of the lute in England. The lute is central to the ensemble. It is Nordstrom's contention that it was as an extension of lute music, especially of the duet, that an ensemble developed to include viol (or violin), lute, flute (or recorder), bass viol, cittern, and bandora. Membership of the consort was important in the development of other instruments in the sextet. The involvement of the violin may have been the instrument's first separation from its traditional role as the soprano member of the violin consort.[69] The need for a cittern and bandora

[66] Allison, *The Solo Lute Music*, pp. x–xi.
[68] I am grateful to Ian Harwood for this point.
[67] Harwood, 'Rosseter's *Lessons for Consort*', 21.
[69] Holman, *Four and Twenty Fiddlers*, 132.

to complete the group would have increased the numbers of them being made, and in the case of the bandora its association as a peculiarly 'English instrument' at this time would have received more prominence.

The ensemble is an important early landmark in the history of instrumentation, since a variety of different but specific instruments were established as a fixed ensemble which composers and arrangers could exploit. Parts written in staff notation were occasionally transferred from one instrument to another—e.g. flute to recorder—but the three parts written in tablature (lute, bandora, cittern) were untransferable. While sets of like instruments may have been the norm throughout the Renaissance, there is plentiful reference to groupings of mixed instruments, especially towards the end of the sixteenth century.[70] As late as 1636 Charles Butler wrote: 'The several kinds of Instruments ar commonly used severally by them selves: as a Set of Viols, a Set of Waits [shawms], or the like: but sometimes, upon some special occasion, many of both Sorts ar most sweetly joined in Consort.'[71] The specific instrumentation of the English mixed consort is strikingly at variance with the principle of like groups or of freely mixed ensembles.

The 'Englishness' of the group of six instruments is important. It was known and admired on the Continent, where English cultural influence was strong. English musicians travelling and living abroad, often as members of theatrical companies, exported the concept of such an ensemble. The Königsberg manuscript contains a significant amount of English lute and bandora music, some of which are consort parts, that may have found its way to the Baltic area through the activities of just such expatriots. There was indeed an English theatrical troupe led by the musician and actor John Spencer based in Königsberg in the years 1604–18. When touring they advertised themselves as 'the Margrave of Brandenburg's servants, the English Comedians', and the Margrave took particular pleasure in Spencer's music.[72] The parallels with Shakespeare's travelling company of players in Hamlet are obvious.

Early seventeenth-century depictions and illustrations of the ensemble exist from the Low Countries and Germany (see Table 6.4).[73] The most famous description of an English consort is that given by Praetorius:

several persons with all sorts of instruments, such as clavicymbal or large spinett, large lyra, double harp, lute, theorbo, bandora, penorcon, cittern, viola de gamba, a small descant fiddle, a traverse flute or recorder, sometimes also a quiet sackbut or racket, sound together

[70] Ernst H. Meyer, *Early English Chamber Music* (2nd rev. edn. by Diana Poulton and the author, London, 1982), 142.
[71] Charles Butler, *The Principles of Musik in Singing and Setting* (London, 1636), 93; Holman, *Four and Twenty Fiddlers*, 131.
[72] Arthur J. Ness and John M. Ward, *The Königsberg Manuscript* (Columbus, Ohio, 1989), 10–11.
[73] *Music for Mixed Consort*, ed. Edwards, p. xxii; Holman, *Four and Twenty Fiddlers*, 137.

Table 6.4. *British and Continental mixed-consort iconography*

Picture	Date and place	Instrumentation
Painting, *Bal Henry III*, after Hieronymus Francken	1540–1610, location unknown	lute, harp, bass viol, violin, cornett, violin, violin, flute
Painting by Lodewyk Toeput (Pozzoserrato)	1550–1606, location unknown	lute, virginals, violin, flute, voices
Unton Memorial painting	1596, National Portrait Gallery	lute, cittern, bandora, violin, bass viol, flute
Frieze on wood panel	c.1575, Great Chamber, Gilling Castle, Yorkshire	lute, cittern, cittern, violin, tenor viol, bass viol
Ceiling painting	1599, Crathes Castle, Aberdeen	lute, violin, harp, bass viol, flute, cittern, clavichord
Engraving by Nicola de Bruyn after a painting by David Vinckboons	c.1601, Gemeentemuseum, The Hague	lute, bandora, violin, bass viol
Watercolour	1602, *album amicorum* of Cellarius of Nuremberg, GB-Lb Add. 27579, fo. 149ˢ	violone, lute, cittern, violin, bandora
Engravings, 'The Arches of Triumph', Stephen Harrison	printed London, 1604	Sig. Fᵛ: harp, violin, bass viol, guitar, small lute, wind band; Sig. Gʳ: voice, recorder, cittern, lyre, cornett, guitar, flute, lute, bass viol
Fresco	c.1610–20, staircase well, Knole, Kent	Group of bass viol, lute, cornett, flute, cittern, and music books
Carvings above fireplace	1603–8, Ballroom, Knole, Kent	lute and viol; lute, cittern, and recorders
Engraved frontispiece Nicolas Vallet	*Regia pietas* (1620),	lute, harp, bass viol, violon, flute, plus boy singer and gentleman obscured by lute

in one company and society ever so quietly, tenderly and lovely, and agree with each other in a graceful symphony.[74]

Praetorius' description includes the usual six instruments plus several others. He may have got his information second-hand, or heard a continentally based English group. In England, at any rate, the surviving musical sources show that the usual six members (with the possible variation of viol or violin, flute or recorder) were to be expected.

[74] Meyer, *Early English Chamber Music*, 143, trans. from Michael Praetorius, *Syntagma musicum* (Wolfenbüttel, 1618), iii. 5.

During the period of its popularity the ensemble was known simply as the 'consort'.[75] In his study of the genre, Warwick Edwards adopted the term 'mixed consort' for the group of six. He did so since the term 'consort' came to be generally used after 1600 for any group of instruments or voices, not specifically a mixed group. Edwards also found it preferable to the appellation 'broken consort', which was widely used last century. This term was never in use in Elizabethan/Jacobean times, but was used for an unrelated group in existence at the Restoration. The term 'broken music' was used by Shakespeare, Bacon, and others in the period before 1630, but refers to diminutions or divisions created by 'breaking' up larger notes into shorter ones.[76] As the lute divisions are a prominent feature of the music for the English mixed-consort music, such references may imply the presence of just such a mixed ensemble of six.

On the title-page of *The First Booke of Consort Lessons* (1599) Morley calls for '*the Treble Lute*, the pandora, the Cittern, the Base-Violl, the Flute & Treble-Violl'. While the type of cittern, pandora, and flute are not specified, the viols (bass and treble) are, as we would expect, referred to by size. The specification of lute as a 'Treble Lute' is something of a surprise, as in terms of tessitura the music would suggest a 'mean' or 'tenor' lute with a top string at a nominal *g'*. There are indications that in England in the period when mixed consort music and duets were popular, there was a particular type of lute associated with the single-line divisions found in such music.[77] A Hardwick manuscript of 1602 lists 'for a bandora 48s, treble lute 20s, bass vyoll 40s, treble vyoll 20s, for the chest to lay them, in 16s'.[78] This suggest the basis of a mixed consort at Hardwick, and it is interesting to note that the bandora was worth twice as much as the lute. In 1575 Francis Willoughby of Wollaton Hall wrote 'to know if Mr. Creme [in London] can find him any treble lutes fit for his purpose'.[79] Peter Forrester has suggested that the lute depicted in the painting *Death and the Maiden* at Stratford may be just such a treble lute.[80]

The Stratford *vanitas* (see Pl. 6.1) includes a lute that is similar to the one seen in the Rizzio engraving (see below, Pl. 13.1). Both instruments are small-bodied, with a long neck relative to the body. Indeed the neck/body joint is at exactly the octave position or 12th fret. Such a neck would facilitate the high fret positions required in many duet trebles and mixed-consort pieces. The small body would improve the response of the upper range of the instrument relative to the bass. This again would improve such a lute's audibility within a mixed consort. Treble lutes

---

[75] *Music for Mixed Consort*, ed. Edwards, p. xiii. See also Warwick A. Edwards, 'The Sources of Elizabethan Consort Music' (Ph.D. thesis, University of Cambridge, 1974), i. 36–57.

[76] e.g. Morley gives an example of a plainsong 'broken in division'. *A Plain and Easy Introduction*, ed. Harman, 178.

[77] Peter Forrester, 'An Elizabethan Allegory and some Hypotheses', *LSJ* 34 (1994), 11–14.

[78] Hardwick MS, 10a, for July 1602, quoted ibid. 13.

[79] *The Willoughby Lute Book*, [p. 2] of the introductory study.

[80] Forrester, 'An Elizabethan Allegory', 13. Doubts remain as to the authenticity of this painting.

PL. 6.1. *Death and the Maiden,* artist unknown. Shakespeare's
Birthplace Trust at Hall's Croft, Stratford-upon-Avon

were in use well into the seventeenth century, as there are several references to such
instruments being acquired for use in Caroline masques.

All the publications of sacred music with mixed consort presuppose a lute
pitched at nominal g' for the top course, as does the surviving instrumental music.
The vocal music with mixed consort is more helpful in establishing an actual workable pitch, and many of the sacred pieces would be unsingable at a pitch much
higher than modern pitch (i.e. $g' = 396$). However, Ian Harwood has suggested that
the instrumental mixed-consort music, though not the sacred published music,
would have been played on instruments pitched significantly higher—something

that may chime in with the specification of a 'treble lute' in the instrumental consort publications. Harwood's contention is that there were two pitch standards used in English instrumental music in the period around 1600, one roughly a tone lower than modern pitch (i.e. $g' = c.349$), and the other a fourth higher than that (i.e. $g' = c.494$).

Harwood bases his argument on inspection of existing instruments from the period, an analysis of the instrumental combinations listed in Tobias Hume's *Captaine Humes Poeticall Musicke* (1607), and the limitations of gut stringing.[81] Harwood suggests that the John Rose instrument in the possession of the Tollemache family of Helmingham Hall in Suffolk is not an orpharion as previously thought, but a bandora at the higher pitch standard. It seems that viols were made in large and small sizes corresponding to these different pitch standards. He refers to the work of Djilda Abbott and Ephraim Segerman, who concluded that the English cittern should be tuned an octave higher than usual, basing their arguments on the small size of the instrument described by Praetorius,[82] though Harwood only sanctions a cittern a fourth above low pitch. The range of a bass flute at the lower pitch standard would then encompass the lowest notes called for in mixed-consort flute parts.[83] Only three sizes of lute are ever mentioned: mean, treble, and bass. For Harwood the mean corresponds to a normal lute at low pitch, the treble to a smaller one a fourth above, and the bass to one a fourth below the mean.

Many writers on the mixed consort have been preoccupied with the connections between the ensemble and the theatre of the day, Thurston Dart and Sydney Beck particularly so.[84] Certainly the earliest apparent reference to the mixed consort is from the play *Jocasta* (1566) by George Gascoigne and Francis Kinwellmarsh. Before the first act there are directions for 'a doleful and straunge noyse of violles, Cythren, Bandurion and such like . . . [to] sounde for the dumme show'.[85] However, as Peter Holman points out, most early references to the mixed consort appear in descriptions of outdoor aristocratic entertainments, several for the queen on her summer progresses.[86] In this context a number of literary accounts survive, the most famous of which are: George Gascoigne's description of a spectacle at Kenilworth in 1575; Bernard Garter's report of a Norwich progress in 1578, part of which is quoted at the start of this chapter; Thomas Churchyard's description of a

[81] Ian Harwood, 'A Case of Double Standards? Instrumental Pitch in England *c.*1600', *EM* 9 (1981), 470–81.

[82] Djilda Abbott and Ephraim Segerman, 'Strings in the 16th and 17th Centuries', *GSJ* 27 (1974), 48–73; 'Gut Strings', *EM* 4 (1976), 430–7. Abbott and Segerman suggest a cittern tuned an octave above the normal pitch.

[83] Harwood, 'A Case of Double Standards?', 478.

[84] Dart, 'Morley's Consort Lessons of 1599'; *Two Consort Lessons Collected by Thomas Morley*, ed. Thurston Dart (London, 1957); *The First Book of Consort Lessons*, ed. Beck.

[85] Ward, 'Sprightly and Cheerful Musick', 22. According to John Stowe's *Annales* (1631), 869, the bandora was invented in 1562 by John Rose. The term 'bandurion' indicates a lack of familiarity with the name bandora, so early in its life.

[86] Holman, *Four and Twenty Fiddlers*, 132.

proposed entertainment as part of the same Norwich progress in 1578; and an anonymous description of an 'Honourable Entertainment . . . at Elvetham' in 1591.[87] While all accounts point to the usual combination of six instruments being heard, only the last is explicit: 'After this speech the Fairy Queene and her maides daunced about the Garden, singing a Song of six parts, with the musicke of an exquisite consort; wherein was the lute, pandora, base violl, citterne, treble viol and flute . . .'

A musician who seems to have been involved directly or indirectly with several of these early spectacles is Edward Johnson, who is not known to have been related to his famous contemporary John Johnson, but probably was. Edward Johnson was the leading musician employed by the Kytson family at Hengrave Hall, Suffolk in the 1570s.[88] Significantly, the Kytson household acquired a 'treable violen' in 1572, most probably for mixed-consort use.[89] It is likely that Johnson, who was paid 10s. in August 1575 'for his charge in awayting on my Lord of Leycester', was loaned to Robert Dudley, Earl of Leicester, for the Kenilworth event of July 1575. Two songs composed for the Elvetham entertainment were written by Edward Johnson, though they survive in settings for voices and viols.[90] It is clear from an inventory of Leicester's household drawn up in 1583 that most of the instruments required for a mixed consort were available to Johnson at Kenilworth.[91]

A section of the famous biographical portrait of Sir Henry Unton's life, now kept at the National Portrait Gallery, shows a banquet at Wadley Manor, the home of Sir Henry and his wife Dorothy. In front of the costumed masquers is a mixed-consort group sitting around a table (see Pl. 6.2). The picture is the only one from the period with the complete set of six instruments. The painting was commissioned by Dorothy after Unton's death in 1596, but the Wadley Manor scenes may record domestic events of the 1580s or even late 1570s. Unton was known to have been a competent musician,[92] and it has been suggested that the lute player in the mixed consort and the bass viol player in the viol consort scene are Sir Henry himself,[93] though this is surely unlikely.

The lute player in the Unton painting plays from a folio-sized book (normally 9″ × 14″) which is nearly twice the height of the quarto-sized books (normally 6.5″ × 8.5″) that all the other players use. This is consistent with the surviving music, where the lute part is normally much the longest, due to the elaborate divisions in

---

[87] See *The First Book of Consort Lessons*, ed. Beck, 15–17. The descriptions are from George Gascoigne, *The Princelye Pleasures* (London, 1576); Robert Laneham, *A letter* (London, 1575); Bernard Garter, *The Ioyful Receyving of the Queenes most excellent Maiestie into hir Highnesse Citie of Norwich* (London, 1578); Thomas Churchyard, *A Discourse of the Queenes Majesties Entertainment* (London, 1579); *The Honourable Entertainment . . . at Elvetham* (London, 1591).

[88] Price, *Patrons and Musicians*, 71–9.   [89] Holman, *Four and Twenty Fiddlers*, 125.

[90] Ibid. 133.   [91] *The First Book of Consort Lessons*, ed. Beck, 16 n. 49.   [92] Ibid. 18.

[93] Anthony Rooley, 'A Portrait of Sir Henry Unton', in *The Companion to Medieval and Renaissance Music*, ed. Tess Knighton and David Fallows (London, 1992), 85–92.

PL. 6.2. Detail from a painted wood panel depicting scenes from the life of Sir Henry Unton, 1557–96. London, National Portrait Gallery, no. 710

repeated sections. The larger size of the lute book may account for the fact that no lute book survives from the published books, apart from a few fragments of Rosseter's 1609 book that were recovered from bookbindings. In great houses where mixed consorts may have been heard, like Kenilworth, Hengrave, Wadley Manor, Sedbury, and Wollaton Hall, one might have expected servants or family members to have provided the easier parts such as the cittern and bass viol, and professional musicians from within or without the household to have played the more difficult parts, especially the lute part. When sets of books were acquired by households they would normally have bound each book into separate leather covers. The larger lute book may have been more likely to have been retained by professionals who had less money, would have needed more recourse to the music as it is much harder, and who it seems did not normally bind up their music into books. Thus the lute book may often have remained unbound and folded over, which would have accelerated its deterioration. Interestingly the Rosseter fragments are consistent with damage through folding over.

From its origins in the great houses of England, music for mixed ensembles was taken up by bands of town waits. These municipal musicians had their origin in the medieval bands of outdoor musicians, playing shawms and other 'haut instruments' to sound curfews and alarms, and to perform for civic functions. By the sixteenth century they also played quiet instruments, and augmented their municipal income by hiring their services out for private functions. It has been assumed that the mixed-consort music for the Norwich royal progress of 1578 involved the Norwich waits. There were only five Norwich waits at the time, but with Edward Johnson they would have been six, including a known lute player. When Edward Jefferies, one of the senior Norwich waits, died in 1617, he bequeathed most of the instruments necessary for the consort. Only the cittern was not mentioned in his will.[94]

The waits most associated with the mixed consort were the London Waits, whom Morley had in mind when publishing his *First Booke*. The work is dedicated to the Lord Mayor and Aldermen of the City of London, and includes the following:

But as the ancient custome is of this most honorable and renowned Cittie hath beene euer, to retaine and maintane excellent and expert Musitians, to adorne your Honors fauors, Feasts and solemne meetings: to those your Lordships Waits. after the commending these my Labors to your Honorable patronage: I recommend the same to your seruants carefull and skilfull handling:

The London Waits were available for private hire, and also performed in the playhouses.[95] They played for some of the court events in January 1600/1, which must have included the first performance of Shakespeare's *Twelfth Night*.[96] Yet the private households were also mentioned by Morley in reference to a gentleman sponsor. The book's title-page states that it was printed 'at the coast & charges of a Gentle-man, for his private pleasure, and for divers others his frendes which delight in Musicke'. The reprinting of Morley's collection in 1611 shows that the set of books achieved a degree of commercial success. One can reasonably suggest that there would have been provincial town waits who followed London fashions by adapting themselves into a mixed-consort band, and thus would have wanted to buy Morley's books.

Discussion of the musical activities of the London Waits in plays leads to the use of the mixed consort by English theatre companies. Mention has already been made of the exporting of the consort abroad through theatre companies. Beck's thesis is that, as theatre companies proliferated, and as more public theatre houses were

[94] Lasocki, 'Professional Recorder Players', i. 237; ii. 734–5.
[95] *The First Book of Consort Lessons*, ed. Beck, 3, 22.   [96] Holman, *Four and Twenty Fiddlers*, 138.

opened, companies relied less on musical actors like Will Kemp and Robert Armin, and more on professional musicians who organized themselves into a 'house band' playing as a mixed consort.[97] There is little surviving evidence to support this idea, and some actors certainly continued to play instruments. There are wills and inventories of actors like Augustine Phillips and Edward Alleyn, which include near complete sets of mixed-consort instruments.[98] In 1598 an inventory for the Admiral's Men had a treble viol, bass viol, bandora, cittern, also three trumpets, a drum, sackbut, chime of bells, three timbrels, and two rackets.

While the employment of music and musicians in the Elizabethan and Jacobean theatre was expected by the audience, the amount varied greatly. The private theatres—like Blackfriars with a tradition of boy players—normally used more music than the public companies, and one report mentions a mixed consort of sorts heard at the Blackfriars in 1602.[99] Schools like St Paul's taught boys to play and sing, and their skills were widely used. In 1609 Philip Rosseter published his *Lessons for Consort*, and became responsible for the troupe, which received a royal patent in that year under the name of 'The Children of the Queen's Revels'.[100] He combined being a royal lutenist (from 1604 to his death in 1623) with an interest in this company in its many manifestations until around 1620. The *Lessons* were dedicated to Sir William Gascoyne of Sedbury Hall, who according to Rosseter had a household which maintained 'such as can lively express them'. In this it seems that Rosseter had private households more in mind for his books, though he clearly had professional interests and connections in the London theatre world as well.

It would be fitting to imagine that Rosseter would have taught his boys to perform mixed-consort music from his books. There are other references that link mixed consorts with children. The Headmaster of the English College of St-Omer, Pas-de-Calais (1600–17) included mixed consorts when describing the musical activities of the school.[101] There are circumstances linking the compilation of the Cambridge consort books with the instrumental tuition of the Christ Church choristers. One must also register that the young Daniel Bacheler (aged 16) spent time in his youth concerning himself with mixed-consort music. And surely he must have played what he arranged and composed.

Public-theatre musicians were usually seated in a special box or music room. In the case of the Globe Theatre it was a rectangular space some 8 by 12 feet on the third stage or tier up—about 23 feet above the stage. The open side of the room facing the audience was crossed by a railing, and was screened by a thin curtain which

[97] *The First Book of Consort Lessons*, ed. Beck, 13.

[98] Ibid. A bass viol, lute, cittern, and pandora are among items left to fellow actors by Augustine Phillips of the King's Company. Alleyn's will, bequeathing a lute, pandora, cittern, and six viols, may have been faked (see Ward, 'Sprightly and Cheerful Musick', 34).

[99] Holman, *Four and Twenty Fiddlers*, 136. [100] Jeffreys, *The Life and Works of Philip Rosseter*, 27.

[101] John H. Long, *Shakespeare's Use of Music* (Gainesville, Fla., 1961), 32.

was usually closed while the musicians performed in the music room. The area could take up to six or eight persons with instruments. On occasion musicians might be needed on stage, in which case they would have to descend, but normally they were used for scene or mood setting, for providing dance music, song accompaniments, or incidental music before or after plays, or between acts—all of which could be done *in situ*.[102]

A rather more unusual venue for the music of the mixed consort may have been on board ship. Musicians were often recruited for long voyages in Elizabethan times. Sir Francis Drake, for example, included nineteen musicians plus sixteen trumpeters among the large fleet of twenty-seven ships and 2,500 men that sailed for the West Indies in 1595. Ian Woodfield suggests that the eleven musicians taken by Drake himself comprised a five-part wind ensemble and a mixed consort of six. A chest of instruments removed from the *Defiance* contained a lute and 'hobboyes sagbutes cornettes and orpharions bandora and suche like', suggesting that they probably had the resources to make up a mixed consort.[103]

With information linking the mixed consort to both the public and private theatre, it is frustrating that it is impossible to locate references that specify the instrumentation of consorts used in plays.[104] Shakespeare uses the term 'broken music' in several plays, and many authors refer to music from a 'consort'. Instruments called for in stage directions in the plays of Shakespeare include lutes, viols, fiddles, and recorders. Other instruments are asked for on occasion: shawms, pipe and tabor, cornetts, sackbuts, rustic instruments (e.g tongs and bones), rebec, fiddle, racket, hunting horn, and trumpets. There are a number of play references to the sounding of instruments with wires, and a few plays by Shakespeare's contemporaries specifically mention the cittern.[105] The overall impression of Elizabethan and Jacobean stage directions is not that a stable consort of the six instruments of Morley and Rosseter's books was expected, but that, as today, music and instrumentation were varied according to the needs and budget of each production. Though plays of this period do not contain large amounts of music, at least as compared with the Restoration period, where there is music, it is often crucial to the action. As the theatre developed it seems that theatre music became more important, especially after the setting up of the Blackfriars theatre.

Among composers of English mixed consort Richard Allison is outstanding (see Table 6.5). His pieces are found in all the four mixed-consort sets of books. His role in the development of the genre can be compared to that of John Johnson with the lute duet. Allison's consort pieces were popular throughout the period from which

---

[102] Long, *Shakespeare's Use of Music*, 32.

[103] Ian Woodfield, *English Musicians in the Age of Exploration* (Stuyvesant, NY, 1995), 13.

[104] Ward, 'Sprightly and Cheerful Musick', 34.

[105] Ibid. 7, 35; *The First Book of Consort Lessons*, ed. Beck, 14.

Table 6.5. *Pieces for mixed consort in the four part-book collections*

Note: In general titles and names have been standardized and modernized. I have not indicated the many instances where missing parts can be supplied from among the four collections, or from other sources.
L = lute, T = viol/violin, F = flute, R = recorder, V =bass viol, B = bandora, C = cittern

A. WALSINGHAM CONSORT BOOKS

1. The Lady Frances Sidney's Goodmorrow [Richard Allison] (FCV)
2. Sir Frances Walsingham's Goodnight [Daniel Bacheler] (TFCV)
3. Sir Frances Walsingham's Goodmorrow [Daniel Bacheler] (TFCV)
4. The Lady Frances Sidney's Goodnight [Richard Allison] (TFCV)
5. The Lady Frances Sidney's Felicity [Daniel Bacheler] (TFCV)
6. Sharp Pavan [Richard Allison] (TFCV)
7. Phillip's Pavan [Peter Philips] (TFCV)
8. The Lady Walsingham's Conceits [Daniel Bacheler] (TFCV)
9. Delight Pavan [John Johnson] (TFCV)
10. Daniel's Trial [Daniel Bacheler] (TFCV)
11. Pavan Dolorosa [Richard Allison] (TFCV)
12. Mr Allison's Knell [Richard Allison] (TFCV)
13. The Bachiler's Delight [Richard Allison] (TFCV)
14. Daniel's Almayne [Daniel Bacheler] (TFCV)
15. The Widow's Mite [Daniel Bacheler] (TFCV)
16. Mr. Allison's Almain [Richard Allison] (TFCV)
17. Squire's Galliard (TFCV)
18. The Lady Frances Sidney's Almain [Richard Allison] (TFCV)
19. The Queen's Dance (FCV)
20. The Battle Pavan (FCV)
21. Proveribus (FCV)
22. The Spanish measure set by Richard Allison (CV)
23. La Vecchia Pavan [John Johnson] (FCV)
24. The Flat Pavan [John Johnson] (TCV)
25. Passing-measures Pavan (title only)
26. Passing-measures Galliard (title only)
27. The Voyce (TFCV)
28. Primero (V)
29. The Quadro Pavan [Richard Allison] (TFCV)
30. The Quadro Galliard [Richard Allison] (TFCV)
31. Mr Marchant's Paven (TFCV)
32. In Pescod time (CV)
33. Go from my Window [Richard Allison] (TFCV)
34. A Pavan of Mr Byrd's [Richard Allison] (FCV)

B. CAMBRIDGE CONSORT BOOKS

(Numbering based on first appearance in Dd.3.18; followed by pieces without a lute part as they appear in Dd.14.24.)

1. The French Volt (fo. 8ʳ) (LRVC)
2. Reade's 7th pavan/Mr Doctor James, Dean of Christchurch's Pavan, made by Mr R. Reade (fo. 12ʳ, fos. 28ᵛ–29ʳ) [Richard Reade] (LRVC)

Table 6.5. *cont.*

3. Reade's 2nd Jigge (fo. 15ʳ) [Richard Reade] (LRV)
4. Lacrimae [John Dowland] (fos. 16ᵛ–17ʳ) (LVFC)
5. Duncomb's Galliard (fo. 17ʳ) (LRVC)
6. Holburn's Farewell (fo. 18ʳ) [Anthony Holborne] (LRVC)
7. Phillip's Pavan (fos. 18ᵛ–19ʳ) [Peter Philips] (LTVC)
8. Reade's Almain (fo. 19ʳ) [Richard Reade/Anthony Holborne] (LRVC)
9. Allison's Pavan (fos. 19ᵛ–20ʳ) [Richard Allison?] (L)
10. The Earl of Oxford's March (fo. 20ʳ) [Byrd? arr. Morley?] (LTR)
11. Johnson's Delight (fos. 20ᵛ–21ʳ, 59ᵛ–60ʳ) [John Johnson] (LRVC)
12. Reade's Galliarde (fo. 22ᵛ, fo. 38ᵛ two versions, the second possibly a duet) [Richard Reade] (LRVC, T from a second lute prt)
13. Nightingale (fo. 22ᵛ) (LTRVC)
14. A Jigg, the first, R. Reade (fo. 24ʳ) [Richard Reade] (LRVC)
15. Reade's Galliard to the 6th Pavan (fo. 27ʳ) [Richard Reade] (LRF)
16. R. Reade's 5th Pavan (fo. 27ᵛ) [Richard Reade] (LRVC)
17. Reade's 6th Pavan (fo. 28ʳ) [Richard Reade] (LRVC)
18. When Phebus First, Richard Reade (fo. 29ʳ) (LRV)
19. Reade's 8th Pavan (fo. 29ᵛ) [Richard Reade] (LRVC)
20. Galliard to the Same [i.e. Reade's 8th Pavan] (fo. 30ʳ) [Richard Reade] (LRV)
21. Reade's 9th Pavan (fo. 30ᵛ) [Richard Reade] (LRFVC)
22. Battel. R. Reade (fo. 31ʳ) [Richard Reade] (L)
23. A Jigg, R. Reade (fo. 31ʳ) [Richard Reade] (LV)
24. Allison's Knell (fos. 31ᵛ–32ʳ) [Richard Allison?] (LVR)
25. Sweet Bryer, A Northern Jigge, R.R. (fo. 32ʳ) [Richard Reade] (LRVC)
26. Primero (fos. 32ʳ–33ʳ) (LRVC)
27. Nutmegs and Ginger (fo. 33ʳ) (LTVC)
28. Reade's Fancy (fos. 33ᵛ–34ʳ) [Richard Reade] (LRC)
29. A Jigg Eglantine (fo. 34ʳ) [Richard Reade] (LRVC)
30. James Harding's Galliard (appears twice, fos. 34ʳ, 58ᵛ) [Richard Reade] (LRV)
31. Go from my Window, Ri. Allison (fos. 34ᵛ–35ʳ) [Richard Allison] (LF)
32. Mousiers Almain (fo. 35ᵛ) (LTVC)
33. Alfonso's Pavan (fo. 36ᵛ) [Alfonso Bassano] (LRVC)
34. Reade's 1st Pavan (fos. 37ʳ–36ᵛ) [Richard Reade] (LRFVC)
35. Reade's 2nd Pavan (fos. 37ᵛ–38ʳ) [Richard Reade] (LRVC)
36. Reade's La Volta (fo. 38ʳ) [Richard Reade] (LRVC)
37. Reade's 3rd or Flatt Pavan (fos. 39ʳ–38ᵛ) [Richard Reade] (LRVC)
38. Reades 4th Pavan (fo. 39ᵛ) [Richard Reade] (LRVC)
39. De la Tromba (fo. 40ʳ) [Richard Allison] (LRVC)
40. Go Merely Wheele (fos. 40ᵛ–41ʳ) (LRVC)
41. La Bergera Galliard (fo. 41ʳ) [Philip Rosseter?] (LRVC)
42. Bacheler's Delight, Ri. Allison (fos. 44ᵛ–45ʳ) [Richard Allison] (LV)
43. De la Tromba, 2nd Treble (fos. 45ᵛ–46ʳ) (L)
44. Dolorosa Pavan Ri. Allison (fos. 46ᵛ–47ʳ) [Richard Allison] (LRV)
45. De la Courte, 1st Parte (fo. 47ʳ) (LRC)
46. The Jew's Dance, R. Nicholson (fo. 48ʳ) [Richard Nicholson] (LR)

47. Porter's Pavan (fos. 48ᵛ–49ʳ) [Walter Porter] (LR)
48. Porter's Galliard (fo. 49ʳ) [Walter Porter] (LF)
49. Emerald Galliard (fo. 52ʳ) (L)
50. My Lady Harcourt's Galliard (fo. 52ᵛ) (L)
51. All night in Venus' Court (fo. 53ʳ) (LV)
52. La Dolce Nenne (fo. 53ʳ) (L)
53. Tarlton Jigg (fo. 53ʳ) (LRVC)
54. Pavan Dolores (fo. 53ᵛ) (L)
55. Reade's 10th Pavan (fos. 55ʳ–56ᵛ) [Richard Reade] (L)
56. Reade's 11th Pavan (fos. 56ᵛ–57ʳ) [Richard Reade] (L)
57. 3rd Jigg, Mr. Reade (fo. 57ʳ) [Richard Reade] (L)
58. Mrs Millicent's Pavan. Ri Allison (fos. 57ʳ–58ᵛ) [Richard Allison] (LV)
59. Flatt Pavan (fos. 60ᵛ–61ʳ) [John Johnson?] (LC)
60. La Vecchio Mrs Lee (fo. 61ᵛ) [John Johnson?] (L)

Without a lute part:
61. Stroger's Paven (FVC)
62. The Sprite's Tune (RVC)
63. My Lo. Chaune Pavane (RVC)
64. The Galliarde (TFVC)
65. The Long Pavan, J. Johnson (RVC) [John Johnson]
66. Do Re Ha Galliard (RVC) [John Dowland]
67. Squire's Galliard (RVC)
68. Complaint/Fortune my Foe [John Dowland] (RVC)
69. The French King's Maske (RVC)
70. In Nomine Pavan (FVC)
71. Galliard to In Nomine Pavan (FVC)
72. The New Medley (C) [John Johnson]
73. A. H. Thought (C) [Anthony Holborne?]
74. Captain Pipers Pavan (FVC) [John Dowland]
75. Pavan (C)
76. Dowland's 1st Galliard (RVC) [John Dowland]
77. La Bergera (C)
78. Dowland's Round Battel Galliard (RVC) [John Dowland]
79. Tremento (RVC)
80. Galliard (C)

C. MORLEY'S *THE FIRST BOOKE OF CONSORT LESSONS* (1599/1611)

1. The Quadro Pavin [Richard Allison] (FCBVT)
2. Galliard to the Quadro Pavin [Richard Allison] (FCBVT)
3. De la Tromba Pavin [Richard Allison] (FCBVT)
4. Captaine Pipers Pavin [John Dowland, arr. Morley?] (FCBVT)
5. Galliard to Captain Pipers pavin [John Dowland, arr. Morley?] (FCBVT)
6. Galliard, Can she excuse [John Dowland, arr. Morley?] (FCBVT)
7. Lacrimae Pavin [John Dowland, arr. Morley?] (FCBVT)
8. Philips Pavin [Peter Philips, arr. Morley?] (FCBVT)
9. Galliard to Philips Pavin [Peter Philips, arr. Morley?] (FCVBT)
10. The Frog Galliard [John Dowland, arr. Morley?] (FCVBT)

Table 6.5. *cont.*

11. Allisons Knell [Richard Allison] (FCVBT)
12. Goe from my Window [Richard Allison] (FCVBT)
13. In Nomine Pavin [Nicholas Strogers, arr. Morley?] (FCVBT)
14. My Lord of Oxenfords Maske [Bryd?, arr. Morley?] (FCVBT)
15. Mounsier's Almaine [John Dowland?, arr. Morley] (FCVBT)
16. Michills Galliard (FCVBT)
17. Joyne Hands [Morley, arr. Morley] (FCVBT)
18. Balowe (FCVBT)
19. O Mistresse mine (FCVBT)
20. Sola Soletta [G. Conversi, arr. Morley] (FCVBT)
21. La Volta (FCVBT)
22. La Coranto (FCVBT)
23. The Lord Souches maske [Giles Farnaby? arr. Morley] (FCVBT)
24. The Batchelars delight [Richard Allison] (1611 edition only) (FBT)
25. Responce Pavin [Richard Allison] (1611 edition only) (FBT)

D. ROSSETER'S *LESSONS FOR CONSORT* (1609)

1. Captain Lester's Galliard [Philip Rosseter] (FC)
2. Pavan [Philip Rosseter] (FC)
3. Prannel's Pavan [Anthony Holborne] (FC)
4. Galliard to Prannel's Pavan [John Baxter] (FC)
5. Now is the month of May [Thomas Morley] (FCLincomplete)
6. The Sacred End Pavan [Thomas Morley] (FCLincomplete)
7. Galliard to the Sacred End Pavan [John Baxter] (FCLincomplete)
8. [Masque Tune, Shows and nightly Revels) [Thomas Lupo] (FCLincomplete)
9. Southern's Pavan [Thomas Morley] (FCLfragments)
10. Infernum [Anthony Holborne] (FC)
11. Spero [Anthony Holborne] (FC)
12. Millicent Pavans [Richard Allison] (FC)
13. Millicent Galliard [Richard Allison] (FC)
14. Cedipa Pavan [John Farmer] (FC)
15. Cedipa Galliard [John Farmer] (FC)
16. A lieta Vita [Giovanni Gastoldi] (FC)
17. Galliard to del la Tromba [Richard Allison?] (FC)
18. La Bergere (FC)
19. The Queen's Pavan [Anthony Holborne] (FC)
20. Move Now [Thomas Campion] (FC)
21. Galliard to the Knell [Richard Allison] (FC)
22. [Time that Leads] [Thomas Lupo] (F)
23. Barrow Faustus Dream [Edmund Kete] (F)
24. Jig [Philip Rosseter] (F)
25. Mall Simms (F)

music for the mixed consort survives. It seems he had a continuing interest in the genre throughout his working life. His eighteen surviving pieces include some of the most elaborate and complex in the repertoire. Of these, nine have extant lute parts. Three of them exist as lute duets, and five in solo-lute versions. It impossible to say in which form the original version of these pieces was conceived. In the Walsingham books there are four pieces 'set' by Allison, suggesting that his role was more as arranger than composer.

We can never be absolutely sure that Allison composed any of his pieces expressly for the mixed consort, though it is likely that he did in some cases, and he was certainly aware of the possibilities of instrumentation within the group. Typical of his longer pieces is the subdividing of the six instruments into quartets, or pairs or trios, which are then contrasted in answering phrases.[106] 'Go from my window' is especially notable in this context. It is unusual for a mixed-consort lesson as it is not a dance form, song, or masque piece, but, like much of the solo-lute repertoire, a set of variations on a popular melody. Luckily the lute part survives in Dd.3.18, so only the bandora part needs to be reconstructed.[107]

There are seven variations in all. Section three opens with lute diminutions with support from cittern and bass viol, while the flute plays the tune. After two bars the treble viol takes the diminutions supported by cittern and bandora(?), with the flute continuing the tune. (See Ex. 6.4.) For the remaining four bars all instruments play: the flute with the tune, the treble viol with a descant, the lute with diminutions, and the rest with harmonic and rhythmic support. The subdivision and answering continues in the next variation with shorter half-bar statements between violin and lute, with the flute taking the tune again. The fifth variation is characterized by triplets in all parts (save the bass and violin, which remain in common time), with diminutions played by flute and lute. In the penultimate section the violin, flute, and lute start in canon, followed by lute and violin in canon. In the last section the violin returns to the tune over fast lute diminutions. This short summary gives an indication of the unusually varied instrumental mixing in this piece, but the same interest in timbre is found in some degree in all Allison's larger pieces for consort.

Of the names associated with the mixed consort, Reade and Bacheler are of importance as composers, and Morley and Rosseter as arrangers, although both these last two may have composed some pieces directly for the consort. Reade is the most prolific, but his music is confined almost entirely to Holmes's manuscripts.[108] One senses that his interest was peripheral, and was maintained only while the Oxford consort was in existence. Only the lute part exists for a number of his consort pieces, suggesting that the Oxford group had other part-books which do not

---

[106] *The First Book of Consort Lessons*, ed. Beck, 24. [107] Dd.3.18, fos. 34ᵛ–35ʳ.
[108] One of Reade's pavans appears in *D-Kl* 4° MS Mus. 125.

Ex. 6.4. *Section 3 of Richard Allison's 'Go from my Window' from Thomas Morley's* Consort Lessons *(1599), bars 17–20 with a lute part from Dd.3.18, fo. 34ᵛ*

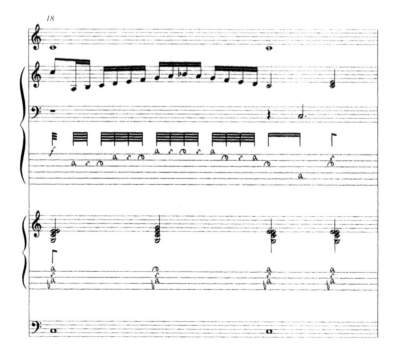

survive. These pieces are identifiable as consort parts, as they have diminutions without supporting harmonies in the repeat sections. While the violin part does not exist for any of Reade's pieces, many of them suggest possible contrapuntal imitation between lute and violin so as to make reconstruction plausible.[109]

Richard Reade's primary interest was not the arrangement of existing music by others, as with Morley and Rosseter, and his music includes only two arrangements of popular tunes. Instead he concentrated on producing pavans (11), galliards (3), and jigs (6), most simply identified by number, rather than given a title. There is also a single fancy, almain, la volta, and an arrangement of a vocal piece. It is likely that many of Reade's consort pieces are arrangements or adaptations of his own music to fit the Oxford consort. The many harmonic discrepancies between the cittern and the lute parts show that in many pieces the cittern part was developed from the bass line in isolation. This fact, plus the rather half-finished nature of many of his lute parts and the clumsiness of his recorder line, suggests that the music was assembled quickly from a variety of sources to suit the mixed consort at hand, then used and discarded soon afterwards without really being sorted out. Pavan 9 is connected to the lute duet 'Drewries accorde', and one of his almains is based on a piece attributed in Dd.2.11 to Anthony Holborne. Perhaps most interesting of Reade's pieces is a long five-part fancy based on the theme of Dowland's most popular solo lute fantasia (*Varietie*, no. 7) in which, almost uniquely, the cittern is given one of the five independent parts. (See Ex. 6.5.)

Reade clearly varied his approach when arranging his music for mixed consort, depending on the type of piece and its genre. Reade's method in pavan 6, for which uniquely we have the model in a five-part version,[110] was only to use the cantus and bassus parts, and most, but not all, of the altus part. An altogether new third part was then created for the recorder, which may on occasion take elements from the tenor and quintus parts (as at the beginning) but most often seems newly composed. This part aims to provide the missing note of the triad at all important points, after looking at the violin and lute top line, and to add rhythmic interest. The part that emerges often seems oddly disjointed and unmelodic, with occasional wide leaps. It uses the very same written range as the violin, and is often the highest written part. The cittern, and we suppose the bandora, was then created from the bass viol part in isolation. This is clear from the many misjudgements that the cittern composer makes in chords, believing the bass viol to be playing the root of the chord when it is actually sounding a first-inversion and vice versa, and minor/major disagreements between the cittern and the rest of the consort. We cannot, of course, be sure it was Reade who made the arrangement; it could have been Holmes himself, or someone else in his musical circle.

---

[109] Nordstrom, 'The Cambridge Consort Books', 77–9.   [110] *D-Kl* 4° MS Mus. 125, no. 39.

Ex. 6.5. *'Richard Reade's Fancy' from the Cambridge consort books; lute part from Dd.3.18, fo. 33ᵛ, bars 1–7*

Ex. 6.5. *cont.*

Some of the pieces by Bacheler display a creativity in design and instrumentation akin to those of Allison. In a number of the pieces the treble viol has important diminutions in the repeat sections. The loss of the bandora part is a pity, but it is lack of the all-important lute parts that will always make reconstruction tentative. The opening of 'The Widows Mite' suggests a contrasting of the treble viol, flute, and cittern (plus bandora?) with flute, lute, cittern, and bass viol six bars later.

Answering between violin and lute throughout this piece is suggested by the many silences in the extant treble viol part, as is the contrasting of instrumental groupings. (See Ex. 6.6.)

Allison produced two major publications during his lifetime: *The Psalmes of David in Meter* (London, 1599) and *An Howres Recreation in Musicke* (London, 1606). *The Psalmes* are of importance in relation to the mixed consort, as the four-part vocal settings have separate tablature parts for lute (or orpharion) and cittern. The sixty-nine psalm settings are all in simple harmony, and with one note to each syllable. Unlike previous psalm harmonizations, Allison put the psalm tune in the cantus, not the tenor. Each piece is printed on one opening of the book as 'table' music. (See Pl. 6.3). The title-page mentions they are 'to be sung and plaide upon the Lute, Orpharyon, Citterne or Base Violl, severally or altogether, the singing part to be either Tenor or Treble to the Instrument, according to the nature of the voyce, or for fowre voyces'. No separate part is given for the orpharion, which is presumably mentioned only as an alternative to the lute as in the title-pages of many books of ayres, and would play from the lute tablature. The bass-viol player, who likewise has no separate part, would play from the bass voice line. The lute part does not attempt to double the vocal parts in a strict intabulation. It provides a simple chordal support and largely avoids the psalm tune. A 7-course lute is required with a seventh course at *D*. In the main the chords involved are technically easy and do not go above the fifth fret. Often the cittern part carries the tune, but needs a bass part to complete the chords. Allison's *Psalmes* need only an easily constructed bandora part to accommodate a full consort of six if the flute plays the alto line and the viol/violin the soprano. The music is intended to be serviceable for a variety of combinations, ranging from a full complement of instruments and voices to a single voice and instrument.

The full mixed consort appears in William Leighton's *The Teares or Lamentacions of a Sorrowful Soule* (1614).[111] Leighton was a Gentleman Pensioner and knight who had been imprisoned for debt. Motives of piety and penitence had subsequently moved him to write a series of 'Himnes and spirituall Sonnets', which he published without music in 1613, promising 'to divuldge very speadely in print, some sweete Musicall Ayres and Tunable Accents'. Leighton was as good as his word and the musical anthology appeared promptly the following year. The surprise is the quality and range of the nineteen composers he recruited to set his words, many of the great names of Jacobean music being present, including some normally associated with secular music.[112]

[111] Verna L. Dimsdale, 'English Sacred Music with Broken Consort', *LSJ* 16 (1974), 39–64; also ead., 'The Lute in Consort in Seventeenth-Century England', 3 vols. (D.Phil. thesis, University of Oxford, 1968), iii. 88–91.

[112] Sir William Leighton, *The Tears or Lamentations of a Sorrowful Soul*, ed. Cecil Hill (Early English Church Music, 11; London, 1970).

Out of a total of fifty-four songs in the anthology, eighteen have consort parts. Eight of these are by Leighton himself, two by John Bull, and one each by John Dowland, John Milton, Robert Johnson, Thomas Ford, Edmund Hooper, Robert Kindersley, Nathaniel Giles, and John Coprario. As in Allison's book all the parts were printed on a single opening, so that one book placed in the centre of a table would serve for all. The three melody instruments are instructed as follows: 'Cantus with a Treble Violl', 'Altus with a Flute', 'Bassus with a Base Violl'. The tenor part is not doubled by any melody instrument. Though most settings are simple and syllabic, there are some pieces that are longer and less homophonic. Only one verse was printed with the music, the others being supplied by the 1613 book. There are

Ex. 6.6. *Opening of first varied repeat from Daniel Bacheler's 'The Widow's Mite', Walsingham consort books, no. 15. Lute and bandora parts reconstructed, bars 1–7*

many clashes between the tablature parts (in particular major/minor discrepancies), and one wonders if the plucked instrumental parts were supplied by the authors, by Leighton, or some other. The tablature parts are not difficult, but frequently awkward to play.

In 1615 Robert Tailour published fifty sacred pieces in his *Sacred Hymns* 'to be sung in Five parts, as also to the Viole, and Lute or Orpharion'. The music in this book is not laid out so that all can play from one opening, and at least two, and sometimes three, books would be necessary for full performance with voice, viols, and lute. Only the treble part has words, under which is placed tablature for the bass viol rather than the lute. The lute part follows after the textless lower parts. The

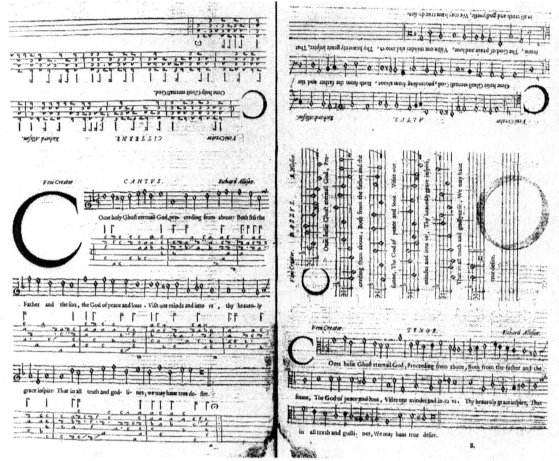

PL. 6.3. Page printed in 'table' format from Richard Allison's *The Psalmes of David in Meter* (London, 1599)

lower parts are more interesting than those of typical psalm settings. In this respect the settings are reminiscent of consort songs, and it may be that viols were primarily intended for the lower parts. Both the tablature parts are effectively short scores of the four lower parts. The lute part is more exacting than those of Allison or Leighton's books, and in following the part-writing provides more than mere chordal support. Tailour writes for a 9-course lute with diapasons on *F*, *D*, and *C*. He gives more importance to the viol tablature than the lute, reflecting, as with lute-song publications, the changing fortunes of the two instruments around this time. The term 'lyra viol' implied a viol part which involved the playing of chords and melody from tablature, and which could give the impression of maintaining distinct polyphonic lines in the manner of a lute. This method of playing the viol became very popular in the Jacobean period.

The popularity of English mixed-consort music is surprising. The three separate published editions would, even on the smallest print runs, have produced many hundreds if not thousands of books. These books, the manuscript collections, and the publications of domestic sacred music with mixed consort, prove that the ensemble, with its seemingly exotic collection of instruments, must be regarded as part of the mainstream of English music in the late Elizabethan and early Jacobean age. The lute has a leading role in many consort lessons, and the fast diminutions that characterize repeat sections show the expectation of a high standard of lute playing in England at this time. The interchange of music for solo lute, lute duet, and mixed consort must have been mutually beneficial to all three forms. At least three of Dowland's solo pieces were turned into duets, and at least three others were arranged for mixed consort, apart from his published duet and the four that Morley arranged and published.[113]

There is one further consort combination to which the lute may have regularly contributed, and that was with a whole consort of viols or violins. Mention has been made of the painting *The Courtiers of Elizabeth*, which depicts a lute with a consort of violins, and there is a further representation, dated *c*.1570, of a lute with a consort of viols, or more likely violins, in an alabaster overmantel of 'Apollo and the Muses' at Hardwick Hall.[114] The combination of lute and viols certainly became common in Jacobean England in the context of song accompaniment. There is one important publication that calls for a lute played with a whole string consort in serious instrumental music: Dowland's *Lachrimae, or Seaven Teares Figured in Seaven Passionate Pavans, with divers other Pavans, Galiards, and Almands, set forth for the Lute, Viols, or Violons, in five parts*. The book is unique in being the only published collection in table-book format in which a consort of viols is grouped around a printed tablature lute part. The lute doubles the string texture most of the time, but has figurations and elaborative devices that are found in none of the other parts, yet the viol parts are performable without the lute.[115] The seven passionate pavans that open the book are a thematically linked unity of extraordinary intensity, developed by Dowland from his famous lute pavan that forms the basis of number one of the 'Lachrimae Antiquae'. Of the other fourteen dance pieces most exist in earlier versions (usually for solo lute), but a few were either newly composed, or were reworkings of music by other composers expressly written for the *Lachrimae* publication.[116] The lute parts in this book are important as they had received 'from

[113] Solo made into a duo: 'Lord Willoughby', 'Lady Rich's Galliard', 'Now oh now/Frog Galliard'; solos in MS consort versions: 'Lady Laiton's Allmain', 'Sir John Smith's Allmaine', and 'Fortune my foe'.

[114] I am grateful to Peter Forrester for alerting me to this.

[115] This is in contradiction to Poulton's opinion in *John Dowland*, 345.

[116] Peter Holman, *Dowland: Lachrimae (1604)* (Cambridge, 1999), 61–74.

me [Dowland] their last foile and polishment'.[117] Clearly they have been arranged to suit a consort setting and are plainly different to the solo versions that Dowland may have played.

The book resembles a typical English lute-song publication in many respects: its table-book format allowing all to play from one large copy; a total of twenty-one items; a prefacing dedication and address to the reader. As Holman points out, however, its real origins lie with Anglo-German instrumental traditions developed in the 1590s by expatriate English musicians working on the Continent, and in particular the cultivation of the serious contrapuntal pavan.[118] Dowland himself states that he began compiling the book in Denmark.[119] The inclusion of violins in the title is important, as professional musicians of the time often played both viols and violins, and varied them according to the occasion. If *Lachrimae* is regarded as more representative of Continental practice, then English evidence that the lute regularly combined with whole consorts of bowed strings for instrumental music in Elizabethan and Jacobean times remains small.

The sacred publications of Allison, Leighton, and Tailour are a testament to the popularity of domestic psalm-singing in Jacobean England. Intended for the homes of the gentry, the inclusion of parts for mixed consorts in these books argues strongly for the continued presence of mixed consorts in the wealthy homes of England from the 1570s well into the Jacobean period. Gradually the mixed consort gave way to consorts of bowed string instruments (viols or violins) with optional support from lutes, theorbos, or keyboard instruments. Whereas in 1590 few great houses had a set of viols, by 1610 many did. Likewise among professional musicians the violin band became ever more popular. The mixed consort with its variety of instruments may have seemed reminiscent of minstrel music and thus archaic. The new types of court string music introduced by John Coprario, and patronized by the Princes Henry and Charles, may have led fashions away from mixed consorts. Certainly by the mid-1620s the musicians of the King's Company at Blackfriars Theatre were employing known violinists.[120] Holman suggests that waits and theatre musicians, who had formerly played mixed-consort instruments, were converting to a four-part string band with theorbos by the 1620s. The new arrangement maintained a six-man line-up. In it the old dual role of the lute, responsible for the alto line with chordal support and single-line divisions in the repeat sections, gave way to that of the more sombre bass line plus sketched-in harmony of the theorbos.

---

[117] John Dowland, *Lachrimae, or Seaven Teares* (London, 1604), sig. A2ᵛ.
[118] Holman, *Four and Twenty Fiddlers*, 160–70; *Dowland: Lachrimae (1604)*, 16–17.
[119] Dowland, *Lachrimae, or Seaven Tears*, sig. A2ʳ.   [120] Holman, *Four and Twenty Fiddlers*, 141.

Chapter Seven

The Golden Age, Part II: 1603–1625

True it is, I have lien long obscured from your sight, because I received a Kingly entertainment in a forraine climate . . . yet I must tell you, as I have beene a stranger; so have I againe found strange entertainment since my returne; especially by the opposition of two sorts of people that shroude themselves under the title of Musitians. The first are some simple Cantors, or vocall singers, who though they seeme excellent in their blinde Division-making, are meerely ignorant, even in the first elements of Musicke, and also in the true order of the mutation of the *Hexachord* in the *Systeme*, (which hath ben approved by all the learned and skilfull men of Christendome, this 800 yeeres,) yet doe these fellowes give their verdict of me behinde my backe, and say, what I doe is after the old manner: but I will speake openly to them, and would have them know that the proudest Cantor of them, dares not oppose himselfe face to face against me. The second are young-men, professors of the Lute, who vaunt themselves, to the disparagement of such as have beene before their time, (wherein I my selfe am a party) that there never was the like of them.

John Dowland, Preface 'To The Reader' in *A Pilgrimes Solace* (1612)[1]

The happy abundance of newly composed English lute music generated in the 1590s began to subside in the Jacobean period. Why this happened is not easily explained. That it did is borne out by the diminishing number of surviving sources, most of which contain much music that was not new. The comments of contemporaries make it clear that it was a time of new styles in the arts, and new and greater influences from abroad. Dowland, in his preface to the reader in *A Pilgrimes Solace* (1612), which is quoted in part above, launched a bitter complaint against two groups of musicians. Dowland had been employed at the Danish court from 1598 to 1606 with significant periods of absence in 1600–1 and 1603–4, when he was probably in London for the most part. In the quotation he is talking about musical developments that he felt had taken place during his absence in Denmark *c.*1604–6, and the reception he received on his return.[2] He attacks two specific groups: certain singers, and some young lute players. In the epistle Dowland pointedly asks why the second group had not answered the challenge to the lute made by Tobias Hume

---

[1] John Dowland, *A Pilgrimes Solace* (London, 1612; repr. London, 1977); modern edn. in *The English Lute Song*, vol. 12, ed. Edmund H. Fellows, rev. Thurston Dart (London, 1968), p. 1.

[2] Poulton, *John Dowland*, 52–66.

on behalf of the lyra viol in *The First Part of Ayres* (1605).[3] Here Hume states that 'the statefull instrument Gambo Violl, shall with ease yeelde full various and as devicefull Musicke as the Lute'. Moreover, Dowland asks why these 'professors' have not challenged the 'divers strangers from beyond the seas, which averre before our owne faces, that we have no true methode of application or fingering of the Lute'.[4]

Dowland does not specify who these young professors of the lute are. If by 'professors' he meant professional players and teachers, it is difficult to know to whom he is referring. Both Daniel Bacheler and Robert Johnson were younger men than Dowland and would seem possible candidates. Bacheler, whose success and royal favour Dowland might have envied, had his music published in *A Musical Banquet* (1610) and in the *Varietie of Lute-Lessons* (1610), where he is styled 'the right perfect Musition'. Although both books were published under Robert Dowland's name, in both cases they owe much to John, and a warm appreciation between the Dowlands and Bacheler is suggested in these publications.

Bacheler died in 1617/18, and Robert Johnson in 1633, only eight years after Dowland. All the remainder of the more important lutenist-composers of solo lute music of the Golden Age period—Robinson, Allison, Collard, Rosseter, Holborne, Francis Cutting, Pilkington, Danyel, and John Johnson—were of Dowland's generation or before, and mostly pre-deceased him. Moreover, as suggested above, some, like Pilkington, Danyel, and Rosseter, who lived into the 1620s and 1630s, probably wrote most, if not all, of their important solo lute music before 1603. Certainly Rosseter, Robert Johnson, and Simon Marson received places as lutenists in the King's Musick during the years 1604–10, and thus before Dowland, who received his place in 1612.[5] It is possible that Dowland, moved by jealousy, may have been deaf to the musical skills of these last-named lutenists, and was aiming his attack at them and their like.[6] Of all native lutenists, Robert Johnson's success in the years preceeding 1612 was the most conspicuous and remunerative. The fact that Johnson was continually called upon to compose for court masques, while Dowland remained excluded, may have been particularly irksome to a composer as capable as Dowland. Alfonso Ferrabosco II might also have been a candidate for Downland's jealousy for similar reasons.

Another plausible answer is that by the term 'professors' Dowland meant those who 'profess' to be competent lute players, but are in fact pretenders and charlatans. Thus he is not talking about those he considers to be good players. Considering the selectivity and elite nature of the musicians in the King's Musick at this time, it is unlikely that any of the these appointees would have been less than reasonably competent executants.

[3] Tobias Hume, *The First Part of Ayres* (London, 1605; repr. London, 1968 and 1985).
[4] Dowland, *A Pilgrimes Solace*, Preface.   [5] Ward, 'A Dowland Miscellany', 108.
[6] Poulton, *John Dowland*, 72–6, for a discussion of Dowland's grounds for jealousy at this stage in his life.

What is clear is that Dowland felt that musicians of a younger generation, who were disparaging of the musical style of Dowland and his contemporaries, were receiving 'most large meanes' and 'such encouragement as I never knew any have'.[7] Possibly he was referring to some of the lutenists employed by Prince Henry during the years 1610–12, all of whom received the generous yearly salary of £40 per annum.[8] Among this group there were three players of renown: Robert Johnson (who was employed by both the king and Prince Henry in the years 1610–12), Thomas Cutting, and John Sturt. There were a number of lutenists active in the early Jacobean period (such as Thomas Cutting and Thomas Sturgon), from whom few if any pieces survive, and about whom we know little.[9] Dowland could have had some or any of them in mind.

The 'divers strangers from beyond the seas' must refer to the younger generation of foreign musicians active in England, among whom were increasing numbers of French lutenists.[10] Certainly the five French musicians employed by Anne of Denmark from 1612 were very well paid. 1612 is also the year of *A Pilgrimes Solace*. Could these be the foreigners that so upset Dowland?

Dowland's lifetime spans and dominates the Golden Age period, and with his death the classical school of English lute composers draws to a close. The bulk of his larger and more serious lute music dates from the 1590s, and all but a few of his pieces can be shown to have been composed before 1610, though pieces were often revised or reworked later. Thus, for instance, of Dowland's seven extant fantasias (save possibly the fantasia published in *Varietie*), most appear in some form in sources that are tentatively dated to before 1600.[11] His *Lachrimae, or Seaven Teares* (1604) was probably a turning point in his composing career. While some of the pieces, particularly the six 'Passionate Pavans' that follow 'Lachrimae Antiquae' at the start of the book, were newly composed, most had been in existence as solo lute pieces for some time. In arranging the pre-existent pieces for the collection, and composing the new ones, Dowland was summarizing his lifelong preoccupation with the serious Pavan, Galliard, and Almain forms. There is little evidence that he composed much more in this genre after 1604. Although later Golden Age sources, such as Add. 38539, Nn.6.36, and the Pickeringe, Board, and Herbert manuscripts, are still rich in the serious pavans, fantasias, and galliards by Dowland and others, a new lighter style of almains, corantos, and masque dances are also apparent. This music is often closely related to the court.

In 1603 James I established himself in London with a wife, two sons, and a daughter, resulting in employment for many more musicians than had been the case

---

[7] Dowland, *A Pilgrimes Solace*.   [8] Price, *Patrons and Musicians*, 224.

[9] Other names are Molsoe, Hewett, Pierce, John Done, George Goselor, William Fregosie [= William Fregozi?], Nicholas Sturt, William Browne, Joseph Sherley, and William Morley.

[10] Hulse, 'Musical Patronage', 55. For instance, Monsieur Lambert and Leucs Fleuron.

[11] Poulton, *John Dowland*, 486–7.

under Elizabeth. During the period 1603–25 the number of 'lutenists in ordinary' employed by the king remained around five.[12] Queen Anne also employed several notable and well-paid musicians up to her death in 1619, some of whom were lutenists.[13] The royal princes, Henry and then Charles, maintained separate musical households (in the years 1610–12 and 1617–25 respectively), and the Princess Elizabeth also had musicians assigned to her.[14] The accession of Charles I in 1625 saw the merging of the king's household with that of the Prince of Wales. This resulted in an increased number of lute players employed directly by Charles, either as members of the new unit of 'lutes, viols and voices', which contained many that he had formerly employed as prince, or as those employed separately as lutenists 'in ordinary' to the king. This number of court lutenists was further enlarged by lutenists in Queen Henrietta Maria's service after 1625. There is no suggestion that among court circles the lute suffered any decline in status or importance in the Jacobean period. Indeed, if numbers alone were the sole criterion, we could conclude the opposite.

While the numbers of lutenists at Court increased, it is clear that the way the instrument was used, and the style of lute music popular in court circles, changed considerably in the late Golden Age. The accelerating extravagance of the Jacobean, and later the Caroline, masques began to dominate the artistic energies of some of the court musicians involved with them, Robert Johnson being a prime example. In such an environment it is understandable that the introspective, melancholic, and essentially private nature of much of the more weighty pieces in the early Golden Age repertoire soon lost favour, and that music associated with the masque, or with Continental styles introduced via the court, rose in importance.

In 1603 there were three royal 'Lutes in ordinary'. The vacant place that had been John Johnson's up to 1594, and momentarily Collard's in 1598–9, went to Robert Johnson in 1604,[15] the year in which Phillip Rosseter succeeded the deceased Walter Pierce. Rosseter died in 1623, and was replaced by Maurice Webster.[16] (See Table 7.1) Mathias Mason's place went first to Simon Marson in 1609, and on his death to Timothy Collins in 1617.[17] In 1612 the long-vacant place of Richard Pike was revived for John Dowland.[18] 1615 marked the outset of the career in royal service of the exceptionally successful singer, lutenist, composer, artist, and art connoisseur Nicholas Lanier III. He was appointed to the place previously held by Robert Hales, as one or the king's lutes in ordinary, at the salary of £40 p.a. plus livery.[19] The Pipe Office copy of the documents of the Exchequer of Audit, which are complete for the years 1600–27, show that these five places were

---

[12] Ward, 'A Dowland Miscellany', 107–8. [13] *RECM* iv. 196–206.
[14] Ibid. 207–9.   [15] Ibid. 79.   [16] Ibid. 112.   [17] Ibid. 85, 101.   [18] Ibid. 89.
[19] PRO E 351/544, mm 52ᵛ. Lanier is first mentioned in accounts ending 29 Sept. 1616 with a payment due to him for the period back to Michaelmas 1615 (*RECM* iv. 44).

maintained at the same respective rates of pay throughout this period with the exception of Maurice Webster's rate, which was altered in 1624.[20]

Queen Anne employed several lutenists among her Grooms of the Privy Chamber.[21] Foremost among them was Daniel Bacheler, who served her until his death, and was the highest paid of her grooms, receiving a total of £160 p.a.[22] From 1607 until Anne's death in 1619 she employed the Italian musician John Maria Lugario at £100 p.a. as another of her grooms. Lugario is normally mentioned in accounts simply as the 'Queens Musician', although he occasionally appears among the Lutes in accounts, suggesting that he played the lute.[23] He seems to have organized music for the queen, as he was reimbursed in 1607 for money he had spent buying a lute, a viol, and various song and consort books.[24] Also among her grooms, Anne counted Robert Hales, the old queen's favourite singer, who was also one of the king's 'lutes in ordinary', and the lutenist and dancing-master Thomas Cardell, Bacheler's uncle.[25]

Of the five French musicians employed by Anne from 1612 some were known singers, who most certainly could at the very least have accompanied themselves on the lute.[26] They returned to France on the queen's death in 1619 after being given the handsome sum of £150 as a gift, plus outstanding wages and rent, by the king.[27] Three of them later returned to the English court to serve Henrietta Maria.[28] Other prominent Frenchmen at the Jacobean court at various times were the violinists Jacques Bochan and Adam Vallet (who was given a place as a lutenist in 1616 while he waited for the next vacancy among court musicians), and the dancing-masters Nicholas Confesse, Nicholas Vielliard (dancing-master to Prince Henry), and Sebastian la Pierre (dancing-master to Prince Charles).[29] A 1619 inventory of Denmark House after Anne's death included seven lutes, all with cases.[30]

Nicholas Confesse is a particularly interesting character as he was responsible for teaching and composing court masque dances in 1610/11, 1612, and 1612/13,[31] and is associated with the popular courante known as Confesse's courante, which exists in several versions for solo lute. Confesse is very much the type of foreign court

---

[20] PRO E 351/543 and 544. Webster was appointed to Philip Rosseter's post at the rate of £20 p.a. on 9 June 1623, yet in accounts ending 29 Sept. 1624, and from then on, he was paid at the rate of 20 pence a day along with John Dowland and Robert Johnson.

[21] *RECM* iv. 196–206.

[22] Anne Batchelor, 'Daniel Bacheler: The Right Perfect Musician', *LSJ* 28 (1988), 3–12 at 6. Bacheler probably received £100 p.a. for his pension, plus a further £60 for wages and livery. See *RECM* iv. 198.

[23] e.g. in PRO E 351/543, mm. 256ᵛ, for Michaelmas 1611–12. He is listed among the 'Lutes' along with Hales, Merson, Rosseter, Johnson, and Dowland (*RECM* iv. 89, 94).

[24] *RECM* iv. 199.   [25] Ibid. 197, 198–9.

[26] PRO E351/543 and 544. See *RECM* iv. 201. Lewes Richard received £155; John Chantard £100; Camille Prevost £130; Peter de la Mare £115; and Claud Oliver £50.

[27] PRO LC 5/135 and IND 6746 for May 1620.

[28] Only Chantard and Oliver did not return in or after 1625.

[29] *RECM* iv, p. x and *passim*.   [30] Ibid. 206.   [31] Ibid. 30, 31, 147, 154.

Table 7.1. *Lutenists in the royal household 1603–1625*

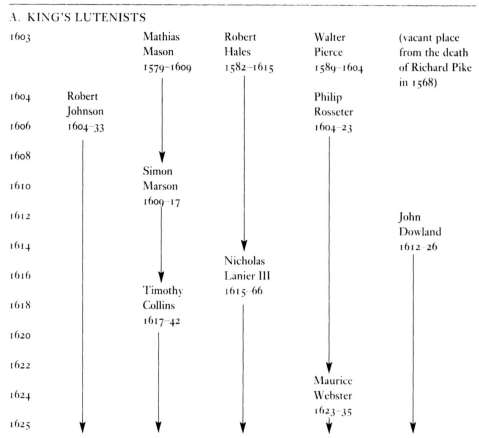

A. KING'S LUTENISTS

1603		Mathias Mason 1579–1609	Robert Hales 1582–1615	Walter Pierce 1589–1604	(vacant place from the death of Richard Pike in 1568)
1604	Robert Johnson			Philip Rosseter	
1606	1604–33			1604–23	
1608		Simon Marson			
1610		1609–17			
1612					John Dowland
1614					1612–26
1616			Nicholas Lanier III		
1618		Timothy Collins	1615–66		
1620		1617–42			
1622					
1624				Maurice Webster	
1625				1623–35	

B. PROBABLE LUTENISTS OR SINGER-LUTENISTS IN PRINCE HENRY'S MUSIC AND PRINCE CHARLES'S MUSIC

Name	Prince Henry	Prince Charles
Robert Johnson	1610–12 £40 p.a.	1617–25
John Miners	1610–12 £40 p.a. (d. 1615)	
Jonas Wrench	1610–12 £40 p.a.	1617–25
Thomas Day	1610–12 £40 p.a.	1617–25
Thomas Cutting	1610–12 £40 p.a. (d. 1614)	
John Sturt	1610–12 £40 p.a.	1617–25 (d. 1625)
Thomas Ford	1610–12 £30 p.a.	1617–25
Angelo Notari	1610–12 £40 p.a.	1617–25
Edward Wormal (singing boy)	1610–12 £20 p.a.	1623–5
Matthew Johnson (singing boy)	1610–12 £20 p.a.	

Name	Prince Henry	Prince Charles
Alphonso Balls		1617–25 £20 p.a.
Richard Balls		1617–22 £40 p.a.
John Coggeshall		1617–25 £40 p.a.
John Drew		1617–25 £40 p.a.
John Daniel		1617–25 £40 p.a.
Robert Marsh		1617–25 £20 p.a.
John Ashbie		1617–20 £20 p.a.
John Ballard		1621–5 £40 p.a.
also:		
Jacques Gaultier	1624–5 £50 (for Spain)	
Nicholas Lanier (Master of the Musick)	1625 £100 p.a.	

C. LUTENISTS TO QUEEN ANNE (D. 1619)

Daniel Bacheler (Groom)	1605–1618/19 £60+ £100 p.a.	
Thomas Cardell (Groom)	1604–19 probably £100 p.a.	
Robert Hales (Groom)	1605–16 £20 p.a.	

personality whose success might have upset Dowland in the years just prior to 1612. The piece appears in Nn.6.36 and so must have been in circulation before 1621, when Holmes died. Several Continental sources attribute the piece to the Parisian lutenist Charles de Lespine, who had been in England in 1610–11, and could well have worked with Confesse.[32] The confusion over authorship highlights the whole problem of attributing masque music as it was so often a joint effort. It could be that Confesse was responsible for only the dance itself, and that Lespine or others produced all the music associated with that dance. Alternatively, Confesse may have produced the basic outline of this masque dance (treble and bass), and Lespine the lute piece. Yet again, Confesse could have produced the lute piece and Lespine the varied repeats, which are quite different in the Continental versions.[33] The piece contains numerous elements that point towards the new *brisé* style developing in Paris at this time, in particular the way that the tonic and dominant chords are spread at the ends of phrases, and the way that the descending motif of bars 40–50 is then broken into continuous quavers in the repeat (bars 60–8), which emphasizes the constituent members of the underlying chord progression, rather than being scale passages. (See Ex. 7.1.)

It is noticeable that several of the more successful and progressive English lutenists of the Jacobean period were either employed by, or in some way associated

[32] Frédéric Lachèvre, *Charles de Lespine* (Paris, 1935). The piece is attributed to Lespine in the Werl and Haslemere MSS.

[33] A similar problem exists with the Board MS, fo. 27ᵛ, 'Antiq Masque per Mr Confesse sett by Mr Taylor', composed for the *Lords' Masque* (1613) for which John Coperario was responsible for the masque music.

Ex. 7.1. *'Coranto Confes', Nn.6.36, fo. 36^v, second section with varied repeat, bars 33–70*

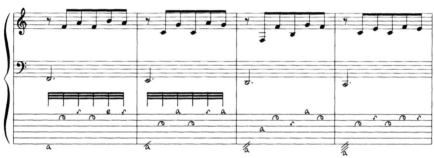

1. Tablature ∿ moved down a line to read *c′* not *f′* .
2. Bass note added.
3. bar 56 is repeated in MS. but the repeat is omitted here.

with, the charismatic young Prince Henry (1583–1612). Shortly after his arrival in England in 1603 at the age of 10, he had a household established for him by James at Oatlands Palace.[34] Despite Henry's leanings towards radical Protestantism, and his early association with the myth of the conqueror as epitomized by Alexander the Great, he was in friendly correspondence with Henry IV of France as early as 1606.

[34] Graham Parry, *The Golden Age Restor'd* (Manchester, 1981), 67.

George Chapman, the established poet at Prince Henry's household, used French subjects for his tragedies at this time, possibly to exploit the Prince's French sympathies.[35]

In 1607 Prince Henry procured from Lady Arabella Stuart the lutenist Thomas Cutting, ostensibly for the service of his uncle, the King of Denmark, but in the event for his own service.[36] In 1609 Henry expressed such an interest in Ben Jonson's *The Masque of Queenes* that the poet prepared an annotated text for the prince.[37] In December of that year Henry brought together the two giants of the Jacobean masque, Inigo Jones and Ben Jonson, for the *Barriers Masque*. On the theme of Arthurian legend, this unusual masque began several days of tilts and military exercises as a prelude to the prince's investiture with the title Prince of Wales.[38] With the Prince's elevation to this new status he established himself with a separate court at St James Palace, and his now independent musical household increased such that it could rival that of the king.[39]

As well as the lutenists Robert Johnson, Thomas Cutting, and John Sturt, there were a number of other musicians in Henry's service who may have sung and/or played the lute, as they later found employment among the 'lutes and voices' after 1625. These included Jonas Wrench, Edward Wormall (described in 1612 as a singing boy), Thomas Ford, and Thomas Day. Other possible singer/lutenists were John Miners (d. 1615) and Matthew Johnson. Michael Cavendish, the lutenist, composer, and member of the Cavendish family, was among Henry's Grooms of the Privy Chamber.[40] The Italian singer and composer Angelo Notari first found a place at the English court among Henry's musicians.[41] His published music suggests that he was important in introducing the new monodic Italian song style that was conceived with a basso continuo primarily intended for the theorbo. Henry may have been leaning more towards Italian culture than French after 1610.[42] With Henry's unexpected death in 1612 the household was disbanded.

In 1616 Charles took his deceased brother's title, and efforts were made to reassemble the same musicians as had formerly been employed by Henry. Most of those named above were found and reinstated by 1618, and the numbers were enlarged by more musicians, some of whom, like John Coggeshall, John Danyel, and Robert Tailor, were most probably lutenists in some capacity. Thomas Cardell, and for a short time his son Francis Cardell, served the Princess Elizabeth up to her marriage to the Elector Frederick of the Palatine in 1613, when she departed with

[35] Graham Parry, *The Golden Age Restor'd* (Manchester, 1981), 67.

[36] The letters concerning these events can be found in *GB-Lbl* Harley 6986, fos. 74, 76, and 78.

[37] Stephen Orgel, *The Jonsonian Masque* (Cambridge, Mass., 1965), 69.

[38] Jerry W. Williamson, *The Myth of the Conqueror: Prince Henry Stuart, a Study of Seventeenth-Century Personation* (New York, 1978).

[39] Documents relating to Prince Henry's musical household can be found in *GB-Lbl* Harley 7009 and 642. It is noticeable that Henry's musicians were generally better paid than those of the king.

[40] I am grateful to Andrew Ashbee for this information.   [41] *RECM* iv. 210–13.   [42] Ibid., p. x.

him for Heidelberg.[43] The protracted celebrations for this event resulted in several lavish court masques. It was for just such events that the body of musicians (in the main lutenists, singers, keyboard and string players), employed by Henry, and later Charles, were required. They were later to become the king's 'lutes, viols and voices', or simply 'lutes and voices'. Henry 'loved Musicke, and namely good consorts of Instruments and voices joyned together'.[44] The many references to Robert Johnson in the household accounts of Prince Charles and the king show that he had special responsibility for acquiring instruments, strings, and books for these musicians.[45] He was also a composer of masque and theatre music. This activity clearly influenced his lute music, and most probably his lighter pieces originated as ensemble music for masque dances. The French lutenist Jacques Gaultier makes his first appearance in Charles's accounts in 1623, and in 1624 he received £100 for his expenses and £50 for his allowance.[46]

The first musician appointed to Prince Henry was Alfonso Ferrabosco II, who in 1604/5 became 'extraordinary groom of the Privy chamber', with duties to instruct Henry 'in the art of music'.[47] In 1604 he bought two viols with cases and strings for Henry.[48] This role Ferrabosco retained when Charles became Prince of Wales. There is every indication that the princes learnt the viol and not the lute from Ferrabosco. This in itself is a break with the Tudors, who favoured the lute, and is symptomatic of the changing fortunes of the lute and viol. Ferrabosco could play the lute—he was listed among the lutes at Elizabeth's funeral[49]—and published a book of lute songs. Yet it is with the viol that he is associated, and it seems he personally did much to establish the lyra viol at the Jacobean court. There is no identifiable solo lute music that survives by Ferrabosco to place alongside his huge output of vocal and viol music.

Prince Charles's household is important for the development of string consort music. In particular John Coprario directed a small group of musicians, referred to in one document as 'Coperario's musique'.[50] Charles himself participated in the music, as John Playford tells us: 'Charles I . . . could play his part exactly well on the Bass-Viol, especially of those Incomparable Fancies of Mr. Coprario to the Organ.'[51] Holman has pointed to the special importance of Coprario and his group in developing the fantasy suite, in mixing viols and violins to the organ, and in using lyra viols.[52] While the organ was the normal accompanying instrument for such mixed consorts in the Caroline period, theorbos were an accepted alternative, and may, in the context of dance movements, have been preferred.

---

[43] Ibid. 207–9.
[44] Roy Strong, *Henry Prince of Wales and England's Lost Renaissance* (London, 1986), 173.
[45] *RECM* iv. 219, 223, 224, 228, 230.   [46] Ibid. 228.   [47] Ibid. 11.   [48] Ibid. 76.
[49] Ibid. 2.   [50] Holman, *Four and Twenty Fiddlers*, 213; *GB-Lbl* Add. 64883, fo. 57ʳ.
[51] Playford, *An Introduction to the Skill of Musick* (1664; 1683), Preface.
[52] Holman, *Four and Twenty Fiddlers*, 213.

The altogether more lavish scale of musical provision found in the households of the royal family are mirrored on a smaller scale in that of some leading courtiers. William Cavendish, 1st Earl of Devonshire, had been a generous patron of musicians at Chatsworth up until 1608 when his mother, Bess of Hardwick, died. Among the musicians were Michael Cavendish and a French lutenist called Lambert. After 1608 William Cavendish spent more time in London, and increased the scale of his musical patronage. In 1613 permanent employment, at the salary of £22 p.a. plus board, was offered to Thomas Cutting, who had lost his royal post on the death of Prince Henry.[53] Cutting had been successively patronized by Lady Arabella Stuart (Cavendish's niece), and by Christian IV in Denmark, where he had succeeded Dowland.[54] A permanent position was also given to the lutenist Mr Molsoe. Employment, intermittent payments, and gifts were extended to John and Robert Dowland, Mr Maynard, Mr Pierce, and a French lutenist, M[onsieur] Louis.[55] At one point around 1613–14 Cavendish may have been patronizing up to six lutenists, from among whom he had a consort of three lutes.[56] It may be that he employed Cutting and this group of lutenists to imitate the band that Prince Henry had put together, with its emphasis on Italianate mixed consorts and singer/lutenists.

Henry Lord Clifford and his father, Francis Clifford, 4th Earl of Cumberland, employed a number of musicians in the years after 1610, including the lutenists Edward Cresset, George Mason, and John Earsdon. Lord Clifford had studied the lute himself at de Pluvinel's Academy in Paris. On his return to England in 1611 he maintained a French lute tutor, a Monsieur Simon.[57] The Earls of Rutland were long-established patrons of music and continued this tradition in the Jacobean period. The lutenist Andrew Marks was resident at Belvoir Castle from 1610 to 1620; he composed some surviving music, and may have made and mended lutes.[58] John Jenkins composed an elegy for Marks.[59] The Belvoir musician was presumably also the Anthony Marks whom William Lawes celebrated in a catch with the words:

> Stand still and listen if you hear with me
> Anthony Markes on his stump,
> I sweare if in this vault he rest his bones,
> His spirit walks and charms these stones.[60]

[53] Hulse, 'Hardwick MS 29'.

[54] For letters concerning Cutting's appointment at the Danish court see Ward, 'A Dowland Miscellany', App. Z, 149–51.

[55] Hulse, 'Hardwick MS 29', 64–5. In her thesis Hulse names M[onsieur] Louis as Leues [Fleuron]; Hulse, 'Musical Patronage', 319.

[56] Hulse, 'Musical Patronage', 222, 319.   [57] Ibid. 55, 224.

[58] Price, *Patrons and Musicians*, 138; music by Marks can be found in *GB-Cu* Nn.6.36 and Dd.5.20, and *EIRE-Dtc* D.1.21.(I and II).

[59] *GB-Och* 736–8.

[60] John Hilton, *Catch that Catch Can* (London, 1652), 93. I am grateful to Andrew Ashbee for this information.

Marks's stump was not a wooden leg, but a wire-strung instrument tuned like a 7-course lute with eight extra basses. It was in effect a theorboed orpharion. A single piece headed 'Alman R. Johnson to the stump by F.P.' survives for this instrument.[61]

The Thynnes of Longleat employed a resident lute teacher in one Mr Wood.[62] Lady Joan Thynne of Caus Castle, Shropshire, was the dedicatee of John Maynard's *The XII Wonders of the World* (1611). John Danyel and his brother, the poet Samuel Danyel, were closely associated with the Seymour family, Earls of Hertford, in the years 1603–6, and were able to help with a masque that the family prepared for the king's enjoyment in 1613.[63] This family also patronized Alfonso Ferrabosco II, and gave an apprenticeship to William Lawes from 1612.[64] Of all the aristocratic households, those of the 1st and 2nd Earls of Salisbury were perhaps the most enthusiastic in their patronage of musicians in the period 1600–14; among them were Anthony Holborne, Robert Hales, Nicholas Lanier, Thomas Robinson, George Mason, and Matthew Johnson.[65]

The polarization of society along religious lines that gathered pace after 1610 may have adversely affected the happy exchange of music between court and country house that had been a feature of Elizabethan life.[66] During the early Golden Age the pleasures of music-making had been shared by many men of all shades of religious and political persuasion. The Reformation and spread of humanist ideas in England had directly encouraged the private patronage of musicians. Country lords, enriched by the dissolution of the monasteries, were able and anxious to underline their new status by employing musicians within the household, some of whom might otherwise have been drawn towards the church.[67] There were strongly musical households on both sides of the religious divide. Musicians so employed were able to foster a high standard of musical literacy and appreciation within the home. The Thynnes of Longleat, who employed the lutenist-composer John Danyel to teach the lute in 1616–17, are an excellent case in point.[68]

A result of this growing musical literacy was the rise of music printing in the late Elizabethan and early Jacobean period. Then the music publishing trade underwent a swift decline. Between 1612 and 1632 only twenty-three first editions were published in England, as compared with forty-eight in the previous twenty years.[69] John Attey's *The First Book of Ayres of Foure Parts* (1622) was the last true lute-song publication. Pilkington's *The Second Set of Madrigals and Pastorals* (1624) was the last significant publication of English madrigals; and 1632, the year in which Walter Porter published his Italianized *Madrigales and Ayres* (which are

---

[61] *GB-Och* Mus. 532. See Robert Johnson, *Complete Works for Solo Lute*, ed. Albert Sunderman (London, 1972).
[62] Price, *Patrons and Musicians*, 130.   [63] Ibid. 127.   [64] Hulse, 'Musical Patronage', 47, 320.
[65] Ibid. 321.   [66] Price, *Patrons and Musicians*, 190.
[67] Ibid. 205.   [68] Ibid. 130.   [69] Ibid. 186–7.

continuo-based compositions), marks the end of music printing in England until the Commonwealth, reprints and psalters with simple harmonizations apart.[70] It may be that music published in London, much of it influenced by court perform-ance and patronage, was unacceptable to disaffected provincial parties.[71] For such men, the more restrained and private music of the late Elizabethan era may have been infinitely preferable, and nostalgic of an age of greater social harmony. An example is John Ramsey, gentleman of Mount in Surrey. His diary written in the 1620s suggests he owned an extensive library of music, and manuscripts of music of a past generation.[72] His son, born in 1622, is advised to learn the lute from Dowland's works, and Dowland and Cavendish are mentioned as excellent musicians.[73]

The breakdown of the Elizabethan religious compromise was exacerbated by the high-handed application of episcopal power, and the suppression of the reforming Puritans by Archbishops Whitgift and Bancroft. Later in the Jacobean and Caroline periods the high-church policy of Bishops Juxon and Laud contributed perhaps more than any other factor to the eventual outbreak of the Civil War.[74] However, the Anglican church, under Laud's programme of encouraging 'the beauty of holi-ness' in worship, may have become more tolerant towards the creative needs of musicians. In the 1620s Tomkins and Pilkington continued to publish secular music of a restrospective nature, and found security in provincial church livings or appointments.

Many musicians continued to exist on private patronage in the Jacobean and Caroline periods, but the attractiveness and supposed security of a court appoint-ment may have increased, especially as some musicians could command extravagant salaries. While it is true that most lutenists aspired to court appointments, several who wrote important lute music before 1605 (e.g. Francis Cutting, Pilkington, and Allison) had no known court positions. Of the lutenists who we know were still composing important solo lute music after this date (Robert Johnson, Daniel Bacheler, John Daniel, and John Sturt), all had court appointments with the king or Prince Henry, although Bacheler, as a Groom of her Majesties Privy Chamber, probably became a gentleman of independent means.

The new lighter style of lute composition, influenced by the Jacobean masque and the developments in French lute music after 1600, is discernable in later Golden Age sources. It may well have been unacceptable to those who had no desire to associate with the court. The instrument itself could thus have become tainted in

[70] Price, *Patrons and Musicians*, 187–8.   [71] Ibid. 190.

[72] Ibid. 187–8. Other examples are *GB-Ob* Mus. Sch. f. 7–10/11–15, compiled c.1630–45 by Mary, Nicholas, and Thomas Hamond of Hawkedon, Sussex, which contains vocal music by Golden Age composers Weelkes, Pilkington, Morley, Gibbons, White, Giles, Mundy, Ravenscroft, and Peerson; ibid. 199.

[73] *GB-Ob* Douce 280, fo. 120ʳ.

[74] For information on the suppression of the reforming Puritan movement see Marshall Mason Knappen, *Tudor Puritanism* (Chicago, 1939), 255–7, 294–7; Patrick Collinson, *The Elizabethan Puritan Movement* (London, 1967), 333–71.

the eyes of such men, and the new tunings and *style brisé* that were introduced into England in the 1620s and 1630s all the more so. For those in society who saw in the court a wasteful extravagance, it was the music of the past that they wished to cultivate. Without the fruitful exchange between court and country house, the Golden Age of lute music passed away. In this parting of the ways those at court still interested in the lute looked increasingly to foreign developments in lute music, and those disaffected from the court to music associated with a previous age. Above all the initiative had passed to viol players and consort composers—a situation all too apparent to Dowland by the close of the first decade of the seventeenth century.

Turning to a consideration of the sources and solo lute music from the Jacobean period (see above, Table 5.3), it is noticeable that, though the numbers are down, the list includes the two largest, and arguably the best, publications: *The Schoole of Musicke* and the *Varietie of Lute-Lessons*. Thomas Robinson published a tutor for the lute in 1603 entitled *The Schoole of Musicke* and followed it six years later with a tutor for the cittern entitled *New Citharen Lessons*. The lute book also promised to teach the 'perfect method, of true fingering of the *Lute, Pandora, Orpharion*, and *Viol de Gamba*; with most infallible generall rules, both easie and delightfull'.[75] In fact Robinson supplied only one set of general rules, and suggested that they could be transferred from one instrument to the other. His *Citharen Lessons* (1609) repeats these rules with only slight alteration to make them suitable for the metal-strung cittern.[76] Robinson's lute book is prefaced by a dedication to James as King of England. In it Robinson states that he 'was thought (in *Denmarke* at *Elsanure*) the fittest to instruct your Majesties Queene'.[77] Robinson must have taught Queen Anne when she was 15, before she married James in Norway in 1589. Little is known of Robinson's life. He probably published other music books than the two that survive. There is some evidence of patronage from the Salisbury household and that of the 1st Earl of Exeter,[78] and he performed in a Merchant Taylor's banquet in 1609 along with many other lutenists. Most likely he made most of his livelihood from teaching.[79]

The Schoole of Musicke is the best source of technical information among the surviving English Renaissance lute tutors. It is framed as a concise and amusing dialogue between a teacher called Timotheus, and a knight who wishes his children to be taught the lute. In the dialogue Robinson deals with posture, how to tie frets onto the lute, learning tablature, fingering for left- and right-hand chord playing, tuning, sight-reading, and ornamentation. The book contains thirty-eight graded pieces, including six duets 'all mine own setting, and the most of them mine own

---

[75] Robinson, *The Schoole of Musicke*, title-page. Modern edn., including tablature and staff notation, ed. David Lumsden (Paris, 1971).

[76] Ian Harwood, 'Thomas Robinson's "Generall Rules"', *LSJ* 20 (1978), 18–22.

[77] Robinson, *The Schoole of Musicke*, sig. A2ʳ.   [78] Hulse, 'Musical Patronage', 319, 321, 322.

[79] Ward, 'A Dowland Miscellany', 119–20.

invention'. The pieces are of excellent quality, and moderate in their technical demands. Sadly, even his simpler pieces have moments of awkwardness that make them unsuitable for the beginner. The five pieces containing left-hand fingerings are particularly interesting, as they show awkward shifts and difficult fingering, possibly to allow for ornamentation, or to give melodic accent to a note.[80]

Robinson wrote for a 7-course lute with a top course comprising two strings tuned at the unison, rather than a single string. This last feature is perhaps a surprise, but was not uncommon at this time, as Continental lute iconography attests. Like Le Roy, Robinson recommends a right-hand technique based on alternation of the thumb and first finger for running passages, though he does allow for running passages in the bass to be played by the thumb alone.[81] He mentions two types of ornaments which he terms 'graces', but fails to link them with an ornament sign. These are the 'fall with a relish' and the 'fall without a relish'.[82] Robinson's book is the first truly English lute tutor, as it owes nothing to Le Roy. Its introduction gives the fullest exposition of a professional lutenist's teaching method that we have from this period, and it contains much good music besides, especially in the delightful toys and settings of popular tunes.

Robert Dowland's *Varietie of Lute-Lessons* (1610) is the last printed lute book of the period (see Pls. 7.1–2). The music it contains is prefaced by two essays: 'Necessarie Observations Belonging to the *Lute*, and Lute playing by *John Baptisto Besardo* of Visonti' (a translation from Besard's *Thesaurus harmonicus* of 1603), and 'Other Necessary Observations belonging to the *Lute* by *John Douland*, Batcheler of Musicke'.[83] The latter essay is limited to advice on stringing, fretting, and tuning, but it is probable that John's role in the preparation of the book was extensive, and that he wished to put his son's name forward. John's contribution is hinted at in the title of the 'Necessary Observations', which jointly credits the two Dowlands with the collection and composition of the musical material. Robert Dowland, in his preface to the readers, indicates that his father was working on a 'greater Worke, touching the Art of Lute-playing'. This work would supersede the instructions contained in *Varietie*, but was clearly never finished.

Besard's advice on right-hand technique differs from that of Robinson and Le Roy. Besard recommends the alternation of the first and second fingers in passages where the bass accompanies a line above, although he too adheres to the thumb and first-finger alternation for passages without bass notes.[84] Besard suggests a right-hand position which allows the thumb to 'stretch out' away from the fingers, which

[80] Susan G. Sandman, 'Thomas Robinson's Interpretive Left-Hand Fingerings for the Lute and Cittern', *JLSA* 11 (1978), 26–35.

[81] Robinson, *The Schoole of Musicke*, sig. B^v–B2^r; see Poulton, *John Dowland*, 390.

[82] Robinson, *The School of Musicke*, sig. C2^r.

[83] Robert Dowland, *Varietie of Lute-Lessons* (London, 1610; repr. London, 1958, ed. Edgar Hunt).

[84] Ibid., sig. C2^r.

PL. 7.2. John Dowland's 'The Right Honourable the Lady Rich, her Galliard', from Robert Dowland, *Varietie of Lute-Lessons* (London, 1610), sig. Nr

PL. 7.1. Frontispiece of Robert Dowland's *Varietie of Lute-Lessons* (London, 1610)

themselves are held 'in a manner of a fist', whereas Robinson preferred the thumb 'behind your fingers'.[85] This change in right-hand position and technique was probably more advanced on the Continent but was gaining ground in England. We know that Dowland himself altered his technique from the thumb inside to the thumb outside during his career.[86] The use of the second finger is normally indicated in sources by two dots under the tablature letter. The first datable English source to show the use of the right-hand ring finger, with three dots under the tablature letter, is in Allison's *Psalmes* of 1599. None of the pieces in *Varietie* contains any fingering signs whatsoever.

Robert Dowland's *Varietie* contains forty-two pieces grouped by genre into fantasias, pavans, galliards, almains, corantos, and voltes, with seven pieces in each group. In organization it parallels the Dutch and German anthologies listed in Table 7.2, and is thus unlike other English manuscript and printed sources which have no such clear divisions, excepting John Dowland's *Lachrimae* (1604). *Varietie* contains a balance between the older, more serious forms of fantasia, pavan, and galliard, and the newer forms of corantos, voltes, and masque dances found among the almains. Eleven foreign lutenists are mentioned in the attributions, reflecting a much keener awareness of Continental lute music than is found in most Golden Age manuscripts.[87] This foreign contribution, along with the 'Necessarie Observations' by Besard that preface the music, doubtless resulted from John Dowland's several foreign peregrinations.

Of the nine contributions made by John Dowland most are pieces that had been in circulation for some time.[88] While the versions of some of the almains, pavans, and galliards in this book have, in some cases, different titles, and in most cases significant musical deviations from the earlier versions, they are more representative of lute music *c.*1600 than 1610. The seven corantos and seven voltes are differentiated from the earlier contents of the book in requiring a ninth course. These pieces mark the first appearance in print in England of music in the lighter French style. The few attributions among these pieces mention only the Parisian lutenists Saman, Perrichon, and Ballard, and represent a French style *c.*1600, comparable to that of Antoine Francisque in the *Trésor d'Orphée* (1600).

The four masque dances in *Varietie*,[89] which can be traced to Ben Jonson's *Masque of Queens* (1609), share a lightness of division texture with the corantos and

[85] Robert Dowland, *Varietie of Lute-Lessons*, sig. C1ᵛ; Robinson, *The Schoole of Musicke*, B2ʳ.

[86] See Poulton, *John Dowland*, 320. This change in technique is described in the MS of Stobaeus of Königsberg, *GB-Lbl* Sloane 1021, p. 24.

[87] I have assumed that 'The Knight of the Lute' (*Varietie*, ed. Hunt, 22) and 'Laurencini' (ibid. 24) are one and the same composer, though this assumption still awaits full substantiation. See *Thirty Pieces for Lute by Laurencini*, ed. Tim Crawford (Lute Society, 1979), 2.

[88] This includes 'The Right Honorable the Lady Cliftons Spirit' (*Varietie*, ed. Hunt, 50), which is wrongly attributed to Robert Dowland (see Poulton, *John Dowland*, 112), and 'Sir Iohn Smith his Almaine', which is unattributed, but clearly by John Dowland (ibid. 159).

[89] Facs., ed. Hunt, 58–60.

Table 7.2. *Principal Dutch and German printed lute books and anthologies 1584–1625*

Anthologies	Title of collection	Comments
Emmanuel Adriaenssen (Antwerp)	1. *Pratum musicum* (1584) 2. *Novum pratum* (1592) 3. *Pratum musicum* (1600) For 7-course lute	Each edition has about 5 fantasias, 50 vocal compositions, for 1 to 4 lutes with 1 to 4 vocal lines, and 30 dances
Adrian Denss (Cologne)	*Florilegium* (1594) For 7-course lute	11 fantasias, 10 passemezzo suites, 22 allemandes, 5 courantes, 2 voltes, 4 branles, 1 ronde, 1 pauvern-tanz, and 84 intabulations
Matthias Reymann (Heidelberg)	1. *Noctes musicae* (1584) 2. *Cythara sacra* (Cologne, 1612, now lost) For 8-course lute	23 preludes, 16 fantasias, 12 passemezzo suites, 5 pavans, 10 galliards, 8 chorea
Johann Rude (Heidelberg)	*Flores musicae* (1600) For 8-course lute	In 2 books: 171 intabulations (over 40 composers), 7 intradas, 1 fantasia, 30 pavans, 2 galliards, 1 chorea. 12 English pieces
Joachim Van den Hove	1. *Florida* (Utrecht, 1601) 2. *Delitiae musicae* (Utrecht, 1612) 3. *Praeludia testudini* (Leiden, 1616) (1) for 7-course lute, (2) and (3) for 8-course lute	Both (1) and (2) include preludes, vocal intabulations and dance types. (1) includes also fantasias and songs; (3) includes only 19 preludes, 2 pavans and 1 echo, all by Hove. Some music for lute duet with voices in (2) and (3)
Jean-Baptiste Besard	1. *Thesaurus harmonicus* (Cologne, 1603) 2. *Novus partus* (Augsburg, 1617) For 7- and 8-course lute	(1) in 10 books; preludes, fantasias, madrigals, French airs, passemezzi, galliards, allemandes, branles, courantes, and miscellaneous pieces. (2) includes music for lute consort and solos
Georg Leopold Fuhrmann (Nüremberg)	*Testudo gallo-germanica* (1615) For 7- or 10-course lute	Includes: preludes, fantasias, vocal intabulations, pavanes, spangnolet, passemezzi, galliards, intradas, branles, allemandes, ballets, courantes, voltes, and others
Elias Mertel (Strasburg)	*Hortus musicalis novus* (1615) For 7- to 9-course lute	235 preludes and 120 fantasias and fugues
Johann Daniel Mylius (Frankfurt)	*Thesaurus gratiarum* (1622) For 10-course lute	Includes songs, preludes, toccatas, fugues, fantasias, galliards, courantes, voltes, allemandes, passemezzi, branles, and choreas
Adriaen Valerius (Haarlem)	*Neder-landtsche gedenck-clank* (1626) For 7- to 9-course lute	Poetic history of Netherlands 1555–1625 with engravings and 76 popular songs for lute (or lutes) and cittern

voltes in the book. These masque dances were almost certainly arrangements for the lute of music originally composed in two parts, treble and bass, which were then filled out according to the instrumentation required for the actual masque. They were the most recently composed pieces in the book, and represent the growing fashion for such pieces in English lute music *c.*1610. The book aims at a balance between the old and the new, and is intended to suit a spectrum of tastes, though no concessions are made to the beginner or less able player. The *Varietie* contains some of the most difficult pieces for the lute, but, incongruously, has instructions suitable for a beginnner who could not possibly play the music. The lack of vocal transcriptions contrasts with most Continental anthologies listed in Table 7.2, yet may have conformed to English taste. The cosmopolitan selection of pieces in the book differs in many ways from that of most English lute manuscripts, not least in its lack of simple toys and ballad-tune settings.

The Sampson lute book (formerly known as the Tollemache lute book) includes twenty-six pieces for 7-course lute (though most need only six courses), sixteen of which are solos, nine are duets, and one is for mixed consort.[90] It was written out by two scribes on paper that dates from *c.*1606. The first scribe, Henry Sampson, copied twelve popular pieces that date from the 1590s and earlier. They include 'The Spanish Pavan', 'Rogero', 'Heaven and Earth', and some early Dowland pieces. The second scribe's repertoire is mainly for two lutes, and is more up to date with pieces by Pilkington, Danyel, and Dowland. Spencer has identified this scribe with one that also appears in Dd.4.22, Dd.9.33, and Add. 15117.[91] It also appears in the Walsingham Consort part books (flute part of no. 9). The Sampson manuscript is most probably provincial and amateur. Its main importance lies in the supplying of several unique duet parts, and an otherwise lost mixed-consort part to an almain by Allison. A manuscript which has some palaeographic characteristics associated with the work of professional copyists is the Euing manuscript now housed in the Library of the University of Glasgow. The book contains a selection of seventy-one popular pieces copied by a scribe whose hand was extremely neat and efficient. There are no identifiable pieces by foreign composers (other than Ferrabosco), and such mistakes as there are remain uncorrected. Against the supposition that the manuscript was the work of a professional scribe is the fact that only three pieces have titles and/or attributions, and that the contents are closely related to the Holmes books, occasionally reproducing some of the mistakes.[92] Possibly the scribe had access to Holmes's work, Dd.9.33 in particular, or did Holmes have access to the Euing manuscript?

---

[90] The book was in the private collection of Robert Spencer. It is published in facsimile as *The Sampson Lute Book*, with an introduction by Robert Spencer (Musical Sources, 4; Leeds, 1974).

[91] Spencer, 'Three English Lute Manuscripts' and 'The Tollemache Lute Manuscript', *LSJ* 7 (1965), 38–9.

[92] Poulton, *John Dowland*, 107.

Most of the pieces in the Euing manuscript are for 6-course lute, but some require a 7-course lute with a bass tuned at *F* or *D*. A small number of pieces require a 9-course lute with diapasons at *F*, *D*, and *C*.[93] Dowland is the favourite composer (19), followed by Cutting (15) and Holborne (8). Ferrabosco the Elder (3), Bacheler (2), John Johnson (1), Robert Johnson (1), and Cavendish (3) are also represented, as are the relatively unknown Bulman and Askue. The selection of pieces is mainstream, with galliards (26) and pavans (24) predominant, and variations (8), almains (4), and fantasias (4) also present. A few pages have short toys, voltes, and tune arrangements as page-fillers. The Euing manuscript is stamped with the royal coat of arms of James I. This and the piece by Robert Johnson suggest a date *c.*1605. The book is entirely for solo lute, save for a set of interesting instructions for realizing a figured bass on the theorbo that dates from a later period and is connected with Matteis.[94]

The so-called 'Cosens' lute book is difficult to date.[95] It contains sixty-nine pieces in a single, tidy, upright hand. It is unusual among contemporary English lute sources as many pieces can be traced to printed collections. From English publications it has a piece from Robinson's *Schoole of Musicke* (1603), a copy of John Danyel's 'The leaves be green' from his song book of 1606, and Bacheler's 'Mounsier's Almaine' from *Varietie* (1610). A section (fos 21ᵛ–32ᵛ) is devoted to Continental preludes and fantasias, many of which also appear in Besard's *Thesaurus harmonicus* (1603), Fuhrmann's *Testudo gallo-germanica* (1615), and Mertel's *Hortus musicalis novus* (1615), as well as many Continental manuscripts like the Hainhofer and Schele. Several of these pieces are by Laurencini, but other composers include Charles Bocquet and Valentine Strobel I.[96]

Another section (fos. 36ᵛ–42ʳ) of the Cosens manuscript contains yet more pieces from foreign publications, including Dowland's 'Lachrimae Pavan' as published by Furhmann.[97] Among the English composers Dowland is the most favoured, but there are also pieces by Bacheler, Danyel, Cutting, Cavendish, Robinson, Thomas Vautor, Thomas Smyth, and William Hollis. The book contains no ornament signs. Most of the pieces require only a 6-course lute, but some need a seventh course.[98]

Table 7.3 lists the contents of the more important English Golden Age manuscript sources believed to have been compiled, at least in part, after 1610. These sources, along with Robert Dowland's *Varietie*, contain a mixture of more modern

[93] Fos. 40ᵛ and 22ᵛ.

[94] Fo. 50ʳ. Nicola Matteis, *The False Consonances of Musick* (1682), ed. James Tyler (Monaco, 1980), p. iv.

[95] Frederick William Cosens owned the book in the 19th c.; otherwise he had no connection with the book. It was presented to *GB-Cu* in 1891.

[96] Laurencini's pieces appear on folios: 21ᵛ, 26ʳ, 28ᵛ–29ʳ, 29ᵛ–30ʳ, 30ʳ, 31ᵛ. The Bocquet piece on fo. 32ᵛ is from Besard (1603), no. 6; Strobel's piece on fo. 28ʳ is from Fuhrmann (Praeludium 8).

[97] Cosens, fos. 36ᵛ–37ʳ; Fuhrmann, pp. 60–1.

[98] One piece (Cosens, fos. 43ᵛ–44ʳ, 'En me revenant') suggests the need for a 10-course lute, but this is a copying error, and the only diapason that is required is a seventh-course *F*.

Table 7.3. *Contents of major post-1610 sources*

Note:

1. Only the earlier sections of the Pickeringe and Board MSS are included. The O.16.2 MS has not been included here although it is possible that part of this MS may have dated from this period.

2. The pieces by Herbert and Hely have been included although they certainly do date from after 1620.

3. The pieces are, in general, listed according to the source attributions; these may be incorrect.

4. Some pieces could be classed under different headings, e.g. some almains could be masque dances. In general MS titles have been followed.

5. Only solo lute music has been included. Duets have been ignored

Manuscript	Pieces	Composers (2 or more attributions)
Pickeringe (fos. 15ʳ-36ʳ)	11 pavans	31 anon.
	8 galliards	10 John Dowland
	2 fantasias	5 Bacheler
	2 corantos	3 Francis Cutting
	2 almains	2 Rosseter
	12 ballad tunes/popular tunes	2 John Johnson
	10 untitled	2 John Whitefield
	13 toys	
	2 hunts-up	
Add. 38539	18 courantes/corantos	9 Robert Johnson
	12 almains	7 John Dowland
	8 galliards	6 Sturt
	7 voltes	2 Kindersley
	7 ballad tune pieces	
	6 masque tunes	
	2 toys/jiggs	
	1 fantasia/canaries/ballet/battel	
Nn.6.36	17 galliards	18 Bacheler
	16 pavans	3 John Dowland
	12 courantes/corantos	2 Sturt
	9 ballad tune pieces	
	3 voltes	
	3 almains	
	2 preludes	
	1 fancy/masque/ballet	
Board (fos. 1ʳ-32ᵛ)	22 ballad tune pieces	47 anon.
	15 almains	10 John Dowland
	14 galliards	8 Allison
	12 corantos	8 Robert Johnson
	10 pavans	8 John Johnson
	8 masque tunes	3 Holborne
	4 toys	2 Robert Dowland
	2 jigs/grounds/studies/preludes	2 Ambrose Lupo
	1 branles/fantasia	
Herbert	86 courantes	28 Jacob (Reys)
	50 fantasias	21 Gaultier

Manuscript	Pieces	Composers (2 or more attributions)
	41 preludes	13 Lorenzino/Cavalier
	22 pavans	11 Sr Danielli Inglesi/Mr Daniel
	19 voltes	11 du Gast genti Provencal
	10 galliards	11 Perrichon
	7 ballad/song-based pieces	11 Diomedes
	3 ballets	10 Herbert
	10 others (chaconne, toccata,	9 Belleville
	fugue, saraband, almain, and	9 La Poulonois
	untitled)	8 Hely
		7 Daniel Bacheler
		7 Saman
		6 Holborne
		5 Robert Johnson
		5 Heart
		4 Bataille
		4 Pietreson
		3 John Dowland
		3 Rosseter
		3 Ballard

lighter pieces (often associated with masque music, and usually of the coranto, volte, or almain type), and music of an older, more serious kind: fantasias, pavans, galliards, and sets of complicated variations. Each of these sources is individual, and reflects the preferences and purposes of its compiler or compilers.

The Pickeringe manuscript has the royal coat of arms of James I on the covers.[99] Probably it was first bound up as a blank book for the use of one of the royal musicians. At some point between 1603 and 1616 it came into the hands of Jane Pickeringe. She entered music, and signed and dated the flyleaf with the inscription 'Jane Pickeringe owe this Booke 1616'. The book also contains an altogether later repertoire of music, which dates from *c*.1630. The main, earlier section of the Pickeringe manuscript (i.e. fos. 4^r–36^r and 52^v–54^r), which is in Jane's hand, contains, in general, a more conservative selection of pieces than those of the other manuscripts in Table 7.3. Indeed this section of the book contains only two corantos and no voltes or masquing tunes. The solo repertoire collected by this compiler is exclusively British, with no known Continental pieces included. The manuscript contains thirteen toys and twelve pieces based on ballad tunes, giving it a strong

[99] See *Jane Pickeringe's Lute Book*, facs. with an introductory study by Robert Spencer (Musical Sources, 23; Clarabricken, 1985).

populist bent.[100] Like the Board manuscript, and probably also Add. 38539,[101] it was compiled by a lady amateur whose technical attainment was admirably high. The criticism of the lute as being a woman's instrument and unsuitable for men may be based on the increasing favour it found with the female members of the gentry from this point onwards.

The Pickeringe manuscript is more representative in content of the lute repertoire in England *c*.1600 than 1616. The manuscript also contains fifteen duets, five of which are ascribed to John Johnson (d. 1594), and one to Richard Allison (d. *c*.1606). It contains only one piece by Robert Johnson. The duet repertoire is similar to that found in the Marsh manuscript of the 1580s and Dd.3.18 of the 1590s. All the duets and quite a number of the solo pieces require only six courses, the remainder requiring seven. A further conservative trait in this source is the use of continuous 'grid system' rhythm signs. By 1610 this older system was gradually being superseded in English sources by mensural rhythm signs, which were added only where rhythmic changes occurred. It must also be said that the old 'grid system' was employed, at least in part, in both Nn.6.36 and the Board manuscript.

There are two theories that would explain the apparent discrepancy between the date of the manuscript and the repertoire. Perhaps Jane Pickeringe dated her book years after compiling her collection. Alternatively, she could have been adding to her collection up to 1616, but her taste in lute music was retrospective. Assuming the latter case, it could be that Jane Pickeringe, about whom nothing is known, was a cultivated gentlewoman, possibly from a provincial family unconnected with the court, who preferred and had access to lute music of an older generation, which she collected and recorded for her and her family's private use.[102]

Add. 38539 is stamped on the binding with the initials 'M.L.' A poem that appears on the flyleaf that begins 'Margareta margarita' has led to the suggestion that this manuscript originally belonged to a woman, but at present the owner's full name and identity are unknown.[103] By contrast with the Pickeringe manuscript, Add. 38539 contains a repertoire of lute music clearly connected with the court, much of it by musicians employed by either the king or Prince Henry. There were two main hands at work on this manuscript, the handwriting changing on fo. 28[v]. The rediscovery in Kraków of Berlin 40641 has made it possible to identify the first hand in Add. 38539 as that of John Sturt, a lutenist employed by Prince Henry from

[100] Thomas F. Kelly, 'Notes on the Jane Pickering Lute Book', *JLSA* 1 (1968), 19–23 at 21.

[101] See *The Board Lute Book*, facs. with an introduction by Robert Spencer (Reproductions of Early Music, 4; Leeds, 1976). See Spencer's commentary, 'The Book and its Date', for the suggestion that Add. 38539 might have originally belonged to a woman.

[102] *Jane Pickeringe's Lute Book*, ed. Spencer. See the introduction for Hughes-Hughes's almost certainly incorrect suggestions as to the identity of Jane Pickeringe.

[103] *The M. L. Lute Book*, facs. with an introduction by Robert Spencer (Musical Sources, 25; Clarabricken, 1985), p. xii.

1610 to 1612, and thereafter a London wait from 1613 to his death in 1625. Add. 38539 was long referred to as the Sturt manuscript, even before the connection could be substantiated. Sturt signed Berlin 40641 on fo. 12ʳ.[104] All twenty-six pieces in Berlin 40641 have French titles, usually just 'Ballet', 'Courant', and 'Volte', or, as in the case of the last four pieces and a few others, individual titles like 'la Duchesse'.

Seven of the pieces in Berlin 40641 are attributable to Robert Johnson, including four pieces written for the *Masque of the Middle Temple and Lincoln's Inn*, known also as the Prince's Masque. This masque was presented on the 15 February 1613 to celebrate the marriage of the Princess Elizabeth, the future 'Winter Queen', to Frederick, Elector Palatine. Sturt played the lute in this masque, along with both Dowlands, Thomas Cutting, Philip Rosseter, Thomas Ford, Robert Taylor, and Thomas Davies. George Chapman wrote the masque, and Johnson was paid £45 for music and songs.[105] Four of the pieces in the mansucript are attributable to John Sturt, and the implication is that some time after 1613 he travelled to the Continent, and was active most probably in France, where he was brought into contact with the latest Parisian styles. There are nine pieces in this manuscript that can also be found in Add. 38539, and five concordances with the Board manuscript. At the start of Berlin 40641 is a watercolour picture graphically illustrating one of the prime reasons for learning the lute, namely to attract a spouse (see Pl. 7.3). Between a man and a woman a lute, flute, and music book are laid out. The lute is held up by an arm descending from clouds. From other clouds at the top right Cupid descends, aiming an arrow at the woman. The lute is the most prominent feature of the picture, and its role as matchmaker is evident. Surely this was inserted to spur on the original owner in his or her musical endeavours.

Although it is not possible to say which manuscript was compiled first, Add. 38539 or Berlin 40641, Sturt probably compiled them for students or private individuals who were well acquainted with fashionable court music. The pieces in both books consistently require a 10-course lute. Sturt has been regarded up to now as a minor figure, but the fact that he probably travelled abroad, was familiar with developments in French lute music, and then presumably returned to England after his travels, suggests that he may have been influential in introducing French styles to England around this time. We have no record that Sturt joined Prince Charles's household around 1618, when most musicians who had held appointments with Prince Henry were reappointed. Could he have been abroad at this time? Add. 38539 is the single most important source of Robert Johnson's lute music, and it is significant that here he supplants Dowland as the most favoured composer.

---

[104] This signature is comparable to that in Add. 38539, fo. 2ᵛ.
[105] Walls, *Music in the English Courtly Masque*, 38–9.

PL. 7.3. An allegory of the reason for learning the lute, watercolour from Berlin Mus. MS 40641 (now in Kraków, Biblioteka Jagiellońska), fo. iᵛ

Six pieces in Add. 38539 can be identified with particular masques, or connections can reasonably be argued.[106] Sturt, who played in the *Masque of the Middle Temple and Lincoln's Inn* in 1613, was clearly connected both with Robert Johnson

---

[106] These masques and associated pieces from Add. 38539 are: (1) *The Lord Hay's Masque* (1607), 'the Lord the hayes Corant' fos. 2ᵛ–3ʳ; (2) *The Masque of Queens* (1609), 'the wiches Daunce' fo. 4ʳ; (3) ?*Oberon* (1611), 'Allmayne by Mr Ro: Johnson', fo. 16ʳ; 'Allmayne by Mr Robert Johnson' fo. 17ʳ; (4) *The Lord's Masque* (1613), 'first tune of the Lordes maske', fo. 30ᵛ; 'second tune of the Lordes maske', fo. 30ᵛ; (5) *The Masque of the Inner Temple and Grays Inn* (1613), 'Mad Tom of Bedlam' fo. 29ʳ, 'grays in maske', fos. 30ʳ and 32ʳ. To these pieces can be added 'the Noble Man' on fo. 19ʳ, which may be from the lost tragi-comedy *The Nobleman* (1612/13) played at court by Cyril Tourneur, which contained a masque. This piece is called 'the noble menes mask tune' in Dd.4.22, fos. 8ᵛ–9ʳ. See Poulton, *John Dowland*, 100.

and the court musical environment in general, and was able to supply the owner of Add. 38539 with much fashionable court music in arrangements for the lute. Apart from one piece by Holborne and one by Francis Cutting, all the composers mentioned in the book were active *c*.1610, and as the masque pieces show, much of its contents date from after 1610. Of the sources considered here, Add. 38539 is most closely associated with the court, containing a fashionable and generally up-to-date repertoire for *c*.1615–20, and one which shows the influence of the French solo music of René Saman, Charles Bocquet, Robert Ballard, Julien Perrichon, Mercure d'Orléans, and Jacques or Ennemond Gaultier.[107]

Nn.6.36 is the last manuscript in the hand of Mathew Holmes, Precentor of Westminster Abbey from 1597 to his death in 1621, and copyist of the great Cambridge lute manuscript collection. The later books in Holmes's hand, particularly Dd.9.33 and Nn.6.36, differ from the earlier ones in being increasingly reliant on music by court composers. Nn.6.36 was probably compiled between 1605 and 1615, and is dominated by the works of Bacheler, the remaining composers having only a few attributable pieces.[108] Only three pieces by Dowland are included, in sharp contrast to Holmes's earlier lute books, where he is generously represented. This perhaps suggests a drop in popularity for Dowland's pieces or, more likely, a degree of personal contact between Bacheler and Holmes. Although galliards and pavans are the mainstay of Nn.6.36, there is a sizeable number of 'currants' and pieces based on popular ballad tunes, and some masque-related pieces.

Two pieces at the end of Nn.6.36 use a tuning similar to Francisque's *cordes avalées* tuning. These pieces, along with John Danyel's 'Mrs Anne Grene her leaves be greene' published in his *Songs for Lute, Viol and Voice* (1616), mark the first appearance of *cordes avalées* tuning in England.[109] Further French influence may be seen in the several voltes and ballets, the piece titled 'a french Toy', and the popular 'Coranto Confes' (Ex. 7.1), which is unusual in that it requires a 10-course lute, the remainder of the manuscript needing only nine or eight courses. The pieces by Bacheler in this source are at variance with these French-inspired pieces, in particular the many long and complicated pavans, several of which are unique.

The first section of the Margaret Board manuscript (i.e. fos. 1ʳ–32ᵛ), compiled by her around 1620–5, is probably somewhat later in date than the manuscripts discussed above. Like Jane Pickeringe's book, it has a later section dating from *c*.1630 in different hands. Although the Board family came from Sussex, Margaret must have had access to court music, as the manuscript is rich in masque almains, corantos, and other dances. It seems that she received some instruction from John

---

[107] See Spencer's inventory in *The M. L. Lute Book.*

[108] Most of these pieces are published in Daniel Bacheler, *Selected Works*, ed. Martin Long (Music for the Lute, Book 5; Oxford, 1970).

[109] Similar version in the Cosens MS, fos. 60ᵛ–61ᵛ.

Dowland himself, as he added a few pieces, and a theoretical table on the first folio.[110] (See Pl. 7.4(*a*).) The theory that Dowland taught was based on the antiquated method of Ornithoparcus (first printed Leipzig, 1517) which Dowland had translated and printed in 1609. The aged Dowland, who was 60 in 1623, could have travelled to Sussex to instruct Margaret Board, but it would seem more likely that she received her tuition in London. The Robert Dowland almain that John Dowland wrote out on fo. 12ʳ is unusually precise in its detailed hold signs, ornamentation, and right-hand fingering. (See Plate 7.4(*b*).)

The repertoire of music in this section of the Board manuscript is very wide-ranging: well-known pavans and galliards are nearly equalled in number by newer corantos, almains, and specific masque dances. Among the attributable pieces those by John Dowland are the most numerous, followed by some by Robert Johnson. Music by the long-dead Richard Allison and John Johnson features prominently. The number of simple ballad-tune settings is high. Many are entered as page-fillers. Their presence suggests that this genre of piece remained popular throughout the Golden Age and afterwards. A few pieces of French origin are included.[111] The Board manuscript should be regarded as a court-related source, although fashionable lighter music is interspersed with more serious older music, perhaps reflecting the contact between Margaret Board and Dr Dowland.

More has been published about the Herbert manuscript than the manuscripts discussed above, and the articles by Thurston Dart, Curtis Price, and Julia Craig-McFeely have thrown much light on the circumstances relating to its compilation and method of organization.[112] Apart from the last fifteen pieces which date from 1640, the manuscript was probably compiled from a loose-leaf collection gathered over many years. The choice of pieces reflects the changing circumstances of Herbert's career. Herbert stayed in Paris in the years 1608–9, travelled widely on the Continent from 1610 to 1617, and was ambassador in Paris from 1619 to 1624, when he was dismissed in disgrace for opposing the marriage of Prince Charles and Henrietta Maria. Thereafter he lived in Britain, first in Montgomery Castle, and from 1632 to his death in 1648 at Richmond. Apart from the eight pieces by Cuthbert Hely (probably copied by Hely himself), there are two scribes at work in the book, one of which was Herbert. It has been suggested that the manuscript was started in 1624, though it may even be that most of the pieces were copied into the book in the 1630s.[113]

---

[110] *The Board Lute Book*. For masque concordances see Spencer's inventory.

[111] e.g. nos. 52, 69, 75 of the Board MS.

[112] Dart, 'Lord Herbert of Cherbury's Lute Book'; Curtis A. Price, 'An Organisational Peculiarity of Lord Herbert of Cherbury's Lute-Book', *LSJ* 11 (1969), 5–27; Julia Craig-McFeely, 'A Can of Worms: Lord Herbert of Cherbury's Lute Book', *LSJ* 31 (1991), 20–48.

[113] Craig-McFeely, 'A Can of Worms', 29–33.

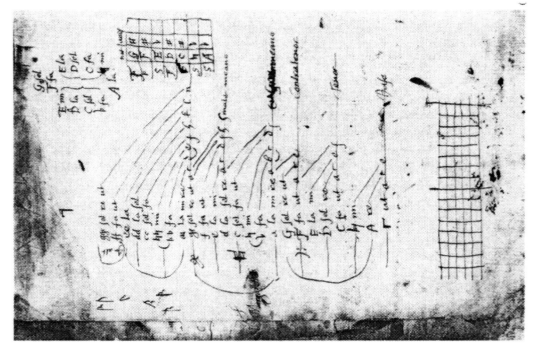

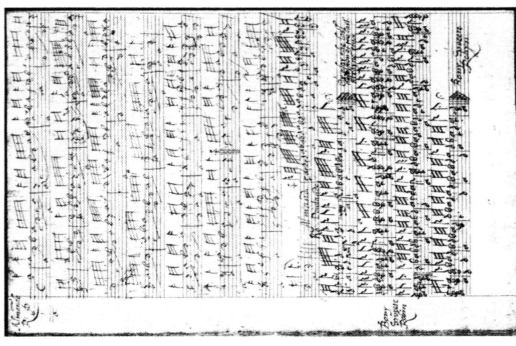

PL. 7.4. John Dowland's handwriting from the Board Lute Book: (a) 'Almande R: D:/Ro: Dowlande'; fo. 12v (b) theoretical tables, fo.iv;

(a)

The Herbert manuscript is perhaps more important as a collection of French lute music from the elusive period leading up to the experimentation with transitional tunings than as a source of English lute music, and reflects Herbert's period of service in Paris. Among English composers, Daniel Bacheler (also called 'Sig. Daniel Inglesi' and 'Mr Daniel' in the book), have the most attributions. Dowland has only three pieces, Robert Johnson and Holborne six. The eight pieces by Cuthbert Hely and the pavans by Herbert himself are clearly later additions to the manuscript, and will be reserved for consideration in the next chapter.

The non-English pieces are representative of Parisian taste in lute music *c.*1600–10. The most favoured composer of all is a certain 'Jacob', who, according to Dart, can be regarded as almost certainly being Jacob Reys (1546–1605). Reys was born in Augsburg, and was lutenist to Henry of Valois. Dart, however, further regarded Jacob Reys as also being the 'Polonois' (Jakob Polak) who received nine attributions in the Herbert manuscript, a supposition that is probably incorrect.[114] The music of Diomedes Cato, Jacob Reys, and Lorenzino link the manuscript with Besard's *Thesaurus*. Several song arrangements are based on Bataille's books of *airs de cour*, and a few pieces come from the books of Vallet and Ballard. Indeed this eclecticism and debt to Continental printed anthologies places the Herbert manuscript as much with Continental manuscript anthologies like the Hainhofer, Montbuysson, Haslemere, and Schele manuscripts as with late English Golden Age sources.

The courante is the most popular form in the Herbert manuscript, but the fifty fantasias indicate a taste for serious pieces, and contrasts with the English manuscripts discussed above, all of which have relatively few fantasias. The repertoire can be compared with the printed anthologies of Besard, Fuhrmann, Mylius, and Van den Hove, but with a pronounced preference towards courantes and fantasias. Unlike the printed books the contents are grouped by key rather than form. The complete lack of English masquing tunes and popular ballad-based pieces indicates both an academic taste and a lack of contact with English court fashions, although the French equivalent is included in the many ballets and courantes.

Viewing the sources in Table 7.3 collectively, there is, by 1610, a marked increase in the number of corantos, courantes, and voltes over earlier English lute sources, a trend mirrored in Continental manuscripts like the Haslemere and Werl. Most of these corantos are unattributed, but of those that are, most are of foreign origin. Although the more serious pavans and galliards of the pre-1600 period, typified by the music of John Johnson, Francis Cutting, Holborne, and John Dowland, main-

---

[114] Dart, 'Lord Herbert of Cherbury's Lute Book', 142. This confusion has resulted from the writings of E. Prinz, who in 1725 claimed that Jakob Polak and Reys were identical. However, according to Sauval's *Historie et recherches des antiquités de la ville de Paris* (1724) Jakob Polak (Le Polonois) was born in Poland, and is thus to be differentiated from Reys.

tained a considerable degree of popularity after 1610 in manuscript collections, surviving sources suggest that little of this type of music was composed for the lute after 1610, with the possible exception of the many pavans by Daniel Bacheler and those by Robert Johnson. A predilection for such music is more pronounced in manuscripts that have little or no known connections with the English Court, such as the Pickeringe and Herbert manuscripts.

Less English solo lute music of the sober intimate type written in the 1590s (and typified by the music in Dd.2.11, Dd.9.33, and Dd.5.78.3) was composed after 1600. Instead there is evidence of the increased importance of masque music, particularly in Add. 38539 and Board. Music intended for masque dances needed to be relatively simple, but robust and extrovert. Much of this music could have been originally intended for string band, and subsequently arranged for the lute. Possibly this new music was of limited appeal to dissaffected sections of the musically educated society.

Very little masque dance music was published in England, though it did appear in print on the Continent and was circulated in manuscript in England. Such music was never written primarily for the lute, but usually for a string consort. It does not always make good solo lute music as the melody range, having been conceived primarily for violins, is often too wide. These musical developments, together with the increasing social divide discussed above, may have decreased the common acceptability and availability of lute music in England from its high point in the 1590s. The increased availability of viols and viol music (both solo and consort), and the passing of the fashion for mixed consort music, would have further eroded interest in the lute in Jacobean England.

Of all the professional English lutenists active in 1612, when Dowland delivered his attack in the Preface to *A Pilgrimes Solace*, the two most important composers of solo lute music, other than Dowland, were Robert Johnson and Daniel Bacheler. Johnson joined the king's service in 1604 among the 'lutes in ordinary' at the age of 21. In 1610 he was also listed among musicians employed by Prince Henry[115] and by Prince Charles in 1617.[116] Charles confirmed this royal appointment in 1625 among the 'lutes and voices', a post Johnson kept until his death in 1633.[117] His appointment to Lutes in Ordinary was at 20d. a day (plus £16. 2s. 6d. a year for livery).[118] This sum was augmented between 1610 and 1612, and in 1617–25 by £40 per year from Prince Henry and then Prince Charles, and then maintained for the rest of his life by his appointment as lutenist among the king's 'lutes and voices'.[119]

[115] *GB-Lbl* Harley 7009, fo. 1ʳ. This list of Prince Henry's musicians is published in Price, *Patrons and Musicians*, 224; also *RECM* iv. 211.

[116] *RECM* iv. 217.   [117] Ibid., iii. 3.   [118] Ibid., iv. 15.

[119] References to payments to Johnson as a musician for the lute can be found in PRO Pipe Office declared account documents at Chancery Lane E351/543 for the years 1605–12, and E351/544 for the years 1612–27 (particularly fos. 3ᵛ, 20ᵛ, 38ᵛ, 52ᵛ, 71ʳ, 83ᵛ, 96ᵛ, 111ᵛ, 128ʳ, 142ʳ, 154ʳ, 169ʳ, 182ᵛ, 201ʳ, 216ʳ), and for arrears E351/545

He also had responsibilities for distributing money for resources among the king's lutes and was regularly given amounts (normally £20 p.a.) for strings.[120] There was a least one disappointment in his career. When Thomas Lupo died in the winter of 1627, Johnson petitioned for his place as composer for the 'lutes and voices', but was unsuccessful, the post going to Theophilus Lupo.

Evidence of the sort of activities that Johnson undertook as an organizer of the royal lutes is seen in Pl. 7.5. This acquittance states at the top that it is for 'Robert Johnson his bill for money laid out for Prince Charles his Musique from Midsomer untill Christmas 1617'. Underneath the various items for buying a lute, strings, mending, and carriage of lutes is a further bill for money paid out for further strings up to midsummer 1618. The huge total sum of £42. 8s. 8d. paid out by Johnson was not reimbursed by Sir Adam Newton, the prince's treasurer, until the bill was countersigned by Sir Robert Carey, the Chamberlain. Only on 11 February 1618/19 was Johnson able to write on the back of the aquittance that he had received the money. Johnson must have been both a good organizer and financially capable to have undertaken this sort of activity.

Not only was Johnson well rewarded financially by his royal patrons, but the instances when he was called upon to provide music for the theatre and masques would have increased his reputation and livelihood considerably.[121] Unlike the other royal lutenists Jacques Gaultier and John Lawrence, he does not seem to have got into debt. Certainly Johnson was better financially rewarded than John Dowland, who in 1612 gained a single appointment at 20d. a day plus livery, and is not known to have received payment for composing music for royal masques.[122] Johnson spent time abroad early in his career as, on 19 April 1605, he was included along with John Danyel among the seven trumpeters and eight other musicians that accompanied the Earl of Hertford's embassy to Albert, Archduke of Austria, in Brussels. Johnson was paid arrears at Michaelmas 1607 for three years back to 1604 and thus was probably away from court for most of this time.[123] Johnson's patron, Sir George Carey, the Lord Chamberlain, was also patron of Shakespeare's company, The King's Men Players. This troupe performed regularly at the Globe and Black Friars theatres. It was probably through the Carey connection that Johnson began his association with the theatre from 1607. Many of his theatre songs survive including a number with words by Shakespeare. George Carey's brother Robert

---

for the years 1617–23; also in Exchequer of Audit declared accounts at Kew PRO Ao 3/129 for the years 1608–9 and 1630.

[120] e.g. *RECM* iv. 102. This role seems to have been taken over by John Coggeshall after 1629 (ibid., iii. 44).

[121] Poulton, *John Dowland*, 82. For instance, Johnson received £45 for 'musicke and songes' in the *Masque of the Middle Temple and Gray's Inn* (1613).

[122] Poulton, ibid. Dowland was, however, paid £2. 10s. for playing the lute in the *Masque of the Middle Temple and Gray's Inn*.

[123] Price, *Patrons and Musicians*, 127; PRO E351/543.

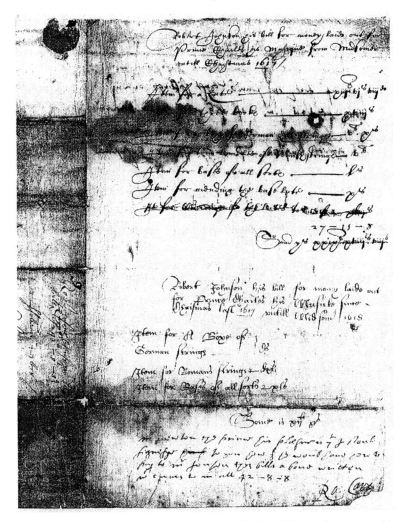

PL. 7.5. Acquittance document belonging to Robert Johnson for sums paid out by him on behalf of the lutes in Prince Charles's household, 1617–18. The Robert Spencer Collection, Royal Academy of Music

Carey was Chamberlain to Prince Charles 1617–25 and his family connection may have helped Johnson's rise to prominence in the prince's music. Johnson's will was proved on 28 November 1633. It indicates that he had a wife Anne, no surviving children, and lived in Acton, where he had lands and tenements.[124] Johnson was a most successful musician. Among Jacobean lutenists only Daniel Bacheler, as a

[124] PRO PROB 11/164, q.97, 15 Nov. 1633.

groom to Queen Anne, received better payment, though Johnson's success was far more conspicuous.

Johnson's output took three main forms: songs, nearly always composed for the stage or masques; dance music for strings; and solo lute music. Much of the dance music is associated with particular masques, as is some of the lute music. Since the publishing of Sundermann's edition of Johnson's solo lute music,[125] several new pieces have come to light via the Board manuscript, and through the research of Peter Holman.[126] It would appear from source evidence that Johnson's surviving lute music, some twenty pieces, with several unattributed but likely additions, was written during the period 1600–15. It is conceivable that the arrangements of masque pieces for lute were not even made by Johnson.

The concordance list supplied by Holman in his article demonstrates the known connection between Johnson's consort masque music and the solo lute pieces adapted from it.[127] *Oberon* (1611) by Ben Jonson, also known as the *Prince's Maske* in honour of Prince Henry, and George Chapman's *Masque of the Middle Temple and Lincoln's Inn* (1613), which was performed to celebrate the wedding of Princess Elizabeth to the Palsgrave Frederick, were possibly the source of six pieces in the known Johnson oeuvre.[128] Johnson is the last of the Golden Age composers to flourish before the adoption of the new tunings in England during the 1630s. His compositions are not only found in the six major manuscripts discussed above, but also in several of the preceding decade and in a few Continental sources, and from the period after 1630 when transitional tunings gradually became the norm.[129] Only those pieces in Richard Mathew's *Lutes Apology* (1652) use tuning no. 10 (arranged by Mathew), but pieces by Johnson in Renaissance tuning appear in the O.16.2 manuscript and the later section of the Board manuscript, both of which are likely to have been copied in the 1630s. Non-lute sources of Johnson's music also indicate that some pieces remained popular up to the mid-century.[130] Finally Mace in 1676 pairs Johnson and Dowland as the most remarkable of the old school.

The number of known almains and masque dances in common time by Johnson which survive in versions for the lute by Johnson has been increased to twelve

[125] *Complete Works for Solo Lute.*

[126] Peter Holman, 'New Sources of Music by Robert Johnson', *LSJ* 20 (1978), 43–52.

[127] Ibid. John P. Cutts, in his article 'Robert Johnson and the Court Masque', *M&L* 41 (1960), 111–26, discusses Johnson's connections with the following masques: *Masque of Queenes* (1609); *Oberon* (1611); *The Lord's Masque* (1613); *The Masque of the Middle Temple and Lincoln's Inn* (1613); and *The Gypsies Metamorphosed* (1621).

[128] Brian Jeffery, 'The Lute Music of Robert Johnson', *EM* 2 (1974), 105–9 at 106. Jeffery suggests that *Complete Works for Solo Lute*, ed. Sundermann, no. VII, 'The Prince's Almain', and no. XI, 'Almain', were originally composed as a C minor/C major pair for *Oberon*.

[129] Foreign lute sources of Johnson's pieces include Berlin 40641; Vallet's *Le Secret des muses: second livre* (1616); Valerius' *Neder-landtsche gedenck-clank* (1626) for lute, voice, and cittern; and the Skene MS for mandore.

[130] Holman, 'New Sources'; in particular MSS *Gb-Och* 379–81 and 1113, and *Gb-Lbl* Add. 10444 for treble and bass versions.

through the discovery of the Board manuscript and Peter Holman's research.[131] The pieces regularly require the highest fret positions on the lute.[132] Clearly many of these pieces are arrangements of dances originally intended for a violin band or massed lutes. This type of lute piece maintained its popularity up to the mid-century, as it appears in the *Lutes Apology*. Playford's keyboard publications continue this trend, starting in 1663 with the first edition of *Musick's Handmaid*, although many English keyboard manuscripts, such as Drexel 5612 and Anne Cromwell's Virginal Book from the 1620–50 period, also reflect their great popularity.

There is a single known coranto by Johnson which is found in the Board manuscript (no. 87, fo. 27^r), entitled 'The Prince his Corranto' (see Ex. 7.2). This coranto has some characteristics more normally associated with his almains and masque dances, particularly in the ascending melodic sequence up to high f'' at the close of the first eight-bar stanza, and the sequences in the second and third stanzas (bars 9–10, 13–14, 17–19, 20–1). Such melodic sequences can also be found in almains nos. VII, VIII, XI, and XII in Sundermann's edition, particularly in their second strains. The simplicity and obvious harmonic direction in this coranto make it an admirable dance tune.[133] It is unusual among corantos in having three strains (nearly all of the other corantos in the Board manuscript have two strains). The two known Johnson galliards, although fine pieces, have no obvious distinguishing features.

Two of Robert Johnson's pavans (ed. Sundermann, nos. II and III) are comparable to those by Daniel Bacheler. It is a trait of Bacheler's style to include divisions which have a great deal of rhythmic variation. Likewise in these pavans by Johnson, although the bass line is adhered to, the divisions over it are very elaborate. However, Johnson's pavan no. IV and his single surviving fantasia stand apart from his other pieces. This fantasia occurs only in the Herbert manuscript, and is unlike the earlier fantasias of Dowland. There is no suggestion of virtuosic display. Instead the piece achieves great expression through the various workings of the opening motif and the excellent use of contrasting tessituras from the very lowest to the highest. (See Ex. 7.3.) The many false relations (as in bar 9), unprepared dissonances (as in bar 10), and three-part descending sequences are stylistic traits that John Wilson was later to employ exhaustively in his solo pieces. The form of this piece, with its many different appearances of the opening theme, each in a different

---

[131] Ibid. These pieces are *Complete Works for Solo Lute*, ed. Sundermann, nos. VII–XII; Board, fo. 28^r, 'Almayne Ro Johnso'; Board, fo. 30^r, 'Almane Mr Johnson'; Board, fo. 30^r, 'An Almayne Mr Johnsonne'; Board, fo. 28^r, 'The Princis Masque'; Nn.6.36, fo. 18^v, 'Maske'; Nn.6.36, fo. 18^v, 'Maske'.

[132] e.g. *Complete Works for Solo Lute*, ed. Sundermann, no. X, and his galliard in Nn.6.36 both use the tenth fret.

[133] It also exists in a five-part consort in William Brade, *Newe ausserlesene liebliche Branden* (Hamburg, 1617) no. 36, 'Coranto Robb Johnson', *a 5*.

Ex. 7.2. *'The Prince his Corranto' by Robert Johnson, Board MS, no. 87, fo. 27ʳ*

Ex. 7.3. *Opening of the Fantasia by Robert Johnson from the Herbert MS, fo. 16ʳ, bars 1–10*

position or voice, drawing to a climax of rhythmic activity around bar 70, has parallels with the pieces by Cuthbert Hely also in the Herbert manuscript.

Johnson's pavan no. IV has even closer links with the solo pieces by Wilson. The final six bars of the second strain bear some similarity to the final passages of Wilson's pieces nos. 8, 9, and 10. (See Ex. 7.4.) The marked preference for the middle and lower registers, and the near continuous stepwise movement of the bass line found in sections of this piece are both characteristics of Wilson's style (see Ex. 10.2), as is the gradual descent by step in three parts in bars 23–4 and 28–30.

Ex. 7.4. *Pavan by Robert Johnson, second strain, Herbert MS fo. 22*ᵛ, *bars 21–32*

Robert Johnson's fantasia is unique, but his pavan no. IV is found in the Herbert manuscript and Add. 38539 (here without divisions). Probably this piece was composed around 1615. Despite the fashion for lighter music in the French style, Johnson could write intense sombre music in a style that was removed from that of earlier Golden Age music, but which was firmly rooted in the English tradition. This style was continued and developed by Hely and Wilson after the Golden Age.

Of all English lutenist-composers Daniel Bacheler was perhaps the most successful in his own lifetime. Research by Anne Batchelor on her own family history shows that the Daniel Bacheler who wrote out the Walsingham part-books, and who composed and put his name to some of the pieces, was one and the same Daniel Bacheler who went on to become lutenist and Groom of the Privy Chamber to Queen Anne from 1603 to his death.[134] On 13 November 1579, Bacheler, at the age

---

[134] Batchelor, 'Daniel Bacheler'. See also ead., *A Batchelor's Delight*. Martin Long in the preface to Bacheler, *Selected Works*, suggested there might have been two Daniel Bachelers. So too does Diana Poulton (*New Grove*, i. 880). More recent research has shown this to be wrong.

of 7, was apprenticed to his uncle, Thomas Cardell, the lutenist and dancing-master at Elizabeth's court.[135] On 7 July 1586, at the age of 14, his apprenticeship was signed over from Cardell to Sir Francis Walsingham, the queen's principal Secretary of State (see above, pl. 5.2(*a*)). Walsingham was responsible for organizing the 1587 funeral procession of his son-in-law, Sir Philip Sidney. This explains Bacheler's presence in Thomas Lant's commemorative funeral roll, where he is seen riding Sidney's war horse and carrying a battleaxe (see Pl. 7.6). Bacheler was 16 in 1588 when he compiled the Walsingham part-books (see above, Pl. 5.2(*b*)). Later he served the ill-fated Robert Devereux, Earl of Essex, from 1594 to 1599, and also his widow Lady Essex. She was Walsingham's daughter, and had been Lady Frances Sidney until her marriage to Essex in 1590. Probably Bacheler was attached to Lady Frances from 1590 through to 1603, serving also Essex during the five years of their marriage. On James's accession Lady Essex was invited to court, where her son could be educated with the young Prince Henry.[136]

Daniel Bacheler was granted many favours by the Crown in the years after 1603, when he first became a Groom of the Privy Chamber, an honour that is mentioned in *Varietie*.[137] He was granted a coat of arms in 1607. He was by far the best paid of the Grooms, receiving £160 p.a., which was even more than any of Anne's well-paid French musicians.[138] He died in January of 1618/19.[139] His solo lute pieces appear in manuscripts of the 1590–1610 period (Cosens, Euing, Dd.2.11, Dd.5.78.3, and Dd.9.33 in particular), but are mostly to be found in two later Jacobean sources: Herbert and Nn.6.36.

Of the eighteen pieces attributed to Bacheler in Nn.6.36, eight pavans and six gal-liards are unique.[140] The style of these pieces, and those in all manuscripts save the Herbert manuscript, are firmly rooted in the English classical style. He shows con-siderable contrapuntal skill, and his division sections are particularly finely worked. Perhaps his greatest gift is the imagination he employs in his variations on 'Monsiers Almain' and 'Une jeune filette'. This last piece is attributed to 'Mr Daniell' in the Herbert manuscript and is anonymous in the Pickeringe manuscript. The pieces in the Herbert manuscript attributed to 'Mr Daniel' or 'Sig. Daniel Inglesi' would appear, on concordance evidence, to be by Bacheler, and not by John Danyel.[141] Bacheler's pieces, of all late Elizabethan and early Jacobean lute music, require an exceptional technique, and the absence of ballad settings, masquing tunes, toys, and other lighter pieces among his surviving works indicates a sober muse.

---

[135] Batchelor, 'The Right Perfect Musician', 3.   [136] Ibid. 5.   [137] Ibid. 6.
[138] *RECM* iv. 197–207. The best paid among the French musicians was Lewes Richard at £155 p.a.
[139] Batchelor, 'The Right Perfect Musician', 7.
[140] *Selected Works*, ed. Long, 47–50.
[141] For example, the pavan in Herbert MS, fos. 3ᵛ–4ᵛ is entitled 'Pavana del St Danielle Ingles', yet in the Pickeringe MS, fo. 27ʳ, it is entitled 'A pavin by Mr Daniell Bachler'. Likewise the 'Pavana del medesima [*sic*]' that follows the above pavan in the Herbert MS is attributed to 'D. Batcher' in the Cosens MS, fos. 80ᵛ–81ʳ.

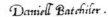

PL. 7.6. Detail from the Funeral Roll by Thomas Lant *Sequitur celebritas* (London, 1587), showing the young Daniel Bacheler, aged 15, riding the dead Sir Philip Sidney's war horse. British Library, C.20, fo. 12, pl. 14

Some of Daniel Bacheler's pieces in the Herbert manuscript suggest the influence of French solo lute music.[142] Four of the known Bacheler courantes are found in the Herbert manuscript, as well as the five unique Bacheler preludes.[143] These Bacheler courantes and preludes suggest a composition date after 1610, and may be among the last pieces he composed. They are stylistically different from the complicated pavans, which probably date from an earlier period. His courantes are comparable to the sober French courantes of the 1610–20 years, especially those by Gaultier in the Herbert manuscript, the Haslemere manuscript, and Basle 53.[144] These courantes share a sombre atmosphere induced by the flat minor keys preferred (only one of Bacheler's courantes is in F major, the others in F minor), a sparseness of texture with odd passages that stay in the low and middle tessitura of the lute, and an expansive and subtle melodic phrasing quite different from most English corantos of the time, which usually approximate to the fast Italian 'corrente' type. (See Ex. 7.5.)

The five preludes by Bacheler compare stylistically to the fantasia and pavan no. IV by Johnson discussed above, and to the solo pieces by Hely and Wilson from the post-Golden Age period. All Bacheler's preludes are in flat minor keys save the E flat major prelude. They share with his courantes a sparseness of texture, interspersed with the occasional full chord, a texture quite different from the Bacheler style in other sources. On balance their tessitura is even lower than in the courantes, with the avoidance of the top course, except for an occasional use for dramatic contrast with the lower registers. That four of the preludes are unbarred throughout or in part indicates a very advanced thinking for the period.[145] (See Ex. 7.6.) Very few of the French preludes in the Herbert manuscript are unbarred, and only Bacheler of all English lute composers of the period makes any significant contribution to the development of the unbarred prelude.[146] The fascination with sonority and the striving for heightened expression by exploiting the lute's sound capabilities displayed in these preludes and courantes brings Bacheler closer to the French experimentalists of the 1610–30 period than any English lutenist of his generation.

During the years 1600–30 the 'coranto' or 'courante' was gaining increasing popularity in England as it was throughout Europe. Morley in 1597 described the courante and volte as:

Like unto this [i.e. the branle] (but more light) be the Voltes and Courantes which being both of a measure, are notwithstanding, danced after sundry fashions, the Volte rising and leaping, the Courante travising and running, in which measure also our Country Dance is

---

[142] Price, 'An Organisational Peculiarity', 22–7.

[143] For concordances for the Bacheler courantes in the Herbert MS, see *Selected Works*, ed. Long, 49.

[144] Some of these pieces were published in tablature by the Lute Society of America in 1981 as *Gautier: 8 Courantes in Renaissance Tuning*, trans. and ed. by Peter J. Danner (n.p., 1981).

[145] Herbert MS, fos. 38ʳ, 42ᵛ, 56ʳ, and 58ᵛ.

[146] This discussion excludes Hely's preludes, as I have regarded them as post-Golden Age pieces.

Ex. 7.5. *Courante by Daniel Bacheler, Herbert MS, fo. 27ᵛ, bars 1–16*

Ex. 7.5. *cont.*

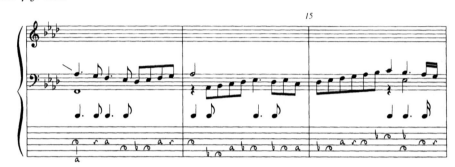

NB. Barlines regularized to $\frac{6}{4}$ not $\frac{3}{4}$.
Diaposon ⅘ tuned at *C* not *D*.

made though it be danced after another form than any of the former. All these be made in strains, either two or three as shall seem best to the maker, but the Courante hath twice so much in a strain as the English Country Dance.[147]

Evidently the 'courante' or coranto in England *c*.1600 was typically a lively dance, both light and somewhat rustic. Only a few of the early Golden Age manuscripts contain many examples, and they are confined in the main to the late sources Add. 38539, Nn.6.36, Board, and Herbert manuscripts. It may be that the increased popularity for the dance throughout Europe after 1600 resulted from its connections with the masque and *ballet de cour*.

The courantes by Bacheler and Gaultier in the Herbert manuscript illustrate the change in the French courante towards a more dignified and complicated dance, with an attendant fascination for hemiola rhythms and an indication of contrapuntal play, and thus away from the lighter, quicker Italian corrente. Corantos in the Board and Nn.6.36 manuscripts approximate more closely to the Italian type. Among these are the single known contributions to the genre by John Dowland (Ex. 7.7) and Robert Johnson in the Board manuscript.

[147] Morley, *A Plain and Easie Introduction*, ed. Harman, 297.

Ex. 7.6. *Prelude in C minor by Daniel Bacheler, Herbert MS, fo. 58ᵛ*

Ex. 7.7. *Coranto by John Dowland, Board MS, fo. 30', bars 1–16*

1. Rhythm sign ⎤ altered to ⎤⎤

The two surviving voltes and single coranto by John Sturt, like all the seven known Sturt pieces, show French influence in their style and texture. The relative wealth of concordances of Sturt's pieces show that, to those close to the court, these pieces were popular. Apart from his court appointments to Princes Henry and Charles, little is known of Sturt's life. He did not join Charles's Lutes and Voices in 1625 as he had died by then.[148] In particular the cadential endings and varied repeats show Sturt's style to be closer to the Parisian style *c*.1600–10 of Saman and Ballard, whose pieces had been published in England in *Varietie*. (See Ex. 7.8.)

Two further masques written for Prince Henry were Samuel Danyel's *Tethys Festival* (1610), presented and performed by Anne of Denmark, and *Oberon* (1611), another Jonson and Jones collaboration, for which Robert Johnson provided music.[149] Prince Henry was a central figure in the development of court taste *c*.1610 not least because he brought together such formidable artistic, musical, and literary talents. A second important figure in the introduction of French and Italian musical styles into England was Anne of Denmark. French influence on the masque did not break through to its full extent until the arrival of Henrietta Maria, though the title-page of Marc de Maillet's *Balet de la revanche du mespris d'Amour* states that it was 'Dancé devant la Royne de la grande Bretaigne. Imprimé a Londres ce 28. Ianvier 1617'. Thus it seems that a French *ballet de cour* was performed for Anne of Denmark as early as 1617.[150]

It is clear from this short study of the last decades of the Golden Age that the English lute style was opened up to French influence, and maintained a continuous, though limited development in the more serious vein of fantasia, pavan, and prelude. The influence of the French lute style was greatly accentuated by the arrival of Jacques Gaultier in 1617, and his subsequent employment in the service of the Duke of Buckingham and later Henrietta Maria. As Gaultier was probably already using the transitional tunings by 1620, he is dealt with in later chapters.

Up to the mid-century some lutenists in England remained faithful to the Renaissance tuning for playing solo lute music. Mathew in the introduction to the *Lutes Apology* (1652) mentions that he had two apprenticeships on the lute, i.e. in both Renaissance and transitional tunings. In the serious music of Robert Johnson, Bacheler, and after 1625 of Hely and Wilson, a purely English style continued to develop, little affected by French music. The increasing social divisions in English society in the Jacobean and Caroline periods may have done much to hinder the happy exchange and acceptability of lute music. The cavalier classes seem to have been the only section of society with a keen interest in the lute after *c*.1625, and most manuscripts whose provenance is known after this date belonged to women of this social group.[151] For them French lute music was the desirable and fashionable thing. For the middle classes and those with Puritan leanings lute music may have seemed increasingly foreign.

---

[148] *RECM* iv. 229. John Sturt, a musician from Churchyard Alley, Fetter Lane, died in Jan. 1624/5 and was buried at St Andrew's Holborn on the 14th.

[149] For this masque Johnson composed dance music which was arranged for the violin band by Thomas Lupo.

[150] Walls, *Music in the English Courtly Masque*, 229.

[151] Such MSS include the Wemyss, Pan 8, Ruthwen, and Longleat MSS.

Ex. 7.8. *Volte by John Sturt, Add. 38539, fo. 21ᵛ, bars 1–34*

In summary, the musical developments at court, especially in the households of the queen and royal children, the interest lavished on the viol, and the influx of foreign musicians makes some sense of Dowland's rage in 1612. He had not only failed to get a court appointment at home, but now the musical agenda of the court had moved on. The lute, the most favoured courtly instrument from early Tudor times, was no longer so esteemed. Further, it is from this point onwards that the lute itself becomes tainted with being 'un-English'. Mace, though writing in the 1670s, learnt the lute in the 1620s, a time when the instrument was still in the transition from being universally admired to one that was regarded by some as effete and affected. For Mace the viol is the quintessentially English instrument. Consorts are admirable because they are democratic. All are equal in volume, and a proper and equitable balance of parts can be maintained. For this reason he objects to the foreign violin, which can outcry the rest and upset the balance. The decline of the lute must be seen alongside the continued flourishing of the viol. While the viol maintained its Englishness the lute lost it. The basic theme of Mace's book is the desire to return to, and connect with, the age of Dowland and Johnson. He hoped to do this by fusing elements of the 'old English lute' (by which he means lutes in Renaissance tuning), with those of the French lute of his day. The association of the lute with the court, and the disaffection of sections of British society with the court in the 1610s and 1620s, certainly contributed to the 'Frenchification' of the lute.

Chapter Eight

The Lute in Song Accompaniment

Pricksong is a faire musicke, so it be done upon the booke surely and after a good sorte. But to sing to the lute is much better, because all the sweetnes consisteth in one alone, and a man is much more heedfull and understandeth better the feat manner, and the aire or veyne of it, when the eares are not busied in hearing any moe than one voice: and beside every litle errour is soone perceived, which happeneth not in singing with company, for one beareth out another.

But singing to the lute with the dittie (me thinke) is more pleasant than the rest, for it addeth to the wordes such a grace and strengh, that it is a great wonder.

From Sir Thomas Hoby's *The Booke of the Courtyer* (1561)

Singing to the lute is as old as lute playing itself. The earliest English sources (mid-sixteenth century) all show that the influence of vocal accompaniment was ever present in the lute repertoire. A good proportion of the surviving pre-1580 pieces are either tablature versions of popular song tunes to be played as solos, or actual accompaniments to songs. This is to be expected, as the early sources like Stowe 389, RA 58, and the commonplace books belonged to amateurs for whom popular songs may have been the most accessible repertoire.

Our perception today of the lute song is coloured by the huge success, both artistic and commercial, of Dowland's *First Booke of Songs* of 1597. The success of this book was made possible by the fashion for singing to the lute evident throughout Elizabeth's reign. Before the onset of published lute songs lutenists adapted a wide variety of material, both sacred and secular, for performance with voice and lute. Most popular were settings of poetry from the Elizabethan anthologies and ballad literature. Some of these settings were complicated intabulations of part-songs or consort songs, others were 'home-made' by amateurs. The simple pieces that resulted consisted of little more than a tune and chordal underpinning, which could accompany a song or be played as a solo.

The earliest of these anthologies, *Songes and Sonnettes* (1557) is better known today as Tottel's Miscellany. It included many courtly lyrics by Surrey and Wyatt. Though these were written in the Henrician period, the *Songes and Sonnettes* remained popular during Elizabeth's reign and was republished six times. From early lute sources we know that a good number of lyrics from the book were set as songs to the lute. Apart from courtly lyrics, the fashion for sung ballads increased greatly in the early Elizabethan period. At this time the lute was the most favoured instrument for accompanying ballad singing.

A Handefull of pleasant delites (1584) was a collection of ballads 'Newly devised to the newest tunes that are now in use, to be sung: everie Sonet orderly pointed to his proper Tune . . . By Clement Robinson and divers others'.[1] Almost certainly a first edition had appeared in 1566. Of thirty-two ballads, twenty-six have tunes that are named. All had appeared as broadsheets before 1584. Such ballads, plus the huge number of registered broadsheets printed and circulated in the Elizabethan period, created a body of songs and associated tunes which amateur and professional lute players drew on for songs and instrumental pieces.[2]

A third anthology, *The Paradyse of daynty devises*, appeared first in 1576. It ran through ten known editions with some change of content over time. Originally it was a manuscript collection compiled by Richard Edwards (Master of the Children of the Chapel Royal, d. 1566). It contained moralizing verse by Edwards himself, William Hunnis, Lord Vaux, Jaspar Heywood, Francis Kinwelmarsh, and others. This collection brought together poems from both the ballad and courtly lyric tradition, its verses 'aptly made to be set'.[3] Lyrics from *The Paradyse* were widely used as part-songs, consort songs, and lute songs. Eight appear in versions for lute in the Dallis manuscript. Other lute settings appear in Add. 15117, the Brogyntyn manuscript, and the later section of the Giles Lodge manuscript. Intabulations of consort-song settings, in particular by William Byrd, appear in Add. 31992, one of the Paston manuscripts. The perception that some lyrics were intended to be sung rather than read is heightened by Anthony Munday's preface to his *Banquet of Daintie Conceits* (1588). In it he apologizes that 'the ditties . . . will seem very bad stuff in reading, but (I perswade me) wyll delight thee, when thou singest them to thine Instrument'.[4]

Lutes were also used to accompany psalms and other religious texts used for domestic purposes. The Dallis manuscript contains much of this sort of material.[5] Along with courtly lyrics it contains fourteen psalm-tune settings, ten workings of the religious song 'Leve le coeur', and two versions of Kinwelmarsh's 'O heavenly God', which is also in the Giles Lodge book. Some of the religious pieces are

[1] *A Handful of Pleasant Delights (1584), by Clement Robinson and Divers Others*, ed. H. E. Rollins (Cambridge, 1924; facs. edn., ed. D. E. L. Crane, Ilkley, 1973). See Ward, 'Music for *A Handefull of pleasant delites*', 177–80 and id., 'Apropos *The British Broadside Ballad and Its Music*', *JAMS* 20 (1967), 28–86.

[2] Diana Poulton, 'The Black-Letter Broadside Ballad and its Music', *EM* 9 (1981), 427–37.

[3] Winifred Maynard, *Elizabethan Lyric Poetry and its Music* (Oxford, 1986), 21–37.

[4] Anthony Munday, *Banquet of Daintie Conceits* (London, 1588), Preface.

[5] *The English Lute Song Before Dowland, i: Songs from the Dallis Manuscript c.1583*, ed. Christopher Goodwin (Lute Society, Albury, 1996).

settings for lute solo; others also supply a vocal line, and in a few cases words as well.

The contents of Table 8.1 can be divided into: the Paston books, the early (pre-1597) lute-song sources, and manuscript sources containing songs from the period of the printed books. Of the early sources the Add. 4900, Dallis, and Brogyntyn manuscripts are significant. Add. 4900 contains a repertoire consistent with the fashions of the 1560s, Dallis and Brogyntyn with the 1570s and 1580s. Of the manuscript sources which contain a post-1597 repertoire Add. 15117 and the Turpyn songbook (*GB-Ckc*, Rowe MS 2)[6] both contain short collections of songs, though they are memorable. Handford's book was never published, but resembles a lute-song publication in every way. Probably it was a presentation copy for Prince Henry. It is remarkable that so few lute-song books survive in manuscript from 1597–1622; it seems that in this period the published books fully satisfied the demand.

There are twenty vocal items in Add. 4900, fifteen of which survive with an accompaniment intabulated for lute. The music is found in a manuscript copy of Francis Godwin's 'Catalogue of the Bishops of England'. The songs are for a single voice with words written beneath the vocal line and, on the opposite page, an intabulation of the lower parts for lute. Originally all the songs probably had lute accompaniments, though five are now lost. Godwin's catalogue of bishops was not printed until 1601, yet the songs come from a period no later than the 1560s. Christopher Goodwin thinks the songs were copied into the source early in the seventeenth century from an older songbook with a collection of early Elizabethan songs.[7] However, the tablature accompaniments themselves, the format, and secretary hand all suggest a date much earlier, probably the 1560s or 1570s.

The musical items in Add. 4900 include madrigals, chansons, and English part-songs, by John Heywood (the poet-courtier and musician to whom Whythorne apprenticed himself), Verdelot, and van Wilder, alongside sacred anthems, motets, and psalms by Taverner, Tallis, and Shepherd.[8] The intabulations are mechanical simplifications of the lower parts, showing little ingenuity in the transfer of medium. Assuming a date before 1570 for the song accompaniments, their existence would confirm the use of the lute to accompany the solo voice by playing a reduction of the other parts decades before the appearance of published lute songs. The range of music is surprising, encompassing a variety of secular genres, and sacred music intabulated for private use in the manner suggested by Tye in 1533 in his dedication to Edward VI of the *Acts of the Apostles*.

---

[6] See Philippe Oboussier, 'Turpyn's Book of Lute-Songs' *M&L* 34 (1953), 145–9.

[7] *The English Lute Song Before Dowland*, ii: *Songs from Additional Manuscript 4900*, ed. Christopher Goodwin (Lute Society, Albury, 1997).

[8] Ward, *Music for Elizabethan Lutes*, i. 33–5.

Table 8.1. *Manuscript sources of songs with tablature lute accompaniment 1550–1620*

Source	Comments
GB-Lbl Add. 29246 (Paston MS)	Vocal music by composers such as Taverner and Fairfax, and In Nomines, fantasias, and hymn settings by Byrd and his contempories
GB-Lbl Add. 29247 (Paston MS)	Similar to Add. 29246
GB-Lbl Add. 31992 (Paston MS)	Largest single source of consort songs by Byrd
GB-Lcm 2089 (Paston MS)	69 settings of mostly Latin sacred music (Lassus, Palestrina, Vittoria, etc.), some Byrd and Ferrabosco. Of the Byrd 3 are in English
GB-Ob Tenbury 340 (Paston MS)	75 intabulations of mostly Latin sacred music, especially motets—mainly by foreign composers, but with 6 by Ferrabosco and 12 by Byrd
GB-Lbl 15117 *c.*1615	The Swarland Song Book. 32 songs, plus lute solos and keyboard music
GB-Ob Tenbury 1019	13 intabulations and one fragment
GB-Ckc Rowe MS 2	The Turpyn Book of Lute Songs. 12 songs all with lute accompaniment
GB-Ctc R.16.29, *c.*1609	George Handfords' Song Book; 20 items. 'Ayres to be sunge to the Lute, and Base Vyole. Newly composed by George Handford'. The last two have two singing parts (a pastoral dialogue). 7-course lute (D)
GB-Lbl Add. 4900, *c.*1560s but copied *c.*1605	20 songs, 15 with lute accompaniment
Dallis MS, *c.*1583–5	19 songs with words; 18 psalm settings (some fragmentary), mostly without words
Brogyntyn MS, *c.*1595–1600	24 consort song accompaniments without a vocal part
Giles Lodge Commonplace Book, *c.*1560–75	1 sketched-out setting of 'Huc tua Penelope' with tablature (lacking rhythm) and vocal part (without words)
Thistlethwaite MS, *c.*1565–75	2 intabulated Italian part-songs with accompanying texts
Osborn Commonplace Book, *c.*1560	2 songs with tablature and a vocal part with words. 2 chanson intabulations and 1 psalm without words

Evidence of the practice of intabulating the consort-song repertoire of the 1570s and 1580s is found in the Brogyntyn manuscript.[9] Along with purely instrumental lute music, the manuscript has a section dedicated to consort-song intabulations. Of the twenty-four intabulations, all but two lack the top line.[10] This was presumably contained in a separate book for a singer. The texts of eight of the songs originate from *The Paradyse of daynty devises*. Elsewhere in the manuscript there is an intab-

[9] See Spencer's introduction to *The Brogyntyn Lute Book*.
[10] For an inventory and notes on the songs see Ward, 'Barley's Songs without Words', 20–2.

ulation of Philip van Wilder's 'Je file' which lacks the uppermost of the five parts. The missing part might also have been in the singer's lost book. These arrangements are for a 6-course lute, but less technically exacting than many in Paston's collection. While it is always possible that the lute was used to double the notes played by a consort of viols to accompany a voice or voices, there is little evidence for this practice in the Elizabethan period. It is more likely that the lute was used instead of viols, either with a solo voice, or to double the lower voices if more were present. The importance of the Paston and Brogyntyn pieces lies not so much in the settings themselves, but as more evidence of the practice of freely intabulating music, both instrumental and vocal, for performance by voice and lute.

Mention has been made of the relatively small number of intabulations of vocal music to be played as solos in the sources of English lute music, and that the majority of those that were in circulation were foreign in origin. The Thistlethwaite manuscript is exceptional in having four long intabulations of vocal music surely intended as solos.[11] There is, however, a group of five important lute manuscripts devoted to over 400 intabulated accompaniments to madrigals, motets, consort songs, fantasias, In Nomines, hymn settings, and extracts from masses.[12] These intabulations could not be played as solos as the uppermost part is normally absent. The five lute books form part of the huge collection of music books owned by Edward Paston (1550–1630), a Norfolk Catholic gentleman.[13] His collection was put together over a long period of time, with music ranging from early sixteenth-century compositions by Fairfax and Taverner to much more contemporary pieces by Merulo and Giovanni Gabrieli. Though some of Paston's books were being copied as late as the second decade of the seventeenth century, in general his taste was very conservative and relates more to the 1560s and 1570s, when he was a young man. Paston had a special preference for the music of William Byrd, and one of the books, Add. 31992, is the largest single source of consort songs by Byrd.[14]

Paston's will mentions not only lute books, but also many printed and manuscript sets of Latin, French, and Italian songs, some of which do not survive.[15] The music contained in the lute books is drawn from a wide repertoire of mainly vocal music, both English and Continental. Many of the lute intabulations are of pieces found elsewhere in part-books from Paston's collection. The intabulations were probably made from the sets of part-books to allow a lute to perform with the voices, or to compensate for any or all of the lower voices that may, on occasion, have been missing. There is a suggestion of personal contact between Paston and Byrd, and also

[11] Thistlethwaite MS, fos. 44ᵛ–47ʳ, 47ᵛ–50ʳ, 67ᵛ–68ʳ, 81ᵛ–84ʳ.

[12] Paston MSS: *GB-Lbl* Add. 29246, 29247, and 31992; *GB-Lcm* 2089; *GB-Ob* Tenbury 340.

[13] For a description of the surviving music collection see Philip Brett, 'Edward Paston (1550–1630): A Norfolk Gentleman and his Musical Collection', *Transactions of the Cambridge Bibliographical Society*, 4 (1964), 51–69.

[14] *Consort Songs by William Byrd*, ed. Stewart McCoy and Bill Hunt (London, 1990), Introduction, pp. i–iii.

[15] Brett, 'Edward Paston', 66–8.

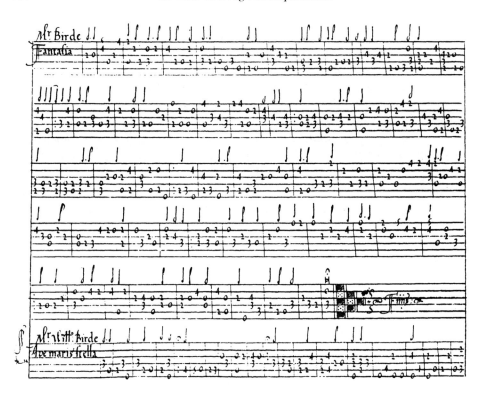

PL. 8.1. Page from Paston manuscript, British Library, Add. MS 29246, fo. 22[v]

between Paston and Thomas Morley.[16] To date the manuscripts have received most attention as sources of Elizabethan consort music, particularly that of Byrd.[17] (For a page from one of them, see Pl. 8.1.)

Paston's books betray considerable Spanish influence in the type of tablature and the directions in Spanish that are found in the books.[18] Edward Paston was fluent in Spanish and spent some of his formative years in Spain.[19] The tablature books were probably not copied out by Paston himself, but by a musical factotum who could well have been Spanish. The books are in Italian tablature, a system which uses numbers instead of letters. This type of tablature was commonly used in Renaissance Spain.[20] Its appearance in the Paston books is unique for English man-

---

[16] Price, *Patrons and Musicians*, 97–8.

[17] *Elizabethan Consort Music I*, ed. Paul Doe (MB 44; London, 1979); William Byrd, *Consort Music*, ed. Kenneth Elliot (The Collected Works of William Byrd, rev. edn., 17; London, 1971).

[18] Stewart McCoy, 'Lost Lute Solos Revealed in a Paston Manuscript', *LSJ* 26 (1986), 21–39 at 21.

[19] Brett, 'Edward Paston', 54.

[20] The exception is Luis Milan, whose system uses numbers as in Italian tablature, but with the top stave line representing the 1st course as in French tablature. In Italian tablature the top line represents the 6th course.

uscripts at this time. While it is difficult to date these sources, they are entirely for 6-course lute, and most of the English repertoire they contain is late Elizabethan, not Jacobean. Many of the pieces appear in more than one book. Such duplication normally involves settings in different keys, but suggests much recopying of music between the books in the collection, and their use over many years. They were probably still in use, and being added to, well into the Jacobean period.

We know from Paston's will that he owned more lute books than the five that survive, that some of these lost books contained solos, and that some were in French tablature. His will includes the following item:

> Item wheras I have many lute bookes prickt in Ciphers after the Spanish and Italian fashion and some in letters of A.B.C. accordinge to the English fashion whereof divers are to bee plaid upon the lute alone and have noe singinge partes and divers other lute bookes which have singing *p*ts sett to them wch must be sunge to the lute and are bound in very good bookes and tied up with the lute parts whereof some have two singinge bookes some three and some fower . . .[21]

Pieces are grouped in the manuscripts roughly according to the number of parts they contain, from three to six. The intabulations are generally very accurate, with little regard for the technical difficulties that arise from a dense texture. As they are for a 6-course lute, some of the lower notes are transposed up an octave. There is also some ordering of pieces by transposition. At the beginning of most pieces in Add. 31992 there is a rubric giving the beginning pitch of the top voice part in tablature. It is clear that many pieces have been transposed from the original viol consort pitch.[22] Where transposition occurred in the lute part, the voice part was left in its original key, allowing the singer to sing his part from a musical text written in a key with one or no accidentals. That this was not the actual performance pitch would have been no problem to a hexachord-trained singer. For the lute player it meant the piece could be intabulated in a practical rather than a difficult key. Such rubrics do not imply that a variety of different lutes at different pitches were used. The frequent transpositions argue against performance with viols, which would have found transposition most inconvenient. The rubrics always indicate that a high voice—either soprano or possibly countertenor—sang the upper part.

Until recently it has been assumed that the intabulations of fantasias, In Nomines, and other purely instrumental music were intended for use with a consort of viols, and not, as the will suggests, with singing books. Stewart McCoy's study of the books has shown that some of these supposedly instrumental pieces may in fact have been used with a voice or voices singing contrapuntal music to solmization syllables without a text to the accompaniment of a lute.[23] He calls this

---

[21] Brett, 'Edward Paston', 66–7. [22] *Consort Songs*, ed. McCoy and Hunt, p. iii.
[23] Stewart McCoy, 'Edward Paston and the Textless Lute-Song', *EM* 15 (1987), 221–7. McCoy's two articles are drawn from his dissertation, 'Some Aspects of the Paston Lute Books' (M.Mus. thesis, King's College, University of London, 1985).

mode of performance the 'textless lute-song'. The music in the part-books which is vocal in origin is a mixture of texted and untexted pieces. Likewise the untexted pieces may not have been played on viols, as has been previously imagined,[24] but simply sung to solmization syllables with possible lute accompaniment. McCoy suggests that many of the songs in Add. 29246 work best with a group of voices and a lute doubling the lower parts. This is because there are instances where the bass note of the final chords are missed out in the intabulation when they fall below the compass of the lute, and are not transposed up an octave as one would expect. Many songs in Add. 31992, however, are quite satisfactory with just a single voice and lute accompaniment. Example 8.1 gives the first four bars of Byrd's three-part Fantasy, no. 3 as a textless lute song with the three vocal parts singing solmization syllables. While the two lower vocal parts are doubled by the lute, and could be absent, the top vocal line must be present as it is not contained in the lute accompaniment, though occasional notes from this part do appear in the lute part.[25]

Like the intabulations in the Brogyntyn lute book, the great majority of the pieces in the Paston manuscripts are not complete in themselves. Normally the part that would be uppermost at any one time in a full score is not present in the lute intabulation. McCoy has shown that the manner in which this has been done in Add. 29246 betrays the existence of a book, or books, containing intabulations of the pieces with all parts intact.[26] From this now-lost book of solos the incomplete version to be played as an accompaniment was made.

In the late Elizabethan era, viol-playing was largely confined to professionals and educational establishments. The lute, bandora, cittern, and virginals had greater popularity in the households of wealthy amateurs than in the succeeding period, when viols became more available. The use of the lute in England as an accompaniment and guide to a group of singers singing textless polyphony was surely not confined to one household, though it may not have been widespread. The existence of Paston's lost solo-lute books containing intabulations of music originally intended for other media shows that, in at least one household, lute intabulations were being produced in large numbers, although these particular intabulations were for home use, and show no signs of ever being in circulation outside the Paston household.

The earliest tablature accompaniments to be printed occur in Barley's *A new Booke of Tabliture* (1596). The book contains four songs for bandora, with voice parts in staff notation, and tablature in parallel below.[27] The songs are not underlaid with the text. Text incipits are printed at the head of each piece, and the text

[24] Byrd, *Consort Songs for Voice & Viols*, ed. Philip Brett (The Collected Works of William Byrd (rev.), 15; London, 1970), p. x.

[25] McCoy, 'Edward Paston and the Textless Lute-Song', 226.   [26] McCoy, 'Lost Lute Solos'.

[27] Ward, 'Barley's Songs without Words'.

Ex. 8.1. *William Byrd, Fantasy à 3, no. 3 as a textless lute song (Add. 41156–8, fo. 9ᵛ) with intabulated accompaniment from Add. 29246, fo. 27ᵛ, bars 1–4*

NB. All sol-fa syllables are editorial. I have assumed a lute with a top string tuned at *á* to match the *á3* version.

of two of the songs appears at the end of the book. The other two songs have no texts, though five unrelated song texts can be found elsewhere in the publication. Ward's conjecture is that the difficulty of printing from woodblocks prevented Barley from placing words with the music, and that the texts found in the book can be made to fit the tunes and accompaniments provided. The practice of using a suitable tune simply as a word carrier was an old one, and out of keeping with the settings of Dowland and the new generation of lute-song composers.[28]

Thomas Morley continued the intabulation tradition in his *Canzonets or Little Short Aers to Five and Sixe Voices* in which he supplied a lute reduction of the lower four voices for the first sixteen pieces with the Cantus part-book.[29] He explains himself in his dedication to Sir George Carey: 'I have also set them Tablature wise to the Lute in the Cantus booke for one to sing and plaie alone when your Lordship would retire your selfe and bee more private.' The book may be a response to Dowland's *First Booke* of the same year. Both books were entered at the Stationers' Register on the same day, and both were dedicated to Carey. Morley's sole patent for printing music with moveable type did not start until 1598 and Byrd's monopoly had expired in 1596. The hiatus in 1597 may help to explain the flurry of music printing of that year.[30] The Morley intabulations are mostly literal, with some elaboration at cadences. With the exception of one song, 'O griefe even on the Bud', David Greer finds the lute and voice versions unsatisfactory as a substitute for five voices, as the contrapuntal interplay is obscured. This may be so, but the presence of Morley's intabulations must argue for the popularity of performance by lute and voice of madrigals and canzonets. Morley must have believed that by offering them in this format he would enhance his sales. (For sources of lute songs at this period see Table 8.2.)

John Dowland's *First Booke of Songes or Ayres of fowre partes, with Tableture for the Lute* of 1597 inaugurated twenty-five years of printed collections of English ayres.[31] Of the thirty-six collections containing printed ayres between Dowland's first book and that of John Attey in 1622 most, but not all, included tablature parts for the lute. Together these books contain some 567 songs with tablature. As such they represent the overwhelming bulk of published English lute tablature, and far

---

[28] Ibid. 13. The practice does continue, as the Swarland MS contains song tunes by Dowland and Morley with new words.

[29] David Greer, 'The Lute Songs of Thomas Morley', *LSJ* 8 (1966), 25–37.

[30] I am endebted to Ian Harwood for this information.

[31] The lute songs are published in facs. by Scolar Press in association with Brian Jordan in the series *English Lute Songs 1597–1632: A Collection of Facsimile Reprints*, 9 vols., ed. F. W. Sternfeld *et al.* (Menston, Yorks., 1968–71). Edited and transcribed versions of most of the lute-song publications are found in the several series of *The English School of Lutenist Song Writers*, ed. E. H. Fellowes, 1–32, in 2 series (London, 1920–32). The collection was partly revised by Thurston Dart as *The English Lute-Songs* (1959–66), including new volumes. The lute-song lyrics are reprinted in Fellowes, *English Madrigal Verse* (Oxford, 1967) and *Lyrics from English Airs*, ed. Edward Doughtie (Cambridge, 1970).

x

outweigh the purely instrumental printed tablatures. Dowland's first book was a great success, and, unlike any of the books that followed, it was reprinted, and not just once, but a remarkable four times (in 1600, 1603, 1609, and 1613), making the book the most successful music publication of the age. In the same way that Morley invented the English madrigal, so it is not an exaggeration to say that Dowland invented the English ayre. The *First Booke* established Dowland's reputation in England, and its success was such that it set in train the outpouring of songs known collectively as the English Lute Song School. Dowland's interpretation of what the ayre was may have been strongly influenced by the French *air de cour*. Adrian Le Roy's *Livre d'airs de cour sur le luth* was published in Paris in 1571, after which publication ceased, only to be recommenced with great vigour in 1603. Between these dates songs were published outside France, including a part-song collection in London entitled *Le Premier Livre de chansons & airs de court, tant en françois qu'en italien & en gascon à 4. & 5. parties* (1597) by the Frenchman Charles Tessier. French *airs de cour* were produced both as lute songs and part-songs, and eight songs from Tessier's published collection survive in an Oxford manuscript for lute and voice.[32] According to Gustav Ungerer, Tessier had been drawn into the cultural circle of the Earl of Essex through Anthony Bacon, brother of Sir Francis Bacon.[33] His song collection was dedicated to Lady Penelope Rich, sister of Essex. While Tessier's music may have made little impression in England outside the Essex circle, Dowland would have certainly become acquainted with the French *air de cour* while in France in 1580–2. Lightness, homophony, and alternative part-song or 'lute and solo voice' versions are characteristics of French airs. Many of Dowland's lute ayres are comparably light; however, his more weighty songs show other influences at work.

A great diversity of styles and approaches are a hallmark of the English ayre. While some composers like Campion and Danyel tended to stick to one interpretation of the genre, Dowland's songs cover a range of styles. One influence was certainly the new style of monodic songs being produced in Italy from the 1590s onwards. Caccini's publication *Le nuove musiche* (1602) contains some of the best-known examples of the early genre. Dowland could have gained direct experience of the emerging style on his travels in Italy. He, or his son Robert, was responsible for the tablature settings of Italian continuo songs in Robert Dowland's *Musicall Banquet* (1610), which included Caccini's famous 'Amarilli mia bella'. English manuscript collections show that the Italian recitative style was known and appreciated

---

[32] *GB-Ob* Mus. Sch. d.237, fos. 7ᵛ–35ʳ. See Frank Dobbins, 'Les airs pour luth de Charles Tessier, luthiste français et compositeur en Angleterre à l'époque de Dowland', in *luths et luthistes en Occident* (Paris, 1999), 169–184.

[33] G. Ungerer, 'The French Lutenist Charles Tessier and the Essex Circle', *Renaissance Quarterly*, 28 (1975), 190–203 at 190; John Ward, 'Tessier and the "Essex Circle"', *Renaissance Quarterly*, 29 (1976), 378–84 at 378; Frank Dobbins, 'The Lute Airs of Charles Tessier', *LSJ* 20 (1978), 23–42 at 23.

Table 8.2. *Published sources of English lute songs 1597–1630*

Date/name/short title	Comments
(1597)(1600)(1603)(1609)(1613) John Dowland *The First Booke of Songes or Ayres*	21 songs, all with lute tablature, one lute duet, 7-course lute
(1598) Michael Cavendish *Madrigals and Airs* (original title not known)	28 items, 20 with lute tablature, 6-course lute
(1600) Thomas Morley *The First Booke of Ayres or Little Short Songs*	Originally 23 items (21 songs and two instrumental pieces), lute tablature parts for 14 survive, 7-course lute
(1600) John Dowland *The Second Booke of Songes or Ayres*	22 songs, all with lute tablature, one piece for lute and viol, 7-course lute
(1600) Robert Jones *The First Booke of Songes or Ayres*	21 songs with lute tablature, 7-course lute
(1601) Philip Rosseter and Thomas Campion *A Booke of Ayres*	21 songs & 21 songs, all with lute tablature, 7-course lute
(1601) Robert Jones *The Second Booke of Songs and Ayres*	21 songs with lute tablature, 7-course lute
(1603) John Dowland *The Third and Last Booke of Songes or Aires*	21 songs with lute tablature, 1 involves a mean lute and a bass lute a fourth below, 7-course lute
(1604) Thomas Greaves *Songes of Sundrie Kindes*	21 items, 9 are songs with lute tablature, 7-course lute
(1605) Francis Pilkington *The First Booke of Songs or Ayres or 4. parts*	21 songs with lute tablature, 1 piece for lute and bass viol, 7-course lute
(1605) Robert Jones *Ultimum Vale*	21 songs with lute tablature, 7-course lute
(1605) Tobias Hume *The First Part of Ayres*	116 items, no real lute tablature (even in 4 songs), mostly lyra viol solos
(1606) John Danyel *Songs for the Lute, Viol and Voice*	20 songs with lute tablature, 1 lute solo; 'Now the earth' has parts for both a bass and a mean lute, 7-course lute(s)
(1606) John Coprario *Funeral Teares*	7 songs with lute tablature, 6-course lute
(1606) John Bartlet *A Booke of Ayres with a Triplicitie of Musicke*	21 songs all with lute tablature, 7-course lute
(1607) Thomas Ford *Musicke of Sundrie Kindes*	10 songs with lute tablature; the remaining 19 items involve lyra viols, 7-course lute
(1607) Tobias Hume *Captaine Hume's Poeticall Musicke*	24 items, no real lute tablature
(1609) Robert Jones *A Musicall Dreame*	21 items, all with lute tablature, 7-course lute
(1609) Alfonso Ferrabosco *Ayres by Alfonso Ferrabosco*	28 items, all with lute tablature, 6-course lute
(1610) Robert Dowland (ed.) *A Musical Banquet*	20 songs with lute tablature, 1 lute solo, 9-course lute
(1610) William Corkine	12 songs with lute tablature, 12 lyra viol

Date/name/short title	Comments
Ayres to Song and Play to the Lute and Basse Violl	solos, 7-course lute
(1610) Robert Jones *The Muses Gardin for Delights*	21 songs with lute tablature, 7-course lute
(1611) John Maynard *The XII. Wonders of the World*	12 songs with lute tablature, 5 pieces for lute and bass viol, 7 for lyra viol and bass viol, 7-course lute
(1612) William Corkine *The Second Booke of Ayres*	28 items, including 5 songs with lute tablature, 7-course lute
(1612) John Dowland *A Pilgrimes Solace*	21 songs with lute tablature, 1 lute solo, 8-course lute
(c.1613) Thomas Campion *Two Bookes of Ayres*	21 & 21 songs all with lute tablature, 7-course lute
(1613) John Coprario *Songs of Mourning*	7 songs all with lute tablature, 6-course lute
(1618) Thomas Campion *The Third and Fourth Booke of Ayres*	29 & 24 songs all with lute tablature, 7-course lute
(1618) George Mason and John Earsden *The Ayres that were Sung and Played*	10 items all with lute tablature, 8-course lute
(1622) John Attey *The First Booke of Ayres of Foure Parts*	14 songs with lute tablature, 10-course lute

in England from soon after 1600.[34] At the root of this style was a desire to express the words of the text in such a way that the listener would be genuinely affected. To do this the melody needed to be declamatory, and follow the accentuation of the words. French writers and thinkers of the group known as *La Pléiade* were also exercised by the same concerns from as early as the 1550s. Naive word painting, instrumental interludes, and counterpoint were to be eschewed. Instead a flexible melody line, always responsive to the text, was to be underpinned by simple, almost static harmonies. In Italy this approach gave rise to the continuo bass line that allowed the singer great rhythmic freedom. Such rubato Caccini termed *sprezzatura*. The influence of the Italian recitative style in England increased in the early years of the seventeenth century, and is more pronounced in the lute-song books produced from 1610 onwards.

Another influence on the English lute ayre was that of the consort song and madrigal intabulation. Here the lute attempted to sketch out the contrapuntal

[34] e.g. *GB-Ob* Tenbury 1018, and *GB-Lbl* Add. 2971.

interplay of parts in an intabulated reduction of the lower parts. This approach, quite at odds with the new Italian style, was characterized by a complicated tablature accompaniment with short preludes and interludes for the lute. In some such ayres—those of Cavendish are an example—one senses that the composer was primarily concerned with the part-song version, and that the lute song was secondary, as the resulting lute part is often far from idiomatic.

A further influence that is particularly strong in Dowland's *First Booke* is that of instrumental dance music.[35] Five of the songs are known to have existed in instrumental versions, particularly for solo lute.[36] Some of these solo pieces certainly predate the song versions. The song 'If my complaints' appears as a lute solo in Dd.2.11, and was later arranged as a consort dance with lute in *Lachrimae* (1604) titled 'Captaine Digorie Piper his Galliard'. Piper was a Cornish pirate who died in 1590. Certainly some of the sources of the lute version of this piece pre-date the published song.[37] (See Ex. 8.2.) However, we know that several of Dowland's songs were composed long before 1597. 'His golden locks' was sung by Robert Hales at a Tiltyard ceremony in 1590.[38] Dowland's most famous piece, his 'Lachrimae' pavan, exists in two versions in Dd.2.11, one in G minor the other in A minor. This suggests that it may have existed as both a lute solo and a string-consort piece from at least the early 1590s. Dowland himself arranged it as a song for two voices and lute in his *Second Booke* of 1600, and for lute and viols in *Lachrimae, or Seaven Teares* (1604).[39] It was also arranged for mixed consort, though probably not by Dowland. The transformation of dance pieces into songs is more a feature of Dowland and his *First Booke* than any other song book.[40]

One innovation of the *First Booke* that was invariably followed in later printed books of ayres was the 'table-book' format (see Pl. 8.2). The print was so arranged that four or five people could read from one book placed in the centre of the table. This format contrasted with the more costly sets of part-books that had been the norm for English music publications up to 1597. In Dowland's book the cantus part was printed on the left page with lute tablature running underneath. On the other side of the opening the altus, tenor, and bassus were printed on the three sides of the page. The words for the first verse were printed below the music of each part. Subsequent verses were simply printed at the bottom of one of the pages, and had to be fitted to the music of the first verse by the singer.

The *First Booke*'s title-page states that it contains 'Songes or Ayres of fowre partes with Tableture for the Lute: So made that all the partes together, or either of them severally [i.e separately], may be song to the Lute, Orpherian, or Viol de

---

[35] Thurston Dart, 'La Rôle de la danse dans l'"ayre" anglais', in Jean Jacquot (ed.), *Musique et poésie au XVIᵉ siècle* (Paris, 1954), 203–9.

[36] Numbers 3, 4, 5, 6, and 19.   [37] Poulton, *John Dowland*, 134–5.   [38] Ibid. 239.

[39] Ibid. 125–6.   [40] John Danyel's 'Rosa Pavan' is the only known example by another composer.

gambo.' While it is clear that Dowland's primary intention was to produce songs for solo voice and lute, he took care to produce reasonable part-song versions, no doubt to increase the book's sales.[41] However, the title is misleading if it suggests that the altus, tenor, or bassus parts would be satisfactory as solos with the lute part. They are not. No bowed instrumental part is provided, and a bass viol player would play the sung bass part. The instruction 'or Viol de gambo' implies the songs could be sung to the bass viol alone and we know that this was a method of performing lute ayres.[42] The title-page allows for a variety of performance depending on what forces are present, though there are some places where the use of the tablature part with

Ex. 8.2. *Comparison of (a) John Dowland's 'If my complaints' (First Booke, 1597, no. 4), and (b) Piper's Galliard, Dd.2.11, fo. 53ʳ, bars 1–8*

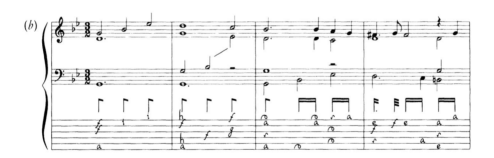

[41] David Greer, 'The Part-Songs of the English Lutenists' *PRMA* 94 (1967–8), 97–110. For part-song versions of Dowland ayres see *John Dowland: Ayres for Four Voices*, ed. Thurston Dart and Nigel Fortune (MB 6; London, 1953, rev. 1963, 1970), and for the other lutenist-composers, *Collected English Lutenist Partsongs: I & II*, ed. David Greer (MB 53–4; London, 1987, 89).

[42] E. H. Jones, '"To sing and play to the Bass-Violl alone"—The Bass Viol in English 17th-Century Song', *LSJ* 17 (1975), 17–23.

Ex. 8.2. *cont.*

1. Tableture ◠ moved up a line to read *f'* not *e'*.
This restores the false relation found in other sources (e.g. 1604 *a5* version).

the part-song is problematical. Dowland's song tablatures are not simply a reduction of the lower parts, and there are some clashes between the lute and lower voice parts, though these discrepancies are not so great as to preclude performance by four voices with lute.

John Dowland produced three more books of songs: *The Second Booke of Songs or Ayres* (1600), *The Third and Last Booke of Songs or Aires* (1603), and *A Pilgrimes Solace* (1612). These later books show a greater diversity of song style than the first book. Unlike the great majority of song books which contain multiples of seven songs (twenty-one being the norm), the second book has twenty-two songs. It opens with eight two-part songs (cantus and bassus), followed by twelve four-part songs. The title-page mentions 'Tableture for the Lute or Orpherian, with the Violl De Gamba', suggesting for the first time that the bass viol be played with the lute. The book is most memorable for the three opening songs of utter melancholy—'I saw my Lady weepe', 'Flow my teares' (Lachrimae), and 'Sorow sorow stay'. The first

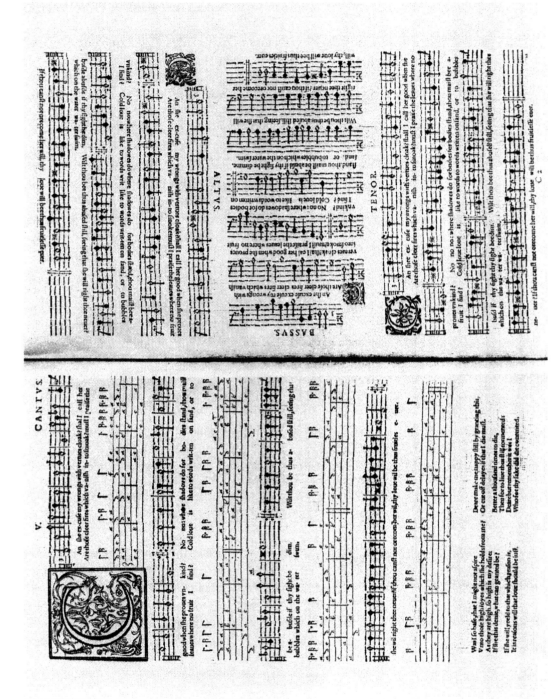

PL. 8.2. Opening of John Dowland's *First Booke of Songs* (1613 edition) showing 'Can she excuse' in table format

of these, with its passages for lute and bass voice, is suggestive of the consort song.

The final two five-part songs have a quinto part marked 'for a treble violl' added to the other four parts. The first of the two songs, 'Cleare or cloudie', also has words for the quinto part. If played as written, this part starts on *d*, the lowest string of the treble viol. Poulton suggests the part would have been sung at the written pitch but played up an octave on a treble viol.[43] It may have been normal practice to transpose up an alto part when played on a treble viol so that it sounds above the voice.[44] The quinto part for the last song, 'Humor say', has no words at all. This piece starts with a basso/canto dialogue accompanied by untexted quinto, tenor, and alto parts. Only in the chorus do four of the parts have texts. Although not clearly stated, this last song implies the use of a consort of viols with the lute. This song, with its greater forces and opening dialogue, must surely have been composed for a masque or similar event. The lute part is melodically uninteresting and comparable to a continuo realization.

The Third and Last Booke of Songs or Aires (1603) is lighter in spirit than *The Second Booke*. Here the title-page instruction reads 'Newly composed to sing to the Lute, Orpharion, or viols', admitting the possibility of viols (plural), instead of lute or orpharion. Numbers 1–4 have parts for cantus, lute, and an untexted bassus for a bass viol. While, for the most part, the bass follows the lute part, there are numerous minor discrepancies between the two. These take the form of octave displacements, passing notes, reiterations and long held notes. Numbers 5–20 have four texted parts plus lute tablature. The last song, 'Come when I call', like the last piece in the previous book, is a complicated masque-type dialogue between two voices with a chorus to end. The lute alone accompanies the three solo phrases of the cantus primus, but the two solo phrases of the 'secunda pars' are accompanied by three untexted lower parts. Here a group of viols is necessary to realize the full texture of the song.[45] The dialogue then is followed by a texted chorus for all five parts. It is described as a '*dia*logue for a base and meane Lute with five voices to sing thereto'. The bass lute is tuned in *d'* a fourth below the mean lute, and accompanies the 'secunda pars'.

The title-page of Dowland's last book, *A Pilgrimes Solace* (1612), has yet another variation on the combinations allowed for. The title reads 'Wherein is contained Musicall Harmonie of 3. 4. and 5. parts, to be sung and plaid with the Lute and Viols'. Instead of the viols being an alternative, Dowland seems to be saying that they are an obligatory addition to the lute. While viols can always double vocal lines, it is in the three three-part songs (nos. 9–11) that a treble and bass viol are essen-

---

[43] Poulton, *John Dowland*, 272.   [44] *Consort Songs by William Byrd*, ed. McCoy and Hunt, p. iv.
[45] The Fellowes edition (1923) and the Dart revised edition (1970) do not include the viol parts, and no mention is made of the omission.

tial. These songs receive extended contrapuntal treatment, which in 'Lasso vita mia' is combined with vocal outbursts in the style of Italian monody. The dialogue 'Up merry Mates' starts with a tenor and bass dialogue followed by four-part chorus. The two final songs of five parts were clearly written for a marriage masque or other such epithalamic celebration. The opening solos are for 'cantus secundus' with lute alone, followed by five-part choruses. 'Welcome black night' opens in true declamatory style, with the lute providing supporting chords in the manner of theorbo realization. (See Ex. 8.3.)

The three songs John Dowland provided for his son's *A Musical Banquet* (1610) have no part-song arrangements. All three have bass parts, but only 'Lady if you spight me' has words for a bass voice. The last, 'In Darkness let me dwell', is justly famous for its intensity. The close of the song where the lute drops out to leave the voice with a suspension that, without accompaniment, can never be completed, is an original and powerful moment. It incorporates a fusion of styles: on the one hand suggested counterpoint in the lute and viol parts with phrases where the instruments play without the voice, and dramatic vocal interjections suggestive of recitative style on the other. It is only in these three pieces and in *A Pilgrimes Solace* that Dowland requires a lute with a minimum of eight courses, rather than the 7-course lute of the earlier books.

Dowland's famous diatribe in his address to the reader in *A Pilgrimes Solace* against the 'two sorts of people' goes on to attack Tobias Hume's presumption on behalf of the viol. Yet it is clear that the viol is made progressively more admissible in Dowland's own directions for performance. It is noticeable that the combinations required for the later songs are more specific than the 'use it how you will' approach of the first book. Unlike many songs by other composers of ayres, the lute part is central to all Dowland's published songs, and to perform them without it, though admissible in *The First Booke*, results in a much impoverished song.

Thomas Campion and Robert Jones both produced five books of ayres, and were thus marginally more prolific in this respect than Dowland. Campion is of special significance, as he has always been justly famous as a poet who presumably composed both the words and music for his songs. He is also presumed to have provided words for other song composers, most notably his close friend Philip Rosseter, and Alfonso Ferrabosco II. He wrote a succession of Jacobean masques for which he contributed the music for a number of songs, some of which were published with lute tablatures.[46] Three of Campion's books contain ayres, all of which were for a solo voice, with lute tablature and an untexted part for bass viol. Part-song versions are present in *Two Bookes of Ayres* (c.1613): the 'Divine and Morall Songs' of the

---

[46] Descriptions of Campion's masques for the Lords Hayes (1607) and the Earl of Somerset (1614) were printed, and together contain three songs by Campion.

Ex. 8.3. *'Welcome black night'*, John Dowland, A Pilgrimes Solace *(1612)*, *no. 20, bars 1-6*

first book has sixteen songs of four parts and four songs of three parts, and the second book has twenty three-part ayres. There can be little doubt that the address 'To the Reader', which prefaces Rosseter's *A Booke of Ayres* (1601), was written by Campion. In this book Campion's twenty-one songs were given pride of place to Rosseter's set of an equal number. In the address he outlines what the ayre should be:

What Epigrams are in Poetrie, the same are Ayres in musicke, then in their chiefe perfection when they are short and well seasoned. But to clogg a light song with a long Praeludium, is to corrupt the nature of it. Manie rests in Musicke were invented either for necessitie of the fuge, or granted as a harmonicall licence in songs of many parts: but in Ayres I find no use they have, unlesse it be to make a vulgar, and triviall modulation seeme to the ignorant strange, and to the judiciall tedious.

Campion goes on to chide those who admit only music that is 'long, intricate, bated with fuge, chaind with sincopation, and where the nature of everie word is precisely exprest in the Note'. Finally he says 'we ought to maintaine as well in Notes, as in action a manly cariage, gracing no word, but that which is eminent, and emphaticall . . .'. Campion's own songs are as we should expect them: short, tuneful, and with a melody carefully married to the text. Sequence and repetition are the hallmarks of his style, characteristics that are underlined by the strophic nature of his songs.

Campion's lute accompaniments are normally modest in their technical demands, though those contained in the 1601 book are harder than those of the later books. They are generally chordal rather than melodic. Occasionally more is required, as in the last two lines of 'When to her lute Corrina sings' when the lute and viol echo the vocal line. (See Ex. 8.4.) Despite Campion's strictures against word-painting, this song is heavy with it: low notes for the words 'leaden strings'; an octave leap with the words 'highest noates'; short gasping rests before the repeated words 'her sighes', and falling minor thirds to sound the sighs; musical portrayal of the words 'the strings do breake' in the lute part, which judders downwards to a tablature 'e' (low $F\sharp$) on the seventh course.

It may be argued that of all lute ayres Campion's lighter songs lose the least if performed by viol and voice without the lute, as the treble and bass are the all-important parts. Yet *A Booke of Ayres* calls for 'Lute, Orpherian, and Base Violl'. The viol frequently strengthens the bass line on the lute at the octave below, and occasionally moves independently, as in the last crotchet of bars 10 and 12 of Ex. 8.4. The songs lose much if the bass viol is not present. A great many of Campion's songs are in G major or minor—easy keys on the lute. 'The Sypres curten of the night' has a lute part in F minor and a vocal part in G minor. This was done simply to avoid the singer being faced with lots of flats. Such apparent discrepancies between voice and tablature pitch does not happen much in the English lute-song repertoire when compared with the French *air de cour*. As with the Paston transcriptions, it does not indicate the use of lutes of different pitches, but is simply a device to help the singer to read his or her part by having it written in a more familiar key. The accompaniments to Rosseter's ayres are in the same mould as those of Campion, and it has been suggested, without foundation, that Rosseter may have helped Campion with his tablature parts.

Jones's *First Booke* (1600) copies the format of Dowland's *First Booke*: twenty-one part-songs for four voices with tablature for the lute. The title-page states they may be sung to the 'Lute, Orpherian or Viol de gambo'. The pieces are not as memorable as those of Dowland's 1597 book, though 'Farewel, dear love' probably

Ex. 8.4. *The last two lines of 'When to her lute', Thomas Campion,* A Booke of Ayres *(1601), no. 6, verse 1, bars 9–14*

1. F♯ in vocal part is editorial. It is altered here to conform to the lute part, though it may be that a clash between lute and voice is intended.

achieved some popularity as snatches of it are sung, with slightly altered words, in the musical clowning of Sir Toby Belch, Sir Andrew Ague-Cheek, and the fool in Shakespeare's *Twelfth Night*.[47] The *Second Booke* (1601) gives the viol far greater opportunity. Gone are the part-songs altogether. Instead the cantus and bassus parts are fully texted for the first verse, and the cantus has a lute part underneath it. On the other side of the opening, at a right angle to the bassus, is an alternative tablature part for lyra viol. This is a significant development, since for the first time in a published English ayre the viol has the opportunity to completely usurp the lute's role. (See Ex. 8.5.) It is noticeable that the texted bass line works well with the lute part but not so well with the lyra viol part. The clashes that occur in the later part of bar 4 are a case in point.

Jones's three later books have fanciful titles. *Ultimum Vale* (1605) is subtitled 'a triplicity of Musicke'. The first part consists of six of the simplest sort of lute ayre for solo voice, lute, and untexted bass. They are all short strophic songs in G minor. Eight songs for 'the Lute, the Viole, and foure partes to sing' make up the second

Ex. 8.5. *'Over these Brookes', Robert Jones, Second Book (1601), no. 11, bars 1–5*

[47] *Twelfth Night*, Act II, Scene iii. See David Greer, 'Five Variations on "Farewel dear loue" ', in John Caldwell, Edward Olleson, and Susan Wollenberg (eds.), *The Well Enchanting Skill: Essays in Honour of F. W. Sternfeld* (Oxford, 1990), 213–29.

Ex. 8.5. *cont.*

1. Lyra viol tablature rhythm signs 𝅗𝅥 ♩ are misplaced in the source. Here they have been moved one place to the left to conform to the lute part.
2. Bass part natural sign is editorial. If the lute is the only accompaniment an F♯ would be required.

part. These are more substantial songs with more variation of key and mood. The third part is described as 'for two Trebles, to sing either to *the Lute, or the Viole or to both, if any please*'. *A Musicall Dreame* (1609) contains a similar triple mix of items, but differently ordered. It contains two Italian songs among the solo-song items. There are many errors in the lute tablature parts and the quality of lute writing is below the standard of Jones's previous books. It is interesting that he makes mention of new lutes of many strings in his address 'To all Musicall Murmurers'. He says that 'as our new come Lutes, being of many strings, not easily used, unlesse in adventure, till practise put forward into deserving Division'. Jones may have been commenting on lutes of eight or more courses coming into vogue, though in his books he only ever employs seven courses.

Jones's last book, *The Muses Gardin for Delights* (1610), is devoted to solo songs for the lute and bass viol. It leads on from the *Musicall Dreame* of 1609, with the reader waking in a muses' garden, where first 'love' and then 'love rejected' are encountered. As with all his books, there is a certain monotony in his songs. In part this is caused by the insufficient key variation. The pieces clearly have a programmatic dimension and, when viewed as a composite, constitute an early form of song cycle. It is a pity that his reputation is so often unfavourably compared with that of either Dowland or Campion, as, from a lutenist's point of view, some of his songs are a joy to play. A good example is 'Over these brookes' from the second book, to words by Philip Sidney. (See Ex. 8.5.) The gently flowing lines, which are built on the ideas of a rising triad in second inversion and a falling triad in root position, give a sense of the restorative power of water. Although the lute part normally consists of only two parts at any one time (occasionally three), the impression of the presence of more parts is given through the many points of imitation, the frequent lute episodes, and the consort-song nature of this song.

Among the published collections of ayres are four which relegate the lute to a cameo role. Both of Tobias Hume's books, *The First Part of Ayres* (1605) and *Captaine Humes Poeticall Musicke* (1607) contain no dedicated lute tablature at all. Hume states that the 1605 book contains some 'Songes to bee sung to the Viole, with the Lute, or better *with the Viole alone*'. The book is mostly filled with solos and duets for viols, and there are only five songs. A lute player would probably want to add some bass notes to the lyra viol tablature provided for the songs to make a workable lute part. The 1605 book is famous for the statement on behalf of the viol that so upset Dowland: '*from henceforth, the statefull instrument* Gambo Violl, *shall with ease yeelde full various as devicefull Musicke as the Lute*'. Hume repeated the statement in his 1607 book, changing the specific reference to the lute to '*shall with ease yield full various deuicefull Musicke as any other instrument*'. Most of the pieces in this book are written in such a way that they may be played as solos, as duets, or as trios. The first two parts are chordal in texture, and are written in tablature; the third part is a single melodic line in staff notation. It contains only three songs. Although 'Principally made for two Basse-Viols', Hume says it is 'so contrived that it may be plaied 8 severall waies upon sundry Instruments with much facilitie'. One of the eight listed ways is 'the fift musicke, for two Lutes and a Basse-Viole'. These pieces, like all lyra viol tablature in *vieil ton* tuning, are technically possible to play on the lute as they stand, but need some alteration to make them more satisfactory. Lyra viol chords have to be bowed across adjacent strings. Chords made up of non-adjacent strings are no problem for the lute, and are often preferable. Hume's pieces, if played on the lute, are made easier and musically improved if chords and sometimes melodies are rearranged so that they fall on non-adjacent strings.

In the two books of ayres by William Corkine, *Ayres to Sing and Play to the Lute and Basse Violl* (1610) and *The Second Booke of Ayres* (1612), Corkine is more even-handed in his preference for lute or viol. The first book has twelve songs with lute tablature and a bass viol part, plus twelve lyra viol solos. The second book has twenty-eight items, only five of which are songs with lute tablature and bass viol parts. This book is interesting for the fourteen songs 'to Sing and Play to the Base-Violl alone'. Here no tablature is given at all. Corkine's lute parts are generally simple, and often consist of little more than two outer parts with extra notes to fill out chords on impor-tant beats. Some of his songs (the more extended ones generally) are written for a high tenor or low alto voice. Thomas Ford's *Musicke of Sundrie Kindes* (1607) is really two books: one of lute ayres, plus a dialogue for two voices and two lyra viols; the other of lyra viol duos. The lute ayres, like those of Campion, are direct and uncom-plicated, though with part-song arrangements in the manner of Dowland's *First Booke*. Ford served both the Princes Henry and Charles. Within these households the fashion for the viol, and in particular the lyra viol, was particularly strong.

The remaining song books can be divided into a group where the approach is more contrapuntal, and another generally later group, which have more declama-tory elements. The former resulted in lute parts that are more complex and techni-cally demanding than the latter, which show the influence of the masque song, and where the bass is more static. Into the first category fall the books of Michael Cavendish (1598), Thomas Morley (1600), Thomas Greaves (1604), Francis Pilkington (1605), John Bartlet (1606), and John Danyel (1606); in the second, those of John Coprario (1606), Alfonso Ferrabosco (1609), John Coprario (1613), George Mason and John Earsden (1618), and John Attey (1622).

One song book that does not fit well into any category is John Maynard's *The XII. Wonders of the World* (1611), which has twelve songs for solo voice, lute, and viol, 'all three joyntly, and none severall'.[48] It also includes six pieces for lute and viol (in two three-piece sets), and seven lyra viol pieces with an optional bass part to go with them. The songs are settings of twelve satirical poems by Sir John Davies, each addressed to a different type of person: widow, merchant, etc., which had been printed as a set in 1608 with the title 'Yet other Twelve Wonders of the World'.[49] Davis and Maynard may have known each other when they were both in Ireland after 1603. What is unusual about Maynard's approach is the degree of divergence between the lute and viol parts. For this reason he indicates that all three (voice, viol, and lute) must be present. The bass of the lute part is shadowed by the

[48] Ian Harwood, 'John Maynard and *The XII Wonders of the World*', *LSJ* 4 (1962), 7–16.
[49] Ibid. 13. They were published in the second edition of Davison's *A Poetical Rhapsody* (1608).

bass viol in almost all other lute ayres with a separate printed bass for the bass viol. In Maynard's pieces the lute and viol are more independent, though they do shadow each other much of the time. Sometimes the viol is silent while the lute accompanies alone. Elsewhere the viol has division-like semiquaver figures not present in the lute line. All the songs are through-composed, and all but one are in G major/minor tonality. They suffer from a lack of tunefulness and instrumental parts that are over-fussy. Their aim is to be humorous in a way that is largely lost to a modern audience.

Michael Cavendish's book of madrigals and airs of 1598 (whose original title is not known) is the most antiquated in style of all the books, and harks back to the consort-song tradition. Of the twenty-eight items, fourteen are 'Ayres in Tabletorie to the Lute expressed with two *voyces and the base Violl or the voice & Lute only*', six are for four voices with lute tablature (no mention of the viol), and a further eight are five-part madrigals without accompaniments. In only three places in the book is a seventh course used, most of the tablature parts requiring only a 6-course lute. In 'Why should my muse' the voice part is really an alto line in the texture, with the lute supplying a higher cantus. (See Ex. 8.6.) This is like many consort songs where the vocal line is the second line down. The piece opens in imitative style and is fully contrapuntal throughout. Presumably the song was conceived as a five-part madrigal and then rearranged for a 6-course lute and voice with a sung or played bass. There are many instances in 'Why should my muse' where the texted bass descends to a low F but the lute jumps to the F above, for example in bars 7 and 11. The closeness of Cavendish's lute ayres to madrigals is indicated by the inclusion in his book of 'Wandering in this place' as both a five-part madrigal and a lute song.

Harder to play, and certainly less idiomatic than Cavendish's lute parts, are those in Thomas Morley's *First Booke of Ayres or Little Short Songs* (1600). We know from the table of contents that Morley's book originally had twenty-three items: twenty-one songs with lute tablature and an untexted bass part for the viol, plus two instrumental pieces (Pavan and Galliard). The only known copy is incomplete. It contains the first thirteen of the songs and most of number 14, though the voice and bass parts of two more of the songs appear in a later manuscript source. Morley was no lutenist. He acknowledges as much in his address to the reader when he says that 'I . . . being no professor thereof [i.e. of lute ayres and by inference the lute], but like a blind man groping for my way, have at length happened upon a method'. He does not explain this 'method', but my suggestion is that Morley conceived his accompaniments at the keyboard and then intabulated them as best he could. From a lutenist's point of view, some of the keys he chooses are unfortunate: 'A painted tale' would be more manageable in G major than A, and 'It was a lover' is technically easier in F major (with a seventh course pitched at *F*) than G. Though the inventive quality of his songs is high, his lute parts are often awkward, with a texture that is too dense.

Thomas Greaves's *Songes of sundrie kindes* (1604) contains nine lute ayres with untexted bass viol parts, together with six consort songs for four viols and voice, and six five-part madrigals. The lute ayres are complex and contrapuntally conceived. Francis Pilkington most certainly was a lutenist, as he states this on the title-page of *The First Booke of Songs or Ayres of 4. parts* (1605). This is very much in the mould of Dowland's *First Booke*, although the full title instruction stipulates 'for

Ex. 8.6. *'Why should my muse'*, Michael Cavendish, 14 Ayres in Tabletorie to the Lute *(1598)*, no. 2, bars 1–11

the Lute or Orpherian, with the Violl de Gamba'. Pilkington aims for a similar blend of songs as in Dowland's first book, with several dance-form songs, but he produces fewer memorable songs. His lute parts are in general quite manageable.

The simpler form of ayre is found in John Bartlet's *A Booke of Ayres with a Triplicitie of Musicke* (1606). They are mostly four-part ayres with lute and viol in the manner of Dowland's first book. It also contains four songs for two trebles to sing to the lute and viol, and three songs for one voice, lute, and viol. A great many of his songs are in G major or minor. While some suffer from a lack of invention, others are enjoyable to play from a lutenist's perspective.

The antithesis to Campion's approach to the ayre is found in some of the songs of John Danyel in his *Songs for the Lute, Viol and Voice* (1606). This is particularly so in his two trilogies 'Griefe, keep within' and 'Can dolefull notes'. The latter has several chromatic passages in all parts to illustrate the words 'No, let Chromatique tunes, harsh without ground, Bee sullaine Musique for a tunelesse hart'. John Danyel was brother to the court poet Samuel Danyel. John may have been something of a poet himself, and was perhaps the author of at least some of the words he set. Campion's warning against ayres that are 'long, intricate, bated with fuge, chaind with sincopation, and where the nature of everie word is precisely exprest in the Note'[50] is directly contradicted in Danyel's song 'Like as the Lute delights', where the text describes a succession of musical effects which are then portrayed musically: 'So sounds my Muse', 'strikes', 'strings high tun'd', 'touch', 'lamentable', 'a wayling descant', 'due reports', 'pleasing relish', 'no ground else', and 'so sweet a touch' are all expressed musically either in the vocal line, or in the lute part, or both. Example 8.7 illustrates three of these effects. The 'wayling descant on the sweetest ground' wails on the D flat over the smoothly rising and then falling ground in the lute part below (bar 17). The 'due reports' introduced in the vocal line (bar 19) with a four-note figure dominates the lute texture until the cadence in bar 23. Most obvious of all is the vocal relish articulated in bar 25 on the words 'relish here I use'.

With the exception of the last two songs, Danyel's ayres are printed with an untexted bass for a viol. The lute parts are highly worked, with space between vocal entries for instrumental interludes. There is also much repetition of words as in a consort song. The last two (nos. 19 and 20) have four sung parts. No. 20, 'Now the earth', also has a second lute part for bass lute (in *e′*, and tuned to a common lyra viol tuning), and a second treble voice part instead of an alto part. Danyel's ayres represent an extreme contrapuntalist approach, yet surprisingly his lute parts are not over difficult. This is achieved by not allowing the texture to become too cluttered.

John Coprario published two sets of elegies: the *Funeral Teares* (1606) for Charles Blount, Earl of Devonshire, and the *Songs of Mourning* (1613) for Prince Henry (with words by Campion). Both contain seven songs. Surprisingly, only a six-course lute is required for both books. His style verges towards the Italianate, but never leaves the constraints of the English lute ayre. In the 1606 book an alto part is provided that is optional for the first six songs, but must be present for the seventh. Coprario's lute parts are simple in the manner of a continuo realization. In the later book each of the first five songs is a lamentation on behalf of someone close to the prince; the sixth is to Great Britain, and the last to the world. Although the accompaniments are simple, the vocal parts are more difficult, and in places approach the *parlando* of the Italian continuo song. All his songs have untexted bass viol parts.

---

[50] See Campion's note 'To The Reader' in Rosseter's *A Booke of Ayres* (1601).

Ex. 8.7. *'Like as the Lute Delights'*, *John Danyel*, Songs for the Lute Viol and Voice *(1606)*, *no. 4, bars 16–23*

Ex. 8.7. *cont.*

The *Ayres* (1609) by Alfonso Ferrabosco display further concrete evidence of Italian influence in the declamatory vocal line and lute parts. The accompaniment is basic, and in a few places pared down to little more than a chord every bar or half bar. (See Ex. 8.8.) This allows the singer the rhythmic freedom to approach a recitative style. All twenty-eight songs have bass parts for a viol. The last three numbers are dialogues. Quite apart from his activities as a composer of consort music, Ferrabosco was much involved in the preparation of court masques, and it is clear that a number of the pieces he published in this book were first composed for masques. Again, only a 6-course lute is required.

Ex. 8.8. '*Yes were the loves*', *Alfonso Ferrabosco*, Ayres *(1609), no. 20, bars 1–5*

George Mason and John Earsden's *The Ayres that were Sung and Played, at Brougham Castle* (1618) is a musical record of the king's entertainment by Francis Clifford, Earl of Cumberland, and his son, Lord Clifford. This is masque music to accompany the king at different times during his short stay at the castle. The ten pieces are complicated, with dialogues and choruses. Together the items make up a greater musical entity. The lute parts, however, are very simple and typical of a recitative accompaniment. An untexted bass part is given for only one of the songs. For the first time in an English song book a 10-course lute is expected. The ayres are in the new declamatory style associated with Nicholas Lanier, Robert Johnson, and John Wilson. They were published as a book of ayres with tablature accompaniments as that was the norm, but were probably first realized and performed from an unfigured bass.

The last book of ayres, John Attey's *The First Booke of Ayres of Foure Parts, with Tableture for the Lute* (1622), is much more in the mainstream of the lute-song school, with fourteen four-part ayres with lute tablature to be performed either as part-songs with lute, or as solo songs with lute, and a viol reading the texted bassus part. Some of the songs are madrigalian, and more comparable to those written before 1610 than those afterwards. In the lute part the basses of the 10-course lute are used much more than in any other song book, and include runs on the open bass diapasons. The lute parts are not easy, and are conceived more in the old contrapuntal style.

Attey's book marks the end of the line for the English ayre with printed lute-tablature accompaniments. By 1622 the more progressive English song composers had abandoned tablature for an unfigured bass line for lute or theorbo. Edward Filmer published a book of *French Court-Aires, with their Ditties Englished* in 1629 by popular French composers of *airs de cour* with tablature. It is noteworthy that the French *air* composers did not abandon tablature in their published books until 1643, and did not provide a bass viol part, as was the norm in England after 1600.[51] The incursion of the viol into the published English books of ayres is one of the most obvious developments. Why a viol was never deemed necessary in France may possibly be because French lutes were louder. More likely the great increase in popularity of viol playing in the years after 1600 made their inclusion desirable. Gentleman amateur players of the viol, epitomized by the likes of Sir Toby Belch, could then be included in music-making with singers and lutenists of greater proficiency. This development is taken a stage further in Martin Peerson's *Private Musicke . . .* (London, 1620). Here there is no tablature, though the lute and virginals are admitted if there are no viols. Peerson states the music is 'for voyces and viols, and for want of viols, they may be performed either to the virginall or lute'.

The lute did continue to appear in lists of possible continuo instruments throughout the century, though as an inferior option. An example is Martin Peerson's *Mottects or Grave Chamber Musique* (1630). By 1625 the theorbo was fast becoming the basic continuo lute. A lute of eight to ten courses could still be used to accompany songs, but its identity is then bound up with, and subsumed under, that of the theorbo.

Published collections of English lute songs are one of the special features of the late Elizabethan/early Jacobean music scene. Taken together, the books show the increased encroachment of the viol as a means of vocal accompaniment, and the changing approach in accompaniment style from one that is either contrapuntal, or basically homophonic but with some melodic interest particularly in the top line, to

---

[51] André Verchaly, 'La Tablature dans les recueils français pour chant et luth (1603–1643)', in Jean Jacquot (ed.), *Le Luth et sa musique* (Paris, 1958), 155–69. Twenty-six collections were published by between 1603 and 1643, numbering together around 1,009 songs.

one that is more perfunctory, like a continuo realization. Yet they are a testament to the special importance of the lute in providing a song accompaniment. The profusion of printed books, in comparison to the small number of published sources of solo music, suggests that for many players at the time, the facility of providing vocal accompaniment was the primary reason for having a lute.

Chapter Nine

From Renaissance to Baroque: A Continental Excursus, 1600–1650

> Vomigny Perrichon and the Polack are furthest Lutinists in the memory of man that deserve to be menconed and to have a Statue upon the Mount of Parnassus for haveing given us the Rudimente of the Lute and cleared the first difficulties that hindered production of this Masterpeece[.] Afterwards Monsieur Mezangeot appeared upon the Stage of Musicke and using the Lute with nyneteene Stringes hath soe polished the Composition and the playing of it that without Contradiction we must give him the praise to have given to the Lute his first perfection . . .
>
> Burwell Tutor, fo. 5^{r-v}

French ideas and fashions were largely responsible for the transformation of the lute and lute music during the first half of the seventeenth century. The famous manuscript of Anne de Chambure entitled 'la Rhetorique des Dieux' by Denis Gaultier of 1652, marks the apogee of French solo lute *brisé* style.[1] Here the music is decked out with pictures and commentaries that build an elaborate web of associations with classical rhetoric, ancient modes, and allegorical personifications of these modes.[2] As the title suggests, the music was held to be of such refinement that it was almost beyond mortal comprehension. The rise of the lute to this exalted position in France in the first half of the century involved a fundamental rethinking of all aspects of the lute and its music. The changes that led to the development of the French Baroque lute style had their origins in the work of Parisian lute makers and players of the first three decades of the century. The magnitude of this change can be seen by comparing Antoine Francisque's *Le Trésor d'Orphée* of 1600, the only source of solo lute music printed in France in the first decade of the century, with Pierre Ballard's *Tablature de luth de différents autheurs, sur des accords nouveaux* (1631). Francisque's book is organized by genre, like the German and Dutch anthologies listed in Table 7.2, and is for a 9-course lute, though many pieces only require eight courses. Ballard's 1631 publication groups pieces according to composer, then tuning, then key, and finally by genre, and requires a 10-course lute. Francisque's book requires only Renaissance tuning, apart from thirteen pieces in a

---

[1] *La Rhétorique des dieux et autre pièces de luth de Denis Gaultier*, ed. André Tessier and Jean Cordey (Paris, 1932).
[2] Robert M. Isherwood, *Music in the Service of the King: France in the Seventeenth Century* (Ithaca, 1973), 6–7.

cordes avalées tuning. Yet Ballard's book makes no use of Renaissance tuning, and requires the transitional tunings nos. 8 and 10 only. Above all the style of the music and the techniques required to play pieces in the respective books are dramatically divergent.

At the root of the stylistic transformation of lute music from 1600 to 1630 was the move away from regarding the lute as a medium that could simulate polyphonic vocal music. The melodic flow of much Renaissance lute music was governed by tunes which were essentially vocal and not particularly well suited to the lute. From this situation French lutenists became predominantly concerned with sonority and expressiveness, and in how the lute's own capabilities could be best exploited to effect the maximum in expressive variation of rhythm, tone, and colour. To achieve these aims their experiments took two main forms: the first with tunings, and the second with significant changes in right-hand, and to a lesser extent left-hand, techniques. Certainly these two developments were concomitant, the latter to exploit the new possibilities opened up by the former.

The lute music of Francisque, Nicolas Vallet, Robert Ballard, and the lute publications of Pierre Ballard are listed in Table 9.1. It is possible to trace the adumbration of the *style brisé* in the music contained in these books. Most of them were printed in Paris under the royal patents of Le Roy and Ballard. The exceptions are the first edition of Vallet's *Le Secret des muses*, published in Amsterdam, and that of the *Œuvres* of Pierre Gaultier, published in Rome in 1638. However, these publications can be considered with those published in Paris. The number of manuscripts that can definitely be said to have been compiled in Paris in the period are not many, although there is evidence that a considerable number of lute makers and players were active in Paris in the years 1600–30.[3]

Louys de Moy's anthology, *Le Petit Boucquet de Frise orientale*, was produced for the marriage of Count Ulrich of East Friesland and Princess Juliana of Hessen in 1631. It connects with the tradition of Dutch and German printed anthologies listed in Table 7.2 in that de Moy was probably Dutch, the book was probably published in East Friesland, and it contains a mixture of solo lute music and music that combines voices and/or instruments with a tablature lute part.[4] However, the style of the solo lute music in *Le Petit Boucquet* is pure French, and all the attributed pieces (excepting those of de Moy himself) are by French lutenist composers. De Moy's own lute compositions are typical of the Parisian style of the 1620s just prior to the exploration of altered tunings, a style exemplified by the music of Robert Ballard.

[3] François Lesure, 'Recherches sur les luthistes parisiens à l'époque de Louis XIII', in Jean Jacquot (ed.), *Le Luth et sa musique* (Paris, 1958), 209–23: see 211–13, list of known makers; and 217–23, list of known players, all of whom were active in Paris 1600–30.

[4] Louys de Moy, *Le Petit Boucquet de Frise orientale* (n.p., 1631; repr. Peer, 1987, ed. Eugeen Schreurs and Martine Sanders, with an introduction by Mijndert Jape).

Table 9.1. *French lute publications 1600–1640*

Composer/publisher	Title of book	Comments
Antoine Francisque (Paris)	*Le Trésor d'Orphée* (1600) For 8- and 9-course lutes, Renaissance tuning and *cordes avalées*	Includes: fantasias, preludes, passamezzi, pavans, galliards branles, gavottes, and vocally inspired pieces
Robert Ballard (Paris)	1. *Diverses pièces mises sur le luth* [Premier Livre] (1611) 2. *Diverses pièces mises sur le luth* [Deuxième Livre] (1614) For 10-course lute in Renaissance tuning only	(1) includes only entrees, ballets, courantes, and voltes; (2) includes ballets, voltes, galliards, branles, and 'pièces diverses'
Nicolas Vallet (Amsterdam)	1. *Le Secret des muses: premier livre* (1615) 2. *Le Secret des muses: second livre* (1616) For 10-course lute in Renaissance tuning	(1) 90 pieces: preludes, fantasias, pavanes, passamezzi, galliards, ballets, courantes, sarabands, and voltes; (2) ballets and branles
Pierre Ballard (Paris)	1. *Tablature de luth de différents auteurs sur l'accord ordinaire et extraordinaire* (1623) For 10-course lute	Lost anthology. Title-page suggests both Renaissance and transitional tunings were employed
Pierre Ballard (Paris)	1. *Tablature de luth de différent autheurs, sur les accords nouveaux* (1631) For 10-course lute, tunings 8 and 10 2. *Tablature de luth de différent autheurs, sur les accords nouveaux* (1638) For 10-course lute, tunings 8, 9, 10, and D minor	87 pieces by R. Ballard (7), Mesangeau (12), Dufaut (13), Chancy (12), Bouvier (20), Belleville (6), Dubuisson (3), and Chevalier (14) 40 pieces: by Mesangeau (19), Dufaut (10), Bouvier (6), Dubut (5). Includes preludes, allemandes, branles, timbres, and canaries
Pierre Gaultier (Rome)	*Les Œuvres de Pierre Gaultier* (1638) For 10-course lute, tunings 6, 8, 9, 10, 11, and D minor	103 pieces: 17 suite-like groups organized by tuning. Includes allemandes, courantes, sarabandes, preludes, ballets, sinfonies, and a single pavan. Contains no fewer than 39 courantes

The book and its music are a testament to the successful export of the new French lute style.

The travels of the lutenist, author, and poet Charles de Lespine, to England, Germany, and Italy in the period 1610 to 1627, the visits of Ennemond Gaultier and of René Mesangeau to England around 1630, together with the activities of the French musicians of Anne of Denmark, Henrietta Maria, and the Cavendish family, suggest that French lutenists were actively contributing to the dissemination of their music abroad.[5] Ennemond Gaultier was usually referred to as 'Vieux' Gaultier, in relation to his cousin Denis Gaultier, who is also known as 'Jeune' Gaultier. Neither is known to have been related to Jacques Gaultier.

By 1630 Paris had become the leading centre in Europe for the teaching and composition of solo lute music. The Englishmen Bullen Reymes, Hender Robarts, and possibly John Rogers studied the lute with French masters in Paris during the period 1630–60. There were no doubt many others. Robert Ballard's position as lute teacher to Louis XIII, and Vieux Gaultier's post as lutenist to Marie de Médicis and lute teacher of Cardinal Richelieu suggest that the instrument had attained high favour with the French Bourbon royal house, which would have undoubtedly boosted the lute's prestige and respectability.[6]

Francisque's book, *Le Trésor d'Orphée* contains stylistic elements that anticipate the *brisé* style. It does not include vocal intabulations, although a long piece based on Lassus' 'Susanne un jour' opens the book. The largest grouping is that of courantes, voltes, and branles. Most significant is the inclusion of thirteen pieces in a *cordes avalées* tuning. This is the first indication that experimentation with lute tuning was under way.[7]

A comparison between the *Trésor d'Orphée* and the near contemporary *Florida* illustrates how French tastes were moving away from those of the rest of northern Europe at the start of the century. Example 9.1 gives the opening of a C minor galliard from each of these books. Both are based on pieces by other composers, Francisque's on a volte by Julien Perrichon, Van den Hove's on John Dowland's 'Can she excuse'. The lightness of texture in Francisque's music and the more infrequent use of full chords contrast with the more ponderous texture of Van den Hove's arrangement, which exhibits a fuller texture than the versions of the Dowland piece found in English sources. (See above, Ex. 5.1.) The bass line in Francisque's pieces moves freely both diatonically and by large intervals. In the *Florida* piece part-writing is less ambiguous, and the bass line has a tendency to move more slowly and keep within an octave compass. In some pieces Francisque

[5] For Lespine, see Lachèvre, *Charles de Lespine*; for Gaultier, see Lesure, 'Recherches', 220.

[6] *Œuvres du Vieux Gautier*, ed. and trans. André Souris, with an introduction and concordances by Monique Rollin (Paris, 1966), p. xii.

[7] The pieces in this tuning are to be found on fos. 22ʳ–24ᵛ (8 branles, 1 gavotte, and 1 pavane) and fos. 31ʳ–31ᵛ (2 voltes and 1 ballet).

approaches a *brisé* texture as a means of variation, particularly in his courantes, branles, and voltes, although this is more usually achieved through Renaissance running divisions. The books of Robert Ballard, Vallet, and Francisque are not anthologies, and in the main contain the works of an individual composer. They are less cosmopolitan in content and rely more on original material than the anthologies listed in Table 7.3.

It may be that Nicolas Vallet (*c*.1583–after 1642) left France after 1614, because as a Huguenot his chances of a successful career as a lutenist were better in the

Ex. 9.1. *Comparison of (a) the opening of Francisque's 'Gaillarde faicte sur une volte de feu Perrichon' (Trésor, fo. 13ᵛ, bars 1–12) with (b) Van den Hove's 'Galiarda' based on John Dowland's 'Can She Excuse' (Florida, fo. 99ʳ, bars 1–11)*

1.   2.

1. The ⌐ rhythm flag has been moved from the second beat to bar 2 second beat.

2. The barring has been regulated from a mixture of $\frac{3}{2}$ and $\frac{6}{2}$ to $\frac{3}{2}$ only.

Netherlands, where the emerging French lute style was becoming fashionable.[8] He had trained and toured in France prior to his departure, and despite spending his remaining working life in the Dutch Republic, must be considered a member of the early seventeenth-century French lute school.[9] Like Van den Hove, Vallet died in misery and poverty after a working life of considerable success.[10]

Vallet's well-documented lute quartets were performed for social functions (weddings and banquets are mentioned), in which they no doubt provided dance music and incidental music. Vallet and another member of his quartet, Edward Hancock, founded a dancing-school for which contracts survive.[11] The fact that this music may have been intended for dancing may explain the clear phrase structure and consistent texture that characterizes much of Vallet's music. Likewise the close connections between Robert Ballard's music and the *ballet de cour* may account for the standardization of phrase lengths and dance forms in much of his music.[12] The dance forms that appear in Pierre Ballard's books of 1631 and 1638 no longer hold to the norms dictated by the dance itself, and constitute abstract art music proper. Herein lies one of the hallmarks of French lute music after 1630. From this point onwards most solo lute music was composed in the form of one or other of the dance movements associated with the suite, although these pieces were unlikely to have been actually danced.

Vallet's published books display a great variety of genre types (see Table 9.1).[13] In this respect his books are comparable to the Dutch and German anthologies of the time, and like them his books are cosmopolitan in outlook, particularly in the many English tunes he arranged.[14] By contrast, Robert Ballard published only entrées, ballets, courantes, and voltes in any number. Despite this divergence in form their respective styles have much in common. In both Vallet's and Ballard's dance pieces simplicity and regularity of phrase and texture are hallmarks of style. Vallet tends more to scalic divisions and rhythmic sequences, whereas Ballard uses *brisé* texture more extensively as a means of variation.

---

[8] *Œuvres de Nicolas Vallet pour luth seul*, ed. and trans. André Souris with a biographical study and critical commentary by Monique Rollin (Paris, 1970), pp. xi–xvii.

[9] Stanley Buetens, 'Nicolas Vallet's Lute Quartets', *JLSA* 2 (1969), 28–36.

[10] *Vallet*, ed. Souris, p. xiv.

[11] Alan Curtis, *Sweelinck's Keyboard Music: A Study of English Elements in Seventeenth-Century Dutch Composition* (London, 1969), 23–4. Curtis prints in full the contract for the quartet and dancing-school drawn up on 12 Nov. 1626 to last for six years.

[12] Much of Robert Ballard's published music would appear to be adaptations of music performed at various *ballets de cour* which Ballard arranged for solo lute. See Robert Ballard, *Premier Livre (1611)*, ed. and trans. André Souris and Sylvie Spycket with a historical introduction and study of concordances by Monique Rollin (Paris, 1963), pp. xii–xiii.

[13] Reprinted in facsimile by The Dutch Lute Society as *The Complete Works of Nicolas Vallet*, 4 vols. (Utrecht, 1994).

[14] English musicians and travelling acting companies as well as English popular music were very popular in Holland in the early 17th c., hence Vallet's arrangements. See Curtis, *Sweelinck's Keyboard Music*, 10–34.

Vallet included in his 1615 book 'La Courante Sarabande'. In this piece bass notes follow full chords placed on the beat. In another piece, 'La moresque', some bass notes anticipate full chords.[15] (See Ex. 9.2.) Ballard used this technique in several of his ballets, as for example in his *Troisieme Ballet de M. de Daufin*. The technique became inseparably associated with the sarabande by 1630. Ballard's books are dominated by his ballets drawn from the *ballet de cour*. In these productions successions of musical *entrées*, which would have accompanied the spectacular entrance of new groups of dancers, follow one another, requiring ingenuity in varying textures. In the reworking of this material Ballard attempted to highlight the differences between *entrées* by contrasting tessitura and more importantly sonority. In this last respect he particularly contributed to the development of the *brisé* style.

The decade of the 1620s was the period in which the advances present in the works of Ballard and Vallet were taken up by the leading Parisian lutenists and transformed into something altogether new. Sadly this transformation is impossible to observe with any clarity due to the lack of surviving manuscript source material

Ex. 9.2. *'La moresque'*, Nicolas Vallet, Le Secret des muses, le premier livre, *p. 84, no. 75, bars 1–7*

---

[15] *Œuvres*, ed. Souris, p. 177, no. 74, bars 23–38 of tablature; p. 178, no. 75, bars 1–5.

from what must have been a most stimulating and exciting period of the lute's development.[16] The key lute book, the *Tablature de luth de différents autheurs sur l'accord ordinaire et extraordinaire* published by Pierre Ballard in 1623 would, if available, certainly illuminate this process of transformation. Unfortunately, all copies are lost save a single title-page.[17] The title suggests that pieces in transitional tunings were included, as well as pieces in Renaissance tuning. It would be interesting to know if these pieces were principally grouped by composer, tuning, or genre, and whether the groupings represent a suite-like ordering of pieces.

One important but little-known source that pre-dates Ballard's 1631 book is Chancy's *Tablature de mandore de la composition du Sieur Chancy*, published in Paris in 1629. It contains six proto suite-type groups, plus a suite of branles.[18] A typical grouping might be allemande, three courantes, sarabande, passemezze, chanson, and volte. However, all these groupings, excluding those of branles, incorporate the fundamental allemande–courante–sarabande sequence, and thus correspond with Pierre Ballard's 1631 book.

On the face of the evidence available to us today it seems that the basic Baroque suite (minus the gigue, which did not take its place until the 1650s)[19] appears ready-formed, without obvious precedent. By 1630 the dances themselves have changed considerably from 1620. The allemande is transformed from the Renaissance, heavy German dance of moderate speed into a slower, stylized, quasi-contrapuntal art form, with comparatively regular phrasing and subtle interplay of rhythmic and melodic motifs. They are generally the most complex movements of the repertoire, and the most difficult to play.[20] The sarabande does not appear in any numbers in French sources before 1630, but assumes an important role as the final, and at this period the fastest, dance movement, drawing its inspiration from the Iberian dance accompanied by guitar and castanets from which it originated.[21] *Brisé* writing is less a feature of this movement-type than in others, and it is marked by regular and balanced phrase structure, generally of four, but also of two and eight bars in length.[22] The two most common types of early saraband are those with a series of strummed

---

[16] Only the French pieces in the Herbert MS associated with Lord Herbert's years in Paris and the Pan 5 and Reymes MSS are definitely of Parisian origin during the years 1600–35.

[17] Lesure, 'Recherches', 216. This title-page was in the private collection of M. Pincherle.

[18] David Fuller in *New Grove*, xviii. 339–40, credits the French lutenists *c.*1620 with the introduction of the allemande–courante–sarabande suite formation. The suite-type groups of movements in Chancy's and Ballard's publications are quoted in David J. Buch's article, 'The Influence of the Ballet de cour in the Genesis of the French Baroque Suite', *Acta musicologica*, 57 (1985), 94–108. This article further investigates the origins of the suite, and the importance of the *ballet de cour* and the French lutenists *c.*1620 in its development.

[19] Wallace J. Rave, 'Some Manuscripts of French Lute Music 1630–1700: An Introductory Study' (Ph.D. diss., University of Illinois at Urbana-Champaign, 1972), 68.

[20] Ibid. 67–8.

[21] David Ledbetter, 'French Lute Music 1600–1650: Towards a Definition of Genres' *LSJ* 30 (1990), 25–47 at 41.

[22] Rave, 'Some Manuscripts', 73.

chords in the opening phrase that recall the guitar dance, and those with the anticipatory bass followed by a chord on the upper courses derived from Ballard and Vallet. This movement rose from obscurity to great popularity during the years leading up to 1630.[23]

The French courante after 1630 epitomizes the *style brisé* and is the most popular dance type of the whole period 1610–80 in the lute repertoire.[24] It is characterized by an absence of regular phrase structure, imitation, or motivic recurrence. The texture is generally thin, with ambiguous part-writing and irregular harmonic rhythm. Courantes are frequently characterized by a 3/2 hemiola rhythm (i.e. ♩.♪|♩♩) particularly at the approach to a cadence. The courante in the decades up to 1630 had been equally popular before joining the allemande and sarabande; several manuscripts in the period 1610–30 contain a high proportion of courantes. However, these earlier courantes, as seen in the works of Montbuysson, Saman, and Perrichon, have a rhythmic pattern similar to the quick 3/4 patterns of the Italian corrente.[25] By 1630 the French courante had become a slower, more subtle dance type with the most consistent use of *brisé* texture. In part these changes, like those affecting the volte and popular-tune settings or *timbres* that are included in the French solo lute sources 1610–40, resulted from the technical exigencies and possibilities of new tunings. It is notable, however, how the advent of transitional tunings saw a considerable drop in the degree of difficulty found in surviving published and manuscript sources, especially as regards the left hand.

The move away from a single standard tuning to a variety of tunings, each of which were suited only to very particular keys, had a bearing on the formation of the suite. Having set a lute in a particular tuning, it made sense to play a succession of pieces, moving from the slowest and most rhythmically free to the fastest and most precise. The variety of tunings a lute might be subjected to within a relatively short space of time may have obliged a lutenist to begin his or her play with a piece that circulated through the basic chord positions pertaining to the desired key and tuning. The unbarred quasi-improvisatory prelude allowed the player to dwell freely on chord positions he or she might have wished to test for tuning imperfections, yet at the same time served to throw into relief the accentuated rhythmic flow of the stylized dance types that were to follow.[26] Some unmeasured preludes of the

---

[23] Ledbetter, 'French Lute Music', 41–6. He lists five main types of lute sarabande in the sources 1630–50.

[24] Ibid. 34–8; also Rave, 'Some Manuscripts', 69–70.

[25] *Œuvres de Vaumesnil, Edinthon, Perrichon, Raël, Montbuysson, La Grotte, Saman, La Barre*, ed. and trans. by André Souris, Monique Rollin, and Jean-Michel Vaccaro (Paris, 1974); for example, Perrichon nos. 15 and 17, Montbuysson nos. 4 and 5, and Saman nos. 1, 2, 4, and 6. The editor shows in his introduction that these early 17th-c. courantes conform in their structure to the description given by Arbeau, *Orchésographie* (trans. Mary Stewart Evans, with a new introduction and notes by Julia Sutton (New York, 1967), 124), suggesting that these pieces were used for dancing.

[26] Ledbetter, 'French Lute Music', 25–31. Preludes, or opening pieces with a similar function and style, also come under the titles 'Entree', 'Point d'Orgue', 'Recherche', and 'Fuge'.

period *c*.1630–50 have no rhythmic indications at all; others are unbarred but have rhythmic signs for some or all of the piece, though even here a regular beat is clearly to be avoided. Preludes usually consist of arpeggiated chords and scale passages with little melodic interest. Cadences are often left incomplete, and harmonic progressions disrupted by abrupt shifts in the harmonic movement.[27] The prelude was often the most adventurous harmonically of a set of movements, frequently including unprepared or unresolved dissonances. The unmeasured prelude was, of all the innovations of the Parisian lutenists of this period, possibly the most successful and far-reaching in its influence on other musical media.

The term *corde avalée* first appeared in mid-sixteenth century French guitar books, such as Guillaume Morlaye's *Quatriesme livre* (1552) (fo. 15ᵛ) and *Second livre* (1553) (fo. 29ᵛ). Here it involved a single altered bass, a practice that can be traced in Italian lute music back to the books of Capirola, Dalza, and Spinacino. Dalza also uses a tuning involving the lowering of the two bottom courses, *g, d, a, f, B♭, F*, and Melchiore de Barberiis (fl. *c*.1545–50) experimented with this and two other 'discordate' tunings, *g′, d′, a, g, d, G* and *a′, e′, a, f, c, G*. *Cordes avalées* tunings in the books of Francisque and Besard involve the retuning of the middle courses of the instrument, with consequent adjustment of the bass courses; for example, from Renaissance tuning *g′, d′, a, f, c, G, F, E, C*, to *g′, d′, b♭, f, B♭, G, F, E♭, B♭′*, or variants on this latter tuning. Often these tunings were used to provide a continuous ostinato bass pattern on open strings for branles or voltes, or as a drone in imitation of the bagpipes or hurdy-gurdy.[28]

By contrast, the transitional tunings popular in France in the 1620s and 1630s involved the lowering of the top three courses to an open chord. Probably the first transitional tuning to evolve was the variously titled 'sharp', 'English Gaultier's tuning', or 'Mersenne's extraordinary tuning', with the top two courses lowered to *e′* and *c′* (tuning no. 8). A close variant of this tuning was to lower the top string to *f′* and the second to *c′* (tuning no. 7), thus producing an F major chord on the top four strings (*f′, c′, a, f*). These two tunings involved no alterations to the basses of a 10-course lute (*G, F, E, D, C*). Probably the next tuning to evolve was tuning no. 10, called the 'Flat French' by Mace in 1676. It was the most popular of all transitional tunings. This tuning involves a further descent of the top string to *e♭′*, the second course to *c′*, and the third to *a♭*. The basses are then altered to run *G, F, E♭, D♭, C*. A close variant of this tuning is tuning no. 9, with the third course raised to *a♮* and the ninth to *D♮*. See Table 9.2.

During the period 1600 to 1630 French lute makers and players experimented with design as well as tuning. It is clear from the published books in Table 9.1 and

---

[27] Rave, 'Some Manuscripts', 65.

[28] e.g. the 'Chorrea rustica a Corde Avalee', *Thesaurus harmonicus*, fo. 169ʳ, has a drone C on the fifth course throughout the piece.

Table 9.2. Cordes avalées *and transitional tunings*

Renaissance tuning (10-course lute): tuning no. 1

Cordes avalées

Sharp tuning: tuning no. 8

Sharp tuning variant (with top course raised a semitone): tuning no. 7

Flat tuning: tuning no. 10

Flat tuning variant (with third and ninth raised a semitone): tuning no. 9

D minor tuning

raised a tone (11-course lute)

manuscript sources that the 10-course lute was standard by 1610. It is the type of lute normally required for the twenty-seven volumes of *airs de cour* published between 1608 and 1632, all but three of which were printed by Pierre Ballard.[29] According to Piccinini it was during this period that the French acquired all the old lutes of Bologna, especially those of Maler and Frei. The makers then used the backs and bellies of these old lutes and fitted them with new necks, pegboxes, and bridges. The conversion of old lutes by French makers at this time may account for the relative lack of surviving French instruments from this period. As a result of this activity the fashion for round-bodied, multi-ribbed instruments in the late sixteenth and early seventeenth centuries gave way to a renewed interest in the 'pearl' shape of the early sixteenth century with only nine or eleven ribs.[30]

The double-headed construction of the 12-course lute is perhaps the easiest conversion to make from an old lute. This is because the existing body and neck of a Renaissance lute can be used, the only alterations necessary being a new pegbox and bridge. It is clear from iconography and musical sources that this type of instrument found lasting favour in England and the Netherlands. The Burwell Tutor also suggests that at some point, presumably during the period 1620–40, the French, like the English, were experimenting with 12-course double-headed lutes. The Burwell Tutor relates that Jacques Gaultier, who left France in 1617 to make his subsequent career in England, 'hath caused twoe heads to be made to the Lute[.] All England hath accepted that Augmentacon and Fraunce att first but soone after that alteracon hath beene condemned by all the french Masters who are returned to theire old fashion keepeing only the small Eleaventh'.[31] Thus the tutor credits Jacques Gaultier with the design and construction of the 12-course lute, although he presumably got an instrument maker to carry out the work, and states that the French masters quickly rejected the instrument.

During the 1640s the French 11-course lute superseded the 10-course lute. An existing 10-course lute could easily be restrung as an 11-course lute by adding a treble rider and altering only the bridge and the nut. A rider is a piece of wood added to the upper edge of the pegbox, cut and drilled to carry a single peg, or a small number of pegs. The preference for the 'small Eleaventh' in the Burwell Tutor extract above refers to the French fashion of using only a single octave eleventh string without a fundamental.[32] This arrangement does not necessitate the use of a treble rider, as, with a single first, second, and eleventh course, the nineteen strings

[29] A minority of these songs require only a 9-course lute. See Jonathan Le Cocq, 'Pitch and Tuning in French Lute Song', *The Lute*, 32 (1992), 46–71 at 49.

[30] Michael Lowe, 'The Historical Development of the Lute in the 17th Century', *GSJ* 29 (1976), 11–25 at 14–15.

[31] Burwell Tutor, fo. 68ʳ.

[32] Ibid., fo. 8ʳ. 'Concerneing the Eleaventh string which is the last Base the good Masters of the Lute doe use onely the octave that is the little one [string] . . .'

of a 10-course lute are simply redistributed on the nut and bridge, while the basic instrument remains unchanged. However, the conversion of an old lute to a 10- or 11-course lute, unlike a conversion to a 12-course lute, required a new neck as well. Lutes in Dowland's time had eight frets on the neck, but by the 1640s nine or ten was the norm.[33] This increase in the length of the neck in relation to the body became possible by replacing the neck on a conversion of an old lute, or a rejected 12-course lute, with a neck suitable for an 11-course lute. This resulted in an increased string length and a slight decrease in pitch. These changes are consistent with the decrease in use of difficult stopped chords in the left hand and the increase in interest in sonority that is part of the *brisé* style.

There is little surviving source evidence that the 12-course lute ever became popular in France.[34] A 10-course lute only is required for both Ballard's 1631 and 1638 books and for Pierre Gaultier's *Œuvres*, also of 1638. Both these last books include the first published pieces requiring the D minor tuning f', d', a, f, d, A, G, F, E, D, C, which in France largely supplanted all other tunings by 1650,[35] although the D major variant of this tuning $f\sharp'$, d', a, $f\sharp$, d, A, G, $F\sharp$, E, D, C remained popular even after the mid-century.[36] To arrive at D minor tuning (transposed down a tone) from tuning no. 10 only the third, fourth, and ninth courses need to be altered, i.e. from $e\flat'$, c', $a\flat$, f, c, G, F, $E\flat$, $D\flat$, C to $e\flat'$, c', g, $e\flat$, c, G, F, $E\flat$, D, C. (See Table 9.2.) Contemporary authorities stress the need to keep an even tension over the whole range of strings. With the continued lowering of the upper course relative to the lower it was necessary to raise the whole tessitura of the instrument. As the 10-course lute gave way to the 11-course lute the nominal tessitura of the instrument was raised a tone, which, when employing the above tuning, resulted in the standard D minor tuning at the normally transcribed pitch.

The transitional tunings and the D minor and related tunings, by increasing the number of adjacent thirds obtained on open strings, can produce a much more sonorous response from a lute than Renaissance tuning, with its reliance on stopped courses for full triads. Even in chords involving stopped courses, the altered tunings gain in sonority over Renaissance tuning through sympathetic vibration of strings not actually sounded. By stopping notes in high positions on low strings and by playing more open strings, altered tunings could produce a richer tone and a

---

[33] Dowland's 'Other Necessary Observations', *Varietie*, sig. D2r; Burwell Tutor, ch. 4.

[34] There are a number of pieces in the Reymes MS which require a twelfth course (fos. 42v, 44r–45r, 56v–60v); however, this MS has strong English associations.

[35] Thomas Mace, writing in 1676, had known the D minor tuning for forty years; *Musick's Monument, or, A Remembrancer of the Best Practical Musik* (London, 1676; facs. edn. Paris, 1966: vol. 1: *Musick's Monument*; vol. 2: trans. and commentary ed. Jean Jacquot and André Souris), 191. Marin Mersenne, *Harmonie universelle* (1636); modern edn. and trans. by Roger E. Chapman (The Hague, 1957) mentions only tunings nos. 8 and 10, p. 115, although he also includes a piece by Mesangeau in tuning no. 9, p. 124.

[36] This tuning is noticeably popular in works of Pinel for 10-course lute. For example, all nine pieces by Pinel in Pan 4 are in this tuning.

greater continuity of sound despite a thinner texture. Scales or melodic passages are produced in such a way that successive notes are not played on the same string, as one would normally expect, but on two or more strings, allowing notes to ring on longer than usual. To achieve these 'campanella' (little bell) effects, the stopped notes usually have to be in high fret positions. Such campanella melodic passages and certain cadential formulae are a feature of the *brisé* style that developed out of the desire to exploit the richer sonority afforded by the new tunings.

It is difficult to chart the basic changes in lute technique after Besard, as there are no surviving tutors from France or England before the Burwell Tutor and Mace's *Musick's Monument* that describe the technique appropriate to the French *style brisé*.[37] It is clear from the music that fundamental changes had taken place by 1630, and that these changes in technique were then refined during the rest of the century, but not altered in substance. At the centre of this change in technique is a rethinking of the division of responsibilities between the thumb and the fingers of the right hand. We have seen how the old technique of 'thumb and index' alternation had given way to one of 'index and middle finger' alternation for melodic passage work. The former tended towards a 'thumb inside the hand' position while the latter allowed a 'thumb outside the hand' position. With the increased number of courses these changes were ever more necessary. The thumb could now be left to concentrate on its responsibility for always playing the bass of all chords or *brisé* passages. Conjunct chords, instead of being plucked by the thumb and individual fingers, normally one to a course to allow arpeggiation, could now be 'raked', so that the thumb brushed across all the strings to meet the middle finger plucking the uppermost string. In this new style difficult chords for the left hand and runs seldom feature. Instead there is greater attention to ornamentation, including slurs and slides, in which the left hand sounds extra notes after the right hand has plucked the string. These technical changes are strongly linked to the use of altered tunings, the increase in the number of courses, and the exploitation of the increased resonance that resulted from the new tunings.

It is difficult to decide who amongst the French lutenist-composers is to be credited with these innovations. The fact that Mesangeau's works appear in generous numbers in both of Pierre Ballard's books, his many manuscript attributions, and the high esteem in which he was held by his contemporaries point to him as a leading figure.[38] Vieux Gaultier wrote a beautiful 'Tombeau de Mesangeau' on the latter's death, and might have been a pupil of Mesangeau.[39] The Burwell Tutor quotation given above singles out Mesangeau as the first master to 'have given to

---

[37] Diana Poulton, 'La Technique du jeu du luth en France et en Angleterre', in Jean Jacquot (ed.), *Le Luth et sa musique* (Paris, 1958), 118.

[38] Besard mentions Mesangeau's skill in his *Novus partus* (Augsburg, 1617) as does Adam Gumpelzhaimer in the *Gymnasma* (Strasburg, 1621).

[39] *Œuvres du Vieux Gautier*, p. xii.

the Lute his first perfection'.[40] This would seem to credit him with many of the innovations of his time. The rest of the group of composers who contributed to Pierre Ballard's books (Chancy, Bouvier, Belleville, Dubuisson, and Chevalier), have little to distinguish between them stylistically. Chancy, however, did publish a book for mandore in 1629, and like Bouvier (a contributor to both the 1631 and 1638 books) may have been an important innovator. Dubut, and more importantly Dufaut, were both major figures at the outset of their careers, and cannot thus be credited with innovations much before 1630.[41]

The active career of Ennemond [or Vieux] Gaultier (1600–31) coincides exactly with the period under discussion. Unfortunately, his music was only published posthumously by his famous nephew Denis, from whose style Vieux Gaultier's music is indistinguishable.[42] It is most likely that Ennemond would have passed through all the transitional phases that led to the consolidation of the *style brisé*, that is through music composed in Renaissance tuning, transitional tunings, and probably D minor tuning also. The Burwell Tutor credits him with having discovered 'The Trumpett Tuneing' and other tunings derived from it such as 'the Goate tuneing', which suggests that he was at the forefront of tuning innovations in the period 1600–40.[43] Certainly the writer of the Burwell Tutor regarded him as the foremost lutenist and teacher of his age. It may be that some or all of the music attributed to Gaultier (or Gautier) in the Prague IV.G.18, Haslemere, Herbert, Montbuysson, and Berlin 40143 manuscripts may be by Vieux Gaultier, but it is also possible that some of these pieces may have been by Jacques Gaultier.[44] Clearly both Gaultiers were important innovators in the period 1600–40.

The main characteristics of the *style brisé* developed by the French lutenists after 1630 can be summarized thus: temporal distribution of chord members, in which notes of different registers or 'parts' are sounded one after another; the deliberate avoidance of textural pattern or regularity of part-writing, resulting in melodic, textural, and linear ambiguity; binary form in all dance movements, and general irregularity of phrase structure with the exception of the sarabande; simple harmonic movement with mid-point cadences to the most closely related keys; a high degree

---

[40] Burwell Tutor, fo. 5ʳ ˅.

[41] The Dubut mentioned here is probably Pierre Dubut (fl. 1640). See *Œuvres des Dubuts*, ed. and trans. by Monique Rollin and Jean-Michel Vaccaro (Paris, 1979), p. xiii. Dufaut was possibly alive until *c*.1680 and thus must have been young in 1631. See *Œuvres de Dufaut*, ed. and trans. André Souris, with an introduciton and concordances by Monique Rollin (Paris, 1965), p. ix.

[42] This disregards pieces ascribed to a 'Gautier' published in Mylius' *Thesaurus gratiarum* (Frankfurt am Main, 1622) or in Louys de Moy's *Le Petit Boucquet de Frise orientale* (1631), which may be by Vieux Gaultier from an early stage in his career.

[43] Burwell Tutor, fos. 14˅, 12ʳ.

[44] See Rave, 'Some Manuscripts', 39–51 for a discussion of the problems of attributing to Jacques or Ennemond works simply entitled Gaultier (or some variant spelling) in MS sources of the period.

of stylistic conformity between composers, making identification of unattributed pieces hazardous.[45]

One might add to these points the importance of ornamentation as an integral part of composition, and a preference for the middle and lower registers of the lute. By 1652, when the *Rhétorique des Dieux* was compiled, these features were firmly established, as was the Baroque suite with the gigue added to the prelude, allemande, courante, and sarabande. From 1625 until the 1680s and 1690s France maintained its hegemony over lute composition and style, the rest of Europe, including England, drawing directly from her for inspiration and compositional models.

---

[45] Jacques or Ennemond works simply entitled Gaultier 38–62; Rave's definition of the *style brisé* is quoted in full in David J. Buch, '*Style brisé, Style luthé*, and the *Choses luthées*', *Musical Quarterly*, 71 (1985), 52–67 at 53. In this article Buch argues against the emphasis in Rave's definition of the *style brisé* on melodic, textural, and linear ambiguity.

Chapter Ten

The Caroline and Commonwealth Periods (1625–1660)

Here is a fellow who comes into *England* with an ill *meen* and thredbare cloaths, and there presently sets up a Court of Judicature, arraigning both *Musick*, Instruments, and Musicians, for not being *a la mode de France*; the twelve ranks of strings oth' Lute, the double neck, the lessons, the method of playing, and almost the hands too, for not being *mangy* about the wrists like his: he belies great masters; and teaches but his own imperfections: And if his fingers be so weak they can scarce crawle o're a Lute, then to play gently and softly is the *mode*, and *doucement* is the word: and if so gouty and child-blained as he rakes the strings worse than if they were grated on by a ragged staff: then *fort* and *Gallyard* is the word, and strong and lusty is the *mode* agen; and if you like not his play, he tells ye at least, that he has the only new method of *Paris*, and that he teaches *a ravir* and *non pareille*, and for his lessons (which he has rakt out of *Gaultier's* dunghill, or collected from the privy-house of *Dufaut*) he keeps them as precious reliques, giving such out for new as were made before the *Avignon* or the *Pope's* coming there:

'Of a Petty French Lutenist in England', from Richard Flecknoe's *Enigmatical Characters* of 1658

The history of lute music in England during the years 1625–42 is dominated by Frenchmen. The arrival of Jacques Gaultier is significant for all the subsequent history of lute playing in England, as it is likely that he was the first to champion the use of transitional tunings in England. In the period 1600–25 the French lute style exemplified by Robert Ballard's music made considerable inroads on English taste. We know from John Danyel's *Songs for the Lute, Viol and Voice* (1606) that *cordes avalées* tunings were known in England before Gaultier's arrival. However, Gaultier's use of an altered instrument (presumably a 12-course lute), tuned in transitional tunings, and played in the early *brisé* style that was developing in France at this time, would immediately set him apart from the English lutenists employed by the Crown in 1625.

Many Englishmen may have been content to play only in Renaissance tuning after 1625, but those who wished to be 'à la mode' and play in the fashionable French style attempted to adapt to the tunings and techniques of the French lute.

After 1630 most extant English solo lute sources have some, if not all, of their contents in new tunings. It is clear, at least as far as we can judge from contemporary documents, that among the noble and gentry classes, the new French style of lute and lute music quickly replaced the older 8- or 10-course lutes played in Renaissance tuning.

Jacques Gaultier's considerable success in England may have been due to the powerful promotion he received from the Duke of Buckingham, his first patron in England. An influential faction in the English court during the 1620s, and especially after the arrival of Henrietta Maria in 1625, looked to France as the arbiter of taste. Gaultier was well placed to ride this tide of fashion. His career is punctuated by scandal and incidents of violence. Never far from trouble, he had to flee to England in 1617, after being accused of murdering a young nobleman. Considerable diplomatic exchange followed with that most accomplished amateur lutenist Lord Herbert of Cherbury, English ambassador to France during the years 1619 to 1624, acting on the Crown's behalf in frustrating the attempts made by the French to extradite Gaultier. The French lutenist may have been imprisoned in the Tower in March 1618 after his flight to England, probably as a result of the extradition proceedings.[1] That he was not returned to France was largely as a result of the powerful protection of Buckingham.[2]

Whether or not Gaultier was already using a 12-course lute on his arrival in 1617 we cannot be sure. The Burwell Tutor credits him with the introduction and success of the distinctive double-headed 12-course lute that remained in use in England at least until the end of the century.[3] The Jan Lievens engraving of Gaultier, which is likely to have been made between 1632 and 1634, when Lievens was in England, shows him with just such an instrument, proving that he was already using it by that date (see Pl. 10.1).[4] Actual evidence of lute-making in England at this time is meagre. No instruments survive, though we know of two foreign names involved with the craft. In 1635 Thomas Mallard, an 'Italian Lute Maker', was living in the parish of St Martin in the Fields. Also in that year, 'John Baptista [Bassano?], lute string maker, Italian' was living in St Margaret's Westminster.[5] Michael Fleming's work on wills and inventories has unearthed a

---

[1] Ian Spink, 'Another Gaultier Affair', *M&L* 45 (1964), 345–7 at 345. The events surrounding the extradition proceedings are collected in *Old Herbert Papers at Powis Castle and in the British Museum, Collections Historical and Archaeological relating to Montgomeryshire issued by the Powys-Land Club* (London, 1886), 97–8, 99, 231–2, 234–5, 240–1, 241–2, 246, 251–3. See also L. de La Laurencie, 'Le Luthiste Jacques Gaultier', *La revue musicale*, 5, no. 3 (1924), 33–9.

[2] For a full account of Gaultier's early career in England see Matthew G. Spring, 'The Lute in England and Scotland after the Golden Age (1620–1750)', 3 vols. (D.Phil. thesis, University of Oxford, 1987), i. 93–112.

[3] Pieces in the Nanki MS that date from the 18th c. show that the 12-course lute was used this late.

[4] Robert Spencer, 'Chitarrone, Theorbo and Archlute', *EM* 4 (1976), 407–23 at 419. It is possible that this engraving was made from an earlier painting.

[5] *Returns of Strangers in the Metropolis 1593, 1627, 1635, 1639*, ed. Irene Scouloudi (Huguenot Society of London, quarto series, 57; London, 1985), 313, 244.

number of interesting references. John Gerard, an Oxford musician, included two lutes, two bandoras, and two citterns among the instruments 'in the shop' when it was inventoried in 1635. A minute of Reading Corporation for 7 November 1634 noted the criticism voiced by four local people against William Hayes for 'annoying them with stinkes by usinge the makinge of lute-stringes with gutte'.[6] There is evidence that lute strings and those for other instruments were made in England and exported, but also that a large number and variety were important at every stage. It seems that the limited making of lutes in England was restricted, with some exceptions, to emigrants and their families (particularly from Italy), but that English instrument makers did mend and possibly supply lutes. Unlike citterns and bandoras, which were produced in England, lutes on the whole were imports.

By 1622 Gaultier had been drawn into the brilliant musical and literary circle of the Killigrew family.[7] Here, in 1622, he made a lifelong friend and correspondent of Constantijn Huygens de Zulichem, the polymath, amateur musician, and Secretary of the United Provinces, who praised his playing in a Latin poem. Huygens was himself an excellent lutenist, and a connoisseur of good musicians. In his portrait of 1627 his own instrument is seen on the table close to him. (See Plate 10.2.) The first mention of Gaultier in royal accounts is in 1623 when he was paid £40 'towards the defreyeng of his Journey into Spayne'.[8] This was most certainly in connection with the ill-conceived visit by Buckingham and Prince Charles to woo the Infanta between March and October 1623. Gaultier visited Madrid and played on his 'most excellent lute' in the Cabinet of the king for the Grandees of Spain.[9] The Grandees were impressed with his playing but suggested he would do better with a guitar! Characteristically Gaultier took offence, but on this occasion resisted the temptation to respond violently, although in a letter to Huygens he relates that he felt like breaking his lute over their ears.[10] At some point Gaultier may have sat for Van Dyck as the Prado has a fine painting titled 'El músico Jacob Gaultier'.[11]

In 1624 and 1625 Gaultier is mentioned in accounts as a musician to Prince Charles.[12] He was granted an annuity for life of £100 on 28 November 1625, which was confirmed in 1629 and 1631.[13] He seems, judging from a letter of 1649 to Huygens, to have remained in royal service until that date without interruption,

[6] Fleming, 'Some Points Arising', 302, 305–6.

[7] *Musique et musiciens au XVIIᵉ siècle: correspondance et œuvres musicales de Constantijn Huygens*, ed. Willem Jozef Andries Jonckbloet and J. P. N. Land (Leiden, 1882), p. ccvi. These events took place at the home of Sir Robert Killigrew (1579–1633), who was a close friend of Buckingham at this time. (*DNB* xxxi. 111.) See also J. P. Van der Motten, *Sir William Killigrew (1606–1695): His Life and Dramatic Works* (Ghent, 1980) and A. G. H. Bacharach, *Sir Constantin Huygens and Britain (1596–1687)* (Leiden and London, 1962).

[8] PRO E101/435/16, quoted in *RECM* iv. 227.

[9] La Laurencie 'Le Luthiste Jacques Gaultier', 36.

[10] *Musique et musiciens*, ed. Jonckbloet and Land, 60–1.   [11] Prado, Madrid, no. 1487.

[12] *RECM* iv. 228, 229.

[13] *DNB* viii. 293. Reference to the appointment can also be found in *Calendar of State Papers Domestic (1625–1626)*, ed. John Bruce (London, 1858), 163; PRO IND 6746 for Nov. 1625, and PRO SO 3/7 for Nov. 1625.

IACOBO GOVTERO INTER REGIOS MAGNÆ BRITANNIÆ ORPHEOS ET AMPHIONES
LYDIÆ DORIÆ PHRYGIÆ TESTVDINIS FIDICINI ET MODVLATORVM PRINCIPI
HANC E PENICILLI SVI TABVLA IN ÆS TRANSSCRIPTAM EFFIGIEM IOANNES LÆVINI
FIDÆ AMICITIÆ MONIMENTVM.L. M.CONSECRAVIT.

PL. 10.1. Jacques Gaultier with 12-course lute, engraving by Jan Lievens (*c.*1632–4). The
Robert Spencer Collection, Royal Academy of Music

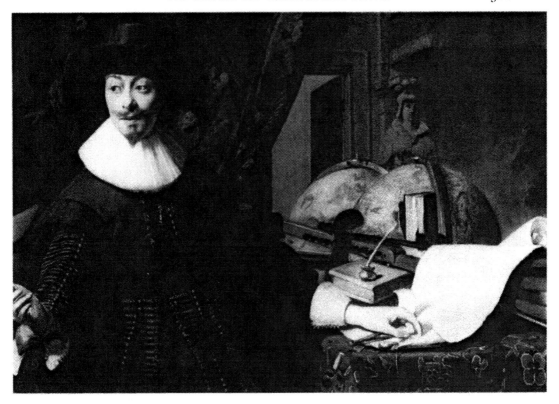

PL. 10.2. Portrait of Constantijn Huygens (1596–1687) by Thomas de Keyser, dated 1627. London, National Gallery

though he does not appear to have followed the court to Oxford in 1642.[14] Exchequer accounts after 1625 always list him as lutenist to Queen Henrietta Maria, whom he taught for a while, and with whom it was rumoured he was having an affair in the winter of 1626–7, an accusation which occasioned a second visit to the Tower.[15] Again he was extricated with his job and reputation intact.

It is likely that Gaultier played in many Caroline masque and court entertainments, particularly the 'pastorales', in which Henrietta Maria liked to perform herself. Two masques, in which we know he appeared, were Shirley's *The Triumph of Peace* (1634) and Davenant's *Britannia Triumphans* (1638). The remarkably detailed papers that survive concerning the arrangements made by Bulstrode Whitelocke for *The Triumph of Peace* show that Gaultier was given pride of place amongst the musicians of 'the Symphony' that performed in the serious part of the antimasque. He

[14] *GB-Lbl* Add. 15944, fos. 46ʳ–47ᵛ; letter dated 28 Aug. 1649.

[15] Spink, 'Another Gaultier Affair'. In this article Spink first drew attention to this scandal, quoting from the Salvetti and Contarini correspondence.

led the processions that accompanied the entrance of the Lord Chamberlain, and was very much in the forefront of the several geometrical arrangements of the symphony when they played.[16] In 1637 a warrant was issued for payment of £10 to 'Mons. Jacques Gaultier, for a treble lute for him to be used in masques'.[17] Most probably this was the lute he played in *Britannia Triumphans*, which was performed on Twelfth Night 1638/9.[18]

The Casebook of Joseph Binnes, a London surgeon, has the following entry for 10 May 1643: 'Mr Ashberrie (a lutanist) at night was bitten by Gottier, the French Luteniste in Covent Garden, had a piece of his cheek bitten out, an inch or more, on the left side at [the] corner of the mouth & neither [= nether] lip, down to the lower part of the jaw. I stiched it & dressed it.'[19] Ashberrie is mentioned as the first lute teacher of Susanna Perwich before Mr John Rogers.[20] The incident seems characteristic of Gaultier, and it suggests that the Frenchman did not leave London with the court in 1642.

The letters between Huygens and Gaultier during the years 1647 to 1649 are concerned with the procurement by Gaultier of a 'lute of Bologna' with nine ribs, made by Laux Maler, for Huygens.[21] Gaultier claims in these letters that there were only fifty of these lutes in all the world, and that England did not have more than half a dozen.[22] Eventually he located such a lute, and suggested a price of £30 for it.[23] Huygens, it seems from a letter from Frederic Rivet, did receive this lute. In his final letter of 1649 Gaultier suggests selling Huygens his own lute, which is all he claims to own after thirty years of royal service, and of which his wife claims part ownership.[24]

Thomas Mace corroborates this assertion when he states, in discussing Laux Maler's lutes, that

> Mr. *Gootiere*, the *Famous Lutenist* in *His Time*, shew'd me *One* of *Them*, which the *King* paid 100*l* [£100] for.

---

[16] Murray Lefkowitz, 'The Longleat Papers of Bulstrode Whitlocke: New Light on Shirley's *Triumph of Peace*', *JAMS* 18 (1965), 42–60.

[17] *RECM* iii. 96. This warrant (PRO LC 5/134, p. 223) is dated 31 Dec. 1637.

[18] Willa McClung Evans, *Henry Lawes, Musician and Friend of Poets* (New York, 1941), 144.

[19] James D. Alsop, 'The Medical Casebook of Joseph Binnes, a London Surgeon', *JAMS* 32 (1979), 367.

[20] John Batchiler, *The Virgins Pattern, in the exemplary life and lamented death of Mrs Susanna Perwich* (London, 1661), 5.

[21] *Musique et musiciens*, ed. Jonckbloet and Land, pp. ccvii–ccx.

[22] Ibid., p. ccviii.

[23] Ibid., p. ccix. The lute for sale belonged to one 'Monsieur Civaif' (*GB-Lbl* Add. 15944, fo. 46ᵛ). See *GB-Lbl* Add. 22953, fo. 203ʳ, dated 1 May 1645, for a letter from Frederic Rivet to Huygens, in which he sends Huygens a lute from London, which he says is recommended by Mr Gaultier. He also encloses 'les 6 parties des Phantasies de Gibbons'.

[24] La Laurencie, 'Le Luthiste', 37, suggests that this lute of Gaultier's originally belonged to Jean [Robert?] Ballard, lutenist to Louis XIII, and that the king of England had acquired it for £100, and given it to Gaultier. In his letter Gaultier actually calls this lutenist Jean Ballard, but La Laurencie noted that Michel Brenet had identified this player as being Robert Ballard.

And Mr. *Edw. Jones* (one of Mr. *Gootiere's Scholars*) had the other, which *He so valued . . .*[25]

The implication of these references is that Gaultier was considered an authority on old lutes, and may even have dealt in lutes. The comments in the Burwell Tutor which connect him with the double-headed 12-course lute, together with references in *Musick's Monument* and the Huygens correspondence, suggest he was active in importing old lutes and converting them into 12-course lutes.[26]

The last mention of Gaultier is in a diary of Lodewijck Huygens, son of Gaultier's long-standing friend, Constantijn Huygens the Elder, written while visiting England in 1651/2. In this diary there are several references to Gaultier between the months of February and July 1652, from which we learn that he was still resident in London, that he was surviving by teaching the lute, and that (according to Gaultier) his wife was insane.[27]

It is not an exaggeration to say that Jacques Gaultier dominated solo lute music at the Caroline court until its removal to Oxford in 1642. He is mentioned by Herrick in several of his poems, and all subsequent writers on lute music in England such as Mace and the author of the Burwell Tutor single him out as the most influential lutenist at the English court at this time. The opinion of Ennemond Gaultier on Jacques Gaultier's playing is interesting, as he is quoted in the Burwell Tutor as saying that 'English Gualtier was fitt to play in a Cabarett because of his thundering way of playing'.[28] This must be due, at least in part, to the additional bass courses and their extra length which the French masters rejected, since they overemphasized the bass, and caused harmonic confusion by ringing on overlong.[29]

Strong French influence is evident in English lute sources from 1610, and French musicians like Adam Vallet,[30] Charles de Lespine,[31] and the French musicians of Anne of Denmark were active in England prior to 1617, but they probably did not influence musical taste to the same extent as Gaultier.[32] His success may in part have been due to the general desire by the English aristocracy to follow French fashions, which increased after Henrietta Maria's arrival. Yet the excellence of his

[25] Thomas Mace, *Musick's Monument*, 48.

[26] Burwell Tutor, fo. 68ʳ.

[27] *Lodewijck Huygens: The English Journal 1651–1652*, ed. A. G. H. Bacharach and R. G. Collmer (Leiden, 1982), pp. 24, 49, 71, 85, 93, 94, 108, 149, 151.

[28] Burwell Tutor, fo. 68ᵛ.

[29] Ibid., fo. 68ʳ: 'if a man hath not a light hand as English Gaultier had one maketh an ugly and confused noise upon them long Bases'.

[30] Adam Vallet's salary was increased in Mar. 1623/4: 'An annuitie of £110 per annum graunted to Adam Vallet during life . . . upon surrender of a petition of £60 formerly granted unto him' (PRO IND 6746). In May 1622 Vallet, with Orlando Gibbons, Thomas Daye, William Heather, and John Clarke, petitioned for the grant of a monopoly for 'all strings for musical instruments, "called Venice, of Romish minikin, and Catlin strings" . . .' (*RECM* iv. 55), though this was ultimately unsuccessful.

[31] Lesure, 'Les Luthistes', 220. Lespine was in England in 1611.

[32] Twelve musicians to Queen Anne and her groom John Maria Lugario were listed among her servants at her funeral in 1618 (*RECM* iv. 48–9). Several of Anne's musicians were also important as dancing-masters (Boucan, de la Pierre), and others went on to serve Henrietta Maria.

playing and the strength of his personality must have been persuasive. Whenever English manuscript sources after 1630 have attributions, a 'Gaultier' (in some spelling or other) is usually mentioned. This may, in certain cases, be because Jacques Gaultier was associated with a particular tuning (no. 8) rather than because he composed the piece. His lute music would seem to have had considerable circulation in manuscript, but was never published.[33]

Gaultier was not the only French lutenist to gain an appointment at the English court. John Mercure was the most noteworthy of the others, but Gaultier was the most influential and successful. A warrant to give Mercure a court appointment was issued on 1 December 1641 in the place of Robert Dowland who had died.[34] All his surviving lute music uses the D minor and related tunings. However, his pieces may be said to be less complex and less *brisé* in style than contemporary Parisian lute music *c.*1640–50, but represent a later development of the French style than those of Jacques Gaultier.

The vignette published by Richard Flecknoe in 1658 on the subject 'Of a Petty French Lutenist in England', quoted above,[35] is fascinating as a cynical reflection of the English attitude to such men as Gaultier, Dufault, and Mercure. While neither of these lutenists, to judge from their reputation and surviving music, was ever a 'mountebank', they certainly would have had less skilful imitators, and no doubt caused considerable resentment among English players of the old school.

The Burwell Lute Tutor relates that Ennemond Gaultier (Le Vieux) was sent to England by his patron Marie de Médicis to represent her at the birth of her first grandson:

he played of the lute before the King and Queene there Maiesties made him presents both worthy of Kinges and of the King of the Lute and the late Duke of Buckingham before whom he played alsoe in imbraceing of him made slide in his pockett Five hundred pounds of Gold to stopp him (as Atalanta did her Sweete-heart with the golden Apples) some few dayes longer in the Courte of England with this pretious burthen . . .[36]

This colourful account cannot be accurate, as Buckingham was assassinated in 1628, and on 29 May 1630 the Queen gave birth to the future Charles II at St James's. It is well documented that Marie de Médicis sent over her midwife to supervise the birth, and it is conceivable, though not proved, that she sent her lutenist as well.[37]

[33] This excludes the piece by 'Goter' in Playford's *Musicks Recreation on the Viol, Lyra-Way* (London, 1661), 'Almain', no. 79, p. 61, which may have been by Gaultier.

[34] *RECM* iii. 111, 112. The exact date of Robert Dowland's death is not known but is likely to have been in 1641 as he is listed in accounts for 1640 (PRO AO 3/129 at Kew).

[35] Adrienne Simpson, ' "Of a petty French lutenist in England" by Richard Flecknoe', *LSJ* 10 (1968), 33. Here Simpson quotes the vignette in full.

[36] Burwell Tutor, fo. 5ᵛ.

[37] Antonia Fraser, *King Charles II: His Life and Times* (London, 1979), 12. The successful midwife received £1,000 for her services.

It is likely that Ennemond's music was known in England before the Burwell Tutor (*c*.1660–72) and the Robarts manuscript (*c*.1654–68), which rest heavily on his teaching and music. Probably in the 1620s and early 1630s Vieux Gaultier would have been using the transitional tunings, and his style would not have been dissimilar to that of Jacques Gaultier at this time. It could well be that some of the 'Gaultier' pieces in English sources are those of Ennemond, and that his direct influence in this country is underestimated.

The researches of Robert Spencer and Francois-Pierre Goy into the life of Bullen Reymes, a junior diplomat attached to the English embassy in Paris in the 1630s, who studied the lute in London and Paris, has shown that one of his teachers was René Mesangeau, and that Mesargeau was in England in December 1631.[38] The Reymes manuscript contains four pieces headed by the note 'Monsieur la flale playd thes tunes in the Queens maske on his harpe'.[39] (Jean de la Flelle was a French harpist among the queen's musicians during the years 1629–40.)[40] This quotation shows that French lute music in transitional tunings had links with the musical style of the queen's masques and *pastorales*. The Burwell Tutor and the Pan 5 and Reymes manuscripts prove that Mesangeau was a most influential teacher and innovator in the early history of the *brisé* style in France, and his presence in England may account for his prominence in English sources *c*.1630.[41] At this visit he possibly met William Lawes, since Lawes set Mesangeau's most popular allemande as a duet by adding a *contrepartie* to it.[42]

The illustrious French lutenist and composer François Dufault was resident in England for some time in the 1660s and probably also in the 1650s. Flecknoe's satirical mention of 'the privy-house of *Dufault*', quoted at the start of this chapter, suggests Dufault's presence in England before 1658, and his music was certainly in circulation in Britain by this date. In Paris in 1662 Huygens entrusted letters to Dufault to take to London where Dufault was about to travel. In the next year Huygens's famous scientist son, Christiaan Huygens, heard both Pinel and, a few days later, Dufault, play in London. Christiaan heard Dufault perform with a 'Mrs Warwick', whose mother (a Mrs Fretwell or Frescheville) had been a Maid of Honour to Queen Henrietta Maria in the 1630s.[43] A letter penned by Constantin Huygens from the Hague on 16 September 1669 to Madame de Warwick

---

[38] Français-Pierre Goy, 'Luth et guitare dans le journal et la correspondence (1631–1636) de Bullen Reymes', *luth et luthistes en Occident* (Paris, 1999), 185–200. See H. A. Kaufman, *Conscientious Cavalier: Colonel Bullen Reymes, M.P., F.R.S. 1613–1672* (London, 1962).

[39] Reymes MS, fo. 59ᵛ. The Queen's masques in the early 1630s were *Love's Triumph through Callipolis* (1631), *Chloridia* (1631), *Albion's Triumph* (1632), *Tempe Restored* (1632), and *Shepherd's Paradise* (1633). De la Flelle took part in the *The Temple of Love* (1634/5).

[40] *RECM* iii. 47, 154; Holman, 'The Harp in Stuart England'.

[41] Sources include Pan 5, Pan 8, and the Wemyss and Pickeringe MSS.   [42] *GB-Ob* Mus. Sch. b. 2, p. 86.

[43] Tim Crawford, 'The historical importance of François Dufault and his influence on musicians outside France', *luths et luthistes en Occident* (Paris, 1999), 201–15 at 201–3.

(presumably the same lutenist who had performed with Dufault in 1663), enquires as to whether Dufault was still alive.[44] Perhaps François Dufault had died by this stage and possibly in England. Dufault's music is well represented in English sources, and his name is often linked with Gaultier's. Huygens, writing to Mlle de Lenclos in London in 1671, recommends 'Les plus belles pieces des Gaultiers, Du Fauts et autres'.[45]

On her arrival from France in 1625 Henrietta Maria was accompanied by a small entourage of Frenchmen and women. Among them was a band of eleven musicians and three singing boys.[46] This number was augmented by several French musicians who were already in England, one of whom was Jacques Gaultier. It is curious that most of the band were issued with passports to leave the country almost as soon as they had arrived.[47] They did not all leave, although many of the Queen's personal servants, including the notorious Mme St George, were forced home by Buckingham and Charles in 1626.[48] The Catholic Chapel of St James (consecrated in 1632), that the Queen had specially prepared for her, aroused suspicion and hatred among the general populace. In 1630 there were riots, and the Chapel and its occupants had to be forcibly protected.[49]

Account books for Henrietta Maria's household have not survived in great number. Among her musicians were three who had previously served Anne of Denmark. Several of Charles's musicians had posts in her household as well.[50] Jacques Gaultier received £120 p.a. for his services to her, quite apart from his pension of £100 p.a. The large sum of £120 p.a. was also paid to eleven others among the fifteen musicians the queen employed in 1629–30, and was well above that enjoyed by the great majority of the king's musicians.[51] Loys Richard heads the surviving lists of the queen's musicians, and probably acted as the 'Master of the Queen's Music'. He received the huge sum of £440 p.a., but this included provision for bringing up a number of French singing boys in his charge.[52] Henrietta Maria employed a female lutenist, as there is a reference in the accounts for 1629/30 to a 'Renee [Ann] de Gowges, Lutanist, for her pension at £40 p.ann'.[53] This woman, who also appears in accounts as 'Rince de Gowges, lutrist', and 'Rince degouges, Lutanist', was brought in to teach the queen the lute as a replacement for Jacques Gaultier in the aftermath of the rumoured scandal of 1626/7.[54] She is exceptional as the only woman who is clearly identified as a musician in the accounts, and who

---

[44] *Musique et musiciens*, ed. Jonckbloet and Land, Letter no. 58.

[45] *Musique et musiciens*, ed. Jonckbloet and Land, 57, letter no. 66.

[46] Ian Spink, 'The Musicians of Henrietta-Maria: Some Notes and References in the English State Papers', *Acta musicologica*, 36 (1964), 177–82 at 178.

[47] Ibid. 177.   [48] Carola Mary A. Oman, *Henrietta Maria* (London, 1936), 46.   [49] Ibid. 68.

[50] These were: Jacques Gaultier, Dietrich Steiffken, Nicholas Duvall, Anthony Robert, Richard Deering (*RECM* iii. 245–6).

[51] Ibid.   [52] Ibid.   [53] Ibid. 245.   [54] Ibid., v. 4, 7.

received payment as part of the royal musical establishment between the years 1485 and 1714.[55]

Among the musicians that Henrietta Maria brought with her in 1625 was the bass singer Nicolas Duvall.[56] In 1633 he was given a further appointment as a musician for the Lutes and Voices to the king in one of the places vacated on the death of Robert Johnson.[57] Duvall sang in the *Triumph of Peace*,[58] and kept his royal appointments until 1642, when accounts are discontinued. In 1634 he was given £15 for a lute for him 'to play in the consort of Mons. le Flelle'.[59] At the Restoration his appointment to the king was given to Captain Cooke, indicating that either Duvall had died or returned to France. Although he was primarily a singer, references suggest that he was also a lutenist.

Anthony Robert (or Roberts), a countertenor singer, was, like Jacques Gaultier, active in England before the queen's arrival, and was appointed to the queen's household on 25 March 1626.[60] Robert was particularly successful in this country, and gained an appointment to the king's Lutes and Voices in 1626, which he kept (apart from the Interregnum) until his death in 1677, as well as his position in the queen's music. His appointment was in the place of Jonas Wrench, a member of Charles's Lutes and Voices, and a reference in the accounts to Robert being given a theorbo suggests that he too was a lutenist.[61] Both Robert and Duvall were among the four Frenchmen chosen by Bulstrode Whitelocke to advise on the musical aspects of the *Triumph of Peace*, indicating their importance at the time.[62]

The French poet Charles de Saint-Évremond (1613–1703), a keen amateur lutenist, lived in exile in England. It seems that there was considerable exchange between musicians and poets in France and England during the Caroline period. The poets Bois-Robert, Voiture, and Saint-Amant all spent time in England.[63] Although some English court lutenists like William Lawes and John Lawrence were quick to adapt to the French lute style, it is plain that the French masters increasingly dominated court lute music during Charles's reign.

In spite of the infiltration of the French lutenists at the English court in the period 1625–42, the number of Englishmen who were musicians for the Lutes and Voices or for the Lutes in Ordinary does not perceptibly decrease, rather it continues to increase. On Charles's accession to the throne in 1625 the formidable musical household that had been assembled for him as Prince Charles in the years 1618–25, many of whom had previously served Prince Henry, was fused with that

[55] Margaret Prevost appears regularly in accounts after the death of her husband in 1637 (*RECM* iii. 14 (2), 16, 17, 19; viii. 130, 132). It is possible that she was a paid musician rather than simply in receipt of a pension.
[56] Spink, 'The Musicians of Henrietta-Maria', 180–2.   [57] *RECM* iii. 73.
[58] Lefkowitz, 'The Longleat Papers', 46.   [59] *RECM* iii. 83.
[60] Spink, 'The Musicians of Henrietta-Maria', 182.   [61] *RECM* iii. 66.
[62] Bulstrode Whitelocke, *Memoirs of the English Affairs* (London, 1682; rev. edn., 1853), 19, Anno 1633.
[63] Jean-Michel Vaccaro, sleeve note to Dufaut record played by Hopkinson Smith (Astrée A8 15).

of the deceased King James.[64] This presented something of a problem for the court's administration. While the old king's five Lutes in Ordinary continued to be paid by the Treasurer of the Chamber, lutenists and singers, who had formerly served Charles as Prince of Wales, were paid directly from the Exchequer.[65] As time moves on all these musicians were grouped together as the Lutes and Voices or occasionally the Lutes, Viols, and Voices.[66] By no means all the members of this group were lutenists in any capacity.

The traditional places as the king's Lutes in Ordinary were maintained at their respective rates of pay until 1642, though gradually subsumed into the larger group. (See Table 10.1.) In 1633 Robert Johnson died, and his place went to the harpist Lewis Evans. On the death of Maurice Webster it would appear that Dietrich Steiffken was appointed to his place as a king's Musician for the Lute on 2 January 1635/6.[67] Webster's father, George, was a lutenist who worked in Bückeburg. George Webster possibly had connections with an expatriate theatre company in Kassel, and Maurice may have been named after the Landgrave Moritz of Hesse-Kassel, who composed lute music. Maurice is important as an early composer of a new type of chamber consort music that developed into the consort suite.[68] Webster was given £5 per year for lute strings for the years 1627 to 1631, so he probably played the lute at this time.[69] Although Steiffken is included as a musician for the lutes,[70] it is unlikely that he served as one for long, if at all, as he is generally mentioned as a viol player, and his surviving music is for the viol.[71] Like Webster before him, Steiffken is spoken of as a musician for 'the consort'.[72] The Consort was a group instituted after Charles's accession in 1625, and originally included both John Dowland and Robert Johnson.[73] Groups drawn from the Lutes and Voices were

---

[64] Seven of Charles's musicians for the 'lutes and voices' had been musicians to Prince Henry in the years 1610–12 (*RECM* iv. 210–15 for Henry's musicians). These were Robert Johnson, Thomas Ford, Thomas Lupo, Thomas Day, Edward Wormall, Angelo Notari, and Jonas Wrench. A list is quoted in Price, *Patrons and Musicians*, 224.

[65] Although the Pipe Office accounts at the PRO are missing for the years 1627–60, the Audit office copy of the accounts of the Exchequer of Audit for the years 1630, 1634, and 1640, together with other accounts, show that the five positions as 'lutes in ordinary' were maintained, three at 20*d.* per day, and two at £40 per year, until 1642, when the accounts cease (Spring, 'The Lute in England', 119). It is noticeable that the Pipe Office accounts always list the 'Musitians for the lute' as a separate entry after the king's trumpets, violins, flutes, and sackbuts, and before the makers and repairers of the king's instruments. This arrangement continues after 1625, and suggests that the king's 'Musitians for the lutes' maintained a separate identity, in the accounts at least, after 1625, when the newer group of the king's 'lutes and voices' came into being.

[66] Ashbee (ed.), *William Lawes*, 1–10.   [67] *RECM* iii. 85.

[68] Holman, *Four and Twenty Fiddlers*, 256–61.   [69] *RECM* iii. 60, 66.   [70] Ibid. 157.

[71] For instance, an entry for 14 Nov. 1637 mentions a payment of £5 to 'Dietrick Steiffkin, one of the musicians for the viol, for strings for the bass viol for a yeare . . .' (*RECM* iii. 93). A large number of viol pieces by Steiffken can be found in the Göess MSS I and II (Göess family private collection, Ebenthal, Klagenfurt, Austria). See Douglas Alton Smith, 'The Ebenthal Lute and Viol Tablatures', *EM* 10 (1982), 462–7.

[72] *RECM* iii. 85. 'A warrant . . . for Dietrich Steiffkyn, musician for the consort in ordinary in the place of Maurice Webster, deceased . . .'. For Webster and Steiffken see ibid. 87, 90, and *RECM* viii. 118.

[73] *RECM* iii. 3. Eleven musicians are mentioned in this group. A Warrant of Apr. 1626 mentions payment to '. . . Robert Dowland, appointed musician in ordinary for the Consort in the place of his father Dr. Dowland, deceased' (ibid. 16).

Table 10.1. *The musicians of the king's Lutes in Ordinary and Lutes, Viols, and Voices 1625–1642*

A. LUTES IN ORDINARY[a]

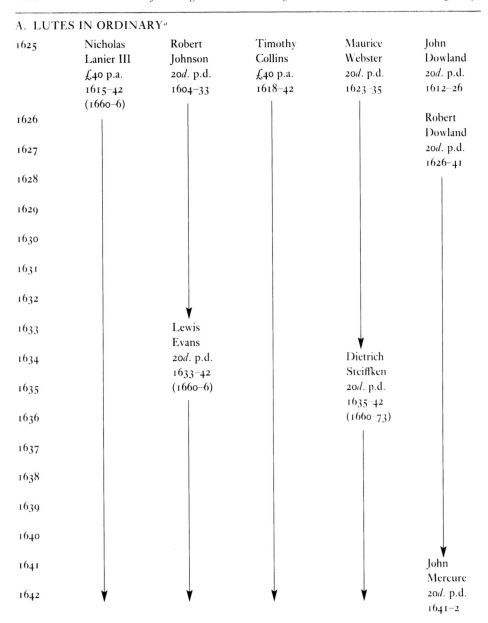

1625	Nicholas Lanier III £40 p.a. 1615–42 (1660–6)	Robert Johnson 20d. p.d. 1604–33	Timothy Collins £40 p.a. 1618–42	Maurice Webster 20d. p.d. 1623–35	John Dowland 20d. p.d. 1612–26
1626					Robert Dowland 20d. p.d. 1626–41
1627					
1628					
1629					
1630					
1631					
1632					
1633		Lewis Evans 20d. p.d. 1633–42 (1660–6)			
1634				Dietrich Steiffken 20d. p.d. 1635–42 (1660–73)	
1635					
1636					
1637					
1638					
1639					
1640					
1641					John Mercure 20d. p.d. 1641–2
1642					

New places:
Jacques Gaultier, £100 p.a. 1625–42
John Fox £40 p.a., 1630–42

Table 10.1. *cont.*

B. LUTES, VIOLS, AND VOICES

1625	1	2	3	4	5	6	7	8	9	10	11	12	13	14	15	16	17	18
1626	1	2	3	4	5	6	19	8	9	10	11	12	13	14	15	16	17	18
1627	1	2	3	4	5	6	19	8	9	10	11	12	13	14	15	16	17	18
1628	1	2	3	4	5	6	19	20	9	10	11	12	21	14	15	16	17	18
1629	1	2	3	4	5	6	19	20	9	10	11	12	21	14	15	22	17	18
1630	1	2	3	4	5	6	19	20	9	10	11	12	21	14	15	22	17	18
1631	1	2	3	4	5	6	19	20	9	10	11	12	21	14	15	22	17	18
1632	1	2	3	4	5	6	19	20	23	10	11	12	21	14	15	22	17	18
1633	1	24	3	4	5	6	19	20	23	10	11	12	21	14	15	22	17	18
1634	1	24	3	4	5	6	19	20	23	10	11	12	21	14	15	22	17	18
1635	1	24	3	4	5	6	19	20	23	10	11	12	21	14	15	22	25	18
1636	1	24	3	4	5	6	19	20	23	27	11	12	21	26	15	22	25	18
1637	1	24	3	4	5	6	19	20	23	27	11	12	21	26	15	22	25	18
1638	1	24	3	4	5	6	19	20	23	27	11	12	21	26	15	22	25	18
1639	1	24	3	4	5	6	19	20	23	27	11	12	21	26	15	22	25	18
1640	1	24	3	4	5	6	19	20	23	27	11	12	21	26	15	22	25	18
1641	1	24	3	4	5	6	19	20	23	27	11	12	21	26	15	22	25	18
1642	1	24	3	4	5	6	19	20	23	27	11	12	21	26	15	22	25	18

1. Nicholas Lanier III (Master)
2. Robert Johnson (lute)
3. Thomas Ford (composer)
4. John Drew (lute, voice)
5. Edward Wormall (lute, voice)
6. Angelo Notari (lute, voice)
7. Jonas Wrench (lute, voice)
8. Thomas Lupo I (viol)
9. Robert Marsh (lute, voice)
10. Robert Taylor (lute, voice)
11. Thomas Day (lute, voice)
12. John Coggeshall (lute)
13. Alfonso Ferrabosco II (viol)
14. Alphonso Balls (lute, voice)
15. John Lanier (lute, voice)
16. Richard Dering (keyboard)
17. John Lawrence (lute)
18. John Kelly (lute)
19. Anthony Roberts (lute, voice)
20. Theophilus Lupo (viol)
21. Alfonso Ferrabosco III (viol)
22. Giles Tomkins (keyboard)
23. Henry Lawes (lute, voice)
24. Nicholas Duvall (lute, voice)
25. William Lawes (lute, voice)
26. John Wilson (lute, voice)
27. John Taylor (viol, voice)

---

a The instrument designation in this table is only a guide. 'Lute' includes all members of the lute family and 'viol' all members of both the viol and violin family.

important for the development of new types of chamber music, such as the harp consorts written by William Lawes.[74]

From 1615 Nicholas Lanier II (see Pl. 10.3) took Robert Hales's place among the king's Lutes in Ordinary, at the salary of £40 per year plus livery, and was also a musician to Prince Charles.[75] These appointments stood him in good stead. With the accession of Charles I he became, in effect, the first 'Master of the King's Musick' at £200 p.a., though the official position was not instituted as early as 1625.[76]

While it is true that most of the king's musicians for the Lutes and Voices were primarily singers, most were also instrumentalists, and some, as far as is known, were purely instrumentalists. Those who are likely to have been principally lutenists include Robert Johnson, John Kelly, John Coggeshall, Edward Wormall, Jonas Wrench, and John Lawrence.[77] Many important singers like Nicholas Lanier, Henry Lawes, William Lawes,[78] Anthony Robert, John Wilson, and Angelo Notari, were probably more than proficient as solo lute players, and were certainly able to accompany themselves on the lute or theorbo. John Coggeshall was given special duties as custodian of the royal lutes, and received an annual sum of £20 each New Year for lute strings,[79] the distribution of which he presumably supervised among the royal lutenists.

The only English lutenists among the king's Lutes and Voices at this time for whom we have any surviving lute music are William Lawes, John Wilson, John Lawrence, and Robert Johnson. Both Lawes and Lawrence were able to compose lute music confidently and idiomatically in the new French style using the transitional tunings. Lawrence, to whom several pieces in the Pickeringe manuscript are attributed, was lutenist to Charles from 1625 until his death in 1635, when William Lawes was appointed in his place.[80] Although the only lute pieces by Lawes that survive are the three fine duets found in his Bodleian autograph score,[81] Lefkowitz suggests in his biography of Lawes that, like Jenkins, he probably composed a lot of

[74] Holman, *Four and Twenty Fiddlers*, 262.

[75] *RECM* iii. 44. Lanier's appointment received the signet warrant on 12 Jan. 1615/16.

[76] Lanier is first mentioned as Master of the King's Music in 1626. See *RECM* iii. 18.

[77] These assumptions are based on the books of Ashbee, Lafontaine, Woodfill, PRO accounts, and the lists of musicians that performed in the *Triumph of Peace*, in Lefkowitz, 'The Longleat Papers'.

[78] Henry and William Lawes were each given £10 to buy lutes on 4 Mar. 1635/6; *RECM* iii. 86. Henry Lawes's theorbo, inscribed with the Earl of Bridgewater's arms and the initials 'H.L.', survived until the 1830s when it was purposely burnt by the Bodleian Library. See R. Poole, 'The Oxford Music School and the Collection of Portraits formerly Preserved There', *Musical Antiquary*, 4 (1912–13), 143–59.

[79] e.g. *RECM* iii. 93 reads 'Warrant for to pay £20 to Mr. John Coggeshall, one of his Majesty's musicians, for strings for the four lutes for one year . . .' (12 Nov. 1637). However, other royal lutenists were also given specific sums for lute strings.

[80] *RECM* iii. 82. Lawrence assigned £18 of his wages to John Banfeild on 20 Mar. 1626/7 (ibid. 24). Lawrence was paid £400 for 'an hattband sett with diamonds, which his Ma⁴ bought of him, and gave to Viscount ffrabone, who was sent to his Ma⁴⁵ from the Queens mother of ffrance'. PRO Ind 6748 for Mar. 1632/3.

[81] *GB-Ob* Mus. Sch. b. 2.

PL. 10.3. Nicholas Lanier (1588–1666), engraved portrait by Jan Lievens, c.1632–4. The Robert Spencer Collection, Royal Academy of Music

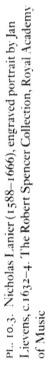

PL. 10.4. John Wilson, from an engraving of 1792 made from a print in the Pepysian Library of Magdalen College, Cambridge. The Robert Spencer Collection, Royal Academy of Music

solo lute music that is now lost.[82] This lost music, we can confidently assume, would have been in the French style, and may have shared characteristics with his music for the lyra viol.

John Wilson's royal appointment in 1635 was to the king's Lutes and Voices in the place of the singer Alphonso Balls [Bales]. Wilson (see Pl. 10.4) had previously been closely involved with the 'King's Men' company, for which he wrote many songs.[83] In 1622 he became a City Wait, and in 1634 he sang as a countertenor and played the theorbo in *The Triumph of Peace*.[84] Wilson suffered nine rejections in his quest for a royal post. His tenth petition was followed up with some biting wit that successfully drew the king's attention, and he gained his appointment in 1635. One contemporary commentator has the following account:

Dr Wilson (the famous musitain and *as great a humorist*) made great and frequent sute to K[ing] Charles, to bee admitted to be one of his private musiq: But by the envie and opposition of some at Court, was still put by. 9 petitions hee had delivered upon for many severall vacancies, and yet still some or other was preferred before him. At length another occasion being offered, hee put in his 10th petition in these words: *Sir I have lived many years only upon commendations of pitie: most men commend mee, and say 'tis pity I am not your servant: soe say Your Majesties etc.* Upon reading hereof the K[ing] sent a nobleman to assure him, that hee should have the next place that fell whereat Wilson swore that hee would not believe the King. Will not believe the K[ing]? No, as long as the K[ing] sees with other mens eyes and heare with other mens eares, I will not believe his answer sent for him; and not long after hee abtained his request.[85]

In Anthony à Wood's vivid accounts of Wilson's lute playing he makes no mention of Wilson as a singer. However, these accounts may well refer to his activities in Oxford after 1642.[86] This apparent discrepancy suggests that Wilson was foremost a singer until after his court appointment, at which point he rose to prominence as a solo lute player. His appointment to the Restoration Chapel Royal proves that he did not cease to be a singer in later life, in name at least.

Caroline court lutenists would have had some playing duties of a domestic nature, where they would have been heard by a private audience, but the only occasions on which they would probably have been assembled 'en masse' would have been in the preparation and performance of the lavish court theatricals in which the Queen herself liked to appear. Henrietta Maria's appearance in *pastorales*, in which she danced on stage, outraged the puritan lawyer Prynne so much that he published

[82] Murray Lefkowitz, *William Lawes* (London, 1960), 137.
[83] *New Grove*, xx. 443.   [84] Lefkowitz, 'The Longleat Papers', 50.
[85] Hulse, 'Musical Patronage', 83–4. From Museum of London, Tangye Collection, manuscript notebook of a society man *c.*1640–60.
[86] Wood, *The Life and Times of Anthony Wood Described by Himself*, i: *1632–1663*, ed. Andrew Clark (Oxford, 1891), 204. Wilson 'sometimes play'd on the lute but mostly presided the consort' (Mar. 1656).

an open condemnation of the practice in his *Histrio-Mastix* (1633).[87] This in turn caused the king to demand a masque from the four Inns of Court jointly as an act of obedience. The result was the most costly masque of all, Shirley's *The Triumph of Peace*.

Bulstrode Whitelocke, who was given responsibility for the musical content of the event, purposefully brought together prominent French, English, German, and Italian musicians to discuss the musical settings.[88] The lavish generosity shown by Whitelocke towards the French musicians of the queen may have been to ingratiate him with her. William Lawes and Simon Ives were responsible for much of the song and recitative music,[89] Davis Mell for the ensemble music, and Estienne Nau and Sebastian de la Pierre composed and taught the dances. In his *Memoirs* Whitelocke boasted that no fewer than forty lutes took part, although many of these players also sang.[90] Those who played the lute in this masque are listed in Table 10.2, and it is most revealing that many prominent singers or players of other instruments, like Thomas Day and Robert Tomkins, also played the lute or theorbo. Clearly a reasonable proficiency on the lute or theorbo was common to most royal musicians of the time.

The Caroline theatrical performances would have given the French players occasion to exercise their technical skills and influence the music in its preparation, thereby giving access to those among the English lutenists, both amateur and professional, who wished to adopt their styles. During the period 1625–42 the court dominated the secular musical life of this country to a greater extent than in the Elizabethan or Jacobean periods. Outside the court there were some in the aristocracy who felt inclined, and had the money required, to mount a Caroline masque. Milton's *Comus*, staged for the Earl of Bridgewater at Ludlow Castle in 1634, is a case in point. The more ambitious and important lutenists would have aspired to court appointments, but some, like Jenkins in particular, never got that far in this period.[91] After being apprenticed to Anne Russell, Countess of Warwick, he may have gravitated to London.[92] He performed in *The Triumph of Peace*, which was put on by the Inns of Court, and may have worked as a teacher and player on the fringes of court and the Inns. Alternatively, he may have been employed in Norfolk by the Derham or L'Estrange families, though it is less likely, since connections with these families cannot be proved before 1642.[93]

---

[87] Whitelocke, *Memoirs*, 18.

[88] Ibid. 19. The French advisors were 'M. La Ware (de la Mare), M. Du Vall, M. Robert and M. Mari'. Gaultier was called in to replace Mari.

[89] Lefkowitz, 'The Longleat Papers', 51.   [90] Whitelocke, *Memoirs*, 19.

[91] *Roger North on Music*, ed. John Wilson (London, 1959), 343 n. 91. North indicates that Jenkins was a court musician in pre-Restoration times; this is most probably incorrect, although he did play in court masques such as *The Triumph of Peace*. See *New Grove*, ix. 596.

[92] Andrew Ashbee, *The Harmonious Musick of John Jenkins*, i: *The Fantasias for Viols* (Surbiton, 1992), 21–2.

[93] Ibid. 24–42.

Table 10.2. *Lutenists and singer-lutenists in the* Triumph of Peace *(1634)*

Name	Instrument/voice	Position in 1634	Amount paid (£)
A. LUTENISTS IN THE 'SYMPHONY'			
Jacques Gaultier	treble lute	Queen's lutenist	40
Peter Jacob	treble lute	foreign musician?	15
John Lawrence	treble lute	King's L. & V.	10
John Kelly	treble lute	King's L. & V.	10
Richard Millar	treble lute	—	10
Robert Keith	treble lute	—	10
William Page (Pagett)	bass lute	—	10
B. SINGERS WHO ALSO PLAYED THE THEORBO			
Charles Coleman	countertenor/ tenor/theorbo	King's L. & V. Consort	10
Thomas Day	tenor/theorbo	King's L. & V. Chapel Royal	30
Nicholas Duvall	bass/theorbo	King's L. & V. Queen's musician	40
John Drew	bass/theorbo?	King's L. & V.	15
Nicholas Lanier	tenor/theorbo?	Master of King's L. & V. King's Lutenist	10
Henry Lawes	countertenor/theorbo	King's L. & V. Chapel Royal	20
Anthony Robert	countertenor/theorbo	King's L. & V. Queen's musician	40
Walter Porter	tenor/theorbo	Chapel Royal	10
Willaim Webb	tenor/theorbo	Chapel Royal	20
John Wilson	countertenor/theorbo	City Wait	20
William Caesar (alias Smegergill)	tenor/theorbo	—	10
Simon Ives	countertenor/theorbo (composer)	—	55
Robert Tomkins	tenor/theorbo	Consort	10
William Lawes	countertenor/theorbo (composer)	—	55
Roger Nightingale	bass/theorbo?	Chapel Royal	10
Thomas Lawton	countertenor/theorbo?	Chapel Royal	10
Thomas Holmes	bass/theorbo?	Chapel Royal	10
John Frost jun.	bass/theorbo?	Chapel Royal	15
Nicholas Horn	countertenor/theorbo?	—	10
John Kellaway	countertenor/theorbo?	—	10
John Lawes	bass/theorbo?	Westminster Abbey	15
C. OTHER LUTENISTS			
Thomas Hutton	lute	Musician at Blackfriars Theatre	10
John Jenkins	lute/theorbo/viol	—	10

Of all the lute music that is lost from this period, the complete loss of the 'multitudes' of lute lessons, that, according to North, Jenkins composed in his early years, is most regrettable.[94] The references to him and his idiosyncratic tuning in the Burwell Tutor suggest that his lute music would have been in the 'airy' French style, though still distinctively English. 'Mr Jenkins Tuning', is a variant on Vieux Gaultier's 'Trumpet Tuning', specifically for the 12-course lute.[95] North suggests that the posthumous reputation of Jenkins as an academic composer of viol fantasy suites is distorted by the loss of his early repertoire, which was greatly indebted to lute music.[96]

Jenkins did not gain a court appointment until 1660, when he took a place as a lute or theorbo player, though he rarely attended to any court duties. Thus his lute music may have been written for country patrons. Many of the sources that originate from provincial family collections, such as the Longleat manuscript and all the Scottish lute sources, contain music of the fashionable French type (from Pierre Ballard's publications in particular), proving that it was available and approved of in aristocratic and gentry country houses.

After the Battle of Edge Hill in 1642 Charles retreated to Oxford, which remained his headquarters until the surrender of his garrison in 1646. During the troubled years after 1642 there was little time or money that could be expended on musical entertainments. Some theatricals were mounted by members of the University to amuse the King and Queen, but in the main such performances were the exception. Some of the king's musicians moved to Oxford, some remained in Parliamentary-dominated London, others dispersed into the country or travelled abroad. No one received regular payment for musical duties after 1642.[97]

As a result of the disbanding of the court, the discontinuation of choral services, and the destruction or removal of the organs from many cathedrals, churches, and chapels, many musicians found their services no longer required, and their means of livelihood removed. The effect of this upheaval was to enrich the musical life of the provincial gentry and middle classes. Whereas the Caroline court dominated the musical life of the country, the Commonwealth period saw a rise in the general level of musical participation among non-aristocratic households. This can be seen in the popularity of music clubs, and in the improved general availability of proficient teachers, many of whom had lost their court employment in the general upheaval.

---

[94] Matthew Spring, 'Jenkins's Lute Music: An Approach to Reconstructing the Lost Multitudes of Lute Lessons', in Andrew Ashbee and Peter Holman (eds.), *John Jenkins and his Time* (Oxford, 1996), 309–23 at 312.

[95] Burwell Tutor, fo. 13ʳ.

[96] *Roger North on Musick*, 347: 'But the unhappyness is, that all his earlyest and most lively compositions are sunk and lost, and none remaine but those of his latter time, when he lived in country familys, and could compose no otherwise than to the capacity of his performers, . . .'

[97] Henry Cart de Lafontaine, *The King's Musick* (London, 1909). There are some entries after 1642, but these are few; see 112–13. *RECM* iii. 114–29.

Playford's music-publishing ventures certainly gained from this dissemination of musical skill. Oxford was particularly fortunate in all these respects through the many college chapel singers and organists ejected from their livings, but who were still active in the town.[98]

In 1642 Charles was joined not only by court musicians, but also by courtiers and ladies, some of whom were enthusiastic musical amateurs. One such lutenist among the ladies at Oxford was Lady Isabella Thynne (1623–57), daughter of Henry Rich, Earl of Holland. Aubrey relates: '[she] would make her entry with her theorbo or lute played before her. I have heard her play on it in the grove myself, which she did rarely.'[99] Lady Isabella became involved in politics with her friend Lady Fanshawe, and probably as a consequence felt it prudent to move to France during the years 1648–54.[100] The magnificent portrait of her by Dobson in the state dining room at Longleat shows her holding her 12-course lute in a wooded grove. (See Pl. 10.5.)

Before the advent of the music clubs the students kept some musical life going in Oxford, as Evelyn speaks of after-dinner music on a visit there in 1653. He writes that he was 'taken up to All Soules where we had music, voices and theorbos performed by some ingenious Scholars'.[101] However, it is in the period after 1656, when William Ellis's meetings were in full session, first meeting every Tuesday and then Thursday at his house on the site opposite the Sheldonian (where the New Bodleian is now situated), that musical life in Oxford really gathered pace.[102]

According to Wood there were four music clubs in Oxford at one time or another during the Commonwealth years. The most important and brilliant club was the one instigated by William Ellis, who had been organist of St John's College until forced to leave his position. Ellis appears as first on the list of 'music masters who were now in Oxford and frequented the said meetings'.[103] Second on the list is: 'Dr John Wilson the public professor the best on the lute in all England. He sometimes play'd the lute, but mostly presided the consort.'[104]

Wood states that he was 'the most curious judge of music that there ever was', and that he was a 'pretender to Buffoonery', as was shown by his singular reaction to the playing of the virtuoso violist Thomas Baltzar at one of Ellis's meetings in 1659. Wilson is reported as having lifted Baltzar's foot to see if he had hooves, as his playing was so miraculous as to have been devilish.[105] The poem entitled 'Dr. Wilson and his lute at Ellis his meeting, Dec. 31, [16]55' by Robert Southwell was

[98] [Anthony Wood], *Athenae Oxoniensis . . . To which are added the Fasti, or Annals of the University of Oxford . . .*, ed. Philip Bliss, 4 vols. (Oxford, 1813–20), ii. 71. John Wilson's *Cheerful Ayres and Ballads* (1659) was published in Oxford.

[99] John Aubrey, *Brief Lives*, ed. Andrew Clark (Oxford, 1898), ii. 24–5.

[100] John Evelyn, *The Diary of John Evelyn*, ed. E. S. de Beer, 6 vols. (Oxford, 1955), iii. 549–50.

[101] Ibid. 106.   [102] Wood, *Life and Times*, 204 (Mar. 1656).   [103] Ibid.

[104] Ibid.   [105] Ibid. 257.

PL. 10.5. Lady Isabella Thynne with her 12-course lute, by William Dobson (*c*.1640).
Longleat House, Wiltshire

inspired by Wilson's playing at one such meeting.[106] It has been observed that those singled out as good players by Wood in his list of musicians at Ellis's meetings in 1656 would exactly make up the consort for which the Bodleian part-books Mus. Sch. e. 431–6 were written.[107]

Wood makes it clear that the clubs collapsed because many of the leading lights, including Wilson, returned to their court appointments, or to positions as organists or singing men.[108] The Oxford clubs may have set a precedent for the many Restoration music meetings and concerts that Pepys in particular comments on, but there seems to be no direct connection between the two. Oxford's musical life in the 1650s probably had parallels in other provincial towns (certainly Cambridge had some important musicians at this time),[109] the result of which was to encourage musical skills and participation among many previously unaffected sections of the public. Wood, Pepys, and Evelyn all seem to have developed their passion for music during the Commonwealth, and it is clear from their experience that, at least until 1660, the lute was prominent amongst the instruments with which they were most familiar.

Roger North, in discussing music during the Civil War, comments that 'when most other good arts languished Musick held up her head . . . for many chose rather to fidle at home, than to goe out, and knockt on the head abroad . . .'.[110] He compounds this in his 'Memoires of Music' by saying that during the Commonwealth professionals from London immigrated to homes of country families and made music 'for the consolation of the cavalier gentlemen'.[111] Not all London professionals did leave the capital, as Playford published a list of London teachers for the voice and viol in his *Musicall Banquet* (1651).[112] Two lute teachers active in London during the Commonwealth were a certain Mr Ashberrie, the victim of Jacques Gaultier's physical attack in 1643, and John Rogers, who served the Cromwell household. Both these men were teachers of that exceptional child Susanna Perwich, who, according to her uncle John Batchiler, her biographer in *The Virgins Pattern* (1661), was unusually gifted in music, as she was in all other matters.[113] Susanna lived in Hackney from the age of 11 until 1661, when she died at 21; thus Rogers was teaching her from 1658 to 1661. Rogers is further mentioned by

[106] Vincent Duckles, 'The "Curious" Art of John Wilson (1595–1674): An Introduction to his Songs and Lute Music', *JAMS* 7 (1954), 93–112 at 95. This poem is taken from *GB-Ob* Eng. poet., fo. 6ʳ.

[107] Richard Rastall, 'Benjamin Rogers (1614–98): Some Notes on his Instrumental Music', *M&L* 46 (1965), 237–42 at 241. These books contain much music by Rogers, who was *informator choristarum* at Magdalen College from 1664 to 1685.

[108] Wood, *Life and Times*, 275.

[109] Percy A. Scholes, *The Puritans and Music in England and New England* (Oxford, 1934), 75–80, 365–6.

[110] *Roger North on Music*, 294.   [111] Ibid., 'Memoirs of Music', 342.

[112] *A Musicall Banquet* (1651), published by Henry Playford. Eighteen teachers are listed for the voice and viol, and nine for organ or virginal.

[113] Batchiler, *The Virgins Pattern*, 5.

Thomas Salmon in his *Essay to the Advancement of Musicke* (1672) as a London teacher of the lute.[114]

The revival of stage music with Shirley's masque *Cupid and Death* (1653, revised 1659) and Davenant's *Siege of Rhodes* (1656) and the musical household that Cromwell maintained give the impression that musical life in the capital quickened pace after the troubled years of the 1640s. Domestic music, as has been suggested, benefited during the Commonwealth by the process of decentralization initiated by the dispersal of the court, and there is no impression that the lute is on the decline at this stage.

That the lute was closely associated with 'gallants and ladys'[115] during the period 1625–60 is confirmed by all contemporary references to the lute. However, the influence of French lute music on English Caroline composers, who, as North states, 'were mostly lutenists', has largely been overlooked.[116] The early lute suites of the 1630s made up of binary dances, exemplified by those in Pierre Ballard's books, and which were developing in the 1620s, may have been the prototypes of the 'setts' to which North refers when discussing the 'flourishing time' of Charles I.[117] North, I believe, is suggesting that French lute music influenced the development of English instrumental suites of the period, from John Coprario (d. 1626), to William Lawes (d. 1645) and John Jenkins (d. 1678), all of whom would have injected 'a spice of the French' from their knowledge of the new French lute idiom.[118]

The view that the early French *brisé* style in transitional tunings took firm root *c*.1630, and continued to be in favour in the next decades, finds strong support in the plentiful iconographical and literary references to the 12-course lute. Pictures of this type of instrument do not seem to occur in French paintings, while they do in great number in Dutch, and, to a lesser extent, in British paintings. The picture by William Dobson (1610–46) of Lady Isabella Thynne with her 12-course lute is an early example of the instrument in an English painting *c*.1635.[119] Less well known is a painting by John Souch (fl. 1616–36) of *Sir Thomas Aston at the Deathbed of his Wife* (see Pl. 10.6), which is dated *c*.1635 which also features the 12-course lute. The deceased young woman is shown surrounded by the possessions with which she was most closely associated in life, including her instrument.

---

[114] *An Essay to the Advancement of Music*, 66.

[115] *Roger North on Music*, 295.

[116] Christopher D. S. Field, 'Matthew Locke and the Consort Suite', *M&L* 51 (1970), 15–25 at 15. In his discussion Field implies that Locke and William Lawes wrote independently of the new French style.

[117] *Roger North on Music*, 295.

[118] *New Grove*, xviii. 339. In his entry on the Suite David Fuller gives credit to the Parisian lutenists, French dancing-masters, and English composers of consort music for the formation of the early Baroque suite *c*.1620.

[119] The picture is hung in the state dining room of Longleat House, Wiltshire. Lady Isabella, née Rich, married Sir James Thynne of Longleat (1605–70). It is reproduced on the cover of *LSJ* 33 (1993).

PL. 10.6. *Sir Thomas Aston at the Deathbed of his Wife* (c.1635), by
John Souch of Chester. Manchester City Art Gallery

PL. 10.7. *Great Picture of the Clifford Family*, commissioned in 1646, artist unknown. The left-hand panel
shows Lady Anne aged 15 in 1605. Appleby Castle, Cumbria

The *Great Picture of the Clifford Family* now hanging at Appleby Castle, commissioned by Anne Clifford in 1646, includes a 12-course lute in the left-hand panel (see Pl. 10.7). In 1605 Anne became heir to her father George Clifford, 3rd Earl of Cumberland, though some of her estate passed to her uncle, Francis, the 4th Earl. The panel shows the young Anne Clifford, aged 15 in 1605, together with possessions that symbolize her education. These include her lute, various books, and portraits of her tutor, the poet Samuel Danyel (brother of the lutenist John Danyel), and her governess. The type of lute in the picture is incorrect for 1605, but correct for 1646. As a girl Anne had learnt music from none other than the young John Jenkins, who had joined the household of Anne Russell, the Countess of Warwick. In her diary for 1603 Anne Clifford wrote: 'I use to wear my hair coloured velvet every day and learnet to sing and play on the bass viol of Jack Jenkins, my aunt's boy.'[120]

In all these three pictures a 12-course lute is seen in the possession of an aristocratic woman. Indeed, on the evidence of the pictures which include lutes from the period, we would conclude that the instrument was played by two classes of society: professional musicians and aristocratic amateur women. The women are generally young, as in the case of the portrait of an unknown girl by Sir Peter Lely, dated *c.*1650 (see Pl. 10.8). Lady Margaret Wemyss was 12 when she started her lute book, and Miss Anne Heydon was 8 when she was painted with her instrument. There is every indication that lute playing was deemed a desirable pre-marriage accomplishment for upper-class girls.

The 12-course lute does occasionally appear in English portraiture and engravings after 1660, but it is in pictures of domestic interiors by Dutch artists that it is most commonly found. Many of this genre of pictures by such artists as Frans van Mieris (1635/6–81), Ferdinand Bol (1616–80), Hendrick Martensz Sorgh (1621–82), Caspar Netscher (1639–84), and Jacob Ochtervelt (*c.*1635–1710) feature 12-course lutes. Of all painters of the seventeenth century Gerard ter Borch (1617–81) undoubtedly featured this type of lute most consistently in his pictures of women playing, or being instructed, on the instrument.[121] Yet there is little in the way of manuscript source evidence from the Netherlands to suggest that their constant depiction in painting was due to anything other than fashion in portraiture.[122] Very few original instruments of this type survive,[123] possibly because they

---

[120] Victoria Sackville-West, *The Diary of Lady Anne Clifford* (London, 1924), 16.

[121] e.g. the picture titled *Young Woman Playing a Lute*, owned by the National Gallery in London.

[122] Of all Continental MSS only the Berlin 40264, Ros 54, Swan, and the Sibley Vault MSS contain any sizeable number of pieces for 12-course lute. Rave states that the first two MSS are of German provenance ('Musical Sources', 140, 215), as is the third, but the Sibley Vault MS might be of Dutch origin as it is found bound as an appendix to a Vallet publication.

[123] The only surviving 12-course lutes known to me are: the small instrument by Raphael Mest, dated 1633, housed in the Library, Linköping, Sweden; the converted Tieffenbrucker in Darmstadt, Hessisches Landesmuseum, Kg: 106; the dubious Jonas Stehelin/Johann Boningk instrument in Leipzig, Instrument Museum, no. 494. See Ole Vang and Ephraim Segerman, 'Two-Headed Lute News', *FoMRHI* 13 (Oct. 1978), 30–8 at 30, Comm. 156.

PL. 10.8. Portrait of an unknown girl with a 12-course lute *c*.1650, by Sir Peter Lely (1618–80). Private collection

were often conversions of lutes that were already old. Their unbalanced shape, with the distinctive double head, together with their weakness in structure caused by the conversion process, produced a fragile lute, ill-suited to lasting 300 years. As such lutes did not find the favour on the Continent that they did in England, many may have been converted yet again into 11-course lutes, and later into 13-course lutes.

Of the music in the sources in Table 10.3, the final pieces from the Herbert manuscript by Cuthbert Hely and Lord Herbert himself, and those by John Wilson in Bodleian Mus. Sch. b. 1, lie outside the mainstream, as the music they contain is in Renaissance tuning only, and seems largely unaffected by contemporary developments in French lute music. The provenance of the Herbert manuscript has already been discussed, and only the final eight pieces by Cuthbert Hely, which probably date from some time after 1630, and the ten pieces by Herbert himself, which are dated between 1626 and 1640, need be considered as post 'Golden Age'.[124]

Table 10.3. *British sources of lute music 1625–1660*

A. PRINCIPAL MANUSCRIPT SOURCES

Herbert (later section)
Wilson
Christopher Lowther
Board (later section)
Pickeringe (later section)
Longleat
O.16.2
Reymes
Pan 5
Wemyss
Pan 8
Robarts
Bodley 410–414

B. FRAGMENTARY SOURCES

Oxford, St Edmund College Library, EE.12 (fragments of 5 pieces for 12-course lute in D minor tuning *c.*1650)
Add. 38539 (duet for 12-course lute, fo. 33ᵛ)
Northampton Public Record Office, FH.3431.c (2 pieces for 11-course lute)
GB-Ob Don.c.57 (Music Collection), fo. 100ʳ (single courante for 10-course lute in Renaissance tuning)

C. PRINTED SOURCES

Richard Mathew, *The Lutes Apology for her Excellency* (London, 1652)

---

[124] In his article 'Lord Herbert of Cherbury's Lute-Book', 146, Dart reads the dating of Herbert's Pavan, piece no. 216, fo. 79ʳ, as 3 Mar. 1619/20(?), though this is probably a misreading of 1629. See Craig-McFeely, 'A Can of Worms', 30.

A further lute source from this period in Renaissance tuning is the Lowther Lute Book.[125] The book's thirty-three pieces were copied in Hamburg *c*.1637 by Christopher Lowther (1611–44) as a result of a series of lessons that he received from a Dutchman. Its foreign provenance would suggest that it has little relevance to lute practice in England at this time. Unusually, an 11-course lute in Renaissance tuning is required.

There is good evidence for the whole-hearted adoption of the early French *brisé* style and use of the transitional tunings by many lutenists in England in the period 1625–60. Some players did remain true to the older, more polyphonic tradition, and eschewed transitional tunings. There was thus a period of overlap, in which the new French-influenced music was being played on lutes in transitional tunings, and solo music that owed little to French developments continued to be played in Renaissance tuning. The late pavans and fantasias by Robert Johnson and Daniel Bacheler that are contained in the Herbert manuscript have much in common, not least in their opening themes, and flat, minor keys.[126] These pieces are the link between the Golden Age polyphonic fantasias of Dowland, Holborne, and Ferrabosco, and the remarkable preludes and fantasias by Cuthbert Hely and John Wilson, which probably date from the 1630s and 1640s. Both Johnson and Bacheler have a single surviving fantasia in which the theme is thoroughly explored in various keys and positions. In the Bacheler piece the texture thins out into a running, florid, semiquaver passage, which broadens out into a more homophonic close.[127] This type of fantasia has many parallels with those of Caroline keyboard and viol composers, and evidently was still being written for the lute after 1625.

The eight pieces by the otherwise unknown Cuthbert Hely, along with the late pavans by Herbert himself, were added to the Herbert manuscript some time after the main bulk of the music in the collection, possibly as late as 1640. The four fantasias by Hely are all monothematic to a degree unmatched in any English lute compositions, save in Dowland's chromatic fantasias. The opening themes used are generally very angular and melodically unusual, making frequent use of accidentals (see Ex. 10.1). In all four pieces a second part is added in imitation in close proximity to the first (usually in the same bar), and for much of the entirety of the four pieces two voices (usually the outer two) move quasi-canonically through the many permutations of the theme. The opening motif of the theme is used extensively in the later development of each piece.

In the Hely fantasia in A major the motif of the theme, a falling minor sixth (or its inversion) followed by a third rising by step, appears seven times in the first

---

[125] See Gwilym Beechey, 'Christopher Lowther's Lute Book', *GSJ* 24 (1971), 51–9.

[126] Compare Herbert MS: Johnson 'Fantasia', fo. 16ʳ, and Batcheler 'Fantasia', fos. 56ᵛ–57ʳ; Johnson 'Pavana', fos. 22ᵛ–23ʳ, and Bacheler 'Pavana', fos. 19ᵛ–20ʳ.

[127] For full transcriptions of these pieces see Daniel Bacheler, *Selected Works*, ed. Long, 41–4, no. 14; and Robert Johnson, *Complete Works for Solo Lute*, ed. Sundermann (London, 1972), 2–3, no. 1.

Ex. 10.1. *Opening bars of Cuthbert Hely's four fantasias from the Herbert MS: (a) A major, fo.
81ᵛ; (b) A minor, fo. 82ᵛ; (c) F minor, fo. 87ᵛ; (d) D minor, fo. 88ᵛ*

(c)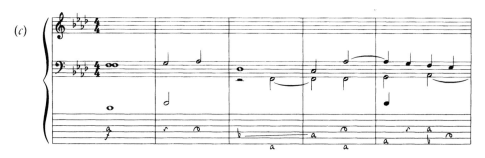

(d)

twenty-two bars, and appears or is implied in many more places later in the pieces.[128] The harmony, while constantly moving, is never taken too far from the home key. Instead, intensity and colour are heightened in the music by the frequent use of unexpected accidentals, which produce many false relations, and occasionally augmented triads. In all the pieces there is a tendency for the opening polyphonic texture to dissolve into continuous running passages towards the close in the Johnson/Bacheler manner. Yet even in these places the theme may still occasionally reappear. As with Wilson's pieces, and the fantasias by Johnson and Bacheler,

[128] The motif appears in bars 1–2, 2–3, 8–9, 12–13, 15–16, 21–2 and also in bars 33–4, 35–6, 40–1, and 44, although there are other places where it is implied.

there is a marked preference for the lower and middle registers, and the top course is used sparingly.

The four remaining Hely pieces are all much shorter in length, and all have key links with other pieces.[129] The preludes in A and D minor precede the fantasias in those keys. They are fully barred, and are characterized by almost continuous step-wise movement of the bass, and harmonic freedom above. Earlier it was suggested that Herbert used the E♭ prelude to preface his own pieces in that key and the F minor saraband to follow the fantasia by Hely in F minor. This saraband and E♭ prelude are remarkable for their total avoidance of the top string. Both show the infuence of French *brisé* style, but are unmistakably English. Cuthbert Hely is an enigma, as his lute music is certainly the most interesting written by an Englishman around 1630 that is extant, yet nothing is known about him, and little of his music survives.[130] It is possible to speculate that Hely served Herbert in his exile in Montgomery Castle, or after his move to Richmond in 1632. In the inscription on the flyleaf of his manuscript, Herbert draws attention to his own compositions in the lines 'The Lutebooke of Edward Lord Herbert of Cherbury and Castle Island, containing diverse selected Lessons of excellent Authors in severall Cuntreys. Wherin also are some few of my owne Composition.' Six of the ten pieces by Herbert are dated,[131] and probably refer to the date of composition rather than insertion in the manuscript. The 1619 dating is questionable, and may be 1627, as it is obscured on the page, and is essentially the same as the piece dated 1627. Sadly, these pieces are of little musical interest apart from the choice of keys (i.e. flat minor), and a very low tessitura similar to those by Hely.

John Wilson's most unusual cycle of thirty pieces for 12-course lute in Renaissance tuning survives in an Oxford manuscript.[132] This source also contains some 226 songs, forty-three of which have a tablature continuo realization under-neath the staves carrying the voice and bass lines. It was presented to the Bodleian Library in 1656 on Wilson's acceptance of the Heather professorship, with the stip-ulation that it was not to be consulted until after his death.[133] The cycle of solo pieces was probably composed in the period 1646–56, when Wilson served Sir William Sarsden in the parish of Churchill after the disbanding of the Court.

---

[129] Herbert MS: fos. 82ʳ A minor prelude ('Prelude Hely'); 88ʳ ('Sarabrand Cut: Hely'); 88ᵛ D minor prelude ('Prelude Hely'); 89ᵛ E♭ minor prelude ('Prelude C. Hely').

[130] Cuthbert Hely's only other known work is a three-part ayre in *GB-Lbl* Add. 18940, fo. 4ᵛ. He may have been related to the 17th-c. musicians Benjamin Hely (fl. 1680–90) and Henry He(a)le.

[131] The pieces are Herbert MS, nos. 28 (1626), 33, 132, 133, 183, 214 (1628), 216 (1619), 225 (1627), 241 (1640), 242 (1639). Numbering according to the inventory in Price, 'An Organisational Peculiarity', 22–7.

[132] *GB-Ob* MS Mus. Sch. b. 1, fos. 3ᵛ–12ᵛ. Pub. in facs. in *Manuscripts at Oxford Part II* (facs. of *GB-Ob* MS Mus. Sch. b. 1.), ed. Elise Bickford Jorgens (English Song 1600–1675: Facsimiles of 26 Manuscripts and an Edition of the Texts, 7; New York and London, 1987). The lute pieces are published as John Wilson, *Thirty Preludes in all (24) Keys for Lute*, ed. Matthew Spring (Utrecht, 1992).

[133] Duckles, 'The "Curious" Art of John Wilson', 96.

The pieces are intended to constitute a set covering every major and minor key. Wilson was not the first person to attempt such a cycle, as Giacomo Gorzanis (*c*.1520–*c*.1575) had written a collection of twenty-four passamezzo–salterello pairs in each major and minor key.[134] However Gorzanis's pieces are all very similar, and, unlike the Wilson cycle, do not constitute a 'well-tempered lute' in which the possibilities of each key are explored.

Some keys in Wilson's cycle have more than one piece (A minor has three, C minor has two, and B♭, E, and D major each have two). The order seems somewhat random, although the pieces get progressively more complex, chromatic, and difficult, moving from the easy and familiar keys on the lute to the unknown. There are two hands at work on these pieces. The first, possibly that of Wilson himself, contributed twenty consecutively numbered pieces. The pieces copied by the second hand are not numbered, and were obviously added where space allowed. This latter hand appears in a tuning chart in the lute volume of the Bodleian part-books Mus. Sch. e. 410–14. These books were connected with Richard Rhodes, an Oxford undergraduate at Christ Church until 1662, who was active as a violinist at Ellis's meetings in 1658.[135]

We have seen how lute composers in the period 1600–25 preferred flat minor keys, and reached such remote keys as E♭ minor. In his songs Wilson is extremely free in his movement from key to key, with little or no proper modulation. Certainly he was known for his bizarre harmonic imagination.[136] In his commendatory poem to Henry Lawes Robert Herrick describes Wilson as 'curious', and Lawes himself wrote a commendatary poem for Wilson's *Psalterium Carolinum* of 1657, which includes the lines:

> For this I know, and must say't to thy praise,
> That thou hast gone, in Musick, unknown ways,
> Hast cut a path where there was none before,
> Like Magellan traced an unknown shore.[137]

To what extent lutenists were aware of writing in remote keys, as opposed to simply basing pieces on unusual stopped-chord positions on the fretboard of the lute, is always difficult to judge, given the variability of lute pitch. However, in Wilson's cycle we can be reasonably sure that definite keys are intended, as the pieces preface songs, some of which have a tablature accompaniment for the same instrument. The vocal pitch establishes the top string as *g*′, thus the key of each piece can be determined.

[134] The MS containing the cycle is *D-Mbs* MS 1511a. Published as *Libro de intabulatura di liuto nel qualle si contengano 24 passa mezi . . .* (1567), ed. B. Tonazzi (Milan, 1975), guitar transcription.
[135] Tim Crawford, 'An Unusual Consort Revealed in an Oxford Manuscript', *Chelys*, 6 (1975–6), 61–8 at 68.
[136] Duckles, 'The "Curious" Art of John Wilson', n. 100.
[137] John Wilson, *Psalterium Carolinum* (London, 1657), sig. A˅.

As Wilson gives no titles to the thirty pieces, it is something of a problem to categorize them. In content and form there exists little comparable lute music, save the late English pieces by Hely, Herbert, and Johnson in the Herbert manuscript. The pieces fall somewhere between the early Baroque free prelude and the late English fantasy tradition. Some pieces have a clear motivic development, and can be quite easily compared with the fantasies by Hely. Others of the very chromatic type, and some of the very simple homophonic type, do not fit this classification at all well. Given this amount of variation, it is best to stick to the more general title 'prelude', despite the fact that some pieces have a structure that is precise and cleverly assembled.

Wilson adopts a different approach towards the flat and sharp keys. While it is true that the pieces get progressively longer and more complex as he moves from the familiar to the remote, the pieces with fully chromatic passages are always those in sharp keys, with the important exception of no. 30 in E♭ minor. The familiar keys like B♭, E♭, and F major get the shortest, simplest, homophonic treatment of all. These pieces have a flow and sonorousness which is often lacking in the pieces in sharp keys, some of which, especially those in remote keys like no. 22 in G♯ minor, are particularly bizarre harmonically, lacking in structure, and arguably less well handled.

No. 30 in E♭ minor is in a class of its own among the pieces in flat keys. It has two extended fully chromatic passages (bars 10–15 and 19–29) in which all three parts descend chromatically. In these two passages one part maintains the rhythmic motif of a crotchet followed by two quavers, while the other parts descend (in the main by minims), the motif being passed from part to part. In these sections the sense of key, though still implicit, is quickly lost, and the music begins to sound almost atonal. (See Ex. 10.2 for the second of these passages.) In the chromatic fantasias of Dowland the structure guides the ear back to the home key. The lack of formal structure in Wilson's piece can leave the listener quite disorientated.

The tendency to avoid the first course is very apparent in the pieces by Hely, Herbert, Johnson, and some of those by Bacheler in the Herbert manuscript. Wilson takes this tendency a step further. Often he uses a higher position on the second course in preference to the first, possibly to gain a more expressive tone, or because the top string was tuned down an octave.[138] The most prominent unifying element in the cycle and the most important compositional device are the diatonic, and occasionally chromatic, bass-line passages, in which the diapasons are fully employed. Wilson's pieces consistently use the diapasons. They are employed far more than in contemporary French lute music, and at least as much as in the nearly contemporary Italian lute music by Bernardo Gianoncelli.[139] Wilson never has

---

[138] e.g. Wilson MS, no. 10, bar 15.   [139] Bernardo Gianoncelli, *Il liuto* (Venice, 1650).

Ex. 10.2. *John Wilson, Prelude in E♭ minor, no. 30, Wilson MS, fo. 12ᵛ, bars 19–29*

recourse to strophic variation as a structural device, and only in some pieces does he fully use thematic development to give the music direction. Instead he relies heavily on long scalar passages in the bass.

Two important late Golden Age manuscripts which contain sizeable collections of pieces in the new French style of *c*.1630, in both Renaissance and transitional tunings, are the Board and Pickeringe manuscripts. Robert Spencer suggests that pieces for 10-course lute, nos. 105–86, in the Board manuscript date from about 1630.[140] Thirty-two of the eighty-one pieces are in transitional tunings. These

---

[140] See Spencer's introductory study to *The Board Lute Book*.

pieces are particularly short and simple, and are representative of the first tentative stages of experimentation with tunings.

At the reverse end of the Pickeringe manuscript there are twenty-nine pieces that are also likely to date from the 1630s, some of which are more substantial than those from the same period in the Board manuscript. There are two hands at work in this section of the manuscript. The first has added seventeen pieces for 10-course lute in various tunings, and a second has contributed twelve more for a 12-course lute.[141] The titles and comments with three of the pieces associate them with the royal musician John Lawrence, who was a musician 'for the Lutes and voices' from 1625 to his death in 1635.[142] Nine pieces are similarly associated with a 'Gaultier' spelt in many variant ways. This may refer to Jacques Gaultier. It may be that in these instances Gaultier and Lawrence are connected with the tunings nos. 8 and 9 respectively, rather than with the composition of these pieces.

Trinity College, Cambridge, MS O.16.2 is a further manuscript that contains a mixture of solo music in Renaissance tunings, probably from the 1620s, and music in transitional tunings that is clearly later.[143] Only the first three folios, the last eighteen, and a single central folio contain music. The remaining folios, as well as many of those containing music, have been used as a notebook for listing past members, rents, and tenancy arrangements of Trinity College, Cambridge. Among the scattering of pieces in five distinct hands, there are thirty-three pieces in Renaissance tuning from the 1620s, eleven pieces for 10-course lute in tunings nos. 8, 9, and 10 that must date from no earlier than the 1630s, and a single exercise based on the 'folies d'Espagna' ground for 11-course lute in D minor tuning from a later period. Many of the pieces in Renaissance tuning are based on masque and ballad tunes, and include solos by Robert Johnson and Daniel Bacheler.

A manuscript for the greater part devoted to music in the French style of the 1630s was found in the library at Longleat House. Longleat 7 contains fifty-seven pieces in both French and Italian lute tablature. It is signed and dated 'Philerenio Scozzese alias Sinciero anno 1634'.[144] Six different scribes added music to the manuscript, and the music dates from the period *c.*1625–35. The pieces are for a 10-course lute using tunings nos. 6, 7, 8, 9, and 10, and a 14-course chitarrone with re-entrant tuning of the top two courses. 'Philerenio Scozzese' most probably was an academic pseudoym adopted by Sir James Thynne (1605–70), and the book was acquired by him in Italy while undertaking a Grand Tour between 1632 and 1634.[145] The book may have already contained exercises and pieces by Kapsperger for theorbo when Thynne acquired it. The French lute pieces were then added

[141] Pickeringe MS, fos. 37ᵛ to 45ᵛ; fos. 51ᵛ to 50ᵛ; fos. 49ᵛ to 46ʳ. See Rave, 'Some Manuscripts', 145–8.
[142] *RECM* iii. 9–10.   [143] Matthew Spring, 'The Lute in England and Scotland', ii. 20–5.
[144] Longleat 7, fo. 82ᵛ.
[145] Daniel Leech-Wilkinson, 'The Thynne Lute Book', *LSJ* 33 (1993), 1–11 at 4–5.

through a course of study with a number of lutenists in Italy, and possibly elsewhere as well. Thynne's wife, Lady Isabella of the Dobson portrait, may also have used the manuscript. It is fascinating that a number of names mentioned in Longleat 7 connect with friends and aquaintances of Bullen Reymes, who travelled in both France and Italy at the same time as Sir James Thynne.[146]

There are four manuscripts with Scottish associations that contain French music from this period. Three of these books form part of the large collection of Panmure House manuscripts owned by the National Library of Scotland and the fourth, the Wemyss manuscript, is also in the National Library. Another manuscript with British connections is the Reymes manuscript. Bullen Reymes was a young diplomat attached to the English Embassy in Paris between June 1631 and September 1633. We are fortunate that a lute manuscript, a journal and a set of letters survive that give a rich account of Reymes's musical activities in the early 1630s.[147] It seems that Reymes had studied the lute with a master, identified by Goy as one 'Hebert', while in London prior to his departure for Paris. This master contributed some 51 pieces to Reymes's book. While in Paris Reymes used his lute in all manner of social events, both formal and informal and in particular to entertain the English ambassador Sir Isaac Wake, and also bought and played the guitar. In Paris Reymes took some lessons from Mesangeau, who contributed 15 pieces to the manuscript and, more successfully, with Merville. Reymes had musical exchanges with a good number of lute players, both French and English, professional and amateur, before departing for a period in Italy and further musical adventures.[148] Reymes copied the remaining pieces into the manuscript himself, probably as late as 1635 or 1636. The Reymes manuscript is for 10-course and 12-course lutes in tunings nos. 6, 7, 8, 9, and 10 and contains 127 pieces. It has much in common with Pan 5 in its contents, tunings, and the fact that they share a principal scribe.[149] Together with Pan 5 it contains French music in transitional tunings that was highly fashionable in England in the 1630s. Three fine duets in this style appear in one of William Lawes's autograph scores, and were probably added to the manuscript as a set *c.*1642–3, although they were likely to have been composed some time during the 1630s.[150] These duets are probably intended for a 12-course lute in tuning no. 9, although only eleven courses are required.

There are three surviving sources that date from the Commonwealth period: the Robarts manuscript, Bodley 410–414, and Richard Mathew's *The Lutes Apology for her Excellency* (1652). Mathew's book is the only source of printed solo lute music in Britain between *Varietie* (1610) and *Musick's Monument* (1676). The Robarts

[146] Goy, 'Luth et guitare', 195. [147] Ibid., 185.

[148] Ibid., 187–91. For Mesangeau see *Œuvres de René Mesangeau*, ed. and trans. André Souris, with a biographical study and critical commentary by Monique Rollin (Paris, 1971), pp. xvii–xx. For a description of the Reymes MS and some of its concordances see Rave, 'Some Manuscripts', 109–14.

[149] Goy, 'Luth et guitare, 187. [150] *GB-Ob* MS Mus. Sch. b. 2.

manuscript resulted from a course of lessons taken by Hender Robarts (1635–85) whilst in Paris from 1654.[151] His master, who compiled the manuscript, and who signed his name 'Bourgaise', was a French lute master in Paris around the middle of the century. Hender Robarts probably brought the manuscript back from France at some point in the 1650s or 1660s. It reflects pure French lute teaching and reper-toire at the mid-century and does not connect with any independent British lute traditions of the time. The manuscript is for an 11-course lute in standard D minor tuning throughout, though with some diapason alterations, and contains sixty-five pieces of the highest quality in seven distinct key groupings.

The old Music School collection of manuscripts in the Bodleian Library includes a set of part-books (Bodley 410–414) for a 'lute consort' with a treble (viol or vio-lin), lyra viol (in tablature), and two unfigured basses (presumably one for a gamba and the other for a theorbo).[152] These thirty-two pieces are found at the reverse ends of Bodley 410–414 that are otherwise known as a source of three- and four-part airs by Coleman, Cooke, and Lawes. Many of the pieces can be shown by con-cordances to have been popular as solo lute pieces as early as the 1630s, although the lute consort for which these books were assembled was probably active in the 1650s or 1660s.

The lute part for nos. 1–20 and 27–32 requires a lute in tuning no. 10 at the pitches g', e', c, a, e, B for the top six courses. Pieces nos. 21–6, however, require a smaller instrument tuned in the 'French B Natural' tuning of the Burwell Tutor (i.e. transposed D major tuning at the pitches $b\flat'$, g', d', $b\flat$, g, d). All thirty-two pieces are unattributed, apart from the last six, which constitute a suite ('Pavan', ayre, courante, allemande, courante, and sarabande). Three pieces of this suite are attributed to John Birchenshaw and there is no reason to suppose that he did com-pose all six.[153] The lute book contains several well-known pieces to which other parts have been added. We know that consorts which feature the lute together with various bowed and plucked instruments were popular in the Caroline and Commonwealth periods.[154] Sadly, these books are the only surviving representa-tives of this genre of lute consort.

The single surviving copy of Richard Mathew's *The Lutes Apology* (1652) (see Pl. 10.9), now owned by the British Library, was found with three other music manu-scripts and other documents that comprised the muniments of Sir William Boteler of Biddenham in Bedfordshire.[155] A staunch Parliamentarian, Boteler served on the

[151] Llanhydrock House, Cornwall, owned by the National Trust. Published as *The Robarts Lute Book*, facs. with an introductory study by Robert Spencer (Musical Sources, 11; Clarabricken, 1978).

[152] For an inventory, examples, and a discussion of the books' provenance see Tim Crawford, 'An Unusual Consort'. Dimsdale lists the pieces in her thesis catalogue, 'The Lute in Consort', ii, incipit nos. 382–413.

[153] Spring, 'The Lute in England and Scotland', i. 270.

[154] See *Lodewijck Huygens*, ed. Bacharach and Collmer, p. xx.

[155] *GB-Lbl* K.1.c.33. See Gerald Hayes, 'Music in the Boteler Muniments', *GSJ* 8 (1955), 43–7, and Adrienne Simpson, 'Richard Mathew and *The Lutes Apology*', *LSJ* 8 (1966), 41–7. Also ead., 'A Study of Richard Mathew's

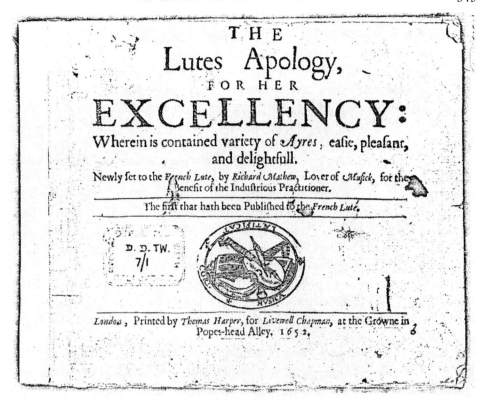

PL. 10.9. Frontispiece from Richard Mathew's *The Lutes Apology* (London, 1652)

County Sequestration Committee during the Commonwealth, and was elected as one of the five members for Bedford County under the Instrument of Government. Sir William died in 1656, and this copy of Mathew's book remained uncut and unused at his death, although his letters reveal a strong musical interest.

There were family connections between Mathew's publisher, Livewell Chapman, the fifth monarchist and seditious pamphleteer, and John Playford the music publisher, through Playford's marriage to Chapman's stepdaughter.[156] Further, the device used for the *Lutes Apology* and the *Dancing Master* is the same. It is that

The Lutes Apology for his Excellency' (M.Mus. diss., King's College, University of London, 1968). Richard Mathew was very probably the quack author of *The Unlearned Alchemist his Antidote, or a more full and ample explanation of the use, verture and benefit of my pill* (London, 1659). For a full account of *The Lutes Apology*, its contents, and provenance see Spring, 'The Lute in England and Scotland', ii. 63–9.

[156] Playford married Hannah Allen, daughter of Benjamin Allen, publisher of Cornhill, *c.*1653, so family contact at this time is very likely. *New Grove*, xv. 1.

adopted by Thomas Harper, from Thomas East, of a lute, violin, and music book, surrounded by the motto 'Laetificat cor musica'. This connection may account for the musical borrowings of Mathew from Playford's books, as Chapman would have been in a good position to draw Mathew's attention to the success of Playford's first books. No doubt Mathew hoped to imitate this success with his *Lutes Apology*.

Mathew's book contains thirty-two pieces for a 12-course lute, all of which are in French flat tuning. The title-page states that it contains a 'variety of *Ayres*, easie, pleasant and delightful' and that they are 'the first that hath been Published to the *French Lute*'. The *Lutes Apology* is prefaced by an epistle addressed 'To the Skilfull and well Accomplisht Masters in Musick' (sig. a2ʳ ˅). This begins as follows: 'Gentlemen: Having served two Apprentiships unto my Lute, and finding my Study well replenished with what were necessary, as to the Body of Musick, after the way of those Worthies, whose Workes live, although they be dead; and finding nothing in Print to the French Lute, which now onely is in Request, . . .' Later in the same epistle he says with reference to the pieces he has prepared: 'As to the French Lute, they are purely my owne; . . . I have made some use of the old tuning, as also of Ayres whose Authours I know not: In some of them I have not followed the proper Basse, nor filled them with inward Parts; because I would not make them hard unto the Schollar.'

From this we can surmise that Mathew was of sufficient age to have learnt the lute prior to 1620, when the Renaissance tuning was still the norm in England, but subsequent changes in fashion led him to then learn the 12-course lute in transitional tunings. Mathew was most probably an amateur, as he speaks harshly of those 'who of right should have saved me from this labour', that is, lute composers and professional players. He admits to having no training in composition, and claims credit for all the pieces 'as to the French lute'.[157] Mathew drew on three types of music: English popular tunes used by Playford in *The English Dancing Master* (1651) and *A Booke of New Lessons for the Cithern & Gittern* (1652); consort pieces and masque tunes by William Lawes, Charles Coleman, Simon Ives, and other unattributed composers; English and Continental lute pieces popular during the 1620s, including two almains by Robert Johnson. In this last category are preludes by Edinthon and Bocquet from Besard's *Thesaurus harmonicus* (1603), a piece by Lespine, and some other anonymous French pieces.[158]

In a second note addressed 'To the Industrious Practitioner in Musick' Mathew promises 'to gratifie you with a Second Part'. The poor quality both of music and printing of the single surviving copy of this publication argues forcibly for the financial failure of Mathew's lute publication. This no doubt led to the breaking of

---

[157] François-Pierre Goy, 'Richard Mathew's Prefatory Epistle and the Contents of *The Lutes Apology*', *LSJ* 31 (1991), 2–7.

[158] Ibid. 6–7; see the 'Table of Contents and Original Versions'.

the promise given in the second epistle. This may have discouraged Playford from publishing any tablatures for the lute.

Surprisingly few of the surviving manuscript sources of French lute music in transitional tunings in Table 10.4 can definitely be proved to have been of French origin. Instead the majority have non-French associations.[159] As mentioned above, the Reymes manuscript resulted at least in part from a course of instruction on the lute taken by the young diplomat Bullen Reymes in Paris and London between 1631 and 1636.[160]

The large Krems L 81, Berlin 40264, and Werl manuscripts are all German or Austrian in origin.[161] If we add the Pan 5 and Reymes manuscripts (as they belonged to Britons) to the remaining group of British sources of this period with pieces in altered tunings, that is, Pan 8, Board, Eg 2046, Longleat, Bodley 410-414, O.16.2, and Wemyss manuscripts, England and Scotland can be seen to have the largest group of surviving manuscript sources and probably the largest currency in terms of numbers of pieces.

The importance of Ballard's printed books of 1631 and 1638 for the understanding of the stylistic development of lute music in Britain and northern Europe in general cannot be overestimated. The concordances in the British lute sources with Ballard's books, though few, are fairly widespread. Music from these books, either via manuscript copies or via the dispersal of the books themselves, more than any other factor would seem, from source evidence, to have introduced and established the French *brisé* style in northern Europe. Surviving British sources of the period contain a body of some 300 pieces in transitional tunings. The majority of these pieces are not masque or popular tunes. They have a high degree of stylistic uniformity, the basis of which was the music introduced into Britain through these Ballard publications, or through manuscripts like the Reymes, which were compiled in part in Paris, and soon after travelled to Britain.

Ballard (1631) uses only tunings nos. 8 and 10 (the so-called Sharp and Flat tunings). The standard D minor tuning appears with these in Ballard (1638), which with Pierre Gaultier's book, also of 1638, marks the first appearance of this tuning in print, as well as of tuning no. 9. This latter tuning is related to both nos. 8 and 10 as it has its basis in the flat tuning (no. 10) but with the third course raised to $a_\natural$ (as in the sharp tuning no. 8), and the ninth to $D_\natural$. *Les Œuvres de Pierre Gaultier* (Rome, 1638) is not of significance to this study as there are no concordances

---

[159] Only the Vm⁷ 6211 MS (which belonged for a time to Sébastian de Brossard) and the Basle 53 MS are clearly of French provenance. The Houghton 174 and Sibley Vault MSS, though unproved, may have been of French origin.

[160] Goy, 'Luth et guitare', 187.

[161] See Rave, 'Some Manuscripts', for provenance information on Krems L 81 and Berlin 40264. The Werl MS originated from South Germany, possibly in the region of Augsburg.

Table 10.4. *Principal British and Continental sources of lute music in transitional tunings 1625–1660*

Country	Source	Approximate number of pieces in transitional tunings[a]
France	Ballard (1623)	contents unknown
	Ballard (1631)	87
	Ballard (1638)	40
	P. Gaultier (1638)	97
	Basle 53	64
	Vm⁷ 6211	63
	Reymes	127
France?	Sibley Vault	37
	Houghton 174	1
	Chicago	187
Germany	Krems L 81	77
	Berlin 40264	79
	Ros 54	15
	Werl	225
	Swan	58
	Ulm 132	10
	Prague IV.G.18	25
	Stobaeus	4
Sweden	L. de Geer	3
Britain	Board	32
	Pickeringe	26
	O.16.2	11
	Longleat	44
	Lawes Duets	3
	Bodley 410–414	32
	Pan 5	106
	Pan 8	42
	Wemyss	41
	Lutes Apology	43

[a] For more information on the tunings in the these sources see Ekkehard Schulze-Kurz, *Die Laute und ihre Stimmungen in der ersten Hälfte des 17. Jahrhunderts* (Wilsingen, 1990), 299–447.

between this book and British sources, only with the German manuscripts Krems L 81, Berlin 40264, and Ros 54. However, it is noteworthy that Pierre Gaultier (1638) uses six different tunings, including D minor, with the majority of pieces in the flat tuning (no. 10).[162]

The picture that emerges from French printed sources is of the establishment by 1630 of the Sharp and Flat tunings (nos. 8 and 10) as the two basic tunings, with a group of subsidiary tunings based around them. These other tunings usually require an alteration by a semitone of one or two courses. The standard D minor tuning first appeared later in the decade. In France in the 1640s it assumed prominence over the others, which became redundant by the mid-century.[163]

This picture is mirrored in British sources up to *c*.1640, the great majority of pieces in transitional tunings being in tunings nos. 8 and 10. (See Table 10.5.) The big difference between the tuning developments in the two countries is that in France in the period approaching the mid-century the D minor tuning was emerging as standard, but in Britain the so-called Flat French or French Flat tuning (no. 10) could make the best claim to being the dominant tuning (discounting sources like the Robarts manuscript that were directly imported from France). Not only are there more pieces in this tuning than any other in the British sources under discussion, but the mid-century Bodley 410–414 uses it for all but six out of thirty-two pieces, and Mathew's *Lutes Apology* uses it exclusively. This trend is already discernible in Pan 8, which probably dates from the 1640s. Of the forty-seven pieces, six are in D minor tuning, five are in tuning no. 9, and the remaining thirty-six are in the Flat tuning (no. 10). Sources after the mid-century from England and Scotland are usually dominated by either tuning no. 10 (Bodley 410–414, *Lutes Apology*, the Nanki manuscript, and *Musick's Monument*), or standard D minor tuning with its major counterpart (all other manuscripts). Indeed, the only sources to feature any of the other transitional tunings apart from the Flat tuning are the Tabley and Balcarres manuscripts, which both have a small number of pieces in other tunings.[164]

The overall picture of tuning developments in England is of a reduction from many tunings *c*.1630 with tunings nos. 8 and 10 most consistently used, to a situation *c*.1650 when the Flat tuning (no. 10) had largely replaced all other transitional tunings. Around the mid-century, under the influence of the French, who now almost exclusively used the D minor tuning, the Flat tuning (no. 10) in England was challenged by the D minor. The Robarts manuscript and Burwell Tutor are testimony to this challenge, as is *Musick's Monument*. However, it would seem that until

---

[162] The tunings used are nos. 6, 8, 9, 10, 11, and D minor (Rave, 'Some Manuscripts', 107).
[163] Ibid. 232.
[164] The Balcarres has a short section (pp. 215–19) in tuning no. 8.

Table 10.5. *Tunings in British sources 1625–1660*

Source	Tuning							
D minor	D major	no. 6	no. 7	no. 8	no. 9	no. 10	no. 11	
SCOTTISH								
Pan 5				37	7	62	1	
Pan 8	6				5	36		
Wemyss				21	1	39	1	
Pan 4	12	11						
ENGLISH								
Pickeringe		1	5	8	9	8		
Board		6	6	14	6			
O.16.2	1			6	1	6		
Longleat		2	1	20	3	17		
Lawes Duets					3			
Lutes Apology						43		
Bodley 410–414		6				26		

Note: This list does not include the Scottish pieces in tuning no. 8 in the Wemyss MS. Pickeringe also has one piece in the tuning *d′, c′, a, f, c, G, F, E♭, D, C, B♭′*, which is not included here.

the end of the century both tunings co-existed in England, and only in the eighteenth century did the D minor tuning reign supreme over the Flat tuning.[165]

The co-existence of these two tunings is largely explained by their strong associations with different instruments: the 12-course lute was particularly well suited to tuning no. 10, with its logical run of diapasons down to the tonic of the major triad on the top three courses;[166] the D minor was ideal for the French 11-course instrument. Indeed, there is little suggestion that the 11-course lute was used much to play in transitional tunings (the Balcarres pieces in tuning no. 8 are exceptional), or that the 12-course lute was much played in D minor tuning, though the Tabley, Pan 8, and Pan 4 manuscripts show that it was to some extent. There is evidence that the 12-course lute was still occasionally played in Renaissance tuning. The Wilson manuscript (1656) and the seven pieces in the Creyghton manuscript (1727), are undoubtedly for a 12-course lute in Renaissance tuning. Nevertheless, it is reasonable to assume that, especially in connection with song accompaniments, the 12-course lute was commonly played in Renaissance tuning between these dates. The 'Theorbo-Lute' or 'Theorboed Lute', referred to as a possible accompanying

---

[165] This is suggested by the Balcarres, Osborne, and Danby MSS.

[166] Mace, *Musick's Monument*, 198. He points out the logicality of this arrangement of diapasons.

instrument for vocal publications from 1650 to 1720, may well be the 12-course lute in Renaissance tuning.

All the pieces in British sources from Ballard's 1631 and 1638 books have rhythmic, and usually also melodic, discrepancies between them and the printed texts. Often chord members are missing or added, and ornamentation is different. The Mesangeau allemande published in Ballard (1638), p. 22,[167] seems to have been unusually popular both in Britain and on the Continent, as it appears in four British sources and a number of Continental manuscripts. The piece requires the less popular tuning no. 9 in the treble strings (described as 'flat save the 3a sharp' in the Wemyss manuscript),[168] and the retuning of the ninth course to $D\natural$, and the tenth to $B\flat'$ in the diapasons if using a 10-course lute—as was envisaged by Ballard the publisher. As three of the British sources that include this piece were intended in part for 12-course lutes, an eleventh course ($B\flat'$) was available without retuning. However, some misunderstanding arose in the Wemyss manuscript version as this bass note is marked both by an eleventh and a tenth course. The only British source to set the piece for a 10-course lute is O.16.2, the version of which is generally faithful to the published text. Here it appears with the addition of left- and right-hand fingering, and of ornamentation signs that include both a comma and a sharp sign, a combination which almost never appears in contemporary French lute sources.

The two versions of the Mesangeau allemande in Scottish sources (Wemyss and Pan 8 manuscripts) both have an extra bass $B\flat'$ added to the opening chord. The version in Pan 8 has some extra dotting consistent with the rest of the manuscript and both books have some rhythmic deviations from Ballard (1638), for example in bar 11. Indeed, in Ex. 10.3, a comparison of the opening bars of the second couplet of the British sources and the published text shows a different discrepancy in every source. This degree of variation, particularly in details of rhythm and ornamentation, is not uncommon among sources of popular pieces from this period and is indicative of what Rave has called 'an extemporary performance manner, rather than a fixed compositional entity'.[169]

Of all the British sources of the Mesangeau allemande, the most interesting is that which appears as the first part (i.e. Lute 1) of the first of the three William Lawes lute duets in his Bodleian autograph score (see Pl. 10.10). It is possible that the first lute part of the other two duets may also be by a composer other than Lawes.[170] The second lute part is thus a *contrepartie* by Lawes to an existing piece by Mesangeau and its appearance in the Lawes autograph score predates by over a

[167] *Tablature de luth de différents autheurs*, pub. Pierre Ballard (Paris, 1638).

[168] Wemyss MS, fo. 33ʳ.

[169] Victor Anand Coelho (ed.), *Performance on Lute, Guitar, and Vihuela* (Cambridge, 1997), 157.

[170] GB-Ob Mus. Sch. b. 2, p. 86, 'For 2 Lutes'. See David Buch, 'On the Authorship of William Lawes's *Suite for Two Lutes*', *JLSA* 16 (1983), 12–14. For transcriptions of these pieces see Spring, 'The Lute in England and Scotland', i. 239–43. These pieces were listed with incipits in Dimsdale, 'The Lute in Consort', iii. 88–91.

EX. 10.3. *Comparison of versions of Mesangeau's allemande, bars 9–13, from British sources:*
(a) Lute I, Lawes Duet, Bodleian Mus. Sch. b. 2, p. 86; (b) O.16.2, p. 109; (c) Wemys MS,
fo. 32ʳ⁻ᵛ; (d) Pan 8, fos. 26ᵛ–27ʳ; and (e) from the French source, Ballard's 1638 book, p. 22

decade any known lute *contrepartie* in French sources.[171] The version of the Mesangeau allemande used by Lawes is reasonably accurate, when compared with the published version, though a few rhythmic variants are to be found and all ornamentation is absent. Although a twelfth course is not required in any of the duets, there can be little doubt that Lawes intended a 12-course lute to be used, as a $B\flat'$ on the eleventh is consistently required, and an 11-course lute in England *c.*1640 would be unlikely.[172]

The *contrepartie* is stylistically a perfect foil to the Mesangeau allemande (titled 'alman' in the manuscript), being no less subtle in its *brisé* texture (see Ex. 10.4). There are three places (bars 5, 9, and 13) in the *contrepartie* not found in the original allemande, where the second lute rests for two or three crotchet beats, which makes the *contrepartie* unsatisfactory as a solo piece, but in all other respects the two parts are completely equal and balanced. While the harmony is only marginally enriched by the addition of the *contrepartie*, the rhythmic flow is made considerably more intricate with the frequent use of dotted quavers in one, and undotted in the other, as on the last beat of the first bar. Occasionally, as in bars 3, 5, and 9, rhythmic or melodic motifs are passed from one lute to the other, but in the main the rhythmic and melodic ambiguity which is synonymous with the style is maintained throughout. Lute 2 usually moves in parallel thirds to Lute 1 at the approach to cadences, and generally shares the same bass line at the octave or unison.

The characteristics noted above in the 'alman' and *contrepartie* are also present in the two courantes that follow. The second lute part of the first courante is notable for the increased rhythmic activity (bars 12 and 21), and harmonic interest (bars 16 and 18). The second corant is remarkable for its use of high frets (up to the ninth fret in bars 1 and 16 of the first lute part), and frequent scale passages. Both these last features are characteristics of English lute practice rather than French. It is clear from these three duets that Lawes had a firm grasp of the new *brisé* style and could compose lute music as fine as that of contemporary French masters.

Among the repertoire of pieces in the new French style in transitional tunings that survive in British sources from 1625–60, the majority have no concordances. This group includes all the preludes, whether measured, unmeasured, or semi-measured. This is typical of almost all manuscript preludes at this time, as they appear to have been particularly personal pieces, which, apart from the few published ones, never achieved any degree of common circulation.[173] Many of this large group of unique pieces are similar to each other, but are sufficiently different to discount true concordances. Of particular importance in this respect are the many

---

[171] Rave, 'Some Manuscripts', 239, states that the earliest known French *contreparties* occur in the Reynaud MS, fos. 100ʳ and 114ᵛ–116ʳ in a layer of the MS that dates from the 1650–70 period.

[172] The Lowther pieces apart, pieces in British MSS for 11-course lute do not exist until *c.*1650.

[173] Rave, 'Some Manuscripts', 66.

PL. 10.10. Three duets for two 12-course lutes from William Lawes's auto-graph MS, Oxford, Bodleian Library, Mus. Sch. b. 2, p. 86

Ex. 10.4. *'Alman', lute duet from William Lawes's autograph MS, Bodleian Mus. Sch. b. 2, p. 86*

Ex. 10.5. *Sarabande, Pan 5, fo. 10ʳ, no. 19*

1. Tablature ↗ altered to read *a* in the upper part, ie. *a* not *b*.

simple sixteen-bar sarabandes, of which Ex. 10.5 is typical. Although there are many very similar pieces with identical phrase structure, including the usual repeated strummed chords on every alternate bar, they normally differ in some respect.[174] Usually the chord members are different, or the tessitura of the top line is different. It is likely that many of this large group of pieces elude concordance

[174] For instance, Pan 5, nos. 8, 15, 22, 28, 33, 36, 37, 41, 44, 79, and 80 are all sarabandes with similar phrase structure and strummed chords.

detection, owing to variant surviving texts. There are also cases of pieces which begin in a very similar fashion but after the opening few bars diverge markedly, and from that point onwards remain different in all respects.[175]

Of all the lute pieces in the early *brisé* style the piece known as 'Old Gautier's Nightingale' achieved the greatest popularity in Britain.[176] The tune on which it is based comes from the song 'O trop heureux' for voice and lute, published by Pierre Ballard in 1623. The anonymous published song was taken from the *Ballet de la Reyne* and is entitled 'Recit de Venus, et des Amours'.[177] The two earliest lute versions of this piece are probably those in Pan 5 (for 10-course lute) and the Pickeringe manuscript (for 12-course lute), which seem to date from the early 1630s. The title given to the piece in the much later Nanki manuscript of 'Old Gautiers Nightinghall' would seem to associate it with Ennemond (le Vieux) Gaultier. A second possibility is that the piece was composed by Jacques Gaultier, whose music might well have been known in France as well as England *c*.1630. Jacques's authorship would help to explain its persistent popularity in Britain in the period 1630–1700. The setting has more in common with the few works that can definitely be ascribed to him than with the works of Vieux Gaultier surviving in mid-century sources like the Robarts manuscript.

Remarkably, 'Old Gautier's Nightingale' appears in sources that span from the 1630s to the early eighteenth century. The varied repetition found in the lute version of Pan 5 and the Pickeringe, Wemyss, and Nanki manuscripts is interesting in that, instead of breaking up the chords into a more continuous *brisé* texture, the usual French treatment for a *double*, the tune is elaborated in semiquavers and quavers, as in the old Renaissance 'division' manner. (See Ex. 10.6.) Such elaboration techniques are rarely found in French sources after *c*.1630, but do appear in British sources.[178] In the Wemyss version of the piece each of the two strains of the tune is followed by a division (AA′BB′). In the Pickeringe, Pan 5, and the Nanki manuscript the divisions follow the two opening unelaborated strains (ABA′B′). On fo. 37ᵛ of the Wemys manuscript a further two divisions are found as a separate piece. These further divisions are also found in the Pickeringe and Nanki manuscript, where yet further divisions, not found in the Wemys manuscript, are also present.

The Bodley 410–414 version of 'Old Gautier's Nightingale' (Ex. 10.7) is the shortest, having no divisions.[179] It is noteworthy that Bodley 410–414 includes four of the most popular lute pieces in the extant British sources of this music (i.e. with

---

[175] For example, Pickeringe MS, fo. 46ᵛ, and Pan 5, fo. 30ʳ, no. 54.

[176] Matthew Spring, 'The Lady Margaret Wemyss Manuscript', *LSJ* 27 (1987), 5–30 at 10.

[177] *Airs de différents autheurs* (11–13th livres) published by Pierre Ballard (Paris, 1623; repr. Geneva, 1985), Livre 11, fos. 3ᵛ–4ʳ.

[178] Rave, 'Some Manuscripts', 46–8. The technique appears in the courante in Pan 8, fos. 22ᵛ–23ʳ (which appears also in Ros 34, p. 288, titled 'Courante de Gautier d'Angleterre').

[179] Tim Crawford, 'An Unusual Consort', 65. The piece is no. 15.

Ex. 10.6. *'Old Gaultier's Nightingale' from the Wemyss MS, fos. 38ᵛ–39ʳ*

1. Rhythm sign ⌐ missing in MS.
2. Rhythm sign ⌐ altered to ⌐.
3. Rhythm sign ⌐ altered to ⌐.

five or more concordances), as well as several other less well distributed pieces. With the exception of the suite of dances associated with 'Mr Birchingshaw' (none of which have any concordances) which end the collection, the manuscript appears to represent a selection of the most popular pieces in this genre of Francophile lute composition in England from the period 1630–60, arranged for a lute to play in consort with others. Many of the pieces, like 'Old Gautier's Nightingale', would have already been twenty years old by the 1650s. The extent to which this tune had

Ex. 10.7. *'Old Gautier's Nightingale' from Bodley 410–414, no. 15*

1. ♪ rhythm sign missing, added here.
2. Rhythm sign dot in MS ignored here.

become established as a popular tune is shown by its presence in several non-lute sources from 1650 to 1700.[180] It is certainly probable that many other popular tunes, especially those published by Playford, and fully established by 1660, had similar origins.

The one consistent genre of piece to be found in British lute sources from all periods is that of simple settings of popular tunes. With the adoption of transitional tunings the manner of tune setting altered to one of great simplicity. The *Lutes Apology* includes five very popular ballad tunes which were often used by Playford.[181] The general confusion, both harmonic and rhythmic, in Mathew's settings often results in badly distorted tunes. For example 'Halloo my Fancy' is obviously in common time, and not, as Mathew attempts to arrange it, in triple time. His setting of 'Bow bels' (Ex. 10.8) is successful up to the rhythm change at bar 9. However, the mixture of unharmonized bars (3, 7, and 8) with those having full chords is unsatisfactory, as are the parallel octaves in bars 5 and 10.

[180] These include John Playford, *Musick's Delight on the Cithren* (London, 1666), sig. C8, no. 38, 'Simphony I.P.'; *A Musicall Banquet in 3 Choice Varieties* (London, 1651), no. 29, 'A simphony' *a 2*; *GB-Och* 1179, p. 1, 'An Allman' (for keyboard). The title 'Simphony' may imply an association with a vocal piece rather than a dance; see Peter Holman, 'The "Symphony" ', *Chelys*, 6 (1975–6), 10–24.

[181] These are: no. 4, [Glory of the] 'West'; no. 8, 'New Rant'; no. 12, 'Gerard's Mistress'; no. 16, [Glory of the] 'North'; no. 17, 'Bowbells'. For Playford concordances of these pieces see Spring, 'The Lute in England and Scotland', ii. 192–7.

Ex. 10.8. *A comparison of 'Bow bels' set by* (a) *John Playford in* A Musicall Banquet *(1651), Part 1, p. 10, no. 12;* (b) *Richard Mathews in* The Lutes Apology *(1651), p. 20, no. 17*

1. Rhythm signs missing in lute version.
2. Rhythm sign in lute version altered from ♩ to ♩.
3. Barline missing in lute version.
4. Barring in both lute and lyra viol versions regularized from here to the end.

Another type of piece found in the manuscripts listed in Table 10.4 is that based on popular masquing tunes, some of which can be traced back to the original masque to which they belonged.[182] Evidently they remained in circulation long after the events for which they were written, and passed into the general currency of popular dance music. One example of this is the piece known by various titles, including 'The Lordes Mask' (*Parthenia In-Violata*, no. 2), 'The turtle dove' (Board, fo. 45ᵛ), and just 'A maske' (O.16.2, p. 132). Like most masque settings for lute it survives in Renaissance tuning only. The Add. 10444 version is called 'Cuperaree or Grays in' (fo. 28ᵛ). It originated from Beaumont's Masque of the *Inner Temple and Gray's Inn* of 20 February 1613.[183] The piece gained great popularity in the period 1613–50, as testified by settings for lyra viol, two trebles, keyboard, virginals, and bass, five-part string consort, and six-part wind consort. The string-consort version appeared in Brade's collection *Newe ausserlesene liebliche Branden* (1617) entitled 'Der Rothschenken Tanz'.[184] The Board manuscript has two versions of the piece (fos. 39ᵛ–40ʳ, and 45ᵛ) and O.16.2 has another (p. 132). These three versions have considerable differences, the O.16.2 version being the least affected by French developments in lute music. Here chords are slightly fuller, the rhythmic flow is less continuous, and the diapasons are only occasionally used.

In spite of the many scribal errors, the first Board version (fos. 39ᵛ–40ʳ) is stylistically the most advanced, with some use of dotted notes and semiquavers, such as at the close of the first strain, and a more flowing two-part texture (Ex. 10.9). The outer two parts of Brade's version conform almost exactly with the two parts of Add. 10444, and it may be that Coprario conceived the piece in these parts only, leaving the inner parts to be created by others. The first Board manuscript lute version follows these lines, but with the occasional appearance of full chords at important points, some use of an added inner part as in bar 4, a *brisé* style cadential ending at bar 8, and frequent octave displacement of the bass line (bars 1, 2, 4, 6, and 8) for rhythmic impetus and continuity to compensate for the lute's lack of sustain. These are the key devices that lutenists used in this period for the adaptation of popular dance pieces into lute solos.

The majority of pieces in the French style from English sources are anonymous and unique. The high degree of stylistic uniformity among the compositions of those Frenchmen who contributed to Ballard's 1631 and 1638 books (with the exception of the conservative Robert Ballard) makes it impossible to attribute pieces in this style to any of them on stylistic grounds alone. Thus the musical personalities of Mesangeau, Chancy, Chevalier, and Dufaut are virtually

---

[182] e.g. the two pieces entitled 'Simphony', which originate from *The Triumph of Peace* (1634).

[183] See *Four Hundred Songs and Dances from the Stuart Masques*, ed. Andrew Sabol (Providence, RI, 1978), nos. 101, 273, and 274.

[184] See *Board*, ed. Spencer, concordances for no. 157.

Ex. 10.9. *Comparison of the masque dance 'Cuperaree or Grays in' (a) by John Coprario from Add. 10444, fos. 28ᵛ–29ʳ and (b) in the Board MS, fos. 39ᵛ–40ʳ, bars 1–8*

1. ♩ Rhythm sign altered to ♩   4. Tablature chord in 3rd and 4th line obscured - here corrected
2. ♪ Rhythm sign absent in MS.   5. Two tablature rhythm signs omitted, here added.
3. Tablature ⌒ obscured in MS.   6. Tablature 'a' a line too low.

indistinguishable.[185] It is sometimes possible to single out on stylistic grounds pieces in British sources which are attempts by British composers to write in the French style of *c.*1630. The 'English' features to be looked for are: a willingness to use high registers; sparse use of *brisé* textures; regular rhythms and phrase lengths; and the inclusion of variations or divisions. Above all there is a conservatism in using the idiomatic clichés that were a standard feature of the *brisé* style, such as the various cadence formulae used most frequently in the final bars of phrases.

Clearly the most popular French lute composers in Britain at this time were Mesangeau and Dufaut, in that order. Although attributions in British sources to Frenchmen are often omitted (or erroneous), concordance evidence leads to a clear preponderance of pieces by these two. This is not surprising, as they were also held to be the leading composers of their day in France. Attributions to Chancy, Merville, Belleville, and Lespine do occasionally appear, but far less frequently.[186] It is perhaps surprising that there is not more music by Mercure in transitional tunings in British sources.[187] However, his activities and whereabouts are uncertain before 1641, when he gained his court appointment, and it is probable that the Burwell Tutor's assertion that he had 'lived a long time in England' refers to the period after 1641.[188] The piece in the Wemyss manuscript entitled 'Curent Lamecure' in the tuning no. 8 has nothing to distinguish it from those attributed to Dufaut and Mesangeau in the manuscript.

The most important French lutenist/composer as regards the development of lute composition in England after 1625 is Jacques Gaultier. Stylistic traits peculiar to Gaultier and that apply generally to the French style in Britain are: lack of consistent use of *brisé* texture; rhythmic predictability, especially the regular succession of quavers and dotted quavers; octave displacement in the melody; thinness of texture; some use of high fret positions; consistently accented position of bass notes; moments of unusual harmony; prominent, 'unaccompanied', melodic passages; use of the 12-course lute.[189] The surfacing of the Wemyss book has considerably enlarged the number of pieces and concordances which may be by Jacques Gaultier. The major part of his known output is seen to have survived in transitional tunings.[190] Possibly the few pieces in D minor tuning found in later sources, particularly Pan 4, were reworked from original versions in transitional tunings. Such a reworking probably accounts for the different versions of the piece found unattrib-

---

[185] Rave, 'Some Manuscripts', 61.

[186] e.g. Wemyss MS, fos. 36ʳ, 41ᵛ, 31ʳ, and 37ʳ respectively.

[187] Attributions to Mercure occur only in the Wemyss, Balcarres, and Ruthwen MSS among British and associated MSS.

[188] Burwell Tutor, fo. 5ᵛ.   [189] Rave, 'Some Manuscripts', 46.

[190] Excluding the many pieces in Renaissance tuning listed from Basle 53, Berlin 40165, and the Montbuysson and Herbert MSS, which may be by Jacques or Ennemond Gaultier.

uted in Pan 8 in tuning no. 10, and in Ros 54 in D minor tuning (attributed to 'Gaultier d'Angleterre').[191]

It is not apparent from the few known works by Gaultier that his style altered much in the period 1630–50, when the French lute style in France developed considerably. This may have resulted from his exile from France after 1617. The dominant position he held at court from 1625, coupled with his stylistic conservatism, probably did much to aid the fossilization of English lute practice in the period 1625–50 in a version of the French style *c.*1630.

In summary, surviving lute sources from 1625 to 1660 suggest that the early *brisé* style, exemplified by the music in Pierre Ballard's books of 1631 and 1638, and played in transitional tunings, can be regarded as the mainstream of serious lute composition in England. Much of Continental Europe also adopted the new French style, especially Germany and Sweden.[192] England seems to have been won over to the new style particularly early on in its development, and with considerable enthusiasm. There is also limited evidence of the continuation of an indigenous English style of lute composition in the pieces by Cuthbert Hely and John Wilson in Renaissance tuning to be found in the Herbert and Wilson manuscripts. The most prominent players of the solo lute in England were Frenchmen like Gaultier and Mercure, and the influence of Parisian lute masters like Mesangeau and Bourgaise was felt at first hand by Englishmen like Reymes and Robarts who studied the lute in Paris. It is during this period that the solo lute begins to become synonymous with the 'French Lute', an instrument that is both foreign and somewhat esoteric. That said, this process was a gradual one, and it is important stress both how popular and influential the new French *brisé* style of lute music was, especially in its earliest phase in 1625–40.

---

[191] Pan 8, fos. 22ᵛ–23ʳ; Ros 54, p. 288.

[192] For the influence of the French *brisé* style in Sweden at this time, see Kenneth Sparr, 'French Lutenists and French Lute Music in Sweden', in Jean-Michel Vaccaro (ed.), *Le Luth et sa musique*, ii (Paris, 1984), 59–67.

Chapter Eleven

The Theorbo

The *Theorboe*, is no other, than *That* which we call'd *the Old English Lute*; and
is an *Instrument* of so much *Excellency*, and *Worth, and of so Great Good Use*,
That in dispite of all *Fickleness*, and *Novelty*, It is still made use of, in the *Best
Performances in Musick, (Namely, Vocal Musick)*

Thomas Mace, *Musick's Monument* (1676), 207

The type of large lute with an extended neck, known in England in the seventeenth
century as the theorbo, originated in Italy in the final decades of the sixteenth century. In Italy the word 'tiorba' was synonymous with 'chitarrone', the name popu-
larly used for the same instrument in the first three decades of the seventeenth
century. The name chitarrone, from the Greek 'kithara', reflects the idea, strong in
the minds of the instrument's inventors, that the instrument was the modern counterpart of the kithara used by the self-accompanying poets of classical antiquity.
The chitarrone is first referred to in the six intermezzi that were part of the theatrical entertainment entitled *La Pellegrina*, performed in Florence in May 1589.
According to one account the singer/composer Jacopo Peri accompanied himself on
a chitarrone in a solo madrigal in the fifth intermezzo.[1] Peri was one of the earliest
of all opera composers, and the connection between opera and the theorbo remained
strong throughout the seventeenth century, the instrument being thought to be
especially suitable for the accompaniment of recitative.

Who exactly invented the theorbo is a question of some controversy, as several
people claim credit. Probably a number of individuals contributed to its invention.
Some contemporary commentators credit Antonio Naldi, who also took part in *La
Pellegrina*, with the invention. The lutenist-composer Alessandro Piccinini makes
no mention of Naldi, but relates a series of stringing experiments which he instigated as leading to the instrument's conception.[2] According to Piccinini large lutes
(presumably bass lutes in D) were restrung to give a resonant accompaniment for
the singers of *bel canto*, and in particular Giulio Caccini. Thinner strings had to be
used to raise the pitch, as much as a fourth or fifth, to that of an ordinary 'mean'
lute in G or A. With the long string length of a bass lute the two highest courses

[1] Kevin Mason, *The Chitarrone and its Repertoire in Early Seventeenth-Century Italy* (Aberystwyth, 1989), 18.
[2] Alessandro Piccinini, *Intavolatura di liuto et di chitarrone* (Bologna, 1623), 8, 'Dell'Arciliuto, e dell'inventore d'esso'.

had to be lowered an octave, giving a 're-entrant' tuning. It may be that the most defining characteristic of the theorbo is the use of a re-entrant tuning. (The term re-entrant refers to any stringing of an instrument in which adjacent strings do not successively rise in pitch).

Piccinini claims credit for having an extended pegbox put on the instrument to allow an additional set of contrabass strings lying off the fingerboard. This new design required the removal of the old, angled pegbox. The extension incorporated a lower set of pegs for the six stopped courses, and an upper set of pegs for the six to eight long unstopped courses.[3]

The Italian theorbo of the early seventeenth century was a hugely successful instrument, if the outpouring of publications of Italian monody is anything to go by. The primary instrument to accompany such songs was the theorbo, and the player was, from the very first, expected to construct his own part from a bass line, with or without continuo figures. Instruments may at first have been conversions from existing bass lutes, but completely new instruments were being constructed in some numbers by 1600. There is considerable variation in size and type of surviving Italian theorboes from the early seventeenth century. However, the typical early theorbo is a large 14-course instrument in A (stopped string length up to 93 cm., and unstopped basses up to 170 cm.), with the top two strings tuned down an octave, a triple rose, and with single courses throughout. Praetorius illustrates just such an instrument, and terms it the 'Lang Romanische Theorba: Chitarron'.[4]

In another woodcut Praetorius illustrates a 16-course 'Paduanische Theorba'. This instrument is altogether shorter, with a central rose, and a larger body relative to the neck. Like the Roman instrument it is tuned in A, with two re-entrant top strings. The Paduan theorbo differs in having eight, not six, stopped courses, and in having a small rose under the bass strings near the bridge.[5] It is noteworthy that even as early as 1619 Praetorius was aware of different types of Italian theorbo. Lutes without extended necks were still played in Italy at least until the mid-century, but gradually lutes with extended necks became the norm. Lutes with extended necks that had a stopped string-length short enough not to require re-entrant tuning were called either 'arciliuto' (archlute) or 'liuto attiorbato' (theorboed lute). The latter name implies that it was in the shape of a theorbo, though this term was only in use in books published between 1614 and 1623.[6] The archlute became increasingly popular as a continuo instrument after the mid-century, often at the expense of the theorbo.

[3] Mason, *The Chitarrone*, 24–30.

[4] Michael Praetorius, *Theatrum instrumentorum* (Wolfenbüttel, 1620), no. 16. For a tuning explanation see Michael Praetorius, *Syntagma musicum: De organographia* (Wolfenbüttel, 1619), 27.

[5] Spencer, 'Chitarrone, Theorbo and Archlute', 409.   [6] Ibid. 414.

In the same period that the chitarrone/theorbo was first developed, Italian solo lute music also underwent great change, and was clearly affected by the new aesthetic values proclaimed by Vincenzo Galilei and the Florentine Camerata. The toccata that replaced the fantasia as the most substantial abstract form in the lute and chitarrone books of Pietro Paolo Melli and Johannes Hieronimus Kapsberger shows the influence of the new monophonic recitative style of Peri and Caccini.[7] Gone is any attempt at strict polyphony. Instead, dramatic chord sequences and prolonged cadences are interspersed with fast, virtuosic, single-line 'passaggi'. The musical innovations first practised by the early monodists, intended primarily as a return to ancient principles, with the aim of allowing the affections of a given text to be expressed, were transposed into a purely instrumental medium. That many of those that advocated the new monodic style, like Vincenzo Galilei and Caccini, were lutenists or chitarrone players, undoubtedly helped this process.

Kapsberger, Melli, Michelangelo Galilei, and Alessandro Piccinini are quite individual in their style and, in the case of Kapsberger and Piccinini, prominently feature their own idiosyncratic techniques.[8] These last two were famous players of the theorbo/chitarrone which began to challenge the lute as a solo instrument after 1600.[9] The content of Italian lute books changed substantially in the period 1600–30, the toccata, corrente, and gagliarda supplanting the old divisions of fantasia, vocal intabulations, and assorted dance types.

Italian Renaissance lute music certainly influenced lute composition in the rest of Europe, but the extent to which Italian lute music absorbed northern influences is less easy to discern. Non-Italians, like Joannes Matelart and Kapsberger, who made their home in Italy, generally adopted the current Italian style when composing for the lute. After 1600 this one-sided exchange decreased, and Italian solo lute music continued its own development until around the mid-century. Italian lutenist composers from the time of Francesco da Milano up to Laurencini received generous representation in north European publications and manuscripts. The post-1600 generation of Italian lutenists received less attention north of the Alps, though there are sizeable numbers of Italian pieces in the Schele, Montbuysson, Haslemere, and Hainhofer manuscripts, and in Fuhrmann's *Testudo Gallo-Germanica* (1615). Melli and Galilei were both for a time attached to foreign courts (at Vienna and Munich respectively), yet by 1620 interest in Italian lute music and lute players was being eclipsed by the popularity of the new French style.

Bernardo Gianoncelli's *Il liuto* (1650) is the last published book for the solo lute in Italy. To be precise, all his pieces are for the 14-course 'liuto attiorbato', which

[7] Melli published five books between 1614 and 1620, and Kapsberger five books between 1604 and 1640.

[8] Stanley Buetens, 'The Instructions of Alessandro Piccinini', *JLSA* 2 (1969), 6–17. Piccinini advocates techniques such as the cadential 'groppo', 'tirate' (single-line runs), and the use of fingernails rather than flesh on the right hand, some of which may have been peculiar to him.

[9] See *New Grove*, iv. 289 for a list of Italian tablature sources for the chitarrone.

was developed and found favour only in Italy, and which was usually tuned in the old Renaissance tuning.[10] The chitarrone and, more particularly, the archlute found favour in Italy well into the eighteenth century. Later Italian tablatures for solo chitarrone and archlute proper appeared respectively in the form of Giovanni Pittoni's *Intavolatura di tiorba* (2 books in 1669), and Giovanni Zamboni's *Sonate d'intavolatura di leuto* (1718). Why the lute should decline so quickly after 1630, when a promising start had been made in the Italian Baroque style, has yet to be explained.[11]

In the first decades of the seventeenth century the theorbo became common as a continuo instrument throughout much of Europe. As the century progressed regional differences became more pronounced, such that Italian, French, and even English traditions of theorbos were recognized as being different. Information on the different types of lute-family instruments around at the end of the seventeenth century can be gleaned from the descriptions and measurements of instruments made by the Englishman James Talbot.[12] Talbot made detailed measurements of a number of lutes. These he divided up into the following categories: French; English; Angelique; Theorbo; Arch Lute; Apollon. The theorbo category was further subdivided into 'French' or 'English', and the French theorbo into 'bigger' or 'lesser'. No information is supplied for either the Apollon lute or larger French theorbo.[13] It is notable that Talbot makes no mention of the Italian theorbo, which by 1700 may have been completely superseded by the success in Italy and elsewhere of the archlute.

Tradition has it that the first theorbo ever seen in England was brought into the country by the architect and connoisseur Inigo Jones, around 1605. Jones designed many of James I's masques, and was the major artistic presence at the early Stuart Court. He returned from one of his Italian artistic sorties with a theorbo. One account has it that, 'at Dover it was thought some engine brought from Popish countries to destroy the king', and that 'he had it sent up to the Council Table'.[14] With such advance publicity the instrument cannot have failed to make an impact at court. Among the first patrons to aquire a theorbo was Henry Lord Clifford, who aquired one in April 1611, and is recorded as having played it himself in April

[10] In his *Intavolatura di liuto* (1623) Piccinini states that the liuto attiorbato was merely a synonym for an archlute, and he claims credit for the instrument's invention. Melli also published music for it in his *Intavolatura di liuto attiorbato, libro secondo* (1614). Gianoncelli includes several pieces in a transitional tuning (no. 6) on pp. 10–12 of his book, although this is an isolated instance of the use of transitional tunings in a work by an Italian lutenist.

[11] Victor Anand Coelho, *The Manuscript Sources of Seventeenth-Century Italian Lute Music* (New York, 1995), 35.

[12] Robert Unwin, 'An English Writer on Music: James Talbot 1664–1708' *GSJ* 40 (1987), 53–72.

[13] Michael Prynne, 'James Talbot's Manuscript: IV. Plucked Strings—The Lute Family', *GSJ* 14 (1961), 52–68.

[14] 'Inigo Jones first br. ye Theorbo in. Engl. circa an 605. at Dover it w. thought sm Engn br. frõ Pop. cuntris to destr. ye K & He & it sent up to Cn Tabl'. Dr Plume's Library, Malden, Essex, pocket-book no. 25. Quotation from Spencer, 'Chitarrone, Theorbo and Archlute', 420 n. 17.

1617.[15] The earliest known depiction of a theorbo in England appears in a portrait of Mary Sidney, Lady Wroth, in Penshurst Place, Kent, dated *c*.1620 (see Pl. 11.1). (For a list of other examples see Table 11.1.) The instrument is similar to Praetorius' Paduan theorbo. It has thirteen single courses, six of which are stopped. Mary Sidney was a niece of the poet Philip Sidney, and daughter of Robert Sidney. Lady Mary was taught the lute and virginals at a young age.[16] She was a woman of some literary pretensions and her *Urania*, a book very much in the mould of her uncle's famous *Arcadia*, caused a court scandal with its thinly veiled allusions to Jacobean court personalities. Possibly the theorbo is present to draw attention to her poetic pretensions.

The Paduan singer, composer, and lutenist Angelo Notari arrived in England around 1610/11, serving first Prince Henry, then Prince Charles. He may have come in the company of Constantine de' Servi, the prince's Florentine architect, who travelled from Paris in June 1611.[17] He was nominally part of the king's music from 1625 until his death in 1663, allowing for a period of absence during the Civil War and interregnum. Before his arrival in England he had been a member of the Venetian Accademia degli Sprovisti (with the nickname 'Il Negligente'), and was an exponent of *bel canto* singing. He published his *Prime musiche nuove* in London in 1613. It contains monodies, duets, and canzonettas of up to three voices with a bass line. The title-page states they are 'per Cantare con la Tiorba, et altri Strumenti'.[18] Although the songs are all in Italian, and may for the most part have been written while in Italy, the preface is in English, and is directed to an English readership. It is a landmark in the introduction of Italian recitative style into England, and argues for the early presence of Italian theorbos in England. Notari's activities as a scribe, writing out large amounts of Italian music throughout much of his long working life in England, is also important, as so much of this material would require theorbos.[19] His autograph manuscript, probably dating from the 1620s, contains a large number of Italian monodies and other music, some with tablature accompaniments for a 10-course theorbo in A.[20]

The rather static non-polyphonic bass lines found in Notari's songs, which are ideal for supporting florid vocal lines, begin to appear in songs by English composers. Notari makes a distinction in his trios between the vocal bass line and the instrumental bass, even though they are printed on the same stave. Lanier's song to

[15] Hulse, 'Musical Patronage', 224.

[16] Price, *Patrons and Musicians*, 172.

[17] Holman, *Four and Twenty Fiddlers*, 201.

[18] Stanley Boorman, 'Notari, Porter and the Lute', *LSJ* 13 (1971), 28–35.

[19] Pamela J. Willets, 'Autographs of Angelo Notari', *M&L* 50 (1969), 124–6; 'A Neglected Source of Monody and Madrigal', *M&L* 43 (1962), 329–39.

[20] *GB-Lbl* Add. 31440. Tablature appears on fos. 20ᵛ, 69ᵛ, and 70ʳ.

PL. 11.1. Mary Sidney, Lady Wroth with theorbo *c.*1620, attributed to
John de Critz (1555–1641). Penshurst, Kent

Table 11.1. *List of English lute/theorbo/theorbo-lute/archlute iconography 1620–1800*

Source	Date and place	Comments
Painting of Lady Mary Wroth	c.1620, Penshurst Place	13-course single-strung theorbo
Engraving by Jan Lievens of Jacques Gaultier	c.1630–33	12-course lute
Drawing by Inigo Jones	1632, collection the Duke of Devonshire	drawing of a masque musician playing a Renaissance-type lute
Painting of Sir Thomas Aston by John Souch	c.1635, Manchester City Art Gallery	12-course lute
Painting of Anne Heydon aged 8	before 1637, Audley End, Essex	neck of instrument obscured
Painting by Dobson of Lady Isabella Thynne	c.1645, Longleat House Wiltshire	12-course lute
Painting of Lady Anne Clifford	1646, Appleby Castle, Cumbria	12-course lute
Painting (*vanitas*)	c.1650, Norwich Castle Museum	12-course lute
Painting of Lady Margaret Hey	Floors Castle, Kelso	12-course lute
Painting by Sir Peter Lely	c.1650, private collection	12-course
Painting of Lady Anne Bruce	c.1660, Stirling Castle	12-course lute
Painting of Robert Robarts	c.1660, Llanhydrock House, Cornwall	double-strung ?French theorbo
Painting by John Michael Wright of unknown lady	c.1670, Columbus Museum of Fine Art, Ohio	11-course lute, the 4 lowest courses each have individual nuts
Painting of Lady Margaret Hay, Countess of Roxburghe	c.1670, Scottish National Portrait Gallery	12-course lute
Engraving	*Musick's Monument*, 1676, p. 32	Thomas Mace's lute-dyphone
Painting by Thomas Murray of Henrietta d'Averqueque, Countess of Grantham	c.1700, Whitfield Fine Art, London	11-course French lute
Engraving of Arabella Hunt	c.1706	11-course French lute
Mezzotint, James McArdell (1728–65) after Allen Ramsey	c.1750, New Haven, Yale arch Centre for British Art	archlute? held by Mary Viscountess Coke
Painting *The Sharpe Family*, by Johann Zoffany	1779–81, National Portrait Gallery	13-course Baroque lute (swan neck)

Ex. 11.1. *'Qual Musico gentil' by Nicholas Lanier, Add. 11608, fo. 27ᵛ, bars 1–12*

an Italian text by Tasso, 'Qual Musico gentil', has a very simple bass line and occasional figures that argue for a theorbo (see Ex. 11.1).[21]

Walter Porter was a member of the Chapel Royal from 1616/17, and famously claimed Monteverdi as 'my good friend and Maestro'. He published his *Madrigales and Ayres* (London, 1632) 'To be performed with the Harpesechord, Lutes, Theorbos, Base Violl, two Violins or two Viols'. This collection of instruments sounds like a typical masque band drawn from the king's Lutes and Voices. Porter sang in a number of court masques, and was one of the singer/theorbo players in the *Triumph of Peace* (1634). There is a clear stylistic distinction between the more contrapuntal madrigals and the more declamatory airs. Many of the pieces have ritornellos, or sinfonias which call for violins or viols, and bass. There are two separate bass part-books, one of which is normally figured. 'Farewell once my delight' is a florid solo song with unfigured bass in the *stilo recitativo*, and would seem ideally suited to a large theorbo.

Theorbos were occasionally heard in Jacobean court masques. *The Masque of Flowers* (1614) incorporated a song 'sung to Lutes and Theorboes' (sig. C2). The earliest court record of payment for a theorbo reads 'To John Kelley, one of his Maᵗˢ Musicons, by warrant dated 30–3–1627, for a Theorbo by him bought and provided for his Maᵗˢ service: £8. 0s. 0d'.[22] In the 1630s it would seem that large numbers of theorbos were being used in court masques. Instruments at £15 each were bought by the Crown for 'Mr Robert' [Anthony Robert] and 'Nicholas Lanier' in 1632 and 1633 respectively.[23] The stage and masque songs of Robert Johnson survive in sources without tablature accompaniments. They are representative of the first

[21] *GB-Lbl* Add. 11608, fo. 27ᵛ.   [22] *RECM* iii. 138.   [23] Ibid. 66, 70.

generation of songs which were composed with a continuo realization in mind, though a lute or theorbo are equally suitable for their performance.

Nicholas Lanier travelled extensively in Italy in the 1620s, and was both familiar with, and impressed by, the Italian recitative style.[24] Lanier's dramatic recitative, 'Nor com'st thou yet, my slothful love' is titled 'Hero's Complaint to Leander. In Recitative Musick' in Playford's *Choice Ayres and Songs* (1683). Roger North tells us that after his return from Italy [in 1628] Lanier 'composed a *recitativo*, which was a poem being the tragedy of Hero and Leander, which for many years went about from hand to hand, even after the Restauration, and at last crept out (wretchedly drest) among Playford's collections in print'.[25] The piece is an early attempt at setting English words in the Italian recitative style, and by far the most appropriate instrument for realizing the continuo bass is a large Italian theorbo in A.

A number of the French musicians of Henrietta Maria certainly played the theorbo—among them Jacques Gaultier, Nicholas Duvall, and Anthony Robert. The influence of French solo music was always present in England, and it is reasonable to suppose that as a separate French theorbo tradition developed, it was imported soon after by Frenchmen and their English admirers. A portrait of Robert Robarts with his theorbo hangs in Llanhydrock House, Cornwall. Robert, like his brother Hender of the Robarts lute manuscript, was sent to Paris to study in 1654. Theorbos may have been relatively rare in France until the mid-century.[26] Until 1643 books of *airs de cour* were published either for unaccompanied voices or for solo voice and lute.[27] After 1643 French *airs* were normally published with a figured or unfigured bass that could be realized on a theorbo. It is only after 1660 that French tutors for the theorbo were produced, and that a solo repertoire emerged.

There is evidence for two sizes of French theorbo: a small instrument for solo music, and a larger one for accompaniment. Talbot measured two lesser French theorbos, one of which was 'fitt for lessons' with eight stopped strings and six diapasons. This instrument was tuned a fourth higher (in D) than the usual French theorbo in A. Typically, it seems that French theorbos had only one rose, were not multi-ribbed, and had shorter diapasons than Italian theorbos. Like Italian instruments they were normally pitched in A with the top two courses tuned re-entrantly. All three French theorbos that Talbot mentions were single strung throughout, although there were exceptions, as shown in the famous picture of the musicians of Louis XIV, painted by Francois Puget in 1687, which shows a double-strung theorbo.[28] The instrument held by the 8-year old Miss Anne Heydon in a painting at Audley End appears to be small, with thirteen single courses and an extended

---

[24] Macdonald Emslie, 'Nicolas Lanier's Innovations in English Song', *M&L* 41 (1960), 13–27; Ian Spink, 'English Cavalier Songs, 1620–1660', *PRMA* 86 (1960), 61–78.

[25] *Roger North on Music*, 294.

[26] Spencer, 'Chitarrone, Theorbo and Archlute', 413.

[27] Le Cocq, 'The Pitch and Tuning of the Lute', 48.   [28] See the front cover of *EM* 4 (Oct. 1976).

neck. Clear identification of the instrument is impossible because the upper neck of the instrument is obscured behind drapery (see Pl. 11.2).

The lute bought for Nicholas Lanier in 1633 for £15 is referred to in accounts as a 'Theorba Lute'. The term 'theorbo lute' continues to appear in English accounts and song publications until the end of the seventeenth century. (See Table 11.4.) This imprecise term has any number of possible meanings. Theorbo lute may imply simply any kind of lute, with or without an extended neck, if used as a continuo instrument. Alternatively it may mean specifically a lute which has been altered such that the old pegbox, and possibly the neck as well, has been removed and a new theorbo-type extension put on; in effect a theorboed-lute. Yet again, it is possible that a double-headed 'English' lute as devised by Jacques Gaultier is implied. Twelve-course lutes were played in Renaissance tuning, and were used to accompany songs. My interpretation is that it is a catch-all term that would incorporate any type of continuo lute, and could be varied according to circumstance. It may be that the most defining characteristic of the term theorbo, consistent with all these different types of instruments, is the use of a re-entrant top course.[29]

Well over fifteen hundred so-called 'Cavalier songs' survive today in over two dozen manuscripts that were produced between 1625 and 1660.[30] (See Table 11.2) Many of these songs, although written much earlier, appeared in print only after 1651, with the commencement of music printing by John Playford following the Civil War period. From what we know of these songs it would seem that some form of lute or theorbo would be the most appropriate instrument for realizing the bass line.[31] Many of the more prolific composers, like the Lawes brothers, Nicholas Lanier, John Wilson, Charles Coleman, William Caesar, and John Jenkins, are known to have been theorbo players. Henry Lawes's theorbo, with the arms of the Earl of Bridgewater, the patron for whom he produced the masque *Comus*, survived until the last century.[32] Few, if any, figures are present in these songs, and the instrumentalist was expected to construct a chordal harmony using the bass and treble lines, and 'the rule of the octave'.[33] Even after the Restoration, the theorbo was still the most popular instrument for song accompaniment, and it is not until the songs of Blow and Purcell that a keyboard becomes more appropriate.[34]

[29] Lynda Sayce, 'Continuo Lutes in 17th and 18th-Century England', *EM* 23 (1995), 667–84.

[30] For a complete facsimile edition see the series English Song 1600–1675, ed. Elise Bickford Jorgens, 26 vols. (New York, 1986–9). For a representative selection see *English Songs 1625–1660*, ed. Ian Spink (MB 33; London, 1971; rev. edn., 1977).

[31] *English Songs 1625–1660*, ed. Spink, p. xix.   [32] Poole, 'The Oxford Music School', 144.

[33] Mace, *Musick's Monument*, 217. See also Nigel North, *Continuo Playing on the Lute, Archlute and Theorbo* (London, 1987), 40, and Wendy Hancock, 'General Rules for Realising an Unfigured Bass in Seventeenth-Century England', *Chelys*, 7 (1977), 69–72.

[34] The best index to this change are the title-pages of printed songbooks listed in Cyrus L. Day and Eleanore B. Murrie, *English Song-Books 1651–1702* (London, 1940).

PL. 11.2. Miss Anne Heydon (aged 8) 1629–1700, painted in 1637 by an unknown artist. Audley End

Table 11.2. *Major manuscript collections of Cavalier songs with bass lines suitable for lute/theorbo accompaniment*

Siglum	Name/date	Description
GB-Lbl Add. 24665	Giles Earle's book dated 1615	lute songs in versions for treble and bass only
GB-Lbl Egerton 2971	c.1620	28 items. Mainly songs with unfigured bass; a few with lyra-viol tablature accompaniments
GB-Ob Tenbury 1018	c.1620	52 solo songs, including 25 in Italian, of which 15 by G. Caccini; most with an unfigured bass
GB-Ob Tenbury 1019	c.1620	2 songs out of 13 with unfigured bass
GB-Och 439	c.1620	83 songs, most with an unfigured bass, plus a few pieces and exercises for lyra viol. Some songs by Byrd and lute-song composers
US-NYp Drexel 4175	Anne Twice's songbook c.1620–30	28 songs (out of original list of 58) 18 have an unfigured bass
GB-Och 87	Mrs Elizabeth Davenant's songbook, c.1624	25 songs, most with an unfigured bass
GB-Ob Don. c.57	1625–40	160 English songs. Most have an unfigured bass
GB-Lbl Add. 53723	Henry Lawes's autograph songbook, c.1625–50	325 songs, most with an unfigured bass
GB-Lbl Add. 29481	c.1630	28 vocal items. Mainly solo songs with an unfigured bass drawn from the lute-song repertoire
GB-Lbl Egerton 2013	c.1630	75 song entries. Over 50 solo songs with an unfigured bass
GB-Lbl Add. 29396	Songs in the hand of Edward Lowe, c.1636–80	105 songs including some dialogues. Most have an unfigured bass
GB-Lbl Add. 31432	William Lawes's autograph songbook, c.1639–41	77 entries. Mainly solo songs with an unfigured bass. Also songs for 3 voices, dialogues, and viol pieces
US-NYp Drexel 4041	c.1640–50	149 songs, most with an unfigured bass
GB-Lbl Add. 11608	Associated with John Hilton, c.1641–56	102 songs, mostly solos songs with unfigured bass. Some songs with more than one vocal part
GB-Lbl Add. 32339	John Gamble's book c.1650–60	77 songs, all but 6 attributed to Gamble. Most have an unfigured bass
GB-Lbl Add. 10337	Elizabeth Rogers Virginal Book, dated 1656	24 songs, 6 with keyboard accompaniment, 18 with an unfigured bass
GB-Ob Mus b. 1.	John Wilson's songbook c.1656	224 items. c.180 are solo songs with an unfigured bass
US-NYp Drexel 4257	John Gamble's songbook c.1659	329 songs, most with an unfigured bass
GB-Eu Dc.1.69	Songs in the hand of Edward Lowe, after 1660	129 songs. One of a set of three books (the cantus secundus being GB-Ob Mus. d.238). Related to Wilson's *Cheerfull Ayres* (1660). Most songs also have an unfigured bass

Table 11.3. *List of English manuscripts containing songs with continuo realizations in tablature for lute, theorbo, or archlute*

Date	Source	Comments
*c.*1630	*GB-Lbl* Eg. 2013	Contains 22 songs (out of 75) with tablature for an 11-course instrument in G and A
*c.*1630	*US-NYp* Drexel 4175 'Ann Twice Her Booke'	Contains 6 songs (out of 28) with lute tablature for a 10-course instrument in G. 4 songs with lyra-viol tablature accompaniments
*c.*1630	*GB-Ob* Mus. Sch. f. 575 Given by William Ives in a large collection of lyra viol music for the use of the Oxford Music School	10 English songs with tablature for a 10-course instrument in G
*c.*1630	*GB-Ob* MS Don c.57	13 songs (out of 160) with a tablature for 10-course instrument in G, 3 of which also have an unfigured bass. One solo lute piece. Also a tablature exercise marked 'Stops on the Theorbo'
*c.*1640	Lambeth Palace 1041 Lady Anne Blount songbook	16 songs for a 13-course theorbo (mainly in A). 11 songs which only use 10 courses (mainly in G), and 11 songs which require 11 courses (mainly in A)
*c.*1656	*GB-Ob* Mus. Sch. b. 1 John Wilson songbook	37 songs (out of 224) for a 12-course instrument in G, the last 23 in Latin
*c.*1690, 1710, and 1720	Tokyo, Nanki Music Library Nanki n-4/42	8 songs with tablature for a 12-course lute in G (not all of which are complete). Also 7 songs and two solos for a 13-course archlute in G

Among the English manuscript collections of songs produced in the period 1625–75 are a number with tablature parts. (See Table 11.3.) Clearly the scribes responsible for these tablature parts had different instruments, and we can be sure that there was no standardized accompanimental lute or theorbo in England at this time. For instance, *GB-Ob* Don c.57 and *GB-Ob* Mus. Sch. f. 575 require only a 10-course instrument, yet some songs in Ann Blount's songbook require up to thirteen courses.[35]

Example 11.2 gives the song 'Sing aloud harmonious spheres' from the Ann Blount songbook. There are five different pitches of lute implied in the twenty-eight songs with tablature in this source, so it is seems clear that the voice part is transposing. The vocal line in this song is written in B flat and it is most unlikely that an instrument in C was used for this song alone. It is noticeable how little the

[35] North, *Continuo Playing*, 296–7.

top course is required in Ex. 11.2. This is true of many of the Cavalier songs with tablature accompaniments in English sources. The great majority of settings suggest an instrument pitched in G, not A. This leads to the proposition that even before the mid-century there was in effect an 'English theorbo', with qualities rather different from foreign instruments. We know that Talbot recognized a distinct 'English Theorbo', and that he had measurements or notes on three instruments, two of which could be single or double strung. There is great variation in the arrangement and number of strings on his English theorbos, but they all have single strings for the top course, which may or may not be re-entrant. The song in Ex. 11.2 suggests a re-entrant course for the top string only, as a re-entrant second course would be unsatisfactory in bar 11. As the English theorbo was normally tuned in G rather than A, this seems the best pitch at which to transcribe this song. The most important characteristic of English instruments, however, is that they have basses of graduated length,[36] and stepped nuts. Two such nuts are seen in the painting by John Michael Wright (see Pl. 11.3). As we might expect, the intabulated accompaniment includes little in the way of true inner parts, the theorbo texture serving to enhance the melodic and dramatic characteristics of the bass line.

As mentioned in Chapter 10, Jacques Gaultier is credited with the invention of the double-headed lute. The second pegbox has a series of stepped nuts, one each for the bottom four courses. The success of this design in England surely explains the incorporation of stepped nuts on English theorbos. Such theorbos are described by both Talbot and Mace, and their use is confirmed in a number of pictures. Approaching the age of 60, Mace was suffering from increasing deafness, such that he could not hear his own lute. His response was to construct his quixotic 'Lute Dyphone' in 1672.[37] Of it he says:

for although I cannot hear the least *Twang* of any other *Lute*, when I *Play* upon It; yet I can hear *This, in a very Good Measure*; yet not so *Loud*, as to *Distinguish Every Thing I Play*, without the *Help of My Teeth*; which when I lay *Close to the Edge of It*, (*There*, where the *Lace is Fix'd*) I hear *All I Play Distinctly*; so that *It* is to Me *(I Thank God) One of the Principal Refreshments, and Contentments I Enjoy in This World.*[38]

The reversible Lute Dyphone (see Pl. 11.4), although a 'one off', is instructive, as it incorporates a 12-course double-headed lute (called the English lute by Talbot), which Mace refers to as 'French', with an English theorbo, referred to by Mace as 'English'. Of its benefits it combines in one instrument the two '*Most Compleat*, and *Useful Lutes* . . . The *Majestick Theorboe*, either for *Voice*, *Organ*, or *Consort*, *etc.* and The *High Improved French Lute*, for *Airy*, and *Spruce, Single* or *Double Lessons*'.[39] The lute end has twelve double courses, the theorbo end thirteen

---

[36] Prynne, 'James Talbot's Manuscript', 58–67.
[38] Ibid. 203.
[37] Mace, *Musick's Monument*, 32.
[39] Ibid. 204.

Ex. 11.2. *'Sing aloud', anonymous song from Ann Blount's Song Book, Lambeth Palace, MS 1041, fo. 5ᵛ*

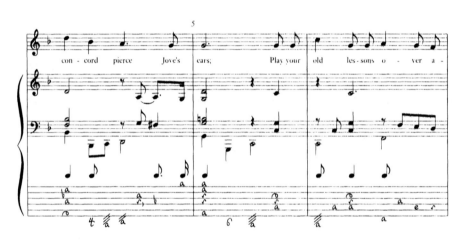

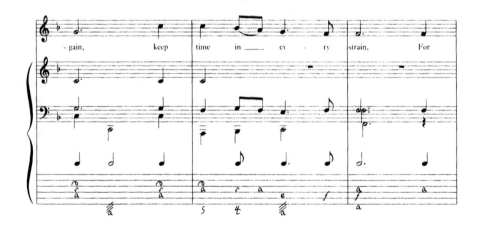

1. These dots indicate a rest and are unique to this scource.

NB. the vocal part has been transposed down a fourth to fit a theorbo in G.

double courses: both are tuned with the top course at *g'*. An advantage for Mace is that 'the *Head* of the *Theorboe* is *much Shorter, than most Theorboes*'.[40] Very long heads he finds troublesome to tune, inconsistent, and unbalanced, 'Whereas *This Instrument* is so *Proportionably* made, that each *Diapason Descends Gradually, Step by Step*; by which means, the whole *Number*, both of *Short*, and *Long, Strings, Speak Uniformly*, and *Evenly* to *Themselves*; which is a very *Considerable Matter*, in any *Instrument*'.[41]

Of the forty-three chapters that make up Mace's '*The Lute made Easie*', which itself is the second and much the largest part of *Musick's Monument*, only the last two chapters are devoted to the theorbo. Chapter 42 deals with its distinctive identity, and supplies a long practice piece.

Chapter 43 deals with realizing a continuo bass and gives a variety of exercises, particularly for cadences and '*Breaking your Parts*'.[42] The long piece covers a number of interesting effects possible on the theorbo, and has much to recommend it for both practice and performance. From the latter chapter it is clear that for Mace a full-sized theorbo normally has thirteen double courses and is tuned in G, although he mentions smaller theorbos in A, and instruments with only twelve courses.[43] That English theorbos could be tuned in A is confirmed by two of Talbot's English theorbos.[44]

At the outset of chapter 42 Mace tells us that '*the Theorboe-Lute is Principally us'd in Playing to the Voice, or in Consort; It being a Lute of the Largest Scize; and we make It much more Large in Sound*, by contriving unto *It a Long Head, to Augment and Increase that Sound, and Fulness of the Basses, or Diapasons, which are a great Ornament to the Voice, or Consort*'.[45] He gives three reasons why it is differentiated from the lute: that it is too large to play solo lessons; that the top string is tuned down an octave (and sometimes the top two strings); that the long diapasons are a great inconvenience, and sound for too long a time in solo lessons. In his one theorbo piece he uses the re-entrant top course sparingly (Ex. 11.3). In the main he is sensitive to the problems of the octave displacement of this course, although there are some places where it seems that little account is taken of it—which results in melodic descents of a seventh where a rising step would be expected. Campanella effects, made easy by re-entrant stringing, and which were fully utilized by Italian chitarrone players, do not appear to have been much used by English theorbo players, if Mace's piece and the few other surviving tablatures are anything to go by. However, Mace's emphasis on 'breaking' chords into arpeggiated patterns suggests it may have been a strong feature of English theorbo continuo realization. It is noticeable in Ex. 11.3 that Mace has recourse to the fifth fret on the second course

---

[40] Mace, *Musick's Monument*, 205.   [41] Ibid.   [42] Ibid. 228.   [43] Ibid. 216–18.
[44] Prynne, 'James Talbot's Manuscript', 60.   [45] Mace, *Musick's Monument*, 207.

PL. 11.3. Lady with a theorbo by John Michael Wright (*c*.1617–1700), painted *c*.1670. The Columbus Museum of Art, Columbus, Ohio

PL. 11.4. The Lute Dyphone in Thomas Mace, *Musick's Monument*, p. 32

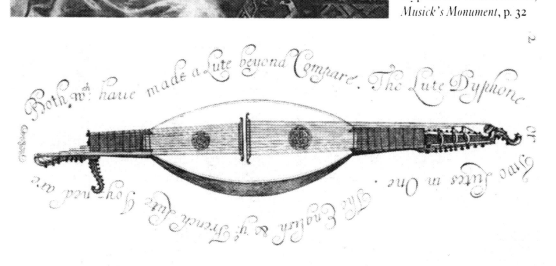

Both, w.ᵗʰ haue made a Lute beyond Compare. The Lute Dyphone or Two Lutes in One. The English & y.ᵉ French Lute ioyned are

W. Fathorne fec.

Concerning this Instrument Reade Pag: 203.

Ex. 11.3. *'A Fancy-Praelude, or Voluntary', by Thomas Mace,* Musick's Monument *(1676),* p. *210, bars 1–8*

in bar 5 to articulate the *g′*, rather than the open top course, which would sound an octave. Arpeggiation becomes the dominant feature of later sections of this piece.

Mace expects figures to be provided for the theorbo player 'in all *Places of Exception*'.[46] There are few if any figures in consort music or song accompaniments before the mid-century. The printing of continuo songs began in 1652 with John

⁴⁶ Mace, *Musick's Monument,* 226.

Playford's *Select Musicall Ayres, and Dialogues, . . . to sing to the Theorbo, Lute, or Basse Violl* (see Table 11.4). Most of the books printed at least until the 1680s specify the theorbo or theorbo-lute as a suitable accompaniment instrument (see Pl. 11.5). The period of the Restoration was perhaps the high-water mark in the use of the theorbo. The Exchequer provided money for seven theorbos (or theorbo-lutes) between 1660 and 1678.[47] Henry Cooke, Pelham Humphrey, and John Blow, successive Masters of the Children of the Chapel Royal from 1660 to 1679, were paid to teach a number of instruments to the children.[48] The theorbo or lute was always among them. Two of the seven theorbos bought by the Crown were for the Children of the Chapel.[49]

As with lute-song publications, the bass viol was sometimes suggested as an alternative to the theorbo, but never as an optional extra in songbook publications after 1650 (see Table 11.4).[50] While most amateurs would have played just the bass line, an experienced viol player might have realized a bass line in lyra viol fashion.[51] Between 1660 and 1680 the harpsichord is often absent from the title-page list of possible instruments for accompaniment, after which point it increasingly heads the list.[52] From 1700 there is far less mention of the lute, theorbo, or theorbo-lute in songbook title-pages, although these instruments and the archlute do occasionally appear. The more complex figures and increased activity and range of the bass lines in the songs of Blow and Purcell, as compared with those of the previous generation, make accompaniment on the theorbo alone quite awkward, and we can assume that by the mid-1680s the harpsichord was the preferred instrument.

A sizeable amount of consort music from the period 1625–70, especially dance music, specifies the inclusion of theorbos (see Table 11.5), and much other instrumental music of the period would benefit from their inclusion.[53] Mace, in his section '*Concerning the Viol*, and *Musick in General*', recommends the theorbo in a number of circumstances: to substitute for the organ in vocal works; in consorts together with the complicated harpsichord-like instrument called the 'pedal'; in instrumental music to balance violins.[54] He has a particular dislike of '*Squaling-Scoulding-Fiddles*',[55] but thought two violins could responsibly be used 'with a *Pair of Lusty Full-Sciz'd Theorboes*'.[56] His reference to theorbos being used in the music meetings of former times is compounded by a mass of evidence of instrumental practice pre-1670.

---

[47] *RECM* i. 37, 39, 124, 128 (2 instruments), 178, 187.

[48] Ibid. 124, 128, 157; v. 118–19, 146–7, 151.   [49] Ibid., i. 128.

[50] Jones, ' "To sing and play to the Base-Violl alone" '. See also Day and Murrie, *English Song-Books*.

[51] Samuel Pepys learnt to sing and play at least two songs in this way. See Pepys, *The Diary of Samuel Pepys*, ed. Robert Latham and William Matthews, 11 vols. (London, 1970–83), i. 59, 76.

[52] Day and Murrie, *English Song-Books*.   [53] North, *Continuo Playing*, 22.

[54] *Musick's Monument*, 235, 236, 246.   [55] Ibid. 204.   [56] Ibid. 246.

Table 11.4. *List of principal song publications from England (1613–1730) which mention lute, theorbo, theorbo-lute, or archlute, it their titles as possible instruments for realizing a continuo bass*

Date	Title/composer	Instrument type
1613	*Prime musiche nuove*, Angelo Notari	la Tiorba et altri strumenti
1632	*Madrigales and Ayres*, Walter Porter	Harpsechord, Lutes, Theorbes, Base Violl
1639/1650	*The first set of psalmes*, William Child	Organ or Theorbo
1652	*Second Book of Ayres* [various]	Theorbo, Harpsicon, or Basse Violl
1652	*Select Musicall Ayres and Dialogues* [various]	Theorbo, Lute, or Base Violl
1653	*Select Musicall Ayres and Dialogues*, pub. John Playford	Theorbo or Basse Violl
1656–7	*Ayres and Dialogues*, John Gamble	Theorbo-Lute or Base-Violl
1657	*Motetts of two voyces*, Walter Porter	organ, harpsycon, lute or viol
1657	*Psalterium Carolinum*, John Wilson	organ or theorbo
1659	*Ayres and Dialogues*, John Gamble	Theorbo-Lute or Basse-Viol
1659	*Select Ayres and Dialogues* [various]	Theorbo-Lute or Basse Violl
1663	*Select Ayres and Dialogues* [various]	Theorbo-Lute
1668	*Poems of Mr Cowley and, others*, William King	Theorbo, Harpsecon or Base-violl
1669	*Select Ayres and Dialogues*, Henry Lawes	Theorbo-Lute or Basse-Viol
1669	*The Treasury of Musick*, Henry Lawes	Theorbo-Lute, or Basse-Viol
1673–9	*Choice Songs and Ayres* [various]	Theorbo-Lute or Bass-Viol
1678	*New Ayres, Dialogues and Trialogues* [various]	Theorbo-Lute or Bass-Viol
1681–4	*Choice Ayres and Songs* [various]	Theorbo-Lute, or Bass-Viol
1685–6	*The Theatre of Music* [various]	Theorbo, or Bass-Viol
1685	*A Third Collection of New Songs* [various]	Theorbo, and Bass-Viol
1687	*A Collection of the Choy[c]est and newest Songs* [various]	Harpsichord Theorbo or Bass-Violl
1687–94	*Comes Amoris* [various]	Harpsichord, Theorbo, or Bass-Violl
1687	*The Theatre of Music* [various]	Harpsichord, Theorbo, or Bass Viol
1687–91	*Vinculum Societatis* [various]	Harpsichord, Theorbo, or Bass-Viol
1688–92	*The Banquet of Musick* [various]	Theorbo-Lute, Bass-viol, Harpsichord or Organ

Date	Title/composer	Instrument type
1688	*Harmonia Sacra*, pub. Henry Playford	Theorbo-Lute, Bass-viol, Harpsichord or Organ
1693	*Harmonia Sacra, the second book* [various]	Theorbo-Lute, Bass-viol, Harpsichord or Organ
1693–1706	*Thesaurus musicus* [various]	Harpsichord, Theorbo or Bass-Viol
1695–6	*Deliciae Musicae* [various]	Theobo-Lute, Bass-Viol, Harpsichord or Organ
1695	*New Treasure of Musick*, pub. Henry Playford	Theorbo, Lute or Bass-Viol; Hapsichord or Spinett
1696–8	*The Banquet of Musick* [various]	Theorbo-Lute, Base-Viol, Harpsichord or Organ
1696	*A collection of new Songs The First Book*, Nicola Matteis	Harpsichord Theorbo or Bass Viol
1696	*A Collection of New Songs* [various]	Harpsichord, Theorbo, or Bass-Viol
1698	*A collection of new songs*, Jean Claude Gillier	Harp, Theorbo, Lute or Spinett
1698–1712	*Orpheus Britannicus*, Henry Purcell	Organ, Harpsichord, or Theorbo-lute
1699	*A collection of new Songs The second Book*, Nicola Matteis	Harpsichord, Theorbo or Bass Viol
1699	*Twelve new Songs* [various]	Organ, Harpsichord, or Theorbo
1700	*Amphion Anglicus*, John Blow	Organ, Harpsichord or Theorbo-Lute
1700	*Harmonia Sacra, a supplement to the second book* [various]	Theorbo-Lute, Bass-viol, Harpsichord or Organ
1704	*A Collection of Songs*, John Eccles	Organ, Harpsichord or Theorbo-Lute
1704	*Harmonia Sacra, Book II. Second edition, enlarged and corrected* [various]	Theorbo-Lute, Bass-viol, Harpsichord or Organ
1716	*Divine Harmony*, John Weldon	Organ, Harpsicord or Arch-Lute
1717	*Divine Harmony, The 2nd Collection*, John Weldon	Organ, Harpsicord or Arch-Lute
1726	*Harmonia Sacra, Book I. Third edition* [various]	Theorbo-Lute, Bass-viol, Harpsichord or Organ
1726	*Harmonia Sacra, Book II. Third edition* [various]	Theorbo-Lute, Bass-viol, Harpsichord or Organ

Mention has been made of the addition of the theorbo to the consort of lutes within the king's Lutes and Voices from the 1630s. Holman argues that waits and theatre musicians of the 1630s onwards, especially if itinerant, used mixed groups of violins and theorbos.[57] Lodewijk Huygens, son of Constantijn, was entertained by a group of six players in a London tavern in January 1651/2. They comprised

[57] Holman, *Four and Twenty Fiddlers*, 142.

PL. 11.5. Title-pages of three seventeenth-century songbook publications listing the theorbo or theobo lute as an accompanying instrument: (a) *Choice Ayres & Songs to Sing to the Theorbo–Lute or Bass–Viol*, Book II (London, 1679); (b) *Deliciae musicae: Being, a Collection of the newest and best Songs . . . with a Thorow–Bass, for the theorbo–Lute*, Book I (London, 1695); (c) *Select Musicall Ayres and Dialogues* (London, 1653)

Table 11.5. *Consort music produced or published in England which specifies lute, archlute, or theorbo*

Date	Title or siglum	Comments
c.1635	*GB-Lbl* 31433	'through-base' part-book for Lawes's Royal Consort for 2 theorboes
c.1650	*GB-Ob* Mus. Sch. e. 413	bass part-book for a mixed consort 'pricked for a theorbo'
1656	*M.L. his little consort of three parts*, [Matthew Locke] pub. John Playford	either for viols and violins alone, or with Theorbos and Harpsichord, according to Playford
?	*Sinfonie für Flote trav., Violine, Viola d'amore*, Johann Christoph Pepusch?	'Klavier, Laute und Basso continuo'
1699	*Six Sonates or Solos*, Mr Croft and an Italian M^r	'Harpsicord Theorboe or Bass-Viol'
1704	*Sonate da Camera*, Matthew Novelle	'Theorbo lute spionett or Harpsicord'
1705	*Opera prima, secunda, terza, quarta*, Arcangelo Corelli	'Organ, Harpsichord or Arch Lute'
1710	*XII Sonates of three parts*, Arcangelo Corelli	'Organ, Harpsichord or Arch Lute'
1712	*XII Sonatas of three Parts*, Mr Valentine at Rome	'Organ Harpsichord or arch Lute'
1712	*Sonates of three Parts*, Michele Mascitti	'Organ Harpsichord or arch Lute'
1720	*Six Sonates for one Flute and two Hoboys, or two Violins* Johann Christian Schickhardt	'Harpsichord & Arch Lute'

two violins, a bass viol, and three theorbos.[58] Samuel Pepys mentions a theorbo player as providing the bass for a group of violins hired for evenings of domestic dancing. One such group, the Duke of Buckingham's players, were paid £3 for Twelfth Night celebrations on the evening of 6 January 1668, to be shared between two violins, a bass violin, and a theorbo.[59]

Some Caroline consort music specifies theorbos. Lawes's 'Royal Consort' is for two trebles, two gambas, and two theorbos.[60] His 'Harp Consorts' require one theorbo. During the Commonwealth much instrumental music was played at the

[58] Holman, *Four and Twenty Fiddlers*, 143.
[59] *Diary*, ix. 12–13. Theorbos for dancing are also mentioned on 23 Mar. 1668 and 26 Mar. 1669 (ix. 128, 464).
[60] Ashbee (ed.), *William Lawes*, 252.

Oxford Meetings, with John Wilson presiding with his theorbo. Here one is reminded of the Burwell Tutor's remark, that 'in a Consort one beates it [time] with the motion of the necke of the Theorbo, and every one must have the eye upon it and follow in playing his motion and keepe the same time with the other players'.[61] Locke's Little Consort can be performed with or without continuo instruments. If played with continuo, 'THEORBO'S and HARPSECORD' are called for. The Oxford set of part-books containing Locke's 'Broken Consort' again suggests three theorbos and the same line-up that Huygens heard described in 1651/2.[62] Much of the dance music of the mid-century period, especially that which includes violins, can quite properly be accompanied by theorbos, even if not explicitly stated by the author.

John Jenkins and John Lilly were employed as theorbo players at the Restoration Court. John Lilly, a very important scribe of consort music, had a very large family to provide for. He was patronized by Lord Keeper North, who employed him for various tasks, amongst them to teach the young Roger North on the 'theorboe lute'.[63] After 1660 theorbos were certainly used along with the harpsichord as continuo instruments for ensembles of violins from the king's Twenty-Four Violins that played in the Chapel Royal and the licensed theatres.[64] This is confirmed in the text of Locke's music to Shadwell's version of the *Tempest* printed in 1674, which calls for a 'Band of 24 Violins, with the Harpsicals and Theorbo's which accompany the Voices'.[65]

Theorbos took part in Banister's concerts, as they are listed several times in *A Parley of Instruments*, along with lutes, guitars, and other plucked instruments.[66] John Crowne's *Calisto; or, The Chaste Nymph* (1675), with music by Nicholas Staggins, though described as a court masque, was a spoken play with parts played by courtiers. The version given at the Hall Theatre involved fifty-one instrumentalists, including two theorbos and four guitars. The less lavish production at court included only one theorbo player, Alfonso Marsh (senior), who received £10 for extraordinary attendance, which probably included money for attending rehearsals along with the harpsichord player.[67] In March 1673 Edmund Flower received £15 for 'a theorbo bought by him for his Majesty's service in the Chapel Royal'.[68] Flower went to play in James II's short-lived Catholic Chapel at St James, where he was joined in 1687 by Seign[o]r Francisco Lodie.[69]

After the Glorious Revolution in 1688, mention of the theorbo is much less frequent. The theorbo's role as the instrument for vocal music was gradually usurped by the harpsichord, although the archlute does continue to appear as a possible con-

[61] Burwell Tutor, fo. 41ʳ.
[62] Holman, *Four and Twenty Fiddlers*, 276.
[63] *Roger North on Music*, 37.
[64] Holman, *Four and Twenty Fiddlers*, ch. 15.
[65] Ibid. 347.
[66] Ibid. 349–52.
[67] Ibid. 367.
[68] *RECM* i. 124. See also Holman, *Four and Twenty Fiddlers*, 400.
[69] *RECM* v. 86–7.

tinuo instrument both for songs and orchestral music. In 1703 a French Master, Mr Dupré, set up a school in London to teach 'the Theorbo in Consort'.[70] The German Gottfried Keller published *A Compleat Method for attaining to play a Thorough Bass upon either Organ, Harpsicord or Theorbo-Lute* in London in 1705. Keller was a composer and harpsichord player, and his method makes no attempt to address the technicalities of playing continuo on the theorbo.

Samuel Pepys's first diary (1660–9) contains many fascinating references to a variety of instruments of the lute family. The circumstances in which the different instruments are mentioned in the diary give us a good idea of what the terms 'lute', 'theorbo', 'French lute', and 'archlute' meant to one particular seventeenth-century amateur musician. Pepys also attempted other instruments, most notably the viol, violin, and later the guitar, but it was to the lute and theorbo that he gave much of his spare time and energy in the years 1660–3. During the years 1663–4 his enthusiasm for practising became distinctly less warm, and after 1664 he seldom played. From 1664 he paid for his 'footboy' Tom Edwards to have lessons on the 'French lute' with 'Mr Caesar', alias William Smegergill, whose songs appeared in several of Playford's printed books. Edwards refused to continue with his lessons in 1667, and from that point onwards Pepys's interest in the lute is passive, taking pleasure in the playing of others, though seldom if ever playing himself.[71]

In 1660 Pepys was required to attend on his patron and protector, Sir Edward Montagu, Earl of Sandwich, aboard the Naseby in the historic voyage to bring Charles home from the Netherlands, and thus to effect the Restoration of the monarchy. Montagu was passionately interested in music, and played several instruments, among them the 'theorbo-lute', which he took on a voyage to Madrid in 1666.[72]

Pepys took ship on 23 March 1660, and did not return until 29 May. For more than two months he was without his 'lute', which was deposited with his manservant at Sandwich's London residence. Pepys did take with him two printed songbooks—Henry Lawes's *Ayres and Dialogues . . . Third Booke* (1658) and one of Playford's editions of *Select Ayres and Dialogues*. During the months of January to March 1660, Pepys had practised fairly regularly, as he did later in November and December, such that on 21 November he 'took much pleasure to have the neighbours come forth into the yard to hear [him]'.[73]

---

[70] Michael Tilmouth, 'A Calendar of References to Music in Newspapers, Published in London and in the Provinces 1660–1719', *RMARC* 1 (1961), 1-107 at 50.

[71] Tom Edwards joined the Pepys family in Aug. 1664. He had been a singing boy at the Chapel Royal until his voice broke, and was introduced by Captain Henry Cooke, Master of Children at the Chapel Royal, and friend of Pepys, to the Pepys household. He was able to read at sight, and was a constant musical companion to Pepys during this diary period (*Diary*, x. 120–1).

[72] Frank Reginald Harris, *The Life of Edward Montagu, K.G., First Earl of Sandwich 1625–1672*, ii (London, 1912), 50.

[73] *Diary*, i. 298.

Exactly what kind of lute (or lutes) Pepys had at this time is never made explicit, but the easy interchange of 'lute' and 'theorbo' that occurs in references to the alterations made to his instrument between 9 and 28 October 1661, and the description of the alterations that were made, give us a rough idea. The entries for 25 and 28 October run as follows:

In my way, I calling at the Instrument-maker's, Hunts, and there saw my Lute, which is now almost done, it being to have a new neck to it and to be made to double Strings.[74]

and so to Pauls churchyard to Hunts, and there find my Therobo done. Which pleases me very well, and costs me 26*s* to the altering—but now he tells me it is as good a Lute as any is in England, and is worth well 10*l*.[75]

Pepys certainly used his instrument to accompany the songs he sang, as he wrote for 24 November 1660: 'And that being done, I fell to entering those two good songs of Mr. Lawes, 'Helpe, helpe, O helpe' &c. and 'O God of heaven and Hell' in my song book—to which I have got Mr. Childe to set the base to the Theorbo.'[76]

As Pepys could not realize a bass, he was in the habit of asking musicians to provide him with tablature realizations, particularly Child, Birchenshaw, and later Cesare Morelli. At first he was delighted with the theory and composition instruction he received from Birchenshaw.[77] For 14 March 1662, whilst undertaking theory and composition instruction from Birchenshaw, he writes:

Then to my lute, upon which I have not played a week or two; and trying over the two songs of *Nulla nulla, &c.* and *Gaze not on Swans*, which Mr Berchinsha set for me a little while ago, I find them most incomparable songs as he hath set them—of which I am not a little proud, because I am sure none in the world hath them but myself, not so much as he himself that set them.

'Gaze not on Swans' was in part 'composed' by Pepys with help from Birchenshaw. Quickly Pepys grew tired of the lessons and engineered a row in order to disassociate himself from his teacher.[78] The term 'lute' is freely interchanged with 'theorbo' for his instrument, both when playing solo, and when accompanying himself. The fact that Pepys constantly used his lute/theorbo for accompanying songs makes it almost certain that it was kept in Renaissance tuning. It is likely that he only played in Renaissance tuning, as it would be impractical for an amateur with limited time to be constantly altering the tuning of his instrument from Renaissance tuning for vocal accompaniment to altered tunings for solo lessons. The practice of accompanying songs on the lute or theorbo in anything other than Renaissance tuning in

---

[74] *Diary*, ii. 201.   [75] Ibid. 203.

[76] Ibid., i. 302. And for 30 Dec. 1660: 'And after dinner Mr. Childe and I spent some time at the lute; and so promising me to prick me some lessons to my Theorbo, he went away to see Henery Laws, who lies very sick.' Ibid. 324.

[77] Ibid., iii. 46.   [78] Ibid. 37-8.

England is rare indeed, and probably would not have been readily familiar to Child and Birchenshaw.[79]

Why did Pepys sometimes call his instrument lute and other times theorbo? Probably the generic term 'lute' could apply in Pepys's day to any member of the lute family. Furthermore, the purpose to which the instrument was put, and by implication the tuning used, was more important than the actual size or shape of the instrument. Thus to Pepys, 'French lute' meant a lute in one or other of the altered tunings, and 'theorbo' meant an instrument in Renaissance tuning, primarily meant for vocal accompaniment, regardless of the type of neck extension or the number of diapasons. This ties in with Mace's statement that the '*The Theorbo*, is no other, than *That* which we call'd the *Old English Lute*'—the old English lute being a lute in Renaissance tuning.

It is possible that Pepys played on two instruments—one a theorbo and the other a lute—however, it seems, as suggested by Richard Luckett, that Pepys's lute and theorbo were 'one and the same instrument'.[80] Although Pepys does on occasion call his instrument a theorbo before the alteration in 1661, when Hunts added a 'new neck . . . to be made to double Strings',[81] the tendency is for him to refer to the instrument as a lute beforehand and a theorbo afterwards. The most likely explanation is that Pepys had an existing 10- or 12-course lute in Renaissance tuning converted to a small theorbo or 'theorbo-lute' by means of a new longer neck and pegbox extension. The altered instrument then might have had 12 to 14 double courses, and a top course which may have required lowering by an octave, depending on its size.

It may be that by the summer of 1664 Pepys could not find sufficient time to make continued study of the lute worth his while. One reason why he was persuaded to accept Tom Edwards as his servant, after the boy had ceased to be of use to the Chapel Royal, may have been that with a solid musical training, Edwards would not only be able to lend service with his voice, but also study the lute with the time, and possibly also the ability, that Pepys lacked. A lute was procured from a Mr Hunt (presumably the instrument maker mentioned in the letter of 25 October 1661), as the entry for 31 August 1664 states: 'After dinner I up to hear my boy play upon a lute which I have this day borrowed of Mr. Hunt; and endeed, the boy would with little practice play very well upon the Lute—which pleases me well.'[82]

On 14 December 1664 we learn that Smegergill is teaching Tom.[83] The boy at first practises hard; sometimes in the early hours when unable to sleep. This instrument may have only been a temporary loan, which for Pepys was quite a normal practice. He himself lent his lute on two separate occasions, once to 'Mr Blagrave'

[79] The Nanki MS contains the only examples of English songs accompanied in flat tuning.
[80] *Diary*, x. 274.   [81] Ibid., ii. 201.   [82] Ibid., v. 258.   [83] Ibid. 344.

and once to his patron, Edward Montagu, Earl of Sandwich.[84] Sandwich played the viol, the keyboard, the guitar, and the lute/theorbo, and Pepys's musicianship may well have been one of the things that recommended him to Sandwich.[85]

It is clear that Tom Edwards was taught the French lute by Smegergill, as Pepys writes for 2 December 1667:

After a little discourse, Mr. Caesar dining there, he did give us some music on his lute (Mr. John Crew being there) to my great content, and then away I; and Mr. Caesar fallowed me and told me that my boy Tom hath this day declared to him that he cared not for the French lute and would learn no more—which Caesar out of faithfulness tells me, that I might not spend any more money on him in vain.[86]

Thus it is possible to see a clear demarcation between the French lute on the one hand (which we may assume was either in D minor or flat tuning, i.e. tuning no. 10), which Pepys mentions as played by others (Smegergill and Edwards), and the lute/theorbo which Pepys himself owned, played, and had altered.

The royal musicians William Child, John Bannister (the famous violinist), and Pelham Humphrey are all mentioned in the diaries as theorbo players.[87] Captain Cooke, who is frequently mentioned in both a professional and social capacity, was a singer well capable of self-accompaniment on the theorbo. The theorbo he acquired in 1662 at the Crown's expense cost £25 with strings,[88] and was more expensive then the usual price of around £15.

In 1667 Humphrey had recently returned from four years' study abroad. The government had paid his expenses expressly to journey to France and Italy. Humphrey was scornful of Louis Grabu, the King's Master of the Music, 'how he understands nothing nor can play on any instrument and so cannot compose, and that he will give him a lift out of his place'.[89] Humphrey belittled Grabu's attempts at emulating the Lullian violin band. Although Grabu was shortly to be relieved of his position, the post never came to Humphrey, who died in 1674. Pepys relates:

I had a good dinner for them, as a venison pasty and some fowl, and after dinner we did play, he on the Theorbo, Mr. Caesar on his French lute, and I on the viol, but made but mean music; nor do I see that this Frenchman doth so much wonders on the Theorbo, but without question he is a good musician; but his vanity doth offend me.[90]

---

[84] On 18 Mar. 1660: 'From thence homewards, and called at Mr. Blagrave's, where I took in my note that he hath of mine for 40s, which he two years ago did give me as a pawne while he had my lute'; ibid., i. 91. (The 'Blagrave' referred to was either Thomas or Robert Blagrave, both later royal musicians). On 10 Aug. 1660 he wrote: 'I went to my Lord's and took Will (who waited for me there) by coach and went home taking my lute home with me [which] hath been all this while since I came from sea at my Lord's for him to play on'; ibid. 218. (Will was William, Pepys's personal manservant.)

[85] Ibid., x. 260.   [86] Ibid., viii. 558.

[87] Child, i. 324 (30 Dec. 1660); Banister, ix. 138 (29 Mar. 1668); Humphrey, viii. 529–30 (15 Nov. 1667).

[88] *RECM* i. 39; another account prices the instrument and strings at £30 (ibid., v. 118).

[89] *Diary*, viii. 529 (15 Nov. 1667).   [90] Ibid. 530.

In his first diary Pepys mentions several other lutenists. Dr Waldegrave is mentioned in the entry for 12 April 1664 as follows: 'And leaving my wife there, I and W. Howe to Mr. Pagets, and there heard some musique, not very good—but only one Dr. Walgrave, an Englishman bred at Rome, who plays the best upon the lute that I ever heard man.'[91]

Dr Waldegrave was personal physician to the Duke of York, later James II. North described Waldegrave as 'a prodigy of an arch-lutinist'.[92] As Waldegrave played the archlute and had spent much time studying in Rome, where the Renaissance tuning had never been supplanted by altered tunings, it is reasonable to suppose that he also played in Renaissance tuning.

Probably the most popular member of the lute family in the eighteenth century was the archlute. This was the type of instrument owned by John Shore, the famous Royal trumpeter, and which he presumably played in the Chapel Royal. His archlute was listed by Talbot, and had 12 courses, all doubled except the top, with g' as the nominal pitch of the top string.[93]

The only tablature source of songs and solos for the archlute from the eighteenth century occurs in a layer of the Nanki manuscript.[94] In this manuscript there are also six complete da capo arias and a recitative, plus two short solo minuets for a 13-course archlute tuned with the top string at g'.[95] One of the arias is from Handel's *Floridante* (1721), the archlute part providing both the bass line with harmony above and the obbligato instrumental line.[96] This part of the manuscript is likely to originate from at least a decade later than the sections discussed elsewhere. The minuets are attractive but lacking in inner parts. The continuo aria accompaniments, such as that for 'E quella quella si la lontananza', are a good guide to a modern player wishing to accompany Handel arias as they are quite practical, with a good separation between bass and harmony, and a cautious use of diapasons (see Ex. 11.4).

The history of the theorbo is distinct from that of the solo 'French' lute in England, and it is noticeable how many musicians of the period 1660–80 had the facility to realize a bass on the instrument. Around 1700 this role seems to have been passed to the archlute, which probably had some enthusiasts until the mid-eighteenth century. Handel used both the archlute and the theorbo in his London theatre orchestras during the 1720s and 1730s. In 1720 a theorbo was used, and in 1728 an archlute.[97] Possibly the players of these instruments would have doubled on other instruments. Handel's scores from the 1730s continue to list archlutes and theorbos on occasion, but such instruments are never mentioned in works

[91] Ibid., v. 119.
[92] *Roger North on Music*, 308, 355.
[93] Prynne, 'James Talbot's Manuscript', 60.
[94] Nanki MS, fos. 11'–20'.
[95] Nanki MS da capo arias and recitative, fos. 11'–20'; solo minuets, fo. 16'.
[96] Nanki MS, fos. 18'–19'.
[97] Donald Burrows, 'Handel's London Theatre Orchestra', *EM* 13 (1985), 349–57 at 355–6.

Ex. 11.4. '*E quella quella si la lontananza*', *Nanki MS, no. 20, fos. 13ᵛ–14ʳ, bars 1–8*

that date from after his return to London from Dublin in 1742.[98] Handel includes a lute part in his aria 'The soft complaining flute' in his *Ode on St Cecilia's Day* (1739). The lute part consists of a mixture of an unfigured bass line, requiring some realization, intermixed with fast solo passages in the middle register of the instrument, for which purposes the archlute is unquestionably best suited. This is perhaps a guide to how Handel might have envisaged the archlute being used in his operas in the 1720s and 1730s, that is, as a continuo instrument which could, on occasion, be called upon to feature in quiet obbligato passages portraying tenderness and pathos.

The theorbo or some kind of lute-family instument was the basic provider of accompaniment for a solo vocal line in England until the 1680s. This fact alone suggests widespread useage and commonly held basic skills. In the same way that a singer today will often have sufficient pianistic skills to accompany himself, so one would have expected a singer in the seventeenth century to have the minimum skills required to realize a bass line on some form of lute, theorbo, or archlute. John Playford's many published songbooks from 1652 to 1684 are aimed at this readership, and the numbers of people using a lute-family instrument in this way would have far exceeded the numbers playing solo lute music.

---

[98] Ibid. 356. For example, *Saul* (1739) specifies a theorbo, and 'Gentle Airs' from *Athalia* (1733) an archlute.

Chapter Twelve

The Decline of the Lute in England after 1660

Lute: Despair *I do*:
Old Dowland *he is* Dead; R. Johnson *too*;
Two Famous Men; Great Masters *in My* Art;
In each of Them *I had more than* One Part,
Or Two, *or* Three; *They were not* Single-Soul'd,
As most our * Upstarts *are, and* too too Bold.
Soon after Them, *that Famous man* Gotiere
Did make me Gratefull *in each* Noble Ear;
He's *likewise* gone: *I fear me much that* I
Am not Long-liv'd, *but shortly too* shall Dye.
    Author. *Chear up*, Brave Soul! *And know that* some
Yet Living, *who for* Thee *will take such* Care, *(there are*
That Thou shalt be Restor'd Thy former Glory,
And be Eterniz'd *to* Eternal Story.
    Lute. *I know I have some* Friends *which yet do* Live,
But are so Few, *can scarcely make me* Thrive:
My Friend Jo. Rogers, *He's* The only Man
of Fame; *He'l do me* All the Good he can:
But He grows Old now; *has not long to stay*;
And when He's gone, *go* Hang my self I may
Upon the Willows, *or where else I list*,
And there may long enough so Hang, *I wist*,
Ere any Take me down.
(* Some Pitifull thin Composers of This Age.)

Thomas Mace, Musick's Monument, p. 34

At the Restoration Charles II initially tried to return the royal household to the situation in 1642 as nearly as possible, and to continue as if there had been no Interregnum. He reinstated as many of the old appointees as could be found, and recommenced their salaries at what they had been in 1642.[1] In instances where musicians had died in the meantime, or were untraceable, new appointments were made.

---

[1] See Andrew Ashbee, *Lists of Payments to the King's Music in the Reign of Charles II (1660–1685)* (Snodland, 1981); *RECM* i, ii, v; Lafontaine, *The King's Musick*, 113.

The one big departure that Charles II made was to reorganize his violins into a band of twenty-four on the French model, and to have them play not only in a secular capacity, but to introduce them (in 1662) into the Chapel Royal. The Chapel's music, under the influence of William Child and Captain Henry Cooke, was steered away from the more austere Jacobean style which prevailed in Caroline times, to the acceptance of a lighter anthem, infused with dance rhythms and furnished with instrumental ritornelli, and thus likely to please the king. In pre-Commonwealth times the royal musicians were loosely grouped into consorts of related instruments. After 1660 the band of twenty-four violins came to dominate court music, playing at court balls, masques, and dinners.[2] The twenty-four were also used in the two playhouses established under royal licence by Davenant and Killigrew in two groups of twelve violins.[3]

Charles is not known to have shown interest in the lute or its music, though several eminent lutenists were appointed to vacant places in 1660, and some returned to places they had occupied in 1642.[4] The remunerative place created for the now deceased Jacques Gaultier at £100 p.a. went to John Rogers, the foremost lutenist in England after Gaultier's demise.[5] Nothing certain is known of Rogers's movements before the Commonwealth. The Burwell Tutor was copied by Mary Burwell from her master's original.[6] This master was probably a pupil of Ennemond Gaultier, and may have been Rogers himself.[7] Rogers's post at the Restoration Court is mentioned in one account as specifically 'musician in ordinary for the French lute'.[8] Sadly, almost none of his music survives.[9]

Of the five places as 'lutes in ordinary' that went back to Elizabethan and Jacobean periods, those of John Mercure and Timothy Collins went to William Howes and John Singleton.[10] Howes was a violinist and wind player. The long-serving John Singleton played violin and sackbut. He also played the theorbo in some capacity in the years after 1660, as an account for October 1662 reads 'warrant to pay £25 to John Singleton, musician, for a theorbo lute and sackbut for his Majesty's service'.[11] Probably his other posts as violinist and sackbut player became paramount by 1670. Lewis Evans (the Irish harpist) and Nicholas Lanier were

[2] *New Grove*, xi. 152.   [3] Ibid. 156.

[4] The royal household did, however, aquire a copy of *Musick's Monument* at some point, as the Spencer collection includes a copy with the royal arms on the binding.

[5] *RECM* v. 26.

[6] Dart, 'Miss Mary Burwell's Instruction Book'.

[7] *The Burwell Lute Tutor*, p. 2. Spencer draws attention to a letter of recommendation sent by William Herbert, 3rd Earl of Pembroke to his cousin, the amateur lutenist Lord Herbert of Cherbury, ambassador in Paris (1619–24), asking him to help the bearer of the letter, a young English lutenist (Spencer suggests John Rogers), who may also have been the author of the Burwell Tutor.

[8] *RECM* i. 137.

[9] Chappell, *Popular Music of the Olden Time*, i. 158. Chappell mentions a manuscript in Rogers's hand which was known to him, the now lost 'Etwall Hall Lute Book'.

[10] *RECM* i. 219–20.   [11] Ibid. 37.

restored to their old places, as was Dietrich Steiffken, who played the viol and probably not the lute.[12] In 1666 both Lanier and Evans died, and their places were given respectively to Pelham Humphrey (who according to Pepys was undistingushed as a theorbo player, though a good musician),[13] and to Henry Brockwell, the violinist and Keeper of the king's Instruments.[14] (See Table 12.1.)

To the places among 'lutes and voices' that originated with the household of Charles I as Prince of Wales, Anthony Robert, Henry Lawes, Nicholas Lanier, and John Wilson were reappointed in 1660. Wilson was given an extra place (probably new), and was admitted to the Chapel Royal in 1662. John Lilly was appointed to the place of John Kelly,[15] and John Jenkins took up John Coggeshall's place, although Jenkins soon became enfeebled by age and seldom attended court.[16] The place of the Frenchman Nicolas Duval went to Captain Henry Cooke.[17]

Table 12.1 confirms that many of the pre-Restoration places as lutenists or members of the 'lutes and voices' were maintained during Charles II's reign. However, as vacated places were filled, posts were often given to men who were already employed as string or wind players, or who were singers in the Chapel Royal. In such cases it is likely that this second post was primarily a sinecure and entailed little or no lute playing. This trend continued after Charles II's reign into the eighteenth century. The distinctions between 'lutes in ordinary', 'lutes and voices', 'viols', and other non-wind instrumental divisions gradually breaks down after 1660. In 1685 James reorganized the court music, abolishing plurality of posts and creating a new group simply called the 'Private Musick', which included violins, viols, harpsichord, some wind instruments, and singers. This group continued well into the eighteenth century but included no individuals identified as solo lute players, though a number of the singers would have been able to accompany themselves on lute or theorbo.[18]

In the years immediately after the Restoration there was in Lawes, Jenkins, Lilly, Wilson, Cooke, Rogers, Marsh, and Lanier a core of men who were, or had been, eminent lutenists or theorbists in some capacity. Lilly in 1662/3 was the last person to receive money (£12) from the court to buy a lute.[19] Pelham Humphrey passed on at least some of his duties of teaching the viol and theorbo as Master of the Children of the Chapel Royal to Lilly in 1673.[20] The only court musician who was definitely a soloist on the French lute was John Rogers. The rest, we can

---

[12] *RECM*: Evans, i. 35; Lanier, i. 6; Steiffken, i. 19.   [13] *Diary*, viii. 530, entry for 15 Nov. 1667.
[14] *RECM*: Humphrey, i. 71; Brockwell, v. 54.
[15] Lafontaine, *The King's Musick*, 121; Ashbee, *Lists of Payments*, 119.
[16] *Roger North on Music*, 298.
[17] *RECM* i. 6; Evelyn, *The Diary*, iii. 144, entry for 28 Oct. 1654: 'also one Cap. Cooke esteem'd the best singer after the Italian manner of any in England: he entertain'd us with his voice & Theorba'.
[18] *Biographical Dictionary*, ii. 1192–8.   [19] *RECM* i. 42.   [20] Ibid. 129–30.

surmise from their reputations, were primarily singer/lutenists, or more likely, singer/theorbists in their role of musicians for the 'lutes and other Private Musick'.

Most members of this very distinguished group of court musicians were old men in 1660. Lawes, Lanier, and Evans were dead by 1667. The rest all died close in time to each other: Cooke died in 1672; Wilson in 1674; Rogers in 1676; both Lilly and Jenkins in 1678; and Robert in 1679.[21] Anne Rogers, the wife of John Rogers, had to petition the crown in 1677 for £525 in unpaid wages, 'which is all that is left to the Pet[itioner] and her Children, who are in a starveing Condicon'.[22] The singer Alphonso Marsh (senior) who died in 1681 could play the theorbo, as he was employed with John Lilly in that capacity for Crowne's *Calisto* (1674/5).[23] None of this group's eventual replacements were distinguished as lutenists or theorbo players, though many of them as children of the Chapel Royal would have been taught the lute and theorbo as boys. The only likely exception was Edmund Flower, who combined as a theorbist, violinist, and sackbut player. Flower was an exceptionally able musician who played the violin with the king's twenty-four violins from as early as 1671, but also had a double sackbut bought for him in 1678 for use in 'his Majesty's service'.[24] He became a musician 'for the theorbo or lute, without fee' in 1670, and had a £15 theorbo bought 'for his Majesty's service in the Chapel Royal' in 1673 and another for £14 in 1679.[25] In 1673 he was promised 'the next place of the musick that shall be voyd either private or wind musick', and received Lilly's job when it became available in 1678.[26] Flower played the theorbo together with Francesco Lodi in the short-lived Catholic Chapel of James II in 1687/8.[27] He survived this period without problems, and was still in royal employment in 1704.[28]

The acclaimed Scottish counter-tenor John Abell was also a violinist and composer. He may have played the lute as among the three places that he received in the king's Musick were those of Alphonso Marsh (lute and voice) and Anthony Robert (Private Musick).[29] Abell had Catholic sympathies, made frequent journeys abroad at royal expense in the years up to 1688, and was a favourite singer of James II, in whose Catholic Chapel he sang. A guitar was bought for him at £10 'for his Majesty's service in his bedchamber', and he was 'Groom to Queen's Privy Chamber' in 1687.[30] After 1688 Abell travelled abroad for ten years but received a pass to return to England in 1698.[31]

The appointment of Thomas Heywood to the lucrative place of John Rogers is a landmark. For 150 years from from 1526 to 1676 the English court had in Philip van Wilder, Anthony de Countie, John Johnson, Daniel Bacheler, John Dowland,

---

[21] Ashbee, *Lists of Payments*, 103–29.   [22] *RECM* viii. 338.
[23] Ibid., i. 145. See Andrew R. Walkling, 'Masque and Politics at the Restoration Court: John Crowne's *Calisto*', *EM* 24 (1996), 27–62 at 34.
[24] *RECM* i. 113, 177.   [25] Ibid. 98, 124, 187.   [26] Ibid. 132, 181.
[27] Ibid., ii. 21.   [28] Ibid. 78.   [29] Ibid., i. 197 (Marsh); i. 185 (Robert).
[30] Ibid., ii. 12; viii. 280; v. 285.   [31] Ibid., viii. 280, 292.

Table 12.1. *Members of the King's Musicians for the Lutes and other private music 1660–1685, with a continuation of the places until 1708*

As of 1642[a]	Year																			
	60	61	62	63	64	65	66	67	68	69	70	71	72	73	74	75	76	77	78	79
Lewis Evans	1	1	1	1	1	1	30	30	30	30	30	30	30	30	30	30	30	30	30	30
Nicholas Lanier III	2	2	2	2	2	2	31	31	31	31	31	31	31	31	31	*place discontinued*				
Timothy Collins	3	3	3	3	3	3	3	3	3	3	3	3	3	3	3	3	3	3	3	3
Dietrich Steiffken[b]	4	4	4	4	4	4	4	4	4	4	4	4	4	3	3	3	3	3	3	3
	5	5	5	5	5	5	5	5	5	5	5	5	5	5	5	5	5	5	5	5
John Mercure	6	6	6	6	6	6	6	6	6	6	6	6	6	6	6	6	38	38	38	38
Jacques Gaultier	7	7	7	7	7	7	7	7	7	7	7	7	7	7	7	7	39	39	39	39
John Fox	8	8	8	8	8	8	8	8	8	8	8	8	8	8	8	8	8	8	8	8
(new place)	9	9	9	9	9	9	9	9	9	9	9	9	9	9	27	27	27	27	27	27
Nicolas Duvall	10	10	10	10	10	10	10	10	10	10	10	10	9	9	27	27	27	27	27	27
Thomas Ford[c]	11	11	11	28	28	28	28	28	28	28	28	28	28	28	28	28	28	28	28	28
Henry Lawes[c]	12	11	11	10	10	10	10	10	10	10	10	10	33	33	33	33	33	33	33	33
John Drew	13	13	13	13	13	13	13	13	13	13	34	34	34	34	34	34	34	34	34	34
Edward Wormall	14	14	14	14	14	14	14	14	14	14	14	14	14	14	14	14	14	14	14	14
Angelo Notari	15	15	15		29	29	29	29	29	29	29	29	29	29	29	29	29	29	29	29
	16	16	16		16															
Anthony Robert	17	17	17	17	17	17	17	17	17	17	17	17	17	17	17	17	17	17	17	43
Theophilus Lupo	18	18	18	18	18	18	18	18	18	18	18	18	18	18	18	18	18	40	40	40
John Taylor	19	19	19	19	19	19	19	19	19	19	19	19	19	35	35	35	35	35	35	35
Thomas Day	20	20	20	20	20	20	20	20	20	20	20	20	20	20	20	20	20	20	20	20
John Coggeshall	21	21	21	21	21	21	21	21	21	21	21	21	21	21	21	21	21	21	41	41
Alfonso Ferrabosco III	22	22	22	22	22	22	22	22	22	22	22	22	22	22	22	22	22	22	22	22
John Wilson	9	9	9	9	9	9	9	9	9	9	9	9	9	9	27	27	27	27	27	27
Henry Lawes	12	12	27	27	27	27	27	27	27	27	27	27	27	27	27	27	27	27	27	27
John Lanier	23	23	23	23	23	23	32	32	32	32	32	32	32	32	32	32	32	32	32	32
Giles Tomkins	24	24	24	24	24	24	24	24	33	33	33	33	33	33	33	33	33	33	33	33
William Lawes	25	25	25	25	25	25	25	25	25	25	25	25	25	25	25	25	25	25	25	25
John Kelly	26	26	26	26	26	26	26	26	26	26	26	26	26	26	26	26	26	26	42	42

Year

Name	80	81	82	83	84	85	86	87	88	89	90	91	92	93	94	95	96	97	98	99
Lewis Evans	30	30	30	30	30	*place discontinued*														
Nicholas Lanier III																				
Timothy Collins	3	3	3	3	3	*place discontinued (d. 1687)*														
Dietrich Steiffken[b]	5	5	5	5	5	5	5	5	5	5	5	5	5	5	5	5	5	5	5	5
John Mercure	38	38	38	38	38	38	38	38	38	38	38	*place discontinued*								
Jacques Gaultier	39	39	39	39	39	39	39	39	*abroad with James II*											
John Fox	8	8	8	8	8	8	*place probably discontinued (d. 1702)*													
(new place)						44	44	44	44	44	44	*place discontinued*								
Nicolas Duvall	37	37	37	37	37	37	*place discontinued (served in Chapel Royal to 1690)*													
Thomas Ford	28	28	28	28	28	28	28	28	28	28	28	28	28	28						
Henry Lawes[c]	33	33	33	33	33	33	33	33	33	33	33	33	33	33	33	33	33	33	33	33
John Drew	34	34	34	34	34	34	34	34	34	34	34	34	34	34	34	34	34	34	34	34
Edward Wormall	14	14	46	46	46	46	46	46	46	46	46	46	46	46	46	46	46	46	46	46
Angelo Notari	29	29	29	29	29	*place discontinued (served in Chapel Royal to 1704)*														
Anthony Robert	43	43	43	43	43	43	43	43	*abroad with James II; place discontinued*											
Theophilus Lupo	40	40	40	40	40	47	47	47	47	47	47	47	47	47	47	47	47	47	47	47
John Taylor	35	35	35	35	35	35	35	35	35	35	35	35	35	35	35	35	35	35	35	35
Thomas Day	20	43	43	43	43	43	43	43	*abroad with James II; place discontinued*											
John Coggeshall	41	41	41	41	41	*not reappointed; place discontinued*														
Alfonso Ferrabosco III	22	22	45	45	45	45	45	45	45	45	45	45	45	45	45	45	48	48	48	48
John Wilson	27	27	*place discontinued*																	
Henry Lawes	27	27	27	*place discontinued*																
John Lanier	32	32	32	32	32	32	32	32	32	32	32	32	32	32	32	32	49	49	49	49
Giles Tomkins	33	33	33	33	33	33	33	33	33	33	33	33	33	33	33	33[d]	33	33	33	33
William Lawes	25	25	25	25	25	*place discontinued*														
John Kelly	42	42	42	42	42	42	42	42	42	42	42	42	42	42	42	42	42	42	42	42

Table 12.1. cont.

	Year 1700	01	02	03	04	05	06	07	08
Lewis Evans									
Nicholas Lanier III									
Timothy Collins									
Dietrich Steiffken[b]	5	5	5	5	5	5	5	5	5
John Mercure									
Jacques Gaultier									
John Fox									
(new place)									
Nicolas Duvall									
Thomas Ford[d]									
Henry Lawes[c]	33	33	33	33	33	33	33	33	33
John Drew	34	34	34	52	52	52	52	52	52
Edward Wormall	46	46	46	46					
Angelo Notari									
Anthony Robert									
Theophilus Lupo	50	50	50	50	50	50	50	50	50 (to 1723)
John Taylor	35	35	35	35	35	35	35	35	35
Thomas Day									
John Coggeshall									
Alfonso Ferrabosco III	51	51	51	51	51	51	51	51	51
John Wilson									
Henry Lawes									
John Lanier	49	49	49	49	49	49	49	49	49 (to 1752)
Giles Tomkins	33	33	33	33	33	33	33	33	33
William Lawes									
John Kelly	42	42	42	42	42	42	42	42	42 (to 1712)

[a] See Table 10.1, of which this is the continuation.
[b] Jointly with Frederick William Steiffken
[c] Shared place.
[d] His place may have been occupied by Henry Purcell in the years 1683–95.

Key (in chronological order of presence, from 1660)

1. Lewis Evans
2. Nicholas Lanier III
3. John Singleton
4. Dietrich Steiffken
5. Frederick William Steiffken
6. William Howes
7. John Rogers
8. Nathaniel Watkins
9. John Wilson
10. Henry Cooke
11. Charles Coleman I
12. Henry Lawes
13. Gregory Thorndale
14. John Harding
15. Angelo Notari
16. Henry Purcell I
17. Anthony Robert
18. Humphrey Madge
19. John Smith
20. Alphonso Marsh
21. John Jenkins
22. John Hingeston
23. Edward Coleman
24. Giles Tomkins
25. John Clement
26. John Lilly
27. Thomas Purcell
28. Charles Coleman II
29. John Goodgrome
30. Henry Brockwell
31. Pelham Humfrey
32. William Clayton
33. John Blow
34. Edward Hooten
35. Francis Cruys
36. Robert Smith
37. Richard Hart
38. Richard Tomlinson
39. Thomas Heywood
40. Jeffrey Ayleworth
41. John Moss
42. Edmund Flower
43. John Abell
44. Nathaniel French
45. Robert Carr
46. John Bowman
47. Charles Powell
48. John Eccles
49. John Shore
50. Charles Smith
51. Thomas Parkinson
52. Charles Hooten

Robert Johnson, Jacques Gaultier, and John Rogers a succession of distinguished lutenists. Before this date named lutenists attached to the English court stretch back to 1285. Heywood is never mentioned as a solo lute player, though he was paid arrears of £183 for his place as lutenist to Charles II between 7 May 1686 and 24 March 1686/7. However, as a singer the ability to accompany himself on some sort of plucked instrument would have been expected. Sometime before 1673 his voice broke, and he was then maintained by Pelham Humphrey at the Crown's expense until a post was available.[32] He was promised Rogers's place in 1674, but had to wait until Rogers died to receive it. Heywood went on to become a successful singer (both as tenor and counter-tenor) in the Chapel Royal, and a page of the 'Back-Stairs' in the Duke of York's household.[33] He disappears from the records in 1688, going abroad with James II, with whom he was closely associated. He is mentioned as serving the Catholic Stuarts, James II, his queen Mary of Modena, and their son James III, as Page of the Bedchamber or Page of the Backstairs until 1717.[34]

The trumpeter John Shore was the last person regularly to play any form of lute in an official capacity for the Crown. He was appointed as a royal trumpeter in 1688,[35] and was probably a member of the royal violins for a while, but from at least December 1705 was paid as 'Lutenist' in the Chapel Royal.[36] He performed many of Purcell's more difficult trumpet parts. From 1705 Shore maintained the lutenist post together with his position as trumpeter, becoming 'Sergeant-trumpeter' in February 1707/8.[37] According to Hawkins he split his lip during his career, making trumpet playing impossible, but he remained as lute player within the Chapel Royal. He is said to have invented the tuning fork for tuning his lute.[38] From the instrument that was owned by Shore and measured by Talbot we can surmise that the 'lute' Shore played in the Chapel Royal was an archlute.[39] Occasionally a lute of some sort was included in the anthems Blow wrote for the Chapel Royal.[40] The Chapel Royal part-books in the Royal Music Library included a lute book (*GB-Lbl* RM. 27.c.14) from which a continuo part was realized, and this may have belonged to Shore. John Weldon included an archlute among the possible continuo instruments for his *Divine Harmony* and a lutenist appears on the frontispiece engraving of the Chapel Royal.[41] Percy Scholes maintained that after Shore died in 1752 a court position as a lutenist was preserved until 1846 in name only.[42]

By 1680 the generation that included John Rogers had all died, and the lute, theorbo, or archlute were unlikely to be heard at court in any capacity other than as an accompanimental instrument, and usually in association with the voice. An instance

[32] *RECM* i. 123.   [33] Ibid., v. 283.   [34] *Biographical Dictionary*, i. 571–3.
[35] *RECM* ii. 19.   [36] Ibid. 85. *Biographical Dictionary*, ii. 1003–5.   [37] *RECM* ii. 93.
[38] *New Grove*, xvii. 282.   [39] Spencer, 'Chitarrone, Theorbo and Archlute', 417.
[40] These anthems are in *GB-Cfm* Mu. MS 240 [31.H.1], fos. 5ʳ–19ᵛ and 21ʳ–29ᵛ.
[41] John Weldon, *Divine Harmony* (London, 1716).
[42] *The Oxford Companion to Music*, ed. Percy A. Scholes; 10th edn., rev. by J. O. Ward (Oxford, 1970), 589.

of the lute being used in this capacity is included in the story told by Hawkins of Mrs Arabella Hunt (d. 1705), the favourite female singer of Queen Mary. Hawkins relates that:

The queen having a mind one afternoon to be entertained with music, sent to Mr. Gostling, then one of the chapel, and afterwards subdean of St. Paul's, to Henry Purcell, and Mrs. Arabella Hunt, who had a very fine voice, and an admirable hand on the lute, with a request to attend her; they obeyed her commands. Mr. Gostling and Mrs. Hunt sang several compositions of Purcell, who accompanied them on the harpsichord; at length the queen beginning to grow tired, asked Mrs. Hunt if she could not sing the old Scots ballad 'Cold and Raw', Mrs. Hunt answered yes, and sang it to her lute. Purcell was all the while sitting at the harpsichord unemployed, and not a little nettled at the queen's preference of a vulgar ballad to his music; but seeing her majesty delighted with this tune, he determined that she should hear it upon another occasion: and accordingly in the next birthday song, viz., that for the year 1692, he composed an air to the words, 'May her bright example chace Vice in troops out of the land', the bass whereof is the tune to Cold and Raw; it is printed in the second part of the Orpheus Britannicus, and is note for note the same with the Scots tune.[43]

The incident is both an example of the popularity of Scots songs in England in the late seventeenth century, and of the lute being used to accompany the voice at court. The Smith engraving of 1706 of Godfrey Kneller's portrait of Mrs Hunt, which appeared in a series of prints of notable court personalities of the William and Mary reign, shows her playing an 11-course French lute and not singing (see Pl. 12.1). This lute was undoubtedly of a type intended for solo playing, and was probably not the same as that with which she accompanied herself.

The Restoration court wanted the latest French orchestral styles, but it seems that the most recently composed lute music of Denis Gaultier, the Gallots, and later Mouton was never in vogue in England.[44] At least there is little manuscript evidence that it was. This may seem odd when in pre-Restoration days French lutenists had been in such demand, and French music in 1660 was still held to be the height of elegance. In truth by 1660 even in France the lute and theorbo were giving way in popularity to the harpsichord, and meanwhile string orchestral music had risen under Lully to an unassailable position such that church, stage, and dance music were all dominated by it.[45] In comparison, the subtle and introverted art of the last generation of French lutenists was of small importance. By 1700 the centre of lute activity had moved eastwards, to Saxony, Bohemia, and the German-

---

[43] Sir John Hawkins, *A General History of the Science and Practice of Music* (London, 1776; rev. edn., 1875), 564. 'Cold and Raw' was first published in *Comes Amoris*, 2nd book (1688) and the tune alone in Playford's *Dancing Master* (1688).

[44] Some music by Denis Gaultier was imported into England as it is found in the Robarts MS and Pan 4 MS. However, the only pieces by Mouton and Gallot that appear in any source that is definitely British are in the Balcarres MS.

[45] Ledbetter, *Harpsichord and Lute Music*, 11–14, 31.

PL. 12.1. *Arabella Hunt with a Lute*, engraving made by John Smith (1652–1742), dated 1706, from a painting by Sir Godfrey Kneller (1646–1723). Owned by the author

speaking lands of the Austro-Hungarian Empire like Silesia, where the music of Mouton and the last generation of French lute composers was enthusiatically collected, and where a new style of Baroque lute music was taking shape in the circle around the composer Count Logy. In the 1680s and 1690s the music of French lutenists no longer found favour in Paris. Instead their music was cultivated in Germany and Bohemia and not, as earlier in the century, in London.[46]

That the Restoration court showed little interest in French lute music, despite a consuming passion for French-style orchestral music, is shown by Pepys's diary of 1660–7, in which no Frenchman is mentioned as a lute master. A reasonable level of accomplishment upon the theorbo was common to many musicians who were masters of other instruments, but those who are mentioned in the diary in connection with the French lute were few indeed: Pepys's footboy Tom Edwards, the

---

[46] A large amount of French lute music by Mouton and his generation is found in early 18th-c. MSS compiled in areas of the Austro-Hungarian Empire, with Vienna, Prague, and Breslau as the main centres of activity.

boy's teacher Smegergill (alias William Caesar), and the amateur Samuel Cooper. Cooper was the foremost English miniaturist of the day, and was engaged to portray Pepys's wife. The entry for 10 July 1668 reads: 'So to Coopers and there found my wife (and W. Hewer and Deb) sitting and painting; and here he doth work finely, though I fear it will not be so like as I expected; but now I understand his great skill in music, his playing and setting to the French lute most excellently—and speaks French.'[47]

Pelham Humphrey taught the lute as well as the theorbo to the children of the Chapel Royal and, with his French experience, it is reasonable to suggest he may have played the French lute.[48]

Evelyn was not the admirer of the lute that Pepys was, despite having some lessons on the lute and theorbo, but he refers to the instrument in several interesting connections after 1660. We know from him that lutes were heard at the Coronation of Charles II in the passage: 'Anthems & rare musique playing with Lutes, Viols, Trumpets, Organs, Voices, &c.'[49] This music was heard after the Crown Imperial was put on the king's head but before the ring was put on his finger.

Evelyn states twice his preference for the Irish harp over the lute, especially when played by his friend, Mr Clarke. For 20 December 1664 Evelyn writes the following passage when talking of Mr Clarke's skill: 'such musique before or since did I never heare, that Instrument neglected for its extraordinary difficulty; but in my judgement far superior to the Lute it selfe, or whatever speaks with strings'.[50] This opinion Evelyn repeats on 14 November 1668.[51] Twice he speaks of Dr Waldegrave, whom Pepys also heard play. On 28 February 1684 he says: 'I din'd at my Lady Tukes, where I heard Dr. Wallgrave (physitian to the Duke & Dutchesse) play most incomparably on the Lute; I know not that ever I heard any to exceede him.'[52]

Evelyn mentions a 'renowned Master', 'Du Prue [Dupré] a *French-man* on the *Lute*', when dining with the Master of the Mint on 20 November 1679.[53] Dupre d'Angleterre was still active as a lutenist and teacher in London as late as 1703.[54] A second Frenchman who played the lute is mentioned in the entry for 19 March 1691: 'Dined at Sir William Farmors who shewed me many good pictures, after dinner had a [french] servant that played rarely on the Lute.'[55] The recurrence of instrumental skills among servants is important, particularly in relation to the lute, and suggests levels of musicianship in persons that are usually ignored in

[47] *Diary*, ix. 259. 'Deb' was Deb Willet, a chambermaid in the Pepys household.

[48] Ashbee, *List of Payments*, 83: 'To Pelham Humphrey, Master of ye Children of his Ma's Chappell Royall, for his paines in learning the Children on the Lute, Violin & Theorbo . . . More to him for 2 base Violls at £5 each, and two Theorboes at £6 each by him bought for teaching the said Children.' (Warrant dated 27 July 1673 though paid after his death.)

[49] *Diary*, iii. 285 (25 Apr. 1661).   [50] Ibid. 92.   [51] Ibid. 518.   [52] Ibid., iv. 370.
[53] Ibid., iv. 186.   [54] Tilmouth, 'A Calendar of References', 80.   [55] *Diary*, v. 44.

contemporary references. Pepys was certainly not the only gentleman to encourage his servants to play instruments. Twice, on 5 January 1660 and on 9–10 November 1660, Pepys was entertained with lute music by Mr Evans, butler to Sir Henry and Lady Wright. On the first occasion, Pepys writes: 'So [to] my Lady Wright to speak with her, but she abroad; so Mr. Evans, her butler, had me into his buttery and gave me sack and a lesson on his lute, on which he played very well.'[56] And on the second: 'Thence I went to Sir Harry Wrights, where my Lord [i.e. Sandwich] was busy at Cards; and so I stayed below with Mrs. Carter and Evans (who did give me a lesson upon the Lute) till he came downe.'[57]

It would appear from the papers of the family of the Duke of Leeds, and advertisements of the period, that musical servants were more highly esteemed than those without such skills.[58] However, the general lack of information on men and women who were personal servants at this time makes impossible any assessment of how widespread such musical accomplishments were.

The masques of the Jacobean and Caroline period had prominently featured lutes 'en masse', and been a strong influence on the solo lute music in the period. After the last masque proper, Davenant's *Salmacida Spolia* (1640), attempts were made in the Commonwealth period by Davenant to introduce an entertainment more in line with Continental operas, most notably in *Cupid and Death* (1653) and *The Siege of Rhodes* (1656). In the Restoration period, before opera was properly established, the king often turned to the two companies patented by the Crown under Davenant and Killigrew for much of his entertainment. The king did much to promote these companies, and lent them his violins divided into two groups of twelve for the purpose.[59] Nevertheless, a number of masque or masque-like entertainments were held at Whitehall in Charles II's reign. In these new court and theatre entertainments it seems the lute had no place, though the theorbo did continue to feature in seventeenth- and early eighteenth-century opera and theatrical entertainments as an established continuo instrument. Among the Restoration masques Crowne's *Calisto* (1675) is the best documented. A large group of over fifty instruments took part. They were divided into two groups: one of two harpsichords, two theorboes, three bass viols, twelve violins, two oboes; the other of twenty violins, five trumpets and drums, two oboes, four guitars.[60] No lutes took part.

Henry Watson, in an article as early as 1909, makes the observation that 'the lute [was] doomed by the transfer of music itself and the instrument along with it, from

---

[56] *Diary*, i. 25.   [57] Ibid. 288.

[58] *GB-Lbl* Egerton 3339, fo. 44. In a letter from Louis Bérard to the 1st Duke of Leeds dated 15/26 Mar. 1708/9. He mentions paying a German footman more than the other footman for his ability to play the flute and bass viol. See Tim Crawford, 'Lord Danby, Lutenist of "Quality"', *LSJ* 25 (1985), 53–68 at 59 and 67 n. 21.

[59] Holman, *Four and Twenty Fiddlers*, 360.   [60] Ibid. 368. Walkling, 'Masque and Politics'.

domestic association to the public arena of the concert room'.[61] While this statement is certainly true, the transfer was not immediate and took much of the period 1650–1750 to come about, during which time small, sometimes private, music clubs and societies flourished. Here professional performers appeared for profit but amateurs might also participate. Although it is never mentioned by Wood, eminent visiting musicians such as Thomas Baltzar from Lübeck, who performed at Ellis's Oxford Music Meetings, may have been paid for their appearances, and would certainly have been entertained lavishly.

The first concerts which were open to the public on payment of an entrance fee were those started by John Banister in 1672, but the playing of music in homes and taverns by professional players was an established practice by 1670.[62] Pepys mentions on several occasions dancing to the music of violins and theorbos, such as the Duke of Buckingham's musicians who provided dance music, and who were paid £3 to be shared between the four of them.[63] Eminent music lovers like the Master of the Mint engaged prominent instrumentalists to entertain their guests. Pepys in later life gave similar home soirées, when famous musicians played for an invited audience.[64]

North relates that the lute was heard at Banister's meetings. The audience heard 'sometime[s] consort, sometimes solos, of the violin, flajolet (one of Banister's perfections), bass violl, lute, and song all'Italliana'.[65] North is disparaging of the enterprise, saying:

Besides the whole was without designe or order; for one master brings a consort with fuges, another shews his guifts in a solo upon the violin, another sings, and then a famous lutinist comes foreward, and in this manner changes followed each other, with a full cessation of the musick between every one, and a gable and bustle while they changed places.[66]

A printed account of one of Banister's performances has survived which is dated 11 December 1676, and titled 'Musick: or a Parley of Instruments'. It advertised a run of performances at Lincoln's Inn Fields starting on 14 December in which a large assortment of instruments were played as part of a semi-theatrical ode to music.[67] Among the several symphonies and consorts various plucked instruments appeared, including lutes, theorboes, guitars, citterns, and harps. Certainly the lute did feature as a solo instrument in the earliest public concerts, the venues being small and intimate. As such enterprises developed, public concert rooms and halls were built

---

[61] Thomas Watson, 'Thomas Mace, The Man; The Book; and the Instruments', *PMA* 35 (Apr. 1908–9), 87–107 at 101.

[62] Scholes, *Oxford Companion to Music*, 9th edn. (1955), 227. John Aubrey mentions taking 'the organs out of Churches to set them up in taverns' during the Commonwealth.

[63] *Diary*, ix. 12.   [64] *DNB* xv. 809.   [65] *Roger North on Music*, 303.

[66] Ibid. 353.   [67] Holman, *Four and Twenty Fiddlers*, 349–52.

expressly for the purpose (such as that built in Villiers Street in about 1680 and known as York Buildings), and the lute would quickly have lost ground.[68]

The Restoration period saw an upsurge in interest in the guitar that may have hastened the decline of the lute. The old four-course Renaissance guitar was popular with English amateurs in the decades after its introduction from France in the 1550s, but is seldom mentioned after the 1570s.[69] The guitar was reintroduced in the mid-seventeenth century in a larger 5-course Baroque form.[70] Ward has shown that Playford when publishing his *A Booke of New Lessons for the Cithern and Gittern* (1652) intended the second part of his book not for the 'small guitar', but for a type of cittern that had been commonly known in England as the 'gittern', and which is unconnected to the medieval gittern in form.[71] Fourteen years later he is scornful of ladies who are anxious to have their daughters 'taught by Monsieur La Novo Kickshawibus on the Gittair',[72] and clearly has in mind the recently introduced 5-course guitar. By 1666 Playford was aware and disparaging of the sudden upsurge of popularity of the guitar. The intrument's rise to prominence in England owed much to the enthusiasm for the instrument of the francophile kings Charles II and James II, both of whom played the guitar, and the appearance at court of the Italian guitar virtuoso Francesco Corbetta (*c.*1615–81) sometime after 1660, hotfoot from his success at the French court of Louis XIV.[73]

Pepys speaks distastefully of the guitar when he heard Corbetta playing it on the 5 August 1667:

After done, with the Duke of York; and coming out through his dressing room, I there espied Signor Francisco tuning his Gittar, and Monsieur du Puy with him, who did make him play to me; which he did most admirably, so well as I was mightily troubled that all that pains should have been taken upon so bad an instrument.[74]

Pepys changed his opinion of the guitar sometime after 1669, as it was for the guitar that Morelli prepared a considerable amount of music for Pepys to play.[75]

Corbetta produced the now lost *Easier Lessons on the Guittar . . . by Seignior Francisco* in the 1670s, and by 1682 Nicola Matteis had published a continuo treatise for the guitar: *The False Consonances of Musick*.[76] Both Evelyn and Pepys make

---

[68] *New Grove*, xi. 202.　　　　　　　　　　　　[69] Ward, 'Sprightly and Cheerful Musick', 16.

[70] James Tyler, *The Early Guitar* (Early Music Series, 4; London, 1980), 44–5.

[71] Ward, 'Sprightly and Cheerful Musick', 6. This contradicts Tyler, *The Early Guitar*, 29.

[72] John Playford, *Musick's Delight on the Cithren* (1666), sig. A^r, 'The Preface'.

[73] Tyler, *The Early Guitar*, 44. Corbetta dedicated *La guitarre royalle* (1671) to Charles II. The 5-course guitar began life in England as an instrument cultivated by high society (Ward, 'Sprightly and Cheerful Musick', 22).

[74] *Diary*, viii. 374.

[75] Pepys left four MSS with guitar accompaniments: *GB-Cmc*, Pepys Library, MSS 2591, 2802, 2803, 2804, and a tutor, MS 2805, dated 1680.

[76] Tyler, *The Early Guitar*, 132 and Ward, 'Sprightly and Cheerful Musick', 20 n. 73. Matteis's work contained only five pieces for solo guitar, but the autograph MS at the Sibley Music Library, Rochester, NY, from which the publication was taken, contains extra pieces.

many references to guitars being played in fashionable circles.[77] The guitar was frequently called for in operatic and theatrical productions of the time (for instance in Purcell's *Dido and Aeneas*), although no music survives associated with particular plays.[78] Corbetta was one of the four costumed guitarists that played in *Calisto*, the others being Messrs Cutom, Deloney, and Delloney.[79] One of these last gentlemen must have been the 'Mr Delawny' who was guitar master to the future Queen Anne in 1682. No lute teacher was among the masters of music, dancing, and singing attached either to Anne or her sister Mary in the years 1676–82.[80]

Newspaper references to lutenists active in London in the early eighteenth century point to the existence of several teachers and players in the first two decades, though they are never heard of outside London. Apart from the already mentioned Mr Dupré, a Mr Cuthbert was active in 1703 accompanying the violinist Mr Latour in a number of concerts.[81] One of the Thomas Deans (father and son) was an archlutenist who appeared in concerts in 1703, 1707, and 1708.[82] The Italian Francesco Conti advertised as a theorbist and mandolin player in 1707.[83] In 1711 the German lutenist Henry von Thornowitz gave several public concerts in London, as did an anonymous Italian master on the French lute and archlute.[84] Between February and June 1718 the great Silesian lutenist Sylvius Leopold Weiss gave weekly concerts in London, and even played before the king.[85]

The many types of lute collected and measured by James Talbot in the period 1685–1701 show that lutes of all kinds were still known in England, and the terminology he uses for particular instruments is interesting.[86] Talbot measured two 'French lutes' with 11 courses, one of which had a string length of over 27 9/16", and an 'English lute' with twelve courses and a stopped string length of only 23" (*c*.58 cm.). The tuning given for both French and English lutes is the D minor tuning with a top string at f'. The shorter string length of the English lute would suggest a top string pitch nearer to about g' than f'.[87] This is the type of instrument introduced to England by Jacques Gaultier *c*.1625, and is persistently called the 'French lute' by Mace.

The two lute manuscripts known as the Osborne and Danby manuscripts were compiled on a Continental tour of 1706–11. This Continental tour, on which lute teachers were found and engaged to teach the young Earl of Danby, in several places they visited, tells us nothing about lute playing in England. Yet it suggests that the lute still could be an acceptable choice of instrument for an aristocratic Englishmen

---

[77] Evelyn, *Diary*, iii. 91, 307; iv. 220, 360; Pepys, *Diary*, vii. 56, 378; ix. 153.

[78] Ward, 'Sprightly and Cheerful Musick', 44.

[79] *RECM* i. 146. Walkling, 'Masque and Politics', 45–6.   [80] *RECM* v. 281, 284.

[81] Tilmouth, 'A Calendar of References', 48.   [82] Ibid. 50, 68, 71.   [83] Ibid. 68.

[84] Ibid. 80.

[85] Douglas Alton Smith, 'Sylvius Leopold Weiss', *EM* 8 (1980), 47–58 at 49.

[86] Prynne, 'James Talbot's Manuscript', 59.   [87] Ibid.

to play, and there may well have been others who similarly learned abroad. Whether or not the Earl of Danby learnt the lute because of the availability of good teachers and the great esteem felt for the lute in Germany and Holland at the time, or because of a family desire for him to study the instrument, we cannot tell.[88]

The last lutenist until the twentieth century to attempt to make a living from his art in England was Rudolf Straube, who arrived *c.*1759 after publishing his *Due sonate a liuto solo* in 1746 in Leipzig,[89] and was active in London until his death *c.*1780.[90] Straube had been a pupil of J. S. Bach at the Thomasschule in Leipzig. He published no music for the lute in England, but turned his attentions to the more fashionable 'English guitar'. Despite its name, this instrument is in fact a form of cittern. The English guitar had six courses of double metal strings, with the bottom two single. It was tuned *g′, e′, c′, g, e, c* and had a considerable vogue during the second half of the eighteenth century in England.[91]

It is likely that Straube was forced to teach and write for the English guitar because he could not attract sufficient pupils for the lute. That he was in very reduced circumstances while in London is proved by the story told of Thomas Gainsborough and a certain unnamed impoverished German lute professor in *The Four Ages of Man together with Essays on Various Subjects* by William Jackson of Exeter (London, 1798).[92] In the story the reluctant lutenist is prevailed upon to relinquish both his instrument and music book by the callous Gainsborough. Straube is never mentioned by name, but there can be little doubt that he was the victim of Gainsborough's musical ambition, since Add. 31698, which in part is in Straube's hand, contains lute music and a version of the story of the Straube–Gainsborough encounter in which Straube's name is used throughout. This manuscript was compiled for a pupil, and there are two distinct main hands. Gainsborough could even have been the pupil. The manuscript contains pieces in tablature as well as mensural notation, and would appear to have still been in circulation in the nineteenth century, as the manuscript is dated on fo. 13ʳ 'copied May 1813' and on fo. 28ᵛ 'copied June 1810'. On the original front cover it was inscribed 'Barry. Harp Maker/King Sᵗ Soho'; he may have been the owner or seller of the manuscript in the early nineteenth century. The music is in the mid-eighteenth-century German style, and does not connect with any living English lute tradition. Evidently there was at least one person learning the lute in London in the early nineteenth century.

---

[88] Many of the papers concerned with this tour are found in *GB-Lb* Egerton 3339. See Crawford, 'Lord Danby'.

[89] Rudolf Straube, *Due sonate a liuto solo* (1746); facs., with introduction by Tim Crawford (Monaco, 1974).

[90] *New Grove*, viii. 204.   [91] Ibid., vi. 199–200.

[92] The extract is on fo. 43ʳ ᵛ of the MS, and is entitled 'Gainsborough the Artist and Rudolph Straube'. It is taken (without reference) from William Jackson of Exeter, *The Four Ages of Man; together with Essays on Various Subjects* (London, 1798), 181. See Tim Crawford's introduction to the facsimile edition of Straube's *Due sonate* (Leipzig, 1746; facs. edn., Monaco, 1981).

A separate report of Straube's reduced circumstances comes from John Marsh's journal for 1777. In it Marsh, a gentleman composer, lends his copy of Mace's *Musick's Monument* to his friend Mr Chafy:

Mr C[hafy] who play'd the guitar a little, desired me to try when in Town to get him one of those exploded instruments [a lute]. I therefore enquir'd at the principal music shops without being able to meet with anything of the kind, but was at length recommended to a Mr Straube a German whom after much trouble & enquir'g I found in a garrett at Pimlico, who had only one which he play'd & wo'd not part with (at least for a second hand price) & as he gave me little or no hope of meeting with one elsewhere I at length gave over the search.[93]

This report would indicate that the encounter with Gainsborough took place after 1777.

The type of lute which Straube played and composed for was the 13-course Baroque lute. This lute was either made with a single pegbox, with bass and treble riders to accommodate the twenty-four strings (eleven double courses with the first and second course single), or in the so-called 'swan-neck' form. This later type was developed in Germany from the 1720s onwards and involved a complicated carved extension to house two sets of pegs. There is evidence that 13-course swan-neck lutes did make an appearance in England as the Victoria and Albert has such a lute on which the marquetary on the back of the neck has the following words: 'Rauche in Chandos Street London 1762'.[94] Michael Rauche was a known instrument maker of the time. However it may be that he imported or modified this instrument, rather than made it from scratch. This type of lute also appears in Johann Zoffany's picture of *The Sharp Family*, dated *c.*1779–81 (see Pl. 12.2). It is for this kind of lute that Add. 31698 is almost certainly intended.

When so little was published or survives in the way of Baroque lute tutors it is ironic that England, where the lute had been in decline for some time, and a backwater as far as lute composition was concerned, should produce two excellent tutors, one printed and one manuscript, while France did not produce even one that is in any way comparable in design or scope that survives. Thomas Mace's *Musick's Monument* (1676) was published only a few years after the Burwell Lute Tutor (*c.*1660–72) was compiled, but they represent two separate schools of thought on lute playing derived from two different traditions.[95] Mace intended 'The Lute made Easie' section of *Musick's Monument* as a tutor for a complete beginner studying without the help of a teacher, but the Burwell Tutor may exist as a result of a series of lessons given by an expert player and teacher to, in all probability, a single

[93] *The John Marsh Journals*, ed. Brian Robins (New York, 1998), 158.

[94] Anthony Baines, *Victoria and Albert Museum, Catalogue of Musical Instruments*, xi: *Non-Keyboard Instruments* (London, 1968), no. 7/7, p. 32.

[95] Some, at least, of *Musick's Monument* was completed by 1672 (see p. 45).

PL. 12.2. *The Sharpe Family*, Johan Zoffany, *c*.1779–81. Hardwicke Court, Gloucester

pupil. Much that is not explained in the Burwell Tutor may have been omitted as practical demonstration made it unnecessary. Mace's book also includes instruction for the theorbo and viol, as well as lengthy observations on how to improve church music.

The Burwell Tutor supplies fourteen study pieces of moderate difficulty, a few of which are dissected bar by bar, along with several exercises, but it is most important as a source of contemporary polemic about the French lute.[96] The pieces

[96] *The Burwell Lute Tutor*, see introductory study by Robert Spencer. See also Dart, 'Miss Mary Burwell's Instruction Book'. Dart's single-stave transcriptions are not altogether satisfactory as he transcribes the pieces into the standard D minor tuning (i.e. f', d', a, f, d, A) instead of raising it to the 'French B flat' and 'French B sharp' tuning pitch specified in the tutor, which results in the pitches $b\flat'$, g', d', $b\flat$, g, d and $b\natural'$, g', d', $b\natural$, g, d (fos. 10$^\text{r}$ and 10$^\text{v}$).

themselves contain a number of uncorrected tablature mistakes and rhythmic inconsistencies,[97] and it may be that Mary Burwell could not play or did not understand the music at the time of copying. The composers mentioned are: Old Gaultier [i.e. Ennemond] (2); Pinel (2); Gaultier of Paris [i.e. Denis] (1); Vincent (1); Gaultier d'Angleterre [Jacques] (1); Marquis of Mortmar (1); Dubut (1); Anon. (5). The pieces are often chosen for a purpose. Example 12.1 demonstrates the stopping

Ex. 12.1. *'Sarabrand of English Gaultier', Burwell Tutor, fo. 27^r*

[97] e.g. in the second half of the Dubut corant on fos. 18ᵛ and 21ᵛ, the notes of bar 5 are a tablature line too low; the final piece, 'The losse of the golden Rose lute', has rhythmic errors in bars 2 and 14.

of the seventh string in bars 5 and 6. This allows the *tirer* and *rabbatre* brushed strokes at the beginning this phrase to traverse across five courses.[98] The piece is transcribed for a lute with a top string at high *bb′* as described in the tutor.

The lute's mythology, history, and metaphysics are discussed at length, as are its abuses and usage. Of the sixteen chapters only chapters 5 to 10 are primarily concerned with the teaching of technique, though chapter 15 supplies six of the pieces. The author of the Burwell Tutor compiled his method from his own experience. The pupil copied into her book sections of text, leaving spaces for the tablature examples, which were then inserted by the teacher himself. The normal Renaissance method of lute-book compilation was for pupils to write their own books from teachers' copies of music, but instances of teachers' copying music into pupils' books are frequent;[99] however, the amount of text Mary Burwell's teacher required her to copy down and absorb is unusual, and has no contemporary parallel.

The most favoured tuning was the 'French B flat', which is none other than the normal D minor tuning though at a high pitch (i.e. with a top string at *bb′* instead of *f′* or *g′*.[100] (See Pl. 12.3.) This high pitch seems unlikely at first, but several other sources, Bodley 410–414 and the tablature transcription in Salmon's *Essay to the Advancement of Music*, show that it was used in England at this time.[101] The author was wholly committed to the pure French school of playing, which in 1650 was at its height in France, and is disparaging of the English practice, introduced *c*.1625 by Jacques Gaultier, of playing on a 12-course lute.[102]

The six tunings introduced in chapter 5 do not deviate very far from the normal D minor/D major tunings which gradually became standardized throughout Europe after 1640, except in the basses. The only tunings to require a retuning of the higher courses are the Trumpet Tuning and its 12-course variant, Mr Jenkins Tuning.[103] These two tunings (*bb′*, *g*, *eb′*, *bb*, *g*, *eb*, *d*, *Bb*, *Ab*, *G*, [*F*], and *bb′*, *g*, *eb*, *bb*, *g*, *eb*, *d*, *C*, *Bb*, *Ab*, *G*, [*F*]), if transposed down a minor third, have much in common with the [French] Flat tuning (tuning no. 10) as used by Mace. The Jenkins tuning shows that Jenkins played on the 12-course lute and preferred a tuning midway between the Flat tuning and the D minor tuning.

---

[98] Ledbetter, *Harpsichord and Lute Music*, 48.

[99] e.g. the Board MS has a piece in Dowland's autograph and the Folger MS has many such teachers' contributions to the MS.

[100] Robert Spencer, in his introduction to *The Burwell Lute Tutor*, gives the pitch an octave down (top string *b*), but in his article 'English Nomenclature of Extended Lutes', *FoMRHI* 23 (1981), Comm. 337, 58, he corrected this to the high pitch (*b′*).

[101] The pieces nos. 28–32 by 'Mr Birchingshaw' in Bodley 410–414 use a lute at this high pitch, as does John Rogers in his 'Arrons Jig' in Salmon's *Essay to the Advancement of Music* (London, 1672), 66. The surviving 12-course instrument (at Linköping in Sweden) is small enough for this pitch.

[102] Burwell Tutor, fo. 68ʳ.   [103] Ibid., fos. 12ᵛ–13ʳ.

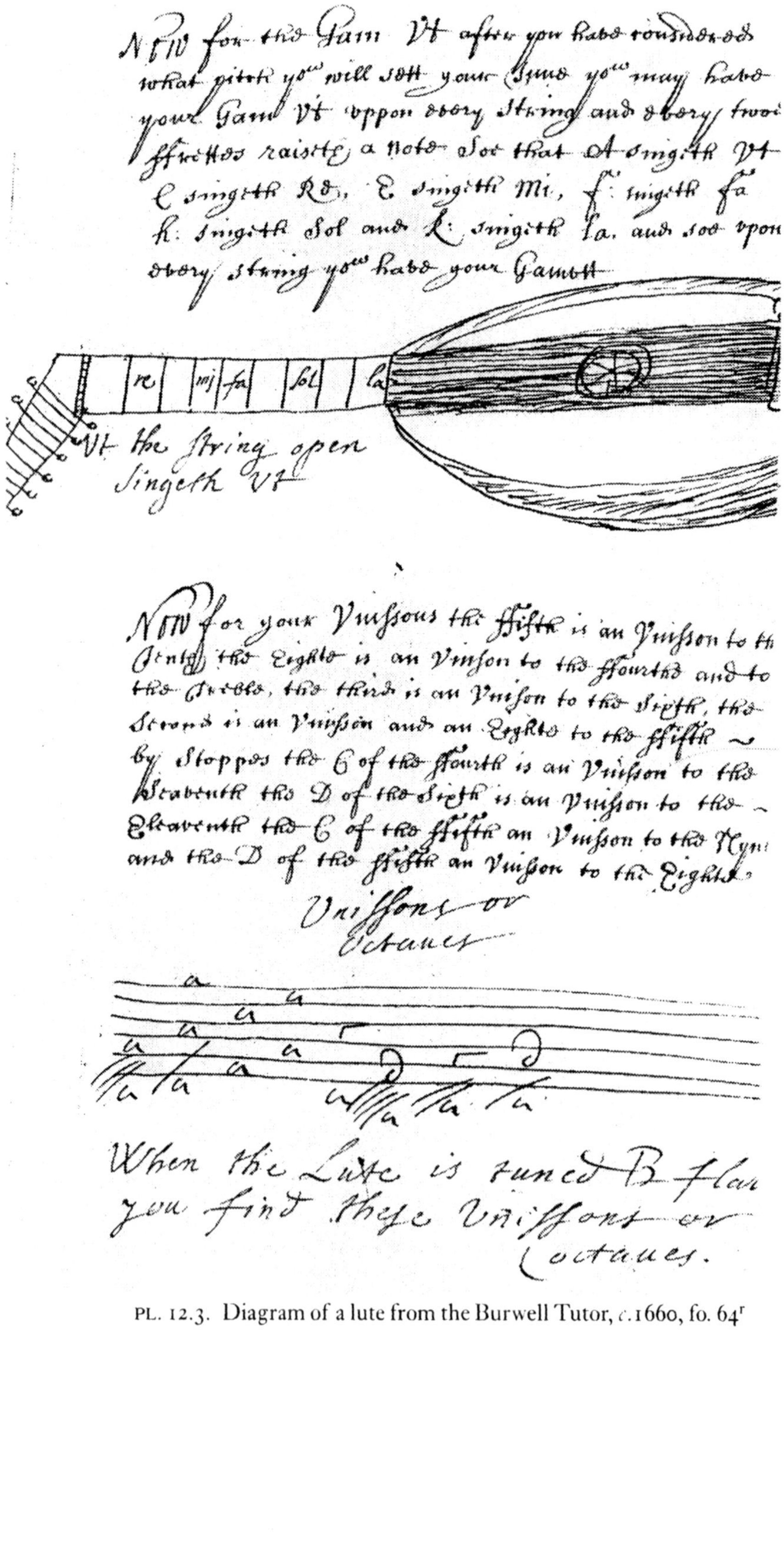

NOW for the Gam Ut after you have considered what pitch you will sett your Treble you may have your Gam Ut uppon every string and every two ffrettes raiseth a note Soe that A singeth Ut C singeth Re, E singeth Mi, f singeth fa h singeth Sol and l singeth la. and soe upon every string you have your Gamutt

re | mi | fa | sol | la

Ut the string open
singeth Ut

NOW for your Unissons the ffifte is an Unisson to the Tenor the Eighte is an Unison to the ffourthe and to the treble, the third is an Unisson to the Sixth, the Second is an Unisson and an Eighte to the ffifte ~ by Stoppes the C of the fourth is an Unisson to the Seaventh the D of the Sixth is an Unisson to the Eleaventh the C of the ffifte an Unisson to the Nyne and the D of the ffifte an Unisson to the Eighte

Unissons or
Octaves

When the Lute is tuned B flat
you find these Unissons or
Octaves.

PL. 12.3. Diagram of a lute from the Burwell Tutor, c.1660, fo. 64^r

Reference is made to classical antiquity and its associated mythology throughout the book, as well as to biblical and Christian history. Pieces in each key or 'moode' are given in chapter 1, though there is no attempt at connecting different modes with different emotional states in the manner of Denis Gaultier's *Rhétorique des Dieux*.[104] The tutor makes very exalted claims for the instrument's status. The lute, it states, is 'without Contradiction the King of Instruments'.[105] It is at pains to dispel the 'Errours & Abuses that are committed about the Lute' (ch. 16). Singled out for criticism here are: the adoption of the 12-course lute—'a bastard Instrument betweene a Lute and a Theorbo'; the compositions of those ill-suited by nature to write lute music; the use of the instrument to play anything other than sober and serious music to select company (i.e. the abuse of using it for singing and dancing, and playing in taverns); and playing too many pieces, on too many tunings, too fast, and without keeping time.[106] There is also the oft-quoted complaint that the lute makes people grow crooked. In reference to this the Burwell Tutor is forthright in saying: 'Those that have said that the Lute maketh people crooked have said it to avoid the Charges in learneing or the paines or the trouble which they have fancied to be in getting that Arte or being crooked before they have learned to play of the Lute to cover there infirmity with that rare quality.'[107]

Later the Burwell Tutor claims that 'For what concerneth the partes of the body the Lute hath a great advantage over other Instruments' because 'The beauty of the Arme, of the hands and of the Necke are advantagiously displayed in playing of the Lute', unlike the virginals, which involve turning the back towards the company or the viol, which 'intangleth one in spreading the Armes and openeth the Legges which doth not become man much lesse woaman'.[108]

This last assertion may seem trivial to us, but there is little doubt in the minds of North and Hawkins that it contributed to the lute's decline. Hawkins includes the following passage on the lute:

The lute, notwithstanding the great improvements which the French had made of it, as well, by varying its form as by increasing the number of chords, thereby rendering it in some respects the rival of the harpsichord was nevertheless declining in the estimation of the World. Waller suggests as a reason for it, an opinion, which, although it is controverted by Mace and other masters, had very probably its foundation in truth; it was suspected that the practice of the lute had a tendency to bring on deformity in ladies and persons of delicate habits, an evil which was not to be feared from the erect and graceful posture required in playing the harpsichord.[109]

---

[104] These 'moodes' are identified by the open bass strings for the tonic of the piece, e.g. 'The last Key or Moode is the Eleaventh Base' (ibid., fo. 63ᵛ).

[105] Ibid., fo. 43ʳ and fo. 68ʳ. [106] Ibid., fos. 68ʳ–70ʳ. [107] Ibid., fo. 16ʳ.

[108] Ibid., fo. 43ᵛ. [109] Hawkins, *A General History*, 706.

North has the following to say on the subject: 'for woman the espinett or harpsichord, lute and guitarr . . . And the harpsichord for ladys rather than the lute; one reason is it keeps their body in a better posture than the other, which tends to make them crooked.'[110]

To a society in which good posture was an important sign of good etiquette such a rumour may have dissuaded many from learning the instrument. Indeed poise and comeliness in playing the lute are constantly emphasized. In marked contrast to Mace, the exalted claims for the lute in the Burwell Tutor would appear to have been made from a position of strength. This is at odds with the true situation. The lute in the England of 1660 was clearly in decline. Probably the tutor's conception goes back to a period when the author himself was a student in France close to Ennemond Gaultier's circle, when the lute was unquestionably the dominant instrument of high society. By 1660 most Englishmen would have disputed the primacy of the lute that is so unhesitatingly stated throughout the book.

The first four chapters of the Burwell Tutor provide some insight into how the history of the lute was taught in mid-century England. The first chapter on the lute's origins draws first on the scene of the holy birth and the music of the angelic host which included 'Lutes and voices'. The Judaic 'Cythara' was believed to have been a kind of lute. Turning to pagan antiquity, the legends of Orpheus, Amphion, and Arion all provide instances of the miraculous powers of the lute.[111] The second chapter, by contrast, says much concerning the development of the instrument which we know to be true, particularly in the increase in size, number of strings and ribs, and the makers of Bologna and Padua.[112]

The third chapter, in dealing with the famous lute masters of old, jumps straight from the time of Julius Caesar, and how the French nation 'ravished' Italian art and science, which included lute playing, to the time of 'Vomigny' [i.e. Vaumesnil], 'Perrichon', and 'the Polack' [Jacob Reys?] (i.e. c.1600–10).[113] From here via Mesangeau, who is given praise for having 'given to the Lute his first Perfection', it moves to Vieux Gaultier, who is given precedence over all the masters, including the other three Gaultiers, Dufault, Dubut, Vincent, Pinel, Mercure, and 'Blanrocher Landas' who are all said to have issued from him, and each of whose style is characterised in words.[114]

The French nation is consistently named as the champion of the instrument: 'as the Violl is the Instrument of England, the Gittarre that of Spaine—the Theorbo that of Italy, the virginall or harpsicall that of Germany the Harpe that of Ireland . . .'.[115] Apart from the admission that 'The first and most famous Lute Masters wee confesse were the Italians'[116] (although the implication is that these Italian lute masters were prominent in classical antiquity rather than a hundred

[110] *Roger North on Music*, 16.   [111] Burwell Tutor, fos. 1ᵛ 2ᵛ.   [112] Ibid., fo. 3ʳ ᵛ.
[113] Ibid., fo. 5ʳ.   [114] Ibid., fo. 5ᵛ.   [115] Ibid., fo. 6ʳ.   [116] Ibid., fo. 5ʳ.

years before), there is no recognition of national schools of lute playing other than that of France. The complete disregard for John Johnson, John Dowland, and the other English masters of the Elizabethan and Jacobean Age argues strongly that the tutor was compiled by someone with a French training and viewpoint of the history of lute music. In fact, as regards history, the Burwell Tutor is only clear in its statements back to about 1610, before which mythology and pseudo-history are freely mixed.

Of much greater interest and importance than the pieces in the Burwell Tutor are the examples and explanations of right- and left-hand fingering and ornament signs, that together form the basis of Baroque lute technique. Here we learn that 'The right hand useth the Thumbe and the twoe next fingers to the Thumb onely'.[117] If there are unplayed strings between the bass of a chord and the higher strings, the upper strings are to be struck with a sliding stroke in which the thumb plays the bass string, and all the others with 'the forefinger onely, sliding from the Treble upward over the Stringes and repeating sometimes the Treble with the middle finger'.[118] This stroke would be used for the opening chord in Ex. 12.1. For chords where there are no unsounded strings between the bass and the higher strings, then the thumb strums down over all the strings, except for the uppermost, which is played by the middle finger.[119] Such a stroke would be used after the double bar in Ex. 12.1. Chords of only two notes are plucked simultaneously by the thumb and middle finger. The Burwell Tutor calls this 'nipping'.[120] Chords in sarabandes are played 'loosely after the manner of the gittarre; not altogether but sometimes with the Thumbe onley sometimes with the forefinger onley'.[121] This last technique would be used for the chords on the second and third beats of the first bar of Ex. 12.1.

The Tutor gives comprehensive instructions for cadences. These are rapid strikings of two notes a tone or semitone apart on conjunct strings, one after the other, followed by a restriking of the first note. Normally a chord will follow if at the end of a phrase or lesson, though the Tutor admits that 'old Gaultier hath intermixed them in all parts of a lesson and that with a great deal of grace'.[122] There are two principal sorts 'although both are compounded of three notes only'.[123] The first is with a sliding stroke where you start on the upper note of the two notes. Here the forefinger slides upwards, striking first the upper and then the lower string, with the upper note reiterated 'with the middle finger as fast after as possibly may be'.[124] The second is begun on the lower of the two strings with 'the first letter to be strucke with the forefinger[,] the second letter with the middle finger[,] and the third with the forefinger again' (Ex. 12.1, bar 11).[125] Cadences with and without a shake [trill] are explained, as are cadences which are played without a sliding

[117] Burwell Tutor, fo. 29ʳ.   [118] Ibid.   [119] Ibid., fo. 32ʳ.   [120] Ibid., fo. 37ʳ.
[121] Ibid., fo. 37ᵛ.   [122] Ibid., fo. 32ʳ.   [123] Ibid.   [124] Ibid., fo. 33ʳ.   [125] Ibid.

stroke.[126] Sometimes only the upper of the two strings of the basses is to be played, sometimes only the lower.[127]

Here then is a comprehensive explanation of Baroque lute right-hand technique which, with its frequent cadences and 'raked' chords, as Mace calls them, is very different from Renaissance technique. The main similarity is in the playing of some melodic phrases in the middle and upper strings without accompanying bass notes.[128] Such phrases are played with the old 'thumb and index' technique that can be traced back to the early Renaissance. Left-hand technique is less revolutionary, though ornamentation and slurring are integral to the style. Instructions on how to 'humour' a lesson by the use of *inégalité* and rhythmically varying the arpeggiation are also given.

Thomas Mace (see Pl. 12.4) is representative of an older school of lute teachers than Rogers. He never travelled abroad, as far as is known. He retained a great affection for the music of the Caroline period, in particular consort music in which all parts were balanced in importance, and in which all parts could be heard. He compares this music favourably to the 'New-Fashion'd Musick' of the post-Restoration era.[129] He is scornful of the guitar ('a Bit of the Old Lute'),[130] and especially wary of the overpowering use of the violin, which he regards as the most injurious of the 'Modes' and 'Fashions' of the times.[131] He speaks of modern violin ayres as 'rather fit to make a Mans *Ears Glow*, and fill his *Brains full of Frisks*, etc. than to *Season and Sober his Mind, or Elevate his Affection* to *Goodness*'.[132]

Mace states that he began to learn the lute fifty-four years before writing his book in 1675. From this we can date his first attempts on the instrument to 1621, when he would have been about 9.[133] It is not known who he was taught by, or if he was self-taught. Few people in England at that time would have been playing the lute in anything other than Renaissance tuning. Like Richard Mathews, he would probably have undergone two apprenticeships on the lute, learning first in Renaissance tuning and then in transitional tunings. His choice of the 'French Flat' tuning no. 10, and the 12-course lute for his book, is understandable given that he was in his prime during the Caroline period. The French style of playing introduced by Jacques Gaultier *c.*1625 is the starting point for an exploration of Mace's style, though much was added in the intervening fifty years, and much invented by Mace himself for the book. The music that Mace composed and included in *Musick's Monument* is very different from the pure French style of *c.*1650 taught by the author of the Burwell Tutor.

---

[126] Ibid., fos. 33ʳ, 39ʳ.   [127] Ibid., fo. 32ᵛ.   [128] Ibid., fos. 32ʳ, 38ᵛ.

[129] Mace, *Musick's Monument*, 236.   [130] Ibid. 237.

[131] Ibid. 236. Mace does allow for the use of violins for '*Extraordinary Jolly, or Jocund Consort-Occasion*', so long as they do not '*Out-cry* the *Rest* of the *Musick*, (the *Basses* especially)', 246.

[132] Ibid. 236.   [133] Ibid. 39.

PL. 12.4. Portrait of Thomas Mace from *Musick's Monument*

Mace mentions Rogers in his '*Praeludium to This Work*' quoted at the beginning of this chapter. Rogers is possibly the 'Old Master-Teacher upon the Lute' who, on looking over Mace's book while it was being printed,

and seeing most of my *Lessons* were in the *Flat Tuning*, seem'd not to be well pleas'd at It, whereupon I took an occasion to *Discourse* the *Business* with him a little, and to *Vindicate It*; but still he seem'd to persist in his *Former Humour*, (of *Opinion* only; for he could give no *Reason* but only 'twas the *Fashion*, and the *New-Tuning*) . . .[134]

Mace is aware of the newer French style but wishes to remain aloof from it. Rather than raking chords with a single right-hand finger he prefers the older English practice of plucked chords, with each chord member being plucked by a different finger.[135] Of all the contemporary fashions in lute playing, he finds most fault with the tendency of lutenists to play in the D minor tuning in preference to French Flat.

England in the 1670s witnessed a debate among musicians, between those who used many tunings, each of which would suit a few related keys only, and those like Matthew Locke who appealed for standardization by the adoption of a single tuning, equally accessible in all keys, but which would lack the special resonances and sonorities of the altered tunings. The debate centred principally on the viol, but was no less applicable to the lute. Mace devotes a whole chapter to proving the superiority of the French Flat tuning over all others, the D minor tuning in particular.[136] This Flat tuning would appear from surviving manuscript sources to have been the most popular of the transitional tunings introduced from France *c.*1630.[137] His argument centres on the assertion that:

This Flat Tuning will give me the Freedom, Naturally, Familiarly, and with Ease and Advantage, to Work, in Fullness of Parts, &c. in all Those 7 keys; And That Other, (call'd the New Tuning) will not so Naturally, Familiarly, and with the like Ease, and Advantages, allow me the like Freedom, to Work with the same Fullness of Parts upon all the 7 Keys.[138]

He supports this with a comparison of all the 'full stops' (i.e. ways of playing full chords containing thirds, fifths, and octaves, and their inversions) possible in each of the seven keys based on the notes of the C major scale in both the French Flat and the D minor tunings.[139] He also points out that the diapasons in tuning no. 10 produce a diatonic major scale beginning on its tonic, which the D minor tuning does not.[140]

---

[134] Mace, *Musick's Monument*, 199.   [135] Ibid. 101.   [136] Ibid. 191–202.

[137] All English post-1620 solo lute MSS that use transitional tunings prominently feature tuning no. 10.

[138] Mace, *Musick's Monument*, 191.

[139] Ibid. 193–6. The results of this comparison are 549 full stops using tuning no. 10, and 350 using D minor tuning.

[140] Ibid. 198–9.

There is some truth in what Mace says, but he overlooks the point that the old Renaissance tuning was more practical in far more keys than even the French Flat. More significantly, as there is little lute music that survives from France after *c*.1640 in tuning no. 10, Mace is cutting his pupils off from the mainstream of French lute music by adhering, in his teaching, to a tuning that was becoming obsolete outside Britain. One reason why Mace's book failed in its object of reviving interest in the lute may have been because he insisted on this tuning, when people would not return to the old ways. This is the very point that was made to him by the old master in the quotation above. He does, begrudgingly, give a suite in the New Tuning (D minor tuning), and a method of converting music from the Flat Tuning to the D minor tuning for the lute, and to Renaisssance tuning for the theorbo.[141]

The foremost reason that Mace gives for the lute's decline is that it is generally held to be difficult to play. To confute this assertion he replies, with questionable reasoning, that the newer lutes with twenty-three strings are much easier than those of old (which had only eleven, twelve, or fourteen strings), as difficult left-hand stops are now much simplified since more open strings are accessible. He reasons that the consequent increase in right-hand difficulty in finding all the diapasons is far less than the benefit in ease for the left hand.[142] Secondly, he suggests that newer lutes are easier to play as they are better laid out for ease of the fingers, and thirdly that great masters, in particular the French, did not reveal the secrets of their art, allowing their skill to die with them—something Mace is prepared to rectify.[143]

The other aspersions against the lute that Mace lists are 'that it will take up the Time of an *Apprenticeship* [i.e. seven years] to play *well*'; next 'That it makes *Young People* grow *awry*' (which we know to have been a common and serious complaint); 'That it is a chargeable instrument' to keep so that 'one had as good keep a Horse as a Lute, for Cost'; that it is a 'women's instrument'; and lastly, that it is 'out of fashion'.[144]

The last three assertions, despite Mace's answer to each, had a large measure of truth in the Restoration period. We know that a set of fine lute strings might cost as much as a third of the instrument itself, and that lutes cost anything between £5 and £100, though a price of between £10 and £20 was normal. Of the manuscripts in the post-1620 period whose provenance is known or can be guessed at, many belonged to women, and by Mace's time no one would dispute that in England, at any rate, the lute was out of fashion.

Mace's primary aim in the lute section of *Musick's Monument* is explained in the title '*The Lute Made Easie*'. It is a guide for a complete beginner working systematically through the basis of technique, with preliminary pieces, plus a full set of suites in each diatonic key, and a supplementary suite in D minor tuning, because, as

---

[141] Mace, *Musick's Monument*, 181–91. [142] Ibid. 39. [143] Ibid. 40. [144] Ibid. 43.

Mace says with some sarcasm, 'I suppose, you may love to be in *Fashion*'.[145] Mace may well have been the first person to have written suites with a prescribed number of movements to be played in a certain order. Until *Musick's Monument*, manuscript sources would indicate that suites were not necessarily put together according to composer. While keeping roughly to the allemande, courante, sarabande (and gigue after 1650) order, their only common characteristic was their key and tuning. Mace's suites, by contrast, stand as unified sets of pieces with more in common than merely a single unifying key and tuning. He also provides six interludes for the player to move without interruption from key to key.

Mace's work as a systematic guide for a complete beginner achieves more than any other lute tutor book ever written, and bears constant rereading. Although the sixteenth-century German tutors of Gerle, Newsidler, Judenkünig, and Waissel are admirable, they do not compare with Mace's book in the fullness of descriptive text which accompanies the musical exercises. It is also a complete handbook for the instrument, with much information on practical matters relating to stringing, fretting, removing the belly, etc.

During the fifty years that Mace played the lute, the instrument in England had undergone a very haphazard development under the influence of French lute music. The English, after a good start in the 1630s, had remained considerably behind fashions in France as regards instruments, tunings, and style. Mace aimed to draw together the best of this half-century-old Anglo-French tradition, update it by the addition to the suites of such forms as the galliard, tattle de moy, and ayre, and thereby put the instrument on a new footing. Mace's tragedy was that by 1676 the lute's decline in popular esteem was irreversible. Even in France the harpsichord had eclipsed the lute as the primary solo instrument for art music. Few people probably ever used Mace's book as an instruction method for the lute, and it seems likely that despite his list of 301 subscribers (which is strongly biased towards members of the University of Cambridge, who would have been Mace's acquaintances, and his family connections in York), many copies remained unsold in 1690.[146] The advertisement licensed on 5 May 1675 (see below), saying that all who bought the book in the first three months of printing (i.e. 10 June to 10 August 1676) would pay only the subscribers' price of 12s., certainly did not succeed in selling off the stock.

Mace's jovial, optimistic style and gift for multiple adjectives hide the increasingly sad circumstances of his old age. At some stage he broke both his arms, which slowed down his shakes.[147] In his first publication, *Profit, Conveniency and Pleasure to the whole Nation, being a short rational discourse lately presented to his Majesty concerning the high ways of England* (1675), to which he added a six-page advertisement

---

[145] Ibid. 181. [146] Rupert M. Thackeray, 'Thomas Mace', *Musical Times*, 92 (1951), 306–7.
[147] Mace, *Musick's Monument*, 103.

for the forthcoming *Musick's Monument*, he includes in the epistle to the king the revealing passage:

> I am no courtier, know not how to Mode
> But bluntly this contrive for public good.
> And though I'm well-nigh Deaf and well-nigh
> Blind;[148]

This is the only reference in all of Mace's works to his loss of sight. References to his increasing deafness, which was probably more upsetting to him as a musician, teacher, and singer, are more common. Certainly his deafness would have made his duties as a singing man of Trinity College difficult in the extreme. On 17 April 1706 a singing man's place was made void by 'Mr Mace' at Trinity College, and there is no suggestion that this is any other than Thomas Mace.[149] Thus it would seem that he kept his place, in name at least, until his death. Possibly he was able to continue singing for a time, despite his deafness, but for how long is not known.

Nothing is heard about Mace from 1676 until 1690, when an advertisement appeared in London which included the following doggerel:

> Men say the times are strange; 'tis True
> 'Cause many strange things hap to be;
> Let it not then seem strange to you,
> To here one strange thing more to see.

In Devereaux Court, next the Grecian Coffee House, at the Temple Back-gate, There is a Deaf Person Teacheth Musick to Perfection; who by reason of his great age v. 77 is come to Town, with his whole stock of rich musical furniture and instruments and books to put off, to whomsoever delights in such choice things; for he hath nothing light or vain, but all substantial and solid music.[150]

There follows a list of articles for sale, including an organ, a pair of viols, a pedal-harpsichord, a single harpsichord, a double lute (Mace's dyphone), several other lutes, viols, and theorboes, and a large collection of music and books, including a number of unsold copies of *Musick's Monument*, which he is prepared to dispose of cheaply.[151]

Mace only stayed for four months in London. Perhaps he did not attract sufficient students to pay his way.[152] The whole expedition sounds like a pathetic attempt to better his lot in different surroundings. In 1698 he published a second

---

[148] Thomas Mace, *Profit, Conveniency and Pleasure* (London, 1675), Introductory Epistle to the King.

[149] Thomas Mace, *Musick's Monument*, ii: trans. and commentary ed. Jean Jacquot and André Souris (Paris, 1966), p. xxvii. Taken from the 'Conclusions Book' of Trinity College.

[150] *GB-Lbl* Harley 5396, no. 386, fo. 129'.

[151] See *Musick's Monument*, ii, pp. xxix–xxx. This advertisement fared little better, since a catalogue announcing the sale of Mace's instruments and music by auction on 17 Dec. 1691 also survives. Ibid. n. 29.

[152] Thackeray, 'Thomas Mace', 307.

and last philanthropic pamphlet, *Riddles, Mervels and Rarities, or, A New Way of Health, from an Old Man's Experience* (published in Cambridge).[153] That this deaf, blind, and aged lute teacher managed to keep himself going into his nineties without an apparent loss of spirit is a testimony to his strength of character.

Much has been made of Mace's musical conservatism. His derisive use of the words 'mode' and 'fashion' underlines this. He looked for gravity and sobriety in music, and upheld the lute and viol against the encroachments of guitar and violin. His concern with tunings and complicated ornamentation, including subtle vibrato and staccato effects, show that he was particularly interested in sonority. In this and other respects Mace was considerably innovative.[154] His care over the organization of movements, variation of dynamics, as well as a whole range of technical effects designed to 'humour' music, show that he was no reactionary. At heart his interest lies in musical rhetoric and spiritual elevation through music, in contrast to the virtuosic display, unrestrained, and arguably unfocused passion of much Italian and some French music fashionable in England in the 1670s and 1680s.

A problem with any assessment of Mace's lute music is that there is little surviving lute music composed in England after 1660 with which to compare his pieces, other than the few English pieces in the Tabley manuscript. He was already an old man when he wrote *Musick's Monument*, and his antiquated ideas are manifest in the book. The lute pieces in the book were intended for students to learn with, and, being didactic in purpose, might be different from other lute music he composed. To imagine that the music in *Musick's Monument* is fully representative of lute composition in England c.1660–70 may be wrong.

A starting point for a stylistic comparison of Mace's lute music is the French music in transitional tunings popular in England from 1630 to 1660. Mace would have been most familiar with this type of composition as it was at the height of its popularity in England while he was a young man. Thus it is not surprising that the basis of his compositional style is that of Mesangeau, Dufaut, and others, as it was known in England c.1630–40. Mace added much that is English to this style, a process that was already at work in the music of lutenists such as Lawes and Lawrence in the pre-Commonwealth period, and much that is purely his own.

Comparison can also be made with mid-century French lute music in D minor tuning, such as that of Denis Gaultier, and the published music of Ennemond Gaultier, and pieces found in the Robarts manuscript. Clearly Mace and his French contemporaries, after having a common starting point in the French *brisé* style c.1630, had moved in different directions. The French had consistently refined the *brisé* style, introducing ever more rhythmic and melodic ambiguities, so that

---

[153] *New Grove*, vi. 422.

[154] See E. D. Mackerness, 'Thomas Mace and the Fact of Reasonableness', *Monthly Musical Record*, 85 (1955), 211–3, 235–9, for an overstatement of Mace's musical conservatism.

part-writing and phrase structures were never clear-cut but always supremely flexible. Mace's music, by contrast with contemporary French music, is much closer to that of Ballard's 1631 and 1638 books, especially in his adherence to the outmoded French Flat tuning (no. 10), one of the most prominent of the transitional tunings of the 1630s. Rhythmic and melodic ambiguity is not a strong feature of Mace's lute music, and much of it is easily defined in terms of treble and bass as well as being rather more tuneful than contemporary French music. These last attributes are hallmarks of the Anglo-French style of lute composers working in England, from Jacques Gaultier onwards, and which give the pieces their Englishness.

Mace's use of the 12-course lute may, in part, explain the wide pitch span between treble and bass. However, his consistent use of the highest frets of the first course (up to frets 'm' and 'n') and the lowest diapasons is directly in contrast to mid-century French lute music, which stays firmly rooted in the lute's middle registers and almost never goes beyond fret 'k' (i.e. the ninth fret).[155] As Mace's texture is often thin, preferring a treble and bass along with the occasional full chord, the result is a rather hollow and 'unhomogeneous' sound, comparable in this respect to that of Mathew's *Lutes Apology*. The highest frets of the middle courses are not exploited as John Wilson does in his pieces, and lower, and thus easier, left-hand positions on these strings are always preferred. The diapasons are fairly consistently employed, more so than in contemporary French lute music, and occasionally for melodic or quick scale passages, which seldom feature in contemporary French lute music.

Indicative of the straightforward nature and lack of rhythmic ambiguity in Mace's lute pieces is the fact that all his preludes are fully barred and rhythmically notated. Dotted passages and pauses are similarly explicit, though these again may only have been included to aid the student. Hemiolas and the constant 6/4:3/2 rhythmic interplay characteristic of French triple-time dances (especially courantes and sarabandes) are at a minimum, although they do occasionally feature.[156] In general Mace's pieces lack subtlety and nuance in their rhythmic flow, in comparison with contemporary French lute music, in which rhythmic ambiguity is of fundamental importance.

Mace's pieces cannot properly be said to be *brisé* in style. While he is always prepared to break up a melodic line between treble and bass (as in the *double* that forms the second part of the second 'coranto' in the '4th Sett') in quasi-*brisé* manner, the

---

[155] 17th-c. French Baroque lutes did not normally have frets on the belly and nine gut frets were the norm. The famous engraving of Charles Mouton by Edelinck after François de Troy's portrait (now in the Louvre, Paris) illustrates this well.

[156] e.g. Mace, *Musick's Monument*, 141, 2nd Sett, 5th Lesson, bars 30–1; and p. 154, 4th Sett, 6th Lesson, bars 1–2, 5–6, 9–10.

general demarcation between the treble and bass line is always unambiguous, contrasting strongly with the French *brisé* style proper. Mace's pieces are generally short and simple to execute. However, they are longer and more involved than most pieces in the 1630–60 period in transitional tunings. Binary form is the basic structure for both Mace and the earlier music, but Mace's strains are usually longer, with an easily defined internal phrase structure.[157]

Mace gives precise descriptions of each type of piece and how it is to be played in terms of speed and 'humour'.[158] He includes more genres than the staple prelude–allemande–courante–sarabande types of the pre-1650 period, and more than in contemporary French lute music. The gigue, which became usual in French lute music after 1650, never appears, though Mace's own invention, the 'Tattle de Moy', has some similarities.[159] The inclusion of 'Interludes' between 'setts', 'Hobnobs' as well as 'Tattle de Moys', are probably peculiar to Mace, but most of the thirteen types he describes were known to his contemporaries. He includes only one popular tune setting (or 'Common Toy' as he describes it), the 'Nightingal'.[160] This genre was a favourite type of lute piece in all periods. Mace's preludes are quite unlike the unmeasured (lacking rhythm signs) or unbarred preludes of the French tradition. In contrast to the French lute prelude, Mace's pieces are harmonically conservative and never include stressed unessential notes. Generally the pieces open with a simple chordal statement, followed by a sequential or motivic idea which is passed between upper and lower parts. Phrases are separated by pause marks, and the final cadence is often preceded by an extended pedal point (see Ex. 12.2). The texture is particularly thin and disjointed in these pieces. As Mace says, it is 'commonly a *Piece of Confused-wild-shapeless-kind of Intricate-Play*'.[161]

Mace's 'Allmaines' are comparable to the French mid-century allemande, being characterized by quasi-imitative motifs, despite Mace's description of them as 'very *Ayrey* and *Lively*'. The 'Ayres', as Mace says, 'differ from *Allmaines*, by being commonly *Shorter*, and of a more *Quick, and Nimble Performance*'. In all other respects they are similar. His 'Corantoes' show little of the rhythmic subtlety of the French courante. Instead they are 'of a *Quicker Triple-Time*', and 'full of *Sprightfulness*, and *Vigour, Lively, Brisk* and *Cheerful*' and thus have much more in common with the quick Italian corrente. The 'Seraband' does not seem to have been such an important or established form of lute composition for Mace, as it appears to have been, from surviving collections, in France or in Britain up to 1660. Mace's first three suites do not include a 'Seraband' at all. His 'Serabands' are intended to be fast,

---

[157] e.g. the 'Coranto' of the 8th Sett (in D minor) runs to 36 bars (*Musick's Monument*, 184).

[158] Ibid. 128–9.　　　　　　　　　　[159] Rave, 'Some Manuscripts', 232.

[160] Mace, *Musick's Monument*, 201. This ballad tune (see Simpson, *The British Broadside Ballad*, 511–13) is, with the exception of the final bars of the first strain, quite distinct from 'Old Gautier's Nightingale'. Other settings of this tune for lute occur in the O.16.2 and Balcarres MSS.

[161] Mace, *Musick's Monument*, 128.

Ex. 12.2. *Prelude by Thomas Mace, 3rd Sett of Lessons,* Musick's Monument *(1676), p. 146*

Ex. 12.2. *cont.*

unlike post-1650 French sarabandes, which had generally become slow. Mace states that they 'are of the *Shortest Triple-Time*; but are more *Toyish*, and *Light*, than *Corantoes*'.[162]

The few 'Galliards' that Mace includes are described as 'perform'd in a *Slow, and Large Triple-Time*, and (commonly) *Grave, and Sober*'.[163] They are characterized by suspensions, pauses, and pedal points, and have no attempt at inner parts or rhythmic ambiguity. Mace includes no examples for lute of the 'Fancy or Voluntary', 'Pavine', 'Chichona', 'Toy or Jigg' or 'Ground', although he gives careful descriptions of them. Most of these forms were no longer composed for the solo lute, yet he does include three similarly outdated 'Galliards'. Their inclusion may be his attempt to link up and draw from the old Renaissance English lute tradition, of which he was well aware.

The 'Tattle de Moy', is Mace's own invention. It is 'much like a *Seraband* . . . *speaking the word, (Tattle de Moy)*'.[164] This underlines the fact that one of the pri-

---

[162] Ibid. 129.   [163] Ibid.   [164] Ibid. 132, 129.

mary concerns of Mace's teaching is with musical rhetoric. Mace is one of the very few Baroque musicians who attempted to convey to his reader the importance and nature of the 'affective' aspect of his music.[165] In learning a piece of music, the pupil is directed to consider its 'fugue', 'form', and 'humour'; the 'fugue' is generally the opening theme; the 'form' the '*Shape of the Whole Lesson*', the 'humour' its projected affect.[166] This last aspect Mace describes in a variety of adjectives such as '*Amiable, Pleasant, Obliging, and Innocent*', or '*Sorrowing, Pittying*, and *Bemoaning*', etc.[167]

The principal means available to the player to 'humour' his music are ornaments, variations of loud and soft, and the judicious application of pauses.[168] Mace supplies his reader with an impressive selection of ornaments, which he describes in great detail.[169] Yet it is apparent from his music that he uses the comma, which he explains as a backfall (i.e. appoggiatura, which may or not be followed by a shake), far more commonly than any other 'grace'.[170] The humour of a piece is not necessarily uniform throughout but may change from strain to strain.[171] By these means the lute is made to 'speak', the rhetorical aspect of the music is brought to life, and the emotions of the listener and player are duly influenced by the music.

Mace does not supply 'loud', 'soft', or pause indications to all his pieces, but it is clear that they are to be added by the student in places where they are appropriate.[172] There are two types, those in full type and those in half type, which presumably indicate a difference of degree.[173] It may be surprising to the modern player how much dynamic variation was expected within a single strain.[174] Other unusual 'affective' directions Mace adds to his music are to 'sobb' and 'crackle', for the accomplishment of which he supplies technical descriptions.[175] The almost 'programmatic' explanations of the 'humouring' he expects in some of his pieces sheds much light on what must be one of the least understood aspects of music of this period. Example 12.3 illustrates the denseness of ideas in Mace's pieces. There are pause marks, dynamics, plentiful ornamentation, a direction to 'crackle', and short phrases that break down into numerous short gestures, all within the first couplet of this Allmaine.

---

[165] Gregory G. Butler, 'The Projection of Affect in Baroque Dance Music', *EM* 12 (1984), 200–7. This article analyses Mace's 'Coranto, I Like my Humour well' (*Musick's Monument*, 131) with regard to Mace's directions as to how to 'humour' the piece.

[166] Mace, *Musick's Monument*, 123, and many other pieces that he gives a detailed commentary on.

[167] Ibid. 124 and 130.   [168] Ibid. 130.   [169] Ibid. 102–9.

[170] Ibid. 104. For example, in the Allmaine on p. 140, there are nine back-falls, one half-fall (one extra note from below) and two beates (lower mordents with or without extra turns).

[171] Butler, 'The Projection of Affect', 201.

[172] e.g. in *Musick's Monument*, 148, he states 'Its *Humour* I will leave to your *Finding out*'.

[173] See ibid. 125, *The Off-spring*, for an example of both types in the same piece.

[174] e.g. *My Mistress*, 121, has five dynamic indications in the last eight bars.   [175] Ibid. 170.

Ex. 12.3. *'Allmaine' by Thomas Mace, 'Sixth sett in B-mi-key'*, Musick's Monument *(1676)*, *p. 177, bars 1–10*

In his *An Essay to the Advancement of Musick* (1672), Thomas Salmon put forward several far-reaching proposals for a rationalization of tablature for the lute and viol, and the standardization of viol (and by inference lute) tuning to a single agreed type. In the last respect there is a direct parallel with Mace's proposal that all lute tunings be abandoned in favour of the French Flat tuning. The comparison is more remarkable in that Salmon proposed the adoption of the altered viol tuning *d′*, *b*, *g*, *d*, *G*, *D* with its minor counterpart *d′*, *b♭*, *g*, *d*, *G*, *D* (usually known as 'harp-way sharp' and 'harp-way flat'), and the discarding of all other tunings, including the old 'viol way' (i.e. *d′*, *a*, *e*, *c*, *G*, *D*), which is analogous to the lute's Renaissance tuning.[176] The viol 'harp-way sharp' tuning is related to the French Flat tuning (no. 10) on the lute, as both have a major triad within the three top open courses. Like Mace, Salmon wished to avoid the confusion caused, especially in consort playing, of using many tunings, but he wanted to keep the increase in resonance and sonority afforded by the use of an altered tuning.

The lute never approached the lyra viol in the number of altered tunings that were tried,[177] but the proposals Salmon put forward for the rationalization of notation apply no less to the lute than the viol. He does not champion a particular lute tuning as he does for the viol, but prints a lute piece ('Arron's Jigg') by John Rogers with the comment, 'I have chose this tuning [French B natural] . . . as 'tis that which the most excellent lutanist Mr John Rogers ordinarily teaches in London to his scholars'.[178] 'French B natural' is none other than D major tuning up a major third. The lute is not specifically included in Salmon's tuning proposals, but it is noticeable that he does not use for his example tuning no. 10, which has more in common with the viol harp-way sharp and harp-way flat tuning than the French B natural.

'Arron's Jigg' is a feeble piece chosen only because it demonstrates Salmon's proposals in the clearest possible light. He intended to replace tablature by a four-line stave in which notes are written in normal mensural notation with basses written alphabetically underneath. Instead of using G, F, and C staves when a melodic line moved freely from one octave to another, he wanted to use only a four-line G clef at different octaves. The abbreviation of Treble, Mean, Tenor, and Bass would be used in the place of clefs to denote the first line of each four-line stave at *g′*, *g*, *G*, and *G′* respectively. This little piece with its transcription into Salmon's new notation is of great importance as it is incontrovertible proof of the existence of small 12-course lutes in England with the top string tuned as high as *b♭′*.

In reply to Salmon's *Essay* Matthew Locke published his *Observations upon a Late Book, Entitled, An Essay to the Advancement of Musick* (London, April 1672), attacking Salmon's proposals in no uncertain terms. Locke's objection as far as the adoption of harp-way sharp and flat tuning for the viol was concerned was that: 'the old Tuning [i.e. *d′*, *a*, *e*, *c*, *G*, *D*] gives her the fair liberty of all sorts of keys in all kinds of Musick for that Instrument, with a far greater advantage to the hand than any

---

[176] Salmon, *An Essay to the Advancement of Music*, 48–54.

[177] Frank Traficante, 'Lyra Viol Tunings: "All Ways have been Tryed to It" ', *Acta musicologica*, 42 (1970), 183–205 at 184. Traficante cites fifty-one different viol tunings.

[178] Salmon, *An Essay*, 66.

other; he confines her to one that can hardly do either.'[179] In discussing the lute and the example provided by Salmon he says much of interest:

His dear Empress the Lute, which his romantic brethren (if he speak truth) do so infinitely admire brings up the rear of his examples; but with the like success (poor dumb thing) as the next: For at first dash (as a true friend to confusion) he gets her at defiance with her sister Instruments by buzzing her in the heed that she is supreme; which is as absolute a Tale of a Tub (how eloquently soever told) as ever wanted bottom or truth: the Harpsichord and Organ far exceeding her in Compass and Parts the Viol and Violin in loudening and softening and continuing a note or sound. Sagbut and Cornett the same; every Instrument having one or other excellency proper to itself. The convenience of its being portable and useful the same time is common to most other Instruments. That true excellency which is peculiarly hers, is the making of a complete consort with the stops of one hand only; which he (notwithstanding all his gay commendation) has absolutely robbed her of in his confounded Example of Arron's Jig, his way of writing being incapable of continuing the Parts of a well-composed lute lesson without all the absurdities before mentioned.[180]

Here is a forthright statement by an eminent non-lutenist musician that the claims put forward by Mace and the author of the Burwell Tutor of the superiority of the lute over other instruments were hollow.[181] We can assume from the defensive attitude taken by Mace towards the lute that by the 1670s the musical establishment mirrored Locke's view rather than Mace's.

Two further publications followed these two. First Salmon's *A Vindication of an Essay to the Advancement of Musick from Mr. Matthew Locke's Observations By Enquiring into the real nature, and most convenient practice of that Science* (London, 1672) and then Locke's final word in *The Present Practice of Musick Vindicated against the Exceptions; and New Way of Attaining Musick lately published by Thomas Salmon* (London, 1673). Despite the increase in abuse heaped on each other's publications, Locke and Salmon contributed little that was new in these further pamphlets to the argument, although, by way of proof, Locke produced a musical composition impossible to play in Salmon's favoured tuning.[182] The suggestion of yet more lost English seventeenth-century lute music comes in the *Present Practice* when Locke states 'I must confess Sir, I have not the Practical Use of the Lute; yet have composed several things for it'.[183] This would place Locke amongst the rare few (like Bach and Vivaldi) who attempted to write specifically for the lute, but

---

[179] Matthew Locke, *Observations*, 33–4.

[180] Lilian M. Ruff, 'Thomas Salmon's "Essay to the Advancement of Musick" ', *The Consort*, 21 (1964), 266–78 at 267.

[181] Salmon also maintains the lute's pride of place over other instruments by saying the 'lute is so generally acknowledged supreme, that it is as needless for me to prove it' (*Essay to the Advancement of Musick*, 60).

[182] Ruff, 'Thomas Salmon's "Essay" ', 267.   [183] Locke, *The Present Practise of Musick Vindicated*, 12.

Table 12.2. *English lute sources after 1660*

Date/source	Lute type/tuning	Comments
c.1660/Burwell Tutor	11-course; D minor transposed trumpet tuning; Jenkins's tuning	13 pieces, plus numerous short exercises and examples
c.1660/Tabley House	12-course lute; D minor tuning, a trumpet tuning version; flat tuning and 'ton Mercure'	69 solos; mostly French composers but 9 by named English composers (Peter Warner, Hubert, Henry Allaby, Mr Charles). 2 solos and 1 song accompaniment for 5-course guitar
1676/*Musick's Monument* by Thomas Mace	12-course lute; flat tuning and D minor tuning	52 pieces in 8 'setts', plus several example pieces and one long exercise piece for theorbo
c.1700/Poznań	11-course lute; D minor and D major tunings	75 solos; arrangements of theatre music, songs, lute solos by French lutenist-composers, and 3 sets of divisions
1690–1710 and 1720/Nanki	12-course lute in flat tuning; renaissance tuning	8 solo lute pieces and operatic arias with intabulated lute and 13-course archlute in parts for 12-course lute. A further layer of the MS has solos and accompaniments for a 13-course archlute
1709–11/Danby	11-course lute; D minor tuning	98 pieces. Continental pieces collected on a Grand Tour
1709–11/Osborne	11-course lute; D minor tuning	42 pieces. Continental pieces collected on a Grand Tour
1727/Creyghton	12-course lute; D minor tuning	17 pieces composed by Robert Creyghton (1636/7–1734). Probably composed much earlier but dated 1727
c.1777–80 and 1810–13/Add. 31698	13-course lute; D minor tuning and mensural notation	Associated with Rudolf Straube and Thomas Gainsborough. In circulation in the early 19th c.

could not play it themselves. (For a list of English sources after 1660 see Table 12.2.)

In 1989 Robert Spencer discovered a lute manuscript together with several other music books at Tabley House, Knutsford, Cheshire.[184] Tabley House was the home

---

[184] The MS was found in 1987 together with a MS book of songs with an unfigured bass.

of Sir Peter Leycester (1614–78), an amateur musician, composer, and something of a music historian. In 1667 he made a list of his impressive collection of some fifty music books and twelve instruments for inheritance purposes. Among them he owned Adriaenssen's *Pratum musicum* (1584), Mace's *Musick's Monument* (1676), and 'one old Lute'.[185] The lute book does not appear to have come from Tabley House itself, nor to have belonged to Leycester, but may have originated with a neighbouring family, and somehow found its way to Tabley later. The Tabley lute book contains sixty-nine solos for 12-course lute, of which forty-four can be played on an 11-course lute, together with two solos and one song accompaniment for 5-course guitar.

The great majority of the lute pieces are in D minor tuning (52). Fourteen pieces are in a version of the Trumpet tuning; two pieces are in the French Flat tuning (no. 10), and two in the 'ton Mercure'. Four or five hands added the lute music, though two of the these hands contributed all but five of the pieces. The first main hand added eighteen pieces, mostly at the beginning of the book, of which seven require a 12-course lute. This hand is very upright and clear, and his repertoire contains eight pieces attributed to English composers. From page 18 the predominant hand changes to that of a more slanted and professional hand. Of the forty-four pieces in this hand none is attributed to an English composer, but some eleven are probably arrangements of English tunes. These include an 'Antic Dance' from Locke's *Cupid and Death* (1659); a piece from *Parthenia*, and a piece entitled 'The Duke of York's Birthday'. There is an intabulation of Lully's 'Sommes-nous pas trop heureux' from the *Ballet de l'impatience* (1661). This information would seem to date the manuscript from the years immediately after the Restoration.

The English pieces are easily distinguishable as they are much less *brisé*, clearly two-part in texture, and rhythmically and melodically unambiguous. They are also more likely to be for 12-course lute, and many are simple tune settings. Example 12.4 shows all these characteristics. This 'toy' is fingered for both left and right hand, and has a full complement of ornaments. It is transcribed here with a top string at $b\flat'$ pitch, as might be expected at this time. It has gigue-like characteristics, though it is similar in form to Mace's 'Tattle de Moys', but with longer phrases. The English composers named are Peter Warner (5), Hubert (2), Henry Allaby (1), and Mr Charles (1). Of these men only Peter Warner is otherwise known. His pieces appear in Peter Leycester's lyra viol book, and he was presumably a local man.

Two-thirds of the contents are by French composers, some of whom, like Nicolas Confesse [Confais], John Mercure, François Dufault, and probably Pinel were

[185] Ward, 'Sprightly and Cheerful Musick' 98–101. The Leycester muniments are now held at the Cheshire Record Office.

Ex. 12.4. '*A Toy Mr Charles*', *Tabley MS, p. 12, bars 1–12*

active in England. Of the French composers nine pieces are by Dufault, eight by Vieux Gaultier, seven by Mercure, six by Denis Gaultier, four by Pinel, three by Confesse, and one each by Heart and Bocquet. This manuscript is of great importance, as it combines locally produced pieces in an Anglo-French style for the 12-course lute with pieces in the mid-century pure French *brisé* style associated with Dufault and Denis Gaultier for the 11-course lute. It shows there were still provincial lutenists collecting such a range of pieces in the 1660s.

The period after the 1670s is an apparent void for surviving seventeenth-century English lute sources. After the Tabley manuscript and *Musick's Monument* nothing survives until the Nanki and Poznań manuscripts, both of which are likely to be from the eighteenth century. The Poznań manuscript was discovered in an attic in the Polish city of Poznań in 1979, and is dated *c.*1700–10. It contains seventy-five pieces for 11-course lute in D minor and major tunings, entered by a single hand, and with titles and directions in a mixture of French and English. There is no obvious ordering of pieces by key or genre in the manuscript, though it contains suites by Laton (Latour?) (21–6), Gaultier (27–33), Hannek (35–42, 45–9), and Paisible (67–72). The manuscript opens with a long orchestral suite by 'Msr Brandcourt' (1–9). This must be the Saxon-born musician Captain François de Prendcourt who came to London in 1686 to be Master of the Children at the Catholic Chapel of James II. He was highly involved in politics after the invasion of William of Orange in 1688 and seems to have changed his allegiance around 1689, as he was convicted as an anti-Jacobite spy by the French that year, and imprisoned in the Bastille until October 1697. On his release he returned to England, where he worked for Thomas Coke, Vice-Chancellor to Queen Anne, and died before 1707.[186] Roger North gained access to two teaching tracts written by Prendcourt.[187] The Poznań lute book also contains arrangements for solo lute of music connected with the London theatre from the period 1680–1700, together with other lute music by Continental composers.

There are similarities between the Poznań and Balcarres manuscripts. Both contain a mixed collection of music adapted from popular violin music, arrangments of instrumental and vocal music—much of it connected with the theatre—and a sprinkling of French lute music. The Poznań source does not have the regional bias of the Balcarres, and is less populist in scope. Instead the theatre music, which is its largest element, shows that the compiler had access to manuscript collections of theatre music, and not just published versions. Several complete overtures and orchestral suites are present. Such adaptations are also found in the Danby manuscript; they are often difficult to play, and arguably do not work as lute music. The most successful piece of this type is the 'Fantasia de Mr Brandcourt', which is most probably adapted from a set of orchestral dance movements. (See Ex. 12.5.) Even here there are moments of harmonic weakness (as in bar 8) that suggest the arranger was not fully competent.

Among the adapted violin music are versions of 'Mr Bannister's ground' and 'Old sir Simon' from Playford's *The Division Violin* (*c.*1705 and 1685), the last of which is also found in the Balcarres manuscript (no. 101), a long set of divisions on

[186] Edward T. Corp, 'Further Light on the Career of "Captain" François de Prendcourt', *M&L* 78 (1997), 15–23 at 15.
[187] *Roger North on Music*, pp. xxiii, 51.

EX. 12.5. *'Fantasia by Mr Brandcourt', Poznań MS, fo. 5ᵛ, bars 1–10*

the Folia d'Espagna, at the end of which is a variation from Corelli's Op. V (1700), and a few Playford *Dancing Master* tunes. Among the theatre pieces is orchestral act music by Finger, Morgan, Solomon Eccles, and Henry and Daniel Purcell. A number of theatre arias are present, which include John Eccles's 'I burn, my brain consumes to ashes' (*Don Quixote*, part 2, 1695), 'A song set by Mr Weldon, sung by Mrs Campion—Panthea all the sences treats' (*The Mad Lover*, 1701), and Purcell's 'The Danger is Over' (*The Fatal Marriage*, 1694).

The Nanki manuscript has at least two distinct layers. The first (fos. 1ʳ–10ᵛ) has solo pieces and operatic arias with intabulated accompaniments for 12-course lute that probably date from the period 1695–1710. A later layer of the manuscript (fos. 11ʳ–20ᵛ) has solo music and operatic arias with intabulations for 14-course archlute that probably date from a period around 1730. There are stylistic similarities between the solo pieces and the vocal accompaniments intabulated for 12-course lute in the earlier layer of the manuscript (in particular the dense texture) that suggests that the arranger in this section of the manuscript set both the vocal music and the solo pieces. These vocal accompaniments call for a 12-course lute with a top string at *f′*. Thus it was a tone lower than the pitch at which Mace normally kept his instrument.[188] The eight pieces for solo lute in the Nanki manuscript represent the most important indication of the style of lute music played in England *c*.1700. Their existence suggests that the 12-course lute and the flat tuning that Mace had championed were still played up to the eighteenth century in Britain.

The songs from Bononcini's *Camilla* date the completion of the earlier layer of the manuscript from not before 1706—the date of the London production with English words, from which this aria comes. Two of the solo lute pieces are 'Sibells', which their titles tell us were 'set upon the lute by C. Morelli'. The first is a version of the 'Old Cibell', which is from Lully's opera, *Atys* (1676). The second is an arrangement of 'Mr. H. Purcell's new Sibell', published in the *Harpsichord Master* (1697). Pepys's musical servant, Cesare Morelli, left England between 1682 and 1686, and is last heard of in Flanders in 1687. Thus there is a gap of ten to twenty years between the last mention of Morelli and the likely date of completion of this part of the manuscript.

The first four solo pieces in the Nanki manuscript appear to constitute a suite in A minor of an allemande, courante, 'Gigue', and 'Toccata'.[189] These pieces, along with the other four, are possibly all lute arrangements of keyboard music. There are usually three distinct parts in all pieces save the gigue and courante. Chords at the beginning and end of phrases can contain up to four, five, and six members. Although the treble and bass parts are dominant, there is no feeling of 'hollowness',

---

[188] Mace, *Musick's Monument*, 198: 'The Order of the Diapasons, in the Flat Tuning'; Nanki MS items nos. 8, 9, 10, 13, and 14 with voice and tablature.
[189] Nanki MS, fos. 1ʳ–2ᵛ.

due to a lack of an inner part, as with Mathew and, to a lesser extent, Mace—despite the often wide pitch span between treble and bass.

A characteristic of these eight pieces that distinguishes them from the repertoire of pre-1650 music in transitional tunings is their greater length. Most of the eight pieces reach twenty-five bars, and several approach forty bars.[190] Admittedly these are not long pieces, but they are much longer than the often minuscule pieces of the pre-1660 period. Their bass lines move rigorously both by step and by larger intervals like a bowed bass line or keyboard left hand, and are more active than those of lute music in general. Neither does the simple stepwise movement characteristic of the Balcarres manuscript, or the melodically ambiguous bass part of *brisé* lute music in general, match the harmonic decisiveness of the bass line of the solo pieces in the Nanki manuscript. The harmonies are neither daring nor complicated, but stylistically appropriate, and full compared with lute music in general. Some use is made of whole-tone or semitone clashes, which are not always resolved, but when arpeggiated might sound like an appoggiatura.[191]

The Nanki pieces make considerable technical demands upon the player, a feature also of the vocal accompaniments. High fret positions are used, involving chord positions of three parts, and the tenth fret is consistently employed. (See Ex. 12.6.) Complex rhythms are an important stylistic feature of this manuscript, particularly in the longer pieces, and it is not always obvious how they are to be executed within the given time, except that they are to be slurred with the left hand.

A piece which exemplifies these general characteristics is the 'Toccata' that finishes the suite of four pieces in A minor at the beginning of the manuscript (see Ex. 12.6). The piece is in four clearly defined sections, which close in E minor, C major, E major, and A minor respectively. Each of these sections is unconnected to the others by way of thematic material. The opening forms a long bravura flourish which descends on the beat from c'' down to $g\sharp$, with a varied rising figure after the main beat, to a cadence in E minor to finish the section. The gradual left-hand position descent from the ninth fret on which the piece opens down to the first position at bar 4, and the first use of diapasons at the close, are most effective.

The Danby manuscript belonged to William Henry Osborne (1690–1711), Earl of Danby from 1694 to his early death in 1711. Like the Osborne manuscript it was purchased part-completed on the European tour made by William and his brother Peregrine Hyde Osborne (1693–1731) during the years 1709–11 that took in many Dutch cities as well as Hanover and Hamburg.[192] William and Peregrine were grandsons of the great Thomas Osborne, 1st Duke of Leeds, who masterminded the Stuart removal and invited William and Mary to take the Crown. A great deal can

---

[190] Nanki MS, 'Toccata che segue' (fo. 2ʳ) has thirty-two bars, 'Another sibell' (fo. 7ʳ) has thirty-nine.

[191] e.g. Nanki MS, no. 1 (untitled Allemande), fo. 1ʳ, bars 11, 19, and 21.

[192] For an account of this tour with excerpts from the correspondence, see Crawford, 'Lord Danby'.

Ex. 12.6. *Toccata, Nanki MS, fo. 2ʳ ᵛ, bars 1–6*

be learnt about these two manuscripts and the circumstances in which they were
compiled in the weekly letters between the young Lord's governor, Louis Berard,
and the old Duke.[193] These letters deal primarily with the progress and developments of the Continental campaigns of Marlborough against France during the War

[193] *GB-Lbl* Egerton 3339.

of the Spanish Succession. Berard meticulously recorded all expenses. Among them are payments for music masters, lute strings, music books, the hiring of musical servants, instruments (including lutes and theorboes), instrument repairs, and tickets for concerts and operas.[194] Sadly, Danby never returned from the tour, as he contracted smallpox on 11 August 1711 in Utrecht, and died nine days later.[195] Danby's younger brother Peregrine succeeded as the 3rd Duke of Leeds in 1729. He was not the enthusiastic lutenist that his elder brother had been (preferring the viol), and there is no suggestion that he continued with any musical activity after 1711.

The Danby manuscript contains ninety-eight pieces and fragments on 137 pages, all for 11-course lute in D minor tuning, and proves to be an important source of music from Handel's Hamburg period. There are several unique dance movements by Handel, and a version of the *Almira* (1707) overture that Handel later adapted for *The Triumph of Time and Truth* production of 1757.[196] Handel apart, it contains all manner of Continental lute music, both French and German, particularly by Losy (eleven definitely attributable pieces plus three probable), and intabulations of popular airs and instrumental pieces by Lully, Purcell, and others. The type of 11-course French lute suitable for the music in the Danby and Osborne manuscripts does occur in British pictures of the early eighteenth century. The Arabella Hunt engraving (see above, Pl. 12.1) and the painting by Thomas Murray of Henrietta d'Averqueque, Countess of Grantham are two examples (see Pl. 12.5).

The Osborne manuscript shares the same origins as the Danby manuscript. It probably also belonged to Lord Danby, although it contains the signatures of Peregrine Hyde Osborne and other members of the Osborne family.[197] The manuscript contains forty-two pieces for 11-course lute in D minor tuning in four key groupings: C major, F major, A minor, and D minor, no. 37 of which is a long 'Folies D'Espagne' (fos. 23ʳ–30ʳ) with fourteen distinct variations, at least eight of which would appear to have been set as duets as they lie on adjacent pages, the second of which is reversed. These pieces are followed by continuo exercises and pieces for a 13-course archlute. No composers are mentioned throughout the thirty-seven folios, and the music is of poor quality. A few pieces concord with the Danby manuscript or with Ox 576, but most are unknown.[198]

---

[194] Crawford, 'Lord Danby', particularly fos. 12, 14, 46, 99, 123, and 178.

[195] *GB-Lbl* Egerton 3339, fo. 200.

[196] Danby MS, pp. 23–4.   [197] See Crawford, 'Lord Danby', 67 n. 32.

[198] Osborne MS, fo. 7ʳ, 'Gigue', concords with Ox 576, fo. 13ᵛ; fo. 3ʳ, 'Lautre Courante', concords with Ox 576, fos. 16ᵛ–17ʳ; fo. 23ʳ, 'les Folier Espanger', concords with Ox 576, fo. 43ᵛ–fo. 6ʳ; fo. 15ᵛ, 'La Bouree', concords with Danby, p. 7.

PL. 12.5. Henrietta d'Averqueque, Countess of Grantham (d. 1724), by Thomas
Murray (1663–1735). Whitfield Fine Art, London

There are seven pieces for 12-course lute found in a manuscript dated 1727 associated with the Revd Robert Creyghton (1636/7–1734).[199] Creyghton was the son of the Revd Creyghton, Professor of Greek at Cambridge, afterwards Dean of Wells, and from 1670 Bishop of Bath and Wells. The younger Creyghton followed his father's career closely, becoming Professor of Greek at Cambridge in 1662. In 1674 he was opted Canon Residentiary of Wells Cathedral. Canon Creyghton composed several services and anthems. He died at Wells in 1734 at the advanced age of 97. Musically his lute pieces are unexceptional, being distinctly two-part with a few quasi-*brisé* clichés improving the flow, and all rather similar. The pieces are pleasant, work well on the lute, and are easy—they require only first position. It is curious that Creyghton at the advanced age of 91 should have contributed a group of pieces to the manuscript for an instrument that was by then all but extinct. He had probably played the lute in his younger days, no doubt the 12-course lute in Renaissance tuning for continuo and vocal accompaniment purposes, and at some point was moved to compose some solo lute pieces in Renaissance tuning. Later in life he decided to add them to this manuscript to preserve them for posterity.

Collectively the English sources of solo lute after 1660 are a mixed bag from which it is difficult to draw conclusions. They are so few and disparate. Mace, the Tabley manuscript, and the Nanki manuscript suggest the continuation of the Anglo-French style in transitional tunings into the eighteenth century. The Poznań manuscript is similar to the Balcarres, Osborne, and Danby manuscripts in containing at least some music by post-1640 French masters, and being in D minor and related tunings. It seems that by 1680 next to nothing was being composed expressly for the lute in England, and such lute players as there were turned to arrangements of music for the violin, orchestra, and theatre songs for material to supplement what little was still circulating in England in the way of real lute music from the Continent.

The history of the solo lute in England after the Restoration is of increasing decline and neglect. By comparison the theorbo, theorbo-lute, or some other form of lute in Renaissance tuning remained the most popular accompanimental instrument for continuo songs to at least 1680. Well into the eighteenth century song publications often included the theorbo, archlute, or lute as a possible continuo instrument. The ability to realize a continuo part on theorboes and lutes in Renaissance tuning considerably outlived the fashion for playing solo lute music in transitional tunings that had been popular until the Restoration. This waning in interest in solo lute music was a gradual process and is difficult to trace with

---

[199] This 18th-c. MS (*GB-Lbl* Add. 37074) contains much other instrumental and vocal music, including lute and keyboard music by Robert Creyghton D.D. Lute pieces nos. 3, 4, and 6 are signed 'R.C.', and nos. 1 and 7 are dated 1727.

precision, but by 1720 the decline was nearly complete. A native Englishman with any proficiency on the lute as a solo instrument after this point was rare indeed. The most favoured member of the lute family in eighteenth-century England was the archlute, although a few Continental players did make a living by playing in the German style on 11- or 13-course lutes in D minor and related tunings. By 1720 the instrument had become 'un-English', and was considered unfashionable and archaic.

Chapter Thirteen

Scottish Lute Music

Was but the sound of laughter heard
Or tinckling of the lute
Would Knox with unction tell
The vengeance that in days of old
Had fallen on Jezebel

Robert Aytoun (1569–1638),
Bothwell

Lutenists were fully established at the Scottish royal court by the late fifteenth century, though the instrument is occasionally mentioned in Scots literature before this time.[1] Sir John Graham Dalyell in his *Musical Memoirs of Scotland* (1849) mentions a number of lutenists belonging to the royal household, the earliest reference being in 1474.[2] Dalyell lists extracts taken from the Household Accounts of the Lords High Treasurers of Scotland showing frequent payments to lutenists during the reign of James III (1460–88) and James IV (1488–1513). Payments were made to a certain Jacob, but also to his fellow lutenists: John Wardlaw, Rankine, Robert Rudman, Adam Dikeson, Robert Hay, John Ledebetar, Craig, 'Lindores', and 'Gray Steil'.[3] The unfortunate James IV married Margaret Tudor in 1503. During the celebrations he entertained his bride by playing the 'clarychordes' and 'lute'.[4] Margaret had been taught the lute as a child. Kenner or Krennar, her 'lutar', is mentioned in English accounts prior to her departure, and was probably English.[5]

Throughout the sixteenth century the Scottish court employed lutenists, as did private families such as the Lords of Ruthven and Kilmawris, the Laird of

---

[1] William Dauney, *Ancient Scotish Melodies* (Edinburgh, 1838), 98. The lute is mentioned in the 'Houlate' (*c.*1450), a poem dating from the reign of James II: 'The lilt pipe and the lute, the fydill in fist'; see *The buke of the Howlat, By Holland*, ed. David Laing (Edinburgh, 1823). Also in the story *Thomas of Erceldoune* (*c.*1475), ed. James A. H. Murray (EETS 61; London 1875), p. 14, v. 259: 'Lutte and rybybe bothe gangande'; James I is also mentioned in a poem as a lute player (Dauney, *Ancient Scotish Melodies*, 97).

[2] Sir John Graham Dalyell, *Musical Memoirs of Scotland* (Edinburgh, 1849), 223–4. The payment of 1474 was to 'Johne Broune, lutar'. Dauney gives a more complete version of these accounts in his appendix no. III, 'Extracts from Documents Preserved in the General Register House at Edinburgh', *Ancient Scotish Melodies*, 355–61.

[3] Henry George Farmer, *A History of Music in Scotland* (London, 1947), 73–5. See also *Music for the Lute in Scotland*, ed. Robert Phillips (Shillinghill, 1995), 7–8.

[4] Farmer, *A History of Music in Scotland*, 74.

[5] *RECM* vii. 20; Farmer, *A History of Music in Scotland*, 74–5.

Johnstoun, and the Countess of Crawford, as well as leading churchmen.[6] As a young man James V (1513–42) played the lute with some enthusiasm, purchasing several lutes for his own use and large numbers of strings.[7] Mary Queen of Scots is reputed to have been a lute player with 'a voice very sweet and good, for she sang very well, blending her voice with the lute which she touched so daintily with a fair white hand'.[8] In 1561 she employed three lutenists, five string players, and a number of grooms of the bedchamber who were also musicians.[9] James Melvill refers to the lute as being practised by students at St Andrews between 1571 and 1574,[10] and Burney speaks of two Scottish lutenists employed at the French court of Henry IV.[11] Helena Mennie Shire notes that the poet Alexander Hume played the lute and left a consort of instruments in his will.[12] Scottish poets like Hume, Robert Aytoun, and William Drummond frequently refer to the lute in their poetry as the preferred courtly instrument.[13]

There is a small amount of Scottish lute iconography from this period to match the literary references. Farmer produces a plate of a lute player from Cowthally Castle described as fifteenth-century, but whose costume must surely be sixteenth.[14] A painted ceiling in Craithes Castle, Kincardineshire, has representations of nine female muses, seven with instruments: lute, fiddle, bass viol, harp, cittern, flute, and clavichord. The castle was built for the Burnetts of Ley, and first occupied in 1596. The room's supporting beams have verses on them, two of which are dated 1599. The mixed ensemble represented is similar to the English mixed consort of Morley.[15] The Wode part-books of *c*.1580 contain drawings of a variety of plucked instruments, including lute and cittern.[16]

The lute represented in engraved copies of a 1564 painting of David Rizzio (see Pl. 13.1) may be an example of the 'treble lute' referred to by Morley and many others.[17] Rizzio was described by James Melville as an Italian musician from Piedmont in the company of the ambassador of Savoy.[18] Many myths surround his activities and death at the Scottish court. It is certain that through his music he became familiar with Mary Queen of Scots, rising to become her secretary for French

---

[6] Dalyell, *Musical Memoirs*, 224; Farmer, *A History of Music in Scotland*, 78–9.

[7] Farmer, *A History of Music in Scotland*, 76–7.

[8] Ibid. 78; also Dauney, *Ancient Scotish Melodies*, 107.

[9] Antonia Fraser, *Mary Queen of Scots* (London, 1969), 206.   [10] Dalyell, *Musical Memoirs*, 225.

[11] Charles Burney, *A General History of Music*, 4 vols. (1776–89); modern edn. by F. Mercer, 2 vols. (London, 1935), ii. 223. These two musicians are named as James and Charles Hedington.

[12] Helena Mennie Shire, *Song, Dance and Poetry of the Court of Scotland under King James VI* (Cambridge, 1969), 81.

[13] *Music for the Lute in Scotland*, ed. Phillips, 7–9.   [14] Farmer, *A History of Music in Scotland*, pl. 4.

[15] Peter Forrester, 'A Scottish Consort', *LSJ* 27 (1987), 38–42.

[16] Farmer, *A History of Music in Scotland*, pl. 7.

[17] Copies are owned by The Scottish National Portrait Gallery and the Spencer Collection at the Royal Academy of Music.

[18] Farmer, *A History of Music in Scotland*, 124.

PL. 13.1. Engraving of David Rizzio by C. Wilkin (published 1814), with the inscription that it was 'from an original picture of 1564'. The Robert Spencer Collection, Royal Academy of Music

correspondence in 1565. By July 1565 it was rumoured that Rizzio was Mary's lover. Having roused the jealousy of her young husband Lord Darnley, Rizzio was attacked in the queen's presence by a gang of disaffected Protestant rebels, and horribly slaughtered outside her chambers in 1566.[19] The close proximity of musical servants to royalty, and their comparative low status, made them useful as spies, but obvious victims of court plots.

There are plentiful literary references to lute playing in Scotland in the late fifteenth, and throughout the sixteenth centuries, but no Scottish lute sources survive from this period. Such sources are a seventeenth- and early eighteenth-century phenomenon only. The earliest examples of lute music that may be Scottish in origin are the few pieces in English Golden Age sources which purport to be Scots in their titles. The earlier part of the Pickeringe and Mynshall manuscripts contain versions of the 'Hunts Up' titled respectively 'The scottish Huntsupe' and 'The Scoth Hunte suppe'.[20] Such pieces were widely disseminated. 'The English Huntsuppe by John Whitfelde' also appears in Pickeringe.[21] Both the English and Scottish 'hunts ups' have lively driving rhythms, the Scottish settings being characterized by a 'double tonic' on C and B flat, the English by a I–I–II–II–IV–I–V–I ground.[22] Imbalance is maintained in the Scottish 'Huntsupe' by fluctuation between 3/2 and 6/4, before moving to an exciting finish with a time change to 2/4. (See Ex. 13.1.) Apart from the continuous oscillation between the scales C major and B flat major, modulation is avoided. This drone-like characteristic is consistently found in Scottish lute music. The Balcarres manuscript has several such pieces.[23]

There are also pieces with a definite Scottish flavour in English sources, like the short untitled piece in the Pickeringe manuscript on fo. 15. This piece (Ex. 13.2) has a single eight-bar strain repeated with some variation. The partial close in bars 2 and 6 on the first inversion of the subdominant, which interrupts the otherwise continuous C pedal, the lack of any perfect cadence, and the simple hexatonic melody all suggest a Scottish origin. It is likely that much European, and especially French lute music, was played in court circles in Scotland during the sixteenth and early seventeenth centuries, as the cultural connection with France was particularly strong at this time, and all existing Scottish lute sources contain a sizeable French contribution.

---

[19] Fraser, *Mary Queen of Scots*, 281.

[20] Pickeringe MS, fos. 15ʳ–16ʳ; Mynshall MS, fo. 5ʳ; see John M. Ward, 'The Hunt's Up', *PRMA* 106 (1980), 1–25, for information on the *Hunt's Up*. However, he makes no mention of the Scottish *Hunt's Up*.

[21] Pickeringe MS, fo. 32ʳ.

[22] Francis Collinson, *The Traditional and National Music of Scotland* (London, 1966), 26. Ward, 'The Hunt's Up', 1.

[23] e.g. Rowallan MS, no. 32, pp. 39–41 shows strong similarities to the Pickeringe MS version.

Ex. 13.1. *'The Scottish Hunt's Up', Pickeringe MS, fos. 15ᵛ–16ʳ, bars 53–74*

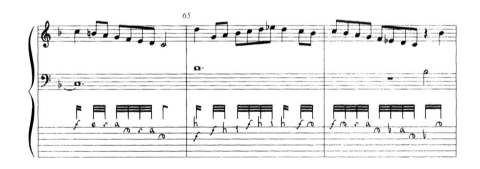

Ex. 13.1. *cont.*

During the period from the disbanding of the Scottish court of James VI in 1603 to the Act of Union in 1706, Scottish music appears to have suffered greatly in comparison with the relatively flourishing courtly musical activity that preceded it. The creative tradition of court song and dance that culminated in the Castalian band of poets that collected around the young James VI in the 1580s, of which Alexander Montgomerie was the leading light, was largely lost after 1606.[24] The view that Scotland lived through a cultural vacuum during the seventeenth century is strengthened when the period is compared with both the preceding era and the eighteenth century.[25] With the removal of the court in 1603, Scots musicians were left to their own resources, with small hope of preferment at home. Wealthy amateurs resorted to private secular music in their own castles and estates. Many Scots nobles and gentry were sent to France as a necessary ingredient in acquiring a liberal education, and musical skills and tastes were often fostered by such experiences. Robert Gordon of Straloch was educated both in France and Aberdeen,

---

[24] Shire, *Song, Dance and Poetry*, 67–116.

[25] David Johnson, *Music and Society in Lowland Scotland in the Eighteenth Century* (London, 1972), 68–84. Johnson highlights the achievements of the Earl of Kelly in the 18th c.

Ex. 13.2. *Untitled piece, Pickeringe MS, fo. 15ʳ*

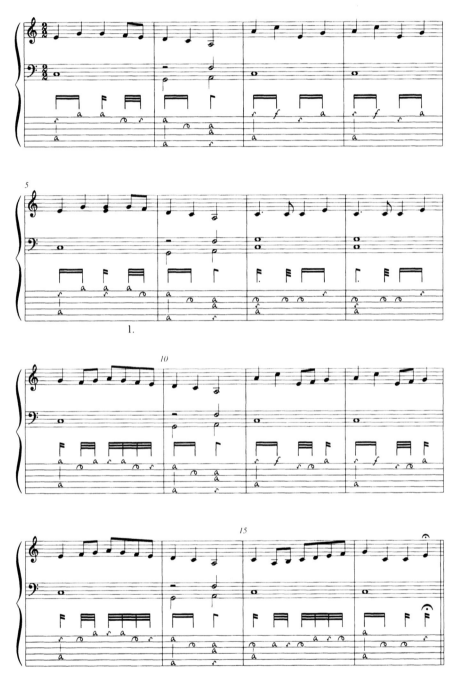

1. Tablature notes appear vertically, one above the other.
I have separated them as *g′ f′*.

where he may have collected pieces for his lute manuscript. Foreign art music as well as popular music was imported in this way. The isolation of the lowland Scots gentry led them to turn increasingly to their own Scots song and dance tradition for suitable melodies for domestic music-making.

Surviving seventeenth-century instrumental manuscripts are for a variety of instruments, particularly lutes and viols, but also for fiddle, mandore, cittern, recorder, and harpsichord. (See Table 13.1.) The fiddle, which was held to be particularly suspect by the Kirk as being licentious and associated with dancing and

Table 13.1. *Manuscript sources of Scottish tunes 1600–1725*

Date	MS siglum (original owner)	Instrument	MS siglum
*c.*1612–28	Rowallan (Sir William Mure)	Lute	*GB-Eu* Laing III.487
1629	Straloch (Robert Gordon)	Lute	(original lost, copy *c.*1847) *GB-En* Adv. 5.2.18
*c.*1630	Skene (John Skene)	Mandore	*GB-En* Adv. 5.2.15
1643–8	Wemyss (Lady Margaret Wemyss)	Lute	*GB-En* Dep. 314, 23
*c.*1650	Pan 11 (Robert Edwards)	Cittern, keyboard, and intrumental ensemble	*GB-En* 9450
*c.*1680	Pan 18 (?)	Keyboard	*GB-En* 9458
*c.*1680	Guthrie (James Guthrie)	Violin	*GB-Eu* Laing III.3
*c.*1680	Pan 7 (?)	Violin	*GB-En* 9454
*c.*1680	Newbattle (?)	Violin	*GB-En* 51778
*c.*1680	Sutherland (?)	Lyra viol and keyboard	*GB-En* Dep. 314, 24
*c.*1692	Blaikie (Andrew Blaikie)	Lyra viol	Central Library, Dundee, Wighton Collection
1694–6	Atkinson (Henry Atkinson)	Violin	Library of the Society of Antiquaries of Newcastle
*c.*1695	Leyden (?)	Lyra viol	*GB-En* Adv. 5.2.19
*c.*1700	Balcarres (?)	Lute	*GB-En* Acc. 9769 (on loan)
1702–20	Thomson (James Thomson)	Recorder and fiddle	*GB-En* 2833
1704	Hume (Agnes Hume)	Viol, keyboard, and voice	*GB-En*, Adv. 5.2.17
*c.*1705	Bowie (George Bowie)	Violin	*GB-En* Acc. 5412 (on deposit). Estate of the late Dr Francis Collinson
*c.*1710	Sinkler (Margaret Sinkler)	Keyboard and violin	*GB-En* 3296 (Glen 143)
1717–40	George Skene (George Skene)	Violin	*GB-En* Adv. 5.2.21
1723–4	Cuming (Patrick Cuming)	Violin	*GB-En* 1667

itinerant vagrant musicians, was not acceptable to gentry amateurs or Scottish society in general until late in the seventeenth century.[26] With the introduction of the violin in Scotland around 1670 the folk tradition of the old medieval and Renaissance fiddle quickly became more acceptable, and transferred itself easily to the new instrument. By 1700 the violin had largely superseded all other stringed instruments as the most favoured instrument for traditional lowland Scots music.[27] No music for the Scottish harp, the 'clarsach', survives. The instrument was particularly associated with blind players, and its music was probably always aurally transmitted. However, some clarsach music did find its way into the general repertoire of Scots melodies, and hence into instrumental collections. The 'Port Rory Dall' found in the Straloch manuscript must refer to the blind Irish harper Rory Dall O'Cahan [or O'Cathain] (1601–50), who spent most of his working life in Scotland.[28] Other pieces in these manuscript collections may have links with the clarsach tradition and would certainly well suit the diatonically strung clarsach.[29]

The titles of a great many old lowland Scots melodies must have originated as songs, though very few have survived with words that are not of the eighteenth century or later. A few Scots songs survive with sixteenth- or seventeenth-century words in the Thomas Wode part-books (1562–92, plus later additions), Rowallan Cantus part-book (1627–37), and John Squyor's music book (1699–1701).[30] Such songs are small in number compared with the hundreds of melodies that remain without associated words, or with words supplied by D'Urfey, Ramsey, Burns, or some other later writer of Scots lyrics. At the time of writing of these seventeenth-century instrumental sources the association of words and melodies would still have been strong in the minds of the compilers.[31] Without exception, the original owners of the manuscripts, where they can be traced, were of the gentry classes, and their books were compiled for domestic music-making in their own home.

The only published secular musical source to come from Scotland in this period was John Forbes's *Songs and Fancies*, first published in Aberdeen in 1662, with later editions in 1666 and 1682.[32] The collection is disappointing as only the Cantus

[26] Mary Anne Alburger, *Scottish Fiddlers and their Music* (London, 1983), 23–4.

[27] David Johnson, *Scottish Fiddle Music in the 18th Century* (Edinburgh, 1984), 3; Alburger, *Scottish Fiddlers*, 24–5.

[28] Farmer, *A History of Scottish Music*, 202.

[29] Collinson, *The Traditional and National Music*, 239–40. This tune also appears in the Skene MS under the title *Port Ballangowne* (Skene, book VIII, pp. 238–44, transcription in Dauney, *Ancient Scotish Melodies*, 229). Collinson quotes from the 'Memoirs of Arthur O'Neill' –taken from Donal O'Sullivan, *Carolan: The Life, Times and Music of an Irish Harper* (London, 1958). O'Neill attributed *Da mihi manum*, *Port Gordon* and *Port Atholl* to O'Cathain.

[30] Wode part-books, e.g. 'Shepherd saw thou not'; Squyors MS (*GB-Eu* Laing III.490), no. 17; and 'The flaming fire' in the Rowallan Cantus part-book (*GB-Eu*, MS Laing III.488).

[31] 'Before the Greeks', no. 55 of the original Straloch MS, was clearly a tune associated with Montgomerie's poem of that name (Shire, *Song, Dance and Poetry*, 144–5).

[32] The full title of the Cantus book is *Cantus, Songs and Fancies: To Thre, Foure, or Five Parts, both Apt for Voices and Viols. With a briefe introduction of Musick, As is taught in the Musick-Schools of Aberdene by T[homas] D[avidson] M[aste]r of Musick.*

part-book was issued, and very few songs of Scots origin are included.[33] The majority are from English madrigal and lute song collections prior to 1603, and from the 'Godly and Spiritual Songs' of the mid-seventeenth century. As such Forbes's collection is representative of music publicly taught at the provincial music schools of seventeenth-century Scotland. At this time musical activity was circumscribed by the musical austerity imposed by the Presbyterian Church.[34] Some teachers at town music schools did provide instrumental tuition, as for instance the Mr Davidson whose system of musical tuition was included by Forbes. Davidson taught the lute and viol, as well as reading, writing, and arithmetic.[35]

The most impressive group of Scots manuscripts collected for domestic music-making was that belonging to the Maule family (Earls of Panmure), now housed in the National Library of Scotland. There are over thirty books surviving, some of which were bought on the Continent, and some compiled in Scotland. The earliest group of manuscripts in the collection, Lady Jean Campbell's book, Clement Matchett's book, Duncan Burnett's book, and Robert Edwards's Commonplace book (Panmure manuscripts 8–11 respectively), were probably acquired for Lady Jean Campbell (b. 1620), the eldest daughter of John, Earl of Loudon and Lord Chancellor of Scotland. Lady Jean married George Maule, who became 2nd Earl of Panmure in 1661.[36] Although much of the music in these books is for keyboard, Lady Jean was probably also the lutenist of the family for whom the lute manuscripts Pan 8 (Lady Jean Campbell's book), Pan 5, and Pan 4 were acquired. Her sons, James and Henry, were good viol players, who turned increasingly to Continental music, which they collected on their visits abroad in 1679–85, and after 1715 when they lived in exile.[37]

The Panmure manuscript collection shows a very active domestic musical tradition in the Maule family, a tradition which embraced not only home-spun Scots melodies and contemporary English music, but also a considerable awareness of Continental, especially French, music (particularly in Pan manuscripts 19, 20, 21, 22, and 23, as well as the earlier lute manuscripts). Although the Maule family may have been exceptional in the richness of its musical life, other Scots gentry encouraged domestic music-making, providing a foundation for the encouragement of public concerts in the eighteenth century.

[33] Possibly 'the Pleugh Song' (1666 edn. only) and 'Shepherd saw thou not' are sufficiently national in character to be classed as Scots song.

[34] Dauney, *Ancient Scotish Melodies*, 24–6.

[35] Ibid. Taken from William Kennedy, *Annals of Aberdeen, from the Reign of King William the Lion* (London, 1818), ii. 135.

[36] Thurston Dart, 'New Sources of Virginal Music', *M&L* 35 (1954), 93–106 at 100–3; Sir James Balfour Paul, *The Scots Peerage*, 9 vols. (Edinburgh, 1904–14), vii. 18.

[37] Paul, *The Scots Peerage*, vii. 25; *DNB* xiii. 86; Patrick Cadell, 'La Musique française classique dans la collection des comités de Panmure', *Recherches sur la musique française classique*, 22 (1984), 50–8. A second family which owned an impressive music collection was the Kerr family of Newbattle Abbey, Midlothian. In this case, most of the MS and printed books of this collection are of 18th-c. origin.

Of the full corpus of Scottish seventeenth-century instrumental sources the seven surviving lute manuscripts and one for mandore form an important part (see Table 13.1). These manuscript sources fall into three groups: the Rowallan and Straloch manuscripts (*c.*1612–28 and 1629), together with the Skene mandore manuscript; the Panmure manuscripts 4, 5, and 8 (from the years 1630–50) and the Lady Margaret Wemyss manuscript (1643–9); the Balcarres manuscript (*c.*1700). Together the these books contain well over 500 individual pieces. Nearly all the lute music in the three Panmure lute manuscripts is in the French style, although they may have been compiled in Britain, and may contain music composed by French lutenists working in Britain.

The remaining four Scottish lute manuscripts span most of the seventeenth century. The earliest two books, the Straloch and Rowallan, are almost contemporary and can be considered together.[38] The solo lute music in the Wemyss manuscript is equally divided between Scottish melodies and French music in transitional tunings. The final source, the Balcarres manuscript, contains a considerable variety of music, much of it drawn from popular fiddle music. All the books have a shared emphasis on Scottish melodies, but also contain a sizeable number of Continental (mostly French) pieces. Whereas the native melodies can often be compared between sources as diverse as the Balcarres manuscript and the Straloch manuscript, despite changing styles of arrangement, the different French repertoires from which each source also draws are unrelated, and reflect the changes through which French lute music progressed during the seventeenth century.

The Rowallan manuscript[39] contains some forty pieces and fragments added, at least in part, by Sir William Mure of Rowallan (1594–1657). Mure was foremost a poet who left a considerable corpus of poetry.[40] He was a grand-nephew of the famous poet Alexander Montgomerie through his mother. To this kinship he refers when he stated that his muse could make but little boast, 'save from Montgomery sche hir birth doth clayme'.[41] The Mure family resided at their castle on the banks of Carmel Water, South of Kilmarnock in Ayrshire. Sir William gained a liberal education, possibly at Glasgow University, which his younger brother attended.[42] Sir William may have been sent abroad, as he undoubtedly knew French well. In

[38] The original Straloch MS was lost after 1842, but several copies remain, the most complete being the Straloch/Graham copy dated 1847 by G. F. Graham. See Spring, 'The Lute in England and Scotland', ii. 6.

[39] *GB-Eu* MS Laing III.487. The pieces on p. 37 and pp. 39–44 would appear to be in a hand different from that associated with Mure, but the poor condition of the MS makes tablature comparisons difficult. The book contains inscriptions mentioning 'Anna Hay' and 'My Lade Bekluch' in the opening folios. Anna was the eldest daughter of the 8th Earl of Errol. She married the Earl of Wintoun in 1609. Her sister Mary married the Earl of Buccleugh in 1616 and died in 1631. Paul, *The Scots Peerage*, iii. 577. Possibly the MS was owned by Anna Hay before her marriage in 1609, and by Mary Hay after her marriage in 1616. How the MS passed from the Hay family to the Mure family is unknown.

[40] *The Works of Sir William Mure of Rowallan*, ed. William Tough (Scottish Text Society, 40–1; Edinburgh, 1989).

[41] Shire, *Song, Dance and Poetry*, 209.   [42] *DNB* xiii. 1225–6.

his early works he attempted to continue Montgomerie's vein of 'Scottis Poessie', and his lute book parallels these light early poems in scope and content. At this time he 'delighted much in building', and 'reformed the house at Rowallan exceedingly'.[43]

Until his father's death in 1639 Mure devoted much time to literature, but then became drawn into an active public life. In 1643 he was a member of Parliament at Edinburgh, and in 1644 he sat on the 'Committee of Warre' for the sheriffdom of Ayr.[44] He was involved in several encounters against the Royalists, and was wounded at Marston Moor, where he had command of a regiment. During his last years he again returned to poetry, though of a more sober religious nature. Mure also had a set of part-books, of which only the cantus remains.[45] Only one song has words, though the remainder do have titles.

Mure's lute book survives in a very decayed and blotched state and many titles seem to have been deliberately blotted out, possibly by Mure himself in his known recantation of courtly aspirations after 1617, and his turning to religious poetry.[46] As far as it may be guessed, more than one hand added to the manuscript, though Mure, who wrote his signature on pages 24 and 25, was probably the principal scribe. At some point the book was chemically treated to help reveal the titles and music.[47] It seems that some of the later Scottish pieces were worked out by Mure himself. Apart from the completed version of 'for Kissing for Clapping for Loving for proving set to the Lute by Mr Mure' (no. 19), there are at least three fragments of workings of this piece in the manuscript. Some of the pieces in the final pages defy all attempts at reconstruction. Like the Straloch manuscript, many of the pieces have problematic rhythmic indications, and inconsistent bar lengths. The pieces require a lute of seven to nine courses in Renaissance tuning throughout.

The original Straloch manuscript was lost in the mid-nineteenth century. David Laing, Librarian of Edinburgh University Library, examined the original early in the nineteenth century and described it as a small octavo with the title: 'An Playing Booke for the lute, wherin ar contained many Currents and other musical things. Musica mentis medicina moestae. At Aberdein. Notted and collected by Robert Gordon. In the yeere of our Lord 1627. In Februaree.' Laing listed the contents, noting that the original had ninety leaves, and was bound into old vellum covers,

[43] *DNB* xiii. 1226.   [44] Ibid.

[45] Shire, *Song, Dance and Poetry*, 213–14; *GB-Eu* MS Laing III.488. The collection is arranged into groups depending on the number of parts, from two to six, and according to English, French, or Scottish origin. Among them are songs set to Montgomerie's words, psalms and works from English published editions from 1595 to 1635, as well as a few native Scots airs. The books were probably compiled after 1627 from the family's music collection.

[46] In 1617 Mure attempted unsuccessfully to gain royal attention with his 'Muse's Welcome' addressed to James at Hamilton; *The Works of Sir William Mure of Rowallan*, Poem xx.

[47] Harry M. Willsher, 'Music in Scotland during Three Centuries', 3 vols. (D.Litt. thesis; University of St Andrews, 1945), ii. 22.

with 'R. Gordon' written in a bold hand on the first page.[48] In 1839 the Straloch manuscript was lent to George Farquhar Graham. Graham 'translated' (i.e. copied) the whole manuscript and transcribed (from tablature to mensural notation) some of the pieces.[49] He also copied excerpts into two separate books: firstly the 'Taphouse copy' dated 1845, and secondly the Straloch/Graham copy dated 1847, which includes pieces not found in the Taphouse copy.[50] Graham bequeathed the Straloch/Graham copy to the Advocates Library, Edinburgh on 25 November 1849.[51] The original was lost after 1842. The pieces in the Straloch/ Graham copy require a lute with up to ten courses in Renaissance tuning.

Robert Gordon of Straloch (1580–1661) came from a lowland Scots gentry background. The second son of Sir John Gordon of Pitlurg (Banffshire), he was educated at Aberdeen, and went on to become the first graduate of Marischal College. In 1598 he went to Paris to complete his studies, remaining there until his father's death in 1600. In 1606 he married, and bought the estate of Straloch. He continued to reside there, even after he succeeded to his father's estate at Pitlurg on the death of his elder brother in 1619.[52] He took up a public role in 1639, acting as one of the commissioners sent to Huntly to treat with Montrose. The service for which he is chiefly known is his contribution to the Scottish section of Blaeu's *Atlas*, which he began in 1630 at the request of Charles I. The Civil War interfered considerably with his work, but part of vol. 6 of Blaeu's *Atlas* is Gordon's work.[53] He was a noted authority on Scottish history.[54]

Graham's extracts in the Straloch/Graham copy are confused, to say the least. In marginal notes he comments that certain pieces in the original are 'very confused and incorrect' (Straloch/Graham copy, p. 15). Occasionally he is altogether defeated and discontinues his attempted copy, commenting that the tablature was 'blotted out', or 'obliterated in the original' (p. 9). In particular the Graham/ Straloch copy is very unclear in its rhythmic intentions, many pieces having few rhythm signs, and unequal bar lengths. Graham included some right-hand fingering indications, and some left-hand ornaments.

A reading of the contents list of the original Straloch manuscript made by David Laing shows that Graham in his partial copy ignored most of the many 'currents',

---

[48] Spring, 'The Lute in England and Scotland', ii. 6–10 for notes on the provenance. Laing's original contents list is found in *GB-Eu*, Laing IV.20, and reproduced in Spring, i. 310–12. A defective and partial contents list was included by Dauney in his *Ancient Scotish Melodies*, 368–9.

[49] Willsher, 'Music in Scotland', ii. 73.

[50] Spring, 'The Lute in England and Scotland', ii. 6–10. The 'Taphouse copy', *GB-En* 349, provided the basis for a copy made by Frank Kidson (now in the Leeds Public Library), which in turn served as the basis for Alfred Moffat's copy (*US-We* M140.G67 P5), made in 1885.

[51] RISM B vii. 99–100.   [52] *DNB* viii. 226.

[53] Willem and Jan Blaeu, *Theatrum Scotia et Hibernia, Theatrum orbis terrarum, sive Atlas novus*, 6 vols. (Amsterdam 1648–55), vi.

[54] *DNB* viii. 226.

'sarabands', 'ballets', and 'braills' that were likely to have been of French origin. The 'current' was the most frequently occuring form in the original manuscript, and Laing for items nos. 53, 73, and 87 gives collective titles such as 'Various other Currants' (no. 53), or, as in the case of item no. 87 which filled five folios, simply 'Other Currents'.[55] These parts of the original contents of the book justify Gordon's note in his title for the original manuscript that it 'contained many Currents and other musical things'. A further ingredient of the original Straloch manuscript were ballad tunes known also in England, such as 'What if a day' and 'Tell me Daphne', and pieces of obvious English origin like the 'Frogges galziart' and 'Lachrymay'. Clearly Graham was more anxious to copy the tunes of likely Scottish origin than those with French or English associations.[56]

Among the pieces of Continental origin in the Straloch/Graham copy and Rowallan manuscripts are some universal favourites like the 'Canaries', 'La Bourre', 'En me revenant', and 'La Spagnoletta'.[57] Versions of these pieces were known throughout much of northern Europe in the first decades of the century, and were certainly known in England at the time.

An important Scottish manuscript, contemporary with the Rowallan and Straloch manuscripts, is the Skene manuscript for 5-course mandore.[58] Dauney used it as the primary source for his *Ancient Scotish Melodies* (1838), including as an appendix transcriptions of eighty-five of the 117 pieces in the manuscript, along with 'notes and illustrations' for each of the tunes. He suppressed certain titles like 'I longe for your virginite', no doubt because he did not wish to upset the sensibilities of his readership.[59] Divided into eight separate books, and requiring two different tunings,[60] the collection is comparable in its mixture of Scottish, French, and English pieces to the Straloch and Rowallan manuscripts, although a larger English presence is discernible in the titles, especially in the first book, which includes four English masque pieces.[61]

---

[55] *GB-Eu* Laing IV.20. This list is reproduced in Spring, 'The Lute in England and Scotland', i. 310–12.

[56] Of the original 114 items listed by Laing only some twenty-five have titles which show possible Scottish associations. Of these almost all were transcribed by Graham.

[57] 'The Canaries' (Straloch/Graham no. 12, pp. 11–12) from Besard's *Thesaurus harmonicus* (1603), p. 168; 'Ostende' (Straloch/Graham, no. 13, pp. 12–14) and 'La Bourre' (Rowallan, no. 11, p. 13) is the 'La Bourree' of Praetorius; 'Brail de Poutou' (Straloch/Graham, no. 11, pp. 8–10) seems unrelated to Le Roy's version published in the *Brief and easye instruction* (1568), fo. 39ʳ; 'Curent' (Rowallan, no. 3, p. 3) is by Santino, Antonio, or Donino Garsi de Parma; 'Sibit Sant nikcola' (Rowallan, no. 7, pp. 8–9) is a version of 'En me revenant de St Nicolas' published by Besard, Fuhrmann, and others; 'Spyenelit reforme' (Rowallan, no. 12, p. 21) is 'La Spagnoletta' of *FVB* and many others.

[58] There is some uncertainty as to the date of this MS. Dauney felt that part at least dated from before 1615. A date nearer 1630 would be more plausible. See Donald Gill, 'The Skene Mandora Manuscript', *LSJ* 28 (1988), 19–33, for a description of the MS, its provenance, and a list of contents.

[59] Dauney, *Ancient Scotish Melodies*, lists 114 pieces in his inventory pp. 5–9, though I make the number 117.

[60] The tunings are *a, d', a', d'', a''* and *c', f', a', d'', g''*.

[61] These are: no. 11, 'Ladie Elizabeths Maske', possibly from one of the masques of 1613 performed to celebrate the marriage of the Princess Elizabeth to the Elector Frederick; no. 15, 'The Comoedians Maske'; no. 17, 'Sommersets Maske', from Coprario's *Masque of Squires* (1613); and no. 24, 'Prince Henreis Maske', from *Oberon* (1610).

Between pages 207 and 225 is a gathering of folios of a smaller size, paginated with the rest of the volume, but not mentioned by Dauney. These pages contain elaborate instructions for tuning a 10-course lute: 'to tune the Lut to the new sharp tune, by the unicent' (p. 221); 'to tune by the Octo' (p. 222); and 'to tune the Flutt [*sic*] to the Flatt tun' (pp. 223–4). The first two sets of instructions give different methods for tuning no. 8 and the third set for tuning no. 10. This indicates that John Skene of Hallyards (d. 1644), the original owner of the manuscript, also played the 10-course lute in transitional tunings, and that the manuscript was not assembled in its present form much before 1630, when such tunings were beginning to appear in English lute sources.

The 'Scottishness' of Lowland melodies has long been a subject of interest, and writings on it have continued to be published since the eighteenth century when Scots songs flooded the British popular song market. In his *Ancient Scotish Melodies* (1838) Dauney included as an appendix a dissertation titled 'Analysis of the Structure of the Music of Scotland. By Mr Finley Dun, Teacher of Singing, &c., In Edinburgh'.[62] This appendix covered the subject in detail. Other nineteenth-century writers on Scots song and popular music in Scotland include G. F. Graham, John Muir Wood, William Stenhouse, William Chappell, and John Glen. These writers took pains to distinguish between popular songs, ballads, and tunes of English origin, and those of Scots origin. A patriotic squabble developed between Chappell and contemporary musicologists over popular tunes which were common to both countries.[63] Glen in his *Early Scottish Melodies* (1900) attempted to claim back some melodies for the Scots that he felt Chappell had erroneously usurped for the English.[64]

The most easily accessible, up-to-date, and understandable discussion of the nature of Scottish melodies can be found in Dr Francis Collinson's *The Traditional and National Music of Scotland* (1966).[65] Collinson discusses the modal, pentatonic, and hexatonic nature of Scottish tunes as well as the familiar 'thumbprints' of Scots melodies, namely scotch snaps, double tonics, wide intervals, frequent ornamentation, melodic clichés, and tunes ending on notes other than the keynote. These characteristics are prominent in the folk music of other countries, but in Scottish melodies they are more consistently used than elsewhere.

Most of the Scottish melodies in the Straloch/Graham copy contain some or many of the characteristics noted above; Table 13.2 lists those pieces which have pentatonic, hexatonic, or modal melodies. Most of this number are hexatonic, and all end on a note or chord other than that at the start. Among the longer pieces,

---

[62] Appendix, no. 1, pp. 315–39.

[63] e.g. 'The Broom of Cowdenknows' was claimed by Chappell (*Popular Music of the Olden Time*, ii. 458–61) as an English tune known as 'The Broom, the bonny Broom' despite the assertion by Stenhouse, Graham, and Wood that it was Scottish. See John Glen, *Early Scottish Melodies* (Edinburgh, 1900), 33–5.

[64] See Glen, *Early Scottish Melodies*, 14–24, on William Chappell.   [65] See pp. 4–31.

where several strains can be distinguished, it is common to have the first basic strain tune elaborated, and sometimes extended in further strains, rather than a second or third strain of new material.[66] The use of a double tonic is not a feature of the Straloch/Graham copy pieces, although no. 30 uses only *G*, *B♭*, and *C* in the bass, and moves between B flat major and C major in bars 6–7, 10–11, and 14–15. However, it is frequently used in the Scottish pieces in the Rowallan manuscript.[67]

Table 13.2. *Pieces in the Straloch/Graham copy with pentatonic, hexatonic, or modal tunes*

Page no.	Piece no.	Title	Comment
5–6	6	Port Preist	Pentatonic beginning on F and finishing on C
6–7	8	I long for the wedding	Hexatonic beginning on C and ending on F
7	9	Gray Steil	Hexatonic beginning on C and ending on F
14–15	14	God be with thee Geordie	Pentatonic on F
15	15	Shoes rare and good in all/Lilt Ladie an Gordoun	Pentatonic on F
16	16	A daunce/Green greus ye rasses	Hexatonic on D
17	18	Its a wonder to see	Pentatonic beginning on F and ending on C
18–19	19	An thou wer myn own thing	First strain hexatonic or A ending on F. Later strains use complete F major scale
19	20	A Port/Port Jean Lindsay	Hexatonic on F ending on D
20	21	Port Rory Dall	Hexatonic beginning on C for first two strains. Final strain uses a complete C major scale ending on G
22	23	Wo betyd thy wearie bodie	Pentatonic on F

The arrangements of Scottish melodies in both Rowallan and Straloch manuscripts are always simple, usually the melody with a bass and an occasional chord. Uninhibited chord movement, especially from the tonic chord to flattened supertonic major, but also to relative major and minor chords, and the frequent use of parallel octaves, make the pieces distinctive. Many of the Rowallan pieces and some of those in the Straloch/Rowallan copy have inconsistent bar lengths, or lack rhythm signs. It may be that the music, as it stands, does represent the intentions of the compilers of the two original manuscripts. Pieces like no. 28 in the Rowallan, and nos. 21 and 28 of the Straloch/Graham copy, can sound acceptable when played with no attempt to alter the rhythm, despite the mixture of 4/4, 6/4, and

[66] Nos. 4, 19, and 25. Single-strain tunes were the norm until late into the 17th c. See Johnson, *Music and Society*, 123.
[67] Rowallan nos. 20, 22, 24, 27, 29, and 33.

3/4 bars. More likely the inconsistencies arise through the omission of rhythm signs above the tablature. These signs may have been unnecessary for the two original owners' performance as they would have known the tunes well, and used the manuscripts only as an aide-mémoire.

That Mure was uncertain and unsatisfied with his versions of some of the Scots melodies in the Rowallan manuscript is shown by the several workings of pieces that fill remaining, otherwise unused, spaces in the pages of his book. Apart from the completed version of 'For Kissing, for clapping, for hugging, for proving, set to the lute by Mr Mure' (Rowallan no. 19), there are at least three fragments of workings on other pages.[68] (See Ex. 13.3.) This piece is remarkable for the consistent use of E♮ in the top octave, and E♭ in the octave below (except in two cases of descending scales). This ambiguity is coupled with the juxtaposition of G major/minor and C major/minor scales. This could have resulted from the basing of this piece on a tune played on the diatonically tuned clarsach with an E♮ in one octave and an E♭ in another. The title suggests the piece was associated with a game, and was influenced by extra-musical associations.

A link between the Rowallan and Straloch manuscripts lies in the 'Port Jean Lindsay', which appears in both.[69] Mure probably wrote poetry to existent tunes. Certainly in Mure's day poems were sung to popular tunes. The 'Battel of Garlan', i.e. 'Battle of Harlaw' (Rowallan no. 23), according to Dauney, was a march tune which by 1600 was already of great antiquity.[70] 'Mary Beaton's Row' (no. 21), refers to the Mary Beatoun who was a lady in waiting to Mary Queen of Scots; Dauney postulates that the tune originated with a ballad, now lost and forgotten, of which she was the subject.[71] The 'Day Dawis' of the Straloch/ Graham copy (no. 4) was a tune known early in the sixteenth century, and Dauney suggests that literary references to the tune hint that it was used as a 'Reveillee' played by a piper or town minstrels in Scotland.[72] 'Gray steil' was a Scottish romance published by Laing in his *Early Metrical Tales*, and goes back to the fifteenth century at least.[73] 'Before the Greeks', which appeared in the original Straloch manuscript (no. 56) but was ignored by Graham in his copy, is associated with the important poem by Alexander Montgomerie (Mure's great-uncle) that opens 'Before the Greeks durst enterpryse'.[74]

---

[68] These workings can be found on pp. 38, 45, and 49, but other pieces have also been reworked.

[69] Shire, *Song, Dance and Poetry*, 211.

[70] Dauney, *Ancient Scotish Melodies*, 138-9, note b. The battle celebrated in the title was fought in 1411 at Harlaw between Highland and Lowland clans.

[71] Ibid., note a.   [72] Ibid. 51, note a.

[73] Ibid. 83, also note c. Included in *Early Metrical Tales*, ed. David Laing (Edinburgh, 1826).

[74] Shire, *Song, Dance and Poetry*, 144-5.

Ex. 13.3. '*for kissing for Clapping for Loving for proving set to the Lute by Mr Mure*', Rowallan
MS, p. 25

1. Crotchet sign ignored and omitted.

The Lady Margaret Wemyss manuscript contains much poetry and song as well as lute music, and has many of the characteristics of a commonplace book.[75] Margaret Wemyss (1630–48) was the eighth of eleven children born to David, 2nd Earl of Wemyss (1610–79), by his first wife Anna Balfour (d. 1649).[76] The second folio of the book carries the line 'begunne june 5 1643' which would mean that Margaret was 12 when she started her book. The first eleven folios of the Wemyss manuscript are taken up by seventeen songs in staff notation, three of which are by Morley, the rest by Campion. Only the cantus and bassus parts are included, the bassus being written, upside down, at the top of the page as an untexted instrumental line only. The cantus tune is written below, the correct way up, with first-verse words under the stave. Subsequent verses follow as text only. The absence of tablature suggests that a solo treble voice was accompanied by a bass viol alone, and the inner part, or parts, were ignored. This was a known mode of performance common in seventeenth-century England. Alternatively, the unfigured bass line was used by a lutenist/theorbist as the basis for a simple accompaniment in the manner of most Cavalier songs.

Eight poems follow the songs, none of which has an attribution save one marked 'composed by S J Sukling' (fos. 13ʳ–14ʳ), but which is not amongst the known works of Suckling. Poems 1 and 5 are accompanied by reference to Scottish tunes. The first 'sings to the air of the lady cromliks liltt', and the second is 'mad on my lady Binny'. A further nineteen poems are contained in the back of the book, which is reversed, the foliation beginning anew from the back. 'Beautie once blasted with the frost' (no. 24), is marked 'This is sung to the tune of when the king shall enjoy his own agane', and on fo. 20ʳ is a piece with the same title as the poem 'Buckingham's Gost', no. 2. These poems were sung to popular tunes which happened to fit the metre and phrase length, but which may also have had associated words of their own, quite different in sentiment. This was an old practice, evidence of which is found as far back as the sixteenth century in the Osborne and Giles Lodge commonplace books. Two of the poems are by Thomas Carew (nos. 16 and 17), and four by Sir Robert Ayton (nos. 12, 15, 20, and 21), with others attributable to Henry Howard, Thomas Cary, Alexander Montgomerie, William Herbert, Henry Hughes and James Graham, first Marquis of Montrose.

There are two separate sections devoted to solo lute music: fos. 17ʳ–27ʳ and 28ʳ–50ʳ. The first group of twenty-eight lute pieces are, in the main, for 10-course lute in Renaissance tuning, the exceptions being the four pieces attributed to 'Gautr' or 'Gutier' (fos. 25ʳ–26ʳ), which are 'on the Sharp tun which is called

[75] The Lady Margaret Wemyss MS is on loan from Lord Strathnaver to the *GB-En*, Deposit 314, no. 23. Patrick Cadell, the Assistant Keeper of the Library, showed me the MS in Jan. 1982. Up to this date it had remained little known as a music source. For a discussion of this MS and a list of contents see Spring, 'The Lady Margaret Wemyss Manuscript'.

[76] Paul, *The Scots Peerage*, viii. 503.

gautirs tune' (i.e. tuning no. 8). This section contains some universal favourites like 'The Spanish Pavane' (fo. 23ʳ), 'Tom of Bedlam' (fo. 18ʳ), and the Garsi de Parma 'Corant' (fos. 19ʳ–20ʳ), but is mainly given over to Scottish tunes. This section of the book is corrupt and inconsistent in its rhythm signs and bar lines, such that reconstruction is difficult. Were these pieces the young Lady Margaret's first attempts at writing down lute music?

In the second section of solo lute music sixty-one pieces fill twenty-two folios. Each piece is titled and supplied with a tuning indication, either 'sharp' (tuning no. 8) or 'flat' (tuning no. 10). All the pieces are for 10-course lute, except 'The King's Masque' on fo. 34ᵛ and an untitled piece on fo. 40ʳ, which are for 12-course lute. The great majority of the attributions are either to 'Gautier', spelt in many different ways, or to 'dafo' (Dufault), though 'Lamercure' (Mercure), 'Delespine' (Lespine), 'Labellvell' (Belleville), and 'Mervell' (Merville) are also mentioned. Many of the attributions can be proved to be erroneous. The French pieces are typical of the transitional style of the 1630s with many concordances with the Reymes and Pan 5 manuscripts.[77] There is a piece each from Ballard's 1631 and 1638 books.[78] There is also a version (under the title 'Almond') of 'Old Gautiers Nightingale', a piece that appears in numerous British sources,[79] and which was also arranged for keyboard, mandore, cittern, and for two viols.[80]

There are twenty-four Scottish lute solos in the Wemyss manuscript, mixed in with thirty-seven French pieces. The Scottish pieces are mostly short, some no more than a dozen bars, and all are written in tuning no. 8 (termed the 'Sharp' tuning throughout the book). Most of them use a hexachord or pentatonic scale based on F.[81] The texture in these pieces is even thinner than that of the Straloch/Graham copy and Rowallan pieces, being seldom more than a single-line melody on the upper courses, with an accompanying bass every few notes. As in the Straloch/Graham copy, two types of ornament sign are employed, the comma and the cross, and these are sometimes used at the beginning and final notes of phrases. The scotch snap (♪♪.) is evident in some of the Wemyss pieces (nos. 9 and 10), though sometimes by implication ♪♪ should be articulated as a scotch snap.[82]

The piece titled 'General Leslys Godnight' (no. 74) is a sarabande, and should be played with the forefinger of the right hand, strumming in the manner of a French sarabande. Two pieces, namely 'Da miche manum' (no. 81), and

---

[77] Spring, 'The Lady Margaret Wemyss Manuscript', 22–6.

[78] Wemyss no. 43, fo. 32ᵛ (Ballard 1638, p. 22); Wemyss no. 52, fo. 36ᵛ (Ballard 1631, p. 36).

[79] Wemyss no. 58, fos. 38ᵛ–39ʳ; Nanki no. 5, fos. 3ᵛ–4ʳ; Bodley 410–414 no. 15; Pickeringe no. 99, fos. 48ᵛ–47ᵛ; Pan 5, fo. 38ᵛ.

[80] *GB-Och* 1179, p. 1; *D-Us* 132, pp. 12–13; John Playford, *Musick's Delight on the Cithren* (1666), no. 36; John Playford, *A Musicall Banquet* (1651), no. 29.

[81] Exceptions include Wemyss MS nos. 53 and 86.

[82] e.g. in the Wemyss MS, *Lilt neidell-eye*, no. 46, in bars 10–15 on the first beat of each bar.

'Goodnight and god be with you' (no. 88), are the only Scottish pieces of any length in the Wemyss manuscript, with sixty and forty bars respectively. Here the opening strains are continually reworked over a static bass. The treatment is akin to that of some of the longer pieces in the Balcarres manuscript, where divisions on a single strain gradually increase in complexity, filling in the notes of the pentatonic melody with weaving divisions in quavers. Many of the Scottish pieces in this source have concordances with the Balcarres manuscript and other Scottish instrumental collections. The wide discrepancies between the Wemyss and Balcarres versions of tunes indicate either the change over time that the tunes underwent, or that a wide variety of interpretation was common during the seventeenth century before published versions were available.

'My Lady Binnis Lilt' (no. 80) of the Wemyss manuscript is the earliest appearance of a Scottish tune that had wide circulation as a lute piece *c.*1650 (see Ex. 13.4). It appears in Mathew's *Lutes Apology* (1652) titled 'Tantarra', in the Ruthwen manuscript as 'Urania', and in the Balcarres manuscript as 'The Lady Binnes Lilt by David Grieve' as well as Scottish sources for other instruments like the Blaikie and Guthrie manuscripts.[83] The tune may be related to the ballad tune in common time 'In January last' which was current in England in the latter half of the seventeenth century,[84] as there are melodic and harmonic similarities. The lute piece is unmistakably of Scottish origin, and is an example of a Scottish tune which became popular as a lute piece outside Scotland.

No attributions or signatures can be found in Pan 5.[85] This manuscript contains some twenty pieces concordant with the Reymes manuscript. Its binding and watermark are also similar to the Reymes manuscript, and it was probably compiled in London or Paris *c.*1630–5. There were possibly two, but more probably three scribes at work on Pan 5.[86] One of the scribes contributed 60 pieces to Pan 5 and was also the same scribe who added 51 pieces to the Reymes manuscript. This scribe is identified by Goy as a lute master of probable French origin named 'Hebert'.[87] The identity of the original owner has not been discovered but the small number of Scottish pieces found amongst all the French suggests an original Scots owner. There are 107 pieces for 10-course lute in tunings nos. 1, 8, 9, and 10 and some exercises for Baroque guitar.

---

[83] See Spring, 'The Lute in England and Scotland', ii. 166, for a full concordance list, and i. 368 for further discussion of this piece.

[84] Simpson, *The British Broadside Ballad*, 365–7.

[85] For notes on the watermarks see *Œuvres de René Mesangeau*, ed. Rollin and Souris, pp. xvii, xix, and n. 18.

[86] For a breakdown of pieces among the three scribes see Rave, 'Some Manuscripts', 115–18, and Spring, 'The Lute in England and Scotland', ii. 57.

[87] Goy, 'luthes et luthistes', 187. See also Rave, 'Some Manuscripts', 114–15; *Œuvres de Mesangeau*, ed. Rollin and Souris, pp. xix–xx.

Ex. 13.4. *'My Lady Binis Lilt', Wemyss MS, fo. 45ʳ⁻ᵛ*

1. Tenor tablature has '*a*' altered to '*r*'.

2. Rhythm sign ♩ ♪ altered to ♪. ♪.

3. ♩ rhythm sign added.

4. Rhythm sign altered to ♪ ♩.

5. Rhythm sign ♪ ♪ altered to ♪. ♪.

Much of the history of Pan 8 is identical with that of Pan 5, though unlike Pan 5, it was probably compiled for Lady Jean Campbell's use, and not acquired by the family second-hand. The forty-eight lute solos are preceded by eight keyboard pieces, two of which are attributed in the manuscript to 'Orlando', but are unlikely to be by Orlando Gibbons.[88] The lute pieces are for 12-course lute in tunings nos. 9, 10, and D minor. Folios 1ᵛ and 2ʳ are signed by Lady Jean Campbell, the later folio also containing the signature of one 'Monsieur Dozell'. Probably Lady Jean added some of the pieces herself. The only attribution among the lute pieces in Pan 8 is to 'Goutier' (fo. 35ʳ), and the only ornament sign in the lute music is the comma, which probably represents either a trill from above on a long note, or an appoggiatura on a short note.

Pan 4 dates from *c.*1650–60 and probably originates from England or Scotland; at least one of the four scribes was English-speaking.[89] It contains twenty-three pieces in standard D minor or D major tunings for 11-course lute, or in the case of pieces nos. 4, 11, 12, and 18 for 12-course lute, and is representative of a later style of French lute music than Pan 5 and 8. The composers mentioned are 'Vincent', 'Vieux Gaultier', 'Bouvier', 'Pinel', 'Hautman', 'Gaultier, d'Angleterre', 'Confesse', and 'Jeune Gaultier'. It has been suggested that there are a number of similarities between Pan 4 and the Ruthwen manuscript, and that the scribe of nos. 18–20 (fos. 17ᵛ–20ᵛ) of Pan 4 and that of the first part of the Ruthwen manuscript (fos. 1ʳ–49ᵛ) are the same.[90] Monique Rollin has suggested that this may be John Mercure's hand, or that of a pupil under his supervision.[91]

The few Scottish portraits that include lutes from this period all show young women holding 12-course lutes. The popularity of this type of instrument in mid-century Scotland is confirmed by these pictures and the presence of pieces for 12-course lute in Pan 4, Pan 8, and the Wemyss manuscripts. (See Pls. 13.2, 13.3, and 13.4.) Like Lady Margaret Wemyss and Lady Jean Campbell, the girls in these portraits would probably have learnt the lute between the ages of 7 and 14 to improve their marriage prospects. For these aristocratic girls the fact that the lute was so strongly associated with France at this time would have been a positive attraction, highlighting the girl's cosmopolitanism and sophistication. Perhaps the most attractive portrait is that of Lady Anne Bruce, daughter of Sir William Bruce (d. 1710) of Kinross, architect in Scotland to Charles II, and a close friend.

The Panmure lute books contain only a handfull of identifiable Scottish or English pieces. They are a testament to the popularity of French lute music in

---

[88] Concerning the virginal pieces in Pan 8, 9, and 10 see Dart, 'New Sources of Virginal Music', 101–3.

[89] Rave discusses Pan 4 on pp. 159–63. Clive Ungless transcribed the complete contents of the MS in his study 'Scottish National Library, MS Panmure 4: A Transcription with an Introductory Essay and Notes' (Honours degree diss., Royal Holloway College, University of London, 1981).

[90] Ungless, ibid. 7.

[91] *Œuvres des Mercure*, ed. and trans. by Monique Rollin and Jean-Michel Vaccaro (Paris, 1977), p. xxiv.

PL. 13.2. Lady Margaret Hey, wife of Henry Lord Ker (married 1644) by Soest, c.1650. Floors Castle, Kelso

PL. 13.3. Lady Margaret Hay, Countess of Roxburghe (1657–1753) with a 12-course lute by Soest. Scottish National Portrait Gallery

PL. 13.4. Lady Anne Bruce, daughter of Sir William Bruce of Kinross, c.1665. Stirling Castle, on loan from Historic Scotland. Crown Copyright

Britain before and around the mid-seventeenth century. The Ruthwen manuscript may have a Scottish provenance.[92] It contains the following remarks: 'Mrs Patricia Ruthwen aught yᵉ Book yᵉ 31 of May 1700'; 'Countess of Kilmarnock july 9 1747'; 'The 10 of october in the year 1656 I have begoon agaien to learn to play on the Leut'.[93] The last of these lines is accompanied on nearby folios by a few lines of doggerel poetry, aphorisms, and a tune in mensural notation which mentions a certain 'Jenny Hill'. Despite the references to these British women, the music is overwhelmingly in the popular French style of *c*.1650, with important pieces by Mercure, Pinel, Vieux Gaultier, Bouvier, and Vincent. The book contains sixty-six pieces on ninety-four folios and has two main sections, the first of which has some indications of original British provenance. Folio 14ʳ contains a version of 'The Lady Binnis Lilt', here entitled 'Urania'. This and the names of two of the women mentioned in the book suggest a Scots connection. The manuscript is for 11-course lute in D minor and related tunings.

The Balcarres manuscript is the largest, and arguably the most important post-1620 British source of lute music. The collection is also possibly the most extensive of all Scottish late seventeenth- and early eighteenth-century instrumental manuscript sources, whether for lute, keyboard, violin, or lyra viol.[94] Among its contents are Scottish tunes common to the Wemyss, Straloch, Rowallan, and Skene manuscripts. Together with native Scottish music, the Balcarres manuscript contains arrangements of violin music, English popular tunes, and French Baroque lute music by mid- and later seventeenth-century masters.

The date of compilation of the Balcarres manuscript cannot be pinpointed, nor its early provenance traced, but it does not date from before the last few years of the seventeenth century, and more probably originates from the first years of the eighteenth. These were the years before the trickle of printed collections of Scots songs, fiddle tunes, and dance music produced for the English and Scottish market became a veritable flood.[95] The popularity of such books, and those that followed, ensured that Scots songs were staple fare for music publishers aiming at the popular market in the eighteenth century. The sheer number of publications that continued throughout the century and into the next which included, or purported to include, old Scots melodies largely ensured that the living and changing body of popular Scots melodies was gradually replaced by more 'tasteful' eighteenth-century

[92] The Ruthwen MS is discussed by Rave, 'Some Manuscripts', 197–203. The Mercure pieces on fos. 2ʳ–13ʳ form the basis of the selection of pieces for the *Œuvres de Mercure*, ed. Rollin and Vaccaro.

[93] Ruthwen MS, fos. 1ʳ, 68ᵛ, 94ʳ.

[94] Matthew Spring, 'The Balcarres Manuscript', *LSJ* 32 (1992) 2–45; for a table of Scottish MS sources (1600–1725), see p. 3.

[95] 1723/4 saw the publication of Ramsey's *The Tea-Table Miscelany*; in 1725 *Musick for Allan Ramsey's Collection of Scots Tunes*, ed. Alexander Stuart was published in Edinburgh, and also the first edition of William Thompson's *Orpheus Caledonius* in London.

arrangements, calculated to sell to the general British public. The Balcarres manuscript is representative of the pivotal years when manuscript circulation, which was responsive to aural tradition, was being increasingly undermined by the scale of popular publications.

In comparison with the arrangements of Scots melodies in contemporary manuscripts the Balcarres manuscript settings are usually longer, often with several different versions of the same tune, and are of a more consistent quality. Though some of the pieces are long (some run to several hundred bars), they have been copied and so arranged that almost no page turns are required.[96] The manuscript is for an 11-course lute tuned primarily in D minor tuning.[97]

Unlike the Rowallan, Straloch, and Wemyss books, the Balcarres manuscript is remarkably free from musical errors, alterations, or omissions and seems to show the presence of a professional musician (or musicians) in the settings of native tunes. Of all the Scottish lute books, its history is the most obscure. All the 158 pages which contain music have entries in a single, clearly legible hand which is probably that of the book's owner and compiler. Whoever the scribe was, he had a reasonable technical skill, and much enthusiasm for collecting lute settings of Scottish tunes, as well as popular English tunes and French lute pieces. (See Pl. 13.5.)

Writers on seventeenth- and eighteenth-century Scottish music who have mentioned the Balcarres manuscript have all assumed that the book originated from the household of one of the Lindsays of Balcarres.[98] Certainly it survives today as part of the Crawford–Lindsay family possessions (until 1988 kept with other Crawford papers at the John Rylands Library in Manchester but since transferred to the National Library of Scotland). However, there is nothing within the manuscript's contents to substantiate this, and it could have been acquired after completion by the Lindsay family. There is also no date to be found within the book. If the lute book was originally connected with the Lindsays of Balcarres family it would have been compiled during the lifetime of Colin, 3rd Earl of Balcarres (1654–1722).[99]

The musical contents suggest an early eighteenth-century compilation date. The great majority of pieces are arrangements of popular tunes, and are thus impossible to date with any accuracy, but a sizeable number of pieces concord closely with pieces from Henry Playford's publications for the violin, in particular *The Division Violin* (1685), *Apollo's Banquet* (1670 and subsequent editions), and, most importantly, *A Collection of Original Scotch-Tunes* (1700 and 1701). The first three pieces of the *Original Scotch-Tunes* appear in the Balcarres manuscript in almost exactly the form as in the publication, the violin part having been transposed down an octave, and a simple bass line added. Of the nineteen pieces in the Balcarres man-

---

[96] The only page turn occurs between pp. 41 and 42 in the first version of *The horsemans Port.*

[97] D major tuning and tunings nos. 8 and 6 are also required for nos. 202–48.

[98] Shire, *Song, Dance and Poetry*, 256; Johnson, *Music and Society*, 26.   [99] *DNB* xi. 1165.

PL. 13.5. Page 144 from the Balcarres MS, showing no. 226, 'The Chancellours farewell, M^r m^claughlans way, by m^r beck'

uscript attributed to the French lute masters, Gallot (which Gallot is never specified), Mouton, Vieux Gaultier, and Mercure, several date from the mid-century.[100] None of the Gallot and Mouton pieces appears in any surviving publications, but they were probably composed well before 1690. Thus they do not contribute any clues as to the date of the book's compilation.

The person who figures most prominently in the arranging of the Balcarres manuscript's contents is a certain 'Mr Beck'. It has been suggested that Beck was a German musician,[101] employed as music tutor at Balcarres House.[102] There is no evidence which clearly substantiates this. David Johnson is perhaps closer to the mark, limiting his description of Beck to that of being 'an Edinburgh lute teacher'.[103] The following extracts from a transcript of a Court of Session roll-book show that Beck did have connections with Edinburgh.[104] This entry runs as follows:

[100] The 'Saraband Mercure' (Balcarres, no. 128) is in the section of the Ruthwen MS which was entered in the 1650s although the piece probably dates from the 1640s. Likewise the Vieux Gaultier pieces (Balcarres nos. 138 and 141) probably date from the 1640s or even the 1630s.

[101] Farmer, *A History of Music in Scotland*, 331.   [102] Johnson, *Music and Society*, 26.

[103] Johnson, *Scottish Fiddle Music*, 16.

[104] Sir John Lauder of Fountainhall, *Decisions of the Lords of Council and Session from June 6th, 1678 to July 30th, 1712*, 2 vols. (Edinburgh, 1759), i. 590. Entry for Jan. 1694.

Halcraig reported Mr. McLean, Dancing-master, and Master of the Revels, against Beck, and the other Musicions who have erected the concert of Musick, craving that they ought to be licensed by him, before they could set up and exact money, seeing his office was to inspect and regulate all games and sports, and see that nothing immoral or indecent should be allowed. The Lords having perused McLean's gift, they found musick indeed contained in it, but that it was insert in that clause anent Tragedies, Comedies, and other theatrical scenes where musick is always used, as also at puppet plays, but that the liberal science of musick itself was not comprehended in his gift especially seeing Musicians were not subject to the Master of the revels abroad, where that place was better known than with us, and that he only used it to drain money from them, without restraining immoralities, if they paid him.[105]

This case, it seems, paved the way for the appearance in Edinburgh of regular public concerts, and hence for the fashionable interest in music and concert life that became a feature of eighteenth-century Edinburgh.[106] With reference to Beck, it confirms that he was a musician who had 'associates' amongst other musicians, and that he was not so tied to any post as to be unable to promote a public concert in Edinburgh. The contents of the Balcarres manuscript suggest that he was probably a lute teacher, and was certainly well able to arrange music for the lute. Of the 252 pieces, Mr Beck is mentioned in connection with 188 of them. In eighty-one cases he is given solo credit for the pieces, either as 'by mr Beck' or more commonly 'mr Beck's way' (very occasionally 'fashion' is substituted for 'way'). In the remaining 107 pieces which mention Beck it is always in connection with another: either 'Jean Mores', 'John Morison', 'Mr Mclaughlan', 'my daughter', 'Jean Burnet', or 'Henrietta Imbries'. An example of such a joint title might be 'Port Atholl, mr mclachlands way, by mr Beck'. In these cases the tune was perhaps played by, or in some way brought to the compiler's attention by Jean Mores, John Morison, Mr Mclaughlan, etc., who thus knew the tune in the form they performed it; Beck was then responsible for the lute arrangement. In the case of the eighty-one titles which mention only Beck, probably the tune was not associated with any individual, but Beck arranged his own, or a commonly known version, for the lute. There is no obvious distinction between 'by mr Beck' and 'mr Becks way', other than that 'by' might imply the particular arrangement of a given tune in which the melody is unaffected, and that 'way' suggests the particular melodic version of a tune that Beck, Mores, Morrison, etc. knew.[107] This loose distinction would allow for the many different versions of the same tune found in the manuscript.

---

[105] Sir John Lauder of Fountainhall, *Decisions of the Lords of Council and Session from June 6th, 1678 to July 30th, 1712*, 2 vols. (Edinburgh, 1759). The second edition of *Domestic Annals of Scotland*, ed. Robert Chambers, drew on the above entry, quoting from it freely (2nd edn., 3 vols., Edinburgh, 1831), iii. 89.

[106] Johnson, *Music and Society*, 32–3. Johnson suggests that following Beck's enterprise, which he dates as Nov. 1693, there followed a grand concert on St Cecilia's Day in 1695, and a weekly series initiated in Nov. 1699.

[107] The inclusion in the title of 'Mr Beck's way', 'David Grieve's way', etc., has no association with any particular tuning, unlike in earlier MSS, where 'harp way', or 'Lawrence way', etc., helped to specify a particular tuning.

It is impossible to say to what extent the compiler of the Balcarres manuscript was responsible for the settings, but the part that Beck played is large. Apart from nos. 112 to 142, where he gives way to David Grieve, Mr Lesslie, and a number of French composers, he is found throughout the manuscript. That Beck was not the book's compiler is proved by the title that follows no. 225 (pp. 142–3), which runs 'The Parliaments Rant, mr macklachlands way, by mr Beck. to want the 10th measure, and to have another in its roome, sent to me by mr Beck all is amended'. Beck had a considerable knowledge of lute technique and composition. Living in or near Edinburgh, he was able to generate a large, popular repertoire for pupils by drawing on Scots fiddle pieces and tune versions favoured by musicians known either to him or the book's compiler. Jean Mores, John Mclaughlan, John Morrison, 'my daughter', Jean Burnett, and Henrietta Imbrie are always mentioned in connection with Beck. Perhaps they were singers or instrumentalists, some of whom were possibly musically illiterate, and hence Beck was required to regularize and arrange the tunes they played. This first group is quite distinct from David Grieve, John Red, and Mr Lesslie, who are always mentioned alone in any attribution. Perhaps these individuals were also lute players, or sufficiently musically literate to make their arrangements available to the compiler without Beck's services. This clear distinction between the two groups follows without exception, and suggests that the compiler's part in arranging tunes was slight.

The one individual in the first group about whom something is known is John Mclaughlan. He was an Edinburgh violinist, and may have been connected with, or was, the 'James McClachlan' listed by Tytler in his detailed description of the St Cecilia's Day concert in Edinburgh in 1695.[108] Several pieces by Mclaughlan appear in Playford's *Collection of Original Scotch-Tunes* (1700), and in the Bowie fiddle manuscript (1705).[109] The cosmopolitan style of his minuets (titled 'J. Mch.') in the last-named sources along with the possible participation in a concert that featured music by [Sir John?] Clerk, Torrelli, Finger, and Bassani, suggests that Mclaughlan was a professional violinist equally at ease with serious art music and native fiddle tunes.[110]

Most probably the compiler of the Balcarres manuscript was an amateur lutenist with a wide musical interest, who employed Beck to help put together a large anthology of lute pieces drawn from popular Scots and English tunes, French lute music, and fashionable dance tunes. The general grouping of pieces by tuning and attribution suggests that the collection was not put together slowly, but was conceived and compiled as a composite whole over a relatively short period of time.[111]

[108] William Tytler, 'On the Fashionable Amusements and Entertainments in Edinburgh in the Last Century, with a Plan of a Grand Concert of Musicians, St Cecilia's Day, 1695', *Transactions of the Society of Antiquarians of Scotland*, 1 (1792), 499–510 at 507–8.

[109] Johnson, *Scottish Fiddle Music*, 22 and 30.   [110] Johnson, *Music and Society*, 12.

[111] See Spring, 'The Balcarres Lute Book', 18–19.

Of the nineteen pieces in the Balcarres manuscript that are ascribed to French lutenist composers, one is by Mercure, four are ascribed to Mouton (one of which is clearly mis-attributed), two to 'Gaultier', and the remaining twelve to Gallot.[112] The single Mercure sarabande in the Balcarres manuscript also appears as the opening piece in the Ruthwen manuscript.[113] The English nature of most of the twelve pieces attributed to Gallot contributes to the suggestion in a Paris guitar manuscript and the Oxford 'de Gallot' guitar book that there was a Gallot d'Angleterre among the illustrious Gallot family of lutenists.[114]

A good example is the simple march-like piece titled 'Dragons, by monsieur Gallot' which is devoid of any *brisé* texture. It may be significant that the only concordances for this piece are found in British sources, namely, Ox 576, titled 'Dragons d'angleterre',[115] and the Sinkler keyboard manuscript, where it is titled 'A March'. A further French tune in the Balcarres manuscript titled 'Belle hereuse, by Mr lesslie' (no. 129), is Lully's 'Sommes-nous pas trop heureux'.[116] Here it is arranged by Mr Lesslie, who was presumably a local musician, as he is responsible for a variety of tune arrangements mostly of a Scottish nature, but he is also credited with an arrangement of 'The Canaries', a simple ground-bass tune which was especially popular in France, but known all over Europe.[117] The French lute pieces are a distinct entity in the manuscript and by comparison with the rest of the contents they are more *brisé* in texture, more idiomatically written for the lute, and contain a full complement of ornaments.

Among the contents of the Balcarres manuscript are nine tune arrangements of English Cavalier or theatre songs.[118] Several of these tunes appear in other Scottish manuscripts like the Leyden and Blaikie manuscripts (for lyra viol), and were popular north of the border. Most of these songs appeared in Playford's song publications, or later in D'Urfey's *Pills*.[119] A conspicuous number of pieces in the Balcarres manuscript, including most of the longer pieces, are lute intabulations of English and Scottish tunes and pieces that had been published by John and Henry Playford during the period 1651–1700. These arrangements and those of the theatre songs

---

[112] Spring, 'The Lute in England and Scotland', i. 324; 'The Balcarres MS', 22–5.

[113] There are several discrepancies between the two sources, especially in the final phrase, but in general the Balcarres version includes a fuller complement of ornaments and rhythm signs when compared with what is thought to be the autograph version in the Ruthwen MS. See Spring, 'The Lute in England and Scotland', ii, pp. vi–vii for notes on the Ruthwen MS.

[114] *F-Pn* Rés. 823; *GB-Ob* Mus. Sch. C94. See Donald Gill, 'The de Gallot Guitar Books', *EM* 6 (1978), 79–87.

[115] This MS may of course originally have been French (Rave, 'Some Manuscripts', 270–5).

[116] From the *Ballet de l'impatience* (1661). Herbert Schneider, *Chronologisch-thematisch Verzeichnis sämtlicher Werke von Jean-Baptist Lully* (Tutzing, 1981), 63.

[117] The Balcarres version is very similar to that of Praetorius' *Terpsichore* (1612), quoted in *New Grove*, iii. 677.

[118] These are: nos. 17, 18, 19, 'Celia that once was blest'; no. 20, 'Celia is my foe'; no. 27, 'From the fair Lavinion shoar'; no. 58, 'Lillybollaro'; no. 77, 'Amarillis told her swannne'; no. 176, 'Adieu to the Pleasures'; no. 189, 'After the Paunges of a desparat lover'.

[119] Thomas D'Urfey, *Wit and Mirth; or, Pills to Purge Melancholy* (London, 1699, with later editions to 1719).

connect the Balcarres with the Poznań manuscript. Some of the Balcarres manuscript versions are similar to those Playford books, particularly the *Division Violin* (1684 and 1685). Others do not concord well with Playford's versions. Probably these tunes had been circulating freely throughout Britain in various forms. A number of Scottish tunes in the manuscript, concord so closely with those in Playford's *Collection of Original Scotch-Tunes* (1700, 1701), that there is every indication that someone involved in the compilation of the book had access to that publication, and that the Balcarres manuscript therefore dates from the years after 1700.

Seventeenth-century England experienced a rise in popularity for the 'raw scots tune' that accelerated throughout the century, and became a positive mania in the eighteenth century.[120] The favour found by many of the Scottish aristocracy and gentry at the Stuart court in London may have encouraged this trend. Playford was quick to see the commercial possibilities of these melodies, and increasingly included 'Scots tunes' in his *Dancing Master* editions, and in his other instrumental publications, especially those for violin. The gradual replacing of old tunes by new tunes of Scottish origin in Playford's books highlights this drift. This is particularly true of the later editions of *Apollo's Banquet*.[121] The third edition of the *Dancing Master* published in 1665 included a supplement titled 'Select New Tunes', which prominently features Scottish violin tunes, most of which were then included with dance instructions in later editions of the *Dancing Master*.[122] Finally, in 1700, Henry Playford published the *Collection of Original Scotch-Tunes*, which was devoted to Scottish melodies, and followed it in 1701 with a second, slightly altered edition.[123]

Five of the many sets of variations in the Balcarres manuscript can be traced back to John Playford's *Division Violin* (1684 and 1685). Four of the pieces, 'Redings ground', 'Old sir simon the king', 'Thomas Tollits ground', and 'John cock thy beaver', appeared in the first edition of the *Division Violin*. The variations on 'Green sleeves' (no. 90) were printed as no. 27, 'Green Sleeves, to a Ground with Divisions', the first of ten additions to the original edition that appeared in the 1685 edition.[124] There are many slight melodic and rhythmic discrepancies between the printed versions and those in the Balcarres manuscript, but for the most part the violin line is simply transposed down an octave to suit the tessitura of the lute, which is the usual method of arranging violin music throughout the Balcarres

---

[120] See Spring, 'The Lute in England and Scotland', i. 148.

[121] In the introduction to the 1690 edition of *Apollo's Banquet* Playford states, 'And now the former Impression being sold off and called upon for more, I here in this Sixth Edition left out some of the old tunes but in their places added twice as many new ones, with divers new Scotch tunes'.

[122] This supplement appears to have given Playford the idea for *Apollo's Banquet* (1670), as many of the 'Select New Tunes' appear in the publication of 1670.

[123] The 1700 edition contained thirty-nine tunes, and the 1701 forty-two tunes. The last tune of the 1700 edition, 'The deal stick the Minster' was dropped from the 1701 edition, and four new tunes added.

[124] See Spring, 'The Balcarres Lute Book', 26.

manuscript. The 'ground base' as set down in the printed source is seldom followed in the manuscript, and Mr Beck shows characteristic ingenuity in varying his bass line with a strong preference for diatonic movement to suit the playing of the lute's diapasons. While for the most part the bass line in the Balcarres versions is also played an octave below the printed pitch, in some strains it moves to the higher octave. It is noticeable in this and the other intabulations of sets of variations originally intended for the violin how little recourse the Balcarres arranger (or arrangers) has to chords of three or more parts to fill out the texture. Instead a clear two-part texture is nearly always discernible.

None of the pieces drawn from the *Division Violin* has an attribution. However, the first and second editions of the publication are dominated by the violinist-composers Davis Mell, John Banister, and, in particular, the Lübecker, Thomas Baltzar, whose division techniques profoundly influenced English violin playing in the mid-seventeenth century.[125] Margaret Gilmore has noted the influence of the *Division Violin* on Scottish fiddle playing in the eighteenth century, and suggests that 'Playford's early collection found its most enduring heritage in Scotland'.[126] The Balcarres manuscript provides ample evidence that this was so. There are sixty-seven pieces which mention John Mclaughlan. They are usually titled 'in mr mclaughlans way, by mr Beck', and are grouped together in two main sections.[127] These pieces include most of those with extended and elaborate variations in the *Division Violin*, and it may be that this Edinburgh violin master was important in bringing the variation techniques developed by Baltzar, Mell, and Banister to Scotland later in the seventeenth century, and partly responsible for their popularity from that point onwards.

Of the thirty-two tunes in the Balcarres manuscript that also appear in Playford's various editions of the *Dancing Master*, several are substantially different but share the same title. Seven of the shared tunes show strong similarities between the *Dancing Master* and Balcarres manuscript versions.[128] Perhaps the most interesting aspect of these tune arrangements are the divisions which follow many of them. 'Donald Couper' has no less than five accompanying variations of both opening strains, but this number is unusual, and most tunes have only one or two. It may be that the various editions of *Apollo's Banquet* were a source for some of the Balcarres tunes. In all these cases the Balcarres tunes are sufficiently divergent to admit only

[125] For information on Baltzar see Peter Holman, 'Thomas Baltzar (?1631–1663), the "Incomparable Lubicer on the Violin"', *Chelys*, 13 (1984), 3–38 at 3.

[126] John Playford, *The Division Violin*, facs. edn. with an introduction by Margaret Gilmore (Oxford, 1980); see the preface.

[127] These are on pp. 88–125 for pieces in D minor tunings (nos. 142–61, 163–89, 192–3), and pp. 139–51 for pieces in D major tunings (nos. 222–39).

[128] Nos. 10, 53, 59, 64, 123, 163, 207.

the indirect influence of the *Apollo's Banquet* versions on those of the Balcarres manuscript.[129]

The publication which contains versions of Scottish tunes concording most exactly with the Balcarres manuscript is Henry Playford's *Collection of Original Scotch-Tunes* (1700, 1701). Concordant pieces from this source have been listed in Table 7.3. Of the fourteen tunes, all of which appear in both the manuscript and printed edition, eight are almost note for note the same in the melody line (after the octave transposition has been allowed for). Example 13.5 shows the similarity of the two sources in the versions of the piece called 'A New Scotch-Measure' by Playford and 'Maulslies scotts measure, mr Becks way' by the compiler of the Balcarres manuscript. A similar arrangement of the tune for keyboard can be found in the Sinkler manuscript. It can be seen from Ex. 13.5 that Mr Beck added a simple bass line to the Balcarres manuscript, plus full chords at the beginning of the first bar and at the end of each of the two strains.

There are slight melodic discrepancies observable in each of the eight closely concordant pieces in Table 13.3, yet the degree of concordance is remarkable, and continues throughout any variations that follow the first strain. The one exception to this is 'Wappat the Widow my Lady' (*Collection of Original Scotch-Tunes*, no. 23; Balcarres MS, no. 210), where the Balcarres manuscript includes all five strains printed by Playford in the same order, but then continues with two extra strains which are not otherwise known. In a further four pieces (*Collection of Original Scotch-Tunes*, nos. 20, 24, 26, and 33) there are strong similarities between the published and Balcarres manuscript versions, at least in the first one or two strains. In each instance the key is the same and the melody line strongly similar. In the case of *Collection of Original Scotch-Tunes*, no. 42, 'And when she came ben she bobbed', and no. 13, 'Sir William Hope's Scotch-Measure', the Balcarres tune which takes the same title is quite different. All the Balcarres manuscript pieces in Table 13.3 were arranged by Mr Beck and five of them mention John McLaughlan. Playford attributed the second piece in Table 13.3 to 'Mr McClauklain', while in the Balcarres manuscript 'Mr Kenneth mcKenzie' is mentioned as well. Both sources are agreed on the title of Playford's first piece, which is credited to a 'Mr McLaine' or 'Macklaine', who is not to be confused with John McLaughlan.[130] These concordances suggest that the Balcarres manuscript and the publication are closely contemporary, and that Beck either had access to the publication or to some of its contributors. The most likely conjecture is that Beck borrowed from the *Collection*

---

[129] 'Peggie I must love the' (no. 145) appeared in the 1687 edition; 'The Shoemaker' (no. 164), 1690 edition; 'I serve a worthie ladie', known also as 'Dumbarton drums' (no. 54), 1687 edition; and 'The Soutors of Selkirk' (no. 238), 1690 edition. None of these tunes featured in any editions of the *Dancing Master*.

[130] Possibly the title could refer to the McLean who was the Edinburgh Master of the Revels in the 1690s (see Spring, 'The Lute in England and Scotland', ii. 95).

Ex. 13.5. *Comparison of (a) 'A New Scotch-Measure', Original Scotch-Tunes (1701), no. 39; (b) 'Maulslies scotts measure, m^r Becks way', Balcarres MS, no. 3, p. 3; and (c) 'Malslys Scots Measure', Sinkler MS, pp. 50–1*

Table 13.3. *Comparison of tune arrangements in the Balcarres MS and Henry Playford's*
A Collection of Original Scotch-Tunes *(1700 and 1701)*

* = close concordance, including any following divisions

Original Scotch-Tunes			Balcarres		
No.	Key	Title/Comments	No.	Key	Title/Comments
1	C	'Mr McLaines Scotch-Measure'	*56	C	'Macklaines scots measure, mʳ Becks way'
2	C	'Mr McClauklaines Scotch-Measure'	158	C	'Mr Kenneth mᶜkenzies scotts measure, mʳ mᶜlaughlans way by mʳ beck'
3	C	'I love my Love in Seacreit'	*26	C	'I love my love in secret, by mʳ beck, morisons way'
13	D	'Sir William Hope's Scotch-Measure'	202	G	'Sir william hopes scotts measure, by mʳ beck' (different melody from that of *Original Scotch-Tunes* version)
14	D	'Stir her up and hold her ganging'	*227	D	'Hold her goeing, mʳ mᶜlaughlans by mʳ Beck'
20	D	'Bess Bell'	*230	D	'Bessie Bell, mʳ Mᶜlaughlans way, by mʳ Beck' (first strain similar, but thereafter differs)
23	G	'Wappat the Widow my Lady' (5 strains)	210	G	'Wapp at the Widdow my ladie, the new way, by mʳ Beck' (7 strains, 2 extra strains not included in *Original Scotch-Tunes*)
24	F	'If love is the cause of my mourning'	153	F	'love is the cause of my mourning, mʳ mᶜlaughlans way, by mʳ beck' (first two strains are very similar, but Balcarres MS includes an extra division)
26	F	'For old long Sine my Joe'	*106	F	'For old lang syne, by mʳ beck' (similar opening strains but with two extra variations)
27	F	'Allen Water'	*57	F	'Alen water, mʳ Becks way'
33	F	'A ways my heart that we mun sunder'	183	F	'Woes the heart that we should sunder, Mʳ McClaughlans way, by Mʳ Beck' (some similarities in first strain only)
38	F	'Holy Even, a Scotch-Measure'	*55	F	'Hallow Even, mʳ Becks way'
39	C	'A New Scotch-Measure' (1701 edn. only)	*3	C	'Maulslies scots measure, Becks way'
42	G	'And when she came ben she bobed'	143	G	'When she came in she bobbed, mʳ mᶜlauchlands way, by master Beck' (1701 edn. only) (dissimilar version with 5 variations)

of Original Scotch-Tunes to generate easy and attractive Scottish pieces for the original owner of the Balcarres manuscript to play on his lute.

Johnson, in his *Scottish Fiddle Music*, suggested that the most characteristic styles of fiddle music in the period 1700–20 were those based on Italian chord progressions, those based on two chords (the so-called double tonic), and those based on five-note scales (i.e. pentatonic melodies).[131] Numerous pieces in each of these categories can be found in the Balcarres manuscript, while many other pieces fall somewhere between the different categories. Several of the sets of variations based on a ground[132] use Italian chord progressions, and most of the other pieces use similar related progressions. 'The Horsemans Port' is both a set of variations on a ground and a piece primarily based on two chords, and thus falls into both categories. Most of the pieces based on a double tonic alternate between F major and G major (only nos. 225 and 229 use a G/A major double tonic), and some do not have a clearly recognizable B strain, thus taking the A A1 A2, etc. form.[133] An example is no. 155, 'Jockie leaped over the dyke, mr mclachlands way, by mr beck', which has six variations of the eight-bar tune. Example 13.6 gives the first two of these variations. It is noticeable in all these pieces that the bass line becomes more animated in subsequent variations as the melody line becomes faster moving.

The third type of piece mentioned by Johnson, that based on a five-note scale, is perhaps the most common type of Scottish piece in the Balcarres manuscript. Of the first 100 pieces, twenty-three are clearly pentatonic in their melody line,[134] and several others (like nos. 73, 87, and 94) are hexatonic. While the fourth and seventh degrees of the scale are generally omitted in the opening strains of these pieces, they are occasionally used for unaccented melody notes, especially in subsequent variations where the melody line becomes more active. The omission of these degrees of the scale does not apply to the harmonization, where they may feature prominently.

Most of the Scottish tunes in the Balcarres manuscript (and many of the English ones too), have a subsequent strain or strains which feature a flowing quaver melody line. Normally there are no more than one or two pairs of subsequent strains (i.e. A B A1 B1 or A B A1 B1 A2 B2), but in some cases they can run to four or six more strains. For example, 'The New Highland ladie, mr becks way', no. 4, has four paired strains, and 'My dearie, an thou dye, John morisons way, by mr Beck', no. 69, has nine strains (A B A1 B1 A2 A3 B3 A4 B4). Comments in the manuscript show that any further strains after the first three pairs of strains were exceptional, and that A B A1 B1 A2 B2 was the norm for less extended pieces.[135] In many of

[131] Johnson, *Scottish Fiddle Music*, 16.   [132] e.g. 'Greensleeves' and 'John come kiss me now'.

[133] Pieces in the MS using a F/G major double tonic are nos. 144, 146, 149, 155, 156, 160, 179, 180, and 181.

[134] These are nos. 4, 5, 8, 13, 36, 37, 43, 48, 49, 56, 57, 68, 69, 71, 72, 75, 78, 79, 80, 90, 93, 96, and 98.

[135] The title of Balcarres MS no. 4, p. 5, has the line, 'it may want the last measure'; no. 69 has the line 'may want the two last measures from this mark', p. 37.

Ex. 13.6. '*Jockie leaped over the dyke, m^r m^clachlands way by m^r beck*', *Balcarres MS, no. 155, p. 99, bars 1–16*

these pieces the bass lines of the A and B sections are fundamentally the same, the B section having been derived as a melodic contrast to the A section, where the melody usually starts on, or moves to, the upper octave.

It can be seen from the Straloch/Graham copy, Rowallan, and Wemyss manuscripts that most Scottish melodies consisted of a single strain repeated with melodic variations.[136] By the end of the seventeenth century many, but not all, melodies had acquired a second derivative strain. For example, 'John Robinsons Park' (no. 117) and 'Green grow the Rushes' (no. 110) remain single-strain tunes in the Balcarres manuscript. Example 13.7 compares the four A strains of 'The New Highland ladie', no. 4. This example illustrates the basic variation principle to be found throughout the Balcarres manuscript, that the variations of the melody line become progressively more animated both in pitch and rhythm as the piece progresses, although the general shape of the melody is still discernible throughout. The last A strain in this piece does not move in completely continuous quavers as in the third A strain, but this is to act as a contrast in preparation for the cascading semiquaver/quaver figure of the final B strain, which moves down the pentatonic scale. The increasing pitch variation is seen when the smooth flow of the second A strain is compared with the third and fourth A strains, where jumps of fourths, fifths, and octaves occur with greater frequency. While the fourth and seventh degrees of the F major scale (Bb and E) are generally omitted in the opening A and B strains, they appear more frequently in later strains. The bass line also becomes more animated in later strains as semibreves and minims give way to crotchets and minims, and as slow-moving intervals of a third or more tend to a faster stepwise movement. The B strain, starting on the upper octave with the same harmonic movement as the A strain (including the F–C cadence in the third bar of each strain), is clearly derived from it, and is developed in later variations in the same way as the A strain. While the harmony is occasionally altered in subsequent variations, and alternative bar lines are inserted (Ex. 13.7, bars 35–6 of A3 and 54–5 of A4), the basic harmonic movement is always the same.

The ending of each strain on a D minor chord (in Ex. 13.7) after the opening in F major is a frequent characteristic of Balcarres tune arrangements, as it is of all early Scottish tune arrangements.[137] The modal nature of many of the Balcarres manuscript pieces is one of their most attractive features. This contrasts with the versions in contemporary manuscripts such as the Sinkler, Blaikie, and Leyden, where the harmonizations are more orthodox.

Comparing versions of Scottish tunes in the Balcarres manuscript with those in manuscripts from early and mid-century (see above, Table 13.1), it is often suprising how little the tunes have altered in the opening strain. Example 13.8 illustrates

---

[136] See Spring, 'The Lute in England and Scotland', i. 317.   [137] Ibid.

Ex. 13.7. *The four A strains of 'The New Highland ladie m' becks way', Balcarres MS, no. 4, pp. 4–5 (the music runs from left to right across the two pages)*

this point with four versions of the tune 'Good night and God be with you', the first from the Skene manuscript (*c*.1630), the second from the Wemyss manuscript (1644–8); the third reconstructed from the Guthrie manuscript (*c*.1680),[138] and the last from the Balcarres manuscript (*c*.1700).

Ex. 13.8. *Four versions of 'Good night and God be with you', bars 1–6: (a) Skene MS, p. 246; (b) Wemyss MS, fo. 49ʳ⁻ᵛ; (c) Guthrie MS, p. 310; (d) Balcarres MS, no. 107, pp. 68–9*

[138] The Guthrie MS is transcribed and reconstructed in Willsher, 'Music in Scotland'.

1. Rhythm sign changed from ⌐ to | to fill the bar.
2. Internal 4 bar repeat sign missing, here added and written out as a repeat of bars 1 and 2.

The melodic shape of the tune is the same in all versions, the Wemyss being the most deviant from the general melodic contour of the four sources, and the Skene and Balcarres manuscripts, the sources furthest apart in time, being possibly the most concordant, especially in the B strain. It is unusual for variations after the opening strain or strains to be similar or identical in pieces drawn from sources that are not contemporary, but it does occasionally occur. Thus all thirty-two bars (eight-bar strain plus three variations), of 'Da mihi manum', Balcarres manuscript no. 168, are very closely similar to the version in the Wemyss manuscript, no. 81, of more than half a century earlier.[139] 'Good night and God be with you' is an example of a tune that appears to have had a B strain from at least the early seventeenth century, and 'Da mihi manum' is one that never acquired a second strain.[140]

A tendency towards increased elaboration and agility in the melodies of Scottish tunes, and also in 'improved' (i.e. more directional) harmony in the tune arrangements, is discernible when manuscripts from the early and late seventeenth century are compared. Both these tendencies continue during the eighteenth century. Not all Scottish tunes in the Balcarres manuscript either originated as songs or were mostly associated with the violin. 'Da mihi manum' may have been a clarsach piece and never a song. 'Lady Binnis Lilt' does not appear to have any associated words, though it does appear in a similar form in English lute and cittern sources.[141] This piece remained principally a lute piece, although lyra viol and violin versions do survive.

Many of the Scots tunes found in the Balcarres manuscript were remorselessly reprinted both for voice and instruments (particularly the violin, flute, and harpsichord) during the century, with many of them finding a place in James Johnson's famous *Scots Musical Museum* (1789–1805), to which Burns added so much.[142] William Stenhouse later added the fruits of early nineteenth-century scholarship in the notes he added to this important work. Even today, most of the Scots tunes found in the Balcarres manuscript are best known in the versions published in the *Scots Musical Museum*.

Scottish lute music has a charm and identity that is quite unique. In these pieces the native tunes of Scotland receive only the most basic and sketchy of harmonies, and none of the pieces can really be said to be highly developed. However, their importance is great in that these lute (and mandore) settings of common tunes are so often the earliest that survive, and as such form part of the bedrock of Scottish national music.

---

[139] This tune, according to O'Neill, was composed by the blind harpist Rory Dall O'Cathain. See Collinson, *The Traditional and National Music of Scotland*, 240.

[140] This tune later appeared in 18th-c. publications (Francesco Barsanti, *A Collection of Old Scots Tunes* (Edinburgh, 1742), and Burk Thumoth, *Twelve Scots and Irish Airs, with Variations* (London, c.1745).

[141] See Spring, 'The Lady Margaret Wemyss Manuscript', 11, 26.

[142] See Johnson, *Music in Society*, 147–9, and also Roger Fiske, *Scotland in Music: A European Enthusiasm* (Cambridge, 1983), 56.

POSTSCRIPT

This book was written in the last decade of the twentieth century, a century which witnessed a gradual revival of interest in and understanding of the lute, in contrast to its obsolescence in the century before. This took place in the context of a revival of early music in general. Since the 1960s there has been a successful revival of the lute with centres of activity established across the globe. New technology has meant that the real costs of printing short-run editions in the form of new tablature or facsimile has plummeted such that even more obscure lute music can be made available to those who are interested. There are now significant organizations and even internet sites and e-mail discussion groups dedicated to the lute and its music, and it is fair to say that it has reclaimed an identity that was almost completely lost in the nineteenth century. Britain's part in this renaissance has been considerable. The south of England in particular has as high a concentration of lute players and makers as anywhere in the world, and London is arguably the performance capital of the lute world. England can boast some two dozen fully professional lute makers, and there is now in place a younger generation of players who developed their skills on dedicated courses at London conservatories, many without ever having studied the classical guitar. Indeed if the guitar was their starting point, it is as likely to have been electric or folk guitar. British composers as diverse as Alan Ridout, James Erber, Stephen Dodgson, and Howard Skempton have also produced a number of new lute works, inspired or commissioned by today's professional players. The break with the past is that these composers are not themselves lute players, as was the norm for lute composers of old.

It is arguable that the lute maintained a niche role in some places in Europe until the later half of the eighteenth century because it was one of the very few domestic instruments capable of touch sensitivity, of playing loud and soft, of self accompaniment, and of polyphonic parts, and that this role was taken from it by the early forms of the piano. On becoming obsolete during the nineteenth century there were still some among the artistic community who maintained an interest in the lute. In particular there were painters of historical events who knew something of the instrument's past through their knowledge of the paintings of the old masters. There were also throughout the nineteenth and twentieth centuries people who reinvented the lute as a form of guitar with a lute-like body shape to fit their romantic notions.

A more practical understanding of the lute developed among the few that had access to lutes in the instrument collections that were developing across the Western world in the nineteenth century. Yet the large number of fakes that museums accumulated did not help this process and are a measure of the pervading ignorance of the time. In England the first real step forward occurred when Arnold Dolmetsch both made and studied the lute himself. His links with the Arts and Crafts movement and in particular with the Art Worker's Guild are significant. It is touching to remember that William Morris asked for Dolmetsch to come and play to him on the virginals as he was dying, and there is even a mention in

James Joyce's *Ulysses* of Dolmetsch and his lute. The Lute Society of Great Britain still meets at the Art Worker's Guild headquarters in London, and Diana Poulton, the most important of Dolmetsch's English lute pupils, had an artistic background and had been a fine art student at the Slade School of Art. While it was said by Poulton that Dolmetsch never really developed a high degree of skill on the lute, he did instil in his pupils the importance of basing their technique on historical sources. Lutes and lute music did periodically appear in concerts of the Dolmetsch family and at the Haslemere Festival from the 1920s onwards. Impetus for rediscovering the lute grew from then on as an offshoot of the Shakespeare industry, from the BBC, and from a respect and awareness of the music of John Dowland. Lute songs in particular were known to the English composers of the generation of Peter Warlock and Vaughan Williams, and from this developed a gradual awareness of some of the lute's solo music. Warlock made and published his own Dowland transcriptions, and Edmund Fellows produced the first series of lute-song editions in the 1920s.

The early music revival that gathered pace after the 1950s produced a new generation of makers and players who were prepared to be more rigorous in their approach to authenticity. The older high-tension lutes intended for stringing with guitar strings, were gradually discarded in favour of lutes of lighter construction like those produced on historical principles by Ian Harwood and John Isaacs in Ely. Up until the 1960s players of the lute were normally first and foremost players of the classical guitar. The brilliance of attack that modern classical guitar technique produced with right-hand nails had overshadowed those few, like Poulton and Desmond Dupre, who played with a more historically aware technique and without nails. The difference in approach was forcefully demonstrated at the groundbreaking seminar 'Le lute et sa musique', of September 1957 organized by Jean Jacquot of the CNRS.

The Lute Society Summer School of 1976 was a turning point for some of those who experienced the playing of the German lutenist Michael Schäffer. A continuous lute tradition stretching back to the medieval period had lasted the longest in German speaking lands, and a significant school of lute playing had surfaced in the 1920s. Schäffer showed that a right-hand technique without nails, with the little finger planted on the belly of the lute, and developed from the Renaissance 'thumb and forefinger' alternation as a starting point, could produce a sound of real integrity and one that could be used in the context of the more esoteric and less accessible lute repertoires, such as that of the French Baroque. The effect of these developments was to separate the lute from the guitar. Some were prepared to sacrifice their nails and thereby give up playing the classical guitar. However, others either gave up playing the lute altogether, or simply adapted lute music for the guitar and carried on playing the music but with no pretence of authenticity. While the effects of these events may have been comparative isolation for lute players in the immediate aftermath, it did mean that in the longer term an appreciation of historical technique could continually develop such that there is now a good understanding of the difference in approach appropriate to the different national repertoires and periods.

My hope is that this book has shown that the lute has had a long and distinguished career in Britain, and that for much of the sixteenth and seventeenth centuries the lute was central to our secular music-making traditions. Within the period 1580-1620 England produced a repertoire of music that was recognized in much of Europe as having a distinct national identity and real integrity. Scotland too had a period in the seventeenth century before the violin became ubiquitously popular, when the lute was a natural instrument for the performance of native music in a domestic setting. My hope is that this book will contribute to a clearer understanding of the part played by the lute in Britain's past music-making, and that lute players of the twenty-first century will better connect with this illustrious past.

BIBLIOGRAPHY

The bibliography excludes the song publications listed in Table 11.4, unless they are cited elsewhere.

Printed Music

ADRIAENSSEN, EMANUEL, *Pratum musicum longe amoenissimum* (Antwerp, 1584; rev. edn., 1600).

——— *Novum pratum musicum* (Antwerp, 1592).

ALLISON, RICHARD, *The Psalmes of David in Meter* (London, 1599).

——— *An Howres Recreation in Musicke* (London, 1606).

——— *The Solo Lute Music of Richard Allison, with Bandora and Cittern Arrangements*, ed. John Robinson and Stewart McCoy, with a biographical sketch by Robert Spencer (Lute Society, Oldham, 1995).

An Anthology of English Lute Music, ed. David Lumsden (London, 1954).

ATTEY, JOHN, *The First Booke of Ayres of Foure Parts, with Tableture for the Lute* (London, 1622).

BACHELER, DANIEL, *Selected Works*, ed. Martin Long (Music for the Lute, Book 5; Oxford, 1970).

BALLARD, PIERRE, *Airs de différents autheurs* (11–13th livres) (Paris, 1623; repr. Geneva, 1985).

——— *Tablature de luth de différents autheurs sur l'accord ordinaire et extraordinaire* (Paris, 1623).

——— *Tablature de luth de différents autheurs, sur les accords nouveaux* (Paris, 1631; repr. Geneva, 1985).

——— *Tablature de luth de différents autheurs sur les accords nouveaux* (Paris, 1638).

BALLARD, ROBERT, *Premier livre* (Paris, 1611), ed. and trans. André Souris and Sylvie Spycket with an introduction and study of concordances by Monique Rollin (Paris, 1963).

BARLEY, WILBURN W., *A new Booke of Tabliture* (London, 1596), ed. Wilburn W. Newcomb as *Lute Music of Shakespeare's Time. William Barley: A New Booke of Tabliture, 1596* (University Park, Pa., 1966).

——— *The patheway to musicke* (London, 1596).

BARSANTI, FRANCESCO, *A Collection of Old Scots Tunes* (Edinburgh, 1742).

BARTLET, JOHN, *A Booke of Ayres with a Triplicitie of Musicke* (London, 1606).

BESARD, JEAN-BAPTISTE, *Thesaurus harmonicus* (Cologne, 1603).

——— *Novus partus, sive concertationes musicae* (Augsburg, 1617).

The Board Lute Book, facs. with an introduction by Robert Spencer (Reproductions of Early Music, 4; Leeds, 1976).

BRADE, WILLIAM, *Newe ausserlesene Paduanen* (Hamburg, 1609).

——— *Newe ausserlesene liebliche Branden* (Hamburg, 1617).

The Brogyntyn Lute Book, facs. with an introductory study by Robert Spencer and Jeffrey Alexander (Musical Sources, 12; Kilkenny, 1978).

The Burwell Lute Tutor, facs. with an introduction by Robert Spencer (Reproductions of Early Music, 1; Leeds, 1974).

BYRD, WILLIAM, *Consort Songs for Voice & Viols*, ed. Philip Brett (The Collected Works of William Byrd (rev.), 15; London, 1970).

—— *Consort Music*, ed. Kenneth Elliot (The Collected Works of William Byrd, rev. edn., 17; London, 1971).

—— *Music for the Lute, Book 6: William Byrd*, ed. Nigel North (London, 1976).

—— *Consort Songs by William Byrd*, ed. Stewart McCoy and Bill Hunt (London, 1990).

CACCINI, GIULIO, *Le nuove musiche* (Venice, 1602).

CAMPION, THOMAS, *The Discription of a Maske, presented before the Kinges Majestie . . .* (London, 1607).

—— *Two Bookes of Ayres* (London, c.1613).

—— *The Third and Fourth Booke of Ayres* (London, 1618).

CAPIROLA, VINCENZO, *Compositione di messer Vincenzo Capriola*, ed. Otto Gombosi (Neuilly-sur-Seine, 1955).

CAVENDISH, MICHAEL, *Book of Madrigals and Airs* (n.p., 1598). Original title not known.

CHANCY, *Tablature de mandore de la composition du Sieur Chancy* (Paris, 1629).

Collected English Lutenist Partsongs: I & II, ed. David Greer (MB 53–4; London, 1987, 1989).

COPRARIO, JOHN, *Funeral Teares* (London, 1606).

—— *Songs of Mourning* (London, 1613).

CORBETTA, FRANCESCO, *La guitarre royalle dediée au roy de la Grande Bretagne* (Paris, 1671).

CORKINE, WILLIAM, *Ayres, to Sing and Play to the Lute and Basse Violl* (London, 1610).

—— *The Second Booke of Ayres* (London, 1612).

DALZA, JOAN AMBROSIO, *Intabulatura de lauto libro quarto* (Venice, 1508; repr. Geneva, 1980).

DANYEL, JOHN, *Songs for the Lute, Viol and Voice* (London, 1606).

DENSS, ADRIAN, *Florilegium* (Cologne, 1594).

DOWLAND, JOHN, *The First Booke of Songes or Ayres of fowre partes, with Tableture for the Lute* (London, 1597, 1600, 1603, 1606, 1613).

—— *The Second Booke of Songs or Ayres* (London, 1600).

—— *The Third and Last Booke of Songs or Aires* (London, 1603).

—— *Lachrimae, or Seaven Teares Figured in Seaven Passionate Pavans, with divers other Pavans, Galiards and Almands, set forth for the Lute, Viols, or Violons, in five parts* (London, 1604).

—— *John Dowland: Ayres for Four Voices*, ed. Thurston Dart and Nigel Fortune (MB 6; London, 1953, rev. 1963, 1970).

—— *A Pilgrimes Solace* (London, 1612; repr. London, 1977); modern edn. in *The English Lute Song*, no. 12, ed. Edmund H. Fellowes, rev. Thurston Dart (London, 1968).

—— *The Collected Lute Music of John Dowland*, ed. Diana Poulton and Basil Lamb (London, 1974).

DOWLAND, ROBERT, *A Musicall Banquet* (London, 1610).

—— *Varietie of Lute-Lessons* (London, 1610; repr. London, 1958, ed. Edgar Hunt).

DUBUT, *Œuvres des Dubut*, ed. and trans. Monique Rollin and Jean-Michel Vaccaro (Paris, 1979).

DUFAULT, FRANÇOIS, *Œuvres de Dufaut*, ed. and trans. André Souris, with an introduction and concordances by Monique Rollin (Paris, 1965).

Elizabethan Consort Music: I, ed. Paul Doe (MB 44; London, 1979).

The English Lute Song before Dowland, i: *Songs from the Dallis Manuscript c.1583*, ed. Christopher Goodwin (Lute Society, Albury, 1996).

The English Lute Song before Dowland, ii: *Songs from Additional Manuscript 4900 and Other Sources*, ed. Christopher Goodwin (Lute Society, Albury, 1997).

The English Lute Songs, 1597–1632: A Collection of Facsimile Reprints, 9 vols., ed. F. W. Sternfeld *et al.*; also pub. as 36 separate vols. (Menston, Yorks., 1968–71).

The English School of Lutenist Song Writers, ed. E. H. Fellowes (2 series, London, 1920–32), rev. Thurston Dart as *The English Lute-Songs* (London, 1959–66).

English Songs 1625–1660, ed. Ian Spink (MB 33; London, 1971; rev. edn. 1977).

Fantasias à3, VdGS anon. nos. 903 and 904, ed. Peter Trent (London, 1984).

FERRABOSCO, ALFONSO, *Ayres by Alfonso Ferrabosco* (London, 1609).

—— *Collected Works for Lute and Bandora*, ed. Nigel North (Music for the Lute, Book 8, Part 1; Oxford, 1974).

—— *Opera omnia*, ed. Richard Charteris (CMM 96; Neuhausen-Stuttgart, 1984–8).

FILMER, EDWARD, *French Court-Aires, With their Ditties Englished* (London, 1629).

The Fitzwilliam Virginal Book, ed. J. A. Fuller Maitland and W. Barclay Squire, 2 vols. (Leipzig, 1899; rev. edn., 2 vols., New York, 1979).

FORBES, JOHN, *Songs and Fancies: To Thre, Foure, or Five Parts, both Apt for Voices and Viols. With a briefe introduction of Musick, As is taught in the Musick-Schools of Aberdene by T[homas] D[avidson] M[aste]r of Musick* (Aberdeen, 1662).

FORD, THOMAS, *Musicke of Sundrie Kindes* (London, 1607).

Four Hundred Songs and Dances from the Stuart Age, ed. Andrew Sabol (Providence, RI, 1978).

FRANCISQUE, ANTHOINE, *Le Trésor d'Orphée: livre de tablature de luth* (Paris, 1600).

FUHRMANN, GEORG LEOPOLD, *Testudo gallo-germanica* (Nuremberg, 1615).

GALILEI, VINCENZO, *Fronimo: Dialogo* (Venice, 1568, rev. edn., 1584).

GAULTIER, *8 Courantes in Renaissance Tuning*, trans. and ed. Peter J. Danner (Lute Society of America, n.p., 1981).

GAULTIER, DENIS, *La Rhétorique des dieux et autre pieces de luth de Denis Gaultier*, ed. André Tessier and Jean Cordey (Paris, 1932).

—— *Œuvres du vieux Gautier*, ed. and trans. by André Souris, with an introduction and concordances by Monique Rollin (Paris, 1966).

GAULTIER, PIERRE, *Les Œuvres de Pierre Gaultier* (Rome, 1638).

GERVAISE, CLAUDE, *Sixième livre de danceries* (Paris, 1555).

GIANONCELLI, BERNARDO, *Il liuto* (Venice, 1650).

GORLIER, SIMON, *Livre de tablature de guiterre* (n.p., c.1560).

GORZANIS, GIACOMO, *Libro de intabolatura di liuto, nel quale si contengono 24 passa mezi . . .* (Venice, 1567), ed. B. Tonazzi (Milan, 1975), guitar transcription.

GREAVES, THOMAS, *Songes of sundrie kindes* (London, 1604).

HILTON, JOHN, *Catch that Catch Can* (London, 1652).

The Hirsch Lute Book, facs. with an introductory study by Robert Spencer (Musical Sources, 21; Clarabricken, 1982).

HOLBORNE, ANTHONY, *The Cittharn Schoole* (London, 1597).

—— *Pavans, Galliards, Almains* (London, 1597).

—— *The Complete Works of Anthony Holborne*, ed. Masakata Kanazawa, 2 vols. (Cambridge, Mass., 1967).

HOVE, JOACHIM VAN DEN, *Florida* (Utrecht, 1601).

—— *Delitiae musicae* (Utrecht, 1612).

—— *Praeludia testudinis* (Leiden, 1616).

HUME, TOBIAS, *The First Part of Ayres* (London, 1605; repr. London, 1968 and 1985).

—— *Captaine Humes Poeticall Musicke* (London, 1607).

Jane Pickeringe's Lute Book, facs. with an introductory study by Robert Spencer (Musical Sources, 23; Clarabricken, 1985).

JOHNSON, ROBERT, *Complete Works for Solo Lute*, ed. Albert Sundermann (London, 1970).

JONES, ROBERT, *The First Booke of Songes or Ayres* (London, 1600).

—— *The Second Booke of Songes and Ayres* (London, 1601).

—— *A Musicall Dreame* (London, 1609).

—— *The Muses Gardin for Delights* (London, 1610).

—— *Ultimum Vale* (London, 1605).

KAPSBERGER, JOHANN HIERONYMOUS, *Libro I[–IV] d'intavolatura di chitarrone* (Venice, 1604, 1616 [lost], 1626, 1640).

—— *Libro I[–II] d'intavolatura de lauto* (1611, 1623 [lost]).

KELLER, GOTTFRIED, *A Compleat Method for attaining to play a Thorough Bass upon either Organ, Harpsicord or Theorbo-Lute* (London, 1705).

The Königsberg Manuscript, ed. Arthur J. Ness and John M. Ward (Columbus, Ohio, 1989).

Das Königsteiner Liederbuch, ed. Paul Sappler (Münchener Texte und Untersuchungen zur deutschen Literatur des Mittelalters, 29; Munich, 1970).

LAURENCINI, *Thirty Pieces for Lute by Laurencini*, ed. Tim Crawford (London, 1979).

LEIGHTON, SIR WILLIAM, *The Teares or Lamentacions of a Sorrowful Soule* (London, 1614), ed. and trans. Cecil Hill (Early English Church Music, 11; London, 1970).

LE ROY, ADRIAN, *Breve et facile instruction pour apprendre la tablature, a bien accorder, conduire, et disposer la main sur le cistre* (Paris, 1551).

—— *A Briefe and easye instru[c]tion to learne the tablature to conducte and dispose thy hand unto the Lute* (London, 1568); facs. pub. as *Fantaisies et danses*, ed. and trans. by Pierre Jansen, with a study of concordances by Daniel Heartz (Paris, 1962; 2nd rev. edn., 1975).

—— *A Briefe and plaine instruction for to learne the Tablature, to Conducte and dispose the hand unto the Gitterne* (London, 1568).

—— *Livre d'Airs de cour* (Paris, 1571).

——— *Œuvres d'Adrian Le Roy: Les Instructions pour le Luth (1574)*, ed. J. Jacquot, P. Y. Sordes, and J. M. Vaccaro, 2 vols. (Paris, 1977).

——— *A briefe and plaine Instruction to set all Musicke of eight divers tunes in Tablature for the Lute. With a brief Instruction how to play on the Lute by Tablature, to conduct and dispose thy hand unto the Lute, with certaine easie lessons for that purpose. And also a third Booke containing divers new excellent tunes* (London, 1574).

——— and BALLARD, ROBERT, *Mellange de chansons* (Paris, 1572).

MACE, THOMAS, *Musick's Monument, or, A Remembrancer of the Best Practical Musik* (London, 1676; facs. edn. Paris, 1966: vol. 1: *Musick's Monument*; vol. 2: trans. and commentary ed. Jean Jacquot and André Souris).

Manuscripts at Oxford Part II (facs. of *GB-Ob* MS Mus. Sch. b. 1.), ed. Elise Bickford Jorgens (English Song 1600–1675: Facsimiles of 26 Manuscripts and an Edition of the Texts, 7; New York and London, 1987).

The Marsh Lute Book, facs. with an introductory note by Robert Spencer (Musical Sources, 20; Kilkenny, 1981).

MASON, GEORGE, and EARSDEN, JOHN, *The Ayres that were sung and played at Brougham Castle* (London, 1618).

MATELART, JOANNES, *Intavolatura de leuto* (Rome, 1559).

MATHEW, RICHARD, *The Lutes Apology for her Excellency* (London, 1652).

MATTEIS, NICOLA, *The False Consonances of Musick* (London, 1682); modern edn. by James Tyler (Monaco, 1980).

MAYNARD, JOHN, *The XII. Wonders of the World* (London, 1611).

MELLI, PIETRO PAOLO, *Intavolatura di liuto, libri I–V* (Venice, 1614, 1616, 1616, 1616, 1620).

The Mellon Chansonnier, ed. Leeman L. Perkins and Howard Garey, 2 vols. (New Haven, 1979).

MERCURE, JOHN, *Œuvres de Mercure*, ed. and trans. by Monique Rollin and Jean-Michel Vaccaro (Paris, 1977).

MERTEL, ELIAS, *Hortus musicalis novus* (Strasburg, 1615).

MESANGEAU, RENÉ, *Œuvres de René Mesangeau*, ed. and trans. André Souris, with a biographical study and critical commentary by Monique Rollin (Paris, 1971).

The M. L. Lute Book, facs. with an introduction by Robert Spencer (Musical Sources, 25; Clarabricken, 1985).

MORLEY, THOMAS, *Canzonets or Litle Short Aers to Five and Sixe Voices* (London, 1597).

——— *The First Booke of Consort Lessons* (London, 1599, rev. 2nd edn., 1611).

——— *The First Booke of Ayres or Little Short Songs* (London, 1600).

——— *Two Consort Lessons Collected by Thomas Morley*, ed. T. Dart (London, 1957).

——— *The First Book of Consort Lessons Collected by Thomas Morley 1599–1611*, ed. Sydney Beck (New York, 1959).

MOY, LOUYS DE, *Le Petit Boucquet de Frise orientale* (n.p., 1631; repr. Peer, 1987, ed. Eugeen Schreurs and Martine Sanders, with an introduction by Mijndert Jape).

The Mulliner Book, ed. and transcr. Denis Stevens (Musica Britannica, 1; London, 1951).

MUNDAY, ANTHONY, *Banquet of Daintie Conceits* (London, 1588).

Music for Mixed Consort, ed. Warwick A. Edwards (MB 40; London, 1977).

Music for the Lute in Scotland, ed. Robert Phillips (Shillinghill, 1995).

Musick for Allan Ramsey's Collection of Scots Tunes, ed. Alexander Stuart (Edinburgh, 1725).

MYLIUS, JOHANN DANIEL, *Thesaurus gratiarum* (Frankfurt am Main, 1622).

The Mynshall Lute Book, facs. with an introductory study by Robert Spencer (Musical Sources, 6; Leeds, 1975).

NOTARI, ANGELO, *Prime musiche nuove* (London, 1613).

Œuvres de Vaumesnil, Edinthon, Perrichon, Raël, Montbuysson, La Grotte, Saman, La Barre, ed. and trans. by André Souris, Monique Rollin, and Jean-Michel Vaccaro (Paris, 1974).

PACOLONI, GIOVANNI, *Longe elegantissima excellentissimi musici . . . tribus testudinibus ludenda Carmina* (Louvain, 1564).

Parthenia In-Violata (London, *c*.1625).

PEERSON, MARTIN, *Private Musicke . . .* (London, 1620).

—— *Mottects or Grave Chamber Musique* (London, 1630).

The Penguin Book of Early Music, ed. Anthony Rooley (Harmondsworth, 1980).

PICCININI, ALESSANDRO, *Intavolatura di liuto et di chitarrone* (Bologna, 1623).

PILKINGTON, FRANCIS, *The First Booke of Songs or Ayres of 4. Parts* (London, 1605).

—— *The Second Set of Madrigals and Pastorals* (London, 1624).

—— *Complete Works for Solo Lute*, ed. Brian Jeffery (Music for the Lute, 3; Oxford, 1970).

PITTONI, GIOVANNI, *Intavolatura di tiorba. Opera prima e seconda* (Bologna, 1669).

PLAYFORD, HENRY, *A Collection of Original Scotch-Tunes* (London, 1700, 1701).

PLAYFORD, JOHN, *A Musicall Banquet in 3 Choice Varieties* (London, 1651).

PLAYFORD, JOHN/HENRY, *The English Dancing Master* (London, 1651; 17 subsequent edns. to *c*.1728 titled *The Dancing Master*).

PLAYFORD, JOHN, *Select Musicall Ayres, and Dialogues* (London, 1652).

—— *Musick's Recreation on the Viol, Lyra-Way* (London, 1661).

—— *Musick's Delight on the Cithren* (London, 1666).

PLAYFORD, JOHN/HENRY, *Apollo's Banquet for the Treble Violin* (London, 1st edn., *c*.1670; 8 subsequent edns. to 1701).

PLAYFORD, JOHN, *Choice Ayres and Songs* (London, 1683).

—— *The Division Violin* (London, 1684; 2nd edn., 1685). Facs. pub. as *The Division Violin*, with an introduction by Margaret Gilmore (Oxford, 1980).

PORTER, WALTER, *Madrigales and Ayres* (London, 1632).

PRAETORIUS, MICHAEL, *Terpsichore* (Wolfenbüttel, 1612).

REYMANN, MATTHIAS, *Noctes musicae* (Heidelberg, 1598).

—— *Cythara sacra* (Cologne, 1612: now lost).

The Robarts Lute Book, facs. with an introductory study by Robert Spencer (Musical Sources, 11; Clarabricken, 1978).

ROBINSON, THOMAS, *The Schoole of Musicke* (London, 1603; repr. Amsterdam and New York, 1973); modern edn., including tablature and staff notation, by David Lumsden (Paris, 1971).

ROSSETER, PHILIP, *Lessons for Consort* (London, 1609).

—— and THOMAS CAMPION, *A Booke of Ayres* (London, 1601).

RUDE, JOHANN, *Flores musicae* (Heidelberg, 1600).

The Sampson Lute Book, facs. with an introduction by Robert Spencer (Musical Sources, 4; Leeds, 1974).

SCHLICK, ARNOLD, *Tablatur etlicher lobgesang und Lidlein uff die Orgeln und Lauten* (Mainz, 1512).

SPINACINO, FRANCESCO, *Intabolatura de lauto, libro primo* (Venice, 1507).

—— *Intabolatura de lauto, libro secondo* (Venice, 1507).

STRAUBE, RUDOLF, *Due sonate a liuto solo* (Leipzig, 1746); facs., with an introduction by Tim Crawford (Monaco, 1981).

Tablature de luth italienne . . . Fac-similé du ms. de la Bibliothèque nationale, Paris, Rés. Vmd. ms. 27 (Geneva, 1981).

TAILOUR, ROBERT, *Sacred Hymns* (London, 1615).

TERZI, GIOVANNI ANTONIO, *Intavolatura di liutto* (Venice, 1593).

TESSIER, CHARLES, *Le Premier Livre de chansons & airs de court, tant en françois qu'en italien & en gascon à 4. & 5. parties* (London, 1597).

THOMPSON, WILLIAM, *Orpheus Caledonius* (London, 1725).

THUMOTH, BURK, *Twelve Scots and Irish Airs, with Variations* (London, *c*.1745).

TOMKINS, THOMAS, *Keyboard Music*, ed. Stephen D. Tuttle (MB 5; 2nd edn., London, 1964).

The Trumbull Lute Book, facs. with an introductory note and guide to concordances by Robert Spencer (Musical Sources, 19; Clarabricken, 1980).

VALDERRÁBANO, ENRIQUEZ DE, *Libro de música de vihuela, intitulado Silva de sirenas* (Valladolid, 1547).

VALERIUS, ADRIAEN, *Neder-landtsche gedenck-clank* (Haarlem, 1626).

VALLET, NICHOLAS, *Le Secret des muses: premier livre* (Amsterdam, 1615).

—— *Le Secret des muses: second livre* (Amsterdam, 1616).

—— *Œuvres de Nicolas Vallet pour luth seul*, ed. and trans. by André Souris with a biographical study and critical commentary by Monique Rollin (Paris, 1970).

—— *The Complete Works of Nicolas Vallet*, 4 vols. (Utrecht, 1994).

VIAERA, FREDERIC, *Nova et elegantissima in Cythara ludenda Carmina* (Louvain, 1564).

The Willoughby Lute Book, facs. with an introduction by Jeffrey Alexander and Robert Spencer (Musical Sources, 13; Kilkenny, 1978).

WILSON, JOHN, *Psalterium Carolinum* (London, 1657).

—— *Cheerful Ayres or Ballads* (Oxford, 1659).

—— *Thirty Preludes in all (24) Keys for Lute*, ed. Matthew Spring (Utrecht, 1992).

The Winchester Anthology, facs. of *GB-Lbl* MS Add. 60577, with an introduction and list of contents by Edward Wilson and an account of the music by Iain Fenlon (London, 1981).

ZAMBONI, GIOVANNI, *Sonate d'intavolatura di leuto* (Lucca, 1718).

Books, Theses, and Articles

ABBOTT, DJILDA, and SEGERMANN, EPHRAIM, 'Gut Strings', *EM* 4 (1976), 430–7.

—— 'Strings in the 16th and 17th Centuries', *GSJ* 27 (1974), 48–73.

Account Rolls of Durham Priory, ed. John Thomas Fowler (Surtees Society, 99, 100, 103; 1898–1900).

AGRICOLA, MARTIN, *Musica instrumentalis deudsch* (Wittenberg, 1529).

ALBURGER, MARY ANNE, *Scottish Fiddlers and their Music* (London, 1983).

ALEXANDER, JEFFREY, 'The English Lute Duet, 1570–1610' (MA thesis, University of Nottingham, 1977).

ALSOP, JAMES D., 'The Medical Casebook of Joseph Binnes, a London Surgeon', *JAMS* 32 (1979), 367.

ANGLÉS, HIGINIO, *Historia de la música medieval en Navarra* (Pamplona, 1970).

—— *La música de las Cantigas de Santa Maria del Rey Alfonso el Sabio*, 3 vols. (Barcelona, 1949–64).

ANGLO, SYDNEY, 'The Court Festivals of Henry VII: A Study Based upon the Account Books of John Heron, Treasurer of the Chamber', *Bulletin of the John Rylands Library*, 43 (1960), 12–45.

ARBEAU, THOINOT, *Orchésographie* (Langres, 1588), trans. Mary Stewart Evans, with a new introduction and notes by Julia Sutton (New York, 1967).

ASCHAM, ROGER, *The Scholemaster* (London, 1570), facs. repr., selected and ed. R. C. Alston (Menston, 1967).

ASHBEE, ANDREW, 'Groomed for Service: Musicians in the Privy Chamber at the English court, *c*.1495–1558', *EM* 25 (1997), 185–97.

—— *The Harmonious Musick of John Jenkins*, i: *The Fantasias for Viols* (Surbiton, 1992).

—— *Lists of Payments to the King's Music in the Reign of Charles II (1660–1685)* (Snodland, 1981).

—— *Records of English Court Music*, 9 vols. (Snodland, 1986–).

—— and LASOCKI, DAVID, assisted by HOLMAN, PETER, and KISBY, FIONA, *A Biographical Dictionary of English Court Musicians 1485–1714*, 2 vols. (Aldershot, 1998).

—— (ed.), *William Lawes (1602–1645): Essays on his Life, Times and Work* (Aldershot, 1998).

AUBREY, JOHN, *Brief Lives*, ed. Andrew Clark (Oxford, 1898).

AWOUTERS, M., 'Snaarinstruementenbouw te Antwerpen: de family Hofmans in de 17de eeuw', in L. Jannssens and M. Kin (eds.), *Handelingen van het eerste Congres van de Federatie van Nederlandstalige Verenigingen voor Oudheidkunde en Geschiedenis van België te Hasselt 19–22 Augustus 1982* (Antwerp, 1990), 319–30.

BACHARACH, A. G. H., *Sir Constantin Huygens and Britain (1596–1687)* (Leiden and London, 1962).

BAINES, ANTHONY, 'Fifteenth-Century Instruments in Tinctoris's *De Inventione et usu musicae*', *GSJ* 3 (1950), 19–26.

—— *Victoria and Albert Museum, Catalogue of Musical Instruments*, xi: *Non-Keyboard Instruments* (London, 1968).

BANKS, JON, 'Performing the Instrumental Music in the Segovia Codex', *EM* 27 (1999), 295–309.

—— 'A Piece of Fifteenth-Century Lute Music in the Segovia Codex', *LSJ* 34 (1994), 3–10.

BATCHELOR, ANNE, *A Batchelor's Delight* (Beverley, 1990).

—— 'Daniel Bacheler: The Right Perfect Musician', *LSJ* 28 (1988), 3–12.

BATCHILER, JOHN, *The Virgins Pattern, in the exemplary life and lamented death of Mrs Susanna Perwich* (London, 1661).

BATES, JONATHAN, and McCOY, STEWART, 'Mercury's Tetrachord', *EM* 10 (1982), 213-15.

BEECHEY, GWILYM, 'Christopher Lowther's Lute Book', *GSJ* 24 (1971), 51-9.

BERNSTEIN, JANE A., 'Philip van Wilder and the Netherlandish Chanson in England', *Musica disciplina*, 33 (1979), 55-75.

BLACHLY, ALEXANDER, review in *Musical Quarterly*, 57 (1971), 330-41.

BLAEU, WILLEM and JAN, *Theatrum Scotia et Hibernia, Theatrum orbis terrarum, sive Atlas novus*, 6 vols. (Amsterdam, 1641-55).

BOORMAN, STANLEY, 'Notari, Porter and the Lute', *LSJ* 13 (1971), 28-35.

BOUTERSE, CURTIS, 'Reconstructing the Medieval Arabic Lute: A Reconsideration of Farmer's "Structure of the Arabic and Persian Lute" ', *GSJ* 32 (1979), 2-9.

BOWLES, EDMUND A., 'Haut and Bas: The Grouping of Musical Instruments in the Middle Ages', *Musica disciplina*, 8 (1954), 115-40.

—— 'The Role of Musical Instruments in Medieval Sacred Drama', *Musical Quarterly*, 45 (1959), 67-84.

BOYD, M. C., *Elizabethan Music and Musical Criticism* (Philadelphia, 1940; rev. edn., 1962).

BRENET, MICHEL (MARIE BOBILLIER), 'Notes sur l'histoire du luth en France', *Rivista musicale italiana*, 5 (1898), 6 (1899); repr. Geneva, 1973.

BRETT, PHILIP, 'Edward Paston (1550-1630): A Norfolk Gentleman and his Musical Collection', *Transactions of the Cambridge Bibliographical Society*, 4 (1964), 51-69.

—— '*Musicae Modernae Laus*: Geoffrey Whitney's Tributes to the Lute and its Players', *LSJ* 7 (1965), 40-4.

BROWN, HOWARD MAYER, 'St Augustine, Lady Music, and the Gittern in Fourteenth-Century Italy', *Musica disciplina*, 38 (1984), 25-65.

BUCH, DAVID J., 'The Influence of the Ballet de cour in the Genesis of the French Baroque Suite', *Acta musicologica*, 57 (1985), 94-108.

—— 'On the Authorship of William Lawes's *Suite for Two Lutes*', *JLSA* 16 (1983), 12-14.

—— '*Style brisé, Style luthé*, and the *Choses luthées*', *Musical Quarterly*, 71 (1985), 52-67.

BUETENS, STANLEY, 'The Instructions of Alessandro Piccinini', *JLSA* 2 (1969), 6-17.

—— 'Nicolas Vallet's Lute Quartets', *JLSA* 2 (1969), 28-36.

The buke of the Howlat, By Holland, ed. David Laing (Edinburgh, 1823).

BULLOCK-DAVIS, CONSTANCE, *Menestrellorum multitudo: Minstrels at a Royal Feast* (Cardiff, 1978).

BURNEY, CHARLES, *A General History of Music*, 4 vols. (1776-89); modern edn. by F. Mercer, 2 vols. (London, 1935).

BURROWS, DONALD, 'Handel's London Theatre Orchestra', *EM* 13 (1985), 349-57.

BURZIK, MONIKA, *Quellenstudien zu europäischen Zupfinstrumentenformen* (Kassel, 1995).

BUTLER, CHARLES, *The Principles of Musik in Singing and Setting* (London, 1636).

BUTLER, GREGORY G., 'The Projection of Affect in Baroque Dance Music', *EM* 12 (1984), 200-7.

BUXTON, JOHN, *Elizabethan Taste* (London, 1963).

BYLER, ARTHUR W., 'Italian Currents in the Popular Music of England in the Sixteenth Century' (Ph.D. diss., University of Chicago, 1952).

CADELL, PATRICK, 'La Musique française classique dans la collection des comités de Panmure', *Recherches sur la musique française classique*, 22 (1984), 50–8.

CALDWELL, JOHN, *English Keyboard Music before the Nineteenth Century* (Oxford, 1973).

Calendar of State Papers Domestic (1611–1618), ed. Mary Anne Everett Green (London, 1858).

Calendar of State Papers Domestic (1625–1626), ed. John Bruce (London, 1858).

Calendar of State Papers and Manuscripts relating to English Affairs, Existing in the Archives and Collections of Venice, and in other Libraries of Northern Italy, ed. Rawdon Brown, vi, part 2: *1556–57* (London, 1881).

CAMDEN, WILLIAM, *The historie of . . . princess Elizabeth, late queene of England*, trans. R. Norton (London, 1635).

CAMPION, THOMAS, *The Discription of a Maske . . . in Honour of the Lord Hayes, and his Bride* (London, 1607).

CASE, JOHN, *Apologia musices* (Oxford, 1588).

CAVE, CHARLES JOHN P., *Medieval Carvings in Exeter Cathedral* (London, 1953).

—— *Roof Bosses in Medieval Churches* (Cambridge, 1948).

CHAPPELL, WILLIAM, *Popular Music of the Olden Time*, 2 vols. (London, 1859; repr. New York, 1965).

CHARTERIS, RICHARD, *Alfonso Ferrabosco (1543–1588): A Thematic Catalogue of his Music with a Biographical Calendar* (New York, 1984).

—— *John Coprario: A Thematic Catalogue of his Music with a Biographical Introduction* (New York, 1977).

—— 'New Information about the Life of Alfonso Ferrabosco the Elder (1543–1588)', *RMARC* 17 (1981), 97–114.

The Chronicle and Political Papers of King Edward VI, ed. W. K. Jordan (London, 1966).

COELHO, VICTOR ANAND, *The Manuscript Sources of Seventeenth-Century Italian Lute Music* (New York, 1995).

—— (ed.), *Performance of Lute, Guitar, and Vihuela: Historical Practice and Modern Interpretation* (Cambridge, 1997).

COLLIER, JOHN PAYNE (ed.), *Trevelyan Papers Prior to AD 1558* (Camden Society, 68; London, 1867).

COLLINS, DAVID, 'A 16th-Century Manuscript in Wood: The Eglantine Table at Hardwick Hall', *EM* 4 (1976), 275–9.

COLLINSON, FRANCIS, *The Traditional and National Music of Scotland* (London, 1966).

COLLINSON, PATRICK, *The Elizabethan Puritan Movement* (London, 1967).

CORP, EDWARD T., 'Further Light on the Career of "Captain" François de Prendcourt', *M&L* 78 (1997), 15–23.

CRAIG-MCFEELY, JULIA, 'A Can of Worms: Lord Herbert of Cherbury's Lute Book', *LSJ* 31 (1991), 20–48.

—— 'English Lute Manuscripts and Scribes 1530–1630', 3 vols. (D.Phil. thesis, University of Oxford, 1994).

CRAWFORD, TIM, 'The historical importance of François Dufault and his influence on musicians outside France', *luths et luthistes en Occident* (Paris, 1999), 201–15.

—— 'Lord Danby, Lutenist of "Quality" ', *LSJ* 25 (1985), 53–68.

—— 'An Unusual Consort Revealed in an Oxford Manuscript', *Chelys*, 6 (1975–6), 61–8.

CURTIS, ALAN, *Sweelinck's Keyboard Music: A Study of English Elements in Seventeenth-Century Dutch Composition* (London, 1969).

CUTTS, JOHN P., 'Robert Johnson and the Court Masque', *M&L* 41 (1960), 111–26.

DALYELL, SIR JOHN GRAHAM, *Musical Memoirs of Scotland* (Edinburgh, 1849).

DANNER, PETER, 'Before Petrucci: The Lute in the Fifteenth Century', *JLSA* 5 (1972), 4–17.

—— 'Dd.4.23 or English Cittern Music Revisited', *JLSA* 3 (1970), 1–12.

DART, THURSTON, 'A Hand-list of English Instrumental Music Printed before 1681', *GSJ* 8 (1955), 13–25.

—— 'Lord Herbert of Cherbury's Lute Book' *M&L* 38 (1957), 136–54.

—— 'Miss Mary Burwell's Instruction Book for the Lute', *GSJ* 11 (1958), 3–62.

—— 'Morley's Consort Lessons of 1599', *PRMA* 74 (1947–8), 1–9.

—— 'New Sources of Virginal Music', *M&L* 35 (1954), 93–106.

—— Review of *Lute Music of Shakespeare's Time. William Barley: A New Booke of Tabliture, 1596*, ed. Wilburn W. Newcomb, in *JAMS* 20 (1967), 493–5.

—— 'La Rôle de la danse dans l'"ayre" anglais', in Jean Jacquot (ed.), *Musique et poésie au XVIe siècle* (Paris, 1954), 203–9.

DAUNEY, WILLIAM, *Ancient Scotish Melodies* (Edinburgh, 1838).

DAVIES, IAN, 'Replete for Three Lutes—The Missing Parts', *LSJ* 24 (1984), 38–43.

DAVIES, SIR JOHN, *The Poems of Sir John Davies*, ed. Robert Krueger (Oxford, 1975).

DAVISON, FRANCIS, *A Poetical Rhapsody* (2nd enlarged edn., London 1608).

DAY, CYRUS L., and MURRIE, ELEANORE B., *English Song-Books 1651–1702* (London, 1940).

DIMSDALE, VERNA L., 'English Sacred Music with Broken Consort', *LSJ* 16 (1974), 39–64.

—— 'The Lute in Consort in Seventeenth-Century England', 3 vols. (D.Phil. thesis, University of Oxford, 1968).

DOBBINS, FRANK, 'The Lute Airs of Charles Tessier', *LSJ* 20 (1978), 23–42.

—— 'Les air pour luth de Charles Tessier, luthistes français et compositeur en Angleterre à l'époque de Dowland', in *luths et luthistes en Occident* (Paris, 1999), 169–184.

Domestic Annals of Scotland, ed. Robert Chambers, 3 vols. (2nd edn., Edinburgh, 1831).

DOWLING, MARIA, *Humanism in the Age of Henry VIII* (London, 1986).

DUCKLES, VINCENT, 'The "Curious" Art of John Wilson (1595–1674): An Introduction to his Songs and Lute Music', *JAMS* 7 (1954), 93–112.

D'URFEY, THOMAS, *Wit and Mirth; or, Pills to Purge Melancholy* (London, 1699); repr. in *Songs Compleat, Pleasant and Divertive* (London, 1719).

The Early English Versions of the Gesta Romanorum, ed. Sidney J. H. Herrtage (EETS/ES, 33; London, 1879).

Early Metrical Tales, ed. David Laing (Edinburgh, 1826).

EDWARDS, WARWICK A., 'The Sources of Elizabethan Consort Music' (Ph.D. thesis, University of Cambridge, 1974).

—— 'The Walsingham Consort Books', *M&L* 55 (1974), 209–14.

ELYOT, SIR THOMAS, *The boke named the governour* (London, 1531).

EMDEN, ALFRED BROTHERSTON, *A Biographical Register of the University of Oxford to A.D.* 1500, 3 vols. (Oxford, 1957–9).

EMMISON, F. G., 'John Petre's Account-Books 1567–77', *GSJ* 14 (1961), 73–5.

—— *The Tudor Secretary: Sir William Petre at Court and Home* (Cambridge, Mass., 1961).

EMSLIE, MACDONALD, 'Nicolas Lanier's Innovations in English Song', *M&L* 41 (1960), 13–27.

EVANS, WILLA MCCLUNG, *Henry Lawes, Musician and Friend of Poets* (New York, 1941).

EVELYN, JOHN, *The Diary of John Evelyn*, ed. E. S. de Beer, 6 vols. (London, 1955).

FALLOWS, DAVID, '15th-Century Tablatures for Plucked Instruments: A Summary, a Revision and a Suggestion', *LSJ* 19 (1977), 7–33.

FARMER, HENRY G., *A History of Arabian Music to the XIIIth Century* (London, 1929).

—— *A History of Music in Scotland* (London, 1947).

—— 'The Influence of Music: From Arabic Sources', *PMA* 52 (1926), 89–124.

—— *An Old Moorish Lute Tutor* (Glasgow, 1933).

—— 'The Origin of the Arabian Lute and Rebec', *Studies in Oriental Musical Instruments* (London, 1931), 89–98.

—— 'Was the Arabian and Persian Lute Fretted?', *Journal of the Royal Asiatic Society*, 103 (1937), 453–60.

FIELD, CHRISTOPHER D. S., 'Matthew Locke and the Consort Suite', *M&L* 51 (1970), 15–25.

FELLOWES, EDMUND H., *English Madrigal Verse* (Oxford, 1967).

FISKE, ROGER, *Scotland in Music: A European Enthusiasm* (Cambridge, 1983).

FLEMING, MICHAEL, 'Some Points Arising from a Survey of Wills and Inventories', *GSJ* 53 (2000), 301–11.

FORRESTER, PETER, 'An Elizabethan Allegory and Some Hypotheses', *LSJ* 34 (1994), 11–14.

—— 'A Scottish Consort', *LSJ* 27 (1987), 38–42.

FORSBROKE, T. D., *Berkeley Manuscripts* (London, 1821).

FOSTER, RICHARD, and TUDOR-CRAIG, PAMELA, *The Secret Life of Paintings* (Woodbridge, 1986).

FOXE, JOHN, *A Book of Martyrs* (Latin edn., Basle, 1559; English rev. edn. London, 1563).

FRASER, ANTONIA, *King Charles II: His Life and Times* (London, 1979).

—— *Mary Queen of Scots* (London, 1969).

GALLO, ALBERTO, *Music in the Castle* (Chicago, 1995)

GALPIN, FRANCIS W., *Old English Instruments of Music* (London, 1910).

GILL, DONALD, 'The de Gallot Guitar Books', *EM* 6 (1978), 79–87.

—— 'The Lute and Musick's Monument', *GSJ* 3 (1950), 9–18.

—— 'The Orpharion and Bandora', *GSJ* 13 (1960), 14–25.

—— 'The Skene Mandora Manuscript', *LSJ* 28 (1988), 19–33.

GIUSTINIAN, SEBASTIAN, *Four Years at the Court of Henry VIII*, trans. Rawdon Brown, 2 vols. (London, 1854).

GLEN, JOHN, *Early Scottish Melodies* (Edinburgh, 1900).

GODWIN, JOYCELYN, ' "Main divers acors": Some Instrument Collections of the Ars Nova Period', *EM* 5 (1977), 148–59.

GOWER, JOHN, *The English Works of John Gower*, ed. George Campbell Macauley (EETS/ES, 82; London, 1901).

GOY, FRANÇOIS-PIERRE, 'Luth et guitare dans le journal et la correspondence (1631–1636) de Bullen Reymes', *luths et luthistes en Occident* (Paris, 1999), 185–200.

—— 'Richard Mathew's Prefatory Epistle and the Contents of *The Lutes Apology*', *LSJ* 31 (1991), 2–7.

GRATTAN FLOOD, W. H., 'Entries Relating to Music in the English Patent Rolls of the Fifteenth Century', *Musical Antiquary*, 4 (1912–13), 225–37.

GREER, DAVID, 'Five Variations on "Farewell dear love" ', in John Caldwell, Edward Olleson, and Susan Wollenberg (eds.), *The Well Enchanting Skill: Essays in Honour of F. W. Sternfeld* (Oxford, 1990), 213–29.

—— 'The Lute Songs of Thomas Morley', *LSJ* 8 (1966), 25–37.

—— 'The Part-Songs of the English Lutenists', *PRMA* 94 (1967–8), 97–110.

GUERRERO LOVILLO, JOSÉ, *Las Cántigas: estudio arqueológico de sus miniaturas* (Madrid, 1949).

GUMPELZHAIMER, ADAM, *Gymnasma* (Strasburg, 1621).

HANCOCK, WENDY, 'General Rules for Realising an Unfigured Bass in Seventeenth-Century England', *Chelys*, 7 (1977), 69–72.

A Handful of Pleasant Delights (1584), by Clement Robinson and Divers Others, ed. Hyder E. Rollins (Cambridge, Mass., 1924; facs. edn., ed. D. E. L. Crane, Ilkley, 1973).

HANHAM, ALISON, 'The Musical Studies of a Fifteenth-Century Wool Merchant', *Review of English Studies*, 8 (1957), 270–4.

HARMON, ROGER, 'Studies in the Cambridge Lute Manuscripts I: "Musica" ', *LSJ* 38 (1998), 29–42.

HARRIS, FRANK REGINALD, *The Life of Edward Mountagu, K.G., First Earl of Sandwich 1625–1672*, ii (London, 1912).

HARWOOD, IAN, 'A Case of Double Standards? Instrumental Pitch in England c.1600', *EM* 9 (1981), 470–81.

—— 'A Fifteenth-Century Lute Design', *LSJ* 2 (1960), 3–8.

—— 'John Maynard and *The XII Wonders of the World*', *LSJ* 4 (1962), 7–16.

—— 'On the Publication of Adrian Le Roy's Lute Instructions', *LSJ* 18 (1976), 30–7.

—— 'The Origins of the Cambridge Lute Manuscripts', *LSJ* 5 (1963), 32–48.

—— 'Rosseter's *Lessons for Consort of 1609*', *LSJ* 7 (1965), 15–23.

—— 'Thomas Robinson's "Generall Rules" ', *LSJ* 20 (1978), 18–22.

HAYES, GERALD, *King's Music* (London, 1937).

—— 'Music in the Boteler Muniments', *GSJ* 8 (1955), 43–7.

HAWKINS, SIR JOHN, *A General History of the Science and Practice of Music* (London, 1776; rev. edn., 1875).

HEARTZ, DANIEL, 'An Elizabethan Tutor for the Guitar', *GSJ* 16 (1962), 3–21.

HELLWIG, FRIEDEMANN, 'Lute-Making in the Late 15th and the 16th Century', *LSJ* 16 (1974), 24–38.

HENNING, UTA, 'The Lute Made Easy: A Chapter from Virdung's *Musica Getutscht* (1511)', *LSJ* 15 (1973), 20–36.

Historia regis Henrici septimi, ed. James Gairdner (London, 1858).

HOBY, SIR THOMAS, *The Booke of the Courtyer* (London, 1561; modern edn., London, 1928). Eng. trans. of Baldassare Castiglione's *Il libro del cortegiano* (Venice, 1528).

HOGWOOD, CHRISTOPHER, *Music at Court* (London, 1977).

HOLMAN, PETER, *Dowland: Lachrimae (1604)* (Cambridge, 1999).

—— 'The English Royal Violin Consort in the Sixteenth Century', *PRMA* 109 (1983), 39–59.

—— *Four and Twenty Fiddlers: The Violin at the English Court 1540–1690* (Oxford, 1993).

—— 'The Harp in Stuart England: New Light on William Lawes's Harp Consorts', *EM* 15 (1987), 188–203.

—— 'New Sources of Music by Robert Johnson', *LSJ* 20 (1978), 43–52.

—— 'The "Symphony" ', *Chelys*, 6 (1975–6), 10–24.

—— 'Thomas Baltzar (?1631–1663), the "Incomperable Lubicer on the Violin" ', *Chelys*, 13 (1984), 3–38.

Household Books of John, Duke of Norfolk and Thomas Earl of Surrey, temp. 1481–1490, ed. John Payne Collier (London, 1844).

HULSE, LYNN, 'Francis and Thomas Cutting: Father and Son?', *LSJ* 26 (1986), 73–4.

—— 'Hardwick MS 29: A New Source for Jacobean Lutenists', *LSJ* 26 (1986), 63–72.

—— 'Musical Patronage of the English Aristocracy c.1590–1640' (Ph.D. thesis, King's College, University of London, 1993).

HUMPHREYS, DAVID, 'Philip van Wilder: A Study of his Work and its Sources', *Soundings*, 9 (1979–80), 13–36.

ISHERWOOD, ROBERT M., *Music in the Service of the King: France in the Seventeenth Century* (Ithaca, 1973).

IVANOFF, VLADIMIR, 'An Invitation to the Fifteenth-Century Lute: The Pesaro Manuscript', in Victor Anand Coelho (ed.), *Performance of Lute, Guitar and Vihuela: Historical Practice and Modern interpretation* (Cambridge, 1996), 1–15.

JACKSON OF EXETER, WILLIAM, *The Four Ages of Man; together with Essays on Various Subjects* (London, 1798).

Jacob's Well, ed. Arthur Brandeis (EETS/OS 115; London, 1900).

JEFFERY, BRIAN, 'The Lute Music of Robert Johnson', *EM* 2 (1974), 105–9.

JEFFREYS, JOHN, *The Life and Works of Philip Rosseter* (Wendover, 1990).

JENKINS, JEAN L., *Musical Instruments* (Horniman Museum and Library Publication; London, 1970).

The John Marsh Journals, ed. Brian Robins (New York, 1998).

JOHNSON, DAVID, *Music and Society in Lowland Scotland in the Eighteenth Century* (London, 1972).

—— *Scottish Fiddle Music in the 18th Century* (Edinburgh, 1984).

JONES, EDWARD H., ' "To sing and play to the Bass-Violl alone"—The Bass Viol in English 17th-Century Song', *LSJ* 17 (1975), 17–23.

JONES, LEWIS, 'The Thibault Lute Manuscript: An Introduction', Part I, *LSJ* 22 (1982), 69–87, and Part II, *LSJ* 23 (1983), 21–6.

KAUFMAN, HELEN ANDREWS, *Conscientious Cavalier: Colonel Bullen Reymes, M.P., F.R.S. 1613–1672* (London, 1962).

KELLY, THOMAS F., 'Notes on the Jane Pickering Lute Book', *JLSA* 1 (1968), 19–23.

KING, H. W., 'Ancient Wills', *Transactions of the Essex Archaeological Society*, 4 (1869).

KLARWILL, VICTOR VON, *Queen Elizabeth and Some Foreigners*, trans. T. H. Nash (London, 1928).

KNAPPEN, MARSHALL MASON, *Tudor Puritanism* (Chicago, 1939).

KNIGHTON, TESS, and FALLOWS, DAVID (eds.), *Companion to Medieval and Renaissance Music* (London, 1992).

LACHÈVRE, FRÉDÉRIC, *Charles de Lespine* (Paris, 1935).

LAFONTAINE, HENRY CART DE, *The Kings Musick* (London, 1909).

LA LAURENCIE, LIONEL DE, 'Le Luthiste Jacques Gaultier', *La revue musicale*, 5, no. 3 (1924), 33–9.

—— *Les Luthistes* (Paris, 1928).

LANE, TODD, 'The Lute Quartets in the Thysius Lute Book', *JLSA* 22 (1989), 28–59.

LANGLAND, WILLIAM, *The Vision of Piers Plowman: A Critical Edition of the B-Text*, ed. A. V. C. Schmidt (London, 1978).

LASOCKI, DAVID, 'The Anglo-Venetian Bassano Family as Instrument Makers and Repairers', *GSJ* 38 (1985), 112–32.

—— 'Professional Recorder Players in England, 1540–1740' (Ph.D. diss., University of Iowa, 1983).

The Laud Troy Book, ed. J. Ernst Wülfing (EETS/OS, 121; London, 1902).

LAUDER OF FOUNTAINHALL, SIR JOHN, *Decisions of the Lords of Council and Session from June 6th, 1678 to July 30th, 1712*, 2 vols. (Edinburgh, 1759).

LAVOIX, HENRI-MARIE F., *Histoire de l'instrumentation depuis le seizième siècle jusqu'à nos jours* (Paris, 1878).

LE COCQ, JONATHAN, 'The Pitch and Tuning in French Lute Song', *LSJ* 32 (1992), 46–71.

LEDBETTER, DAVID, 'French Lute Music 1600–1650: Towards a Definition of Genres', *LSJ* 30 (1990), 25–47.

—— *Harpsichord and Lute Music in 17th-Century France* (London, 1987).

LEFKOWITZ, MURRAY, 'The Longleat Papers of Bulstrode Whitlocke: New Light on Shirley's *Triumph of Peace*', *JAMS* 18 (1965), 42–60.

—— *William Lawes* (London, 1960).

LEECH-WILKINSON, DANIEL, 'The Thynne Lute Book', *LSJ* 33 (1993), 1–11.

LESURE, FRANÇOIS, 'Recherches sur les luthistes parisiens à l'époque de Louis XIII', in Jean Jacquot (ed.), *Le Luth et sa musique* (Paris, 1958), 209–23.

Letters and Papers, Foreign and Domestic, of the Reign of Henry VIII, ed. James Gairdner, vi (London, 1882).

Letters and Papers, Foreign and Domestic, of the Reign of Henry VIII, ed. John Sherren Brewer, vi (London, 1882).

Letters of Denization and Acts of Naturalisation for Aliens in England (1509–1603), ed. William Page (Publications of the Huguenot Society of London, 8; Lymington, 1893).

LOCKE, MATTHEW, *Observations upon a Late Book, Entitled, An Essay to the Advancement of Musick* (London, 1672).

LOCKE, MATTHEW, *The Present Practice of Musick Vindicated against the Exceptions; and New Way of Attaining Musick lately published by Thomas Salmon* (London, 1673).

LOCKWOOD, LEWIS, 'Pietrobono and the Instrumental Tradition at Ferrara in the Fifteenth Century', *Rivista italiana di musicologia*, 10 (1975), 115-33.

Lodewijck Huygens: The English Journal 1651-1652, ed. A. G. H. Bacharach and R. G. Collmer (Leiden and London, 1982).

LONG, JOHN H., *Shakespeare's Use of Music* (Gainesville, Fla., 1961).

LOWE, MICHAEL, 'The Historical Development of the Lute in the 17th Century', *GSJ* 29 (1976), 11-25.

LUMSDEN, DAVID, 'The Sources of English Lute Music (1540-1620)', 3 vols. (Ph.D. thesis, University of Cambridge, 1955).

LUNDBERG, ROBERT, 'Historical Lute Construction: The Erlangen Lectures, Day One', *American Lutherie*, 12 (Winter, 1987), 37-47.

LYDGATE, JOHN, *Lydgate's Reason and Sensuallyte*, ed. Ernest Sieper (EETS/ES, 84; London, 1901).

—— *The Minor Poems of John Lydgate*, ed. Henry Noble MacCracken (EETS/ES, 107; London, 1911).

Lyrics from English Airs, ed. Edward Doughtie (Cambridge, Mass., 1970).

Lyrics in Anglia (*c.*1500), ed. Frederick Morgan Padelford (Anglia, 31; 1908).

McCOY, STEWART, 'Edward Paston and the Textless Lute-Song', *EM* 15 (1987), 221-7.

—— 'Lost Lute Solos Revealed in a Paston Manuscript', *LSJ* 26 (1986), 21-39.

—— 'Some Aspects of the Paston Lute Books' (M.Mus. thesis, King's College, University of London, 1985).

MACE, THOMAS, *Musick's Monument, or, A Remembrancer of the Best Practical Musik* (London, 1676); facs. edn., vol. i: *Musick's Monument*; vol. ii: trans. and commentary ed. Jean Jacquot and André Souris (Paris, 1966).

—— *Profit, Conveniency and Pleasure to the whole Nation, being a short rational discourse lately presented to his Majesty concerning the high ways of England* (London, 1675).

—— *Riddles, Mervels and Rarities, or, a New Way of Health, from an Old Man's Experience* (Cambridge, 1698).

MACKERNESS, E. D., 'Thomas Mace and the Fact of Reasonableness', *Monthly Musical Record*, 85 (1955), 211-13, 235-9.

MACRAY, WILLIAM DUNN, *A Register of the Members of St. Mary Magdalen College Oxford*, 8 vols. (London, 1894-1915).

MALDEN, HENRY ELLIOT (ed.), 'Devereux Papers with Richard Brouhton's Memoranda (1575-1601)', *Camden Miscellany*, 13 (1923), pub. in Camden 3rd ser., 34; London, 1924).

MASON, KEVIN, *The Chitarrone and its Repertoire in Early Seventeenth-Century Italy* (Aberystwyth, 1989).

MATHEW, RICHARD, *The Unlearned Alchemist his Antidote, or a more full and ample explanation of the use, verture and benefit of my pill* (London, 1659).

MAUNSELL, ANDREW, *The first (seconde) part of the catalogue of English printed bookes* (London, 1595).

MAYNARD, WINIFRED, *Elizabethan Lyric Poetry and its Music* (Oxford, 1986).

The Medieval Treasury: The Art of the Middle Ages in the Victoria and Albert Museum, ed. Paul Williamson (London, 1986).

MERES, FRANCIS, *Palladis tamia (Wits Treasury), the Second part of Wits Commonwealth* (London, 1598).

MERSENNE, MARIN, *Harmonie universelle* (1636); modern edn. and trans. by Roger E. Chapman (The Hague, 1957).

MEYER, ERNST H., *Early English Chamber Music* (2nd rev. edn. by Diana Poulton and the author; London, 1982).

The Middle English Dictionary, ed. Hans Kurath, 10 vols. (Ann Arbor, 1952–).

Middle English Metrical Romances, ed. Walter Hoyt French and Charles Brockway Hale, 2 vols. (New York, 1964).

MONTAGU, JEREMY, *The World of Medieval and Renaissance Musical Instruments* (Newton Abbot, 1976).

—— and GWEN, *Minstrels and Angels* (Berkeley, 1998).

MORLEY, THOMAS, *A Plaine and Easie Introduction to Practicall Musicke* (London, 1597); modern edn. as Thomas Morley, *A Plain and Easy Introduction to Practical Music*, ed. R. Alec Harman (London, 1952).

MUMFORD, IVY L., 'The Identity of "Zuan Piero" ', *Renaissance News*, 11 (1958), 179–82.

MUNDAY, ANTHONY, *A Banquet of Daintie Conceits* (London, 1588).

MURE, SIR WILLIAM, *The Works of Sir William Mure of Rowallan*, ed. William Tough (Scottish Text Society, 40–1; Edinburgh, 1989).

Musique et musiciens au XVII⁵ siecle: correspondance et œuvres musicales de Constantijn Huygens, ed. Willem Jozef Andries Jonckbloet and J. P. N. Land (Leiden, 1882).

NEBRIJA, ELIO ANTONIO DE, *Vocabulario español-latino* (Salamanca, c.1495).

NEUBAUER, ECKHARD, 'Der Bau der Laute und ihre Besaitung nach arabischen, persischen und türkischen Quellen des 9. bis 15. Jahrhunderts', *Zeitschrift für Geschichte der arabisch-islamischen Wissenschaften*, 8 (1993), 259–378.

NEWTON, RICHARD, 'English Duets for Two Lutes', *LSJ* 1 (1959), 23–30.

—— 'English Lute Music of the Golden Age', *PRMA* 45 (1938–9), 63–90.

NICHOL, J. G., *Literary Remains of King Edward the Sixth* (London, 1857).

NORDSTROM, LYLE, 'Albert de Rippe, Joueur de luth du Roy', *EM* 7 (1979), 378–95.

—— 'The Cambridge Consort Books', *JLSA* 5 (1972), 70–103.

—— 'The English Lute Duet and Consort Lesson', *LSJ* 18 (1976), 5–22.

—— 'The Lute Duets of John Johnson', *JLSA* 9 (1976), 30–42.

NORTH, NIGEL, *Continuo Playing on the Lute, Archlute and Theorbo* (London, 1987).

NOTT, GEORGE F., unpublished 'Songs and Sonnets' (1814?) in the library at Arundel Castle.

OBOUSSIER, PHILIPPE, 'Turpyn's Book of Lute-Songs', *M&L* 34 (1953), 145–9.

Old Herbert Papers at Powis Castle and in the British Museum, Collections Historical and Archaeological relating to Montgomeryshire issued by the Powys-Land Club, ed. M. C. Jones (London, 1886).

OMAN, CAROLA MARY A., *Henrietta Maria* (London, 1936).

ONGARO, GIULIO M., 'The Tieffenbruckers and the Business of Lute-Making in Sixteenth-Century Venice', *GSJ* 44 (1991), 46–54.

ORGEL, STEPHEN, *The Jonsonian Masque* (Cambridge, Mass., 1965).

O'SULLIVAN, DONAL, *Carolan: The Life, Times and Music of an Irish Harper*, 2 vols. (London, 1958).

The Oxford Companion to Music, ed. Percy A. Scholes (9th edn., Oxford, 1955); 10th edn., rev. J. O. Ward (Oxford, 1970).

PAGE, CHRISTOPHER, 'The 15th-Century Lute: New and Neglected Sources', *EM* 9 (1981), 11–21.

—— 'Fourteenth-Century Instruments and Tunings: A Treatise by Jean Vaillant? (Berkeley, MS 744)', *GSJ* 33 (1980), 17–35.

—— 'French Lute Tablature in the 14th Century?', *EM* 8 (1980), 488–92.

—— 'String-Instrument Making in Medieval England and Some Oxford Harpmakers, 1380–1466', *GSJ* 31 (1978), 44–67.

The Paradise of Dainty Devices (1576–1606), by Richard Edwards and Others, ed. Hyder E. Rollins (Cambridge, Mass., 1927).

PARRY, GRAHAM, *The Golden Age Restor'd* (Manchester, 1981).

PAUL, SIR JAMES BALFOUR, *The Scots Peerage*, 9 vols. (Edinburgh, 1904–14).

PAYNE, IAN, *Provision and Practice of Sacred Music at Cambridge Colleges and Selected Cathedrals c.1547–c.1646* (New York and London, 1993).

PEPYS, SAMUEL, *The Diaries of Samuel Pepys*, ed. Robert C. Latham and William Matthews, 11 vols. (London, 1970–83).

PICKEN, LAURENCE, 'The Origin of the Short Lute', *GSJ* 8 (1955), 32–42.

The Pilgrimage of the Life of Man, ed. Frederick J. Furnivall (EETS/ES, 83; London, 1901).

PIRROTTA, NINO, 'Music and Cultural Tendencies in Fifteenth-Century Italy', *JAMS* 19 (1966), 127–61.

PLAYFORD, JOHN, *An Introduction to the Skill of Musick* (London, 1664, 1683, 1687).

POOLE, R., 'The Oxford Music School and the Collection of Portraits formerly Preserved There', *Musical Antiquary*, 4 (1912–13), 143–59.

POULTON, DIANA, 'The Black-Letter Broadside Ballad and its Music', *EM* 9 (1981), 427–37.

—— 'The Early History of the Lute', *JLSA* 20–1 (1987–8), 1–21.

—— *John Dowland* (London, 1972; rev. edn., 1982).

—— 'The Lute in Christian Spain', *LSJ* 19 (1977), 34–49.

—— 'Notes on the Spanish Pavan', *LSJ* 3 (1961), 5–16.

—— 'La Technique du jeu du luth en France et en Angleterre', in Jean Jacquot (ed.), *Le Luth et sa musique* (Paris, 1958), 107–20.

PRAETORIUS, MICHAEL, *Syntagma musicum* (Wolfenbüttel, 1618; rev. edn., 1619).

—— *Theatrum instrumentorum* (Wolfenbüttel, 1620).

PRICE, CURTIS A., 'An Organisational Peculiarity of Lord Herbert of Cherbury's Lute-Book', *LSJ* 11 (1969), 5–27.

PRICE, DAVID C., *Patrons and Musicians of the English Renaissance* (Cambridge, 1981).

The Privy Purse Expenses of the Princess Mary, ed. F. Madden (London, 1831).

PRIZER, WILLIAM F., 'Lutenists at the Court of Mantua in the Late Fifteenth and Early Sixteenth Centuries', *JLSA* 13 (1980), 5–34.

Promptorium parvulorum, ed. Albert Way (Camden Society, 25, 54, 89; London, 1843–65).

PRYNNE, MICHAEL J., 'James Talbot's Manuscript: IV. Plucked Strings—The Lute Family', *GSJ* 14 (1961), 52–68.

—— 'A Note on Marx Unverdorben', *LSJ* 1 (1959), 58.

—— 'The Old Bologna Lute-Makers', *LSJ* 5 (1963), 18–31.

PULVER, JEFFREY, *A Dictionary of Old English Music and Musical Instruments* (London, 1923).

Queene Elizabethes Achademy, a Booke of Precedence, ed. Frederick J. Furnivall (EETS/ES, 8; London, 1869).

RADKE, HANS, 'Beiträge zur Erforschung der Lautentablaturen des 16.–18. Jahrhunderts', *Die Musikforschung*, 16 (1963), 34–51.

RAMOS DE PAREJA, BARTOLOMÉ, *Musica practica* (Bologna, 1482).

RAMSEY, ALLAN, *The Tea-Table Miscelany* (London, 1723/4).

RASTALL, RICHARD, 'Benjamin Rogers (1614–98): Some Notes on his Instrumental Music', *M&L* 46 (1965), 237–42.

—— 'The Minstrels of the English Royal Households, 25 Edward I–1 Henry VIII: An Inventory', *RMARC* 4 (1964), 1–41.

—— 'Some English Consort-Groupings of the Late Middle Ages', *M&L* 55 (1974), 179–202.

RAVE, WALLACE B., 'Some Manuscripts of French Lute Music 1630–1700: An Introductory Study' (Ph.D. diss., University of Illinois at Urbana-Champaign, 1972).

The Regulations and Establishment of the Household of Henry Algenon Percy, the Fifth Earl of Northumberland, at his Castles of Wressil and Lekinfield in Yorkshire, ed. Thomas Percy (1st edn., London, 1770).

REMNANT, MARY, *English Bowed Instruments from Anglo-Saxon to Tudor Times* (Oxford, 1986).

—— 'The Gittern in English Medieval Art', *GSJ* 18 (1965), 104–9.

—— 'Notes and Queries: "Opus Anglicanum" ', *GSJ* 17 (1964), 111–13.

—— and MARKS, RICHARD, 'A Medieval Gittern', *Music and Civilization: The British Museum Yearbook*, 4 (1980), 83–134.

Returns of Strangers in the Metropolis 1593, 1627, 1635, 1639, ed. Irene Scouloudi (Huguenot Society of London, quarto series, 57; London, 1985).

RIBERA Y TARRAGÓ, JULIÁN, *La música de las Cantigas: estudio sobre su origen y naturaleza* (Madrid, 1922); trans. Eleanor Hague and Marian Leffingwell in *Music in Ancient Arabia and Spain* (Stanford, 1929; repr. New York, 1970).

Roger North on Music, ed. John Wilson (London, 1959).

The Romance of Sir Degrevant, ed. L. F. Casson (EETS/OS, 221; London, 1949).

Le Roman de la Rose, ed. Félix Lecoy, 3 vols. (Paris, 1965–70).

ROOLEY, ANTHONY, 'A Portrait of Sir Henry Unton', in *Companion to Medieval and Renaissance Music*, ed. Tess Knighton and David Fallows (London, 1992), 85–92.

—— and TYLER, JAMES, 'The Lute Consort', *LSJ* 14 (1972), 13–24.

ROY, ADENET LE, *Cleomadès*, ed. A. Van Hasselt (Brussels, 1865–6).

RUBSAMEN, WALTER H., 'The Earliest French Lute Tablature', *JAMS* 21 (1968), 286–99.

RUFF, LILIAN M., 'Thomas Salmon's "Essay to the Advancement of Musick" ', *The Consort*, 21 (1964), 266–78.

RUSSELL, RAYMOND, *The Harpsichord and Clavichord* (London, 1959).

SACKVILLE-WEST, VICTORIA (LADY NICHOLSON) (ed.), *The Diary of Lady Anne Clifford* (London, 1924).

SALMON, THOMAS, *An Essay to the Advancement of Music* (London, 1672).

—— *A Vindication of an Essay to the Advancement of Musick from Mr. Matthew Locke's Observations By Enquiring into the real nature, and most convenient practice of that Science* (London, 1672).

SANDMAN, SUSAN G., 'Thomas Robinson's Interpretive Left-Hand Fingerings for the Lute and Cittern', *JLSA* 11 (1978), 26–35.

SARRAZIN, GREGOR IGNATZ (ed.), 'Octavian Imperator', *Altenglische Bibliothek*, 3 (Heilbron, 1885).

SAYCE, LYNDA, 'Continuo Lutes in 17th- and 18th-Century England', *EM* 23 (1995), 667–84.

SCHLICK, ARNOLT, *Spiegel der Orgelmacher und Organisten* (Mainz, 1511).

SCHNEIDER, HERBERT, *Cronologisch-thematisch Verzeichnis sämtlicher Werke von Jean-Baptist Lully* (Tutzing, 1981).

SCHOLES, PERCY A., *The Puritans and Music in England and New England* (London, 1934).

SCHULZE-KURZ, EKKEHARD, *Die Laute und ihre Stimmungen in der ersten Hälfte des 17. Jahrhunderts* (Wilsingen, 1990).

SCOTT, DAVID, 'Elizabeth I as Lutenist', *LSJ* 18 (1976), 45.

SHEPHERD, MARTIN, 'The Interpretation of Signs for Graces in English Lute Music', *LSJ* 36 (1996), 37–84.

SHIRE, HELENA MENNIE, *Song, Dance and Poetry of the Court of Scotland under King James VI* (Cambridge, 1969).

SIMPSON, ADRIENNE, ' "Of a petty French lutenist in England" by Richard Flecknoe', *LSJ* 10 (1968), 33.

—— 'Richard Mathew and *The Lutes Apology*', *LSJ* 8 (1966), 41–7.

—— 'A Study of Richard Mathew's *The Lutes Apology for his Excellency*' (M.Mus. thesis, King's College, University of London, 1968).

SIMPSON, CLAUDE M., *The British Broadside Ballad and its Music* (New Brunswick, NJ, 1966).

SMITH, DOUGLAS ALTON, 'The Ebenthal Lute and Viol Tablatures', *EM* 10 (1982), 462–7.

—— *A History of the Lute from Antiquity to the Renaissance* (Lexington, 2001).

—— 'Sylvius Leopold Weiss', *EM* 8 (1980), 47–58.

SÖHNE, GERHARD CHRISTIAN, 'On the Geometry of the Lute', *JLSA* 13 (1980), 35–54.

SOUTHWORTH, JOHN, *The English Medieval Minstrel* (Woodbridge, 1989).

SPARR, KENNETH, 'French Lutenists and French Lute Music in Sweden', in Jean-Michel Vaccaro (ed.), *Le Luth et sa musique*, ii (Paris, 1984), 59–67.

SPENCER, ROBERT, 'Chitarrone, Theorbo and Archlute', *EM* 4 (1976), 407–23.

—— 'English Nomenclature of Extended Lutes', *FoMRHI* 23 (1981), Comm. 337, 57–9.

—— 'Three English Lute Manuscripts', *EM* 3 (1975), 119–24.

—— 'The Tollemache Lute Manuscript', *LSJ* 7 (1965), 38–9.

—— 'The Weld Lute Manuscript', *LSJ* 1 (1959), 48–57.

SPINK, IAN, 'Another Gaultier Affair', *M&L* 45 (1964), 345–7.

—— 'English Cavalier Songs, 1620–1660', *PRMA* 86 (1960), 61–78.

—— 'The Musicians of Henrietta-Maria: Some Notes and References in the English State Papers', *Acta musicologica*, 36 (1964), 177–82.

SPRING, MATTHEW, 'The Balcarres Manuscript', *LSJ* 32 (1992), 2–45.

—— 'Jenkins's Lute Music: An Approach to Reconstructing the Lost Multitudes of Lute Lessons', in Andrew Ashbee and Peter Holman (eds.), *John Jenkins and his Time: Studies in English Consort Music* (Oxford, 1996), 309–23.

—— 'The Lady Margaret Wemyss Manuscript', *LSJ* 27 (1987), 5–30.

—— 'The Lute in England and Scotland after the Golden Age (1620–1750)', 3 vols. (D.Phil. thesis, University of Oxford, 1987).

STARKEY, DAVID, *The English Court, from the Wars of the Roses to the Civil War* (London, 1987).

—— (ed.), *Henry VIII: A European Court in England* (London, 1991).

STERNFELD, FREDERICK W., *Music in Shakespearean Tragedy* (London, 1963).

STEVENS, JOHN, *Music and Poetry in the Early Tudor Court* (London 1961; rev. edn., 1979).

STONE, LAWRENCE, *The Crisis of the Aristocracy (1558–1641)* (Oxford, 1967).

STRONG, ROY, *Henry Prince of Wales and England's Lost Renaissance* (London, 1986).

The Text of The Canterbury Tales, by Geoffrey Chaucer, ed. John M. Manly and Edith Rickert, 8 vols. (Chicago, 1940).

THACKERAY, RUPERT M., 'Thomas Mace', *Musical Times*, 92 (1951), 306–7.

Thomas of Erceldoune (c.1475), ed. James A. H. Murray (EETS, 61; London, 1875).

Three Middle English Sermons from the Worcester Chapter MS F.10, ed. Dora Mortimer Grisdale (Leeds University School of English Language, Text & Monographs, 5; Kendal, 1939).

TILMOUTH, MICHAEL, 'A Calendar of References to Music in Newspapers, Published in London and the Provinces (1660–1719)', *RMARC* 1 (1961), 1–107.

TOFFOLO, STEFANO, *Antichi strumenti veneziani: 1500–1800* (Venice, 1987).

Tottel's Miscellany 1557–1587, ed. Hyder E. Rollins (rev. edn., Cambridge, Mass., 1965).

TRAFICANTE, FRANK, 'Lyra Viol Tunings: "All Ways have been Tryed to do it" ', *Acta musicologica*, 42 (1970), 183–205.

TURNBULL, HARVEY, 'The Origin of the Long-Necked Lute', *GSJ* 25 (1972), 58–66.

Two Coventry Corpus Christi Plays, ed. Hardin Craig (EETS/ES, 87; London, 1902).

TYLER, JAMES, *The Early Guitar* (Early Music Series, 4; London, 1980).

TYTLER, WILLIAM, 'On the Fashionable Amusements and Entertainments in Edinburgh in the Last Century, with a Plan of a Grand Concert of Musicians, St Cecilia's Day, 1695', *Transactions of the Society of Antiquarians of Scotland*, 1 (1792), 499–510.

UNGERER, GUSTAV, 'The French Lutenist Charles Tessier and the Essex Circle', *Renaissance Quarterly*, 28 (1975), 190–203.

UNGLESS, CLIVE, 'Scottish National Library, MS Panmure 4: A Transcription with an Introductory Essay and Notes' (Honours degree diss., Royal Holloway College, University of London, 1981).

UNWIN, ROBERT, 'An English Writer on Music: James Talbot 1664–1708', *GSJ* 40 (1987), 53–72.

VACCARO, JEAN-MICHEL, sleeve note to *Dufaut* recording played by Hopkinson Smith (Astrée A8 15).

VERCHALY, ANDRÉ, 'La Tablature dans les recueils français pour chant et luth (1603–1643)', in Jean Jacquot (ed.), *Le Luth et sa musique* (Paris, 1958), 155–69.

VIOLLET-LE-DUC, EUGÈNE-EMMANUEL, *Dictionnaire raisonné du mobilier français*, 6 vols. (Paris, 1858–75).

VIRDUNG, SEBASTIAN, *Musica getutscht* (Basle, 1511).

VAN DER MOTTEN, J. P., *Sir William Killigrew (1606–1695): His Life and Dramatic Works* (Ghent, 1980).

VANG, OLE, and SEGERMAN, EPHRAIM, 'Two-Headed Lute News', *FoMRHI* 13 (1978), Comm. 156, 30–8.

WALKLING, ANDREW R., 'Masque and Politics at the Restoration Court: John Crowne's *Calisto*', *EM* 24 (1996), 27–62.

WALLS, PETER, *Music in the English Courtly Masque 1604–1640* (Oxford, 1996).

WARD, JOHN M., 'Apropos *The British Broadside Ballad and its Music*', *JAMS* 20 (1967), 28–86.

—— 'Barley's Songs without Words', *LSJ* 12 (1970), 5–22.

—— 'The "Dolfull Dumps" ', *JAMS* 4 (1951), 111–21.

—— 'A Dowland Miscellany', *JLSA* 10 (1977), 5–151.

—— 'The Fourth Dublin Lute Book', *LSJ* 11 (1969), 28–46.

—— 'The Hunt's Up', *PRMA* 106 (1980), 1–25.

—— 'The Lute Books of Trinity College, Dublin: Preface', *LSJ* 9 (1967), 17–18.

—— 'The Lute Books of Trinity College, Dublin, II: MS D.1.21 (The So-called Ballet Lute Book)', *LSJ* 10 (1968), 15–32.

—— 'Music for *A Handefull of pleasant delites*', *JAMS* 10 (1957), 151–80.

—— *Music for Elizabethan Lutes*, 2 vols. (Oxford, 1992).

—— 'The So-called "Dowland Lute Book" in the Folger Shakespeare Library', *JLSA* 9 (1976), 5–29.

—— 'Sprightly and Cheerful Musick: Notes on the Cittern, Gittern and Guitar in Sixteenth- and Seventeenth-Century England', *LSJ* 21–3 (1979–81).

—— 'Tessier and the "Essex Circle" ', *Renaissance Quarterly*, 29 (1976), 378–84.

—— and Music 200, 'The Lute Books of Trinity College, Dublin: MS D.3.30/I, The So-called Dallis Lute Book', *LSJ* 9 (1967), 19–40.

WATSON, HENRY, 'Thomas Mace: The Man; The Book; and the Instruments', *PMA* 35 (1908–9), 87–107.

WHITELOCKE, BULSTRODE, *Memoirs of the English Affairs* (London, 1682; rev. edn., 1853).

WHYTHORNE, THOMAS, *The Autobiography of Thomas Whythorne*, ed. James M. Osborn (Oxford, 1961).

WILLETS, PAMELA J., 'Autographs of Angelo Notari', *M&L* 50 (1969), 124–6.

—— *The Henry Lawes Manuscript* (London, 1969).

—— 'A Neglected Source of Monody and Madrigal', *M&L* 43 (1962), 329–39.

WILLIAMS, NEVILLE, *Henry VIII and his Court* (London, 1971).

WILLIAMSON, JERRY W., *The Myth of the Conqueror: Prince Henry Stuart, a Study of Seventeenth-Century Personation* (New York, 1978).

WILLSHER, HARRY M., 'Music in Scotland during Three Centuries', 3 vols. (D.Litt. thesis, University of St Andrews, 1945).

WINTERNITZ, EMANUEL, *Musical Instruments and their Symbolism in Western Art* (London, 1967).

WOOD, ANTHONY À, *Athenae Oxoniensis . . . To which are added the Fasti, or Annals of the University of Oxford*, ed. Philip Bliss, 4 vols. (Oxford, 1813–20).

—— *The Life and Times of Anthony Wood Described by Himself*, i: *1632–1663*, ed. Andrew Clark (Oxford, 1891).

WOODFIELD, IAN, *The Early History of the Viol* (Cambridge, 1984).

—— *English Musicians in the Age of Exploration* (Stuyvesant, NY, 1995).

WOODFILL, W. L., *Musicians in English Society from Elizabeth to Charles I* (Princeton, 1953).

WRIGHT, LAWRENCE, 'Medieval Carvings of Musical Instruments in St. Mary's Church, Shrewsbury', *FoMRHI* 12 (1977), Comm. 74.

—— 'The Medieval Gittern and Citole: A Case of Mistaken Identity', *GSJ* 30 (1977), 8–42.

WYATT, THOMAS, *Collected Poems of Sir Thomas Wyatt*, ed. Kenneth Muir and Patricia Thompson (Liverpool, 1969).

INDEX

CPSIA information can be obtained at www.ICGtesting.com
Printed in the USA
LVOW11s1617240114

370874LV00011B/574/A

9 780195 188387